McGraw-Hill's Certified Quality Engineer Examination Guide

McGraw-Hill's Certified Quality Engineer Examination Guide

Jagdish Vani

McGraw-Hill, Inc.

New York   San Francisco   Washington, D.C.   Auckland   Bogotá
Caracas   Lisbon   London   Madrid   Mexico City   Milan
Montreal   New Delhi   San Juan   Singapore
Sydney   Tokyo   Toronto

Library of Congress Cataloging-in-Publication Data

Vani, Jagdish.
    McGraw-Hill's certified quality engineer examination guide /
    Jagdish Vani.
          p.   cm.
    Includes index.
    ISBN 0-07-067064-1
    1. Industrial engineers—United States—Examinations—Study guides.
  2. Quality control—United States—Examinations—Study guides.
  I. Title. II. Title: Certified quality engineer examination guide.
  TS23.V36   1994
  620′.0076—dc20   94-35051
                                                          CIP

1 2 3 4 5 6 7 8 9 0 DOC/DOC 9 0 0 9 8 7 6 5

ISBN 0-07-067064-1

*The sponsoring editor for this book was Harold Crawford and the production
supervisor was Pamela A. Pelton.*
Printed and bound by R. R. Donnelley & Sons Company.

McGraw-Hill books are available at special quantity discounts to use as pre-
miums and sales promotions, or for use in corporate training programs. For
more information, please write to the Director of Special Sales, McGraw-Hill,
Inc., 11 West 19th Street, New York, NY 10011. Or contact your local book-
store.

To my loving wife Maya
and children Konark and Palak.
This book is dedicated to you for believing in me
and sharing my enthusiasm, for your caring support,
encouragement, patience, and understanding.

To the American Society for Quality Control (ASQC)
for providing me a sound and healthy environment
and opportunities for professional development
and continuous improvement.

Contents

Preface

Many people have asked me over the last two years, how and why I decided to write this book and when will it be over? It sounds like a long distance drive and the cry of kids of "how much more." I was introduced to the concepts of listening to the voice of the customer (VOC) and developing strategic methods for deploying the VOC in the organization for new products during my MBA studies in the early 1980s. It was my preliminary and informal exposure to the upcoming era of quality improvement methods, strategic role of quality in today's business, quality as a competitive tool, and understanding the sound techniques of systematic deployment of VOC into every level of the organization.

In Detroit, working in the automotive field, I came across the quality system and quality improvement requirements from leading automotive customers and joined the American Society for Quality Control (ASQC) to better understand the two important areas:

1. Tactical methods, i.e., the tools and methods in the field of quality improvement which constitute the technical side of the quality and micro level applications of such tools and methods.

2. Strategic issues, i.e., the role of leadership in developing sound business strategies to achieve the highest levels of customer enthusiasm, excitement, and delight and thereby gain market leadership. This means, understanding the use of basic principles of quality and management to design the quality into the products and to manage the quality at a macro management level.

As a Vice Chair for Education of the Greater Detroit Section of ASQC, I faced the challenging task of meeting the requirements of refresher course participants effectively and providing a well balanced education program for the Section's customers. During this time, like any other growing business, Detroit Section's Refresher course programs for various certification examinations of ASQC were in a period of tremendous growth. The organization and advance quality planning activities to handle this fast growth were not in place. At that moment I realized that education and learning are also processes like any other manufacturing process and the principles of quality planning and improvement apply equally to them.

As an instructor for many subjects in different refresher courses for certification examinations, I have come across many participants and instructors.

They include everyone from fresh college graduates to highly experienced engineers and managers with diverse backgrounds. They all have been very hungry for knowledge and learning, and for becoming professionally recognized as certified. Many of them have approached me from time to time with their individual difficulties in various areas of body of knowledge (BOK).

I have gained first hand experience of the problems and difficulties faced by many students of the refresher courses as I have taken these certification examinations (CQE, CRE, and CQA). I have been teaching, counseling, and answering questions ranging from what is CQE and how to apply for it, to highly technical questions on the subject matter of BOK.

I have been developing educational materials for many such subject areas for the last several years. Hence I decided to write a book that answers such questions in a simple, easy to understand, step-by-step manner and contains in-depth solutions, cautions, and cross references for more detailed reading for each area of the new BOK. The book contains multiple choice questions dealing with the subject areas of the new BOK and the answers in an appropriate level of detail. It provides complete solutions for many analytical situations.

This is not a textbook or a handbook in quality control. This is not a stand-alone, all inclusive book or reference. This book can act as a valuable study guide and a "how to" book for the CQE examination. It covers the new BOK subjects for the new CQE certification examination and some of the BOK for other certification examinations. The readers are continuously directed to many reference materials in the footnotes and bibliogrpahy in each chapter for a more detailed and thorough understanding. The book is most useful when used along with some of the reference materials and books.

I did not realize the magnitude, the challenge, and number of hours of work this project required. Years of study, consulting, problem solving, experience of developing quality improvement methods and training materials have gone into making this book. Many people have helped and encouraged me during this never ending project, i.e., from the concept phase to a finished product as a complete book. It is not possible to list and recognize each of them but I will try to list a few.

My special thanks are due to:

- The customers of this book, i.e. the past, present, and future participants of certification examinations for pursuing the personal and professional excellence by achieving ASQC's certifications, for their support, suggestions, and feedback for continuous improvement. Most of them have shared their difficulties in various areas of BOK, helping me to prioritize the content of the book.

- Sally M. Harthun, Manager, Certification, ASQC, Milwaukee, Wisc., for granting permission to reprint the previously published certification examination questions in CQE, CRE, and CQT, as well as the BOK and other information from the certification examination brochures. I also thank the many hardworking and courteous customer service representatives of ASQC, who have very promptly responded to my questions, and supplied or mailed me the necessary information from time to time.

- The Copyrights and Permissions department, McGraw-Hill, Inc., New York, for granting the permission to reprint statistical tables in this book.

- Harold B. Crawford, editor, Sybil P. Parker, publisher, Mary Ellen Haramis, secretary, Jim Halston, editing supervisor, Professional and Reference division, and many other people at McGraw-Hill, Inc., New York, for their professionalism, patience, caring, and constructive criticism and guidance during the entire book development and editing process. Their support throughout the editing process has resulted in a book that readers will find very useful.

- Members of the Executive Board of the Greater Detroit Section of ASQC for their support.

- My superiors, mainly Jay Reidsma, and Robert Brain of Dimensional Management department, Midsize Car Division, General Motors Corporation, for their approval, consideration, and support. In addition, many colleagues and employees at my job have been very helpful during the preparation of the book.

- My relatives and personal friends for accommodating me and my family.

I wish to express my sincere thanks to Doug Berg, Richard A. Ganfield, Don Mitchell, Ken Molloy, Mary Ann Ritter, William J. Wiechec, and Robert Zaciewski of General Motors Corporation; Robert L. Danek, William W. Scherkenbach, William Harral, Arch Associates; George Mouradian, A.M. General Corporation; Jim Ireland, Kay Automotive Graphics; Arun Kapur, and Roderick A. Munro of Ford Motor Company, and Hans Bajaria, Multiface, Inc. They have continuously encouraged me, believed in me, and enthusiastically supported my aggressive goals and contributed significantly in my professional career over the years.

Last but not the least, my loving wife Maya, son Konark, and daughter Palak have my deepest appreciation and gratitude for their empathy and compassion. They have smilingly sacrificed their personal priorities and endured my late hours of typing every single day. My children have allowed me to close the doors of my study room (i.e., a bedroom) so that "dad" could complete the book successfully.

If this book helps you in pursuing your goals and initiatives, all the people above deserve and share the credit. If it does less than you expected, I take the responsibility to continuously improve it further.

Jagdish Vani
Troy, Michigan

McGraw-Hill's
Certified
Quality
Engineer
Examination
Guide

CHAPTER 1

ADVANCE QUALITY PLANNING FOR THE CQE EXAMINATION

You have made a significant decision and commitment if you have decided to appear for the Certified Quality Engineer (CQE) or Quality Engineer In Training (QEIT) examination. This is a very important milestone in your professional and personal career and hence it is very important that you plan for this event most effectively. We use principles of advance quality planning for many quality improvement efforts. The same principles are also applicable to planning for the examination.

This chapter provides important advance quality planning suggestions to prepare effectively for the CQE (or QEIT) examination. These suggestions are generic and descriptive but not specific or prescriptive to any specific individual. You need to review them and select applicable items, if any, for your particular case.

The following tips and suggestions are based on the most recent policy changes in the administration of the CQE Examination published by the Certification Committee of the American Society for Quality Control.[1] The policies and rules published for the Certification Examinations are subject to change in the future. The users of this book must note this. It is your responsibility to contact ASQC for the latest rules and information for the Certification Examinations and follow the latest rules.

IMPORTANT CHANGES IN THE CQE EXAMINATION

- The CQE Body of Knowledge (BOK) is completely revised and has been adopted by the ASQC Divisions and approved by the Certification Committee after a rigorous enhancement process.

- The CQE Examination will be a *one-part* examination and will have a *five-hour* time limit.

- The new BOK consists of six main areas and the CQE Examination will consist of 160 questions (including case studies).

- The first administration of the "new" CQE Examination is scheduled for June 1995.

- Contact the ASQC Certification committee for QEIT Guidelines.

MEMBERSHIP AND EXAMINATION FORMS

- Obtain ASQC's membership application form if you are not currently a member, and the CQE

---

[1] Revised CQE Body Of Knowledge, New CQM Body Of Knowledge, Sally Harthun, Manager of Certification, ASQC, Milwaukee, WI, January 20, 1995.

examination application brochure from ASQC in Milwaukee, Wisconsin by calling toll free **1-800-248-1946 or (414) 272-8575; Fax # (414) 272-1734.** You should become a member of the society to obtain a wide variety of membership benefits in the quality field. Contact the membership department of ASQC to obtain more details and get contact names and phone numbers of the local Section officers. Contact the Certification department of ASQC to obtain the details about the Certification program.

● Read the CQE Examination booklet/brochure thoroughly. It provides the details of the CQE Certification requirements and answers very clearly all important questions. For any questions, call ASQC at the above toll-free number or your local ASQC Section officers.

● Complete membership and/or examination application forms as soon as possible. Mail the forms with appropriate fees **before the last date** for the examination application to: **ASQC, 611 East Wisconsin Avenue, P. O. Box 3005, Milwaukee, WI 53201-3005.**

BODY OF KNOWLEDGE

● Study the **Body of Knowledge** (BOK) for Quality Engineering thoroughly as it lists the subject areas used to design the examination questions. You can use the BOK as a source for self assessment against each item [e.g., a rating scale 1(low) through 5 (high)] or develop a Pareto chart of the weakest subject categories. Use this as a check sheet to help you prioritize the planning and time allocation for preparation on the weakest subjects. You need to continuously balance study efforts between your strengths and weaknesses in different subjects.

● Decide if you will need additional help in specific (weaker) subjects, e.g., a refresher course, additional classes from local colleges, seminars, etc.

BIBLIOGRAPHY/REFERENCE MATERIALS

● Refer to the bibliography in the CQE Examination booklet. Identify the books that you already have and develop plans to buy or borrow additional books from colleagues or libraries.

● Add visual controls to your study materials to make your study efforts more VISIBLE. Organize and label your reading material for quick and easy access to various subjects. Highlight or mark up important pages, tables, charts, figures, and formulas by visual signs such as tabs, color coding, and bookmarks. You may make cross-reference notes in various books to trace information.

● Refer to ASQC's policy for allowable and restricted materials. In the examination, bring only the materials that meet ASQC's policy for the examination.

● Do not take too many books (a full cart load), as you may not have that much time to refer to them in the examination. Take only a few that you are going to use and are familiar with.

ASQC'S PUBLISHED EXAMINATION SETS

- ASQC has published a total of four CQE Examinations in the 1972, 1974, 1978, and 1984 issues of *Quality Progress* magazine. Review them as a reference or a practice set only. Please do not depend on them completely as the BOK is revised and the questions are updated continuously. This book includes these examination sets with solutions or explanations for most of the questions.

- Prepare continuously and consistently for the examination. Do not depend on any single reference or source. You must refer to specific materials for different areas and be well prepared.

CHECKLIST OF THINGS TO BRING

- You should make a checklist of things to bring with you to the examination, so that you do not forget some important items. This may sound silly and too simple, but the author has seen many students forget calculators, books, and supplies, etc. Table 1-1 lists a few items (not all inclusive) and you may add other specific items.

Table 1-1 Checklist of things to bring for the examination

No.	ITEM DESCRIPTION	Check X	Comment
1	Personal ID		
2	Seating pass and map for the examination location		
3	Class manual/material		
4	*Quality Control Handbook*, by Juran		
5	*Glossary and Tables for SQC*, by ASQC		
6	*MIL-STD -105E, MIL-STD-414, MIL-STD-9858A*		
7	Regular and/or scientific dictionaries		
8	Pencils/pen/highlighters/markers, etc.		
9	Pencil sharpener/eraser		
10	Calculator and calculator manual		
11	Batteries for calculator (extra new set)		
12	Scale /ruler		
13	Food, coffee, etc.		
14	Personal hygienic needs / medicines if any		list them
15	Scratch papers		
16	List other reference books below		
17			

REFRESHER COURSES / STUDY GROUPS

- Many ASQC sections provide refresher courses or preparatory courses locally. You may need to contact them for information. Some of these courses are of the overview type and provide limited coverage of the subject in a short period. These courses can help you focus and organize properly but may not provide an in-depth detailed understanding of basic concepts and methods. However, you need to know the subjects in the BOK thoroughly.

- Make a list of all contacts and develop good networking with other people. Form small study groups to study and solve mutual difficulties. In the author's CQE teaching experience, many students have indicated that forming small study groups has been very beneficial to them.

- Be familiar with the examination site. Plan to be at the site well in advance so that you can get good parking, seating, etc. Contact your local section for examination site details.

SUGGESTIONS FOR THE EXAMINATION (The examination day)

- Do not wait till the last day or last minute. Plan well and prepare thoroughly before the examination day. You should take sufficient rest and be fresh.

- Follow the proctor's instructions for registration and examination rules. You will be given one examination test set and one answer sheet. Verify the total number of questions and ensure that you have received a complete set with all pages and no page is missing or unstapled. Read instructions provided on the front of the examination test set and follow them thoroughly.

- Read each question carefully as it may contain some key terms as shown in Table 1-2.

Table 1-2 Commonly used key terms in test questions

Is	Is not	True	False
Least	Most	Correct	Incorrect
(more) likely	(Less) or not likely	All of the above	None of the above
Below	Beyond	Except	All
Equal to	Not equal to	a and b only, b and c only,	
More than	Less than	i and ii only,	
		Exactly	

Now read the question carefully again to get the true meaning.

STORY QUESTIONS

- Many test questions in statistical methods and tools are in the form of a story which generally does not provide a straight or clear definition of the problem. You have to read the story and decide what is unknown that needs to be solved, and what data is directly available from the story and which formula or equation to use to solve the question. The story problems are not generally easy to answer quickly. It requires a very high level of practice and ongoing study effort. Remember: **practice, practice, and practice.**

Let's call the test question the Voice Of Examination (VOE). First try to convert the VOE into some simple language that you can understand such as in the form "**Given**" and "**Find**."

Example: A process is producing a material which is 40% defective. Four pieces are selected at random for inspection. What is the probability of exactly one defective piece being found in the sample?

a.   0.870
b.   0.575
c.   0.346
d.   0.130

Key: c.   0.346   (Ref. Applications Question 80, October 1974)
Given: $p = 0.40$, $n = 4$, $r = 1$ defective, attribute data
Find: P(exactly one defective) = $P(r = 1)$

You can see now how simple the data look as compared to the story information. It can now help you analyze the data and decide the distribution that is applicable and the formula or statistical table to be used, etc. In the above case, one sees that it meets the conditions of binomial probability distribution and then one tries to solve it.

This means you should try to translate the story language of the VOE into a simple, easy-to-understand and remember "Given" and "Find" format. Most of the story-type questions are solved in this book using this approach.

This process is shown in Table 1-3.

Table 1-3 Steps for story questions

1.	**READ THE STORY/QUESTION CAREFULLY.**
2.	**LIST EACH "GIVEN"** using conventional notations where possible.
3.	**CLEARLY DEFINE THE UNKNOWN AS "FIND."**
4.	**THINK ABOUT THE POSSIBLE SUBJECT THAT FITS THE "GIVEN" AND/OR "FIND." DECIDE THE PROPER FORMULA OR METHOD.** (Use reference material to verify the equation or formula, if necessary.)
5.	**DO CALCULATIONS CORRECTLY AND BE FAST.** (Be familiar with your calculator and various function keys. Practice with your calculator for various applications.)
6.	**SELECT THE MOST APPROPRIATE ANSWER.** Make sure you study each answer choice before you finalize your choice, as there could be a more appropriate choice. Do not fall for the obvious choice every time.
7.	**BLACKEN OR DARKEN CIRCLE, OVAL OR BOX PROPERLY IN THE ANSWER SHEET FOR EACH QUESTION.**

• Each individual has different analytical skills and strengths or weaknesses. Hence these are only suggested steps that can help some of you. You do not have to follow them if you already use a different method or approach.

- Some questions provide answer choices up to four decimal points and some are rounded off to two decimals. In some cases, the answers are given as simple fractions, e.g., 14/39, and not as a decimal. Hence be careful in selecting the most appropriate answer.

ANSWER SHEET

- The answer sheet is a typical scanned form that requires darkening the small circles, ovals, or rectangular boxes using the appropriate lead pencil. It is important that you darken each item properly and completely as the answer sheets are scanned electronically. Make sure you complete the answer sheet with details such as your name, section number, examination, section, etc., correctly and thoroughly by darkening appropriate boxes, circles, or ovals, and follow the same practice when answering each question.

- You must use the answer sheet to document your answers. Do not document your answers in the test set by circling the choice. Your answers must appear in the answer sheet.

- Make sure you follow the answer sheet carefully and blacken the answer correctly, i.e., in the right row and column. For example, if you are answering question #21, make sure that you are blackening the answer for question #21 (row) and not in the row for #20 or for #22. It is easy to misalign your eyesight with the answer sheet, resulting in an incorrect series of all subsequent answers. This is a very costly error.

  Similarly, follow the column properly, i.e., the column in the answer sheet describes the choices in the form of 1, 2, 3, 4, 5 or a, b, c, d, e, etc.

  This may again sound too simple and silly, but I have seen this error too often and this is one of the most costly errors. You miss one row/column and all the other answers fall in the wrong spaces even though you may have solved them correctly.

TIME MANAGEMENT

- Remember the TIME. Time can be your enemy and it starts clicking away fast. Do not waste time. There are several ways to save time depending upon your style and preparations for multiple-choice-type tests. Some ways are described in the next few tips.

- You should know what subject matters are your strengths. Keep going down the list of questions and answer the ones which are your strengths. It can boost your speed and motivation. You may find some questions simple and easy to answer and therefore can be solved quickly.

● You should know your weakness, i.e., the subject matter that you are not very comfortable with, you may not be confident in, you did not prepare well, etc. You should not try to answer them first. Make a note and do not waste your time researching in the books. You can come back to them later if the time permits.

● Be **POSITIVE**. Do not get discouraged or frustrated. It is very natural to feel that way but you are not the only one feeling that way.

● **BEST OF LUCK**

CHAPTER 2

HOW TO USE THIS GUIDE FOR THE
CQE EXAMINATION

The guide is prepared in the form of questions and solutions. This is not intended to be a textbook. It is not meant to be the only reference but it is a strong tool for preparation and practice. You must follow and refer to the bibliography provided at the end of each chapter or other sources for more detailed discussion on many basic concepts.

- The questions are organized in a logical pattern. The questions based on a particular concept or subject category are sorted from past examinations and are grouped together in each chapter. This will provide you with an opportunity to study and solve many possible types of questions from each subject/concept at one time. It will expose you to different language, choices, and question patterns.

- This guide book contains a lot of material on each subject, i.e., it contains 13 chapters based on the six main areas of the new BOK for the CQE examination. Please do not try to overdo it in a short time. This can be frustrating and overwhelming. Pace yourself and manage your preparation time effectively. If you are attending refresher courses or other courses, you may follow each chapter accordingly in that order. You must prioritize your study efforts and concentrate on your weakest subjects.

- Each chapter contains the author-generated new questions and some questions from ASQC's published examinations from the October 1972, October 1974, August 1978, and July 1984 issues of *Quality Progress* magazine. These questions are marked with proper cross-referencing in each chapter indicating the source of the question, e.g., Ref. Principles Question 44, October 1972. The choices for these questions are changed from numeric numbers as Choice 1, 2, etc., to alphabetic letters as Choice a , b, etc., to be consistent with some of the newer changes in the examination. As per the most recent changes in the policy, the "new" CQE Examination will be a *one-part* examination and not a two part or section examination.

- Chapters 3 through 8 focus on the statistical subjects and require significant practice. The application of statistical methods and tools is very important in quality engineering and hence there is considerably higher emphasis on these subjects in the CQE examination.

- Do not merely read solutions of statistical questions, but try to solve them on your own first without referring to the solution. You need to test yourself to see how well you know the question and how correctly you can answer it or solve it. If you get frustrated, then look at the book and study the solution, then redo the question, and all calculations on your own. Do not read calculations, practice them using your calculator and be thoroughly familiar with the functions in your calculator. The point is, you need to prepare yourself for the examination.

Do not memorize the questions from the book or any other reference as they are not generally repeated in the examination. There may be similar types of questions but they may contain different data, values, choices, etc. The question data bank is continuously updated and new questions are added for each subject. Hence your focus should be on sound understanding of concepts and applications which will enable you to solve or answer the variety of questions that can be asked from a given subject. You should develop generic and descriptive thinking and an understanding of principles and applications of the BOK subjects for a broader range of areas.

Most of the questions provide detailed discussion or explanation for selecting one of the choices as the correct choice. In some cases, it also provides the reasons for not selecting other choices.

Some questions do not provide more details if the questions are too simple or easy to understand.

It is necessary that you understand some basic concepts and get more detailed understanding of the subject matter. It is also not possible to provide full detail about each question. Hence many questions have a footnote with the name of the reference book, the page numbers, etc., that can lead you to appropriate information. Most of such references are commonly available in libraries or bookstores.

This guide book considers the *Quality Control Handbook* by J. M. Juran, 4th edition, McGraw-Hill, Inc., as a very important, simple-to-use textbook or reference book. It provides significant coverage of each subject area in one book as compared to buying many other books. Hence the author has used this handbook as an important resource to answer many questions and cross-referenced it in the footnotes repeatedly.

● Chapters 16 through 19 include the complete set of the ASQC's past 4 published examinations from the October 1972, October 1974, August 1978, and July 1984 issues of *Quality Progress* magazine. These questions are in their natural order of publication and are cross-referenced to respective chapters for solution and discussion, e.g., Refer to Question 32 in Chapter 4, Statistical Inference and Hypothesis Testing. You should practice these tests to get a real experience of the examination, since they are not necessarily grouped in any logical order.

● The statistical questions in probability, distributions, hypothesis testing, design of experiments, etc., are story-type questions generally. They are defined in terms of the **"Givens"** and **"Find"** approach discussed in Chapter 1.

Past examinations have repeated many questions. They are shown by a footnote reference. If the question is repeated from the past, you should give more attention to it during your preparation.

Some questions in statistics, SPC, quality management, quality auditing, etc., indicate over-lapping categories of BOK and hence the solution refers to different chapters and references.

- There is an obvious repetition in some solutions. It is intended to provide you more detailed practice and understanding of the concepts. You should pay more attention to such questions.

- Some questions from the past examinations may be obsolete depending upon changes in the BOK, technology and application, or changes in quality theories. Some new concepts such as deployment of voice of customer, robust designs, new tools of quality, error proofing, lean manufacturing, etc., are briefly discussed in some questions.

- Make sure that you are familiar with how to use the statistical tables, such as normal, binomial distribution, etc. Most of the commonly used statistical tables are provided in the Appendix in this book; refer to them to obtain proper values for various questions. In the case of Chapter 8, Acceptance Sampling, the tables shown are generally partial tables for respective questions. You can mail your order for MIL-STD-105E, MIL-STD-414, and MIL-STD-9858A to:

    Standardization Document Order Desk, 700 Robbins Ave.,
    Building # 4, Section D, Philadelphia, PA 19111-5094

    (Please verify the address in the future in case of an address change or changes in the ordering process.)

- Calculator use: You should have a scientific calculator with statistical functions. Contact ASQC for questions on any particular type or brand of calculator and follow the examination guidelines. Make sure that you know how to use the statistical function keys properly and correctly, as different calculator brands use slightly different notations for some of the statistical terms. Many students waste considerable time in referring to the calculator owner's manual during the examination to try to understand the function keys. You may answer some simple statistical questions incorrectly if you use the wrong keys. This can be a very expensive error. The author finds this to be one of the most common weaknesses in students. Remember that there are some questions that are a *bonus* that can be answered very quickly if you know how to use the statistical functions in the calculator.

CHAPTER 3

FUNDAMENTAL CONCEPTS OF PROBABILITY AND STATISTICS

ASQC'S BODY OF KNOWLEDGE (BOK) FOR THE CQE EXAMINATION

This chapter focuses on the following selected subject areas of BOK from *Section III, Statistical Principles and Applications.*

Terms and Concepts

1.   Definitions of basic statistical terms
2.   Enumerative and analytical studies
3.   Levels of measurement (e.g., nominal, ordinal, interval, ratio)
4.   Descriptive statistics (e.g., measures of central tendency and variation, histograms, exploratory data analysis)
5.   Basic probability concepts (e.g., independence, mutually exclusive)
6.   Theoretical expected value
7.   Assumptions and robustness of tests

Distributions

1.   Frequency and cumulative
2.   Probability distribution functions
3.   Binomial, Poisson, normal, exponential

1.   Statistic is

        a.   the collection, organization, analysis, interpretation, and presentation of data
        b.   a science or a tool for decision making under uncertainty
        c.   the characteristics of sample(s) and is used to make some inferences about its population
        d.   all of the above

Key: d.   all of the above

2.   A statistic is

        a.   the solution to a problem
        b.   a population value
        c.   a positive number between 0 and 1 inclusive
        d.   a sample value

Key: d.   a sample value   (Ref. Principles Question 44, October 1972)
        The statistics such as the sample mean ($\overline{X}$) or the sample standard deviation (S) describe the sample value. Statistics is merely the collection of the raw facts or data and not necessarily the solution to a problem. The analysis of data may enable you to estimate the population values and may help solve a problem or make a decision. Hence choice a is inappropriate. The parameter, such as μ, describes the population value for the population mean. Hence choice b is incorrect. Probability takes the value between 0 and 1; but the statistics can take practically different values based on the type of data, and not necessarily the value between 0 and 1. Hence choice c is incorrect.

3.   A number derived from sample data which describes the data in some useful way is called a

        a.   constant
        b.   statistic
        c.   parameter
        d.   critical value

Key: b.   statistic   (Ref. Principles Question 2, July 1984)
        We take various samples from a population and calculate, for example, its sample mean $\overline{X}$, sample standard deviation S, etc. These numbers are called statistics for that sample that describes the sample data. Choices a, c, and d are incorrect as they represent the population data and not the sample data.

4.   A number resulting from the manipulation of some raw data according to certain specified procedures is called

        a.   a sample
        b.   a population

       c.   a constant
       d.   a statistic
       e.   a parameter

Key: d.   a statistic   (Ref. Principles Question 47, October 1974)
Statistics is the collection, organization, analysis, interpretation, and presentation of data. It means we collect raw data or facts and try to organize them in some format, and then analyze or manipulate the data to make conclusions.

You might think that this can apply to a population parameter, i.e., the data can be of population. However, the key word is *some* raw data which indicates that it is a sample value. Choices b, c, and d are incorrect as they represent the population data and not the sample data.

5.   Data are

       a.   coded test / inspection measurements
       b.   computer-prepared summaries
       c.   collected raw facts
       d.   the output after processing that management wishes to know

Key: c.   collected raw facts   (Ref. Principles Question 67, October 1974)

6.   Population characteristics are

       a.   statistics
       b.   parameters
       c.   constant values
       d.   b and c both
       e.   a and c both

Key: d.   b and c both
A parameter is the true value of the characteristic, it represents the population value of the characteristic and it is a constant value, e.g., the population mean μ is a parameter. The term statistics in choice a describes the sample values and not the population values.

7.   In statistical quality control, a parameter is

       a.   a random variable
       b.   a sample value
       c.   a population value
       d.   the solution to a statistical problem

Key: c.   a population value   (Ref. Principles Question 62, October 1974)

A parameter is the true value of the characteristic, it represents the population value of the characteristic, and it is a constant value, e.g., the population mean μ is a parameter.

8.   A parameter is

        a.   a random variable
        b.   a sample value
        c.   a population value
        d.   the solution to a statistical problem

Key: c.   a population value   (Ref. Principles Question 37, October 1972)
        Please refer to the comments in the previous questions.

9.   Which of the following is/are true?

        i.   The characteristic of a population is a statistic
        ii.   The characteristic of a sample is a parameter
        iii.   The characteristic of a population is a parameter
        iv.   The characteristic of a sample is a statistic

        a.   i and ii
        b.   ii and iii
        c.   iii and iv
        d.   iv and i

Key: c.   iii and iv
        This is a repeat question. Please refer to various questions above for comments.

10.   We use sample data to draw conclusions about the population. This describes

        a.   a probability situation
        b.   a statistic situation
        c.   a random situation
        d.   all of the above

Key: b.   a statistic situation
        This is a repeat question. Please refer to various questions above for comments.

11.   We use some known characteristic of the population and try to analyze the sample data. This describes

        a.   a probability situation
        b.   a statistic situation
        c.   a random situation

      d.   all of the above

Key: a.   a probability situation

The characteristic of the population is known, e.g., the proportion nonconforming for the process is given as p'= 0.10, and we try to analyze the data of the sample to determine the probability of observing or finding r = 0, or 1, etc., of nonconforming items in the sample. This describes a probability situation.

12.   In determining a process average fraction defective using inductive or inferential statistics, we are making inferences about _____ based on _____ taken from the _____ .

      a.   statistics, samples, populations
      b.   populations, samples, populations
      c.   samples, statistics, populations
      d.   samples, populations, samples
      e.   statistics, populations, statistics

Key: b.   populations, samples, populations   (Ref. Principles Question 4, October 1974)

To make an inference about the population, we first take some samples from the population, calculate the statistics such as mean, standard deviation, etc. Then based on statistics of the sample, we can make inferences about the population parameter or we can estimate the population value.

Be careful with the language of such a question. Read it carefully a few times, place your answers in blanks, and make sure that it reads logically and meaningfully.

13.   In determining a process average fraction defective using inductive or inferential statistics, we use _____ computed from _____ to make the inferences about _____

      a.   statistics, samples, populations
      b.   populations, samples, populations
      c.   samples, statistics, populations
      d.   samples, populations, samples
      e.   statistics, populations, statistics

Key: a.   statistics, samples, populations   (Ref. Principles Question 9, August 1978)

When we use inferential statistics, we draw a sample from a population. Then we calculate statistics from the sample to make some inferences or assertions about the population.

Be careful with the language of such a question. Read it carefully a few times, place your answers in blanks, and make sure that it reads logically and meaningfully.

14.   The distributions for continuous probability distributions are described by its

    a.   Probability Mass Functions
    b.   Probability Density Function
    c.   Cumulative Density Function
    d.   a and b both
    e.   b and c both

Key: e.   b and c both

The continuous probability distributions are based on the data of the continuous random variable and normally are defined by its appropriate "Probability Density Function" (pdf). The cumulative probabilities are defined by the "Cumulative Density Function" (cdf).

The choice a defines the probability distribution based on the Attribute data, i.e., discrete random variable.

15.   Continuous data

    a.   can take practically any value depending upon the sensitivity of the measuring equipment.
    b.   can take only specific values in jumps and not any value.
    c.   form continuous distribution.
    d.   a and c both.
    e.   b and c both.

Key: d.   a and c both.

The continuous data can take practically any value depending upon the sensitivity of the measuring equipment, e.g., if the diameter of a hole is 10 ± 0.50 mm, it can take any value depending upon the sensitivity of the measuring equipment. This hole diameter will not take only specific values in jumps because it is a variable characteristic or a continuous data. This type of random variable forms a continuous probability distribution.

Choice b defines the attribute data and a discrete distribution where the data take only a specific value, e.g., a single throw of a fair die can take only a specific values of 1 or 2 or 3 ... etc.

16.   A random variable

    a.   may be either discrete or variable
    b.   is called "random" because it depends on the normal distribution
    c.   is called "variable" because it refers to the variance
    d.   is all of the above

Key: a.   may be either discrete or variable   (Ref. Principles Question 34, October 1972)

A random variable (rv) is any rule that associates a number with each outcome in the sample space S where sample spaces S may contain discrete or variable outcomes. An rv can be defined as a numerically valued function over a sample space S, whose value is determined by a random experiment.[1]

17.   Random selection of a sample

        a.   theoretically means that each item in the lot had an equal chance to be selected in the sample
        b.   assures that the sample average will equal the population average
        c.   means that a table of random numbers was used to dictate the selection
        d.   is a meaningless theoretical requirement

Key: a.   theoretically means that each item in the lot had an equal chance to be selected in the sample   (Ref. Principles Question 84, October 1972)
        Choice b is incorrect because sample average is not a constant value, it is likely to vary from sample to sample whereas the population value is a constant value. Choice c is incorrect because the use of a random numbers table is recommended to generate random numbers but it is not dictated.

18.   Probability is defined as

        a.   a measure of the degree of uncertainty
        b.   likelihood, a chance, a trend
        c.   a study of randomness and uncertainty
        d.   all of the above

Key: d.   all of the above

19.   Which of the following is/are not true?

        a.   Probability is expressed from -1 to $+1$.
        b.   Probability of zero means the certainty that an event will definitely not occur.
        c.   Probability of 1 means the certainty that an event will definitely occur.
        d.   Probability is expressed as a number between 0 & 1 or 0 % to 100 %.
        e.   b, c, and d above.

Key: a.   Probability is expressed from -1 to $+1$.
        The key phrase is *"not true."* The probability is a nonnegative number and it can be as low as zero and as high as 1. The probability is expressed as $0 \leq P(x) \leq 1$. Probability of zero means the certainty that an event will definitely not occur and 1 means the certainty that an event will definitely occur. Only choice a is incorrect as the probability cannot be a negative number.

20.   All probabilities are

---

[1] *Fundamental Concepts of Probability, Statistics, Regression and DOE* by Jagdish Vani, 3rd edition, April 1993, Section 1.

    a.   all negative but they add up to unity

    b.   nonnegative but they do not add up to unity

    c.   are nonnegative and add up to unity

    d.   none of the above

Key: c.   are nonnegative and add up to unity

The word *unity* indicates a value of 1. Refer to Question 19 above for a detailed discussion.

21.   A probability of zero means

    a.   the degree of certainty that an event will occur.

    b.   the degree of uncertainty that an event will occur.

    c.   the degree of certainty that an event will not occur.

    d.   the same as the probability of 1.

Key: c.   the degree of certainty that an event will not occur.

Probability is expressed as a number between 0 and 1. The probability of 0 indicates the degree of certainty that the event will not occur.

22.   The probability can be expressed as

    i.   percentages (0 to 100%)

    ii.   proportions   (0 to 1)

    iii.   odds

    iv. $-\infty$ to ∞

    a.   i and ii only

    b.   ii and iii only

    c.   i, ii, and iii

    d.   iv only

Key: c.   i, ii, and iii

The probability is a nonnegative number between 0 and 1 and can be expressed as percentages (0 to 100%), proportions (0 to 1), and as odds or chances.[2] Item iv above is incorrect because probability is not a negative number but it is given as $0 \le P(x) \le 1$.

23.   The sum of all relative frequency is

    a.   zero

    b.   1

    c. $0 \le f \le 1$

    d. $-\infty \le f \le \infty$

---

[2] *Fundamental Concepts of Probability, Statistics, Regression and DOE* by Jagdish Vani, 3rd edition, April 1993, Section 1.

Key: b.   1
       The relative frequency is defined as the ratio of the number of observations in a particular category to the total number of observations. Hence the sum of all such relative frequencies or cumulative values or probabilities will add up to unity or 1 as a fundamental rule.

24.   A box of parts contains some good (G) and some bad (B) parts as shown below. What is the probability of obtaining a bad item in a single random drawing of one part?

       G G G B G B G B
       G B G G G G G G
       B G G B G G G G
       G G G G G G G G

       a.   1
       b   26/32
       c.   0.1875
       d.   Zero

Key: c.   0.1875
       Given: Box containing n = 6 bad (B) and 26 good (G) parts, i.e., total of N = 32 parts
       Find: P(obtaining a bad part)
       Each of the 32 parts in the box has an equally likely chance of being selected.

       P (one bad part) = $\dfrac{n}{N} = \dfrac{6}{32} = 0.1875$

25.   As a quality manager, you are looking to hire a quality technician. The personnel manager brings 7 candidates for an interview. What is the probability that the 5th candidate will be selected as the quality technician if every candidate has an equal opportunity of being selected?

       a.   1/8
       b.   3/7
       c.   1/7
       d.   1

Key: c.   1/7
       Given: N= 7 candidates and each has an equal opportunity of being selected
       Find: P(5th candidate is selected)
       This is the case of an equally likely probability where there are N=7 possible employees.

       Using the relative probability we get P(5th candidate selected) $= \dfrac{n}{N} = \dfrac{1}{7}$

26.   What is the probability of not obtaining a 5 on the first roll of a (6-sided) die?

       a.   1/6
       b.   0.1667

    c.   5/6

    d.   0.5

Key: c.   5/6

Given: One roll of a die, i.e., n = 1, 6 sides, i.e., total possible outcomes N = 6

Find: P(not obtaining a 5)

Event A = obtaining the 5 on the first roll of the die;

$$P(A = \text{getting 5 on first roll}) = \frac{n}{N} = \frac{1}{6}$$

Complement of event A is denoted as A' = not obtaining a 5.

Using the theorem for the probability of the complement[3] of an event A, we get

$$P(A' = \text{not getting a 5 on first roll}) = 1 - P(A) = 1 - \frac{1}{6} = \frac{5}{6}$$

27.   If probability of an event A occurring is 0.9, the probability of event A not occurring is

    a.   0.9

    b.   0.0

    c.   0.1

    d.   1.0

Key: c.   0.1

Given: P(A) = 0.90

Find: P(event A not occurring)

This is the case of the complement of an event A, and P(A' = event A not occurring) is given as:

P(A') = 1 − P(A) = 1 − 0.9 = 0.1

28.   A random variable X takes on the values of 1, 2, or 3 with probabilities of $\frac{(1+r)}{3}$, $\frac{(1+2r)}{3}$, and $\frac{(0.2+3r)}{3}$, respectively. Hence the value of r is

    a.   0.2667

    b.   0.3322

    c.   − 0.1333

    d.   0.1333

Key: d.   0.1333

Given: Random variable X takes different values x_i = 1, 2, and 3 and $P(x = 1) = \frac{(1+r)}{3}$,

$P(x = 2) = \frac{(1+2r)}{3}$, and $P(x = 3) = \frac{(0.2+3r)}{3}$

Find: value of r

Total probability is always 1.00 or 100%, i.e.,

---

[3] *Fundamental Concepts of Probability, Statistics, Regression and DOE* by Jagdish Vani, 3rd edition, April 1993, Section 1.

$P = P(x =1) + P(x =2) + P(x =3) = 1$ and substituting the values of each probability,

$\frac{(1+r)}{3} + \frac{(1+2r)}{3} + \frac{(0.2+3r)}{3} = 1$

Now simplify this equation $\frac{(1+r)+ (1+2r)+ (0.2+3r)}{3} =$

$1 + r + 1 + 2r + 0.2 + 3r = 3$. Now we can solve this for r as $6r = 0.80$

Hence $r = 0.1333$

29.   Based on the data in Question 28, the probabilities for each of the values 1, 2, and 3 of the random variable are :

   a.   0.1333, 0.2666, 0.3999, respectively
   b.   0.3778, 0.4222, 0.2000, respectively
   c.   0.1, 0.2, 0.3, respectively
   d.   0.3, 0.4, 0.3, respectively

Key: b.   0.3778, 0.4222, 0.2000, respectively

   Given: Random variable takes values x =1, 2, and 3; $P(x = 1) = \frac{(1+r)}{3}$, $P(x = 2) = \frac{(1+2r)}{3}$, and

   $P(x = 3) = \frac{(0.2+3r)}{3}$; and from Question 28, $r = 0.1333$

   Find: Find Probabilities P(x =1), P(x = 2) and P(x = 3)

   $P(x = 1) = \frac{(1+r)}{3} = \frac{(1+0.1333)}{3} = 0.3778$

   $P(x = 2) = \frac{(1+2r)}{3} = \frac{(1+2 \times 0.1333)}{3} = 0.4222$

   $P(x = 3) = \frac{(0.2+3r)}{3} = \frac{(0.2 +3 \times 0.1333)}{3} = 0.2000$

30.   The mean for the data in Question 28 is

   a.   1.0000
   b.   0.3333
   c.   1.8882
   d.   2.0000

Key: c.   1.8882

   Given: Random variable takes values xi = 1, 2, and 3; from Question 28, r = 0.1333; and from Question 29, P(x = 1) =0.3778, P(x = 2) = 0.4222, and P(x = 3) = 0.2000

   Find: Find the mean

   mean $\mu = E(X) = \sum x_i \times P(X= x_i)$

   $= (1) (0.3778) + (2) (0.4222) + (3) (0.2000)$

   $= 1.8222$

31.   A pair of fair dice is tossed. What is the probability of obtaining a sum of 6?

        a.   1/18
        b.   5/36
        c.   7/36
        d.   1/6

Key: b.   5/36
        Given: Sum of the values from a pair of dice
        Find: P(sum of 6)
        Each die has 6 total outcomes. Total possible outcomes when 2 die are tossed are:
        $N = n_1 \times n_2 = 6 \times 6 = 36$, i.e., the sample space will be these 36 sum values.

Table 3-1 Sum of the outcomes of two die in one toss

		DIE 1					
		1	**2**	**3**	**4**	**5**	**6**
D	**1**	2	3	4	5	6	7
I	**2**	3	4	5	6	7	8
E	**3**	4	5	6	7	8	9
2	**4**	5	6	7	8	9	10
	5	6	7	8	9	10	11
	6	7	8	9	10	11	12

Each outcome as the sum of the values from two die is shown in Table 3-1. There are n = 5 favorable outcomes (1, 5); (2,4); (3,3), (4,2); and (5,1) which have a sum of 6 as shown in the shaded boxes in Table 3-1.

Hence the probability of obtaining a sum of 6 is P(sum of 6) $= \dfrac{n}{N} = \dfrac{5}{36}$

32.   A pair of fair dice is tossed. What is the probability of obtaining a sum of 9?

        a.   4/36
        b.   1/9
        c.   0.111
        d.   all of the above

Key: d.   all of the above
        Given: Sum of the values from a pair of dice
        Find: P(sum of 9)
        Be careful here. Did you pick choice a, 4/36, as your answer? This is an obvious choice but other choices such as 1/9 and 0.111 are also correct. Hence the answer is *all of the above*.
        Each die has 6 total outcomes. Total possible outcomes when 2 dice are tossed are:
        $N = n_1 \times n_2 = 6 \times 6 = 36$, i.e., the sample space will be these 36 sum values.

Table 3-1 in Question 31 shows that there are n = 4 favorable outcomes (3, 6); (4, 5); (5, 4); and (6,3) which have a sum of 9.

The probability of obtaining a sum of 9 is P(sum of 9) = $\frac{n}{N} = \frac{4}{36} = \frac{1}{9} = 0.111$

The correct choice is d, all of the above.

33.   The probability of drawing a red card from a deck of ordinary playing cards in a random draw is

   a.   0.25
   b.   0.50
   c.   13/52
   d.   0.00

Key: b.   0.50
       Given: deck of ordinary cards, i.e., 52 cards
       Find: P(A = finding a red card in a single draw)
       Table 3-2 gives the total sample space or total number of outcomes.

Table 3-2 Deck of 52 cards

Denomi- nation	SUIT				Total
	Spade (Black)	Club (Black)	Heart (Red)	Diamond (Red)	
1 Ace	♠ A	♣ A	♥ A	♦ A	4
2 Deuce	♠ 2	♣ 2	♥ 2	♦ 2	4
3	♠ 3	♣ 3	♥ 3	♦ 3	4
4	♠ 4	♣ 4	♥ 4	♦ 4	4
5	♠ 5	♣ 5	♥ 5	♦ 5	4
6	♠ 6	♣ 6	♥ 6	♦ 6	4
7	♠ 7	♣ 7	♥ 7	♦ 7	4
8	♠ 8	♣ 8	♥ 8	♦ 8	4
9	♠ 9	♣ 9	♥ 9	♦ 9	4
10	♠ 10	♣ 10	♥ 10	♦ 10	4
Jack 'J'	♠ J	♣ J	♥ J	♦ J	4
Queen 'Q'	♠ Q	♣ Q	♥ Q	♦ Q	4
King 'K'	♠ K	♣ K	♥ K	♦ K	4
Total	13	13	13	13	52

Watch out! *Did you pick choice a: 0.25 or choice c:13/52 ? Did you pick only 13 Diamonds or 13 Hearts as the number of favorable outcomes as Red* and not a total of 26? If so, then it is not true. The number of red colored cards n = 13 Diamond +13 Heart cards = 26 red cards

Hence P(A = drawing a red card) = $\frac{n}{N} = \frac{26}{52} = 0.50$

34.   Find the probability of drawing a king of spades from a deck of playing cards in a single draw?

      a.   4/52
      b.   13/52
      c.   1/52
      d.   1/5

Key: c.   1/52

Given: Deck of playing cards, i.e., 52 cards; k = 4 kings; s =13 spade cards

Find: P(king of spades ♠K)

Refer to Table 3-2 in Question 33 above for the matrix of 52 cards. We can solve this 2 ways.

Method 1:   There is only one king of spades in a deck of 52 cards, i.e.,

P(king of spades) = number of favorable outcomes / total outcomes = $\dfrac{n}{N} = \dfrac{1}{52}$

Method 2:   Use the multiplication law for independent events.

Drawing a king is an independent event from drawing a spade. We can determine the probability of joint occurrence of both events as P(K and S).

P(K= drawing a king) = $\dfrac{k}{N} = \dfrac{4}{52}$ and P(S = drawing a spade) = $\dfrac{s}{N} = \dfrac{13}{52}$

Hence P(Drawing both, i.e., king of spade ♠K) = P(K and S) = P(K) × P(S)

P(K and S) = $\dfrac{4}{52} \times \dfrac{13}{52} = \dfrac{1}{52}$

35.   In case of mutually exclusive events,

      a.   P(A or B) = P(A) + P(B)
      b.   P(A and B) = 0
      c.   P(A and B) = P(A) × P(B)
      d.   a and b only
      e.   b and c only

Key: d.   a and b only

Mutually exclusive events mean that the occurrence of one event prevents the occurrence of the other event. The probability theorem for the mutually exclusive events is given as P(A or B) = P(A) + P(B). Also the joint probability P(A and B) = 0. Hence the choice c is incorrect because the joint probability P(A and B) is not possible for mutually exclusive events.

36.   If two events A and B are not mutually exclusive but are independent, the probability of either event A or B occurring is

      a.   the sum of the individual probabilities, i.e., P(A) + P(B)
      b.   the multiplication of the individual probabilities, i.e., P(A) × P(B)
      c.   the sum of the individual probabilities minus the probability of both occurring together, i.e., P(A) + P(B) − P(A) × P(B)
      d.   zero

Key: c.   the sum of the individual probabilities minus the probability of both occurring together,
             i.e., P(A) + P(B) − P(A) × P(B)
        The two events A and B are independent and not mutually exclusive events. Based on the
        theorems of probability, for two independent events A and B, the probability of A or B is given
        as: P(A or B) = P(A) + P(B) − P(A) × P(B)

        Hence choice a is incorrect for independent events as it does not subtract the joint probabilities
        P(A) × P(B) from the sum. Choice b of P(A) × P(B) is incorrect, because it describes only the
        joint probability of both events occurring together and not the probability of either A or B
        occurring.

37.   "Independent events" means

        a.   the occurrence of one event makes the occurrence of the other event impossible.
        b.   two events cannot occur at the same time.
        c.   the occurrence of one event has no bearing on the occurrence of the other event(s).
        d.   Both a and b above.

Key: c.   occurrence of one event has no bearing on the occurrence of the other event(s).
        Be careful here. You are likely to select choice d which is incorrect because the definitions in
        choices a and b are for mutually exclusive events and not for independent events.

38.   For two events A and B, one of the following is a true probability statement

        a.   P (A or B) = P (A) + P (B) if A and B are independent.
        b.   P (A or B) = P (A) + P (B) if A and B are mutually exclusive.
        c.   P (A and B) = P(A) × P(B) if A and B are mutually exclusive.
        d.   P (A or B) = P(A) × P(B) if A and B are independent.

Key: b.   P (A or B) = P (A) + P (B) if A and B are mutually exclusive.
        (Ref. Principles Question 19, July 1984)
        Mutually exclusive events are ones where if event A occurs, event B cannot occur. For two
        mutually exclusive events A and B, the probability that both will occur at the same time is zero,
        i.e., P(A and B) = 0. This will eliminate choice c. Choices a and d are incorrect because the
        formula should read as: For two independent events A and B, the probability that event A or B
        will occur is given as P(A or B) = P(A) + P(B) − P(A) × P(B). Hence P(A or B) = P(A) + P(B) if
        A and B are mutually exclusive events is a true statement.

39.   Which one of the following is a true statement of probability?

        a.   P(E and F) = P(E) + P(F)
        b.   P(E or F) = P(E) + P(E/F)
        c.   P(E or F) = P(E) + P(F) − P(E and F)
        d.   P(E and F) = P(E) + P(F) − P(E and F)

Key: c. $P(E \text{ or } F) = P(E) + P(F) - P(E \text{ and } F)$ (Ref. Principles Question 35, October 1972)
Choice c is the correct theorem of probability for independent events E and F. Choices a and d
are incorrect because the joint probability between E and F is given as the multiplication of the
two events as $P(E \text{ and } F) = P(E) \times P(F)$ and not the sum as in choice a. Choice b is an incorrect
statement of probability for any rule. It is not applicable for independent, mutually exclusive
events, conditional probabilities, or joint probabilities.

40.   A plant has two machines A and B. Based on the maintenance history, machine A's availability is
       90% and B's availability is 80%. What is the probability that on a given day machine A or B
       may not be available?

       a.   10%
       b.   2%
       c.   20%
       d.   28%

Key: d.   28%
       Given: Machine A is available: $P(A) = 0.90$ and B is available: $P(B) = 0.80$
       Find: P(A or B not available)
       Using the complement of the event,
       $P(A' = \text{machine A is not available}) = 1 - 0.90 = 0.10$ and
       $P(B' = \text{machine B is not available}) = 1 - 0.80 = 0.20$
       Events A and B are independent events as the availability of machine A does not affect or depend
       on the availability of machine B or vice versa. Similarly the events A' and B' are independent
       events. Hence the probability that machine A or B will not be available, i.e., P(A' or B') can be
       described by using the probability theorem for the independent events as follows:

       $$P(A \text{ or } B \text{ not available}) = P(A' \text{ or } B') = P(A') + P(B') - P(A') \times P(B')$$
       $$= 0.1 + 0.2 - (0.10)(0.20) = 0.28 \text{ or } 28\%$$

41.   A plant has two machines A and B. Based on the maintenance history, machine A's availability is
       90% and B's availability is 80%. What is the probability that both machines will be available at a
       given time ?

       a.   0.0
       b.   85%
       c.   72%
       d.   28%

Key: c.   72%
       Given: Machine A is available: $P(A) = 0.90$ and B is available: $P(B) = 0.80$
       Find: P(both machines A and B are available), i.e., P(A and B)
       Events A and B are independent events as the availability of machine A does not affect or
       depend on the availability of machine B or vice versa.

The joint probability for independent events is given by the multiplication rule as:
$P(A \text{ and } B) = P(A) \times P(B) = 0.9 \times 0.8 = 0.72$ or 72%

42.   Probability that car A will fail completely in 10 years is 0.9 and that car B will fail completely in 10 years is 0.95. What is the probability that both cars will fail in 10 years?

        a.   0.900
        b.   0.950
        c.   0.855
        d.   0.995

Key: c.   0.855
        Given: $P(A = \text{car A fails}) = 0.9$, $P(B = \text{car B fails}) = 0.95$
        Find: P(both cars will fail)
        Event A = car A fails in 10 years, Event B = car B fails in 10 years. Both events A and B are independent events as the failing of car A does not depend or affect the failing of car B.
        The joint probability for independent events A and B is given using the multiplication theorem.
        $P(A \text{ and } B) = P(A) \times P(B) = 0.9 \times 0.95 = 0.855$

43.   The editor of a newsletter on quality found that 70% of the members of a quality society subscribe to magazine A and 80% subscribe to magazine B. If she (he) selects a member at random, what is the probability that that member subscribes to at least one of the two magazines?

        a.   0.94
        b.   0.8
        c.   0.7
        d.   0.6

Key: a.   0.94
        Given: $P(A = \text{subscribing to magazine A}) = 70\%$ or 0.70
                $P(B = \text{subscribing to magazine B}) = 80\%$ or 0.80
        Find: P(at least one magazine)
        The key phrase is *at least one magazine* which means magazine A or B or both magazines. Hence we need to find P(A or B or both). This is given by the probability theorem of two independent events because the event A and B are two independent events.
        $$P(\text{magazine A or B or both}) = P(A) + P(B) - P(A \text{ and } B)$$
        $$= P(A) + P(B) - P(A) \times P(B)$$
        $$= 0.8 + 0.7 - (0.8) \times (0.7) = 0.94$$

44.   A process is turning out end items which have defects of type A or type B in them. If the probability of a type A defect is 0.10 and of a type B defect is 0.20, the probability that an end item will have no defect is

        a.   .02

b.   .28
c.   .30
d.   .72
e.   .68

Key: d.   .72   (Ref. Applications Question 14, August 1978)
Given: Two types of defects A or B; $P(A) = 0.10$; $P(B) = 0.20$
Find: P(no defects), i.e., P(no defects of A and B)
No defects means both defects A and B are not present. The complement of probabilities gives:
$P(\text{no defect A}) = P(A') = 1 - P(A) = 1 - 0.10 = 0.90$
$P(\text{no defect B}) = P(B') = 1 - P(B) = 1 - 0.20 = 0.80$
$P(\text{no defects}) = P(\text{no A and B defects}) = P(A') \times P(B') = 0.90 \times 0.80 = 0.72$

45.   A box contains 40 good and 20 bad parts of which half the good and half the bad are red-colored parts and the others are blue. Find the probability that a part chosen at random is good or is red-colored.

a.   50/60
b.   5/6
c.   0.833
d.   all of the above

Key: d.   all of the above
Given: Good = 40 parts; bad = 20 parts; total = 40 + 20 = 60 parts
        Half are red and half are blue, i.e., 30 are red and 30 are blue parts.
Find: P(choose a good part or a red-colored part)
Watch out! Did you pick either choice a or b or c at first sight? This is a common and psychological reaction to jump to an obvious answer, you have to be careful and must evaluate each choice. The correct answer is choice d, *all of the above.*

Table 3-3 The matrix of parts

	Red	Blue	Total
Good	20	20	40
Bad	10	10	20
Total	30	30	60

Refer to Table 3-3 to calculate different probabilities.

$P(\text{good part}) = P(G) = \dfrac{40}{60}$ and $P(\text{red part}) = P(R) = \dfrac{30}{60}$

Selecting a part as good or red are two independent events.

P(a good or a red part) = P(G or R) = P(G) + P(R) − P(G and R)

$$= \frac{40}{60} + \frac{30}{60} - \left(\frac{40}{60}\right) \times \left(\frac{30}{60}\right) = \frac{50}{60} = \frac{5}{6} = 0.833$$

Hence the appropriate answer will be *d, all of the above.*

46.   In the final audit area, you find two boxes of parts. Box A contains 200 parts, 60 of which are nonconforming, and box B has 150 parts, 40 of which are nonconforming. If you draw a part at random from each box, what is the probability that both items are nonconforming?

   a.   0.57
   b.   0.30
   c.   0.08
   d   0.29

Key: c.   0.08
   Given: Box A has 60 nonconforming out of 200 parts
          Box B has 40 nonconforming out of 150 parts
   Find: P(A and B both are nonconforming)

   Finding a nonconforming part from box A: $P(A) = \dfrac{60}{200} = 0.30$

   Finding a nonconforming part from box B: $P(B) = \dfrac{40}{150} = 0.267$

   The events A and B are independent events and hence the probability of finding both parts A and B as nonconforming is given by joint probability formula:
   $P(A \text{ and } B) = P(A) \times P(B) = 0.30 \times 0.267 = 0.08$ or 8%

47.   In the final audit area, you find two boxes of parts. Box A contains 200 parts, 60 of which are nonconforming, and box B has 150 parts, 40 of which are nonconforming. If you draw a part at random from each box, what is the probability that one item is conforming and one is nonconforming?

   a.   0.30
   b.   0.27
   c.   0.08
   d.   0.41

Key: d.   0.41
   Given: Box A has 60 nonconforming out of 200 parts
          Box B has 40 nonconforming out of 150 parts
   Find: P(one conforming and one nonconforming)
   We can solve this using two methods: 1: probability theorems and 2: binomial probability distribution.

   Method 1: Finding a nonconforming part from box A $P(A) = \dfrac{60}{200} = 0.30$, then a conforming part from box A: $P(A') = 1 - 0.30 = 0.70$

   Similarly, finding a nonconforming part from box B $P(B) = \dfrac{40}{150} = 0.267$, then a conforming part from box B: $P(B') = 1 - 0.267 = 0.733$

   There are four possible outcomes when we draw one part from each box, as shown in Table 3-4.

Table 3-4 Four types of outcomes

	B: part B conforming	B': part B nonconforming
A: part A conforming	P (A and B)	**P(A and B')**
A': part A nonconforming	**P(A' and B)**	P(A' and B')

There are two outcomes that have one conforming and one nonconforming outcome shown as P(A' and B) and P(A and B')

$$P(A' \text{ and } B) \quad = P(A \text{ conforming and B nonconforming})$$
$$= P(A') \times P(B) = 0.70 \times 0.267 = 0.19$$
$$P(A \text{ and } B') \quad = P(A \text{ nonconforming and B conforming})$$
$$= P(A) \times P(B') = 0.30 \times 0.733 = 0.22$$
$$P(\text{one conforming and one nonconforming}) = P(A' \text{ and } B) + P(A \text{ and } B')$$
$$= 0.19 + 0.22 \quad = 0.41 \text{ or } 41\%$$

Method 2: Using a Binomial Probability distribution as follows:
Total number of nonconforming parts = 60 + 40 = 100
Total number of parts = 200 + 150 = 350
Hence probability of finding a nonconforming part at any random draw is

$$p = P(\text{nonconforming}) = \frac{100}{350} = 0.286 \text{ which will be constant for each draw and}$$
$$q = 1 - p = 1 - 0.286 = 0.714$$

If we draw n = 2 parts at random, we can get r = 0 nonconforming, or 1 nonconforming or 2 nonconforming parts.

If we get *r = exactly 1 nonconforming* out of 2 draws, means one part is nonconforming and one will be a conforming part which can be expressed as follows:

$$P(r = 1) = \frac{n!}{r!(n-r)!} p^r q^{n-r} = \frac{2!}{1!(2-1)!} (0.286)^1 (0.714)^{2-1} = \frac{2}{1} (0.286)(0.714) = 0.41 \text{ or } 41\%.$$

48.   There is a 90% probability that each of your machines in next operation is busy, i.e., occupied with jobs at any moment. What is the probability that machine 1 and 2 both are busy at the same time?

    a.   0.9
    b.   0.10
    c.   0.01
    d.   0.81

Key: d.   0.81
Given: P(each machine busy) = 0.90, i.e.,
        P(A = machine 1 is busy) = 0.90 and P(B = machine 2 is busy) = 0.90
Find: P(machine 1 and machine 2 both are busy)
Both events A and B are independent events. Hence probability that both machine 1 and 2 are busy is given by the multiplication rule for two independent events as follows:

P(A and B both) = P(A & B) = P(A) × P(B) = 0.90 × 0.90 = 0.81

49.   Suppose that 5 bad electron tubes get mixed up with 8 good tubes. If 2 tubes are drawn simultaneously, what is the probability that both are good?

    a.   8/13
    b.   14/39
    c.   7/12
    d.   7/13
    e.   36/91

Key: b.   14/39   (Ref. Applications Question 9, August 1978)
    Given: 5 bad tubes, 8 good tubes, total N = 5+8 =13, r –2 tubes drawn.
    Find: P(both tubes are good)
    The key word is *simultaneously,* meaning two items are selected at the same time and there is *no replacement* of the items in the box. It means the probability changes for each trial.
    Event A= 1st draw of tube is good, i.e., $P(A) = \frac{8}{13}$.
    For the second draw, we have 8 –1 = 7 good tubes remaining out of total 13 –1 = 12 tubes.
    The "event B = 2nd draw of the tube is good| given that first tube was good" = $P(B|A) = \frac{7}{12}$

    This is a case of conditional probability theorem: $P(B|A) = \frac{P(A \text{ and } B)}{P(A)}$
    To find the joint probability of both tubes are good, rearrange the terms in the form of P(A and B) as follows: P(both tubes are good) = P(A and B) = $P(B|A) \times P(A) = \frac{7}{12} \times \frac{8}{13} = \frac{14}{39}$

50.   From a deck of playing cards, find the probability of obtaining a heart on the second draw, given that the first draw was also a heart without replacement.

    a.   4/17
    b.   13/52
    c.   1/16
    d.   1/4

Key: a.   4/17
    Given: Deck of 52 cards; 13 hearts, A = first draw heart, B = second draw heart, *no replacement*
    Find: P(2nd draw is heart given that the first was heart without replacement).
    The key phrase is *no replacement* indicating probability is not constant from draw to draw and hence use conditional probability.
    We can define P(A = first draw is heart) = $\frac{13}{52} = \frac{1}{4}$

Given that we have a heart card on the first draw and there is no replacement, it now contains 12 heart cards out of a total of 51 cards left. Hence the conditional probability of getting the second draw as heart, given that the first draw was a heart, is given as: $P(B|A) = \dfrac{12}{51} = \dfrac{4}{17}$

51.   From a deck of playing cards, what is the probability that two consecutive draws will be hearts without any replacement?

    a.   1/4
    b.   4/17
    c.   1/17
    d.   1/16

Key: c.   1/17

Given: Deck of 52 cards, 13 hearts, A = first draw heart; B = second draw heart, *no replacement*
Find: P(both are hearts in a consecutive draw) = P(A and B)

The key words are *no replacement* indicating probability is not constant from draw to draw and hence use conditional probability.

Refer to Question 20: $P(A = \text{first draw is a heart}) = \dfrac{13}{52} = \dfrac{1}{4}$ and the conditional probability of

2nd draw as a heart| given that first draw was a heart: $P(B|A) = \dfrac{12}{51} = \dfrac{4}{17}$.

The conditional probability theorem is given as $P(B|A) = \dfrac{P(A \text{ and } B)}{P(A)}$.

Hence the joint probability that both consecutive draws are hearts is as follows:

$$P(A \text{ and } B) = P(B|A) \times P(A) = \dfrac{4}{17} \times \dfrac{1}{4} = \dfrac{1}{17}$$

52.   If the probability of 1 or more defectives is 0.75, 2 or more defectives is 0.40, 3 or more defectives is 0.15, and 4 or more defectives is 0.06, what is the probability of 2 or less defectives?

    a.   0.25
    b.   0.85
    c.   0.60
    d.   0.15

Key: b.   0.85

Given: P(1 or more defectives) = 0.75   P(2 or more defectives) = 0.40
            P(3 or more defectives) = 0.10   P(4 or more defectives) = 0.60
Find: P(2 or less defectives)

The fundamental rule[4] is $P_0 + P_1 + P_2 + P_3 + P_4 \ldots + P_n = 1.0$

---

[4] *Fundamental Concepts of Probability, Statistics, Regression and DOE* by Jagdish Vani, 3rd edition, April 1993, Section 2.

$$P_0 + P_1 + P_2 + P_3 + P_4 \,.....\, + P_n = 1.0$$

$|\rightarrow\rightarrow\rightarrow\rightarrow\rightarrow\rightarrow\rightarrow\rightarrow$ indicates 1 or more defectives

$|\rightarrow\rightarrow\rightarrow\rightarrow\rightarrow\rightarrow\rightarrow$ indicates 2 or more defectives

$|\rightarrow\rightarrow\rightarrow\rightarrow\rightarrow\rightarrow$ indicates 3 or more defectives

$|\rightarrow\rightarrow\rightarrow$ indicates 4 or more defectives

P(1 or more defectives) means	$P_1 + P_2 + P_3 + P_4 + P_5 \,...+ P_n$	$= P(r \geq 1) = 0.75$
P(2 or more defectives) means	$P_2 + P_3 + P_4 + P_5 .... + P_n$	$= P(r \geq 2) = 0.40$
P(3 or more defectives) means	$P_3 + P_4 + P_5 \,...+ P_n$	$= P(r \geq 3) = 0.15$
P(4 or more defectives) means	$P_4 + P_5 ... + P_n$	$= P(r \geq 4) = 0.06$

$$P_0 + P_1 + P_2 + P_3 + P_4 +_{P5} \,..... \, P_n = 1.0$$

$\leftarrow\leftarrow\leftarrow\leftarrow\leftarrow \mid \rightarrow\rightarrow\rightarrow\rightarrow\rightarrow\rightarrow$

2 or less? | 3 or more

P(2 or less defectives) $= P_0 + P_1 + P_2 = 1 - (P3 + P4 + ...+ P_n)$

$= 1 - P(3 \text{ or more defectives})$

$= 1 - 0.15 = 0.85$

Make a habit of arranging the data in this manner and position yourself properly using the fundamental rule of probability. Decide which side is given by the available data and which needs to be calculated.

53.   In Question 52 above, what is the probability of finding exactly 2 defectives?

a.   0.25
b.   0.85
c.   0.60
d.   0.15

Key: a.   0.25

Given: P(1 or more defectives) = 0.75   P(2 or more defectives) = 0.40

P(3 or more defectives) = 0.10   P(4 or more defectives) = 0.60

Find: P(exactly 2 defectives)

The fundamental rule: $\mathbf{P_0 + P_1 + P_2 + P_3 + P_4 \,......P_n = 1.0}$

$|\rightarrow\rightarrow\rightarrow\rightarrow\rightarrow\rightarrow\rightarrow$ indicates 2 or more defectives

$|\rightarrow\rightarrow\rightarrow\rightarrow\rightarrow$ indicates 3 or more defectives

P(2 or more defectives) means	$P_2 + P_3 + P_4 + P_5 .... + P_n$	$= P(r \geq 2) = 0.40$
P(3 or more defectives) means	$P_3 + P_4 + P_5 \,...+ P_n$	$= P(r \geq 3) = 0.15$

$$P_0 + P_1 + P_2 + P_3 + P_4 +_{P5} \,..... \, P_n = 1.0$$

$|\rightarrow\rightarrow\rightarrow\rightarrow\rightarrow\rightarrow\rightarrow\rightarrow$ $P(r \geq 2)$

$|\leftrightarrow| \rightarrow\rightarrow\rightarrow\rightarrow\rightarrow\rightarrow\rightarrow$ $P(r \geq 3)$

$\mathbf{P_2}$

P(exactly 2 defectives) $P(r = 2) = P(r \geq 2) - P(r \geq 3) = 0.40 - 0.15 = 0.25$

54.   In case of permutation

      a.   the order of the arrangement is important
      b.   the order of the arrangement is not important
      c.   a collection of items is not in a particular sequence
      d.   all of the above

Key: a.   the order of the arrangement is important
A permutation is an arrangement of items in a particular order. Here the order of arrangement is important. A permutation is a collection of items distinguished by which way each item is arranged and by their sequence.

55. $\dfrac{n!}{(n-r)!}$ defines the

      a.   binomial probability distribution
      b.   combination of r items from a collection of n items
      c.   hypergeometric probability distribution
      d.   permutation of r items from a collection of n items

Key: d.   permutation of r items from a collection of n items
This is a simple and a basic concept. You need to understand the construction of various formulas for basic concepts. The formula represents the permutation of r items from a collection of n items, i.e., $P_r^n = \dfrac{n!}{(n-r)!}$. It can be misleading at first sight as a formula for combination because combination of r items given n items is expressed as $C_r^n = \dfrac{n!}{r!(n-r)!}$

56.   Given 6 books, how many sets can be arranged in lots of 3 but always in a different order

      a.   18 sets
      b.   54 sets
      c.   108 sets
      d.   120 sets

Key: d.   120 sets   (Ref. Principles Question 31, August 1978)
Given: n = 6 books, taking r = 3 books at a time, different order
Find: Number of book sets of 3 each in different order.
Here the order is important. It means it is a case of **permutation**
The permutation of n objects taken r at a time is given as $P_r^n = \dfrac{n!}{(n-r)!} = \dfrac{6 \times 5 \times 4 \times 3!}{3 \times 2 \times 1!} = 120$
Hence we can arrange a total of 120 sets of 3 books in different order.

57.   How many different ways can you make a team of 5 from a total of 10 players in any order?

        a.   30240
        b.   50
        c. $(10)^5$
        d.   252

Key: d.   252
        Given: n = 10 players, r = 5 players selected for a team.
        Find: Number of arrangements *in any order*
        This is a case of combination of n=10 players, r = 5 taken at a time as the order of arrangement is
        not important. The combination is given by the following formula.

$$C_r^n = \frac{n!}{r!(n-r)!} = \frac{10!}{5! \times 5!} = \frac{3,628,800}{120 \times 120} = 252$$

        where n! reads as n factorial and n! = n × (n-1) × (n-2) × (n-3) × .... × 0! and 0! =1
        For example, 5! = 5 × (5-4) × (5-3) ×........× 0 ! = 120

        *The breakdown of n! given above is to understand the concept. This function key is normally
        available on most of the scientific pocket calculators. You must read your calculator manual for
        details and practice it. You can get a straight answer for n! factorial by using the proper
        function key in the calculator. Also some of the calculators have function keys for both
        permutation and combination, then you can directly calculate the values in fewer steps without
        using the formula or equation.*

        *Questions of this type are simple and easy to solve by maximizing the use of the calculator and
        hence you must score correct. You cannot afford to lose points on such simple questions. You
        must practice more and more and capitalize on as many simple questions as possible.*

58.   A plant has 6 operators and only 3 machines operating on a particular day. In how many ways
        can you select 3 operators in any order to run each of the available machines ?

        a.   18
        b.   120
        c.   20
        d.   216

Key: c.   20
        Given: n = 6 operators and only 3 operators are selected to run the available machines
        Find: number of ways 3 operators can be selected in *any order*
        This is a case of *combination*, as the 3 operators can be selected in *any order* from 6 operators.

$$C_r^n = \frac{n!}{r!(n-r)!} \quad \text{i.e.} \quad C_3^6 = \frac{6!}{3!(6-3)!} = 20$$

59.   How many different ways can you arrange or display 5 books at a time out of 10 in any order?

    a.   30240
    b.   50
    c. $(10)^5$
    d.   252

Key: d.   252

Given: n = 10 books, r = 5 books arranged

Find: number of different arrangements of books in *any order*

This is a case of *combination,* as the order of arrangement is not important.

$$C_r^n = \frac{n!}{r!(n-r)!} = \frac{10!}{5! \times 5!} = \frac{3{,}628{,}800}{120 \times 120} = 252$$

60.   In nonparametric statistics

    a.   no assumptions are made concerning the distribution from which the samples are taken.
    b.   the parameters of the distribution must have no parameters in common.
    c.   the sample and the distribution must have no parameters in common.
    d.   none of the above.

Key: a.   no assumptions are made concerning the distribution from which the samples are taken.

(Ref. Principles Question 30, August 1978)

In the case of nonparametric statistics, we do not make any assumptions about the shape of the population distribution and it is called *distribution free*.

61.   An ungrouped frequency distribution is preferred when

    i.   we have a large number of observations.
    ii.   we have few observations.
    iii.   individual details are of importance.

    a.   i only
    b.   ii only
    c.   iii only
    d.   i and ii only
    e.   ii and iii only

Key: e.   ii and iii only

Ungrouped frequency distribution involves each observation individually instead of grouping them into cells of equal width. The ungrouped frequency distribution is preferred when we have only a few observations and individual details are of importance or sensitive. Hence grouping the data into cells does not provide meaningful information.

Watch i where we have a large number of observations. It is very difficult to use ungrouped frequency distribution just because of the mere size of the data. Also, it may not show a meaningful shape and size of the distribution as the frequency associated with each individual value may not be high. In such a case, grouping the data into cells will provide meaningful frequencies under each cell.

62.   When we arrange a set of measurements in order of magnitude and indicate the frequency associated with each measurement, we have constructed

        a.   a grouped frequency distribution
        b.   a cumulative frequency distribution
        c.   an ungrouped-grouped frequency distribution
        d.   a bar graph
        e.   a histogram

Key: c.   an ungrouped-grouped frequency distribution (Ref. Principles Question 6, October 1974)
        The key phrase is "*each measurement*." An ungrouped frequency distribution is the one where each individual measurement is recorded with its frequency. Here we do not create the cells of equal width for the different values of the characteristic but each measurement is recorded in order and its corresponding frequency is plotted.

63.   A frequency distribution described with cells or classes for data instead of individual data value is

        a.   ungrouped frequency distribution
        b.   grouped frequency distribution
        c.   a histogram
        d.   a bar graph

Key: b.   grouped frequency distribution
        Choice a is incorrect because it represents the ungrouped frequency distribution. Choices c and d are incorrect because a histogram can be used for either grouped or ungrouped frequencies. Also refer to Questions 61 and 62 above for additional discussion.

64.   The tabulation of the number of times a given quality characteristic measurement occurs within the sample of product being checked is called a

        a.   histogram
        b.   normal distribution
        c.   control chart
        d.   random function

Key: a.   histogram (Ref. ASQC CQT Examination, Core portion, Question 11)
        Choice b is incorrect because the tabulation of data in the form of the frequencies may or may not show a normal distribution.

65.   A histogram

    a.   does not explain the skewness
    b.   does not explain the spread of the distribution
    c.   does not explain the central tendency of the data
    d.   does not show the order in which the data were collected

Key: d.   does not show the order in which the data were collected
       A histogram shows the frequency of occurrence of the data but it loses the order of occurrence or
       data collection. It also does not provide any information on the time of occurrence. Such
       information can be preserved and analyzed through control charts or run charts.

66.   A frequency polygon

    a.   is a plot of connected points whose ordinates are proportional to cell frequencies
    b.   is also known as a cumulative relative frequency graph
    c.   is also known as a sample distribution function
    d.   applies only to discrete random variables

Key: a.   is a plot of connected points whose ordinates are proportional to cell frequencies
       (Ref. Principles Question 52, October 1972)
       A frequency polygon is a type of histogram where the frequencies of different values of a
       characteristic are shown as points instead of vertical bars. All such points are connected using a
       line chart. It only shows individual frequencies or relative frequencies and not the cumulative
       frequencies. It can be used for both random or discrete random variables.

67.   The relative frequency is

    a.   the number of the observations in a particular category
    b.   the number of cells in the histogram
    c.   the cell width in the histogram
    d.   the ratio of the number of the observations in a particular category to the total number
          of the observations

Key: d.   the ratio of the number of the observations in a particular category to the total number
             of the observations
       The relative frequency can be described simply as n/N where n is the frequency of observations
       and N is the total number of observations.

68.   The Y axis of a cumulative probability function shows

    a.   the incremental probability of events
    b.   the probability of an event for a given X
    c.   the relative frequency of events

  d. the relative frequency of events equal to or less than a given X
  e. all of the above

Key: d. the relative frequency of events equal to or less than a given X
(Ref. Principles Question 22, October 1974)
The Y axis on a cumulative probability function is the cumulative frequency or cumulative relative frequency data. Hence for any characteristics of interest, the Y axis shows the total / cumulative frequency of events equal to or less than a given X.

69. Figure 3-1 shows:

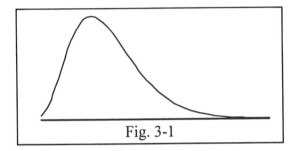
Fig. 3-1

  a. a normal distribution
  b. a positively skewed distribution
  c. a negatively skewed distribution
  d. an exponential distribution

Key: b. a positively skewed distribution
Figure 3-1 shows a positively skewed distribution where the tail runs toward the right side more.

70. Figure 3-2 shows:

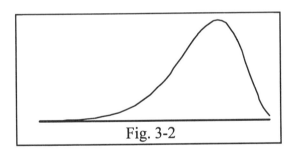
Fig. 3-2

  a. a normal distribution
  b. a positively skewed distribution
  c. a negatively skewed distribution
  d. an exponential distribution

Key: c. a negatively skewed distribution
Figure 3-2 shows a negatively skewed distribution where the tail runs toward the left side more.

71. Figure 3-3 shows the following distributions:

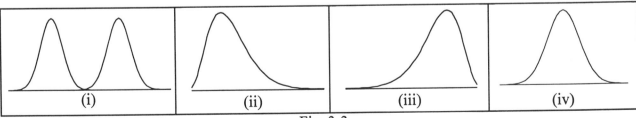
Fig. 3-3

     a.   i: normal, ii: positively skewed, iii: negatively skewed, iv: bimodal
     b.   i: bimodal, ii: positively skewed, iii: negatively skewed, iv: normal
     c.   i: positively skewed, ii: negatively skewed, iii: normal, iv: bimodal
     d.   i: bimodal, ii: negatively skewed, iii: positively skewed, iv: normal

Key: b.   i: bimodal, ii: positively skewed, iii: negatively skewed, iv: normal

This is a simple question based on the properties of distributions.[5] Some distributions are bimodal (i), positively skewed (ii), negatively skewed (iii), and others may be normal (iv).

72.   Figure 3-4 shows

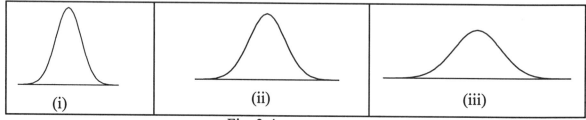

Fig. 3-4

     a.   i. leptokurtic, ii. platykurtic, iii. mesokurtic
     b.   i. platykurtic, ii. leptokurtic, iii. mesokurtic
     c.   i. leptokurtic, ii. mesokurtic, iii. platykurtic
     d.   i. mesokurtic, ii. platykurtic, iii. leptokurtic

Key: c.   i. leptokurtic, ii. mesokurtic, iii. platykurtic

73.   _____ is a location parameter

     a.   standard deviation
     b.   mean
     c.   variance
     d.   range

Key: b.   mean

The mean indicates the location where most of the data is grouped or concentrated.

74.   _____ describes the magnitude, i.e., location of the distribution.

     a.   the mean
     b.   the median
     c.   the mode
     d.   the standard deviation

---

[5] *Fundamental Concepts of Probability, Statistics, Regression and DOE* by Jagdish Vani, 3rd edition, April 1993, Section 2.

Key: a.   the mean
        Mean is the location parameter and describes the magnitude of the data as the average value.

75.   What is the mean height of five men who have the following heights: 5'6", 5'9", 5'4", 5'11", 5'8".

       a.   6'0"
       b.   5'5"
       c.   5'6 1/2"
       d.   5'7 3/5"

Key: d.   5'7 3/5"   (Ref. ASQC-CQT Examination, Core portion Question 4)

76.   If you multiply all the data by a constant

       a.   the mean becomes double.
       b.   mean decreases by the same magnitude of the constant.
       c.   mean increases by the same amount as the constant.
       d.   it does not affect the value of the mean at all.

Key: c.   mean increases by the same amount as the constant.
       Example: Assume that we are given this data: 5, 3, 4, 4, 3, 5
                   The mean = (5 + 3 + 4 + 4 +3 + 5)/6 = 24/6 = 4
                   Now multiply each value by a constant 2.
                   New data is 10, 6, 8, 8, 6, 10.
                   New mean = (10 + 6 + 8 + 8 + 5 +10)/6 = 48/6 = 8
                   New mean of 8 is two times the original mean and it is increased by the same amount
                   as the constant 2.
       Note: *Use the statistical function for calculating mean in your calculator and be familiar with
               the key entry by practicing a few questions given here.*

77.   If you add a constant to each data value,

       a.   the mean increases because it gets multiplied by the same value as a constant.
       b.   the mean decreases because it gets multiplied by the same value as a constant.
       c.   the constant value gets added to the mean and the mean is increased in the value by
             adding the same constant value.
       d.   it does not affect the value of the mean at all.

Key: c.   the constant value gets added to the mean and the mean is increased in the value by
             adding the same constant value.
       Example: Assume that we are given this data: 5, 3, 4, 4, 3, 5
                   Mean = (5 + 3 + 4 + 4 + 3 + 5)/6 = 24/6 = 4
                   Add a constant of 3 to each value
                   New data is 8, 6, 7, 7, 6, 8

New mean is $(8 + 6 + 7 + 7 + 6 + 8)/6 = 42/6 = 7$

New mean is increased to 7 from 4, i.e., the constant 3 is added to the mean, and the new mean is increased in value by adding the same constant value.

78. _____ describes the most likely value of the distribution

   a.   the mean
   b.   the median
   c.   the mode
   d.   the standard deviation

Key: c.   the mode
The mode is defined as the most frequently occurring value and hence is the most likely value of the distribution.

79.   The most frequently occurring value of the random variable x is called

   a.   the median
   b.   the mode
   c.   the mean
   d.   the range

Key: b.   the mode

80.   The mean and median of the following data are: 1, 2, 3, 4, 5

   a.   Mean = 3 median = 3.5
   b.   Mean = 0, median = 3
   c.   mean = 3, median = 3
   d.   mean = 3, median = 2.5

Key: c.   mean = 3, median = 3
Given: Data of n = 5 samples
Find: Mean and median
Mean $\overline{X} = \dfrac{\sum X_i}{n} = \dfrac{1+2+3+4+5}{5} = \dfrac{15}{3} = 3$
Data: 1, 2, 3, 4, 5 indicates that the middle value is the 3rd value, i.e., median =3

81.   Which of the following is true?

   a.   The mean divides the area of a distribution into two equal halves.
   b.   The median divides the area of a distribution into two equal halves.
   c.   The mode divides the area of a distribution into two equal halves.

d.   The mean is not sensitive to extreme values of data.

Key: b.   The median divides the area of a distribution into two equal halves.
The median *always* divides the distribution in two halves, i.e., 50% of the data is below and 50% of the data is above the median, regardless of the type of distribution. All other choices are incorrect.

82.   The mean, median, and mode for the following data set is: 3, 5, 2, 6, 5, 9, 5, 2, 8, 6.

    a.   5,   5,   5.1
    b.   5,   5.1, 5
    c.   5.1, 5.1, 0
    d.   5.1, 5,   5

Key: d.   5.1, 5,   5
Given: The raw data set for 10 values.
Find: The mean, median, and mode.

Mean $\quad \overline{X} = \dfrac{\sum X_i}{n} = \dfrac{3+5+2+6+5+9+5+2+8+6}{10} = 5.1$

Median: Rearranging the data in increasing order and then taking the average of 5th and 6th data values: 2, 2, 3, 5, **5, 5**, 6, 6, 8, 9
The 5th and 6th values are 5 and 5. Hence the median is the average of $(5+5)/2 = 5$.
Mode: The most frequently occurring number is 5.

83.   The median for the following data is: 30, 29, 27, 34, 35, 26, 31.

    a.   30.29
    b.   30
    c.   29 + 30 / 2
    d.   no median

Key: b.   30
Given: n = 7 data.
Find: Median.
Median is defined as the midpoint of the data if we rearrange the data in an increasing manner. From the given data: 26, 27, 29, **30**, 31, 34, 35, the midpoint is 4th data = 30.

84.   If a distribution is skewed to the left, the median will always be

    a.   less than the mean
    b.   between the mean and mode
    c.   greater than the mode
    d.   equal to the mean
    e.   none of the above

Key: b.   between the mean and mode   (Ref. Principles Question 6, August 1978)
        Median is always in the middle of mean and mode irrespective of type of distribution, i.e.,
        whether it is skewed, normal, etc.

        Refer to Figure 3-5 (c) which shows a distribution skewed to the left, i.e., negatively skewed
        distribution. It shows that the median is greater than the mean, i.e., choice a is wrong. Also it is

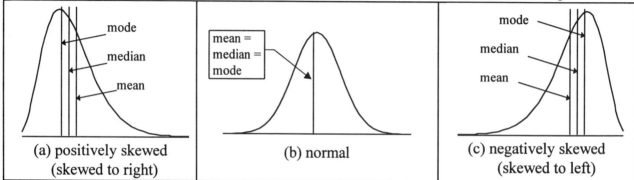

        (a) positively skewed   (b) normal   (c) negatively skewed
            (skewed to right)   (skewed to left)

Fig. 3-5 Mean, mode, and median for various distributions.

        less than the mode, i.e., choice c is wrong. Only in the case of a normal distribution, the mean,
        median, and mode are the same which makes choice d wrong because it is not a normal
        distribution but it is skewed to the left.

85.   Which one of the following is always true?

        a.   The mean of the distribution is always the fiftieth percentile of the distribution.
        b.   The mode of the distribution is always the fiftieth percentile of the distribution.
        c.   The median of the distribution is always the fiftieth percentile of the distribution.
        d.   Standard deviation of the distribution is always the fiftieth percentile of the distribution.

Key: c.   The median of the distribution is always the fiftieth percentile of the distribution.
        The key phrase in the question is *always true*. The median *always* divides the distribution in two
        halves, i.e., 50% of the data are below and 50% of the data are above the median, regardless of
        the type of the distribution.

        Watch for choice a because the mean is the average of all the data and it is the fiftieth percentile
        of the distribution in case of *normal distribution* only and therefore *not always*. But if the
        distribution is nonnormal or skewed, the mean is pulled away in the direction of the tail.
        Similarly watch for choice b where mode represents the most frequently occurring value; and
        like mean, it is the fiftieth percentile of the distribution only if it is *normal distribution* and
        therefore *not always*.

86.   The mean of either a discrete or a continuous distribution can always be visualized as

        a.   the point where 50% of the values are to the left side and 50% are to the right side
        b.   its center of gravity

c.   the point where the most values in the distribution occur

d.   all of the above

Key: b.   its center of gravity   (Ref. Principles Question 21, August 1978)
The mean of a distribution is the location parameter and it is also called the first moment of the distribution. It locates the point where the distribution will balance, i.e., its center of gravity.

87.   In case of normal distribution,

a.   mean is the fiftieth percentile of the distribution
b.   mode is the fiftieth percentile of the distribution
c.   median is the fiftieth percentile of the distribution
d.   a, b, and c only

Key: d.   a, b, and c only
In case of the normal distribution, mean, mode and median are at the same value and they divide the distribution into two equal halves, i.e., as the fiftieth percentile.

88.   For the normal distribution the relationships among the median, mean, and mode are that

a.   they are all equal to the same value.
b.   the mean and mode have the same value but the median is different.
c.   each has a value different from the other two.
d.   the mean and median are the same but the mode is different.

Key: a.   they are all equal to the same value   (Ref. Principles Question 5, July 1984)

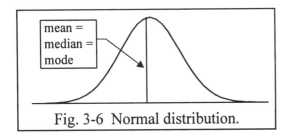

Fig. 3-6 Normal distribution.

The normal distribution is symmetrical on both sides of the mean. Hence the mean, median, and mode are all equal to the same value and they divide the distribution into two equal halves as shown in Figure 3-6.

89.   When performing calculations on sample data

a.   the cumulative relative frequency graph that is often used is called a histogram.
b.   rounding the data has no effect on the mean and standard deviation.
c.   coding the data has no effect on the mean and standard deviation.
d.   coding and rounding affect both the mean and standard deviation.

Key: d.   coding and rounding affect both the mean and standard deviation.
(Ref. Applications Question 37, October 1972)

Choice a is wrong because histogram shows the actual or relative frequencies of occurrence and not the cumulative frequencies. Choice b is incorrect because rounding off the data affects both the mean and the standard deviation.

For example, assume the data are: 5.14, 5.21, 5.17, 5.18, 5.12, 5.16, 5.14
This data gives a mean = 5.16 and sample standard deviation S = 0.03
Now round off above data to 1 decimal: 5.1, 5.2, 5.2, 5.2, 5.1, 5.2, 5.1
This rounded data gives a rounded off mean = 5.2 and S = 0.1. This example shows a significant effect of rounding off on mean and standard deviation.

Choice c is wrong because the coding does affect the mean. The mean gets reduced or increased by the amount of coding. Standard deviation does not change if data are coded.
For example, assume the data are: 5.14, 5.21, 5.17, 5.18, 5.12, 5.16, 5.14;
the mean = 5.16, S = 0.03 and code the above data by subtracting 5.00 from the data,
we get new coded data as : 0.14, 0.21, 0.17, 0.18, 0.12, 0.16, 0.14
New mean = 0.16 and S = 0.03 which indicates that the standard deviation has remained the same as 0.03, but mean has been reduced from 5.16 to 0.16.

90.   Which one of the following is a true statement?

    a.   the mean is very sensitive to extreme values
    b.   the mode is very sensitive to extreme values
    c.   the median is sensitive to extreme values
    d.   mean, mode, or median are not sensitive to extreme values

Key: a.   the mean is very sensitive to extreme values
The key phrase in the question is *true statement*. The mean is always sensitive to extreme values and gets pulled away from the point of central tendency in the direction of the extreme values or skewness.[6] Mode is the most frequently occurring value and hence is not sensitive to extreme values. Median is the midpoint or middle value that divides the data into two halves and hence is not sensitive to extreme values.

91.   A bin contains 40 pills with a weight of 3.1 grams each, 30 pills weighing 3.2 grams and 10 pills weighing 3.3 grams. The weight of an average pill is found from

    a. $\dfrac{3.1 + 3.2 + 3.3}{3}$

    b. $\dfrac{3.1(40) + 3.2(30) + 3.3(10)}{3}$

    c. $\dfrac{(3.1 + 3.2 + 3.3)(10 + 30 + 40)}{80}$

    d. $\overline{X} = \dfrac{3.1(40) + 3.2(30) + 3.3(10)}{80}$

---

[6] *Fundamental Concepts of Probability, Statistics, Regression and DOE* by Jagdish Vani, 3rd edition, April 1993, Section 2.

Key: d. $\overline{X} = \dfrac{3.1(40) + 3.2(30) + 3.3(10)}{80}$ (Ref. Applications Question 15, August 1978)

Given: Number of pills having different weights $f_1 = 40$ pills with $X_1 = 3.1$ grams; $f_2 = 30$ pills with $X_2 = 3.2$ grams; and $f_3 = 10$ pills with $X_3 = 3.3$ grams

Find: The average weight of a pill

This is the case of a weighted average and not a simple arithmetic average. A weighted average is used instead of a simple arithmetic mean when different samples do not have the same frequency or sample size or all values do not have equal weight.

If we denote X_i as the weight and f_i as the number of observations or frequency of data, we can calculate $\overline{X} = \dfrac{\sum X_i \times f_i}{\sum f_i} = \dfrac{X_1 f_1 + X_2 f_2 + X_3 f_3 \ldots \ldots X_n f_n}{f_1 + f_2 + f_3 \ldots \ldots f_n}$

$$\overline{X} = \dfrac{3.1(40) + 3.2(30) + 3.3(10)}{40 + 30 + 10} = \dfrac{3.1(40) + 3.2(30) + 3.3(10)}{80}$$

92.   There are 15 students having less than 2 years college education, 20 with 4 years BS education, and 5 having 6 years MS education. The mean number of years of education of the students is

   a.   3.5
   b.   3.33
   c.   13.33
   d.   46.67

Key: a.   3.5

Given: $f_1 = 15$ students $X_1 = 2$ years education
           $f_2 = 20$ students $X_2 = 4$ years education
           $f_3 = 5$ students $X_3 = 6$ years education

Find: The mean number of years education

This is a case of weighted average because the number of students is not the same for each type of college education.

$$\overline{X} = \dfrac{\sum X_i \times f_i}{\sum f_i} = \dfrac{X_1 f_1 + X_2 f_2 + X_3 f_3}{f_1 + f_2 + f_3} = \dfrac{15 \times 2 + 20 \times 4 + 5 \times 6}{15 + 20 + 5} = 3.5 \text{ years}$$

93.   During a self-assessment for an audit, a quality engineer assigned a rating of 5 to 18 items, 4 to 20 items, 3 to 33 items, 2 to 16, and 1 to the remaining items from a total of 100 items. The mean rating is

   a.   0.15
   b.   6.667
   c.   1
   d.   3.14

Key: d.   3.14

Given: $f_1 = 18$ items $X_1 = $ rating of 5
          $f_2 = 20$ items $X_2 = $ rating of 4
          $f_3 = 33$ items $X_3 = $ rating of 3
          $f_4 = 16$ items $X_4 = $ rating of 2
          $f_5 = 13$ items $X_5 = $ rating of 1,   Total 100 items

Find: The mean rating.

This is a case of weighted average where the number of items is not the same for each rating of X_i. The mean of audit ratings is given as follows:

$$\overline{X} = \frac{\sum X_i \times f_i}{\sum f_i} = \frac{X_1 f_1 + X_2 f_2 + X_3 f_3}{f_1 + f_2 + f_3} = \frac{18 \times 5 + 20 \times 4 + 33 \times 6 + 16 \times 2 + 13 \times 1}{18 + 20 + 33 + 16 + 13} = 3..14$$

94.   Standard deviation is expressed as

   a.   a unitless quantity
   b.   the same unit as the original unit of measure
   c.   the square of the original unit of measure
   d.   the square root of the original unit of measure

Key: b.   the same unit as the original unit of measure

Standard deviation is calculated from the measurements of some characteristic, and it gives a measure of the variability of the data in the same unit as the original unit.

The formula is: $S = \sqrt{\sum (X_i - \overline{X})^2 / n - 1}$

For example, a characteristic is diameter in millimeters (mm). You can calculate the average $\overline{X}$ in mm. To calculate its standard deviation, first square the deviation of individual measurement from its mean as mm^2, add all these squares, and then take the square root of this sum of squares which will make the unit mm. Hence the standard deviation will also be in mm, the same as the original unit of measure.

It is neither the square nor the square root of the original unit of the measure. Watch for choice c or d as a possible obvious choice on the first thought, but they are not true when you understand the composition of the formula.

95.   Standard deviation represents

   a.   the location of the data
   b.   the scatter of the data
   c.   both the location and scatter of the data
   d.   the shape of the data

Key: b.   the scatter of the data

Standard deviation indicates the variability or the dispersion of the data, i.e., the scatter of the data. Watch choice a because the mean represents the location of the data and not the standard deviation.

96. $\sqrt{\dfrac{\sum X^2 - n\overline{X}^2}{n-1}}$ is an expression for

    a.   the population standard deviation
    b.   the sample variance
    c.   the sample standard deviation
    d.   the confidence interval for the population mean

Key: c.   the sample standard deviation
This is the shortcut formula for the sample standard deviation based on the individual values.

97.   A vending machine is filling the coffee cups. A random sample of 12 cups was measured in fluid ounces to determine the variability. Calculate the sample average and sample standard deviation of the following data.

          12.1   12.2   11.9   12.3   11.9   12.0
          11.8   11.9   12.0   12.0   12.1   11.8

    a.   12,   0.1537
    b.   12,   0.1472
    c.   12,   0.0236
    d.   12,   0.0217

Key: a.   12,   0.1537
Given: n = 12 cups sample data.

Find: Sample average $\overline{X}$ and sample standard deviation S.

This is a simple bonus question, and solve it using the calculator. Get $\overline{X}$ = 12 and sample standard deviation S = 0.1537.

Most of the commonly available scientific calculators have two separate function keys for calculating sample and population standard deviation. Most of them use S, or s, or σ_{n-1}, or S_{n-1} notations or the symbols for sample standard on the function key. Refer carefully to your calculator manual for proper key notation and steps to enter the data. Be careful to use the proper function key for sample standard deviation and not the population standard deviation function key. Also be careful in data entry.

98.   What is the standard deviation of the following sample: 3.2, 3.1, 3.3, 3.3, 3.17? (The answer was corrected by ASQC.)

    a.   3.2

      b.   0.0894
      c.   0.10
      d.   0.0498
      e.   0.20

Key: b.   0.0894 (This is the corrected answer.) (Ref. Applications Question 6, July 1984)
Given: n = 5 sample data.
Find: Sample standard deviation S.
Hence you should enter the data using the calculator and you should get S= 0.0894.

99.   Calculate the standard deviation of the following set of five sample observations: 1.5, 1.2, 1.1, 1.0, 2.4.

      a.   0.756
      b.   0.858
      c.   0.568
      d.   0.500

Key: c.   0.568   (Ref. ASQC-CQT Examination, Core portion Question 3)
Given: 5 samples data.
Find: Sample standard deviation.
Use your calculator to calculate sample standard deviation S= 0.568. (The fifth data value was not given in the original question. Author has added the value to match the answer.)

100.   Calculate the standard deviation of the following complete set of data : 52, 20, 24, 31, 35, 42.

      a.   10.8
      b.   11.8
      c.   12.8
      d.   13.8

Key: a.   10.8   (Ref. Applications Question 52, October 1972)
Given: n = 6 raw data of the population, the key phrase is *complete set* indicating population
Find: The population standard deviation σ.
Use your calculator and you should get population standard deviation σ = 10.8 (rounded off).
Watch out! Looking at n = 6 data values, you are likely to jump to calculate this as sample standard deviation S which is 11.8, choice b, but it is incorrect. The question uses the key term *complete set* which means this is all the data that you have. It represents the entire population and not a sample data. The population can be as small as a few units in case of space shuttles, prototype parts, etc.

101.   Variance is

      a.   the difference between actual and assumed values

     b.   equal to 1.0 in most normal distributions

     c.   the square root of the standard deviation

     d.   the square of the standard deviation

     e.   the standard error of the mean

Key: d.   the square of the standard deviation (Ref. ASQC CQT Examination, Core Question 14)
Choice a is incorrect because the difference between actual and assumed values is normally called the deviation or the gap. Choice b is wrong because variance equals 1.0 only for standardized normal distribution where the raw data are transformed or converted into Z values. Choice c is easy to rule out based on the formula of variance.
Choice e is incorrect because the *standard error of the means* σ_x is defined by the central limit theorem (CLT) as follows: *If the sample size of a random sample is n, then the sample mean* $\overline{X}$ *has a normal distribution with mean* μ *and standard deviation* $\sigma_x = \sigma/\sqrt{n}$ *where* μ *and* σ *are the population mean and population standard deviation, respectively.*

102.   Quality control has been labeled as the science and art of identifying and controlling variability. One measure of variability as used in this context is

     a.   the arithmetic mean

     b.   the size of a lot

     c.   the mode

     d.   the variance

     e.   the geometric mean

Key: d.   the variance   (Ref. Principles Question 12, October 1974)
Variance is the sum of the squared deviations divided by the sample size n and is denoted as σ^2,

i.e., $\sigma^2 = \dfrac{\sum (X_i - \mu)^2}{n}$. This is one of the most widely used measures of variability. The remaining items, such as the arithmetic mean, the mode, and the geometric mean, represent the different measures of central tendency and not the variability. The size of the lot indicates the sample size only and not the variability of the sample data.

103.   The sum of the squared deviations of a group of the measurements from their mean divided by the number of the measurements equals

     a. σ

     b. σ^2

     c.   zero

     d.   X

     e.   the mean deviation

Key: b. σ^2 (Ref. Principles Question 8, August 1978)

Variance is defined as $\sigma^2 = \dfrac{\sum(X_i - \mu)^2}{n}$; where the numerator $\sum(X_i - \mu)^2$ is the sum of the squared deviations of the observations from their mean and it is divided by n measurements. Choice a is σ, which is incorrect because it is the standard deviation and not the variance. The rest of the choices are incorrect because they do not meet the definition of σ^2.

104.   The variance for the following sample data is: 43, 34, 40, 49, 37, 44, 51, 39.

    a.   5.4414
    b.   29.609
    c.   5.8171
    d.   33.8392

Key: d.   33.8392
        Given: 8 samples data.
        Find: Sample variance.

This is the case of sample variance $S^2 = \dfrac{\sum(X_i - \overline{X})^2}{n-1}$ and not the population variance σ^2.

Any simple calculator with statistical function keys can give you the value of sample standard deviation S. Then square it to get variance S^2. Refer carefully to your calculator manual for the proper steps to enter the data.

Using a calculator, you should get S = 5.817 and hence $S^2 = (5.817)^2 = 33.8392$.

105.   Estimate the variance of the population from which the following sample data came: 22, 18, 17, 20, 21.

    a.   4.3
    b.   2.1
    c.   1.9
    d.   5.0

Key: a.   4.3   (Ref. Applications Question 47, October 1972)
        Given: Sample data for 5 samples
        Find: S^2
        The key word is *variance* and not the standard deviation. Use your calculator and you should get
        S = 2.0736 and $S^2 = (2.0736)^2 = 4.3$.

106.   What is the best estimate of the variance of the population from which the following sample came: 17, 20, 18, 22, 21?

    a.   3.44
    b.   4.3

      c.   5.00
      d.   2.10

Key: b.   4.3   (Ref. Applications Question 63, October 1974)
      Given: raw data of n = 5 samples
      Find: S^2
      Using a scientific calculator, $S^2 = (2.074)^2 = 4.3$ (See Question 105 above.)

107. Which of the following statistical measures of the variability is not dependent on the exact value of every measurement?

      a.   interquartile range
      b.   variance
      c.   range
      d.   coefficient of variation
      e.   none of the above

Key: c.   range   (Ref. Principles Question 10, August 1978)
      The key phrase is *not dependent*. Be careful in selecting the answer.
      Range is defined as a difference between the highest value and the lowest value, i.e.,
      R = High − Low. Hence it does not depend on the exact value of every measurement.

      The interquartile range is the difference between the third quartile Q_3 (i.e., 75th percentile) and the first quartile Q_1 (i.e., 25th percentile).[7] It depends upon the exact value of every measurement to calculate the 25th percentile and 75th percentile. Hence choice a is not the correct choice.

      Variance depends upon each X_i, i.e., exact value of every measurement. Hence choice b is not the correct choice. Coefficient of variation[8] (CV) also depends on exact value of every measurement as it is the ratio of standard deviation S to its mean and is given as $CV = s/\overline{X}$. Hence choice d is wrong.

108. Which of the following measures of variability is *not* dependent on the exact value of every measurement?

      a.   mean deviation
      b.   variance
      c.   range
      d.   standard deviation
      e.   none of the above

Key: c.   range   (Ref. Principles Question 19, October 1974)

---

[7] *Theory and Problems of Statistics* by Murray R. Spiegel, Schaum's Outline Series, 2nd edition, McGraw-Hill, New York, Chapter 4, pg. 87.
[8] *Juran's Quality Control Handbook* by J. M. Juran, 4th edition, McGraw-Hill, New York, pg. 23-18.

Please refer to comments in Question 107, which covers all the terms except mean deviation.

The mean deviation[9] or the average deviation is given as MD = $\dfrac{\sum \left| X_i - \overline{X} \right|}{n}$. You can see that here the deviation of each individual X_i from the sample mean $\overline{X}$ is added as an absolute value but it is not squared. That is the major difference in MD and variance or standard deviation formula. Hence MD also depends on exact value of each measurement.

109.   A sample of n observations has a mean $\overline{X}$ and standard deviation $s_x > 0$. If a single observation which equals the value of the sample mean $\overline{X}$ is removed from the sample, which of the following is true?

   a. $\overline{X}$ and s_x both change.
   b. $\overline{X}$ and s_x remain the same.
   c. $\overline{X}$ remains the same but s_x increases.
   d. $\overline{X}$ remains the same but s_x decreases.

Key: c. $\overline{X}$ remains the same but s_x increases.   (Ref. Principles Question 7, July 1984)
   Example: Assume that you are given the following data: 5, 4, 5, 3, 3. n = 5
   Mean $\overline{X}$ and s_x are $\overline{X} = 4$ and $s_x = 1$ for n = 5.
   Now, remove the data value X = 4, which equals the sample mean $\overline{X}$, from the sample.
   Hence the sample will be 5, 5, 3, 3 and n = 4 as we removed one observation value of 4.
   The new mean $\overline{X}$ and s_x are $\overline{X} = 4$ and $s_x = 1.1547$ for n = 4. (You should be able to do this type of calculation of mean and sample standard deviation or population standard deviation using most of the scientific calculators. Hence formulas for $\overline{X}$ and s_x are not used here.) We can see that $\overline{X} = 4$ did not change when the value of one observation $X_i = 4$ is removed from the data, but its s_x increased from $s_x = 1.00$ to $s_x = 1.1547$.

110.   Sample data is as follows: 5, 4, 5, 3, 3. It was later found that the observation value of 4 in this sample was not correct and it was dropped. This means

   a.   the mean will reduce but standard deviation S will remain the same.
   b.   the mean will remain the same but standard deviation S will increase.
   c.   both mean and standard deviation S will increase.
   d.   both mean and standard deviation S will decrease.

Key: b.   the mean will remain the same but standard deviation S will increase.
   Given: n = 5 sample values, and a sample value of 4 was dropped.
   Find: Effect of dropping the data on sample mean and standard deviation.
   Before data: n = 5 samples, $\overline{X} = 4$ and S = 1

---

[9] *Theory and Problems of Statistics* by Murray R. Spiegel, Schaum's Outline Series, 2nd edition, McGraw-Hill, New York, Chapter 4, pg. 88.

After data: n = 4 samples, $\overline{X}_{new}$ = 4 and S_{new} = 1.1547
Hence the mean remains the same but S has increased.

111.   The standard deviation as a percent of the mean is called

    a.   relative precision
    b.   coefficient of variability
    c.   standard deviation of the mean
    d.   standard error

Key: b.   coefficient of variability   (Ref. Principles Question 89, October 1972)
Coefficient of variation CV is defined as a ratio of standard deviation to its mean and is given as $CV = S/X$. It describes the relative measure of variation and explains the mutual relationship between the standard deviation and the mean. CV is a good signal for the design engineer to balance the magnitude of the allowable design tolerances to the nominal values of the design based on the knowledge of the process variation, i.e., process capability.

112.   The ratio of the standard deviation to the mean is called

    a.   regression coefficient
    b.   coefficient of correlation
    c.   coefficient of variation
    d.   process capability ratio

Key: c.   coefficient of variation
Coefficient of variation is defined as a ratio of standard deviation to its mean, i.e., $CV = S/\overline{X}$.

113.   Determine the coefficient of the variation for the last 500 pilot plant test runs of high-temperature film having a mean of 900° Kelvin with a standard deviation of 54°?

    a.   6%
    b.   16.7%
    c.   0.06%
    d.   .31%
    e.   the reciprocal of the relative standard deviation

Key: a.   6%   (Ref. Applications Question 1, August 1978)
Given: N = 500 test runs, $\overline{X}$ = 900K, σ = 54K
Find: C.V.

$$\%C.V. = \frac{\sigma}{\overline{X}} \times 100 = \frac{54}{900} \times 100 = 6\%.$$

Be careful with choice c since it shows 0.06% and not 6%.

114.   If X and Y are distributed normally and independently, the variance of X–Y is equal to

a. $\sigma_x^2 + \sigma_y^2$

b. $\sigma_x^2 - \sigma_y^2$

c. $\sqrt{\sigma_x^2 + \sigma_y^2}$

d. $\sqrt{\sigma_x^2 - \sigma_y^2}$

Key: a. $\sigma_x^2 + \sigma_y^2$ (Ref. Principles Question 20, August 1978)

The variance of the difference between two independent variables X and Y is given as follows: $\sigma_{x-y}^2 = \sigma_x^2 + \sigma_y^2$ and this is the same as the variance of the sum of two variables.[10]

115. If X and Y are dependent random variables, and if X has variance 4 and Y has variance 3, then the variance of 5X−Y is

a.   103
b.   23
c.   17
d.   Unknown

Key: d.   Unknown   (Ref. Applications Question 87, October 1972)

Given: $\sigma_x^2 = 4$, $\sigma_y^2 = 3$, X and Y are dependent variables

Find: Variance of 5X−Y.

The variances are additive if they are normally and independently distributed. The key word in the question is "dependent" which means the changes in variable X will affect the variable Y, or in simple words, they may interact with each other. Hence the variance for 5X−Y is unknown from the given data. Be careful with choice a, which assumes that X and Y are independent and are additive, i.e., $\sigma_{5x-y}^2 = (5)^2 \, \sigma_x^2 + (-1)^2 \, \sigma_y^2 = (5)^2 \, (4) + (-1)^2 \, (3) = 103$ but this is an incorrect choice.

116. If we draw a large number of samples from a controlled process, we would not be surprised to discover

a.   some differences among the values of the sample means
b.   a distribution of sample means around some central value
c.   that many sample means differ from the process average
d.   all of the above
e.   none of the above

Key: d.   all of the above   (Ref. Principles Question 10, October 1974)

This represents the concept of sampling distribution of means where it is likely that the sample means will have different values, but all these sample means will form a normal distribution

---

[10] *Statistical Quality Control* by E. L. Grant and R. S. Leavenworth, 6th edition, McGraw-Hills, New York, pg. 369.

around some central value. The sample means can be different from each other or from the process average. This is based on the central limit theorem (CLT) as follows: *If the sample size of a random sample is n, then the sample mean* $\overline{X}$ *has a normal distribution with mean* μ *and standard deviation* $\sigma_x = \dfrac{\sigma}{\sqrt{n}}$ *where* μ *and* σ *are the population mean and population standard deviation, respectively.* The $\overline{X}$ chart from $\overline{X}$ and R control chart in statistical process control is based on this concept of sampling distribution of means.

117.   When small samples are used to estimate the standard deviation through use of the range statistic, sample subgroup sizes larger than 20 should not be used because:

   a.   the number 20 causes calculation difficulties
   b.   the efficiency of the range as an estimator of the standard deviation falls to 70%
   c.   the distribution for n = 20 is skewed
   d.   n = 20 adversely affects the location of the mean
   e.   the variance is a biased estimate

Key: b.   the efficiency of the range as an estimator of the standard deviation falls to 70%
        (Ref. Applications Question 21, August 1978)
        This can best be explained by its definition: Range is the difference between the high and low; or maximum and minimum values from the data. Hence it does not consider all values in the data set. It only looks at the two values. Hence the range statistic is not very effective as an estimator of standard deviation if the sample size becomes larger.

        Juran[11] indicates that range is more effective when we have 10 or fewer samples or small sample sizes. You can try to validate the effectiveness of the standard deviation calculated using $S = \dfrac{R}{d_2}$ by gradually increasing sample size, and compare with the standard deviation calculated using the formula $S = \sqrt{\dfrac{\sum(Xi - \overline{X})^2}{n-1}}$ to see if its efficiency has fallen to 70%.

118.   Interquartile range is defined as

   a.   first quartile Q_1 of the distribution of the data
   b.   second quartile Q_2 of the distribution of the data
   c.   third quartile Q_3 of the distribution of the data
   d.   the measure of the variability as the difference between the third quartile and first quartile

Key: d.   the measure of the variability as the difference between the third quartile and first quartile
        Interquartile range is abbreviated as IQR and is given as IQR = $Q_3 - Q_1$. A quartile is the observation which indicates where 25% of the observations fall as first quartile Q_1; 50 % as second quartile Q_2; or 75% of the observations as third quartile. Hence IQR is another way of

---

[11] *Juran's Quality Control Handbook* by J. M. Juran, 4th edition, McGraw-Hill, New York, pg. 23.17.

representing a measure of variability. Other more commonly used indicators of variability are range (R) and standard deviation(s).

119.   When using a handhold programmable calculator to compute the adjusted sum of squares for a variable, the formula $[\Sigma(X^2) - (\overline{X})(\Sigma X)]$ is preferred to $[\Sigma(X^2) - (\Sigma X)^2/N]$ because

     a. $\overline{X}$ has already been calculated.
     b.   the preferred formula is significantly easier to compute
     c.   there is less chance of under flow or overflow
     d.   division by N may produce a rounding error.

Key: c.   there is less chance of under flow or overflow (Ref. Principles Question 83, July 1984)

120.   Figure 3-7 shows three distributions. We can conclude that

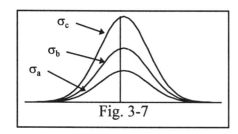

Fig. 3-7

     a. $\sigma_a^2 = \sigma_b^2 = \sigma_c^2$
     b. $\sigma_a^2 < \sigma_b^2 < \sigma_c^2$
     c. $\sigma_a^2 > \sigma_b^2 > \sigma_c^2$
     d. $\sigma_a^2 > \sigma_b^2 \quad \sigma_b^2 < \sigma_c^2$

Key: c. $\sigma_a^2 > \sigma_b^2 > \sigma_c^2$

121.   Figure 3-8 shows three distributions for a characteristic; we can conclude that

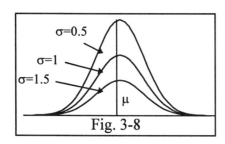

Fig. 3-8

     a.   they have the same mean but different variability
     b.   they have the same variability but different means
     c.   they have the same mean and same variability
     d.   they have a different mean and different variability

Key: a.   they have the same mean but different variability

122.   Figure 3-9 shows three distributions for a characteristic, we can conclude that

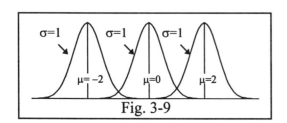

Fig. 3-9

     a.   they have the same mean but different variability
     b.   they have the same variability but different means
     c.   they have the same mean and same variability
     d.   they have a different mean and different variability

Key: b.   they have the same variability but different means

123.   A random sample of 10 items were taken from lot A, 20 from lot B, and 30 from lot C. The three lots contained the same type of material. Each of the samples yielded the same mean. Which of the following statements is true concerning the standard deviation of the samples?

        a.   The standard deviation of the lot C sample is the largest.
        b.   The standard deviation of the lot A sample is the largest.
        c.   The standard deviation of the lot C sample is three times as large as that of the lot A sample.
        d.   None of the above statements can be made.

Key: d.   None of the above statements can be made.
        (Ref. Applications Question 28, October 1974)
        The question gives only the information of sample size for each lot A, B, and C and the mean of each sample is the same. But it does not give any information about its individual values or range. The larger sample size may give a more accurate estimate of the standard deviation (S) but this does not mean that it will give a larger value of S for the larger sample. You need to have actual raw data or the measurement values from each sample, then you can compare the actual standard deviations. Sample size alone is not enough information for calculating the standard deviation of each lot.

124.   _____ is a variability parameter in case of a normal distribution.

        a.   standard deviation
        b.   mean
        c.   variance
        d.   median

Key: c.   variance
        The parameters of the normal distribution are mean μ and the variance σ^2.

125.   The unit for the Z in normal distribution is

        a.   same as mean
        b.   same as individual data
        c.   same as standard deviation
        d.   unitless

Key: d.   unitless

        The term Z is a standardized normal variable given as $Z = \dfrac{(x-\mu)}{\sigma}$. It is a unitless quantity because units for the random variable X and its standard deviation are the same and they get canceled out in the above formula.

If X is a random variable that is normally distributed with mean μ and standard deviation σ, the standardized variable $Z = \dfrac{(x-\mu)}{\sigma}$ has the normal distribution with mean = 0 and variance = 1.

126.   If we express the variable X in terms of its standardized units of $Z = (X-\mu)/\sigma$ we can say that the Z is normally distributed with

    a.   mean 0 and variance 0
    b.   mean 0 and variance 1
    c.   mean 1 and variance 0
    d.   mean 1 and variance 1

Key: b.   mean 0 and variance 1
The parameters of the normal distribution are mean $\mu = 0$ and the variance $\sigma^2 = 1$.

127.   The parameters of normal distribution are
    a.   sample $\overline{X}$ and range
    b. $\overline{X}$ and standard deviation of sample
    c. μ and σ^2
    d.   sample $\overline{X}$ and σ^2

Key: c. μ and σ^2
The normal distribution is described by its parameters μ and σ^2.

128.   In a normal distribution what is the area under the curve between +0.7 and +1.3 standard deviation units.

    a.   0.2930
    b.   0.7580
    3.   0.2580
    d.   0.1452

Key: d.   0.1452   (Ref. Applications Question 50, October 1972)
Given: $Z_1 = 0.7$, $Z_2 = 1.3$, normal distribution
Find: The area under the curve *between* Z_1 and Z_2 standard deviation units, i.e., $P(0.7 < Z < 1.3)$

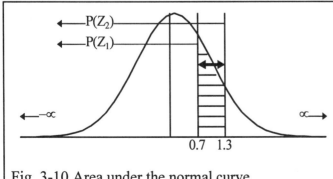

Fig. 3-10 Area under the normal curve.

First draw the picture of normal distribution with the given $Z_1 = 0.7$ and $Z_2 = 1.3$. You have to find the shaded area *between* the two lines as shown in Figure 3-10. The Z table gives $P(Z_1) = 0.7580$ and $P(Z_2) = 0.9032$.
The shaded area = $P(0.7 < Z < 1.3)$
                 = $P(Z_2) - P(Z_1)$
                 = $0.9032 - 0.7580$
                 = 0.1452

129.   Find the area under the normal distribution curve for a Z value of greater than 2.

    a.   – 0.0228
    b.   0.0228
    c.   0.0454
    d.   0.9773

Key: b.   0.0228

Given: Normal distribution and the Z value of greater than 2.
Find: The area under the curve $P(Z > 2)$.
First draw the picture of the normal distribution. This is a case of finding the area *beyond* the given value of Z, i.e., (probability) from Z to $+ \infty$ as shown in the shaded area in Figure 3-11.

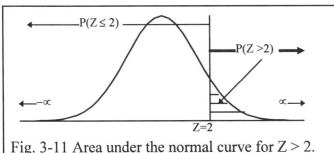

Fig. 3-11 Area under the normal curve for Z > 2.

The normal table gives $P(Z \le 2) =$ 0.9772 as the area on the left of the line (i.e., from $- \infty$ to Z = 2).
Hence area $P(Z > 2) = 1 - P(Z \le 2)$
$$= 1 - 0.9772$$
$$= 0.0228$$

130.   How many standard deviation units will span a total area of 40% symmetrical about the mean, under a normal curve?

    a.   ± 0.84
    b.   ± 0.52
    c.   ± 1.28
    d.   – 0.25

Key: b.   ± 0.52   (Ref. Applications Question 85, October 1972)

Given: normal distribution; 40% total area symmetrical about the mean.
Find: Number of standard deviation units, i.e., corresponding Z value.

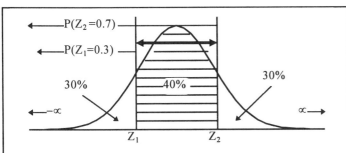

Fig. 3-12 40% area symmetrical about the mean under the normal curve between $Z_1 = 0.3$ and $Z_2 = 0.70$.

First draw the picture of normal distribution with 40% symmetrical area *between* the two Z_1 and Z_2 lines as shown in Figure 3-12. Since it is a symmetrical distribution, the area outside the shaded area on each side of the mean is 30%. Refer to the Z table to find Z_1 and Z_2 values that gives the $P(Z_1) = 0.30$ and $P(Z_2) = 0.70$. You should be able to get $Z_1 = - 0.52$ and $Z_2 = 0.52$.

Hence Z = ± 0.52 will give a total area of 40% symmetrical about the mean.

131.   What value in the Z table has 5% of the area in the tail beyond it?

   a.   1.960
   b.   1.645
   c.   2.576
   d.   1.282

Key: b.   1.645   (Ref. Applications Question 14, July 1984)
   Given: Z table, i.e., normal distribution.
   Find: The value of Z that gives a 5% area in the tail *beyond* it, i.e., P(Z > ?) = 0.05
   Here **watch out** for a most common mistake. It is necessary that you make a habit of drawing the
   figure or graph to understand similar problems. You are likely to think the 5% area *beyond* the
   tail as a two tail case, i.e., a total 5% area outside as shown in Fig. 3-13 (a). That is incorrect.
   Hence use Fig. 3-13 (b) to get a 5% area *beyond* the tail. The Z table gives the 95% area (i.e., 5%
   area outside the right tail) at Z = 1.645. Hence choice b of Z = 1.645 is the correct answer and not
   choice a, 1.96.

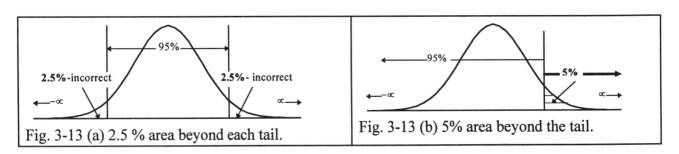

Fig. 3-13 (a) 2.5 % area beyond each tail.   Fig. 3-13 (b) 5% area beyond the tail.

132.   Find P(–3 ≤ Z ≤ 3)

   a.   0.0027
   b.   0.9546
   c.   0.9974
   d.   0.99865

Key: c.   0.9974
   Given: Normal distribution and the Z values of –3 to +3.
   Find: The area under the curve for P(–3 ≤ Z ≤ 3), i.e., area *between* z_1 and z_2 lines.

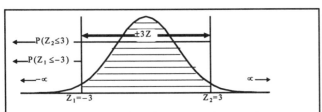

Fig. 3-14 Area under the normal curve between
$Z_1 = -3$ and $Z_2 = 3$.

First draw the picture of normal distribution
and decide the area of interest. This is a case of
finding the area under the curve from
$Z_1 = -3$ through $Z_2 = 3$ as shown in the shaded
area *between* two lines in Fig. 3-14. Refer to the
Z table for $Z_1 \le -3$ and $Z_2 \le 3$. We get the
following probability values.

$P(Z_1 \le -3) = 0.0013$, and $P(Z_2 \le 3) = 0.9987$.
Hence $P(-3 \le Z \le 3) = P(Z_2 \le 3) - P(Z_1 \le -3) = 0.9987 - 0.0013 = 0.9974$.

This is also the most commonly used term for process capability, i.e., $\pm 3\sigma$ includes 99.73% area under the normal distribution curve. You should remember the areas for $\pm 1\sigma$, $\pm 2\sigma$, and $\pm 3\sigma$ values.

133. Approximately what percentage of the area under the normal curve is included within ± 3 standard deviations about the mean?

  a.   50.0%
  b.   68.0%
  c.   90.0%
  d.   95.0%
  e.   99.7%

Key: e.   99.7%   (Ref. ASQC-CQT Examination, Core portion Question 1.)
  Please refer to Question 132 for a detailed explanation.

134. The lengths of a certain bushing are normally distributed with a mean $\overline{X}$. How many standard deviation units symmetrical about the $\overline{X}$ will include 80% of the lengths?

  a. ± 1.04
  b. ± 0.52
  c. ± 1.28
  d. ± 0.84

Key: c. ± 1.28 (Ref. Applications Question 10, August 1978)
  Given: Mean $\overline{X}$, normal distribution, 80% area under the normal distribution curve symmetrical about the mean $\overline{X}$.
  Find: Standard deviation units that include 80% of the bushing lengths.

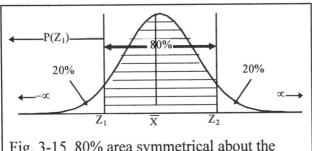

Fig. 3-15 80% area symmetrical about the mean under the normal curve.

First draw the picture of normal distribution and decide the area of interest. This is a case of finding the area under the curve *between* the two lines from Z_1 through Z_2 as shown in the shaded area in Fig. 3-15. The area under each tail is hence 10%. Refer to Z table for area under the curve for $P(Z_1) = 0.10$, and you will get $Z_1 = -1.28$.

Since it is a symmetrical distribution, it will have the same value, i.e., $Z_2 = +1.28$ for 90% area under the curve. Hence $Z = \pm 1.28$ indicates the 80% area under the curve, symmetrical about the mean, i.e., between the two lines.

135. The lengths of a certain bushing are normally distributed with mean $\overline{X}$. How many standard deviation units symmetrical about $\overline{X}$ will include 70% of the lengths?

   a. ± 1.04
   b. ± 0.52
   c. ± 1.28
   d. ± 0.84

Key: a.   ± 1.04   (Ref. Applications Question 53, October 1974)
   Given: Mean $\overline{X}$, normal distribution, 70% area under the normal distribution curve symmetrical about the mean $\overline{X}$.
   Find: Standard deviation units that include 70% of the bushing lengths.

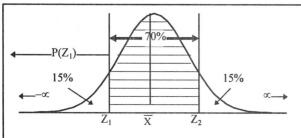

Fig. 3-16 70% area symmetrical about the mean under the normal curve.

First draw the picture of normal distribution and decide the area of interest. This is a case of finding the area under the curve *between* the two lines from Z_1 through Z_2 as shown in the shaded area in Fig. 3-16. The area under each tail is hence 15%. Refer to Z table for area under the curve for $P(Z_1)$ = 0.15, and you will get $Z_1 = -1.04$.

Since it is a symmetrical distribution, it will have the same value, i.e., $Z_2 = +1.04$ for 70% area under the curve. Hence $Z = \pm 1.04$ indicates the 70% area under the curve, symmetrical about the mean, i.e., between the two lines.

136. You are a quality engineer taking the measurement of the length of a part which has an average length of 10 mm with a standard deviation of 0.6 mm. What is the probability of your process producing parts bigger than 11.5 mm?

   a. 0.9983
   b. 0.0454
   c. 0.0062
   d. 0.0227

Key: c.   0.0062
   Given: $\mu = 10$ mm average length, and $\sigma = 0.6$ mm, X = 11.5 mm
   Find: $P(X > 11.5)$, i.e., probability of parts *beyond* X = 11.5 mm.
   This is a case of finding the probability or the area under the curve *beyond* X = 11.5 mm value, as shown in the shaded area in Fig. 3-17.

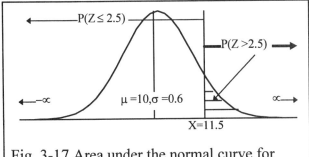

Fig. 3-17 Area under the normal curve for
X > 11.5 mm.

We need to convert X = 11.5 to a standardized value of Z as follows:

$$Z = \frac{X - \mu}{\sigma} = \frac{11.5 - 10}{0.6} = 2.5.$$

From the Z table, we get P(Z = 2.5) = 0.9938.
Hence P(Z>2.5) = 1 − P(Z ≤ 2.5)
$$= 1 - 0.9938 = 0.0062.$$

137.   If the specification on the part in Question 136 is 10 mm ±1.5, what is the probability that the parts will meet the specification?

  a.   0.9983
  b.   0.9876
  c.   0.0062
  d.   0.9973

Key: b.   0.9876
    Given: μ = 10 mm average length, and σ = 0.6 mm, and the specification is 10 mm ±1.5.
    Find: The probability that the part will meet the specification of 8.5 mm to 11.5 mm, i.e.,
        P(8.5 mm ≤ X ≤ 11.5 mm).
    This is a case of finding the probability or the area under the curve *between* X_1 = 8.5 mm to X_2 = 11.5 mm as shown in the shaded area in Fig. 3-18.

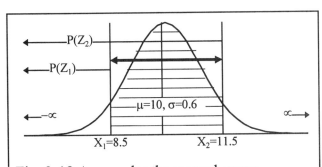

Fig. 3-18 Area under the normal curve
between X_1 = 8.5 and X_2 = 11.5 mm.

First calculate the Z values for both X_1 and X_2.

$$Z_1 = \frac{X_1 - \mu}{\sigma} = \frac{8.5 - 10}{0.6} = -2.5 \text{ and}$$

$$Z_2 = \frac{X_2 - \mu}{\sigma} = \frac{11.5 - 10}{0.6} = 2.5$$

From the normal table, for Z_1 = −2.5, we get
P(Z_1 ≤ −2.5) = 0.0062 and Z_2 = 2.5 gives
P(Z_2 ≤ 2.5) = 0.9938.
P(−2.5 ≤ Z ≤ 2.5) = P(Z_2 ≤ 2.5) − P(Z_1 ≤ −2.5)
$$= 0.9938 - 0.0062 = 0.9876$$

Hence the probability that the parts will meet the specification is 0.9876 or 98.76%.

138.   The diameter of a part is normally distributed with a mean of 0.501 in. and a standard deviation of 0.001 in. The customer specification on the drawing requires the diameter to be 0.500 ±0.003 in. The percentage of parts produced that will meet the customer requirement is:

  a.   68.26%
  b.   95.46%
  c.   97.72%

d.   99.73%

Key: c.   97.72%
    Given: $\mu = 0.501$ in. diameter and $\sigma = 0.001$ in., and the specification is 0.500 ± 0.003
    Find: The probability that the part will meet the specification of 0.500 ± 0.003, i.e.,
        $P(0.497 \leq X \leq 0.503$ in.$)$.
    This is a case of finding the probability or the area under the curve *between* $X_1 = 0.500 - 0.003 =$
    0.497 and $X_2 = 0.500 + 0.003 = 0.503$ as shown in the shaded area in Fig. 3-19.

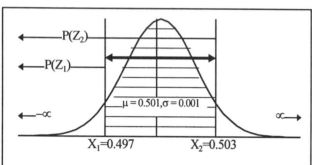

Fig. 3-19 Area under the normal curve between
$X_1 = 0.497$ and $X_2 = 0.503$ in.

First calculate the Z values for both X_1 and X_2.
$$Z_1 = \frac{X_1 - \mu}{\sigma} = \frac{0.497 - 0.501}{0.001} = -4 \text{ and}$$
$$Z_2 = \frac{X_2 - \mu}{\sigma} = \frac{0.503 - 0.501}{0.001} = 2.0$$
From the normal table, we get $P(Z_1)$ and $P(Z_2)$.
For $Z_1 = -4.0$, $P(Z_1 \leq -4.0) = 0.0000$ and
for $Z_2 = 2.0$, $P(Z_2 \leq 2.0) = 0.9772$.
$P(-4.0 \leq Z \leq 2.0) = P(Z_2 \leq 2.0) - P(Z_1 \leq -4.0)$
              $= 0.9772 - 0.0000 = 0.9772$

    Hence the probability that the parts will meet the requirements is 0.9772 or 97.72%.

139.   The quality engineer in the above case (Question 138) made some adjustments to the process and
    the process is now producing parts with a mean of 0.500 and with a standard deviation of 0.001.
    Determine the percentage of the parts that conforms to the specification of 0.500 ± 0.003 inch.

    a.   68.26%
    b.   95.46%
    c.   97.77%
    d.   99.73%

Key: d.   99.73%
    Given: $\mu = 0.500$ in. diameter and $\sigma = 0.001$ in., and the specifications are 0.500 ± 0.003
    Find: The probability that the part will meet the specification of 0.500 ± 0.003, i.e.,
        $P(0.497 \leq X \leq 0.503$ in$)$.
    This is a case of finding the probability or the area under the curve *between* $X_1 = 0.500 - 0.003 =$
    0.497 and $X_2 = 0.500 + 0.003 = 0.503$ as shown in the shaded area in Fig. 3-20.
    First calculate the Z values for both X_1 and X_2.
$$Z_1 = \frac{X_1 - \mu}{\sigma} = \frac{0.497 - 0.500}{0.001} = -3 \text{ and } Z_2 = \frac{X_2 - \mu}{\sigma} = \frac{0.503 - 0.500}{0.001} = 3$$

    From the normal table, we get $P(Z_1)$ and $P(Z_2)$. For $Z_1 = -3$, $P(Z_1 \leq -3) = 0.00135$ and
    for $Z_2 = 3.0$, $P(Z_2 \leq 3.0) = 0.99865$.

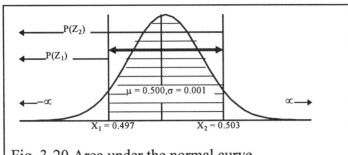

Fig. 3-20 Area under the normal curve
between $X_1 = 0.497$ and $X_2 = 0.503$ in.

Hence, $P(-3 \leq Z \leq 3) = P(Z_2 \leq 3) - P(Z_1 \leq -3) = 0.99862 - 0.00135 = 0.9973$.

This is also given by the fact that the $\mu \pm 3\sigma$ gives 99.73 area under the normal distribution curve.

140.   Select the incorrect statement from among the following: The IDs of a certain piece of tubing are normally distributed with a mean of 1.00 in. The portion of the tubing with IDs less than 0.90 in. is

a.   less than the proportion of IDs greater than 0.90 in.
b.   less than 50%
c.   less than the proportion with IDs greater than 1.10 in.
d.   less than the proportion with IDs greater than 1.00 in.

Key: c.   less than the proportion with IDs greater than 1.10 in.
(Ref. Applications Question 9, October 1974)
Given: Mean ID = 1.00 in., X_i = 0.90 in. and IDs are normally distributed.
Find: Proportion or percentage of tubings with ID less than 0.90 in.
The key phrase to remember is *incorrect statement.*
Draw the picture, i.e., normal distribution as shown in Fig. 3-21 and identify each area.

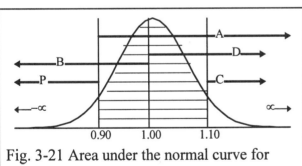

Fig. 3-21 Area under the normal curve for
different proportions.

In Fig. 3-21, P indicates the proportion (area) of the tubings with IDs less than 0.90 in. Now let us compare each choice with this area P.

a: A indicates the proportion of the IDs greater than 0.90 in. and one can easily see that area P is less than area A. Hence choice a is not an incorrect statement.

b: B indicates the proportion (area) less than 50%. Area P is less than area B or 50%. Hence choice b is not an incorrect statement.

c: C is the proportion (area) of the tubings with IDs greater than 1.10 in. Please study this area carefully. Since normal distribution is symmetrical about the mean, area P is the same as area C and not less. Hence choice c is an incorrect statement.

d: D indicates the proportion (area) of the tubings with IDs greater than 1.00 in., i.e., it is 50% area. The area P is less than area D or 50%. Hence choice d is not an incorrect statement.

141.   If the distribution of defectives among various lots is found to follow the laws of chance, we can

conclude that

    a.   all lots should be accepted
    b.   all lots should be rejected
    c.   the product was well mixed before dividing into lots
    d.   the manufacturing process is not predictable

Key: c.   the product was well mixed before dividing into lots
(Ref. Applications Question 54, October 1974)
If the product is well mixed, then no biases are introduced in drawing a sample. It makes the lot homogeneous, i.e., each item or part has an equally likely chance of being selected or it follows the laws of chance. Choice a or b is obviously not correct, as we do not know the customer requirements or specifications to make accept-reject decisions. Choice d is incorrect because if the distribution was following the laws of chance, it has only the random variation or common cause variation. It means the process will be actually in statistical control and one can predict the manufacturing process.

142.   Suppliers A and B each have sent us samples of 50 items to examine for us to choose between them to award a contract. The samples have the same mean and range. However, the standard deviation of A's product is 15 and B's is 5. We may conclude that

    a.   A's product is grouped closer to the mean than B's.
    b.   B's product is grouped closer to the mean than A's.
    c.   there are three times as many measurements from −1 standard deviation to +1 standard deviation in A's product as in B's.
    d.   there are one-third as many measurements from −1 standard deviation to +1 standard deviation in A's product as in B's.
    e.   cannot say anything unless we know the value of the common mean.

Key: b.   B's product is grouped closer to the mean than A's.
(Ref. Applications Question 10, October 1974)
The standard deviation of B is 5, which is a smaller standard deviation compared to 15 of A, as shown in Fig. 3-22. Lower standard deviation means lower variation and hence B has a narrower distribution than A, i.e., B's product is grouped closer to the mean than A's.

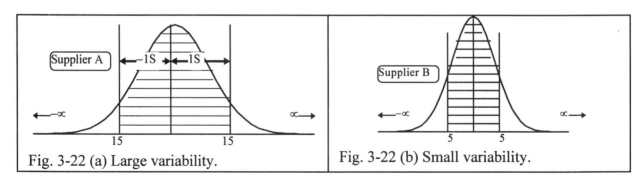

Fig. 3-22 (a) Large variability.   Fig. 3-22 (b) Small variability.

143.   The controlled process has a mean of 50 and a standard deviation of 5. What is the probability

that a random sample of 16 items yields a mean greater than 53?

    a.   0.99
    b.   0.01
    c.   0.49
    d.   0.58
    e.   0.42

Key: b.   0.01   (Ref. Applications Question 48, October 1974)

Given: Mean $\mu = 50$ (controlled process), $\sigma = 5$, $n = 16$, $\overline{X} = 53$.

Find: $P(\overline{X} > 53) = $ P(mean of the sample will be greater than 53), i.e., area *beyond* $\overline{X} = 53$.

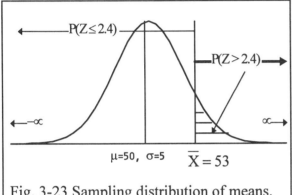

Fig. 3-23 Sampling distribution of means.

Refer to Fig. 3-23. This is a case of "central limit theorem," i.e., of sampling distribution of means $\overline{X}_i$ and not of individual X_i's since we are interested in finding the probability of mean $\overline{X}_i > 53$ and not an individual $X_i > 53$. The random variable $\overline{X}_i$ follows a sampling distribution of means and it is a normal distribution with a mean μ and standard deviation $\sigma_X = \dfrac{\sigma}{\sqrt{n}}$ where μ and σ are population mean and standard deviation, respectively.

First we need to calculate σ_x and Z value for $\overline{X} = 53$ as follows.

Standard error of mean is $\sigma_x = \dfrac{\sigma}{\sqrt{n}} = \dfrac{5}{\sqrt{16}} = 125$ and $Z = \dfrac{\overline{X} - \mu}{\sigma_x} = \dfrac{53 - 50}{1.25} = \dfrac{3}{1.25} = 2.4$

From Z table, for Z = 2.4, get the value of $P(Z \le 2.4) = 0.9918$. This is the unshaded area in Fig. 3-23, but we are interested in the area *beyond* Z = 2.4.

Hence $P(Z > 2.4) = 1 - P(Z \le 2.4) = 1 - 0.9918 = 0.0082 \approx 0.01$

144.   A process is in control at $\overline{\overline{X}} = 100$, $\overline{R} = 7.3$ with n = 4. If the process level shifts to 101.5 with the same $\overline{R}$, what is the probability that the next $\overline{X}$ point will fall outside the old control limits?

    a.   0.016
    b.   0.029
    c.   0.122
    d.   0.360

Key: a: 0.016   (Ref. Applications Question 12, July 1984)

Given: $\overline{\overline{X}} = 100$, $\overline{R} = 7.3$ with n = 4, $\overline{\overline{X}} = 101.5$

Find: The probability that the next $\overline{X}$ point will fall outside the old control limits.

This is a case of $\overline{X}$ and R chart and sampling distribution of means.

We need to first find the control limits for the $\overline{X}$ chart based on the given $\overline{R}$ values.

The upper control limit (UCL) and lower control limit (LCL) for the $\overline{X}$ chart are given by the following formula:

$$UCL = \overline{\overline{X}} + A_2 \overline{R} \quad (a) \qquad LCL = \overline{\overline{X}} - A_2 \overline{R} \quad (b)$$

where $\overline{\overline{X}}$ is the center line (CL), A_2 is a constant and a multiplier to $\overline{R}$ to define the $\pm\,3$ standard deviation limits above and below the center line $\overline{\overline{X}}$. Table 3-5 gives the values of some constants for different sample sizes to compute the control limits. (Refer to any statistical quality control book or reference to obtain commonly used constants in control charts.)

Table 3-5 Constants for control charts

Sample Size **n**	**A₂** factor for control limits for chart for the averages	**d₂** factor, i.e., divisors for estimate of standard deviation
2	1.880	1.128
3	1.023	1.693
4	*0.729*	*2.059*
5	0.577	2.326

For n = 4, we get $A_2 = 0.729$.

$UCL = \overline{\overline{X}} + A_2 \overline{R} = 100 + 0.729 \times 7.30 = 105.32$

$LCL = \overline{\overline{X}} - A_2 \overline{R} = 100 - 0.729 \times 7.30 = 94.68$. This is shown in Figure 3-24.

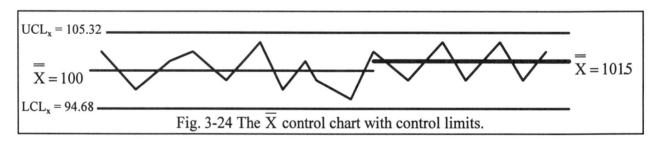

$UCL_x = 105.32$

$\overline{\overline{X}} = 100$

$\overline{\overline{X}} = 1015$

$LCL_x = 94.68$

Fig. 3-24 The $\overline{X}$ control chart with control limits.

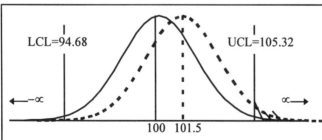

Fig. 3-25 Sampling distribution of means and the mean shift.

Refer to Figures 3-24 and 3-25 where the control limits are the same as the old limits and only mean $\overline{\overline{X}}$ has shifted from 100.0 to 101.5. The probability that next point $\overline{X}$ will be outside the control limit will be more on the UCL side shown in dashed area which can be calculated using Z statistic and Z table.

Calculate the standard deviation S of the process using the range $\overline{R}$ values and d_2 factor where d_2 is a divisor to estimate the standard deviation, i.e., $d_2 = 2.059$ from Table 3-5.

$$S = \frac{\overline{R}}{d_2} = \frac{7.3}{2.059} = 3.5 \quad \text{and standard error of mean } S_x = \frac{S}{\sqrt{n}} = \frac{3.55}{\sqrt{4}} = 1.77 .$$

Let us now calculate the Z_U and Z_L using the Z formula as follows:

$$Z_U = \frac{UCL - \overline{\overline{X}}new}{s/\sqrt{n}} = \frac{105.32 - 101.5}{1.77} = 2.16 .$$

From the Z table, the probability $P(Z_U \leq 2.16) = 0.9846$. Hence the probability of finding the next $\overline{X}$ point falling outside the old upper control limits of 105.32 will be:
$P(Z > 2.16) = 1 - P(Z_U \leq 2.16) = 1 - 0.9846 = 0.0154 \approx 0.016$.

Similarly, $Z_L = \frac{94.68 - 101.5}{1.77} = -3.86$, and from the Z table, $P(Z_L = -3.86) \approx 0$. Hence the probability of finding the next $\overline{X}$ point falling outside the old lower control limits of 94.68 will be a very small or zero probability. Hence the total probability of finding the next $\overline{X}$ point falling outside the old control limits of 105.32 and 94.68 will be: $0.016 + 0 = 0.0016$. Choice a is correct.

This question requires understanding of many basic concepts, e.g., probability theory, normal distribution, control charts, and sampling distribution of means. It is a time consuming and more difficult question because it requires many more calculations. You must do proper and balanced time allocation for the entire test. Try not to spend too much time on one question. You should keep going down the list to the next question and not stay stuck on one question for too long a time. Some students may even prefer to pass such a question, and leave it for the end, if time permits. Do not get frustrated with such questions, because the test has both, easy and hard questions. The trick is to find the easy ones quickly, answer them fast, and work your way through the difficult ones, one by one, case by case. Prioritize the difficult questions and allocate your time depending on the total remaining time. You need to decide which approach can work best for you, but your objective is to answer correctly as many questions as possible in the shortest time.

145.   To test for normality, which one of the following is not a useful method?

    a.   histogram
    b.   skewness and kurtosis
    c.   probability plots
    d.   chi-square goodness of fit test
    e.   scatter plots

Key: e.   scatter plots
All other items above except scatter plots are commonly used tools or methods to test for normality. Scatter plots are used to determine the relationship between any two variables and indicate the line or curve of best fit or lack of fit. They are not used to test for normality.

146.   Recognizing the nature of process variability, the process capability target is usually

      a.   the same as product specifications
      b.   independent of product specifications
      c.   looser than product specifications
      d.   tighter than product specifications

Key: d.   tighter than product specifications   (Ref. Principles Question 56, October 1974)
The process capability is defined as $\pm3\sigma$, i.e., ±3 standard deviations which accounts for 99.73% probability under a normally distributed data as shown in Fig. 3-26. If this $\pm3\sigma$ process capability is the same as the product specifications then the product is 99.73% capable, i.e., the process is producing 0.27% or 2700 parts per million outside of the specifications.

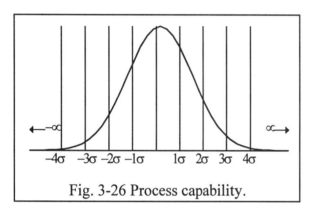

Fig. 3-26 Process capability.

This may not sound too high at first, but in today's competitive customer-driven markets, it is still a high percentage of parts outside the specification. Hence the effort is to achieve $\pm4\sigma$ (i.e., 60 parts per million outside of the specifications), $\pm5\sigma$ (i.e., 2 parts per million outside of the specifications), and even $\pm6\sigma$ capabilities instead of barely meeting the specifications with $\pm3\sigma$ capability.

The process variation σ must be reduced significantly to achieve high targets of process capability. Hence the process capability targets are generally more aggressive and tighter than the product specifications.

147.   The permissible variation in a dimension is the

      a.   clearance
      b.   allowance
      c.   tolerance
      d.   measurement

Key: c.   tolerance   (Ref. Principles Question 87, October 1972)
Tolerances are set by engineering to define the allowable maximum and /or minimum values for the product to perform or operate properly.

148.   Tolerances are

      a.   determined from the process data to calculate the limits of the random variable around some central or mean value.
      b.   are set by engineering to define the allowable maximum and /or minimum values for the product to perform or operate properly.
      c.   the interval within which the population parameter lies at a given confidence level.

d.   determined from the process data to define the amount of process variation, and these limits will contain a specified proportion of the total population.

Key: b.   are set by engineering to define the allowable maximum and /or minimum values for the product to perform or operate properly.

Choice a defines the control limits, choice c defines the confidence limits, and choice d defines the process capability or statistical tolerance limits.

149.   Three parts are additive in an assembly. Their design specifications for length and tolerance are 0.240 ±0.006, 0.3200 ±0.0006, and 1.360 ±0.003, respectively. Assume that each of the distributions is normal. Combine these dimensions statistically to give a final length and tolerance to three decimal places

   a. 1.360 ± 0.006
   b. 0.799 ± 0.565
   c. 0.640 ± 0.010
   d. 1.920 ± 0.007

Key: d. 1.920 ± 0.007 (Ref. Applications Question 42, October 1972)

Given: 0.240 ±0.006, 0.3200 ±0.0006, and 1.360 ±0.003, respectively; normal distribution

Find: Statistically determine the assembly length and tolerances

Nominal dimensions are denoted as N_a, N_b, and N_c. The individual component tolerances are T_a, T_b, and T_c.

N = assembly nominal length = $N_a + N_b + N_c$ = 0.240 + 0.320 + 1.360 = 1.920 and statistically the assembly tolerances are given as root sum of squares (RSS) formula:

$$T = \sqrt{T_a^2 + T_b^2 + T_c^2} = \sqrt{0.006^2 + 0.0006^2 + 0.003^2} = 0.0067 \approx 0.007$$

Hence the assembly nominal and tolerances are 1.920 ± 0.007, respectively.

150.   The minimum proportions of the observations that lie within ± 3 standard deviations for a continuous random variable is

   a.   95%
   b.   99.73%
   c.   89%
   d.   75%

Key: c.   89%

Can you think why? Did you fall into the trap of picking the *obvious choice b of 99.73%* ? The key terms are *minimum proportions* and *a continuous random variable,* and it also does not say that the random variable follows a normal distribution. It means the random variable can follow any continuous distribution, but we do not know the type of distribution. Hence choices a, b, and d are incorrect because they represent the proportions of the points or the area under the curve for normal distribution. Also, the phrase *minimum proportions of the points* is not true for normal distribution. Area under the normal distribution curve represents the actual or cumulative % of the area and not the minimum area, e.g., ±3σ includes a total of 99.73% of points or parts and not a minimum of 99.73% points.

The question requires conceptual understanding of *Chebyshev's inequality theorem*, which indicates the importance of standard deviation for any continuous random variable. Chebyshev's theorem states that[13] *"For any continuous random variable, the proportions of the observations falling within the ± k standard deviations of the mean are at least 1 – 1/k²."*

If k = 3 standard deviations, the percentage of the points falling within ± 3 standard deviations of the mean will be $1 - 1/3^2 = 1 - 1/9 = 1 - 0.11 = 0.89$ or 89%. Hence choice c is correct.

151.   The minimum proportions of the points falling within ± 2 standard deviations of the mean for any distribution is

        a.   95.46%
        b.   68.26%
        c.   99.73%
        d.   75%

Key: d.   75%
        The question requires conceptual understanding of **Chebyshev's** inequality theorem, as discussed in Question 150.

        Chebyshev's theorem states that:[14] *For any continuous random variable, the proportions of the observations falling within the ± k standard deviations of the mean are at least 1 – 1/k².*

        If k = 2 standard deviations, the percentage of the points falling within ± 2 standard deviations of the mean will be $1 - 1/2^2 = 1 - 0.25 = 0.75$ or 75%. Hence choice d is correct.

        You should not fall into the trap of picking the obvious choice a of 95.46%. Choices a, b, and c are incorrect as they represent the total area under the curve for ± 2; ± 1, and ± 3 standard deviations for the normal distribution, respectively. Also, the term *minimum proportions of the points* is not true for normal distribution. Area under the normal distribution curve represents the *actual or cumulative % of the area* and not the minimum area, e.g., ± 2σ includes a total of 95.46% of points or parts and not a minimum of 95.46% points.

152.   How many outcomes are possible when performing a single trial of a binomial experiment?

        a.   One
        b.   Two
        c.   Three

Key: b.   Two   (Ref. Principles Question 28, July 1984)
        This is one of the fundamental assumptions for binomial distribution, i.e., there are only two

---

[13] *Fundamental Concepts of Probability, Statistics, Regression and DOE* by Jagdish Vani, 3rd edition, April 1993, Section 4.
[14] *Fundamental Concepts of Probability, Statistics, Regression and DOE* by Jagdish Vani, 3rd edition, April 1993, Section 4.

outcomes possible such as success or failure, accept or reject, good or bad, etc.

153.   The probability of observing at least one defective in a random sample of size ten, drawn from a population that has been producing on the average ten percent defective units is

   a. $(0.10)^{10}$
   b. $(0.90)^{10}$
   c. $1 - (0.10)^{10}$
   d. $1 - (0.90)^{10}$
   e. $(0.10)(0.90)^{9}$

Key: d. $1 - (0.90)^{10}$ (Ref. Principles Question 32, August 1978)
   Given: $n = 10$ samples; $p = 0.10$, at least one defective = one or more defectives, i.e., $r \geq 1$.
   Find: P(at least one defective) =?
   The data indicates this as binomial distribution because sample size $n = 10 < 16$, $p = 0.10$,
   $q = 1 - p = 1 - 0.10 = 0.90$, and there are two outcomes as defectives or nondefectives.

   The fundamental rule[15] is $P_0 + P_1 + P_2 + P_3 + \ldots\ldots + P_{10} = 1$

   P(at least one defective) $= P(r \geq 1) = P_1 + P_2 + P_3 + \ldots\ldots + P_{10} = 1 - P_0$

   $$P(r \geq 1) = 1 - \frac{n!}{r!(n-r)!} p^r q^{n-r} = 1 - \frac{10!}{(0!)(10-0)!}(0.10)^0 (0.90)^{(10-0)} = 1 - (0.90)^{10}$$

154.   The expression $\dfrac{x!}{x!(x-n)!} p'^x (1-p')^{n-x}$ is the general term for the

   a.   Poisson distribution
   b.   Pascal distribution
   c.   hypergeometric distribution
   d.   binomial distribution
   e.   none of the above

Key: e.   none of the above   (Ref. Principles Question 43, October 1974)
   Watch out. Your immediate reaction can be choice d as binomial distribution. But if you carefully examine each letter in the formula it will immediately show the inconsistencies in the combination portion of the equation. The correct form of the equation should be

   $$P(x) = \frac{n!}{x!(n-x)!} p'^x \times (1-p')^{n-x}$$

   Any such equation can be rewritten by using different letters or nomenclature without changing the meaning of the equation. You need to be familiar with the composition of the equation and what it means to answer such simple questions on basic concepts or equations.

---

[15] *Fundamental Concepts of Probability, Statistics, Regression and DOE* by Jagdish Vani, 3rd edition, April 1993, Section 2.

155.   The expression $\dfrac{n!}{x!(n-x)!}p'^x(1-p')^{n-x}$ is the

      a.   general term for the Poisson distribution
      b.   general term for the Pascal distribution
      c.   general term for the binomial distribution
      d.   general term for the hypergeometric distribution

Key: c.   general term for the binomial distribution (Ref. Principles Question 88, October 1972)

The binomial distribution is defined by the equation $P(X = x) = \dfrac{n!}{x!(n-x)!}p'^x(1-p')^{n-x}$

156.   The binomial distribution is a discrete distribution and may be used to describe

      a.   sampling without replacement from a finite population
      b.   the case of n independent trials with probabilities constant from trial to trial
      c.   the case of n independent trials with several outcomes for each trial
      d.   sampling without replacement from a finite population where there are several outcomes for each trial

Key: b.   The case of n independent trials with probabilities constant from trial to trial
(Ref. Principles Question 85, October 1972)
Binomial distribution is a discrete distribution. It defines the probability of r occurrences in n independent trials when probability of an occurrence p is constant for each of the n trials. It involves only two outcomes for each trial. Choice b meets these criteria. Choices a, c, and d are the criteria for hypergeometric distribution, respectively.

157.   One defective is

      a.   an item that is unacceptable to the inspector
      b.   the same as one defect
      c.   a characteristic that may be unacceptable for more than one reason
      d.   an item that fails to meet quality standards and specifications

Key: d.   an item that fails to meet quality standards and specifications
(Ref. Principles Question 86, October 1972)
Today, *a nonconforming unit[16] is a term used instead of the term defective, which means a single unit or item that contains one or more nonconformities (defects). A nonconformity is a single occurrence of a nonconformance to a given quality standard or specification.* Such evaluation should be made objectively and not subjectively.

158.   If the probability of success in a single trial is 0.3, and two trials are performed, what is the probability of at least one success?

---

[16] *Fundamental Statistical Process Control Reference Manual,* © AIAG 1991, published in collaboration with ASQC Automotive division and Chrysler Corporation, G. M. Corporation and Ford Motor Co., pg. 151.

  a.   0.910
  b.   0.410
  c.   0.510
  d.   0.490
  e.   0.030

Key: c.   0.510   (Ref. ASQC CQE Examination Brochure, Application Question 18)
Given: p = 0.30 as probability of success,   n = 2 trials
Find: P(at least one success), i.e., P(r ≥ 1).
Use binomial probability distribution[17] here because the sample size is n = 2 < 16, and each event has only two outcomes, i.e., either a success or failure. This is a case of "at least"[18] 1 success. The fundamental rule is:

$$\mathbf{P_0 + P_1 + P_2 + P_3 + P_4 ...+ P_n = 1.0}$$
$$|\!\rightarrow\!\rightarrow\!\rightarrow\!\rightarrow\!\rightarrow\!\rightarrow\!\rightarrow\!\rightarrow \text{ indicates at least one success, i.e., 1 or more success}$$

P(at least one success) = $P_1 + P_2 + P_3 + P_4 + P_5 ..+ P_n = P(r \geq 1)$
                  = $1 - P(r=0)$

From binomial table: at p = 0.3, r = 0, n = 2, we get P(r = 0) = 0.490.
P(at least one success)   =1 – 0.490 = 0.510
This is a relatively simple question if you use the fundamental rule, decide which side you want to find, and then use the appropriate statistical table. You must practice how to read the statistical table. There are many similar questions in this section, with big story text, but they require only one or two steps like this one. Practice these questions carefully and understand the basic rules and concepts.

159. What is the probability of 3 fours in 5 tosses of a die?

  a.   0.03215
  b.   0.0046
  c.   0.0032
  d.   0.9954

Key: a.   0.03215
Given: n = 5 tosses, r = 3 fours
Find: P(3 fours in 5 tosses)
There is a total of N = 6 outcomes from a die. Hence each toss has a constant probability of p = 1/6 of obtaining a 4 as an equally likely event. Use binomial probability distribution because the sample size is small, i.e., n = 5 < 16, each event has only two outcomes, i.e., either a 4 is obtained (success) or not obtained (failure), and p=1/6 = 0.167 >0.10; and q = 5/6 of not obtaining a four. This is a case of *exactly*[19] 3 fours, i.e., r = 3.

$$P(r = 3) = \frac{n!}{r!(n-r)!}\, p^r \times q^{n-r} = \frac{5!}{3!(5-3)!}\left(\frac{1}{6}\right)^3 \left(\frac{5}{6}\right)^{5-3} = 0.03215$$

---

[17] *Juran's Quality Control Handbook* by J. M. Juran, 4th edition, McGraw-Hill, New York, pg. 23.27.
[18] *Fundamental Concepts of Probability, Statistics, Regression and DOE* by Jagdish Vani, 3rd edition, April 1993, Section 2.
[19] *Fundamental Concepts of Probability, Statistics, Regression and DOE* by Jagdish Vani, 3rd edition, April 1993, Section 2.

Generally, you should use the binomial table for such problems and not the formula, but here the value of $p = 1/6$ is not a commonly used value like 0.1, 0.15, 0.20, etc. Hence the table does not provide such probability.

An important reminder! You should practice to solve this level of degree of difficulty and be very familiar with the function keys of your calculator to solve such problems.

160. A process is producing material which is 30% defective. Five pieces are selected at random for the inspection. What is the probability of exactly two good pieces being found in the sample?

    a.   0.868
    b.   0.309
    c.   0.436
    d.   0.132

Key: d.   0.132   (Ref. Applications Question 10, July 1984)
Given: $p = 30\%$ defective, i.e., $p = 0.30$, $n = 5$ pieces
Find: Probability of *exactly two good* pieces, i.e., P(exactly two good pieces).
Read this question very carefully. You are asked to find *exactly two good and not two bad* pieces. You are likely to solve the question as two bad pieces and it will be wrong!!
Here $n = 5$, i.e., $n < 16$ pieces, and $p = 0.30$, i.e., $p > 0.10$ and there are only two outcomes possible, i.e., good or defectives. All these conditions meet the binomial probability distribution assumptions.[20]
This problem can be solved in 3 different ways. Follow only one method that you find easy.

[1] We use p as the probability of defectives and q as the probability of good pieces, i.e., $q = 1-p$, and hence we use r as r = number of defectives or occurrences for a given p.
    $$P_0 + P_1 + P_2 + P_3 + P_4 + P_5 = 1.0$$
    $\leftarrow\leftarrow\leftarrow\leftarrow\leftarrow\leftarrow\leftarrow|$ indicates that $P_0 + P_1 + P_2 + P_3 = $ P(3 or less) $= $ P($r \leq 3$)
    $\leftarrow\leftarrow\leftarrow\leftarrow\leftarrow|$ indicates that $P_0 + P_1 + P_2 = $ P(2 or less) $= $ P($r \leq 2$)
"Exactly two good pieces is the same as exactly three bad pieces from a sample of 5 pieces."
P(exactly two good pieces) = P(exactly three bad pieces)
                $= $ P(r = 3 bad)
                $= $ P($r \leq 3$) $-$ P($r \leq 2$)
                $= 0.9692 - 0.8369$ (values from binomial distribution table)
                $= 0.1323$

[2] You can use the binomial equation for probability mass function, i.e., the formula for exact values of probability. (You must practice the calculations.)
$n = 5$, $p = 0.3$, $q = 1 - p = 1 - 0.30 = 0.70$, and $r = 3$ then $P(x = r) = \dfrac{n!}{r!(n-r)!} p^r q^{n-r}$

$$P(r = 3) = \frac{5!}{3!(5-3)!}(0.30)^3(0.70)^{5-3} = \frac{5!}{3! \times 2!}(0.30)^3(0.70)^2 = 0.1323.$$

---

[20] *Juran's Quality Control Handbook* by J. M. Juran, 4th edition, McGraw-Hill, New York, pg. 23.27.

[3] If you are confused by the two good is the same as the three bad approach, try this method. As you know, in the case of a binomial distribution, the term p is the probability of occurrence of an event, i.e., occurrence of good or bad, pass or failure, etc. Here good or bad is assigned arbitrarily. Normally we denote p = probability of defectives then q = probability of good but if we say p = probability of good, then we can consider q = probability of bad.

Hence we denote q = probability of defectives which is given as 0.30 and r = 2 good, then, p = 1− 0.30 = 0.70 will be probability of the good. Using the equation for r = 2 good:

$$P(x = r) = \frac{n!}{r!(n-r)!} p^r q^{n-r} \qquad P(r = 2) = \frac{5!}{2!(5-2)!}(0.70)^2(0.30)^{5-2} = 0.1323$$

161. A process is producing material which is 40% defective. Four pieces are selected at random for the inspection. What is the probability of exactly one good piece being found in the sample?

    a.   0.875
    b.   0.575
    c.   0.346
    d.   0.130
    e.   0.154

Key: e.   0.154   (Ref. Applications Question 12, August 1978)
Given: p = 40% defective, i.e., p = 0.40; n = 4 pieces.
Find: the probability of finding **exactly 1 good** piece.
Read this question very carefully. You are asked to find **exactly one good** and not one bad piece. You are likely to solve the question as one bad piece and it will be wrong!
Here n = 4, i.e., n < 16 pieces, p = 0.40, i.e., p > 0.10 and there are only two outcomes possible, i.e., good or defectives. All these conditions meet the binomial probability distribution assumptions.[21] This problem can be solved in the same three ways as shown in Question 160, above. Follow only one method that you find easy.

[1] We use p as the probability of defectives and q as the probability of good pieces, i.e., q = 1− p, and hence we use r as r = number of defectives or occurrences for a given p.
    P_0 + P_1 + P_2 + P_3 + P_4 = 1.0

$$P_0 + P_1 + P_2 + P_3 + P_4 = 1.0$$

    ←←←←←←←| indicates that $P_0 + P_1 + P_2 + P_3 = P(3 \text{ or less}) = P(r \le 3)$
    ←←←←←←| indicates that $P_0 + P_1 + P_2 = P(2 \text{ or less}) = P(r \le 2)$

"Exactly one good piece is the same as exactly three bad pieces from a sample of 4 pieces."
P(exactly one good piece)   = P(exactly three bad pieces)
                   = P(r = 3 bad)
                   = $P(r \le 3) - P(r \le 2)$
                   = 0.9744 − 0.8208   (values from binomial distribution table)
                   = 0.1536 ≅ 0.154

[2] You can use the binomial equation for probability mass function, i.e., the formula for exact

---

[21] *Juran's Quality Control Handbook* by J. M. Juran, 4th edition, McGraw-Hill, New York, pg. 23.27.

values of probability. (You must practice the calculations.)

$n = 4$, $p = 0.4$, $q = 1-p = 1- 0.40 = 0.60$, and $r = 3$

$$P(x = r) = \frac{n!}{r!(n-r)!}p^r q^{n-r}$$

$$P(r = 3) = \frac{4!}{3!(4-3)!}(0.40)^3(0.60)^{4-3} = \frac{4!}{3! \times 1!}(0.40)^3(0.60)^1 = 0.1536 \cong 0.154 \quad \text{(You must}$$

practice the calculations.)

[3] If you are confused by the one good is the same as the three bad approach, try this method. As you know, in case of binomial, the term p is the probability of occurrence of an event, i.e., occurrence of good or bad, pass or failure, etc. Here good or bad is assigned arbitrarily.

Normally we denote p = probability of defectives then q = probability of good, but if we denote p = probability of good, then we can consider q = probability of bad.

q = probability of defectives, i.e., $q = 0.40$ and $r = 1$ good, then $p = 1 - 0.40 = 0.60$

$$P(x = r) = \frac{n!}{r!(n-r)!}p^r q^{n-r} = \frac{4!}{1!(4-1)!}(0.60)^1(0.40)^{4-1} = 0.1536 \cong 0.154$$

162.   A large lot of parts is rejected by your customer and found upon screening to be 20% defective. What is the probability that the lot would have been accepted by the following sampling plan: sample size =10; accept if no defectives, reject if one or more defectives?

    a.   .89
    b.   .20
    c.   .80
    d.   .11
    e.   None of the above

Key: d.   .11   (Ref. Applications Question 18, July 1984)

Given: p = 20% or p = 0.20, n = 10, r = 0 then accept, otherwise reject.

Find: The probability that the lot will be accepted, i.e., the probability that the lot has r = 0 defectives

Here n = 10 < 16 pieces, and p = 0.20, i.e., p > 0.10 and there are only two outcomes possible, good or defectives. All these conditions meet the binomial distribution assumptions.[22]

[1]   We use p as the probability of defectives, q = 1- p = 0.80; and r = 0. We can easily solve this by using the binomial probability table and we get P(r = 0) = 0.1076 ≈ 0.11.

[2]   p = 0.20 then q = 1- p= 0.80; the formula for binomial probability distribution is as follows.

$$P(x = r) = \frac{n!}{r!(n-r)!}p^r q^{n-r}, \text{ i.e., } P(r = 0) = \frac{10!}{10!(10-0)!}(0.20)^0(0.80)^{10-0} = 0.1073 \approx 0.11$$

163.   A large lot of parts is rejected by your customer and found to be 20% defective. What is the

---

[22] *Juran's Quality Control Handbook* by J. M. Juran, 4th edition, McGraw-Hill, New York, pg. 23.27.

probability that the lot would have been accepted by the plan: sample size = 10; accept if no defectives and reject if one or more defectives?

    a.   0.89
    b.   0.63
    c.   0.01
    d.   0.80
    e.   0.11

Key: e.   0.11   (Ref. Applications Question 22, August 1978)
Refer to Question 162 above, because it is a repeat question. The data given is the same, only some of the choices are changed. However the answer is the same value. You have to be careful with similar looking questions and read the data of the question carefully each time.

164.   If the probability of the success on a single trial is 0.30, and two trials are performed, what is the probability of at least one success?

    a.   0.910
    b.   0.410
    c.   0.510
    d.   0.490
    e.   0.030

Key: c.   0.510   (Ref. Applications Question 5, October 1974)
Given: $p = 0.30$ as probability of success, $n = 2$ trials, $r =$ at least one success.
Find: P(at least one success)
The key phrase is *at least*. Here $n = 2 < 16$ and $p = 0.30 > 0.10$. All these conditions meet the binomial probability distribution assumptions.[23]
The fundamental rule for total probability is given as follows:

$$P_0 + P_1 + P_2 = 1.0$$

$|{\rightarrow}{\rightarrow}{\rightarrow}$ indicates 1 or more than 1 correct guesses, i.e., $P(r \geq 1)$

$$
\begin{aligned}
\text{P(at least one success)} &= \text{P(one or more success)} \\
&= P(r \geq 1) \\
&= P_1 + P_2 \\
&= 1 - P_0 \\
&= 1 - 0.49 = 0.51 \text{ (values from binomial distribution table)}
\end{aligned}
$$

165.   If the probability of a success on a single trial is 0.20 and 3 trials are performed, what is the probability of at least one success?

    a.   0.008
    b.   0.384
    c.   0.488
    d.   0.600

---

[23] *Juran's Quality Control Handbook* by J. M. Juran, 4th edition, McGraw-Hill, New York, pg. 23.27.

Key: c.   0.488   (Ref. Applications Question 28, October 1972)
Given: $p = 0.20$ for success; $n = 3$ trials
Find: P(at least 1 success) = P(1 or more successes) = P($r \geq 1$)
The key phrase is *at least*[24] one success.
Here $n = 3$, i.e., $n < 16$ pieces, and $p = 0.20$, i.e., $p > 0.10$ and there are only two outcomes
possible, i.e., good or defectives. All these conditions meet the binomial probability distribution
assumptions.[25]
The fundamental rule is $P_0 + P_1 + P_2 + P_3 = 1$

$|\rightarrow\rightarrow\rightarrow\rightarrow\rightarrow$ indicates at least 1 success, i.e., 1 or more successes

$$
\begin{aligned}
\text{P(at least 1 success)} = \text{P(1 or more success)} &= \underline{P_1 + P_2 + P_3} \\
&= 1 - P_0 \\
&= 1 - 0.5120 \text{ (value from binomial table)} \\
&= 0.488
\end{aligned}
$$

166. Suppose that you are blindfolded and five items are placed before you, each of which is either
      defective or nondefective. The probability that you will identify all items correctly is
      approximately

      a.   1.000
      b.   0.170
      c.   0.200
      d.   0.500
      e.   0.030

Key: e.   0.030   (Ref. Applications Question 49, October 1974)
Given: $n = 5$ items; two possible outcomes: defective or nondefective
Find: P(correct items) = P(success)
Method 1: p = Number of successful outcomes / total outcomes = $1/2 = 0.5$
P(all 5 items are correctly identified) = P(success) = $P_1 \times P_2 \times P_3 \times P_4 \times P_5$
$$= (1/2) \times (1/2) \times (1/2) \times (1/2) \times (1/2) = (1/2)^5 = 0.03125$$

Method 2: Use the binomial probability distribution with $n = 5$, $r = 5$, $p = q = 0.50$

$$\text{P}(r = 5) = \text{P (exactly 5 correct items)} = \frac{n!}{r!(n-r)!} p^r \cdot q^{n-r} = \frac{5!}{5!(5-5)!} 0.5^5 \times 0.5^0 = 0.5^5 = 0.03125$$

167. A process is producing a material which is 40% defective. Four pieces are selected at random for
      inspection. What is the probability of exactly one defective piece being found in the sample?

      a.   0.870
      b.   0.575
      c.   0.346
      d.   0.130

---

[24] *Fundamental Concepts of Probability, Statistics Regression and DOE* by Jagdish Vani, 3rd edition, April 1993, Section 2.
[25] *Juran's Quality Control Handbook* by J. M. Juran, 4th edition, McGraw-Hill, New York, pg. 23.27.

Key: c.   0.346   (Ref. Applications Question 80, October 1974)
          Given: p = 0.40, n = 4, r = 1 defective
          Find: P(exactly one defective) = P(r = 1)
          The key word is *exactly* one defective.[26] Here n = 4 <16 and p = 0.40 > 0.10. All these
          conditions meet the binomial probability distribution assumptions.[27]
          The fundamental rule for total probability is $P_0 + P_1 + P_2 + P_3 + P_4 = 1$
                          one or less defectives ←←←|
                             zero defectives ←←←|

          Method 1: Use binomial table which gives cumulative probabilities for r or fewer occurrences.
          Hence P(r = 1) = P(r ≤ 1) − P0 = 0.4752 − 0.1296 = 0.3456 ≈ 0.346

          Method 2: Use binomial probability mass function for n = 4, p = 0.40, q =1 -0.40 − 0.60, r = 1

$$P(r = 1) = \frac{n!}{r!(n-r)!} p^r \times q^{n-r} = \frac{4!}{1!(4-1)!} 0.4^1 \times 0.6^{4-1} = \frac{4!}{3!} \times 0.4 \times 0.6^3 = 0.3456 \approx 0.346$$

168.   The appropriate mathematical model for describing the sampling distribution of outcomes in
          samples of ten from a process which is 5% defective is

          a.   the normal curve with mean 0.05
          b.   the binomial distribution with p' = 0.05
          c.   the hypergeometric distribution with mean 0.05
          d.   the Poisson distribution with np' = 0.05

Key: b.   the binomial distribution with p'=0.05 (Ref. Applications Question 23, October 1974)
          Here, p = 0.05 as constant, there are only 2 outcomes, n = 10 < 16 which meet the binomial
          distribution assumptions.[28] It describes the percent defectives. It is the underlying distribution
          for the p chart in SPC.

169.   A quiz of 10 questions is designed such that the probability of guessing a correct choice is 0.20
          for any question. What is the probability that a student will guess correctly no more than six
          questions?

          a.   0.0009
          b.   0.9991
          c.   1.0000
          d.   0.0055

Key: b.   0.9991
          Given: n = 10 questions, p = 0.20 of obtaining a correct answer, r ≤ 6 questions correctly
                    identified
          Find: P(no more than 6 questions correctly identified), i.e., P(r ≤ 6)

---

[26] *Fundamental Concepts of Probability, Statistics, Regression and DOE* by Jagdish Vani, 3rd edition, April 1993, Section 2.
[27] *Juran's Quality Control Handbook* by J. M. Juran, 4th edition, McGraw-Hill, New York, pg. 23.27.
[28] *Juran's Quality Control Handbook* by J. M. Juran, 4th edition, McGraw-Hill, New York, pg. 23.27.

This is a case of binomial distribution[29] with a constant p = 0.20, i.e., q = 0.80, the sample size is small n =10<16, and there are only two outcomes, i.e., a correct guess or an incorrect guess. This is also a case of not more than 6 occurrences , i.e., *r or less than r occurrences.*[30]
The fundamental rule is

$$P_0 + P_1 + P_2 + P_3 + P_4 + P_5 + P_6 + P_7 + ... + P_{10} = 1.0$$
$$\leftarrow\leftarrow\leftarrow\leftarrow\leftarrow\leftarrow\leftarrow\leftarrow\leftarrow\leftarrow\leftarrow\leftarrow\leftarrow \mid$$
no more than 6 correct guesses

P(no more than 6 correct guesses) $= P_0 + P_1 + P_2 + P_3 + P_4 + P_5 + P_6 = P(r \le 6)$.
Binomial table gives the probability of finding 2 or fewer than r items with n = 10, p = 0.20.
P(no more than 6 correct guesses) = P (r ≤ 6) = 0.9991.

170.   In Question 169, what is the probability that the student will get more than two questions right by guessing?

   a.   0.6778
   b.   0.3758
   c   0.3222
   d.   0.3020

Key: c.   0.3222
       Given: n = 10 questions, p = 0.20 of obtaining a correct answer, r > 2 questions correctly identified
       Find: P(more than 2 questions correctly identified), i.e., P(r > 2)
       This is a case of binomial distribution[31] with a constant p = 0.20, i.e., q = 0.80, the sample size is small n =10 < 16, and there are only two outcomes, i.e., a correct or incorrect guess.
       $$P_0 + P_1 + P_2 + P_3 + P_4 + P_5 + P_6 + P_7 + ... + P_{10} = 1.0$$
       $$\mid\rightarrow\rightarrow\rightarrow\rightarrow\rightarrow\rightarrow\rightarrow\rightarrow \text{ indicates more than 2 correct guesses, i.e., } P(r > 2)$$
       $$P(2 \text{ or less}) \leftarrow \mid$$

   P(more than 2 correct guesses) $= P_3 + P_4 + ... + P_{10} = P(r > 2)$
                                       $= 1 - P(r \le 2)$
                                       $= 1 - 0.6778$ (from binomial table at n = 10, r = 2, p = 0.20)
                                       $= 0.3222$

171.   The expression $P(x) = \dfrac{\mu^x e^{-\mu}}{x!}$ is the general term for

   a.   Poisson distribution
   b.   Pascal distribution

---

[29] *Juran's Quality Control Handbook* by J. M. Juran, 4th edition, McGraw-Hill, New York, pg. 23.27.
[30] *Fundamental Concepts of Probability, Statistics, Regression and DOE* by Jagdish Vani, 3rd edition, April 1993, Section 2.
[31] *Juran's Quality Control Handbook* by J. M. Juran, 4th edition, McGraw-Hill, New York, pg. 23.27.

      c.   Hypergeometric distribution
      d.   Binomial distribution

Key: a.   Poisson distribution   (Ref. Principles Question 26, July 1984)
This is the fundamental equation for the Poisson distribution. The commonly used equation for the Poisson distribution uses the notation λ which is the same as mean μ and variance σ^2, i.e., $\lambda = \mu = \sigma^2$

We can rewrite the equation as $P(x) = \dfrac{\lambda^x e^{-\lambda}}{x!}$

172.   The expression $\dfrac{v^x \cdot e^{-\mu}}{x!}$ is the general term for the

      a.   hypergeometric distribution
      b.   Pascal distribution
      c.   Poisson distribution
      d.   binomial distribution
      e.   none of the above

Key: c.   Poisson distribution   (Ref. Principles Question 15, August 1978)
This question has an error (may be a typo) in the formula for Poisson distribution which can lead towards choice e "none of the above," as the answer. However ASQC's published answer is choice c "Poisson distribution." The corrected formula for Poisson distribution should be

$P(x) = \dfrac{\mu^x e^{-\mu}}{x!}$ where the symbol v is replaced by the symbol μ.

173.   The assumed probability distribution for the control chart for the number of defects is the

      a.   binomial distribution
      b.   Poisson distribution
      c.   normal distribution
      d.   student t distribution

Key: b.   Poisson distribution   (Ref. Principles Question 43, October 1972)
The key phrase is *number of defects,* which is described by the Poisson distribution. Binomial distribution describes the percent defectives or fraction defectives. The normal and student t distributions are *continuous distributions* and not the *attribute or discrete distributions.*

174.   You have been asked to sample a lot of 500 (this is ASQC's correction in this question) units from a vendor whose past quality has been about 2% defective. A sample of 40 pieces is drawn from the lot and you have been told to reject the lot if you find two or more parts defective. What is the probability of finding 2 or more parts defective?

      a.   0.953

   b.   0.809
   c.   0.191
   d.   0.047

Key: c.   0.191   (Ref. Applications Question 4, July 1984)
   Given: N = 500 samples, p = 0.02 or 2%, n = 40 piece samples
   Find: Probability of finding two or more defectives, i.e., $P(r \geq 2)$.
   Here N > 10n, n = 40, i.e., n > 16 p = 0.02 < 0.10 and np = 40×0.02 = 0.80. This meets the
   conditions for Poisson distribution as an approximation.[32]

$$P_0 + P_1 + P_2 + P_3 + P_4 + P_5 + P_6 + P_7 + ... + P_{40} = 1.0$$

   $|\rightarrow\rightarrow\rightarrow\rightarrow\rightarrow\rightarrow\rightarrow\rightarrow$ indicates 2 or more than 2 defectives, i.e., $P(r \geq 2)$
   P(1 or less) $\leftarrow|$

   P(2 or more than 2 defectives) $= P(r \geq 2)$
                                        $= 1 - P(r \leq 1)$
                                        $= 1 - 0.809$ (from Poisson table for np = 0.80, r = 2)
                                        $= 0.191$

175.   What is the probability of finding no defective items in a random sample of 100 items taken from
   the output of a continuous process which averages 0.70% defective items?

   a.   0.49
   b.   1.74
   c.   0.10
   d.   0.74
   e.   0.33

Key: a.   0.49   (Ref. Applications Question 5, July 1984)
   Given: n=100 items, p= 0.70% defectives, i.e., p = 0.007
   Find: Probability of finding no defectives, i.e., $P(r = 0)$.
   Here n =100, i.e., n >16, p = 0.007, i.e., p < 0.1, and np = 100 × 0.007 = 0.70, and it is a
   continuous process, i.e., we can safely assume N > 10n. This meets the conditions for Poisson
   distribution as an approximation.[33]
   From Poisson table, for np = 0.7 and r = 0, the probability of finding no defectives is given as
   follows: $P(r = 0) = 0.497 \approx 0.49$ as the nearest choice.

176.   An inspection plan is set up to randomly sample 3 ft² of a 1000 ft² carpet and to accept the carpet
   only if no flaws are found in the 3 ft² sample. What is the probability that a roll of a carpet with
   an average of one flaw per square foot will be rejected by the plan?

   a.   0.05
   b.   0.72

---

[32] *Juran's Quality Control Handbook* by J. M. Juran, 4th edition, McGraw-Hill, New York, pg. 23.29.
[33] *Juran's Quality Control Handbook* by J. M. Juran, 4th edition, McGraw-Hill, New York, pg. 23.29.

c.   0.90
d.   0.95

Key: d.   0.95   (Ref. Applications Question 11, July 1984)
Given: n = 3 ft² sample, p = 1 flaw/ft² , N = 1000 ft² and number of flaws = n×p = 3 × 1 = 3
flaws.
Find: Probability of rejecting the carpet with 1 flaw/ft².
This is the case of Poisson probability distribution where it focuses on number of defects. Here p
is not the proportion of defectives but reflects the average number of defects. Hence it can be a
number larger than 1. We accept the carpet if it has no flaws and reject the carpet if it has one or
more flaws.
Total number of flaws = np = 3 × 1 = 3
P(rejecting the carpet) = P(r ≥ 1) = 1– P(r = 0) = 1 – 0.05 = 0.950 (values from Poisson table)

177.   An inspection plan is setup to randomly sample 3 ft of a 100 ft cable and accept the cable if no
flaws are found in the 3 ft length. What is the probability that a cable with an average of 1 flaw
per foot will be rejected by the plan?

a.   0.05
b.   0.95
c.   0.72
d.   0.03
e.   0.10

Key: b.   0.95   (Ref. Applications Question 13, August 1978)
Refer to Question 176 above for a detailed solution. This is a repeat question for a Poisson
distribution case involving the average number of defects.

178.   The number of repair jobs arriving at a repair line is averaging 4 per shift. What is the probability
that there will be no repair jobs arriving today?

a.   0.018
b.   0.982
c.   0.0302
d.   0.01

Key: a.   0.018
Given: λ = np = 4 number of repair jobs, i.e., an average of 4 repair jobs per shift.
Find: P(no repair jobs)
The arrival pattern of the repair jobs generally follows a Poisson distribution with average
number of repair jobs λ = np = 4. The probability of no repair jobs P(r = 0) is given using the
probability mass function for the Poisson distribution as follows:

$$P(r = 0) = \frac{\lambda^r \times e^{-\lambda}}{r!} = \frac{4^0 \times e^{-4}}{0!} = 0.0183$$

Or using the Poisson table: for np = 4 and r = 0, you will find P(r = 0) = 0.018

179.   Large panes of plate glass contain, on the average, 0.25 flaws per pane. The standard deviation of the distribution of the flaws is

    a.   0.25
    b.   0.05
    c.   0.50
    d.   0.75
    e.   none of the above

Key: c.   0.50   (Ref. Applications Question 6, August 1978)

Given: Average number of flaws /pane, i.e., $\overline{C}$=0.25 flaws/pane
Find: The standard deviation of the distribution

The average number of flaws follow a Poisson distribution with np = $\overline{C}$=0.25
The variance V(X) is given as $\mathbf{V(X) = np} = 0.25$
Hence the standard deviation $\sigma = \sqrt{np} = \sqrt{0.25} = 0.50$

180.   When using a Poisson as an approximation to the binomial, the following conditions apply for the best approximation:

    a.   larger sample size and larger fraction defective
    b.   larger sample size and smaller fraction defective
    c.   smaller sample size and larger fraction defective
    d.   smaller sample size and smaller fraction defective

Key: b.   larger sample size and smaller fraction defective
(Ref. Applications Question 28, August 1978)
The criteria[34] for binomial distribution are smaller sample size of n < 16 and larger fraction defectives. For Poisson distribution, it is the reverse case, i.e., it requires larger sample size, i.e., n > 16, and smaller probabilities of occurrence.

181.   Assume a large lot contains exactly 4% defective items. Using the Poisson distribution, what is the probability that a random sample of 50 items will not reflect the true lot quality?

    a.   27%
    b.   73%
    c.   82%
    d.   67%

Key: b.   73%   (Ref. Applications Question 21, October 1972)
Given: p = 4% or 0.04 defective items; it follows the Poisson distribution, n = 50 items
Find: P(lot does not reflect the true lot quality)
The key word is *not*.

---

[34] *Juran's Quality Control Handbook* by J. M. Juran, 4th edition, McGraw-Hill, New York, pg. 23.27.

Method 1: Poisson distribution: np $= 50 \times 0.04 = 2$ defective items

If the lot contains *exactly*[35] r $= 2$ defective items, it reflects the true lot quality.

The fundamental rule is $\mathbf{P_0 + P_1 + P_2 + ... + P_n = 1}$

P(r $= 2$ exactly defective items) $= $ P(r ≤ 2) $-$ P(r ≤ 1) $= 0.677 - 0.406 = 0.271$

Hence P(lot does not reflect the true lot quality) $= 1-$ P(r $= 2$ exactly defective items)

$= 1 - 0.271 = 0.729 \approx 0.73$

Method 2: Use the Poisson distribution formula for *exact* probabilities of mass function.

$$P(r = 2 \text{ exactly}) = \frac{(np)^r \times e^{-np}}{r!} = \frac{2^2 \times e^{-2}}{2!} = 0.271$$

P(lot does not reflect the true lot quality) $= 1 -$ P(r$=2$) $= 1 - 0.27 = 0.73$.

182.   Which of the following distribution requires a finite population or fixed population size to draw samples?

    a.   binomial

    b   hypergeometric

    c.   exponential

    d.   Poisson

Key: b.   hypergeometric

The key phrases are *finite population or fixed population* which is an important criteria for hypergeometric distribution.

183.   The hypergeometric distribution is

    a.   used to describe sampling without replacement from a finite population where there are several outcomes for each trial

    b.   a continuous distribution

    c.   a discrete distribution with its expected value equal to its variance

    d.   the limiting distribution of the sum of several independent discrete random variables

Key: a.   used to describe sampling without replacement from a finite population where there are several outcomes for each trial   (Ref. Principles Question 56, October 1972)

Hypergeometric distribution criteria are: Finite population, samples are drawn without replacement, probability is not constant for each trial, and there are several outcomes of each trial.[36] It is a discrete distribution and not a continuous distribution.

184.   A lot of 50 pieces contains 5 defectives. A sample of two is drawn without replacement. The probability that both will be defective is approximately

    a.   0.4000

    b.   0.1000

    c.   0.0010

---

[35] *Fundamental Concepts of Probability, Statistics, Regression and DOE* by Jagdish Vani, 3rd edition, April 1993, Section 2.

[36] *Fundamental Concepts of Probability, Statistics, Regression and DOE* by Jagdish Vani, 3rd edition, April 1993, Section 2.

d.   0.0082
e.   0.0093

Key: d.   0.0082   (Ref. Applications Question 5, August 1978)

Given: N = 50 pcs, d = 5 defectives, n = 2 samples, r = 2 defectives, without replacement

Find: P (both pieces will be defective)

This can be solved in two different ways.

Method 1: Using conditional probability theorem:

Event A = 1st draw of the part is defective; and Event B = 2nd draw of the part is defective

$$P(A = \text{1st draw is defective}) = \frac{5}{50} = \frac{1}{10}$$

$$P(B|A) = P(\text{2nd part is defective | 1st part was defective}) = \frac{4}{49} \text{ with no replacement}$$

The conditional probability theorem is given as $P(B|A) = \dfrac{P(A \text{ and } B)}{P(A)}$

Rearrange above equation to get the joint probability P(A & B), i.e., the probability that both consecutive draws are defectives, as follows:

$$P(A \text{ and } B) = P(B|A) \times P(A) = \left(\frac{4}{49}\right) \times \left(\frac{1}{10}\right) = 0.00816 \approx 0.0082$$

Method 2: Using hypergeometric distribution because of two criteria[37] : *Finite lot size* of 50; and *no replacement*. N = 50, d = 5, n = 2, r = 2

$$P(r = 2) = \frac{[C_r^d] \times [C_{n-r}^{N-d}]}{[C_n^N]} = \frac{[C_2^5] \times [C_{2-2}^{50-5}]}{[C_2^{50}]}$$

$$P(r = 2) = \frac{[\frac{5!}{2! \times (5-2)!}] \times [\frac{45!}{0! \times (45-0)!}]}{[\frac{50!}{2! \times (50-2)!}]} = \frac{[10] \times [1]}{[25 \times 49]} = 0.00816 \cong 0.0082$$

This requires significant practice, so make sure that you know how to use the statistical function keys on your calculator properly. It can be a time-consuming question. Allocate and prioritize your time in the examination for such questions and make sure that you do not spend too much time on one question.

185.   Which of the following is/are true?

a.   The frame is a description of the sampling units that compose the universe.
b.   The frame provides an identified list of the N sampling units that compose the universe.
c.   Some frames may cover the universe completely and some leave a gap; a portion of the universe may not be covered.
d.   all of the above.

---

[37] *Fundamental Concepts of Probability, Statistics, Regression and DOE* by Jagdish Vani, 3rd edition, April 1993, Section 2.

Key: d.   all of the above
        Deming[38] provides detailed discussions on the frame and the elements of a sampling plan. The frame is made of sampling units, e.g., an industrial product, purchasing records, lab test records, number of suppliers, parts lists, etc. The frame can be thought of as a list of sampling units that compose or make up the universe.

The frame must show a definite location, boundary, address, or a set of rules for the creation and definition of the sampling unit. A frame should provide further statistical information for each sampling unit.

It is sometimes difficult to provide a suitable frame during sampling. Each piece, item, or material covered by the frame will have a certain probability of belonging to any given sampling unit. Without a frame, there cannot be a probability sample and we cannot know the probability of selecting any sampling unit. A list of all parts used in an automobile model A, a list of types of raw materials, a list of members of a professional society, etc., are examples of a frame. In problem solving exercises, a frame may consist of a list of causes or factors based on a brain-storming of ideas. Once a list is made, describing the sampling units, a random sample can be drawn with some known probabilities.

If we draw a sample of all the sampling units in the frame, it will provide complete coverage of the frame, i.e., a 100% sample. However, the frame may or may not cover the entire universe. Some frames leave a gap and may not cover a portion of the universe. A frame may fail to include a portion of the universe, i.e., the universe may cover more material or items and only a portion of the universe lies in the frame, e.g., how to find a frame or frames to discover all problems or failures that customers may experience from a totally new product. There are test data, design reviews, and historical data, etc., which can help in identifying a list of potential failures during early stages of product design. However, there can be some intangible or qualitative problems which may not be known and hence not included in such a list.

Hence sometimes it is advisable to use a combination of frames. For example, in the sampling of types of problems faced by the customers of a certain product, we can use two separate frames.
1. A list of most frequently occurring problems with their description and cost, history, etc.
2. A list of sample cities or regions of the country to study and make a list of other problems, that
    are not on the list.

The concepts discussed in this question and in the following few questions of enumerative and analytic studies are new and difficult to understand. They are not taught or discussed in most of the conventional statistical studies. However, they are very important concepts to help develop sound statistical thinking. You should read these concepts in more detail and develop strong understanding of these concepts.

186.   Which of the following is/are true?

---

[38] *Some Theory of Sampling* by W. E. Deming, Dover Publications, Inc., New York, 1966, pg. 27, 83; *Sample Design in Business Research* by W. E. Deming, John Wiley and Sons, Inc., New York, pg. 39-42.

a.   Enumerative study is the one in which the action will not be taken on the material in the frame studied.

b.   Enumerative study is the one in which the action will be taken on the material in the frame studied.

c.   Enumerative study is the one in which the aim is to find out why and not how many, i.e., why there are so many or so few items or products in a particular category and not merely how many.

d.   all of the above.

Key: b.   Enumerative study is the one in which the action will be taken on the material in the frame studied.

Deming[39] has discussed the importance of distinguishing between the enumerative and analytical use of the data. We collect statistical data to provide a rational basis for action. Such an action may be based on the enumerative interpretation of the data or analytic interpretation of the data. Let us define these two terms in more detail here.

Enumerative study is one in which the action will be taken on the material in the frame studied. Hence choice a is incorrect. It mainly focuses on the question "how many?" Here some action needs to be taken because frequency of count of some characteristic of the universe exceeds some critical value, e.g., number of defectives in a lot exceeds acceptable quality limits, number of the members that do not renew a membership in a professional society, etc. Such problems or situations depend purely on the numbers, counts, or percentages, and hence they are descriptive and enumerative in nature. They do not involve the analytic question of interpretation of "why?"

Choice c is incorrect because it describes the "analytic study."

187.   Which of the following is/are true?

a.   Analytic study is the one in which the action will be taken on the process or cause-system that produced the frame studied; the aim being to improve practice in the future.

b.   Analytic study is the one in which the action will be taken on the material in the frame studied.

c.   Analytic study is the one in which the aim is to find out why and not how many, i.e., why there are so many or so few items or products in a particular category and not merely how many.

d.   a and b above

e.   a and c above

Key: e.   a and c above

Refer to Question 186 for comments on Deming's discussion of distinction between the

---

[39] *Some Theory of Sampling* by W. E. Deming, Dover Publications, New York, Chapter 7 - *Distinction Between Enumerative And Analytic Studies*, pg. 249; *On Probability as a Basis for Action* by W. E. Deming, The American Statistician, Volume 29, No. 4, 1975, pg. 146-152; *On the Use Of the Judgment Samples* by W. E. Deming, a paper delivered in Tokyo, 28 November 1975 before the Japan Statistical Association, Reports of Statistical Applications, volume 23, March 1976, Union of Japanese Scientists and Engineers, pg. 25-31.

enumerative and analytic studies. Choice b is incorrect because it defines the enumerative study. Hence choice d is also incorrect.

Analytic study is the one in which the action will be taken on the process or cause-system that produced the frame studied, the aim being to improve practice in the future. Analytic study is the one in which the aim is to find out why and not how many, i.e., why there are so many or so few items or products in a particular category and not merely how many. The aim of any statistical study in the analytic study is to learn the cause systems and thereby decide what actions on the system or process will bring improvements in the future.

In the case of the analytic study, when one takes the data on some critical product characteristic that is important for customer satisfaction, the aim of the study is to aid the prediction of the process that produced the product. The intention is to improve the units that will be produced in the future.

The enumerative study focuses on the actions on the material or the lot, i.e., to accept it or to reject it regardless of the reasons or causes. The question is what should we do with this batch or the lot of the product just made? The statistical theory of the estimation and tests of significance such as t-test, F-test, chi-square test, etc., are based on the study of the past, i.e., of the lot that is already produced. They do not provide a prediction of the process in the future.

The analytic study focuses on the root cause system, i.e., on "why" and not merely on "how many?" Which of the variable(s) caused it? Should we adjust the process or leave it? Should we change the material? Shewhart's control charts provide analytic studies of the statistical data and they tell when to take action on the process. Analytic study is based on the fact that the processes are dynamic and not static. It requires that the process is in a state of statistical control and is stable, and that any special cause detected by the statistical signal is identified and removed. It enables you to predict the output of the process in the future based on the stability of the process.

Deming has provided a simple criterion by which to distinguish between the enumerative and analytic studies. If you take a 100% sample of the frame, such as 100% parts made today, it provides the complete answer to the question "how many?" posed for an enumerative study. However, it does not provide the answer to the analytic study question "why?" Hence there is no such thing as a 100% sample in the analytic study.

188.   Whenever we use numbers only to categorize the outcomes of a variable, it represents

        a.   the ordinal scale of measurement
        b.   the interval scale of measurement
        c.   the nominal scale of measurement
        d.   the ratio scale of measurement

Key: c.   the nominal scale of measurement

When we use numbers to represent categories or attributes, it is considered the nominal scale of measurement. If we code some information for data processing, we get nominal data. For example, we may use code 10 for CQE examinees, 20 for certified quality auditor (CQA) examinees, and 30 for certified reliability engineer (CRE) examinees. Such data should not be treated as numerical, since the relative size has no meaning. We can assign code 30 to CQE and vice versa.

189.   Whenever we rank items or data by importance, strength, or severity, it represents

   a.   the ordinal scale of measurement
   b.   the interval scale of measurement
   c.   the nominal scale of measurement
   d.   the ratio scale of measurement

Key: a.   the ordinal scale of measurement
The ordinal scale of measurement differs from the nominal data in that the ordering of the numbers has a specific meaning, e.g., a customer satisfaction survey uses the following rating scale:

Strongly disagree 1	Disagree 2	Uncertain 3	Agree 4	Strongly agree 5

Here the numerical assignment of scales 1 through 5 indicates the degree of agreement or importance. The important point here is that 1 represents stronger disagreement than 2, but the difference between a scale of 1 and 2 may or may not be the same as between 4 and 5. One should not apply simple arithmetic operations to such ordinal data.

190.   If we use a scale where the relative order of numbers and also the difference between them is important, it represents

   a.   the ordinal scale of measurement
   b.   the interval scale of measurement
   c.   the nominal scale of measurement
   d.   the ratio scale of measurement

Key: b.   the interval scale of measurement
Here the relative order of numbers as well as the difference between them is important. It expresses the difference between two numbers in the form of the number of units. It requires a zero point which may be assigned arbitrarily, e.g., Fahrenheit and Celsius scales have zero points but both are different zero points and have different unit distances between two intervals of data. It requires the same amount of heat to raise the temperature from 40 to 50 as from 80 to 90 degrees Celsius. However, 80 is not twice as hot as 40 degrees Celsius and hence the ratio of 80/40 does not provide any meaningful conclusions.

Ratio data are used for ranking. They allow for the arithmetic operations of addition and subtraction.

191.   Whenever we allow for all basic arithmetic operations, including division and multiplication, it
        represents

        a.   the ordinal scale of measurement
        b.   the interval scale of measurement
        c.   the nominal scale of measurement
        d.   the ratio scale of measurement

Key: d.   the ratio scale of measurement
        Ratio data allow for all basic arithmetic operations as a ratio. Here the ratio between two
        numbers has a meaning, i.e., one number in the numerator being twice as large as another in the
        denominator. A typical ratio scale of measurement is used when we describe revenue, profit,
        physical measurements of length, height, weight, etc.

192.   The expected value of a discrete random variable is given by the formula

        a. $E(X) = \dfrac{\sum\limits_{i=1}^{r} X_i}{n}$

        b. $E(X) = \sum\limits_{i=1}^{r} [x_i - E(X)]^2\, P(x_i)$

        c. $E(X) = \sum\limits_{i=1}^{r} x_i P(x_i)$

        d. $E(X) = \int\limits_{a}^{b} x f(x) dx$

Key: c. $E(X) = \sum\limits_{i=1}^{r} x_i P(x_i)$

        The key phrase is *discrete random variable*. It does not provide any information on the type of
        probability distribution the random variable follows.

        Choice a is incorrect as it describes the arithmetic mean of the data. The question does not
        indicate that it is a continuous random variable. Hence choice d is incorrect because it describes
        the expected value of a continuous and not of a discrete random variable.

        Choice c defines the expected value of a discrete random variable as follows. "Let X be a
        discrete random variable that assumes finite values x_1, x_2, x_3 .... x_i. The mean or expected value

of the random variable denoted by E(X) is given by the formula: $E(X) = \sum_{i=1}^{r} x_i P(x_i)$, where $P(x_i)$ is the probability that the random variable X assumes the value x_i."

Choice b is incorrect because it defines the variance V(X) of the discrete random variable and not the expected value E(X).

193.   The variance of a discrete random variable is given by the formula

a. $V(X) = \dfrac{\sum_{i=1}^{r} X_i}{n}$

b. $V(X) = \sum_{i=1}^{r} [x_i - E(X)]^2 P(x_i)$

c. $V(X) = \sum_{i=1}^{r} x_i P(x_i)$

d. $V(X) = \int_{a}^{b} x f(x) dx$

Key: b. $V(X) = \sum_{i=1}^{r} [x_i - E(X)]^2 P(x_i)$

It also can be further simplified as $V(X) = \sum_{i} x_i^2 P(x_i) - [E(X)]^2$.

Please refer to Question 192 for a detailed discussion of each formula.

194.   The mean or expected value for the following data of the discrete random variable X and the probability $P(x_i)$ is

x_i	$P(x_i)$
0	0.85
1	0.13
2	0.02

a.   0.33
b.   0.15
c.   0.075
d.   0.17

Key: d.   0.17
        Given: Raw data of x_i and $P(x_i)$.

Find: E(X).

Table 3-6 Expected value data

x_i	$P(x_i)$	$x_i\,P(x_i)$
0	0.85	$0 \times 0.85 = 0.00$
1	0.13	$1 \times 0.13 = 0.13$
2	0.02	$2 \times 0.02 = 0.04$
		$\sum = 0.17$

The key phrase is *discrete random variable*.

The E(X) is given by the formula: $E(X) = \sum_{i=1}^{r} x_i P(x_i)$.

Refer to Table 3-6 to calculate E(X), i.e., $E(X) = \sum_{i=1}^{r} x_i P(x_i) = 0.17$.

195.   The variance for the following data of the discrete random variable X and the probability $P(x_i)$ is

x_i $P(x_i)$
0   0.85
1   0.13
2   0.02

a.   0.1811
b.   0.17
c.   0.21
d.   0.33

Key: a.   0.1811
Given: Raw data of x_i and $P(x_i)$.
Find: V(X).

The V(X) is given by the formula: $V(X) = \sum_{i}^{r} x_i^2 P(x_i) - [E(X)]^2$. We need to rearrange the data to calculate V(X) as shown in Table 3-7.

Table 3-7 Variance V(X) data

x_i	$P(x_i)$	$E(X) = x_i\,P(x_i)$	$(x_i)^2$	$(x_i)^2\,P(x_i)$
0	0.85	$0 \times 0.85 = 0.00$	$0^2 = 0$	$0 \times 0.00 = 0.00$
1	0.13	$1 \times 0.13 = 0.13$	$1^2 = 1$	$1 \times 0.13 = 0.13$
2	0.02	$2 \times 0.02 = 0.04$	$2^2 = 4$	$4 \times 0.02 = 0.08$
		$\sum = 0.17$		$\sum = 0.21$

Hence $V(X) = \sum_{i}^{r} x_i^2 P(x_i) - [E(X)]^2 = 0.21 - (0.17)^2 = 0.1811$.

196.   The mean for the binomial probability distribution is given as

      a.   p
      b.   np
      c.   npq
      d. $\sqrt{npq}$

Key: b.   np
The key phrase is *binomial distribution*. If X is a binomial random variable, then $E(X) = np$, where n is the sample size and p is the constant probability of occurrence. Both n and p are the parameters of the binomial distribution. Hence choice b is correct.

Choice a is an incorrect formula. Choices c and d represent variance $V(X)$ and standard deviation, respectively, for the binomial case. Hence they are not the correct choices.

197.   A process is producing material that is 40% defective. Five pieces are selected at random for the inspection. What is the expected number of defective pieces among the five samples selected?

      a.   0.4
      b.   5
      c.   2
      d.   1.2

Key: c.   2
Given: n = 5 <16, two outcomes, i.e., defectives p = 0.40 and nondefectives q = 1 – 0.4 = 0.60.
Find: E(X).
The data meet the criteria for the binomial distribution.
The $E(X)$ for binomial distribution is given as $E(X) = np = 5 \times 0.40 = 0.20$.

198.   A process is producing material that is 40% defective. Five pieces are selected at random for the inspection. What is the expected standard deviation, assuming the binomial distribution?

      a.   1.095
      b.   1.2
      c.   2.0
      d.   1.41

Key: a: 1.095
Given: n = 5 <16, two outcomes, i.e., defectives p = 0.40 and nondefectives q = 1 – 0.4 = 0.60.
Find: Expected standard deviation S(X).
The variance for binomial distribution is given as $V(X) = npq$. Hence the expected standard deviation $S(X)$ will be $S(X) = \sqrt{npq} = \sqrt{5 \times 0.4 \times 0.6} = 1.095$.

199.   For Poisson distribution

        a.   E(X) = np
        b.   V(X) = np
        c.   both expected value of mean and variance are the same
        d.   all of the above

Key: d.   all of the above
        This is a fundamental concept. The mean and the variance of the Poisson random variable are given by $E(X) = V(X) = np$. Some books use λ as a parameter, i.e., λ is the average number of occurrences. Then $E(X) = V(X) = \lambda$.

200.   For an exponential distribution, the mean E(X) is given as

        a. $E(X) = \lambda$
        b. $E(X) = \lambda^2$
        c. $E(X) = e^{-x/\lambda}$
        d. $E(X) = np$

Key: a. $E(X) = \lambda$
        This is a fundamental concept for an exponential distribution where λ is the parameter of the distribution. Choice b represents the $V(X) = \lambda^2$ for exponential distribution. Choice c is incorrect as it represents the reliability formula for exponential distribution. Choice d is incorrect as it represents the binomial and/or Poisson distribution formula for E(X).

201.   Which of the following is not a graphical tool to show the data?

        a.   Histogram
        b.   Scatter plot
        c.   Stem and Leaf plot
        d.   mean

Key: d.   mean
        Mean is the numerical representation of the data and it indicates where most of the data is centered. Histogram is a widely uscd graphical tool in quality and shows graphically the distribution of the data. Scatter plot shows the scatter of observations on the x-y axis and indicates if there is any relationship between the two variables. The Stem and Leaf plot is also a graphical plot to show the data and is used in descriptive statistics. It contains a stem of one or more leading digits and a leaf with the remaining numbers. Here you can see the shape, spread, and mode easily. Also the original data are not lost.

202.   In the case of stem and leaf displays each observation is split into which of the following two parts?

   a.   a leaf consisting of one or more leading digits and a stem consisting of one or more remaining digits
   b.   a stem consisting of one or more leading digits and a leaf consisting of one or more . remaining digits
   c.   all digits are equally divided into stems and leafs
   d.   all of the above

Key: b.   a stem consisting of one or more leading digits and a leaf consisting of one or more remaining digits

A stem and leaf display is a graphical representation of the data set. If we have a data set, consisting of at least two digits in each observation, we can split it in two parts to construct a stem and leaf display. A stem consists of one or more leading digits. A leaf consists of the remaining digits. If the data set consists of the age of the members, then an age of 35 can be split into a stem as 3 and a leaf as 5. Each observation will be split in this manner to construct a stem and leaf graphical display. The display is constructed by arranging the stem data in the left margin or left side. All leaves for each observation are listed beside each stem respectively in the order they were found originally. As a result the original data are not lost, as compared to a histogram. Also see Question 201 above for additional discussion.

ASQC - CQE BIBLIOGRAPHY AND OTHER REFERENCES ON FUNDAMENTAL CONCEPTS OF PROBABILITY AND STATISTICS

1. *Advanced Quality Planning and Process Control Plan Methodology Reference Manual*, 1st ed., published jointly by GM/Ford/Chrysler, 1994.
2. *ANSI/ASQC A1-1987 Definitions, Symbols, Formulas, and Tables for Control Charts*, Milwaukee, ASQC Quality Press, 1987.
3. ASQC Statistics Division, *Glossary and Tables for Statistical Quality Control*, 2nd ed., Milwaukee, ASQC Quality Press, 1983.
4. Braverman, Jerome D., *Fundamentals of Statistical Quality Control*, Englewood Cliffs, NJ, Prentice-Hall, 1981.
5. Deming, W. E., *Out of the Crisis*, Massachusetts Institute of Technology, Center for Advanced Engineering Study, Cambridge, MA, 02139.
6. Deming, W. E., *Some Theory of Sampling,* New York, Dover Publications, 1966, pg. 27, 83, 249.
7. Deming, W. E., *Sample Design in Business Research,* New York, John Wiley and Sons, pg. 39-42.
8. Deming, W. E., *On Probability as a Basis for Action,* The American Statistician, Volume 29, No. 4, 1975, pg. 146-152;
9. Deming, W. E., *On the Use of the Judgment Samples,* a paper delivered in Tokyo, 28 November 1975 before the Japan Statistical Association, Reports of Statistical Applications, Volume 23, Union of Japanese Scientists and Engineers, March 1976, pg. 25-31.
10. Dovich, Robert A., *Quality Engineering Statistics*, Milwaukee, ASQC Quality Press, 1992.
11. Duncan, A. J., *Quality Control and Industrial Statistics*, 5th ed., Homewood, IL, Irwin Inc., 1986.
12. *Fundamental SPC Reference Manual*, 1st ed., Southfield, MI, published jointly by ASQC Automotive Division and AIAG, GM/Ford/Chrysler, 1991.

13. Grant, Eugen L. and Richard Leavenworth, *Statistical Quality Control*, 6th ed., New York, McGraw-Hill, 1988.

14. Juran, Joseph M., *Juran's Quality Control Handbook*, 4th ed., New York, McGraw-Hill, 1988.

15. Kane, Victor, *Defect Prevention*, New York, Marcel Dekker, Inc., and Milwaukee, WI, ASQC Quality Press, 1989.

16. Keats, J. Bert and Douglas C. Montgomery, *Statistical Process Control in Manufacturing*, New York, Marcel Dekker, 1991.

17. McWilliams, Thomas P., *How to Use Sequential Statistical Methods*, Volume 13, Milwaukee, ASQC Quality Press, 1989.

18. Phadke, Madhav S., *Quality Engineering Using Robust Design*, Englewood Cliffs, NJ, Prentice Hall, 1989, pg. 32, 67-93, 108-120, 180, 213.

19. Shewhart, W. A., *Economic Control of Quality of Manufactured Product*, Milwaukee, WI, Quality Press, republished as the 50th Anniversary edition by the American Society for Quality Control, 1980.

20. Schooling, Edward G., *Acceptance Sampling in Quality Control*, New York, Marcel Dekker, 1982.

21. Shapiro, Samuel S., *How to Test Normality and Other Distributional Assumptions*, Volume 3, revised, Milwaukee, ASQC Quality Press, 1990.

22. Stephens, Kenneth S., *How to Perform Continuous Sampling*, Volume 2, Milwaukee, ASQC Quality Press, 1990.

23. Stephens, Kenneth S., *How to Perform Skip Lot and Chain Sampling*, Volume 4, Milwaukee, ASQC Quality Press, 1990.

24. Vani, Jagdish, *Fundamental Concepts of Probability, Statistics, Regression and DOE*, 3rd ed., Troy, MI, Quality Quest Inc., 1993.

25. Western Electric, *Statistical Quality Control Handbook*, Indianapolis, AT&T, 1956.

CHAPTER 4

STATISTICAL INFERENCE AND HYPOTHESIS TESTING

ASQC'S <u>BODY OF KNOWLEDGE (BOK)</u> FOR CQE EXAMINATION

This chapter focuses on the following selected subject areas of BOK from *Section III, Statistical Principles and Applications.*

Terms and Concepts

1.   Central limit theorem
2.   Inferential statistics (e.g., t-tests)
3.   Assumptions and robustness of tests

Distributions

1.   Sampling
2.   Chi-square, Student's t, and F

Statistical Inference

1.   Point and interval estimation
2.   Tolerance and confidence intervals, significance level
3.   Hypothesis testing/Type I and Type II errors

1. Let X be any random variable with mean μ and standard deviation σ. Take a random sample of size n. As n increases and as a result of the Central Limit Theorem

    a. the distribution of the sum $S_n = X_1 + X_2 + ... + X_n$ approaches a normal distribution with mean μ and standard deviation $\sigma / \sqrt{n}$
    b. the distribution of $S_n = X_1 + X_2 + ... + X_n$ approaches a normal distribution with mean μ and standard deviation $\sigma / \sqrt{n}$
    c. the distribution of X approaches a normal distribution with mean μ and standard deviation $\sigma / \sqrt{n}$
    d. none of the above

Key: d. none of the above (Ref. Principles Question 78, October 1972)
    The key concept is the **central limit theorem (CLT)**: "**If the sample size of a random sample is n, then the sample mean $\overline{X}$ has a normal distribution with mean μ and standard deviation $\sigma_x = \sigma / \sqrt{n}$, where μ and σ are population mean and standard deviation, respectively.**" This theorem describes the sampling distribution of averages or means $\overline{X}$ and not the individuals or the sum of individuals. Be careful with choice c, which is incorrect because it refers to the distribution of individuals and not to the sample averages $\overline{X}$. The concept of CLT is an important theorem and try to remember it for additional similar questions in this chapter.

2. Random selection of a sample

    a. theoretically means that each item in the lot had an equal chance to be selected in the sample
    b. assures that the sample average will equal the population average
    c. means that a table of random numbers was used to dictate the selection
    d. is a meaningless theoretical requirement

Key: a. theoretically means that each item in the lot had an equal chance to be selected in the sample (Ref. Principles Question 84, October 1972)
    Choice c is incorrect because there are different ways to generate random numbers. The use of a random numbers table is recommended as one of the many methods to generate random numbers but it is not dictated as the only method.

3. The basic reason for randomness in sampling is to

    a. make certain that the sample represents the population
    b. eliminate personal bias
    c. guarantee to reduce the cost of inspection
    d. guarantee correct lot inferences

Key: b. eliminate personal bias (Ref. Principles Question 24, October 1972)
    A random sample means that each unit or item has an equal chance of being selected and no personal bias is introduced. Be careful with choice a, which is also true, but choice b is more

appropriate and the fact that no personal biases are introduced ensures that the samples represent the population. There are some contemporary views challenging the concept of the "random sample" theory. However, for all practical purposes, the above statement is true.

4.   Which one of the following is not true for the distribution of individuals?

   a.   Its mean is the same as the mean of the sampling distribution of means.
   b.   It is generally wider than the sampling distribution of means.
   c.   It may or may not be normal.
   d.   The standard deviation of the distribution of individuals is given as $\sigma_x = \dfrac{\sigma}{\sqrt{n}}$.

Key: d.   The standard deviation of the distribution of individuals is given as $\sigma_x = \dfrac{\sigma}{\sqrt{n}}$.

The key phrase is **not true**. The term $\sigma_x = \dfrac{\sigma}{\sqrt{n}}$ does not define the standard deviation of the individuals, but it defines the standard error of the mean for sampling distribution. The

standard deviation for the distribution of the individuals is given as $\sigma = \sqrt{\dfrac{\sum (X_i - \overline{X})^2}{n}}$.

5.   The sampling distribution of means or averages

   a.   has the center of the distribution the same as the center of the distribution of individuals
   b.   tends to be approximately normal even when the distribution of the individuals may or may not be normal
   c.   is narrower than the distribution of the individuals
   d.   has the standard error of the mean which is given as $\sigma_x = \dfrac{\sigma}{\sqrt{n}}$
   e.   all of the above

Key: e.   all of the above

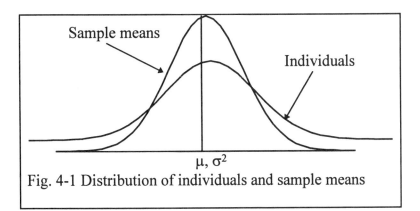

Sample means

Individuals

μ, σ^2
Fig. 4-1 Distribution of individuals and sample means

Fig. 4-1 shows the relationship between the individuals and the sample means and both have the same mean as the center of the distribution. The narrow curve is the sample mean curve and the wider curve is the curve for individuals. The sample mean curve is narrower because the extreme values are offset and averaged out in each sample.

Whether the distribution of individuals is normal or not, the distribution of sample means tends to be normal. The fact that the averages tend to have a normal distribution is the basis of the central limit theorem (CLT) as discussed in Question 1.

6.   Which one of the following is true for the distribution of the sample means?

        a.   It is generally wider than the distribution of the individuals.
        b.   Its standard deviation is given as $\sigma = \frac{\sigma_x}{\sqrt{n}}$.
        c.   It tends to be approximately normal even when the distribution of the individuals may or
                may not be normal.
        d.   It is not based on the central limit theorem.

Key: c.   It tends to be approximately normal even when the distribution of the individuals may or
                may not be normal.
        The key word is **true.** Please refer to Fig. 4-1 in Question 5 above. Choice a is incorrect because
        the distribution of the sample means is generally a narrower curve than the distribution of the
        individuals. Be careful with choice b as the formula looks similar but it is incorrect. The correct

        formula for the standard error of mean σ_x should be $\sigma_x = \frac{\sigma}{\sqrt{n}}$. Choice d is not true because the

        distribution of the sample means is based on the central limit theorem.

7.   Which one of the following is true?

        a.   The sample average is always constant from sample to sample.
        b.   The sample average is an estimator of the population mean.
        c.   The population mean is an estimator of the sample average.
        d.   The sample mean and population mean are the same regardless of the sample size.

Key: b.   The sample average is an estimator of the population mean.
        The key word is **true.** The question requires sound understanding of the fundamental concepts of
        the central limit theorem and the sampling distribution of means. We take samples of size n from
        a population and calculate the sample statistics, such as the sample average, which is an
        estimator of its parameter population mean μ. Choice a is incorrect because the sample averages
        are likely to vary from sample to sample and form a sampling distribution of means. Choice c is
        incorrect because the sample average is used to estimate the population mean μ using proper
        statistics. Choice d is incorrect because the sample means and the population means are not the
        same when the sample size is small. The sample mean varies from sample to sample and depends
        on the sample size. As the sample size increases, and becomes larger, the sample average gets
        closer to the population mean μ.

8.   If we denote $\overline{X}$ as the average of a sample, i.e., a point estimate of the mean μ, which of the
        following is/are true?

        i.   the average and mean are the same thing
        ii.   the average is a parameter
        iii.   the average is constant from sample to sample

      iv.   mean is the parameter

      a.   i and ii only
      b.   ii and iii only
      c.   iii and iv only
      d.   iv only

Key: d.   iv only

The mean μ is the population parameter, i.e., it is a true value of the population. The μ is constant from sample to sample. The sample average $\overline{X}$ is the average of a sample and it represents the sample statistic and not a parameter. It varies from sample to sample, which can be described by the sampling distribution of means. Hence the average $\overline{X}$ and the mean μ are not the same thing. Please refer to Question 7 for additional discussion.

9.   The distribution of a characteristic is negatively skewed. The sampling distribution of the mean for large samples is

      a.   negatively skewed
      b.   approximately normal
      c.   positively skewed
      d.   bimodal
      e.   Poisson

Key: b.   approximately normal   (Ref. Applications Question 24, August 1978)

A distribution of individuals may be normal or skewed, the distribution of sample means tends to be approximately normal. This is the basis of the central limit theorem: "If the sample size of a random sample is n, then the sample mean $\overline{X}$ has a normal distribution with mean μ and standard deviation $\sigma_x = \sigma / \sqrt{n}$, where μ and σ are population mean and standard   deviation, respectively."

10.   The sampling distribution of the means

      a.   is almost normal
      b.   is the same as the population standard deviation
      c.   is not normal at all
      d.   cannot be determined unless you know the population distribution

Key: a.   is almost normal

Whether the distribution of individuals is normal or not, the distribution of sample means tends to be normal and it is the basis of the central limit theorem discussed in Question 1.

11. $\sigma_x = \dfrac{\sigma}{\sqrt{n}}$ defines

a. the sample standard deviation
b. the population standard deviation
c. the standard error of mean
d. the coefficient of variation

Key: c.   the standard error of mean
Can you recollect the concept by looking at the formula? The term σ_x is called the standard error of mean. You should have had enough practice using the central limit theorem discussed in Question 1. Table 4-1 lists the formulas or equations for the terms in this question.

Table 4-1 List of equations for some important terms

Standard error of mean	$\sigma_x = \dfrac{\sigma}{\sqrt{n}}$
Sample standard deviation	$S = \sqrt{\dfrac{\Sigma(X_i - \overline{X})^2}{n-1}}$
Population standard deviation	$\sigma = \sqrt{\dfrac{\Sigma(X_i - \overline{X})^2}{n}}$
Coefficient of variation (CV)	$CV = \dfrac{\sigma}{\mu}$

Questions such as this require that you understand both the name or the title of the concept and its formula equation. Here an equation is given, and you are asked to find the term or the title. In another question, you may be given a definition, title, or statement and be asked to find the correct formula equation.

12.   For a certain make of a car, the factory installed brake linings have a mean lifetime of 40,000 miles with a 5000 mile standard deviation. A sample of 100 cars has been selected for testing. Assuming that the finite population correction may be ignored, the standard error of $\overline{X}$ is

a. 50 miles
b. 500 miles
c. 400 miles
d. 4000 miles

Key: b.   500 miles   (Ref. Applications Question 3, July 1984)
Given: $\overline{X}$ = 40,000 miles as mean lifetime; σ = 5000 miles and n = 100 cars, normal distribution.
Find: Standard error of mean σ_x.

If we ignore the finite correction factor, σ_x is given as $\sigma_x = \dfrac{\sigma}{\sqrt{n}} = \dfrac{5000}{\sqrt{100}} = 500$ miles.

13.   If the sample size is increased by a factor of 4, the standard error of mean

a. increases by a factor of 4

     b.   decreases by a factor of 4
     c.   increases by a factor of 2
     d.   decreases by a factor of 2

Key: d.   decreases by a factor of 2

This question can be easily answered by studying the formula of the standard error of mean $\sigma_x = \dfrac{\sigma}{\sqrt{n}}$ where the sample size n is in the denominator. If the sample size is increased by a factor of 4, then $\sqrt{n}$ increases by a factor of 2, and hence σ_x decreases by a factor of 2. Let's take an example. If the sample size $n_1 = 40$ with $\sigma = 4$, then $\sigma_x = \dfrac{\sigma}{\sqrt{n_1}} = \dfrac{4}{\sqrt{40}} = 0.632$. If we increase the sample size by a factor of 4, i.e., new $n_2 = 4 \times 40 = 160$, then $\sigma_x = \dfrac{\sigma}{\sqrt{n_2}} = \dfrac{4}{\sqrt{160}} = 0.316$.

This shows that σ_x is decreased from 0.632 to 0.316 by a factor of 2.

14.   A large normally distributed population has a mean of 50 mm and standard deviation of 4 mm. If a sample of size 40 is randomly selected, find the probability that the sample mean is less than 51 mm.

     a.   0.94
     b.   0.60
     c.   0.68
     d.   0.9973

Key: a.   0.94

Given: Population mean $\mu = 50.0$ mm, $\sigma = 4.0$ mm, $n = 40$, and sample mean $\overline{X} = 51$ mm, normal distribution.

Find: Probability that $\overline{X} < 51$ mm.

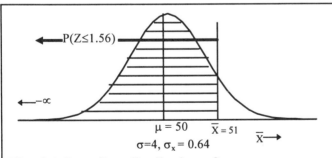

Fig. 4-2 Sampling distribution of means - area under the curve for $\overline{X} < 51$

First draw a picture of normal distribution based on the given data and highlight the area that is of interest as shown in Fig. 4-2. This is a case of sampling distribution of means. The standard error of mean is given as

$$\sigma_x = \frac{\sigma}{\sqrt{n}} = \frac{4}{\sqrt{40}} = 0.64 \text{ and Z will be}$$

$$Z = \frac{\overline{X} - \mu}{\sigma_x} = \frac{51 - 50}{0.64} = 1.56$$

We need to find the area *below[1]* the value $Z = 1.56$, i.e., find $P(Z < 1.56)$. From the Z table, $P(Z < 1.56) = 0.9406$ (see note below).

---

[1] *Fundamental Concepts of Probability, Statistics, Regression and DOE* by Jagdish Vani, 3rd edition, April 1993, Section 2.

Note: The question should ask to find the area or the probability that the sample mean is *less than or equal to 51 mm, i.e.,* $\overline{X} \leq 51$ *mm*, instead of $\overline{X} < 51$ mm. The Z table does not give directly the area for P(Z < 1.56) but it provides the area for P(Z ≤ 1.56).

15.   The controlled process has a mean of 50 and a standard deviation of 5. What is the probability that a random sample of 16 items will yield a mean greater than 53?

   a.   0.99
   b.   0.01
   c.   0.49
   d.   0.58
   e.   0.42

Key: b.   0.01   (Ref. Applications Question 48, October 1974)
   Given: Mean μ = 50 (controlled process),   σ = 5, n = 16, $\overline{X}$ = 53.
   Find: $P(\overline{X} > 53)$ = P(mean of the sample will be greater than 53) = ?

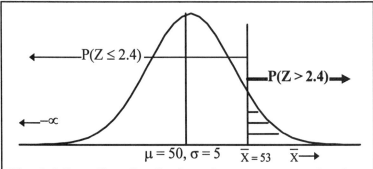

We will assume normal distribution for the data, as the question does not specify it. First draw a picture of normal distribution based on the given data and highlight the area that is of interest as shown in Fig. 4-3. This is a case of sampling distribution of means.

Fig. 4-3 Sampling distribution of means - area under the curve for $\overline{X}$>53

The standard error of mean is $\sigma_x = \dfrac{\sigma}{\sqrt{n}} = \dfrac{5}{\sqrt{16}} = 1.250$, and $Z = \dfrac{\overline{X} - \mu}{\sigma_x} = \dfrac{53 - 50}{1.25} = \dfrac{3}{1.25} = 2.4$

We need to find the area *beyond*[2] the value Z = 2.4, i.e., find P(Z > 2.4).
From the Z table, P(Z ≤ 2.4) = 0.9918 and hence, the area beyond 53 is given as
P(Z >2.4) = 1– P(Z ≤ 2.4)
                = 1 – 0.9918
                = 0.0082 ≈ 0.01

16.   A point estimate means

   a.   two points are used to define the confidence interval of the population parameter
   b.   the confidence limits of the mean
   c.   the estimation of the confidence limits of the population parameter
   d.   a single number or a value computed from the sample data to make an inference about the

_____

[2] *Fundamental Concepts of Probability, Statistics, Regression and DOE* by Jagdish Vani, 3rd edition, April 1993, Section 2.

population parameter

Key: d.   a single number or a value computed from the sample data to make an inference about the
              population parameter
The point estimate is a single value and it is the center of the interval estimate. It is less
preferable than the interval estimate as it provides only a single value estimate of the population
parameter. The remaining choices describe the interval estimate concepts, such as confidence
interval or limits.

17.   The confidence limits are defined as

       a.   an interval between two numbers which is likely to include the population value
       b.   the high and low values or the upper and lower boundaries of the confidence interval
       c.   the degree of uncertainty or degree of confidence that an estimation about the value of the
             population parameter is correct
       d. $1 - \alpha$ where α is the level of significance

Key: b.   the high and low values or the upper and lower boundaries of the confidence interval

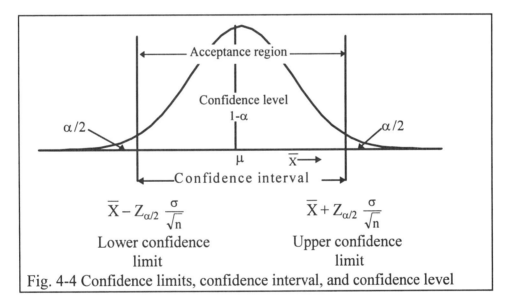

Fig. 4-4 Confidence limits, confidence interval, and confidence level

Watch out for similar looking terms here. Choice a defines the *confidence interval* (C.I.), and
choice c represents the *confidence level*. Choice d indicates the confidence level $1 - \alpha$. Fig. 4-4
graphically shows the relationship of these terms used in interval estimates and the formulas of
C.I. for the Z statistic.

18.   The degree of certainty or degree of confidence that an estimation about the value of the
       population parameter is correct is called

       a.   the confidence limits
       b.   the confidence interval
       c.   the confidence level

        d.   all of the above

Key: c.   the confidence level
        The confidence level is defined as the degree of certainty that an estimation about the value of the population parameter is correct. Fig. 4-4 graphically shows the confidence level as $1 - \alpha$.

19.   When finding a confidence interval for mean μ based on a sample size of n

        a.   increasing n increases the interval
        b.   having to use s_X instead of σ decreases the interval
        c.   the larger the interval, the better the estimate of μ
        d.   increasing n decreases the interval

Key: d.   increasing n decreases the interval (Ref. Principles Question 36, October 1972)
        This can be easily understood by studying the confidence interval formula. If the population standard deviation σ is known, then the C.I. is given as C.I. $= \overline{X} \pm Z_{\alpha/2} \dfrac{\sigma}{\sqrt{n}}$. If n increases, $\dfrac{\sigma}{\sqrt{n}}$ becomes smaller as n is in the denominator and hence it results in a smaller confidence interval. Hence choice a is incorrect. Choice b is incorrect because, if we use $s_x = \dfrac{s}{\sqrt{n}}$ instead of σ, generally the t statistic is used to calculate C.I., e.g., C.I. $= \overline{X} \pm t_{\alpha/2} \dfrac{s}{\sqrt{n}}$. The term s_x is a slightly larger value than σ, because of the $n - 1$ term used to calculate sample standard deviation s, and the value of t from the t table is higher than Z for a given confidence level and sample size n. This will result in an increase in C.I. Choice c is incorrect because, if the interval is larger, it represents more error or a less accurate value. Hence it does not give a better estimate of μ.

20.   If sample size n is increased, keeping all the data as constant, the confidence interval will

        a.   remain unchanged
        b.   will increase
        c.   will decrease
        d.   all of the above

Key: c.   will decrease
        Refer to Question 19 for explanation.

21.   Suppose that given X = 50 and Z = ±1.96, we established 95% confidence limits for μ of 30 and 70. This means that

        a.   the probability that $\mu = 50$ is 0.05
        b.   the probability that $\mu = 50$ is 0.95
        c.   the probability that the interval contains μ is 0.05
        d.   the probability that the interval contains μ is 0.95
        e.   none of the above

Key: d. the probability that the interval contains μ is 0.95
(Ref. Principles Question 17, August 1978)
In the interval estimation, we try to define the confidence interval for the population parameter such as mean μ for a given confidence level $1 - \alpha$. The confidence interval specifies both lower and upper limits for the population parameter μ and not for the sample statistics $\overline{X}$. The limits 30 and 40 define the 95% probability that the given interval contains the population mean μ. Hence Choice d is correct. Choices a and b are not correct because they refer to the point estimate instead of the interval estimate, i.e., they give the probability that the mean $\mu = 50$ is 0.05 or 0.95 instead of an interval that contains μ. Choice c is incorrect because it describes a 5% and not a 95% confidence level. (Note: The question states X = 50 which seems to be an error, it should be corrected to read $\overline{X} = 50$.)

22. Suppose that given $\overline{X} = 35$ and $Z_{0.01} = \pm 2.58$, we established confidence limits for μ of 30 and 40. This means that

   a. the probability that $\mu = 35$ is 0.01
   b. the probability that $\mu = 35$ is 0.99
   c. the probability that the interval contains μ is 0.01
   d. the probability that the interval contains μ is 0.99
   e. none of the above

Key: d. the probability that the interval contains μ is 0.99
(Ref. Principles Question 58, October 1974)
Refer to Question 21 above for an explanation, as the question is repeated with only slight changes in the value of the sample mean, the confidence level, and the confidence limits.

23. Given $Z_{0.05} = \pm 1.96$, the mean of a sample as 30, and the standard error of the mean as 5, the lower limit of the interval that would include the population mean with probability 0.95 is

   a. 20.20
   b. 28.04
   c. 15.31
   d. 25.00
   e. 24.00

Key: a. 20.20 (Ref. Applications Question 74, October 1974)

Given: $Z_{0.05} = \pm 1.96$, $\overline{X} = 30$; the standard error of mean $\sigma_x = \dfrac{\sigma}{\sqrt{n}} = 5$; $\alpha = 0.05$.

Find: The lower confidence limit on population mean μ at a 95% confidence level.
First draw the picture of the normal distribution as shown in Fig. 4-5 for the given data. This is a simple case of finding the confidence limits using the C.I. formula and Z statistic.

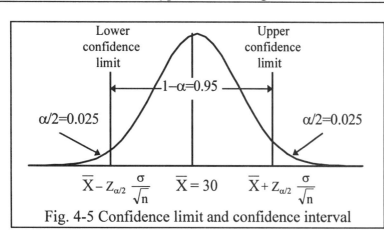

Lower confidence limit is given as:

$$LCL = \overline{X} - Z_{\alpha/2}\frac{\sigma}{\sqrt{n}}$$

$$= 30 - 1.96 \times 5 = 20.2$$

In some questions, you may be asked to find the upper confidence limit which is given as

$$UCL = \overline{X} + Z_{\alpha/2}\frac{\sigma}{\sqrt{n}}$$

$$= 30 + 1.96 \times 5 = 39.8$$

Fig. 4-5 Confidence limit and confidence interval

24.   The sample of 100 parts shows an average diameter of 1.5 mm with a population standard deviation $\sigma = 0.25$. The confidence interval for mean diameter of a part at 5% level of significance is

    a.   ±0.049
    b. 1.5 ± 0.49
    c.   (1.451, 1.549)
    d.   (1.4589, 1.5411)

Key: c.   (1.451, 1.549)

Given: $\overline{X} = 1.5$ mm, $\sigma = 0.25$ mm, n = 100, $1 - \alpha = 0.95$ or 95% confidence level.
Find: Confidence interval for the mean diameter.
We will assume normal distribution for the data, as the question does not specify it.

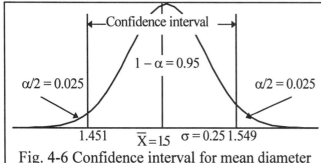

Fig. 4-6 Confidence interval for mean diameter

First draw the picture of the normal distribution as shown in Fig. 4-6 for the given data. The standard error of mean is:

$$\sigma_x = \frac{\sigma}{\sqrt{n}} = \frac{0.25}{\sqrt{100}} = 0.025$$

As σ is known, i.e., $\sigma = 0.25$ mm, we use the Z statistic for normal distribution. For $1 - \alpha = 0.95$, the Z table gives $Z = \pm 1.96$.

Hence the C.I. on μ will be $\mu = \overline{X} \pm Z \sigma_x = 1.5 \pm 1.96(0.025) = 1.5 \pm 0.049$, i.e., C.I. on μ is (1.451, 1.549).

25.   For a sample of 30 parts, the sample average is 12 with a standard deviation of 1.2. The confidence interval for the mean at a 99% confidence level is

    a.   (11.3964, 12.6036)
    b.   (11.4361, 12.5639)
    c.   ±0.5639

      d.   (8.4, 15.36)

Key: a.   (11.3964, 12.6036)

Given: n = 30, $\overline{X}$ = 12 and sample standard deviation S = 1.2, α = 1 – 0.99 = 0.01, symmetric.
Find: C.I. on the mean.
The data provide the sample standard deviation and not the population σ. Hence the standard

error of mean is calculated using sample data: $S_x = \dfrac{S}{\sqrt{n}} = \dfrac{1.2}{\sqrt{30}} = 0.219$.

As σ *is unknown,* we use the t statistic. From the t table for 1 – α = 99%, df = n –1= 30 – 1 = 29,
we get $t_{0.995}$ = 2.756. Hence the C.I. on μ will be

$\mu = \overline{X} \pm t \times S_x = 12 \pm 2.756(0.219) = 12 \pm 0.6036$, i.e., (11.3964, 12.6036).

26.   Find the confidence interval for the mean of a product characteristic having the sample average
      of 50, sample size of 64, and sample standard deviation of 8 at a 95% confidence level.

      a. 50 ± 2.5
      b. 50 ± 1.96
      c. 50 ± 1.75
      d 50 ± 3.00

Key: b. 50 ± 1.96

Given: $\overline{X}$ = 50, n = 64 items, S = 8, 95% confidence level.
Find: The 95 % confidence interval.
As sample size increases, the t value approaches normal distribution. Here the data from 64
samples indicate that t statistics for 63 df should be obtained, which most of the t tables do not
provide. The t value will be approximately 1.998, which is very close to the value of the Z = $\pm$
1.96, and hence use the Z statistic instead of t.

Hence C.I. on μ will be C.I. = $\overline{X} \pm Z_{\alpha/2}\ \dfrac{\sigma}{\sqrt{n}} = 50 \pm \dfrac{8}{\sqrt{64}} = 50 \pm 1.96$.

27.   Find the confidence interval for the mean of a product characteristic having the sample average
      of 50, sample size of 64, and sample standard deviation of 8 at a 100% confidence level.

      a. 50 ± 2.5
      b. 50 ± 1.96
      c. $50 \pm \infty$
      d 50 ± 3.00

Key: c. $50 \pm \infty$

Given: n = 64, S = 8, confidence level = 1– α = 100, $\overline{X}$ = 50.
Find: Confidence interval at a 100% confidence level.

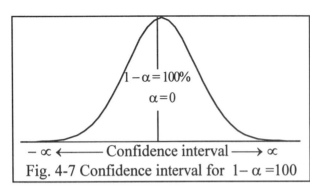

Fig. 4-7 Confidence interval for $1-\alpha = 100$

First draw the picture of normal distribution as shown in Fig. 4-7. The confidence level is 100%, i.e., the acceptance region is the complete area and there is no rejection region, or $\alpha = 0\%$. Hence the 100% confidence interval for the population mean is $-\infty \leq \mu \leq \infty$. The population mean lies between $-\infty$ and $+\infty$ with a 100% confidence level.

28.   Based on the following data, determine the confidence interval for the mean:
$\sigma = 0.30$, n = 10, $\overline{X}$ = 15 and 5% level of significance.

     a.   (14.756, 15.244)
     b.   (14.814, 15.186)
     c.   (14.869, 15.131)
     d.   (14.827, 15.173)

Key: b.   (14.814, 15.186)
Given: The data above, σ *known.*
Find: C.I. for the mean at 5% level of significance, i.e., $1 - \alpha = 0.95$.
We will assume normal distribution for the data, as the question does not specify it. First draw the picture of the normal distribution as shown in Fig. 4-8 for the given data.

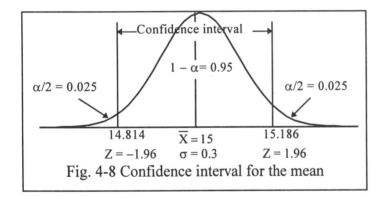

Fig. 4-8 Confidence interval for the mean

As σ *is known,* use the Z statistic to determine the C.I. For the 95% confidence level, the Z table provides $Z = \pm 1.96$.

$$\text{C.I.} = \overline{X} \pm Z_{\alpha/2} \frac{\sigma}{\sqrt{n}}$$

$$= 15 \pm 1.96 \frac{0.3}{\sqrt{10}} = 15 \pm 0.186,$$

i.e., 14.814 and 15.186.

29.   Consider the following data: $\sigma = 0.30$, n = 10, $\overline{X}$ = 15, and the C.I. for the mean at a 95% confidence level is (14.814, 15.186). What will be the effect on the C.I. if the confidence level is increased from 95% to 99%?

     a.   C.I. will remain unchanged.
     b.   C.I. will decrease.
     c.   C.I. will increase.
     d.   Cannot calculate the C.I. value for a 99% confidence level.

Key: c.   C.I. will increase.
Given: $\sigma = 0.30$, n = 10, $\overline{X}$ = 15, the C.I. is (14.814, 15.186) at a 95% confidence level.

Find: Effect on C.I. for the mean at a 99% confidence level.

We will assume normal distribution for the data, as the question does not specify it. First draw the picture of the normal distribution as shown in Fig. 4-9 for the given data. It shows the 99% values in italics.

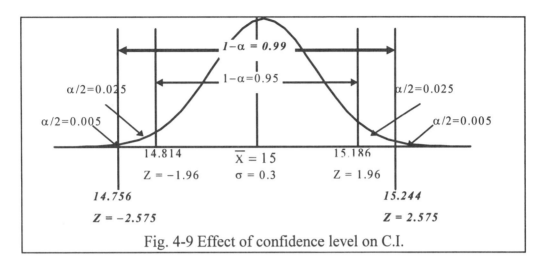

Fig. 4-9 Effect of confidence level on C.I.

As σ *is known*, use the Z statistic to find the C.I. at the 99% confidence level, i.e., Z = ± 2.575.

$$\text{C.I.} = \overline{X} \pm Z_{\alpha/2} \frac{\sigma}{\sqrt{n}} = 15 \pm 2.575 \frac{0.3}{\sqrt{10}} = 15 \pm 0.244, \text{ i.e., } 14.756 \text{ and } 15.244.$$

This proves that the C.I. is *increased* from ±0.186 to ±0.244, i.e., from (14.814, 15.186) to (14.756, 15.244) when the confidence level is increased from 95% to 99%.

30.   Consider the following data: σ = 0.30, n = 10, $\overline{X}$ = 15, and the C.I. for the mean at a 95% confidence level is (14.814, 15.186). What will be the effect on the C.I. if the sample size is increased from 10 to 20?

    a.   C.I. will remain unchanged.
    b.   C.I. will decrease.
    c.   C.I. will increase.
    d.   Cannot calculate the C.I. value for a 99% confidence level.

Key: b.   C.I. will decrease.

Given: σ = 0.30, n = 10, $\overline{X}$ = 15, the C.I. is (14.814, 15.186) at a 95% confidence level.

Find: The C.I. for the mean at a 95% confidence level for n = 20 instead of n = 10.

We will assume normal distribution for the data, as the question does not specify it. First draw the picture of the normal distribution as shown in Fig. 4-10 for the given data.

As σ *is known*, use the Z statistic to determine C.I. for the 95% confidence level, i.e., Z = ± 1.96.

$$\text{C.I.} = \overline{X} \pm Z_{\alpha/2} \frac{\sigma}{\sqrt{n}} = 15 \pm 1.96 \frac{0.3}{\sqrt{20}} = 15 \pm 0.131, \text{ i.e., } 14.869 \text{ and } 15.131.$$

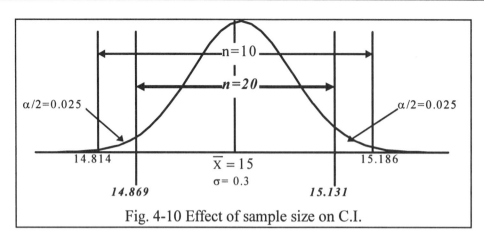

Fig. 4-10 Effect of sample size on C.I.

This proves that the C.I. is *decreased* from (14.814, 15.186) to (14.869, 15.131) when the sample size is increased from n = 10 to n = 20.

31.   If the sample size n is increased, keeping all the data constant, the confidence interval will

   a.   remain unchanged
   b.   will increase
   c.   will decrease
   d.   all of the above

Key: c.   will decrease

The C.I. for the population parameter μ is given as C.I. $= \overline{X} \pm Z_{\alpha/2} \dfrac{\sigma}{\sqrt{n}}$. Here as n increases, the

term $Z_{\alpha/2} \dfrac{\sigma}{\sqrt{n}}$ becomes smaller because the term 'n' is in the denominator. This results in an

overall smaller C.I. as shown in Question 30 above.

32.   If it was known that a population of 30,000 parts had a standard deviation of 0.05 seconds, what size sample would be required to maintain an error no greater than 0.01 second with a confidence level of 95%?

   a.   235
   b.   487
   c.   123
   d.   96
   e.   78

Key: d.   96   (Ref. Applications Question 16, August 1978)
   Given: N = 30,000 parts; σ = 0.05 second; E = error = ± 0.01 second, 1 − α = 95% confidence
         level, i.e., α = 5%.
   Find: Sample size n.
   We will assume normal distribution for the data, as the question does not specify it. First draw

the picture of the normal distribution as shown in Fig. 4-11 for the given data. The term error may seem like a new term at first, but it is easy to understand using the formula for the C.I. on μ.

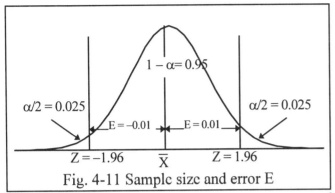

Fig. 4-11 Sample size and error E

Here at the $(1-\alpha)$ confidence level, the C.I. on μ is C.I. $= \overline{X} \pm Z_{\alpha/2} \dfrac{\sigma}{\sqrt{n}}$ where the term $Z_{\alpha/2} \dfrac{\sigma}{\sqrt{n}}$ is the error or precision in estimating the population mean μ. It is shown as E in Fig. 4-11, i.e.,

$$E = Z_{\alpha/2} \frac{\sigma}{\sqrt{n}}.$$

And solving for the sample size we get $n = \dfrac{Z^2 \sigma^2}{E^2}$.

As σ *is known,* use the Z statistic to determine C.I. for the 95% confidence level, i.e., $Z = \pm 1.96$.

Hence, $n = \dfrac{(1.96)^2 (0.05)^2}{(0.01)^2} = 96.04 \cong 96.$

33.   The standard deviation for a part is $\sigma = 0.25$. How large of a sample must we take to be 95% confident of getting a precision of 0.025 of the true mean?

    a.   100
    b.   385
    c.   96
    d.   358

Key: b.   385

Given: $\sigma = 0.25$; precision $E = \pm 0.025$; $\alpha = 1 - 0.95 = 0.05$.

Find: Sample size n.

For a 95% confidence level, $Z = \pm 1.96$. Sample size n is given as $n = \dfrac{Z^2 \sigma^2}{E^2}$

Hence $n = \dfrac{(1.96)^2 \times (0.25)^2}{(0.025)^2} = 384.16 \cong 385.$

34.   If the precision in Question 33 above is changed to 0.05 of the true mean, what will be the sample size at a 95% confidence level?

    a.   100
    b.   385
    c.   358
    d.   97

Key: d.   97
        Given: $\sigma = 0.25$; precision $E = \pm 0.05$, $\alpha = 1 - 0.95 = 0.05$.
        Find: Sample size for a 95% confidence level.

        For a 95% confidence level, $Z = \pm 1.96$, and hence $n = \dfrac{Z^2 \sigma^2}{E^2} = \dfrac{(1.96)^2 \times (0.25)^2}{(0.05)^2} = 96.04 \cong 97$.

35.   Which table should be used to determine a C.I. on the mean when σ is not known and the sample size is 10?

        a.   z
        b.   t
        c.   F
        d. χ^2

Key: b: t   (Ref. Applications Question 20, July 1984)
        Here the population standard deviation σ *is not known*, and the sample size is n = 10, which is a very small sample size. Hence the t table is used instead of the Z table.

36.   Two machines gave the following results on a product characteristic. The first machine with a population variance of 0.25 gave a mean of 11 from a sample of 5 parts. The second machine with a population variance of 0.16 gave a sample mean of 9 from a sample of 10 parts. Find the C.I. on the difference of the two means at a 95% confidence level.

        a. 2 ± 0.50
        b. 11 ± 0.51
        c. ± 0.51
        d. 10 ± 0.51

Key: a. 2 ± 0.50
        Given: $n_1 = 5$, $\overline{X}_1 = 11$, $\sigma_1^2 = 0.25$, $n_2 = 10$, $\overline{X}_2 = 9$, $\sigma_2^2 = 0.16$, and $1 - \alpha = 95\%$.
        Find: C.I. on the difference of the two means at a 95% confidence level.

        We will assume normal distribution for the data, as the question does not specify it. Here σ_1^2 and σ_2^2 are known. The C.I. on the difference of two means, with two population variances known, is given by the formula:

        $$\mu_1 - \mu_2 = (\overline{X}_1 - \overline{X}_2) \pm Z\sqrt{\dfrac{\sigma_1^2}{n_1} + \dfrac{\sigma_2^2}{n_2}} = (11 - 9) \pm 1.96\sqrt{\dfrac{0.25}{5} + \dfrac{0.16}{10}} = 2 \pm 0.50$$

        Note: Be careful with the σ_1^2 and σ_2^2. They are already given as variances or squares, hence do not square them again when you substitute them in the formula.

37.   t distribution is

        a.   the same as normal distribution

      b.   a skewed distribution

      c.   bell shaped and more spread out than the normal distribution

      d.   bell shaped and less spread out than the normal distribution

Key: c.   bell shaped and more spread out than the normal distribution

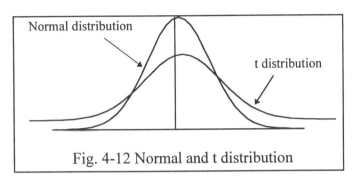

Fig. 4-12 Normal and t distribution

Fig. 4-12 shows the relationship between normal and t distribution. The t distribution is a bell shaped and symmetric distribution. It is flatter and wider than the normal distribution. The t statistic is used when the *population standard deviation σ is unknown* and is found using n – 1 degrees of freedom where n represents the sample size.

38.   The standard deviation S_x of Student t distribution is

      a.   the same as normal distribution

      b. $S_x = 1$

      c.   greater than 1

      d.   smaller than 1

Key: c.   greater than 1

This is the property of Student t distribution which has a standard deviation of greater than 1, whereas the standardized normal distribution has the standard deviation of $\sigma = 1$ and $\mu = 0$.

39.   If the population standard deviation σ is not known and sample size is small, you should use

      a.   Z statistic and normal distribution

      b.   t distribution

      c.   binomial distribution

      d.   α level of significance

Key: b.   t distribution

The t distribution is used when the population standard deviation σ is unknown and the sample size is generally smaller. As the sample size n increases, at a given confidence level, the t distribution approximates the normal distribution.

40.   At what sample size does the value of the t statistic approach approximately normal distribution conditions?

      a.   sample size of n = 6

      b.   sample size of n = 11

      c.   sample size of n = 21

      d.   sample size of n = ∝

Key: d.   sample size of n = ∝
       The t distribution is defined by its degrees of freedom (df = n − 1) at a given confidence level.
       Refer to Table 4-2 for the t value at the 97.5% confidence level and 5, 10, 20, and ∝ df, for the
       sample sizes given in the question. You can see that as the sample size n reaches ∝, i.e., the df
       reaches ∝, the value of t decreases and it becomes the same as that of the Z statistic value of
       normal distribution.

Table 4-2 t values at 97.5% confidence level

df	$t_{0.975}$
5	2.571
10	2.228
20	2.086
:	:
:	:
120	1.980
∝	**1.960**

For 95% area on a two-tail t test, at df of 5, 10, and 20, the t values are much higher than 1.96. At df = 120, we get t = 1.98. For df = ∝, the value of t is 1.96, which is the same as the Z value for 95% area under the normal curve.

41.   One use for a Student t test is to determine whether or not differences exist in

       a.   variability
       b.   quality costs
       c.   correlation coefficients
       d.   averages
       e.   none of the above

Key: d.   averages   (Ref. Principles Question 27, August 1978)
       The Student t distribution is used to test the differences in the averages or means of two
       populations when the population standard deviations σ_1 and σ_2 are unknown and the sample
       sizes are small.

42.   For a test of hypothesis,

       a.   only the null hypothesis Ho needs to be defined
       b.   only the alternate hypothesis Ha or H₁ needs to be defined
       c.   both the null hypothesis Ho and the alternate hypothesis Ha need to be defined
       d.   the alternate hypothesis considers the two tail test condition only

Key: c.   both the null hypothesis Ho and the alternate hypothesis Ha need to be defined
       In a test of hypothesis, the null hypothesis Ho indicates that *there is no change*, or there is no
       significant difference, whereas the alternate hypothesis Ha indicates that there is a change or a
       significant difference. If Ho is rejected, then Ha is accepted. Ha also helps define whether it will
       be a two tail or one tail test of hypothesis and its acceptance region.

43.   In a test of hypothesis, 1 − α defines

    a.   the acceptance region
    b.   the level of significance
    c.   the rejection region
    d.   the 95% confidence level

Key: a.   the acceptance region

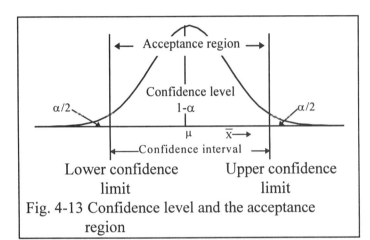

Fig. 4-13 Confidence level and the acceptance region

In a test of hypothesis, $1-\alpha$ indicates the confidence level and it defines the acceptance region for the statistics used such as the Z or t statistic, etc. as shown in Fig. 4-13. It shows a two tail test and each tail indicates the rejection region at the $\alpha/2$ level of significance. Choices b and c indicate the term α, which is the level of significance, and it defines the total rejection region.

44.   A null hypothesis requires several assumptions; a basic one of which is

    a.   that the variables are dependent
    b.   that the variables are independent
    c.   that the sample size is adequate
    d.   that the confidence interval is ±2 standard deviation
    e.   that the correlation coefficient is − 0.95

Key: b.   that the variables are independent   (Ref. Principles Question 26, August 1978)

45.   Which of the following cannot be a null hypothesis?

    a.   The population means are equal.
    b. $p' = 0.5$.
    c.   The sample means are equal.
    d.   The differences in the population means is 3.85".

Key: c.   the sample means are equal   (Ref. Principles Question 23, July 1984)
    The key phrase is ***cannot be***. The test of hypothesis is for the population parameter such as mean μ, proportion defectives p', etc., and not for the sample statistic such as sample mean $\overline{X}$. We want to test the hypothesis that the assertion about the population parameter is true. Choices a, b, and d are statements for the test of the hypothesis for population parameters, but choice c is a statement for the sample means. Hence choice c is not a correct statement for defining the null hypothesis.

46.   Which of the following cannot be a null hypothesis?

    a.   The population means are equal.
    b. $p' = 0.5$.
    c. $p' = 0.25$.
    d.   The sample means are equal.
    e.   The differences in the population means from which the samples were drawn is 3.85".

Key: d.   The sample means are equal. (Ref. Principles Question 29, October 1974)
    Please refer to Question 45 for comments.

47.   In a statistical hypothesis, a Type I error is committed by

    a.   rejecting the null hypothesis when it is false
    b.   rejecting the null hypothesis when it is true
    c.   accepting the null hypothesis when it is true
    d.   not rejecting the null hypothesis when it is false

Key: b.   rejecting the null hypothesis when it is true
    Refer to Table 4-3 which shows a total of four outcomes, of which two are errors called Type I
    and Type II errors. The Type I error occurs if you reject a null hypothesis when it is true. If this
    happens, it is called the *producer's risk* α.

Table 4-3 The outcomes of a hypothesis testing experiment

DECISION	NATURE OF HYPOTHESIS	
	Ho TRUE	*Ho FALSE*
DO NOT REJECT Ho, i.e., ACCEPT Ho	Good / Correct Decision Probability = $1 - \alpha$	**TYPE II ERROR** **Bad / Wrong Decision** **Probability = β** ***CONSUMER'S RISK***
REJECT Ho	**TYPE I ERROR** **Bad / Wrong Decision** **Probability = α** ***PRODUCER'S RISK***	Good / Correct Decision Probability = $1 - \beta$
TOTAL PROBABILITY	1	1

48.   The beta risk is the risk of

    a.   selecting the wrong hypothesis
    b.   accepting a hypothesis when it is false
    c.   accepting a hypothesis when it is true
    d.   rejecting a hypothesis when it is true

Key: b.   accepting a hypothesis when it is false (Ref. Principles Question 53, October 1972)
    Refer to Table 4-3 in Question 47 for both Type I and Type II errors. *The Type II error means*

accepting a hypothesis when it is false, resulting in an incorrect decision. Simply stated, beta, denoted as β, is the risk of accepting bad parts as good and it results in a *consumer's risk.*

49.   Probability (not rejecting Ho | Ho is false) is called

   a.   the Type I error α
   b.   the Type II error β
   c.   the Type I error $1 - \alpha$
   d   the Type II error $1 - \beta$

Key: b.   the Type II error β
Refer to Table 4-3 in Question 47 for both Type I and Type II errors. *The Type II error β occurs if we accept a null hypothesis Ho when Ho is not true.* It is also called *consumers' risk.*

50.   A null hypothesis assumes that a process is producing no more than the maximum allowable rate of defective items. The Type II error is to conclude that the process

   a.   is producing too many defectives when it actually isn't
   b.   is not producing too many defectives when it actually is
   c.   is not producing too many defectives when it is not
   d.   is producing too many defectives when it is

Key: b.   is not producing too many defectives when it actually is
(Ref. Principles Question 1, July 1984)
Let's assume that the maximum allowable rate of defective items is $p = 0.10$. The null hypothesis is: Ho: $p = 0.10$ or 10% and Ha: $p > 0.10$. The Type II error means accepting the hypothesis when it is false, i.e., accepting the process as a good process when it is actually producing more than 10% defectives ($p > 0.10$). If the process is actually producing more than 10% (too many defectives) and we conclude that the process is good and not producing too many defectives, it will result in a Type II error.

51.   If two sigma limits are substituted for conventional three sigma limits on a control chart, one of the following occurs

   a.   decrease in alpha risk
   b.   increase in beta risk
   c.   increase in alpha risk
   d.   increase in sample size

Key: c.   increase in alpha risk   (Ref. Principles Question 54, October 1972)
The control limits on a control chart normally represent ±3 sigma limits, i.e., a 99.73% confidence level or 0.27% alpha risk of a Type I error. If ±2 sigma limits are used instead of ±3 sigma limits, it will result in a 95.46% confidence level or 4.54 % alpha risk of a Type I error.

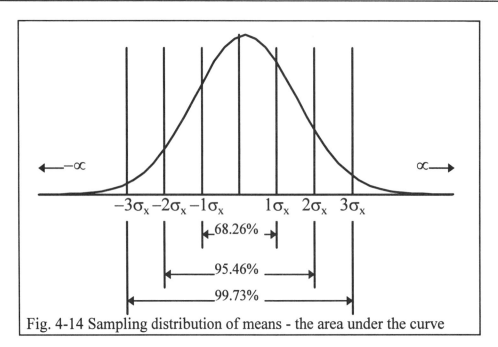

Fig. 4-14 Sampling distribution of means - the area under the curve

This means the alpha risk is increased to 4.54%. Fig. 4-14 shows the area under the curve for $\pm 1\sigma_x$, $\pm 2\sigma_x$, and $\pm 3\sigma_x$ standard deviations for sampling distribution of means.

52.   A process calls for the mean value of a dimension to be 2.02". Which of the following should be used as the null hypothesis to test whether or not the process is achieving this mean?

     a.   The mean of the population is 2.02".
     b.   The mean of the sample is 2.02".
     c.   The mean of the population is not 2.02".
     d.   The mean of the sample is not 2.02".
     e.   All of the above are acceptable null hypotheses.

Key: a.   The mean of the population is 2.02".   (Ref. Principles Question 25, October 1974)
The term null means '*no change.*' We use hypothesis testing to make assertions or estimations about a population parameter. Here the population parameter given is the mean = 2.02". Hence choice a is correct as the null hypothesis Ho: μ = 2.02". Choices b and d refer to a sample which is incorrect. Choice c is incorrect because it represents an alternate hypothesis Ha.

53.   If, in a t test, alpha is 0.05,

     a.   5% of the time we will say that there is no real difference but in reality there is a difference
     b.   5% of the time we will make a correct inference
     c.   5% of the time we will say that there is a real difference when there really is not a difference
     d.   95% of the time we will make an incorrect inference
     e.   95% of the time the null hypothesis will be correct

Key: c.   5% of the time we will say that there is a real difference when there really is not a
              difference   (Ref. Principles Question 25, July 1984)
      Refer to Table 4-3 which shows the alpha (α) as a Type I error, i.e., we reject the hypothesis
      when it is true. In the above case, we are testing the null hypothesis Ho so that there is no
      difference in some population parameter, e.g., Ho: $\mu = \mu o$. If the level of significance is 5%, it
      means 5% of the time we are likely to make a Type I error of rejecting the hypothesis, or we are
      likely to conclude that there really is a difference in the population parameter when actually there
      is no real difference. This question is repeated in the October 1974 examination.[3]

      *You may find the language very confusing, hence, read the question again and use the concepts
      defined in Table 4-3.*

54.   If in a t test alpha is 0.01,

      a.   1% of the time we will say that there is a real difference, when there really is not a
              difference
      b.   1% of the time we will make a correct inference
      c.   1% of the time we will say that there is no real difference but in reality there is a
              difference
      d.   99% of the time we will make an incorrect inference
      e.   99% of the time the null hypothesis will be correct

Key: a.   1% of the time we will say that there is a real difference, when there really is not a
              difference   (Ref. Principles Question 16, August 1978)
      Refer to Question 53 above for discussion. The only difference is that the value of alpha is 0.01
      or 1% as the level of significance instead of 5%.

55.   The difference between setting alpha equal to 0.05 and alpha equal to 0.01 in hypothesis testing
      is

      a.   with alpha equal to 0.05 we are more willing to risk a Type I error
      b.   with alpha equal to 0.05 we are more willing to risk a Type II error
      c.   alpha equal to 0.05 is a more "conservative" test of the null hypothesis (Ho)
      d.   with alpha equal to 0.05 we are less willing to risk a Type I error
      e.   none of the above

Key: a.   with alpha equal to 0.05 we are more willing to risk a Type I error
              (Ref. Principles Question 64, October 1974)
      When $\alpha = 0.05$, the Type I error or the risk will be 5%, i.e., 5% of the time we will reject the
      hypothesis when it is true. If $\alpha = 0.01$, the Type I error or the risk will be 1%. Hence with $\alpha =$
      0.05, we are more willing to risk a 5% Type I error, i.e., 5% of the time we will reject the
      hypothesis instead of 1%.

56.   The appropriate mathematical model for describing the sampling distribution of the fraction

---

[3] *ASQC CQE Examination*, Quality Progress, October 1974, Principles Section, Question 51.

defective in samples from a controlled process in which p' = 0.05 is

    a.   the normal curve
    b.   the binomial distribution in which p' = 0.05
    c.   the binomial distribution in which p' = 0.95
    d.   the alpha level

Key: b.   the binomial distribution in which p' = 0.05 (Ref. Principles Question 44, October 1974)
The binomial distribution is based on the attribute data of fraction defectives. Hence the sampling distribution of the fraction defectives in samples from a controlled process in which p' = 0.05 is best described by the binomial distribution p' = 0.05. Choice c is incorrect because the value of the fraction defectives given is p' = 0.05 and not 0.95.

57.   The degrees of freedom for the test of hypothesis used to test the difference between the two means when population standard deviations of the two populations are not known and not equal, are

    a. $n_1 + n_2 - 2$
    b. $n_1 - 1$
    c. $(n_1 - 1)(n_2 - 1)$
    d.   minimum of $n_1 - 1$ and $n_2 - 1$

Key: d.   minimum of $n_1 - 1$ and $n_2 - 1$

Given: This represents testing the difference between the two means when σ_1^2 and σ_2^2 are
unknown and unequal,[4] i. e., $\sigma_1^2 \neq \sigma_2^2$
Test Ho: $\mu_1 = \mu_2$, i.e., the means of two populations are equal.

Find: Degree of freedom (df)

Use t statistics as σ_1 and σ_2 are unknown and are unequal. $t_{\alpha/2} = \dfrac{(\overline{X}_2 - \overline{X}_2)}{\sqrt{\dfrac{S_1^2}{n_1} + \dfrac{S_2^2}{n_2}}}$ and refer to the t

table at df = minimum of $n_1 - 1$ and $n_2 - 1$. X_1 and X_2 are normally distributed and the standard deviations of the population are estimated by the sample standard deviations S_1 and S_2.

58.   A test of hypothesis can be

    a.   left-tailed test
    b.   two tailed test
    c.   right-tailed test
    d.   all of the above

Key: d.   all of the above

Depending on the statement of null hypothesis Ho and alternate hypothesis Ha, the test of

---

[4] *Fundamental Concepts of Probability, Statistics, Regression and DOE* by Jagdish Vani, 3rd edition, April 1993, Section 4.

hypothesis can be either a one tailed (left-tailed or right-tailed) test or a two tailed test.

59.   It is hypothesized that the average starting salary of a quality engineer is $30,000 and the population standard deviation is assumed to be $2000. If a random sample of 100 in a survey indicates the average salary to be $28,000, test the hypothesis with a 95% confidence level.

    a.   Reject the null hypothesis Ho: μ = 30,000.
    b.   Reject the alternate hypothesis Ha: $\mu \neq$ 30,000.
    c.   Accept the null hypothesis Ho: μ = 28,000.
    d.   Accept the null hypothesis Ho: μ = 30,000.

Key: a.   Reject the null hypothesis Ho: μ = 30,000.

Given: n = 100, $\overline{X}$ = $28,000, σ = $ 2000, confidence level = 0.95.
Find: Test the hypothesis Ho: μ = $30,000 and Ha: $\mu \neq$ $30,000.
We will assume normal distribution for the data, as the question does not specify it. First draw the picture of the normal distribution as shown in Fig. 4-15 for the given data. Here σ = 2000 is known, and hence, to test the hypothesis, we will use the Z statistic for the 95% confidence level.

$$Z = \frac{\overline{X} - \mu}{\sigma_x} = \frac{\overline{X} - \mu}{\sigma / \sqrt{n}} = \frac{28,000 - 30,000}{2000 / \sqrt{100}} = -10.0.$$

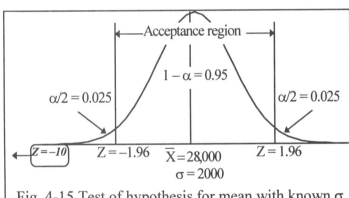

From the Z $_{table}$ for the 95% confidence level, $Z_{0.95}$ = ± 1.96. Hence $Z_{cal} > Z_{table}$, i.e., the Z calculated is outside the acceptance limit as shown in Fig. 4-15. Hence we reject the null hypothesis Ho: μ = 30,000 and accept the alternate hypothesis of Ha: $\mu \neq$ 30,000, which means that the mean salary is not $30,000 and there is a significant difference in the mean salary of the quality engineers.

Fig. 4-15 Test of hypothesis for mean with known σ

60.   A material is found to have a mean breaking strength of 1500 psi and a standard deviation of 100 psi. The company is using new techniques for controlling processes. You, as a quality manager, would like to see if these new techniques have increased the mean breaking strength. Hence a sample of 50 parts is taken which yields an average breaking strength of 1550 psi. What can you conclude with a 1% level of significance?

    a.   Reject the null hypothesis Ho: μ = 1500.
    b.   Reject the null hypothesis Ho: μ = 1550.
    c.   Accept the null hypothesis Ho: μ = 1500.
    d.   Accept the null hypothesis Ho: μ > 1550.

Key: a.   Reject the null hypothesis Ho: μ = 1500.
    Given: μ = 1500 psi; σ = *100 psi known*, n = 50, $\overline{X}$ = 1550 psi, α = 1% or 0.01.

Find: Test the hypothesis that the new mean strength is better than the existing material.
Ho: $\mu = 1500$ psi, i.e., there is really no change in the strength;
Ha: $\mu > 1500$ psi, i.e., new mean strength is better than existing mean strength 1500.

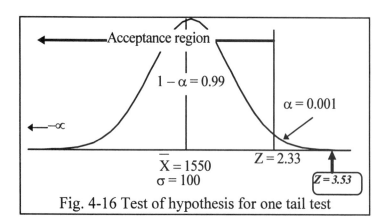

This indicates a *one tail test* and it gives the rejection region in the right tail. We will assume normal distribution for the data, as the question does not specify it. First draw the picture of the normal distribution as shown in Fig. 4-16 for the given data. As $\sigma = 100$ *psi known,* we use the Z statistic.

Fig. 4-16 Test of hypothesis for one tail test

$$Z_{cal} = \frac{\overline{X} - \mu}{\sigma_X} = \frac{\overline{X} - \mu}{\sigma / \sqrt{n}} = \frac{1550 - 1500}{100 / \sqrt{50}} = 3.53$$

From the Z table at a 99% confidence level and a rejection region of 1% as one tail area, $Z_{table} = \pm 2.325$. Hence $Z_{cal} > Z_{table}$, i.e., the Z_{cal} is outside the acceptance region and it falls in the rejection region in the right tail area. So we reject the null hypothesis that mean strength is 1500 psi at 1% level of significance. It means we accept the alternate hypothesis that there is significant difference, i.e., there is a significant increase in the breaking strength of the material because of the new techniques.

Note: This is a one tail and not a two tail test and hence be careful in referring to the Z table for 99% area. If you picked the value of Z = ± 2.575, it will give you an area of 0.005 in each tail, which is incorrect.

61.   A machine is designed to make parts of the size of 10 mm. The company has been receiving too many complaints from its major customer that the parts are shorter than 10 mm. The company's field engineer finds that a sample of 20 parts has an average size of 9.5 mm with a standard deviation of 0.50 mm. Should you accept the complaint and adjust your machine with a 5% level of significance?

    a.   Reject the null hypothesis that the machine produces the parts smaller than 10 mm.
    b.   Reject the null hypothesis that the machine produces parts 10 mm or larger.
    c.   Accept the null hypothesis that the machine produces parts smaller than 9.5 mm.
    d.   Accept the null hypothesis that the machine produces parts 9.5 mm or larger.

Key: b.   Reject the null hypothesis that the machine produces parts 10 mm or larger.

Given: $\mu = 10.0$ mm, n = 20 parts, $\overline{X} = 9.5$ mm, S = 0.50 mm, σ *is unknown*, $\alpha = 0.05$.
Find: Test the hypothesis   Ho: $\mu \geq 10$ mm, i.e., parts are larger than 10 mm.
                                   Ha: $\mu < 10$ mm, i.e., parts are shorter than 10 mm.
First draw the picture of the normal distribution as shown in Fig. 4-17 for the given data.

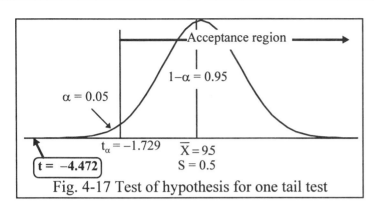

Fig. 4-17 Test of hypothesis for one tail test

Here σ is unknown but only sample standard deviation is known, and the sample size n = 20 < 30, we use the t statistic. As the company is receiving the complaints that the parts are short, we use *one sided t test* to test the null hypothesis Ho: μ ≥ 10 mm, i.e., parts are larger.

The acceptance region is the 95% area to the right of the tail. This indicates a *one tail test* and it gives the rejection region in the left tail as shown in Fig. 4-17.

For n = 20, S = 0.50 mm, and $\overline{X}$ = 9.5 mm, we get $t_{cal} = \dfrac{\overline{X}-\mu}{S_x} = \dfrac{\overline{X}-\mu}{S/\sqrt{n}} = \dfrac{9.5-10}{0.5/\sqrt{20}} = -4.472$

For n = 20, i.e., df = 20 – 1 = 19; one sided 95% level, the t table gives t_{table} = – 1.729. Hence $t_{cal} < t_{table}$, i.e., t_{cal} of – 4.472 lies outside of the t_{table} = –1.729. Hence the null hypothesis that parts are larger than 10 mm is rejected. It means the alternate hypothesis Ha, that parts are shorter than 10 mm, is accepted. The company should adjust the machine.

Note: This is a one tail and not a two tail test and hence be careful in referring to the t_{table} for 95% area. If you picked the value of t = ±2.093, it will give you an area of 0.025 in each tail, which is incorrect.

62.   A purchaser wants to determine whether or not there is any difference between the means of the convolute paperboard cans supplied by two different vendors A and B. A random sample of 100 cans is selected from the output of each vendor. The sample from A yielded a mean of 13.59 with a standard deviation of 5.94. The sample from B yielded a mean of 14.43 with a standard deviation of 5.61. Which of the following would be a suitable null hypothesis to test?

    a. $\mu_A = \mu_B$
    b. $\mu_A > \mu_B$
    c. $\mu_A < \mu_B$
    d. $\mu_A \neq \mu_B$

Key: a. $\mu_A = \mu_B$ (Ref. Applications Question 28, July 1984)
Given: Two vendors A and B. $\overline{X}_a$ = 13.59, S_a = 5.94; $\overline{X}_b$ = 14.43, S_b = 5.61; N = 100.
Find: A suitable statement for the null hypothesis.
We are given here all quantitative data for the samples A and B. But we do not need all the statistical data to write the null hypothesis. The null hypothesis is always for a population parameter indicating *that there is no change or no significant difference*. Hence the most suitable null hypothesis is choice a: $\mu_A = \mu_B$, i.e., the two means are the same and there is no significant difference in them. Choices b and c are incorrect as they do not indicate that two means are the same. Choice d is incorrect because it states that the two means are not the same.

63.   A supplier of cotton yarn claims that his product has an average breaking strength of 90
        pounds. To test his claim, you select a random sample of 16 pieces of yarn. If the standard
        deviation of his process is unknown and you use the normal curve theory instead of t distribution
        theory to test the null hypothesis, you would

        a.   increase the risk of Type I error
        b.   decrease the risk of Type I error
        c.   increase the risk of Type II error
        d.   both b and c
        e.   none of the above

Key: a.   increase the risk of Type I error   (Ref. Applications Question 32, October 1974)
        Given: Average breaking strength $\mu = 90$ pounds, n = 16 pieces of yarn.
        Find: Effect of normal vs. t distribution on the Type I or II error.

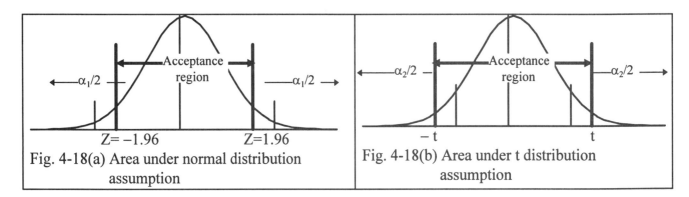

Fig. 4-18(a) Area under normal distribution
assumption

Fig. 4-18(b) Area under t distribution
assumption

        Fig. 4-18(a) shows the area under the assumption of *normal distribution* with Type I error of α_1
        and Fig. 4-18(b) shows the area under the assumption of *t distribution* with Type I error of α_2. If
        you assume normal distribution instead of t distribution, the area under t distribution is larger
        than the area in normal distribution because the t distribution is flatter than the normal
        distribution.

        Let us use the 95% confidence level as an example. The Z value for 95% is ±1.96, however the t
        value for n −1 = 16 − 1 = 15 degrees of freedom will be t = ±2.131. We can see that the t value is
        always greater than the Z value at different degrees of freedom and will reach to 1.96 at ∝
        degrees of freedom. The area in Fig. 4-18(a) is larger than that in Fig. 4-18(b) and hence if we
        use normal distribution and the Z statistic, we would have rejected the hypothesis at $Z_{cal} > 1.96$
        instead of 2.131 eventhough Ho may be true. It means the probability of rejecting the hypothesis
        is higher using the Z statistic than the t statistic and the Type I error increases with normal
        distribution.

64.   In order to test whether the outputs of two machines were yielding the same average value or
        one was larger than the other, a sample of 10 pieces was taken from each. The t value turned
        out to be 1.767. Using a level of significance of 0.05, one tailed test, we conclude that

        a.   the obtained t ratio does not fall within the critical region

b.   there was no significant difference between the means
c.   the null hypothesis was rejected
d.   the null hypothesis was accepted
e.   the question cannot be answered unless we know the standard deviations

Key: c.   the null hypothesis was rejected (Ref. Applications Question 45, October 1974)
Given: Two machines, $n_1 = n_2 = 10$, $t_{cal} = 1.767$; $\alpha = 0.05$, one tail test.
        Ho: $\mu_1 = \mu_2$, i.e., the means of two machines are the same.
        Ha: $\mu_1 > \mu_2$, i.e., the mean of one machine is better than the other.
Find: Test the hypothesis and make a conclusion for the means of two machines.
The population standard deviations σ_1 for machine 1 and σ_2 for machine 2 are not known. The question does not clearly indicate whether two standard deviations should be assumed to be equal. The answer changes significantly depending on this assumption.

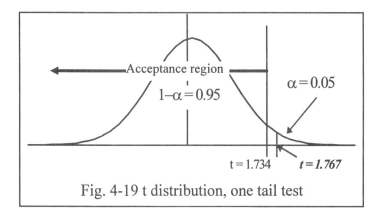

Fig. 4-19 t distribution, one tail test

Assumption I: $\sigma_1 = \sigma_2$, then the degrees of freedom[5] will be given as:
$df = n_1 + n_2 - 2 = 10 + 10 - 2 = 18$.
The t table value will be $t_{0.95,18} = 1.734$, and $t_{cal} = 1.767$, hence $t_{cal} > t_{0.95,18}$.
Fig. 4-19 shows that t_{cal} falls outside the critical region or acceptance region which is given in choice a. This means that the null hypothesis is rejected as shown in choice c.

Now you can see that choice a is also correct because the obtained t ratio does not fall within the critical region. However, choice c is a more appropriate choice as compared to choice a, because it provides the final conclusion about the hypothesis.

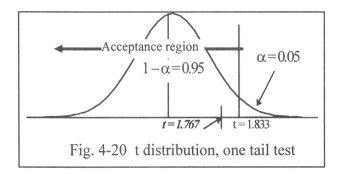

Fig. 4-20 t distribution, one tail test

Assumption II: $\sigma_1 = \sigma_2$, then the degrees of freedom[6] will be given as:
$df = \min (n_1 - 1, n_2 - 1) = 10 - 1 = 9$ (and not 18). The t_{table} value will be $t_{0.95, 9} = 1.833$ and $t_{cal} = 1.767$. Hence $t_{cal} < t_{0.95, 9}$.
Fig. 4-20 shows that t_{cal} falls inside the $t_{0.95, 9}$ critical region or the acceptance region, indicating that we fail to reject it.

In other words, we accept the null hypothesis. This matches choice d and also choice b as possible correct answers but not choice c.

ASQC's published answer is *choice c: null hypothesis was rejected which is true with assumption I only*. You can now see how much difference such an assumption makes in the overall

---

[5] *Juran's Quality Control Handbook* by J.M. Juran, 4th edition, McGraw-Hill, New York, pg. 23. 66, Table 23.29 Test 2(b).
[6] *Juran's Quality Control Handbook* by J.M. Juran, 4th edition, McGraw-Hill, New York, pg. 23. 66, Table 23.29 Test 2(d).

conclusion. You can get two opposite answers. Also there are two possible correct answers for any of the two assumptions.

Hence the best choice left is choice e which states "the question cannot be answered unless we know the standard deviations."

Note: You may contact the proctor in the examination and explain any such ambiguity or error. The proctor or chief proctor will document your concern in the proctor's report and forward it to the certification committee for further evaluation and action.

65.   In an experiment designed to compare two different ways of measuring a given quantity, it was desired to test the null hypothesis that the means were equal at the 0.05 level of significance. A sample of five parts was measured by method I and a sample of seven parts with method II. A t ratio of 2.179 was obtained. We should

    a.   reject the null hypothesis
    b.   fail to reject the null hypothesis
    c.   assert that there is no difference between the two methods
    d.   conclude that $\overline{X}_1$ is significantly greater than $\overline{X}_2$
    e.   conclude that we must know the sample means in order to answer the question

Key: b.   fail to reject the null hypothesis (Ref. Applications Question 13, October 1974)
       Given: Ho: $\mu_1 = \mu_2$, i.e., means of two measuring systems are equal;
              Ha: $\mu_1 \neq \mu_2$, $\alpha = 0.05$ or 95% confidence level; $n_1 = 5$ parts for method I, $n_2 = 7$ parts for method II, $t_{cal} = 2.179$.
       Find: Test the hypothesis and decide to fail to reject (in simple words accept it) or reject the Ho. The population standard deviations σ_1 for method I and σ_2 for method II are not known. The question does not clearly indicate whether two standard deviations should be assumed to be equal. The answer can change significantly depending on this assumption and the data.

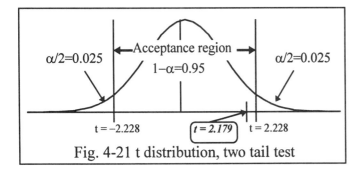
Fig. 4-21 t distribution, two tail test

Assumption I: $\sigma_1 = \sigma_2$, then the degrees of freedom[7] will be given as:
$df = n_1 + n_2 - 2 = 5 + 7 - 2 = 10$.
The t table value will be $t_{0.975, 10} = 2.228$, and $t_{cal} = 2.179$; hence $t_{cal} < t_{0.975,10}$. Fig. 4-21 shows that t_{cal} falls inside the critical region or acceptance region, i.e., we fail to reject the null hypothesis Ho.

This matches choice b. This also means that there is no significant difference in the two methods which matches choice c. ASQC's published answer is choice b.

Assumption II: $\sigma_1 = \sigma_2$; then the degrees of freedom[8] will be given as:

---
[7] *Juran's Quality Control Handbook* by J.M. Juran, 4th edition, McGraw-Hill, New York, pg. 23. 66, Table 23.29 Test 2(b).

$df = \min (n_1 - 1, n_2 - 1) = 5 - 1 = 4$ (and not 10). The t_{table} value will be $t_{0.975, 4} = 2.776$ and $t_{cal} = 2.179$. Hence $t_{cal} < t_{0.975, 4}$.

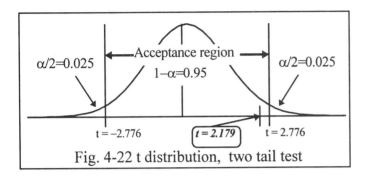

Fig. 4-22 t distribution, two tail test

Fig. 4-22 shows that t_{cal} falls inside the $t_{0.975, 4}$ critical region or acceptance region indicating that we fail to reject it, i.e., we accept the null hypothesis. This also means that there is no significant difference in the two methods which matches choice c. ASQC's published answer is choice b and not choice c.

Note: In a test of hypothesis, the conclusion is written as reject Ho. If the calculated value falls within the acceptance region, instead of stating that we accept the Ho, it is recommended to state that "we fail to reject Ho."

In this question, we are fortunate that both assumptions gave the same conclusion. But in the previous Question 64 we found an opposite conclusion from each assumption. You can now see how much difference such an assumption makes in the overall conclusion. Also there are two possible correct answers for any of the two assumptions.

66.   Two balance scales are to be compared by weighing the same five items on each scale, yielding the following results:

	Item 1	Item 2	Item 3	Item 4	Item 5
Scale A	110	99	112	85	99
Scale B	112	101	113	88	101

The sharpest test comparing mean effects is obtained by using which one of the following?
a.   Paired data test of significance with 4 degrees of freedom.

b. $t = \dfrac{\overline{X}_A - \overline{X}_B}{S_p / \sqrt{n}}$ for 8 degrees of freedom.

c.   Analysis of variance for randomized blocks.

d.   Determining the correlation coefficient r.

Key: a.   Paired data test of significance with 4 degrees of freedom.
            (Ref. Applications Question 55, October 1972)
       Given: Data of weight from scale A and scale B. $n_a = n_b = 5$ samples from each scale.
       Find: The test statistic to be used for comparing the mean effects, i.e., to test if there is a significant difference in two scales.
       This is the case of a test of the hypothesis for the difference between the two means as a paired t test. We have 5 samples from each scale. But it does indicate any data on the population standard deviations σ_a or σ_b, and whether they are equal. (If the values of sample standard deviations are

[8] *Juran's Quality Control Handbook* by J.M. Juran, 4th edition, McGraw-Hill, New York, pg. 23. 66, Table 23.29 Test 2(d).

available, we can run the F test of the hypothesis to determine if both σ_a and σ_b, are equal.) In the absence of any such data, let's assume that the population standard deviation of the two scales are not equal, i.e., $\sigma_a \neq \sigma_b$. Hence the degrees of freedom df = min $(n_a - 1; n_b - 1) = 5 - 1 = 4$.

67.   The parameters of F distribution are

   a.   the S_1^2 and S_2^2 where S_1 and S_2 are two sample standard deviations as estimators for population standard deviations
   b.   the degrees of freedom from each sample, i.e., υ_1 and υ_2
   c.   the mean and σ^2
   d. σ_1^2 and σ_2^2 where σ_1 and σ_2 are the population standard deviations

Key: b.   the degrees of freedom from each sample, i.e., υ_1 and υ_2
        F distribution is described by the ratio of two sample variances of a normal population, i.e.,

$$F = \frac{S_1^2}{S_2^2}$$ and it has υ_1 and υ_2 degrees of freedom in the numerator and denominator, respectively.

68.   The ratio of two variances drawn from the same normal population are described by which one of the following distributions?

   a.   F
   b.   Student t
   c.   chi-square
   d.   normal

Key: a.   F   (Ref. Principles Question 58, October 1972)
        F distribution is described by the ratio of two sample variances of a normal population, i.e.,

$$F = \frac{S_1^2}{S_2^2}$$. The chi-square is used to test the standard deviation of a single population, and sample

standard deviation S is used to estimate the population standard deviation.

69.   To test the hypothesis if the standard deviations or variances of two populations are equal, you will use

   a.   chi-square (χ^2) distribution
   b.   t distribution
   c.   F distribution
   d.   ANOVA

Key: c.   F distribution
        F distribution is used to test the hypothesis if the two standard deviations of two populations are equal. Chi-square distribution is used to test the hypothesis for a single standard deviation. ANOVA and t test are used to test for means and not for standard deviations.

70.   Determine whether the following two types of rockets have significantly different variances at the 5% level.

Rocket 1	Rocket 2
61 readings	31 readings
1346.89 miles²	2237.29 miles²

   a.   significant difference because $F_{calc} < F_{table}$
   b.   no significant difference because $F_{calc} < F_{table}$
   c.   significant difference because $F_{calc} > F_{table}$
   d.   no significant difference because $F_{calc} < F_{table}$

Key: b.   no significant difference because $F_{calc} < F_{table}$
   (Ref. Applications Question 20, August 1978)

Given: $n_1 = 61$, $S_1^2 = 1346.89$ miles², $n_2 = 31$, $S_2^2 = 2237.29$ miles², F test at $\alpha = 0.05$.

Find: Test the hypothesis Ho: $\sigma_1^2 = \sigma_2^2$, i.e., no significant differences between two variances
   Ha: $\sigma_1^2 \neq \sigma_2^2$.

This is a simple question based on the F distribution concept and involves only a small calculation, but you may get confused with the discussion because of the errors in the choices.

Error: There seems to be a few typographical errors in the answers, e.g., choices b and d are the same. Maybe choice d could be corrected to read "no significant difference because $F_{cal} > F_{table}$" which will balance the choices. Also the question does not indicate whether it is the one tail or two tail case for the 5% level. Hence we will test for both. The choices indicate that F_{cal} is either smaller or greater than F_{table}, which may indirectly suggest we use the one tail test.

The F_{cal} will be the same for both cases as: $F_{cal} = \dfrac{S_2^2}{S_1^2} = \dfrac{2237.29}{1346.89} = 1.661$.

   (1)   One tail test: The degrees of freedom for the numerator will be $df_2 = n_2 - 1 = 31 - 1 = 30$, for the denominator it will be $df_1 = n_1 - 1 = 61 - 1 = 60$. From the F table, we get $F_{0.05, 30, 60} = 1.65$. Hence $F_{cal} > F_{0.05, 30, 60}$ which indicates that there is significant difference between the two variances, i.e., meets choice c; however ASQC's answer is choice b. So the one tail test assumption gives an opposite and incorrect answer.

   (2)   Two tail test: The F table at $F_{0.025}$ and $F_{0.975}$ should give $\alpha = 0.05$ total area in two tails. $F_{0.975, 30, 60} = 1.82$; $F_{0.025, 30, 60} = 1/1.94 = 0.515$.
   Here F_{cal} is between two F_{table} values: $0.515 < F_{cal} < 1.82$. Hence the two tail test proves that there is no significant difference between the two variances. This meets choice b or d only *partially* because F_{cal} is less than F_{table} at the upper limit of 1.82, but it is higher than the F_{table} value at the lower limit of 0.515. However the choices given in the question do not indicate an interval for F_{cal}.

71.   If, in a designed experiment, you obtained an F-ratio of 0.68 with 2 and 20 degrees of freedom, you would conclude that

   a.   there were no significant differences among the means

  b. you had made an error
  c. the variances were equal
  d. the null hypothesis was rejected
  e. all of the above

Key: a. there were no significant differences among the means
  (Ref. Applications Question 14, October 1974)
  Given: $F_{cal} = 0.68$, $df_1 = n_1 - 1 = 2$ for the numerator, $df_2 = n_2 - 1 = 20$ for the denominator
    test of hypothesis or null hypothesis for treatment means.
  Find: What is your conclusion for the hypothesis?
  Error: Test of hypothesis steps require: "Choose Type I error, i.e., the level of significance of α,
  for the test." However the data do not specify the required level of significance of α without
  which one cannot test the hypothesis. Also the data do not indicate if it is a one tail or two tail
  test.

  In the case of the designed experiment, generally we perform an analysis of variance (ANOVA)
  calculation and try to determine the significant differences for means using the F test of
  significance. Let's assume a one tail test for simplicity for $df_1 = 2$ and $df_2 = 12$.
  The null hypothesis is Ho : $\mu_1 = \mu_2 = \mu_3 \ldots \mu_k$.

  Table 4-4 F table values for 2 and 12 df at different confidence levels

$1 - \alpha$	F_{table}	F_{cal}	Comment
0.95	3.49	0.68	$F_{cal} < F_{table}$
0.975	4.46	0.68	$F_{cal} < F_{table}$
0.99	5.85	0.68	$F_{cal} < F_{table}$

  In each case of α, in Table 4-4, the $F_{cal} < F_{table}$. Hence F_{cal} is inside the critical region or
  acceptance region. Hence the F ratio is not significant and we accept the null hypothesis that
  there were no significant differences in the means.

72. The values of χ^2 can be

  a. $-\alpha$ to $+\alpha$
  b. zero or positive
  c negative or positive
  d. all of the above

Key: b. zero or positive
  The chi-square distribution has the following properties.
    - it is not symmetrical
    - the value of χ^2 can be zero or positive but cannot be negative
    - the χ^2 distribution depends on the degrees of freedom $df = n - 1$

73. You have been doing precision testing on a special order micrometer delivered by a vendor.
  The sample size in your test was 25 readings. The acceptance specification requires a precision

sigma of 0.003 inch. Your observed precision sigma was 0.0033 inch. Although the observed precision did not meet the requirements, you are reluctant to reject it because you need it badly. You should

    a.   accept it because it is close enough
    b.   reject it because it did not meet the criteria
    c.   apply the chi-square test to see if the micrometer should be accepted.
    d.   apply the F test to see if the micrometer should be accepted
    e.   send the micrometer to the gage lab for adjustment

Key: c.   apply the chi-square test to see if the micrometer should be accepted
(Ref. Principles Question 24, July 1984)
The question describes the precision sigma of 0.003 inch. To test for the standard deviation (sigma) of the population we need to use the chi-square test. The null hypothesis is described as

Ho: $\sigma = \sigma_0$ and the test statistic chi-square is given as: $\chi^2 = \dfrac{(n-1)s^2}{\sigma_o^2}$.

Here we can test the null hypothesis Ho: $\sigma = 0.003$ inch at a given level of confidence, where $s = 0.0033$ inch as the sample standard deviation. The F test is the ratio of two variances but the question provides the data about only one standard deviation and not two variances; hence, it is not a correct choice.

74.   The critical value of χ^2 for a sample size of 15 with a 95% confidence level for a two tail case is

    a.   2.7 and 19.023 respectively
    b.   6.26 and 27.49
    c.   5.63 and 26.12
    d.   none of the above

Key: c.   5.63 and 26.12
Given: χ^2 distribution, sample size n = 15, 95% confidence level, i.e., $\alpha = 5\%$, two tail test.
Find: Critical value of χ^2, i.e., the table value of χ^2.

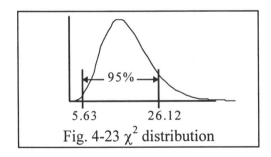

Fig. 4-23 χ^2 distribution

Fig. 4-23 shows the χ^2 distribution at the 95% confidence level and df = n − 1= 15 − 1 = 14. Refer to the χ^2 table for df =14. *Make sure that you are referring to the df value and not the sample size n value.* The critical values for 14 df are 5.63 and 26.12.

75.   The results of a designed experiment are to be analyzed using a chi-square test. There are five treatments under consideration and each observation falls into one of two categories (success or failure). The calculated value of chi-square is compared to the tabulated chi-square with how many degrees of freedom?

a.   10
b.   9
c.   5
d.   4

Key: d.   4   (Ref. Applications Question 21, July 1984)
       Given: 5 treatments, two outcomes: success or failure.
       Find: The number of degrees of freedom.
       Refer to Table 4-5 χ^2 contingency table where the rows indicate the results or outcomes and the columns indicate the treatments.

Table 4-5 χ^2 contingency table

Treatment → Outcome ↓	1	2	3	4	5
Success					
Failure					

Number of rows r = 2 and the number of columns c = 5.
Hence degrees of freedom = $(r-1)(c-1) = (2-1)(5-1) = 4$.

76.   Three trainees were given the same lots of 50 pieces and asked to classify them as defective or nondefective with the following results:

	Trainee 1	Trainee 2	Trainee 3	Total
Defective	17	30	25	72
Nondefective	33	20	25	78
Total	50	50	50	150

In determining whether or not there is a difference in the ability of the three trainees to properly classify the parts

a.   the value of chi-square is about 6.9 (This is ASQC's correction.)
b.   using a level of significance of 0.05, the critical value of chi-square is 5.99
c.   since the obtained chi-square is greater than 5.99, we reject the null hypothesis
d.   all of the above
e.   none of the above

Key: d.   all of the above   (Ref. Applications Question 31, July 1984)
       Given: The raw data of 3 trainees, 50 pieces, defective vs. nondefective items.
       Find: If there is a significant difference in the ability of the three trainees, i.e., Ho: $p_1 = p'_2 = p'_3$.
       The choices given above already indicate the use of χ^2 distribution.
       Develop the χ^2 contingency table first with **r** rows and **c** columns. The analysis can become a two-way classification or r × c contingency table in which the observed frequency f_e will occupy the r rows and c columns.

We now need to calculate the expected frequency f_e for each observed frequency. The row total is denoted as R_T and the column total as C_T for total frequencies in each row or column as shown in Table 4-6 below.

Table 4-6 Contingency table for χ^2 distribution

	Trainee 1 C_1	Trainee 2 C_2	Trainee 3 C_3	Row total R_T
Row R_1 Defective	f_{o11} f_{e11}	f_{o12} f_{e12}	f_{o13} f_{e13}	$R_{T1} = f_{o11} + f_{o12} + f_{o13}$
Row R_2 Nondefective	f_{o21} f_{e21}	f_{o22} f_{e22}	f_{o23} f_{e23}	$R_{T2} = f_{o21} + f_{o22} + f_{o23}$
Column total C_T	$C_{T1} = f_{o11} + f_{o21}$	$C_{T2} = f_{o12} + f_{o22}$	$C_{T3} = f_{o13} + f_{o23}$	$G_T = R_{T1} + R_{T2}$ $= C_{T1} + C_{T2} + C_{T3}$

f_o: observed frequency f_o is given as f_{oij} in the table or the raw data.

$$f_{eij} = \frac{(R_{Ti})(C_{Tj})}{G_T} \qquad i = 1,2...m \text{ row}; \quad j = 1, 2...n \text{ column}.$$

$$f_{e11} = \frac{(R_{T1})(C_{T1})}{G_T} = \frac{72 \times 50}{150} = 24 \text{ , } f_{e12} = \frac{(R_{T1})(C_{T2})}{G_T} = \frac{72 \times 50}{150} = 24$$

and similarly we can calculate the remaining f_{eij} as follows:

$f_{e13} = 24;$ $f_{e21} = 26;$ $f_{e22} = 26;$ $f_{e23} = 26.$

These data are now shown in Table 4-7.

Table 4-7 Contingency table data for χ^2 distribution

	Trainee 1 C_1	Trainee 2 C_2	Trainee 3 C_3	Row total R_T
Row R_1 Defective	17 24	30 20	25 25	$R_{T1} = 17 + 30 + 25 = 72$
Row R_2 Nondefective	33 26	20 26	25 26	$R_{T2} = 33 + 20 + 25 = 78$
Column total C_T	$C_{T1} = 17 + 33 = 50$	$C_{T2} = 30 + 20 = 50$	$C_{T3} = 25 + 25 = 50$	$G_T = 72 + 78 = 150$

The χ^2 measures the extent to which the observed frequency f_o, and the expected frequency f_e agree and it is given by

(a) $\chi^2 = \sum\limits_i^r \sum\limits_j^c \frac{(f_{oij} - f_{eij})^2}{f_{eij}} = \frac{(17-24)^2}{24} + \frac{(30-24)^2}{24} + \frac{(25-24)^2}{24} + \frac{(33-26)^2}{26} + \frac{(20-26)^2}{26} + \frac{(25-26)^2}{26}$

This χ^2 meets choice a, i.e., the value of chi-square is about 6.9 (This is ASQC's correction)

(b) df $= (r-1)(c-1) = (2-1)(3-1) = 2$ and for a level of significance of $\alpha = 5\%$, one tail test, $\chi^2_{0.05, 2} = 5.99$ from the χ^2 table, which meets choice b.

(c) Based on (a) and (b) above, we can conclude that the χ^2 calculated value is 6.9, which is greater than the table value of $\chi^2 = 5.99$. Hence we reject the null hypothesis that all trainees are the same. This meets choice c.

(d) Hence the best answer is choice d as "all of the above."

Watch for your impulse or immediate reaction to choice a or b as the correct answer, just because your calculations give you the same values as a or b etc. In this type of question, the important thing to remember is *not to react to the obvious answer* but evaluate each answer carefully because other answers also could be equally true. This is a very time-consuming question, be careful in the examination and manage your time with the remaining questions.

This question is repeated in the August 1978 and October 1974 examinations.[9]

77. Given that random samples of process A produced 10 defective and 30 good units, while process B produced 25 defectives out of 60 units. Using the chi-square test, what is the probability that the observed value of chi-square could result, under the hypothesis that both processes are operating at the same quality level?

    a.   less than 5%
    b.   between 5% and 10%
    c.   greater than 10%
    d.   50%

Key: b.   between 5% and 10%   (Ref. Applications Question 1, October 1972)
    Given: Process A: 10 defective and 30 good; process B: 25 defectives out of 60 units, use of χ^2 distribution; same quality level, i.e., $p_A = p_B$ where p indicates percentage nonconforming.
    Find: The probability, i.e., the confidence level $1 - \alpha$ based on the calculated value of χ^2.

Table 4-8 Contingency table for χ^2 distribution

	Process A C_1	Process B C_2	Row total R_T
Row R_1 Defective	f_{o11} f_{e11}	f_{o12} f_{e12}	$R_{T1} = f_{o11} + f_{o12} +$
Row R_2 Good units	f_{o21} f_{e21}	f_{o22} f_{e22}	$R_{T2} = f_{o21} + f_{o22} +$
Column total C_T	$C_{T1} = f_{o11} + f_{o21}$	$C_{T2} = f_{o12} + f_{o22}$	$G_T = R_{T1} + R_{T2}$ $= C_{T1} + C_{T2}$

Develop the χ^2 contingency table first with r rows and c columns. The analysis can become a two-way classification or $r \times c$ contingency table in which the observed frequency f_e will occupy the r rows and c columns.

---

[9] *ASQC - CQE Examination*, Quality Progress, August 1978, Applications section, Question 11 and October 1974, Applications Section, Question 60.

We now need to calculate the expected frequency f_e for each observed frequency f_o in each cell of the contingency table. The row total is denoted as R_T and the column total as C_T for total frequencies in each row or column as shown in Table 4-8.

f_o: observed frequency f_o is given as f_{oij} in the table or the raw data.

$$f_{eij} = \frac{(R_{Ti})(C_{Tj})}{G_T} \qquad i = 1,2...m \text{ row}; \quad j = 1, 2...n \text{ column}.$$

Hence Table 4-9 gives the values of f_o and f_e.

Table 4-9 Contingency table for f_o and f_e values

	Process A C_1	Process B C_2	Row total R_T
Row R_1 Defective	10 14	25 21	$R_{T1} = 10 + 25 = 35$
Row R_2 Good units	30 26	35 39	$R_{T2} = 30 + 35 = 65$
Column total C_T	$C_{T1} = 10 + 30 = 40$	$C_{T2} = 25 + 35 = 60$	$G_T = R_{T1} + R_{T2}$ $= C_{T1} + C_{T2} = 100$

$$f_{e11} = \frac{(R_{T1})(C_{T1})}{G_T} = \frac{35 \times 40}{100} = 14, \qquad f_{e12} = \frac{(R_{T1})(C_{T2})}{G_T} = \frac{35 \times 60}{100} = 21;$$

and similarly we can calculate the remaining f_{eij}, i.e., $f_{e21} = 26$; $f_{e22} = 39$.
The χ^2 measures the extent to which the observed frequency f_o, and the expected frequency f_e agree and is given by

$$\chi^2 = \sum_i^r \sum_j^c \frac{(f_{oij} - f_{eij})^2}{f_{eij}} = \frac{(10-14)^2}{14} + \frac{(25-21)^2}{21} + \frac{(30-26)^2}{26} + \frac{(35-39)^2}{39} = 2.93$$

$df = (r-1)(c-1) = (2-1)(2-1) = 1$.
From the χ^2 table, we get $\chi^2_{0.90} = 2.71$ and $\chi^2_{0.95} = 3.84$ which indicates that our χ^2 calculation of 2.93 lies between a 90% and 95% confidence level or 5% and 10% level of significance.

78.   How many degrees of freedom should you use in the above problem?

    a.   1
    b.   2
    c.   3
    d.   4

Key: a.   1   (Ref. Applications Question 2, October 1972)
    For χ^2, the degrees of freedom $df = (r-1)(c-1) = (2-1)(2-1) = 1$.

79.   On the basis of the data in the previous problem, what could you conclude?

     a.   Nothing. The facts involving the consequences of a wrong decision are unknown.
     b.   The two processes are comparable.
     c.   The two processes are significantly different.
     d.   Reject the null hypothesis.

Key: a.   Nothing. The facts involving the consequences of a wrong decision are unknown.
(Ref. Applications Question 3, October 1972)
The question above does not define the associated level of significance α. Hence we do not know the confidence level or the risk associated with the wrong decision.

80.   A process is acceptable if its standard deviation is not greater than 1.0. A sample of four items yields the values 52, 56, 53, and 55. In order to determine if the process should be accepted or rejected, the following statistical test should be used.

     a.   t test
     b.   chi-square test
     c.   Z test
     d.   none of the above

Key: b.   chi-square test   (Ref. Applications Question 29, October 1972)
The variable of interest is the standard deviation and not the mean, i.e., accept the process if the standard deviation is not more than 1.0. The best applicable test statistic is the chi-square test where the sample standard deviation S is used to estimate the population σ.

χ^2 given as $\chi^2 = \dfrac{(n-1)S^2}{\sigma_0^2}$ with $n - 1$ degrees of freedom.

81.   A value of 0.9973 refers to the probability that

     a.   the process is in control
     b.   a correct decision will be made as to control or lack of control of the process
     c.   the process is unstable
     d.   a point will fall inside the three sigma limits for an $\overline{X}$ chart if the process is in control

Key: d.   a point will fall inside the three sigma limits for an $\overline{X}$ chart if process is in control
         (Ref. Applications Question 57, October 1972)
The upper and lower control limits (UCL and LCL) of a control chart represent the $\pm\, 3\sigma_x$ limits. It indicates a confidence or probability of 0.9973 or 99.73%. It means that there is 0.9973 probability that a point will fall inside the $\pm\, 3\sigma_x$ limits of the $\overline{X}$ chart if the process is in control.

ASQC-CQE BIBLIOGRAPHY AND OTHER REFERENCES ON STATISTICAL INFERENCE AND HYPOTHESIS TESTING

1. *ANSI/ASQC A1-1987 Definitions, Symbols, Formulas, and Tables for Control Charts*, Milwaukee, ASQC Quality Press, 1987.
2. ASQC Statistics Division, *Glossary and Tables for Statistical Quality Control*, 2nd ed., Milwaukee, ASQC Quality Press, 1983.
3. Braverman, Jerome D., *Fundamentals of Statistical Quality Control*, Englewood Cliffs, N.J., Prentice-Hall, 1981.
4. Dovich, Robert A., *Quality Engineering Statistics*, Milwaukee, ASQC Quality Press, 1992.
5. Duncan, A. J., *Quality Control and Industrial Statistics*, 5th cd., Homewood, IL, Irwin Inc., 1986.
6. Grant, Eugen L. and Richard Leavenworth, *Statistical Quality Control*, 6th ed., New York, McGraw-Hill, 1988.
7. Juran, Joseph M., *Juran's Quality Control Handbook*, 4th ed., New York, McGraw-Hill, 1988.
8. Keats, J. Bert and Douglas C. Montgomery, *Statistical Process Control in Manufacturing*, New York, Marcel Dekker, 1991.
9. McWilliams, Thomas P., *How to Use Sequential Statistical Methods*, Volume 13, Milwaukee, ASQC Quality Press, 1989.
10. Schooling, Edward G., *Acceptance Sampling in Quality Control*, New York, Marcel Dekker, 1982.
11. Shapiro, Samuel S., *How to Test Normality and Other Distributional Assumptions*, Volume 3, revised, Milwaukee, ASQC Quality Press, 1990.
12. Stephens, Kenneth S., *How to Perform Continuous Sampling*, Volume 2, Milwaukee, ASQC Quality Press, 1990.
13. Stephens, Kenneth S., *How to Perform Skip Lot and Chain Sampling*, Volume 4, Milwaukee, ASQC Quality Press, 1990.
14. Vani, Jagdish, *Fundamental Concepts of Probability, Statistics, Regression and DOE*, 3rd ed., Troy, MI, Quality Quest Inc.,1993.
15. Western Electric, *Statistical Quality Control Handbook*, Indianapolis, AT&T, 1956.

CHAPTER 5

REGRESSION AND CORRELATION ANALYSIS

ASQC'S BODY OF KNOWLEDGE (BOK) FOR CQE EXAMINATION

This chapter focuses on the following selected subject areas of BOK from *Section III, Statistical Principles and Applications.*

Terms and Concepts

1.   Descriptive statistics (e.g., scatter diagrams)

Correlation and Regression Analysis

1.   Linear models
2.   Least-squares fit
3.   Correlation and regression statistics (e.g., R, R^2, standard error of estimate)
4.   Time series analysis
        a. Run charts
        b. Trend analysis
5.   Pattern analysis

1.   The correlation coefficient can take any value between

        a.   0 and 1 only
        b. $-\alpha$ to α
        c. -1 to 1
        d.   none of the above

Key: c. -1 to 1
        The correlation coefficient r lies between -1 and $+1$. The value of $r = -1$ indicates a negative or inverse relationship and $r = 1$ indicates a positive or direct relationship between two variables.

2.   If two variables show good correlation, it does not mean that

        a.   the change in one of the variables can cause the other to change
        b.   there is a causation
        c.   you can predict the change in the dependent variable if there is a change in the independent variable
        d.   all of the above

Key: d.   all of the above
        This is an important difference between correlation and regression. Correlation only indicates if there is some degree of positive or negative, or no correlation. It does not mean that there is a cause-and-effect relationship between the two variables, i.e., it does not mean that there is some causation. Correlation also cannot be used to predict the proportional change in the dependent variable for a change in the independent variable.

3.   If the scatter of different points is much wider, then r will

        a.   be reaching to a perfect correlation of 1
        b.   be reaching to a perfect correlation of -1
        c.   will not be affected
        d.   will become smaller

Key: d.   will become smaller

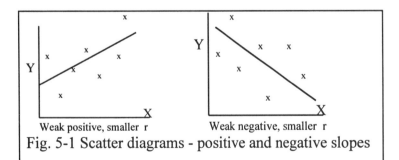

Weak positive, smaller r   Weak negative, smaller r

Fig. 5-1 Scatter diagrams - positive and negative slopes

First draw the scatter plots as shown in Fig. 5-1. If the scatter of the points becomes wider, it indicates a weaker relationship between the two variables. If the slope is positive, then it will be a weak positive relationship because of the wider scatter of points and vice versa. It results in a smaller correlation coefficient, r.

4.   If the variable Y tends to increase as X increases, the correlation is

        a.   positive

      b.   negative

      c.   zero

      d.   nonlinear

Key: a.   positive

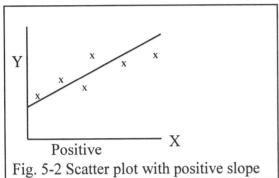

Refer to Fig. 5-2 which shows the positive correlationship or a positive slope. In case of positive correlation, as X increases, the value of Y also increases and it has a direct relationship. The relationship may become a strong or weak positive relationship depending on the slope of the best-fit line.

Fig. 5-2 Scatter plot with positive slope

5.   The correlation coefficient r is

      a.   not affected by which variable is called x or y

      b.   used to measure the strength of a linear relationship. It is not designed to measure the strength of a relationship that is not linear

      c.   always between −1 and +1

      d.   all of the above

Key: d.   all of the above

The choices above indicate the basic properties of the correlation coefficient r.

6.   If we use averages instead of individual data to calculate the correlation coefficient r, the value of r

      a.   remains the same for individual data or averages data

      b.   is the same as the standard error of mean

      c.   decreases significantly

      d.   gets inflated significantly

Key: d.   gets inflated significantly

When we use averages instead of individual data, the extreme value in the data gets averaged out. Hence the effect of variation is underestimated or suppressed. This is likely to inflate the value of r significantly and may indicate that there is higher correlation than there actually is.

7.   Which of the following statements is correct?

      a.   The higher the correlation, the better the regression equation estimate.

      b.   The lower the correlation, the better the regression estimate.

      c.   Regression estimates are better made with positive than with negative correlation.

d.   The lower the correlation, the greater is the likelihood that homoscedasticity exists with respect to the predicted variable.

e.   The better the regression estimate, the greater is the likelihood that homoscedasticity exists with respect to the predicted variable.

Key: a.   The higher the correlation, the better the regression equation estimate.
(Ref. Principles Question 75, October 1974)
The correlation coefficient is between -1 and $+1$, i.e., $r = -1$ means strong negative correlation and $r = 1$ means strong positive correlation. Therefore, the higher correlation value or stronger r will indicate the better estimate for the regression equation estimate.

Choice b is incorrect as correlation and regression estimates are directly related to each other and not inversely because in the case of a simple linear regression, $r^2 = R^2$. Choice c is incorrect because the negative or positive value of r will indicate the slope of the regression equation in the case of linear regression but one is not a better estimate of regression than the other. Choices d and e use the term homoscedasticity, meaning equal variances, a term that is used in ANOVA.

8.   A correlation problem

a.   is solved by estimating the value of the dependent variable for various values of the independent variable

b.   considers the joint variation of two measurements, neither of which is restricted by the experimenter

c.   is the one case where the underlying distributions must be geometric

d.   is solved by assuming that the variables are normally and independently distributed with mean = 0 and variance = σ_e^2.

Key: b.   considers the joint variation of two measurements, neither of which is restricted by the experimenter   (Ref. Principles Question 19, October 1972)
The correlation is not used for estimating or predicting the dependent variable based on the values of an independent variable. It does not depend on which variable is X or Y, and it is based on the joint variations of all (X_i, Y_i) pairs. It is not necessary that the distributions be geometric. Choice d represents an assumption of equal variances in ANOVA and not for correlation.

9.   Which of the following statements concerning the coefficient of simple linear correlation r is *not* true?

a. $r = 0.00$ represents the absence of a relationship.

b.   The relationship between the two variables must be nonlinear.

c. $r = 0.76$ has the same predictive power as $r = -0.76$.

d. $r = 1.00$ represents a perfect relationship.

Key: b.   The relationship between the two variables must be nonlinear.
(Ref. Principles Question 42, October 1974)
The key term is ***not true.*** The statement clearly describes simple linear correlation r, which means the relationship between two variables is linear. Hence choice b is not a true statement

and, therefore, it is the correct answer. All other choices are true statements, but we are not interested in true statements.

10.   A correlation coefficient of 0.975 for two variables X and Y indicates

i.   there is a weak relationship between variables X and Y
ii.   there is a strong relationship between variables X and Y
iii.   we can predict the value of Y based on the relationship Y= 0.975X

a.   i and iii both
b.   ii and iii both
c.   ii only
d.   iii only
e.   none of the above

Key: c.   ii only
The correlation coefficient of 0.975 is a high correlation which indicates a strong and not a weak relationship between variables Y and X. Hence item i is not correct. The correlation coefficient r cannot be used to predict Y because a high correlation does not mean that there is a cause and effect relationship. Also the equation of a straight line is generally given as $Y = a_o + a_1X$. Here we do not know the coefficients a_o, which is the Y intercept, and a_1, which is the slope of the line. The coefficient r = 0.975 is not the same as the slope nor the Y intercept. Hence Y = 0.975X shown in item iii is not a correct equation.

11.   The correlation coefficient r for the following coded data is

X	1	1	2	3
Y	1	5	4	2

a.   0.81
b. -1
c.   1
d. -0.191

Key: d. -0.191
Given: Raw data on X_i and Y_i from n = 4 pairs.
Find: The correlation coefficient r.

Table 5-1 Correlation data

X_i	Y_i	X_iY_i	X_i^2	Y_i^2
1	1	$1 \times 1 = 1$	1	1
1	5	$1 \times 5 = 5$	1	25
2	4	$2 \times 4 = 8$	4	16
3	2	$3 \times 2 = 6$	9	4
$\sum X_i = 7$	$\sum Y_i = 12$	$\sum X_iY_i = 20$	$\sum X_i^2 = 15$	$\sum Y_i^2 = 46$
$(\sum X_i)^2 = 49$	$(\sum Y_i)^2 = 144$			

The correlation coefficient r is given as follows $r = \dfrac{n\sum X_i Y_i - (\sum X_i)\sum(Y_i)}{\sqrt{\left[n\sum X_i^2 - (\sum X_i)^2\right]\left[n\sum Y_i^2 - (\sum Y_i)^2\right]}}$

Table 5-1 shows the data in a tabular form to get various values to calculate r.

$r = \dfrac{4(20) - (7)(12)}{\sqrt{[4(15) - 49][4(46) - (144)]}} = -0.191$

*You must practice to make the table shown above and calculate individual elements of the formula first, and then substitute them in the formula carefully. Also do not make the mistake of squaring the values again. Keep in mind that $(\sum X_i)^2$ and $\sum X_i^2$ are not the same. The term $(\sum X_i)^2$ represents the "**square of the sums**"and is equal to 49 in the data, whereas $\sum X_i^2$ represents the "**sum of the squares**" and it is equal to 15.*

12.   In the manufacture of airplane fuselage frames, thousands of rivets are used to join aluminum sheets and frames. A study of the number of oversized rivet holes and the number of minor repairs on a unit yielded a correlation coefficient of ±1.08. This means

    a.   the number of oversized rivet holes on a unit is a good predictor of the number of minor repairs that will have to be made
    b.   you have made serious errors in calculating r
    c.   the number of oversized rivet holes is a poor predictor of the number of minor repairs
    d.   a large number of oversized rivet holes means that a small number of minor repairs will have to be made
    e.   a large number of oversized rivet holes means that a large number of minor repairs will have to be made

Key: b.   you have made serious errors in calculating r
The data show that the value of $r = \pm 1.08$, which is not possible as r should always be between -1 and $+1$. That is, r will always be $-1 \le r \le 1$ and not greater than 1. Hence there is a serious error in the calculation of r.

13.   The _____ variable is the one which is used to predict the _____ variable in the case of simple linear regression.

    a.   dependent, independent
    b.   independent, dependent
    c.   slope, Y intercept
    d.   response, factor

Key: b.   independent, dependent
A regression equation is used to estimate or predict the proportional difference in the dependent variable based on the change in the independent variable.

14.   In the case of the simple linear regression equation $Y = a_0 + a_1 X$, the coefficients a_0 and a_1 are

a.   slope and Y intercept, respectively
b.   Y intercept and slope, respectively
c.   X abscissa and slope, respectively
d.   slope and error I, respectively

Key: b.   Y intercept and slope, respectively

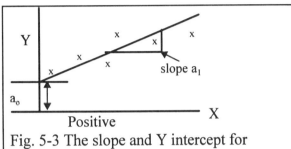

Fig. 5-3 The slope and Y intercept for
simple linear regression

Fig. 5-3 shows the equation of a straight line. The equation is described by two coefficients a_0, which is the Y intercept, and a_1, the slope, respectively. The slope a_1 represents the proportional change in Y with the change in X, i.e., slope $a_1 = \Delta Y/\Delta X$.

15.   If the equation of a line is given by the simple linear regression equation $Y = a_0 + a_1 X$, the resulting line is called a

a.   regression of X on Y
b.   regression of Y on X
c.   regression of both X and Y
d.   all of the above

Key: b.   regression of Y on X
Regression strongly depends on which variable you call Y and which X. Y is the dependent variable on X and hence the resulting line is called a regression of Y on X. This is not the same as regression of X on Y. Do not treat these two types as the same. Correlation differs from regression because in correlation it does not matter which variable is called X or Y.

16.   Regression of Y on X is the same as regression of X on Y.

a.   false
b.   true

Key: a.   false
Refer to Question 15 above.

17.   For a linear regression, $y = b_0 + b_1 x$

a.   shows y is a dependent and x is an independent variable
b.   shows y is an independent and x is a dependent variable
c.   shows regression of x on y
d.   shows a second order equation

Key: a.   shows y is a dependent and x is an independent variable

In regression, an independent variable is the variable which is used to predict the variable of interest and the dependent variable is the variable which is being predicted.

Choice b is incorrect because y is a dependent variable and not independent. Similarly, x is an independent variable and not a dependent variable. Hence choice a is correct.

Choice c is incorrect because the equation shows regression of y on x and it is not the same as the regression of x on y.

Choice d is incorrect because it is a first order linear equation and not a second order parabolic equation.

18. All of the following statements are true except

    a. in multiple regression, extrapolation beyond the region of observation can lead to erroneous predictions
    b. at least three variables are involved in multiple regression
    c. multiple regression involves one independent and two or more dependent variables

Key: c. multiple regression involves one independent and two or more dependent variables
(Ref. Principles Question 17, July 1984)
Choice c is an incorrect statement because multiple regression can have more than one independent variable, such as X_1, X_2, and X_3, etc., to estimate one or more dependent variables.

19. The coefficient of determination is

    a. the ratio of standard deviation and its mean
    b. the ratio of total variation to the explainable variation
    c. the ratio of explainable variation to the total variation
    d. the ratio of mean squares of error to the mean squares between the treatments

Key: c. the ratio of explainable variation to the total variation
The coefficient of determination R^2 is given as[1] **R^2 = Explainable variation / Total variation**

SST: The total variation of the dependent variable Y is defined as the sum of squares for total (SST), and is given as $\mathbf{SST} = \Sigma(Y_i - \overline{Y})^2$. It is composed of two types of sources of variation defined as follows.

SSR: Sum of squares due to regression. $SSR = \Sigma(Y_i' - \overline{Y})^2$ where Y_i' is the estimated value of Y using the linear regression equation. This is called *explainable variation* because it follows a definite or fixed pattern in the form of a straight line.

SSE: Sum of squares for the error term. $SSE = \Sigma(Y_i - Y_i')^2$ where Y_i' is the estimated value of Y using the linear regression equation. This is called unexplainable variation because it is the error variation and does not have a definite pattern or it behaves in a random manner.

Hence we can rewrite the equation as follows: $R^2 = \dfrac{SSR}{SST}$.
Please refer to Question 20 for additional comments.

[1] *Fundamental Concepts of Probability, Statistics, Regression and DOE* by Jagdish Vani, 3rd edition, April 1993, Section 7.

20. The ratio of $\dfrac{\text{SSR}}{\text{SST}}$, where SSR is the sum of squares for regression and SST is the sum of squares for total, is defined as

    a.   the correlation coefficient r
    b.   the coefficient of determination R^2
    c.   the F ratio for the ANOVA table
    d.   the coefficient of variation, CV

Key: b.   the coefficient of determination R^2

The coefficient of determination R^2 is used to measure the adequacy of the prediction equation by determining the proportion of the variation that can be explained by the linear regression equation. This is done by separating the total variation (SST) into its components, i.e., variation due to regression (SSR) and variation due to error (SSE), in the form of its sum of squares,[2] which are defined as follows.

$$\text{SST} = \text{SSR} + \text{SSE} \qquad\qquad \text{SSR} = \text{SST} - \text{SSE}$$

SST: The sum of squares for total is the total sum of the squared deviations of the Y_i observations about their mean, i.e., $\text{SST} = \Sigma(Y_i - \overline{Y})^2$.

SSE: The sum of squares for the error term. $\text{SSE} = \Sigma(Y_i - Y_i')^2$ where Y_i' is the estimated value of Y using the linear regression equation.

SSR: The sum of squares due to regression. $\text{SSR} = \Sigma(Y_i' - \overline{Y})^2$

$$R^2 = \frac{\text{SST} - \text{SSE}}{\text{SST}} = \frac{\text{SSR}}{\text{SST}} = \frac{\text{Explainable variation}}{\text{Total variation}}, \text{ or we can express it in another way as}$$

$$R^2 = \frac{\text{SST} - \text{SSE}}{\text{SST}} = 1 - \frac{\text{SSE}}{\text{SST}} = 1 - \frac{\text{Unexplainable variation}}{\text{Total variation}}$$

It is necessary that you understand the relationship of these components of variation in a linear regression equation and then judge the effectiveness of the linear equation.[3]

21. In the case of a linear regression equation of one independent variable,

    a.   the coefficient of determination R^2 is greater than the square of the coefficient of correlation r^2, i.e., $R^2 > r^2$
    b.   the coefficient of determination R^2 is smaller than the square of the coefficient of correlation r^2, i.e., $R^2 < r^2$
    c.   the coefficient of determination R^2 is the same as the square of the coefficient of correlation r^2, i.e., $R^2 = r^2$
    d.   none of the above

Key: c.   the coefficient of determination R^2 is the same as the square of the coefficient of correlation r^2, i.e., $R^2 = r^2$

---

[2] *Fundamental Concepts of Probability, Statistics, Regression and DOE* by Jagdish Vani, 3rd edition, April 1993, Section 7.
[3] *Juran's Quality Control Handbook* by J. M. Juran, 4th Edition, McGraw-Hill, New York, pg. 23.101-103.

In the case of a simple linear regression equation, the coefficient of determination R^2 is equal to the square of the coefficient of correlation[4] r^2, i.e., $R^2 = r^2$.

22.   In the case of a linear regression equation, the least squares property means

   a.   the sum of the squares of the horizontal deviations of the sample points from the regression line is the smallest possible
   b.   the sum of the squares of the vertical deviations of the sample points from the regression line is the smallest possible
   c.   the sum of the squares of the horizontal deviations of the sample points from the Y axis is the smallest possible
   d.   the sum of the squares of the vertical deviations of the sample points from the X axis is the smallest possible

Key: b.   the sum of the squares of the vertical deviations of the sample points from the regression line is the smallest possible

The key difference between choices a and b is the term horizontal deviations vs. vertical deviations of the sample points from the regression line.

Fig. 5-4 shows a line of best fit. It shows a point Y_i' as an estimated value for each observed Y_i. The vertical deviation of the actual (observed) value of Y_i from the estimated value of Y_i' (based on the equation), i.e., $Y_i - Y_i'$, is called the estimate of the error term or residuals. The objective is to minimize these errors and get the best fit of the line. Hence we use the *least squares estimate* because they minimize the sum of squared deviations between the observed value Y_i and the predicted or estimated value Y_i', i.e., minimize $\Sigma(Y_i - Y_i')^2$.

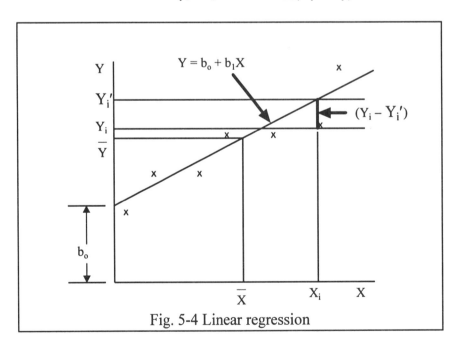

Fig. 5-4 Linear regression

23.   In linear regression, when you plot the equation of a straight line over the data,

   a.   the equation should exactly pass through all (X_i, Y_i) points

___
[4] *Juran's Quality Control Handbook* by J. M. Juran, 4th Edition, McGraw-Hill, New York, pg. 23.103.

b.   the equation should exactly pass through the point ($\overline{X}$, $\overline{Y}$)

c.   the equation should not pass through the point ($\overline{X}$, $\overline{Y}$)

d.   the equation should not pass through all (X_i, Y_i') points where Y_i's are the estimated values of Y from the equation

Key: b.   the equation should exactly pass through the point ($\overline{X}$, $\overline{Y}$)

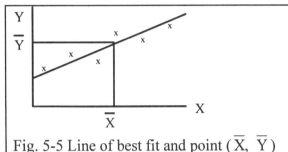
Fig. 5-5 Line of best fit and point ($\overline{X}$, $\overline{Y}$)

The line passes through the common point ($\overline{X}$, $\overline{Y}$) as shown in Fig. 5-5. The point ($\overline{X}$, $\overline{Y}$) represents the average of sample values of all raw data of X_i and Y_i, as well as the average for the estimated values of Y_i' calculated from the equation of the best-fit line for each X_i value.

24.   The regression line always passes through

a.   all points in the data
b.   only the first and last X and Y data points
c.   no points
d.   ($\overline{X}, \overline{Y}$)

Key: d.   ($\overline{X}, \overline{Y}$)

This is a repeat question. Please refer to Question 23 above.

25.   The least squares method is used in

a.   the central limit theorem
b.   calculating σ^2
c.   calculating σ^2 from σ^2
d.   calculating a best-fit regression line
e.   inspecting hole locations

Key: d.   calculating a best-fit regression line (Ref. Principles Question 28, August 1978)
The least squares criterion requires that a line be chosen to fit the data of the two variables (one dependent and one independent variable) so that the sum of squares of the vertical deviations separating the points from the line will be a minimum. The deviations are shown by the vertical line segments that connect the points to the estimated regression line in the scatter diagram in Question 22 above.

The remaining choices are totally incorrect. Choice a, the central limit theorem, is about the sampling distribution of means and does not use the least squares method. The population variance σ^2 is calculated using the sum of squared deviations of individual observations from its

mean divided by the number of observations, i.e., $\sigma^2 \dfrac{\sum (X_i - \overline{X})^2}{n}$ but it does not try to minimize the sum of squared deviations. Hence choices b and c are incorrect. Also choice c, calculating σ^2 from σ^2, seems to be an incomplete statement. Inspecting hole locations also has no direct meaning or relation with the least squares method.

26.   In the regression equation $y = mx + b$, y increases with x in all cases

     a.   if b is positive
     b.   if b is negative
     c.   if m is positive
     d.   if m is negative

Key: c.   if m is positive   (Ref. Principles Question 79, October 1972)
The coefficient m in the above equation represents the slope of the line. If m is a positive slope, a small change in X will result in proportional change in the response variable Y, i.e., if X increases, Y increases proportionately or vice versa.

27.   If $Y = -2 + 3X$ is the simple linear regression equation, the value of Y when $X = 2$ is

     a.   6
     b.   4
     c.   -2
     d.   3

Key: b.   4
Given: The straight line equation $Y = -2 + 3X$, $X = 2$.
Find: Value of Y.
The equation is $Y = -2 + 3X$,
          if $X = 2$, $Y = -2 + 3(2) = 4$.

28.   If $Y = -2 + 3X$ is the simple linear regression equation, the slope of the line is

     a. -2
     b. $-2/3$
     c.   3
     d.   0

Key: c.   3
The straight line equation is given as $Y = a_o + a_1X$ where a_o and a_1 are the Y intercept and slope, respectively. In the above equation, the Y intercept $a_o = -2$ and the slope $a_1 = 3$.

29.   The equation of the straight line whose slope is -5 and the Y intercept is 8, is given as

     a. $Y = -5 + 8X$
     b. $X = -5 + 8Y$
     c. $Y = 8 - 5X$
     d. $X = 8 - 5Y$

Key: c. $Y = 8 - 5X$
       Given: Y intercept $a_0 = 8$, slope $a_1 = -5$.
       Find: The equation of the line.
       The general model of the linear equation is $Y = a_0 + a_1 X$. Hence, substituting the values of a_0
       and a_1, $Y = 8 - 5X$.

30.   Consider the data below where Y is a dependent variable and X is an independent variable. The
       linear regression equation is shown as $Y = b_0 + b_1 X$, where b_0 is the Y intercept and b_1 is the
       slope of the line.

X	1	1	2	3
Y	1	5	4	2

       The value of b_1 is

       a. -0.191
       b. -0.364
       c.   3.637
       d.   0.364

Key: b. -0.364
       Given: Raw data on X_i and Y_i from $n = 4$ pairs.
       Find: The constant b_1, i.e., the slope of the line.
       The data were used in Table 5-1 in Question 11 on pg. 5-5 to calculate correlation coefficient r.
       The same table is used here as Table 5-2 to calculate the regression constant b_1.

Table 5-2 Regression data

X_i	Y_i	$X_i Y_i$	X_i^2	Y_i^2
1	1	$1 \times 1 = 1$	1	1
1	5	$1 \times 5 = 5$	1	25
2	4	$2 \times 4 = 8$	4	16
3	2	$3 \times 2 = 6$	9	4
$\sum X_i = 7$	$\sum Y_i = 12$	$\sum X_i Y_i = 20$	$\sum X_i^2 = 15$	$\sum Y_i^2 = 46$
$(\sum X_i)^2 = 49$	$(\sum Y_i)^2 = 144$			

       $\sum X_i = 7$ $\sum Y_i = 12$ $\sum X_i Y_i = 20$ $\sum X_i^2 = 15$ and $(\sum X_i)^2 = 49$

       The constant b_1 is given as: $b_1 = \dfrac{n \sum X_i Y_i - (\sum X_i)(\sum Y_i)}{n \sum X_i^2 - (\sum X_i)^2} = \dfrac{4(20) - (7)(12)}{4(15) - 49} = -0.364$

31.   From the data in Question 30 above, the value of the Y intercept b_0 is

       a.   3.637
       b.   0.364
       c. -0.364
       d.   1.75

Key: a.   3.637

> **Given:** Raw data on X_i and Y_i from $n = 4$ pairs.
> **Find:** The Y intercept b_0.
>
> The Y intercept is given as $b_0 = \overline{Y} - b_1 \overline{X}$
> Refer to Question 30 above. We have $b_1 = -0.364$, $\Sigma X_i = 7$, $\Sigma Y_i = 12$, and $n = 4$.
>
> This gives $\overline{X} = \dfrac{\Sigma X_i}{n} = \dfrac{7}{4} = 1.75$ and $\overline{Y} = \dfrac{\Sigma Y_i}{n} = \dfrac{12}{4} = 3$.
>
> The constant b_0 is given as $b_0 = \overline{Y} - b_1 \overline{X} = 3 - (-0.364)(175) = 3.637$.

32.   From the data in Questions 30 and 31, the equation of the line can be expressed as

  a. $Y = 3.637X + 0.364$
  b. $Y = 3.637 - 0.364X$
  c. $Y = 0.364 - 3.637X$
  d. $Y = 0.364 + 3.637X$

Key: b. $Y = 3.637 - 0.364X$

> **Given:** The data of Questions 30 and 31, i.e., $b_0 = 3.637$ and $b_1 = -0.364$.
> **Find:** The equation of the line.
> The regression equation of the line is $Y = b_0 + b_1 X$, substituting the values of b_0 and b_1 we can
> write the equation of the line as $Y = 3.637 - 0.364X$.

33.   From the data in Questions 30 and 31, the coefficient of determination R^2 is

  a. 3.637
  b. 0.364
  c. -0.364
  d. 1.75

Key: b.   0.364

> **Given:** The data of Questions 30, 31, and 32, i.e., $b_0 = 3.637$ and $b_1 = -0.364$ and $Y = 3.637 -$
> $0.364X$.
> **Find:** The coefficient of determination R^2.
> Table 5-3 shows the data to calculate R^2.

Table 5-3 Regression data

X_i	Y_i	$(X_i - \overline{X})$	$(Y_i - \overline{Y})$	$(X_i - \overline{X})(Y_i - \overline{Y})$	$(Y_i - \overline{Y})^2$
1	1	$(1-1.75) = -0.75$	-2	$(-0.75)(-2) = 1.5$	$(-2)^2 = 4$
1	5	-0.75	2	-1.5	4
2	4	0.25	1	0.25	1
3	2	1.25	-1	-1.25	1
$\Sigma X_i = 7$	$\Sigma Y_i = 12$			$\Sigma(X_i - \overline{X})(Y_i - \overline{Y})$	$\Sigma(Y_i - \overline{Y})^2 = 10$
$(\Sigma X_i)^2 = 49$	$(\Sigma Y_i)^2 = 144$				
$\overline{X} = 1.75$	$\overline{Y} = 3$				

The coefficient of determination R^2 is given as

$$R^2 = \frac{b_1 \sum (X_i - \overline{X})(Y_i - \overline{Y})}{\sum (Y_i - \overline{Y})^2} = \frac{(-0.364)(-1)}{10} = 0.364.$$

And from Question 11, we calculated $r^2 = (-0.191)^2 = 0.364$ which proves that $r^2 = R^2$ in the case of a linear regression.

34. If the value of the coefficient of determination $R^2 = 0.90$, we can conclude that

   a. 90% of the total variation is not explainable by the linear regression equation
   b. 10% of the total variation is explainable by the linear regression equation
   c. 90% of the total variation is explainable by the regression linear equation
   d. 95% of the total variation is explainable by the linear regression equation

Key: c. 90% of the total variation is explainable by the regression linear equation
   The coefficient of determination R^2 is expressed as a ratio, i.e.,
   $R^2 =$ Explainable variation / Total variation $= 0.90$, which means 90% of the total variation is explained by the linear regression equation and 10% is unexplained.

35. A study was conducted on the relationship between the speed of different cars and their gasoline mileage. The correlation coefficient was found to be 0.35. Later it was discovered that there was a defect in the speedometers and they had all been set 5 miles per hour too fast. The correlation coefficient was computed using the corrected scores. Its new value will be

   a. 0.30
   b. 0.35
   c. 0.40
   d. -0.35

Key. b. 0.35 (Ref. Applications Question 1, July 1984)
   Given: $r = 0.35$, two variables: speed of the cars and gas mileage, the speed setting 5 miles per hour too fast.
   Find: The effect of corrected speed on the correlation coefficient r.

   The correlation coefficient $r = \dfrac{\sum (X_i - \overline{X})(Y_i - \overline{Y})}{\sqrt{[\sum (X_i - \overline{X})^2][\sum (Y_i - \overline{Y})^2]}}$ and it will remain the same.

   Table 5-4 shows X = speed of the car with the old data and the new (correct) data.

Table 5-4 Correlation data

X_i	$X_i - \overline{X}$	new X_i	new $X_i - \overline{X}$
35	35-50= −15	30	30−45= − 15
45	− 5	40	− 5
55	5	50	5
65	15	60	15
$\sum X_i = 200$	$\sum (X_i - \overline{X}) = 0$	$\sum X_i = 180$	$\sum (X_i - \overline{X}) = 0$
Avg. $\overline{X} = 50$		45	

These numbers are arbitrary but will make the point clear that if all X_i are reduced by 5 miles per hour, the factor $\sum(X_i - \overline{X})$ does not change. Hence the value of r does not change even with the corrected speed data.

36.   Trend analysis is useful because

      a.   it allows us to describe the historical pattern in the data
      b.   it permits us to project the past patterns and/or trends in the future
      c.   it helps us to understand the long term variation of the time series
      d.   all of the above

Key: d.   all of the above

37.   Time series analysis is useful to understand which of the following characteristic movements?

      a.   irregular or unnatural movements
      b.   cyclic movements
      c.   seasonal variations
      d.   secular or long term movements
      e.   all of the above

Key: e.   all of the above
Time series is a process of collecting observations at regular intervals at specific times, e.g., analysis of the warranty data at every three months, number of accidents in a plant every year. The time series analysis indicates that some characteristic movements or variations are present in most of the time series data at some varying degrees. Each item in choices a through d is an example of a type of time series variation. It is important to understand such time series variations for meaningful interpretation of the data and forecasting future movements.

38.   If a time series data shows a general direction (upward or downward) of all the observations taken over a period of time, it is considered as

      a.   irregular or unnatural movements
      b.   cyclic movements
      c.   seasonal variations
      d.   secular or long term movements

Key: d.   secular or long term movements

39.   If a time series data shows some sporadic or unnatural variations, it is called

      a.   irregular or unnatural movements
      b.   cyclic movements
      c.   seasonal variations
      d.   secular or long term movements

Key: a.   irregular or unnatural movements

40. If a time series data shows identical patterns at certain months or periods each year, it is called

   a. irregular or unnatural movements
   b. cyclic movements
   c. seasonal variations
   d. secular or long term movements

Key: c. seasonal variations

41. If a time series shows long term cyclic behavior, or swings about a trend line or curve, it is called

   a. irregular or unnatural movements
   b. cyclic movements
   c. seasonal variations
   d. secular or long term movements

Key: b. cyclic movements

ASQC-CQE BIBLIOGRAPHY AND OTHER REFERENCES ON REGRESSION AND CORRELATION ANALYSIS

1. ASQC Statistics Division, *Glossary and Tables for Statistical Quality Control*, 2nd ed., Milwaukee, ASQC Quality Press, 1983.
2. Braverman, Jerome D., *Fundamentals of Statistical Quality Control*, Englewood Cliffs, N.J., Prentice-Hall, 1981.
3. Dovich, Robert A., *Quality Engineering Statistics*, Milwaukee, ASQC Quality Press, 1992.
4. Duncan, A. J., *Quality Control and Industrial Statistics*, 5th ed., Homewood, IL, Irwin Inc., 1986.
5. Grant, Eugen L. and Richard Leavenworth, *Statistical Quality Control*, 6th ed., New York, McGraw-Hill, 1988.
6. Juran, Joseph M., *Juran's Quality Control Handbook*, 4th ed., New York, McGraw-Hill, 1988.
7. Keats, J. Bert and Douglas C. Montgomery, *Statistical Process Control in Manufacturing*, New York, Marcel Dekker, 1991.
8. Vani, Jagdish, *Fundamental Concepts of Probability, Statistics, Regression and DOE*, 3rd edition, Troy, MI, Quality Quest Inc., 1993.
9. Western Electric, *Statistical Quality Control Handbook*, Indianapolis, AT&T, 1956.

CHAPTER 6

DESIGN OF EXPERIMENTS (DOE)

ASQC'S BODY OF KNOWLEDGE (BOK) FOR CQE EXAMINATION

This chapter focuses on the following selected subject areas of BOK from *Section III, Statistical Principles and Applications.*

Terms and Concepts

1. Inferential statistics (e.g., ANOVA)
2. Assumptions and robustness of tests

Experimental Design

1. Terminology (e.g., independent and dependent variables, factors, levels, treatment, error, randomization, confounding, replication)
2. Power and sample size
3. Design characteristics (e.g., balance, replication, efficiency, fit)
4. Types of designs
   a. One-factor
   b. Full and fractional factorial
5. Taguchi robustness concepts

1.   A factor

      a.   is something under study
      b.   can be quantitative or qualitative
      c.   can be controllable or uncontrollable
      d.   all of the above

Key: d.   all of the above
       A factor[1] is an element that needs to be studied or investigated for its effect on the result. It
       contributes to the accomplishment of the result and it can have different settings or levels. A
       factor can be controllable or uncontrollable, it may be quantitative, e.g., temperature or
       dimension, and can be uncontrollable, e.g., qualitative, i.e., operator A, B; supplier A and B, etc.

2.   When you assign a single level or version to a single factor during an experimental run, it is
      called a

      a.   block
      b.   randomization
      c.   treatment
      d.   replication

Key: c.   treatment
       A treatment means assigning a single level or version to a single factor in any experimental
       run.[2] In the case of a single factor, treatments and levels are used interchangeably, e.g., fertilizer
       type A is one treatment, and fertilizer type B is the second treatment. Refer to Question 13 for
       the definition of a block, Question 3 for replication, and Question 6 for randomization.

3.   Replication

      a.   means a repeated number of measurements or observations
      b.   increases precision
      c.   is the same as randomization
      d.   a and b both

Key: d.   a and b both
       Replication means performing the experiments more than once, i.e., replicating the experiment
       for all treatment combinations of the design. It means we can have a larger number of
       experiments and more data, which can provide more meaningful analysis of main effects and
       interactions, if any. It provides a better estimate of the experimental error and increases the
       precision and accuracy of the experimental results because the analysis will not be distorted by
       the outliers of extreme values. The analysis helps to determine which factors have significant
       effects on the mean of the process and which factors have significant effects on the variability of
       the process.

---

[1] *Fundamental Concepts of Probability, Statistics, Regression and DOE* by Jagdish Vani, 3rd edition, April 1993, Section 8.
[2] *Juran's Quality Control Handbook* by J. M. Juran, 4th edition, McGraw-Hill, New York, pg. 26.3.

Randomization is not the same as replication. It means a process of assigning or selecting levels of factors such that no biases are introduced during the experimentation. All trials or runs are conducted in a random order to minimize the risk of effects of biases. There are several methods of randomizing the runs, e.g., use of random number tables. We can use various experimental designs, e.g., completely randomized design, completely randomized block design, etc.

4.   Which of the following purposes are served by replicating an experiment?

        i.   Provide a means for estimating the experimental error.
        ii.   Increase the number of treatments included in the experiment.
        iii.   Improve the precision of estimates of treatment effects.

        a.   i and ii only
        b.   i and iii only
        c.   ii and iii only
        d.   i, ii, and iii

Key: b.   i and iii only   (Ref. Applications Question 30, July 1984)
        Replication means repetition of experiments for each of the treatment combinations. This allows the experimenter to include all elements that contribute to the experimental errors. It hence provides a means for estimating the experimental error and improves the precision of the estimates of the treatment effects.

        Be careful with "i and ii only" types of grouped choices where you have to match two choices with the question and then select the correct group. This sometimes adds more complexity, a higher degree of difficulty, and sometimes confusion.. Read the question statement and each group carefully and thoroughly and look for key terms or concepts.

5.   When you perform *one experiment* with *forty-nine repetitions*, what are the fifty experiments called?

        a.   randomization
        b.   replications
        c.   planned grouping
        d.   experimental pattern
        e.   sequential

Key: b.   replications   (Ref. Applications Question 17, August 1978)
        Replication is defined as performing the experiment more than once, i.e., replicating the experiment in all designed conditions for all treatment combinations. Please refer to Question 3.

6.   Randomization

        i.   enables us to balance out the effect of uncontrollable variables

ii.   means assigning different experimental runs to various treatment combinations in a purely chance manner

iii.   improves the effectiveness of the estimates of error variance in the experiment

a.   i and ii only

b.   ii and iii only

c.   iii and i only

d.   i, ii, and iii above

Key: d.   i, ii, and iii above

The term randomization means assigning different experimental runs to various treatment combinations in a purely chance manner.[3] Randomization is an important step in any experimental design, to get unbiased estimates of effects and it balances out the effects of uncontrollable variables in the run. All trials or runs are conducted in a random order to minimize the risk of effects of biases. There are several methods of randomizing the runs, e.g., use of random number tables, and one can use various experimental designs, e.g., completely randomized design, completely randomized block design, etc.

Be careful with the "i and ii only" type of grouped choices where you have to match two choices with the question and then select the correct group. This sometimes adds more complexity, a higher degree of difficulty, and sometimes confusion. Read the question statement and each group carefully and thoroughly and look for key terms or concepts.

7.   If we have included all possible levels of a factor in the experimental design, it is called

a.   random effects model

b.   fixed effects model

c.   mixed effects model

d.   none of the above

Key: b.   fixed effects model

In a fixed effects model,[4] levels of a factor are all the possible levels of that factor and no other level could be possible, e.g., raw material as a factor may only have 3 types available and you can only select these 3 types as 3 levels but no other levels are possible.

In the case of a random effect model, a factor has many possible levels and you can select the number of levels needed for the experiment. Here you are not constrained by few fixed choices but you have a larger population. For example, temperature is a factor at two levels, then we can select two levels practically from many different levels such as 200°F, 250°F, 300°F, 400°F, and so on; or any such levels.

In the case of a mixed effects model, the experimental design contains some factors as fixed

---

[3] *Juran's Quality Control Handbook* by J. M. Juran, 4th edition, McGraw-Hill, New York, pg. 26.4, and Glossary and tables for Statistical Quality Control prepared by ASQC, Statistics Division, 2nd edition, pg. 65-6.13.

[4] *Fundamental Concepts of Probability, Statistics, Regression and DOE* by Jagdish Vani, 3rd edition, April 1993, Section 9.

effects and others as random effects factors.

8.   To state that the levels of a factor are fixed indicates that

   a.   the levels are to be set at certain fixed values
   b.   the equipment from which the data are collected must not be moved
   c.   the factors under consideration are qualitative
   d.   the levels were chosen from a finite population

Key: a.   the levels are to be set at certain fixed values (Ref. Principles Question 25, October 1972)
This defines the concept of the fixed effects model in the design of experiments. A fixed effects model means levels of a factor are the only possible levels and there are no other levels possible. For example, if a plant has only 3 machines and the machine is a factor, then one can use a maximum of 3 levels of machine in the experimental design and no more. The factor machine is a fixed effect factor with 3 levels. Refer to Question 7 above for additional discussion.

9.   To state that a model in the experimental design is fixed indicates that

   a.   the levels used for each factor are the only ones of interest
   b.   the levels were chosen from a fixed population
   c.   the equipment from which the data are collected must not be moved
   d.   the factors under consideration are qualitative

Key: a.   the levels used for each factor are the only ones of interest
(Ref. Principles Question 22, July 1984.) This is a repeat question with slight changes in text. Refer to Questions 7 and 8 above for discussion.

Choice a "the levels used for each factor are the only ones *of interest*" is ASQC's answer, but if we study it harder, it indicates that there are more levels possible, and we are selecting the levels of each factor as per our interest. Hence it does not meet the definition of the fixed effects model. It should state that "the levels used for each factor are the only ones *available* or *possible.* "

10.   When considering qualitative and quantitative factors in the same designed experiment

   a.   the sum of squares for the qualitative factors can still be calculated even though no numerical scale can be attached to the levels
   b.   tables of orthogonal polynomials do not apply because no numerical scale can be attached to one of the factors
   c.   the interactions between qualitative and quantitative factors no longer make sense
   d.   the tables of orthogonal polynomials apply to both types of factors if the levels of each are equally spaced

Key: a.   the sum of squares for the qualitative factors can still be calculated even though no numerical scale can be attached to the levels (Ref. Principles Question 26, October 1972)
Whether the factor is qualitative or quantitative, when each factor is changed from one level to

the other level, the effect of each factor on the response variable Y is calculated in the form of main effect. Hence the sum of squares for the qualitative factors can still be calculated even though no numerical scale can be attached to the levels.

11.   Information generated in a designed experiment

    a.   always results in an analysis of variance table
    b.   is based on the fact that 'the variance of the sum is the sum of the variances'
    c.   must always be quantitative
    d.   may be based on values which are not necessarily numerical

Key: d.   may be based on values which are not necessarily numerical
(Ref. Principles Question 49, October 1972)
The designed experiment may involve a fixed effect model with all possible levels of a factor, a random effect model with some levels from many possible levels, or a mixed effect model containing both effects. It may also have quantitative factors such as temperatures at 200°F and 300°F and/or qualitative factors such as machines A, B, and C. Also the response variable can be qualitative or quantitative. Hence some of the information generated about the factors and their levels and the response variable can be qualitative in nature and not numerical.

12.   The main objection of designed experimentation in an industrial environment is

    a.   obtaining more information for less cost than can be obtained by traditional experimentation
    b.   getting excessive scrap as a result of choosing factor levels that are too extreme
    c.   verifying that one factor at a time is the most economical way to proceed
    d.   obtaining data and then deciding what to do with it

Key: b.   getting excessive scrap as a result of choosing factor levels that are too extreme
(Ref. Applications Question 68, October 1972)
The key phrase is **main objection** indicating the cautions for designing an experiment. The size of the experiment depends on the number of factors, their levels, and replication, if any. When the experiment is run, it produces the parts or products from each run that may or may not be the optimum quality. Hence it can create the scrap or parts that are not acceptable. This is one of the main objections. The other objections could be resources, production downtime, cost, etc.

13.   A block in the experimental design means

    a.   a heterogeneous unit
    b.   a relatively homogeneous unit
    c.   a relatively nonuniform unit
    d.   an arbitrary grouping

Key: b.   a relatively homogeneous unit
In experimental design, the term block means a relatively homogeneous experimental unit. It

subdivides the experimental space into smaller homogeneous or uniform units. This results in greater precision and a smaller error of estimation. The term block in agriculture means a portion of land which has common conditions such as proximity to river, wind conditions, soil type, etc.

14.   The experimental design which is appropriate when one factor is under investigation and the experimental environment is divided into homogeneous units is called

        a.   Yoden square
        b.   fractional factorial
        c.   completely randomized
        d.   randomized block

Key: d.   randomized block
        The randomized block design is the one where all levels of the treatment variable are assigned randomly within each block. The blocking provides a more homogeneous situation for evaluating the effects of the treatment variable and results in greater precision.

15.   A completely randomized design

        a.   is appropriate when only one experimental factor is being investigated
        b.   is used to investigate one factor by allocating experimental units at random to treatments
        c.   does not require any blocking
        d.   all of the above

Key: d.   all of the above
        Completely randomized design is a simple analysis. It provides flexibility of assigning the number of treatments in the experiment. It is generally a one-factor design with no blocking. Here all the experimental units are randomly allocated and we try to estimate the effects of treatments.[5]

16.   Sensitivity in the experimentation is

        a.   getting the true result
        b.   extreme care in data analysis
        c.   using the best measuring devicc
        d.   ability to distinguish differences in the response variables

Key: d.   ability to distinguish differences in the response variables
        (Ref. Principles Question 9, October 1974) This question is repeated in the October 1972 examination.[6]

17.   In every experiment, there is experimental error. Which one of the following statements is true?

---

[5] *Juran's Quality Control Handbook* by J. M. Juran, 4th edition, McGraw-Hill, New York, pg. 26.7 and 26.10.
[6] *ASQC - CQE Examination*, Quality Progress, October 1972, Principles section Question 45.

a. This error is due to lack of uniformity of the material used in the experiment and to inherent variability in the experimental technique.
b. This error can be changed statistically by increasing the degrees of freedom.
c. The error can be reduced only by improving the material.
d. In a well designed experiment, there is no interaction effect.

Key: a. This error is due to lack of uniformity of the material used in the experiment and to inherent variability in the experimental technique.
(Ref. Principles Question 74, October 1972)
Every process has some inherent variability or common causes which are calculated as an error term in the experiment. The analysis helps decompose the total variation into its three main components of variation: *the treatment variation for each treatment variable, effect of interactions if any, and the error variation.* ANOVA uses this concept of inherent variability as homoscedasticity, i.e., an assumption of common or equal error variances σ_e^2 for the treatments. In every experiment, this error is calculated as the sum of squares for the error term (SSE); it is also called the *within treatment error (SSW).* It is then used to test for significance in the F test.

18. The error term ε_{ij} of the population model $\chi_{ij} = \mu + \tau_{ij} + \varepsilon_{ij}$ is usually considered

a. normally and independently distributed with mean = 0 and variability = 1
b. normally and randomly distributed with mean = 0 and variance = 1
c. randomly distributed with mean = 0 and variance = σ_e^2
d. normally and independently distributed with mean = 0 and variance = σ_e^2

Key: d. normally and independently distributed with mean = 0 and variance = σ_e^2
(Ref. Principles Question 33, October 1972)
ε_{ij} is the error term in the model and is normally and independently distributed with mean = 0 and variance = σ_e^2. This is the fundamental assumption in ANOVA, that the variances within the treatment groups are equal.

19. The power of efficiency in designed experiments lies in the

a. random order of performance
b. the sequential and cyclical procedure of conjecture to design to analysis and back to conjecture
c. hidden replication
d. the large number of possible combinations of factors

Key: c. hidden replication   (Ref. Principles Question 66, October 1972)
A designed experiment involves a wide range of treatment combinations of many factors. Depending upon the design, different levels of a factor will be treated with other levels of all remaining factors several times. This can result in hidden replication of experiments for levels of factors which makes the designed experiment a powerful tool for quality improvement at low cost. Because of the hidden replication in the design, one can minimize or optimize the number

of experimental runs resulting in cost and time savings, e.g., three factors A, B and C at two levels. Let us consider a factorial case, i.e., we have $2 \times 2 \times 2 = 8$ total runs as shown in Table 6-1.

Table 6-1 A 2^3 factorial experiment

Expt. No.	Run No.	A	B	C	Response Y
1	5	1	1	1	Y_1
2	8	1	1	2	Y_2
3	1	1	2	1	Y_3
4	7	1	2	2	Y_4
5	3	2	1	1	Y_5
6	4	2	1	2	Y_6
7	6	2	2	1	Y_7
8	2	2	2	2	Y_8

You can see that we have a total of eight runs and no additional replication in the total experiment. However factor A is run a total of four times at level 1 and four times at level 2, with all the levels of factors B and C, which indicates the hidden replication in the design. In the same way factors B and C are run four times at level 1 and level 2, respectively.

20.   An incomplete block design may be especially suitable when

    a.   there is missing data
    b.   there is need for fractional replication
    c.   it may not be possible to apply all treatments in every block
    d.   there is a need to estimate the parameters during the experimentation

Key: c.   it may not be possible to apply all treatments in every block
(Ref. Applications Question 44, October 1972)
In an incomplete block design, all treatments cannot be accommodated within a single block[7] and there are not enough experimental units to run a complete replication of all experimental runs.

21.   For a two-factor experiment with n observations per cell run as a completely randomized design

    a.   the degrees of freedom cannot be determined because of the interaction term in the mathematical model
    b.   if both factors are fixed, all tests of significance are made using the error mean square
    c.   the interaction term cannot be calculated by subtracting the main effects sum of squares from the cell sum of squares
    d.   when the interactions effect is significant, it becomes obvious that one of the main effects is also significant
    e.   all of the above

---

[7] *Juran's Quality Control Handbook* by J. M. Juran, 4th edition, McGraw-Hill, New York, pg. 26.59-60.

Key: b.   if both factors are fixed, all tests of significance are made using the error mean square
               (Ref. Principles Question 8, October 1974)

22.   The following data are based on an experiment.

       Table 6-2 Factor A and B response values

		Factor B	
		B_1	B_2
Factor A	A_1	8	12
	A_2	14	18

       The main effect of factor B is

       a.   4
       b.   6
       c.   11
       d.   15

Key: a.   4
       Refer to Table 6-3 for the main effects of factors A and B.
       The average response of factor B at B_1 is $\overline{B}1 = 22/2 = 11$.
       The average response of factor B at B_2 is $\overline{B}2 = 30/2 = 15$.
       The main effect of factor B is $\overline{B}2 - \overline{B}1 = 15 - 11 = 4$.

       Table 6-3 Main effects of A and B

		Factor B		
		B_1	B_2	Avg.
Factor A	A_1	8	12	$\overline{A}1 = 20/2 = 10$
	A_2	14	18	$\overline{A}2 = 32/2 = 16$
	Avg.	$\overline{B}1 = 22/2 = 11$	$\overline{B}2 = 30/2 = 15$	

23.   In the above example (Question 22), we can say that

       a.   There is an interaction between factor A and factor B
       b.   There is no interaction between factor A and factor B
       c.   The main effects for each factor are zero
       d.   all of the above

Key: b.   There is no interaction between factor A and factor B
       Fig. 6-1 (a) and (b) shows the response charts for A×B interaction. Fig. 6-1(a) shows the   parallel
       lines for the responses of B from B_1 to B_2 at A_1 as one line and at A_2 as the other line. Similarly
       Fig. 6-1(b) shows parallel lines for responses of A from A_1 to A_2 at B_1 as one line and at B_2 as
       the other line. This means that there is no interaction between the two factors A and B.

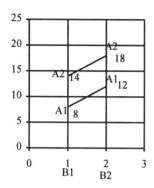

Fig. 6-1(a) Response chart-interaction A×B

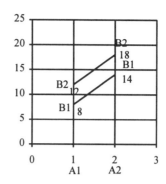

Fig. 6-1(b) Response chart-interaction B×A

24.   A factorial experiment is one in which

    a.   there is only one factor under study
    b.   all levels of a given factor are combined with all levels of every other factor in the experiment
    c.   levels of one factor are nested within and cannot be used with all levels of other factors
    d.   the number of rows and the number of columns are the same

Key: b.   all levels of a given factor are combined with all levels of every other factor in the experiment

The factorial experiment is one in which the experiment runs are performed for all possible combinations of all levels of each factor with all levels of every other factor. The term factorial only refers to the type of experiment and not a particular design or layout. Please refer to Question 19 above for an example of a 2^3 factorial experiment.

25.   When constructing a factorial experiment, one of the following is true:

    a.   factorial experiments may not contain any number of levels per factor; they must be the same for each factor.
    b.   confounding takes place in factorials when we run a fractional part of the complete experiment
    c.   contrasts and treatment combinations are the same
    d.   in factorials, the factors must be quantitative

Key: b.   confounding takes place in factorials when we run a fractional part of the complete experiment   (Ref. Principles Question 28, October 1972)

Confounding[8] means the combining of the main effects of a factor with the effect of any other factor in the experiment. When fractional factorial experiments are run, we have a smaller number of total runs. It results in the confounding of main effects of treatments with the interaction of two or more factors and/or confounding of main effects of one interaction with another interaction. When confounding takes place, you cannot recover the main effects of the factors or the interactions from the design. Even in the case of the (full) factorial experiment,

---

[8] *Fundamental Concepts of Probability, Statistics, Regression and DOE* by Jagdish Vani, 3rd edition, April 1993, Section 9.

e.g., the 2^k factorial experiment, confounding[9] is likely to occur if we want to analyze main effects of all factors and all their possible interactions without any replication.

Full factorial experiments do not require every factor to be at the same number of levels, i.e., one factor may be at 2 levels with quantitative values (e.g., temperature at 200°F and 300°F) and another at 3 levels which are qualitative, e.g., machines A, B, and C. Contrasts are used to calculate the mean effects whereas the treatment combination defines the levels of different factors in each experimental run in the experiment.

26.   An experiment with two factors in which all levels of one variable are run at each level of the second variable is called a

        a.   one-way experiment
        b.   Latin square experiment
        c.   factorial experiment
        d.   fractional factorial experiment

Key: c.   factorial experiment   (Ref. Principles Question 27, July 1984)
        A factorial experiment is one in which the experimental runs are performed for all possible combinations of all levels of one factor with all levels of every other factor.

        Choice a is incorrect because a one-way experiment means there is only one factor and not two factors under study at different levels. In a Latin square design, the combination of levels of any one factor with the versions of the other two appears once and only once.

        In the case of a fractional factorial experiment, only a selected number of treatment combinations, i.e., only a fraction of the total number of a (full) factorial experiment, are run and not all possible combinations.

27.   When considering a factorial experiment, observe that

        a.   this experiment cannot be used when complete randomization is necessary
        b.   a main effect may be confounded
        c.   this type of the design is not encountered in the industrial experiments
        d.   one of the advantages is that an exact test always exists for all effects

Key: b.   a main effect may be confounded (Ref. Principles Question 64, October 1972)
        Confounding[10] means the combining of the main effects of a factor with the effect of any other factor in the experiment. The concept of confounding is very important in factorial experiments as many times many replications of an experiment may not be possible or a complete factorial cannot be run in one block or at one time. It may result in blocking the experiment,[11] and you can recover only some but not all high-order interactions.

---

[9] *Design and Analysis of Experiments* by Douglas C. Montgomery, John Wiley and Sons, 1991, Chapter 9.
[10] *Fundamental Concepts of Probability, Statistics, Regression and DOE* by Jagdish Vani, 3rd edition, April 1993, Section 9.
[11] *Design and Analysis of Experiments* by Douglas C. Montgomery, John Wiley and Sons, 1991, Chapter 9.

28.   If there are 5 levels of a factor A and 4 levels of a factor B, then the total number of experiments in a factorial experiment will be

    a. 5^4
    b. 4^5
    c. 5×4
    d.   9

Key: c. 5×4
    In the case of factorial experiments, the total number of experimental runs are given by multiplication of levels of each factor, i.e., 5×4.

29.   A 3^2 experiment means that we are considering

    a.   Two levels of three factors
    b.   Two dependent variables and three independent variables
    c.   Two go/no go variables and three continuous variables
    d.   Three levels of two factors

Key: d.   three levels of two factors   (Ref. Principles Question 13, July 1984)
    This is a factorial experiment of 2 factors at 3 levels each resulting in $3 \times 3 = 9$ total experimental runs. This question is repeated in the October 1972 examination.[12]

30.   A test of significance using a given value of α is performed on the yield data from a process using a standard material and a proposed substitute. Which of the following conclusions is not possible from this test?

    a.   The standard material is better than the substitute material.
    b.   We have an interaction between the two materials.
    c.   The probability of Type I error is α.
    d.   The sample size is too small to detect the difference necessary to justify a material change.
    e.   The proposed material is better than the standard parts/material.

Key: b.   We have an interaction between the two materials.
    (Ref. Principles Question 79, October 1974)
    Here the material is the only factor or variable of interest and is set at two levels, i.e., standard material and a proposed substitute. It means it is a single factor ANOVA and there is no second variable in the experiment, hence the question of interaction does not exist. All other choices are possible conclusions from this test.

31.   The design in which the number of treatments equals the number of rows and number of columns is

---

[12] *ASQC - CQE Examination*, Quality Progress, October 1972, Principles section Question 48.

    a.   Latin square design
    b.   nested design
    c.   factorial design
    d.   fractional factorial design

Key: a.   Latin square design

The Latin square design is a square arrangement; i.e., it has the same number of rows and columns and is represented as an n × n design, e.g., 3 × 3 or 4 × 4 Latin square design. It contains the same number of versions for the main factor under study and for all other factors in the experiment.

The nested design is a hierarchical design,[13] i.e., an experiment where the number of levels of a factor are all different across the levels of other factors, and we cannot use a level of one factor with all levels of another factor.

The factorial experiment is one in which the experiment runs are performed for all possible combinations of all levels of each factor with all levels of every other factor. The term factorial only refers to the type of the experiment and not a particular design or layout.
A fractional factorial experiment only includes a few selected treatment combinations or a few runs from all possible combinations.

32.   The Latin square design means

    i.   the number of treatments must equal the number of rows and columns
    ii.   that each treatment occurs only once in each row and once in each column
    iii.   the number of rows, columns, and treatments need not be the same
    iv.   no interactions exist

    a.   i, ii, and iii only
    b.   ii, iii, and iv only
    c.   iii, iv, and i only
    d.   iv, i, and ii only

Key: d.   iv, i, and ii only

Only choice c does not apply because it includes item iii which indicates a condition in Yoden square design and not Latin square design. In the case of Yoden square design, the number of rows and columns need not be the same.[14] All other items meet the conditions of the Latin square design.

33.   The primary advantage of the Latin square design compared to factorial design is

    a.   it requires less data
    b.   it eliminates the need for interactions

---

[13] *Fundamental Concepts of Probability, Statistics, Regression and DOE* by Jagdish Vani, 3rd edition, April 1993, Section 9.
[14] *Juran's Quality Control Handbook* by J. M. Juran, 4th edition, McGraw-Hill, New York, pg. 26.9.

c.   it allows higher significance levels
d.   it does not require homogeneity of variance

Key: a.   it requires less data   (Ref. Principles Question 18, July 1984)
The Latin square is an n × n square design, e.g., if we have factor A at 3 levels, B at 3 levels, and C at 3 levels, then using Latin square, we will have a total of 3×3 = 9 experimental runs as compared to 3×3×3 = 27 runs in the case of a factorial experiment. Hence it requires less data.

34.   A Latin square design is an experiment design which

a.   cannot be used when an estimation of the interaction effects is desired
b.   affords a good estimate of interaction effects
c.   is useful because the underlying distributions need not be normal
d.   avoids the need to assume that the effects are additive

Key: a.   cannot be used when an estimation of the interaction effects is desired
(Ref. Principles Question 4, October 1972)
In Latin square design, the combination of levels of any one factor with the versions of the other two appears once and only once. Latin square design is a square n×n fractional design and does not provide enough degrees of freedom for interaction. It does not provide an estimation of any interaction effects.

35.   A Latin square design is noted for its straightforward analysis of the interaction effects. The above statement is

a.   true in every case
b.   true sometimes, depending on the size of the square
c.   true only for Greco-Latin squares
d.   false in every case
e.   false except for Greco-Latin squares

Key: d.   false in every case   (Ref. Principles Question 23, August 1978)
This is false because the Latin square design does not allow any interaction between the variables.

36.   In the case of ANOVA, which of the following is/are not true?

i.   The response variable is normally distributed in each of the populations being compared.
ii.   The distributions of the dependent variable in each population have the same variance.
iii.   The degrees of freedom are not additive.
iv.   The F ratio is used to determine if there is significant difference between the treatment means.

a.   only i
b.   only ii

c.   only iii
d.   all of the above

Key: c.   only iii

The ANOVA is based on some important assumptions: the degrees of freedoms are additive and treatment distributions are normal and have equal variances. Hence choice c is not true.

37.   The test used for testing significance in an analysis of variance table is

a.   The Z test
b.   The t test
c.   The F test
d.   The Chi-square test

Key: c.   The F test   (Ref. Principles Question 6, July 1984)

In analysis of variance (ANOVA), the ratio of mean squares of treatments to mean squares of error is compared against the F statistic using the F table for the test of significance.

38.   In a single-factor analysis of variance, the assumption of homogeneity of variance applies to

a.   the variance within the treatment groups
b.   the variance of the treatment means
c.   the total variance
d.   all of the above

Key: a.   the variance within the treatment groups   (Ref. Principles Question 9, July 1984)

This is a fundamental assumption in ANOVA that the variances within the treatment groups are equal. This is a repeat question with slight changes from the October 1974 and August 1978 examinations.[15]

39.   Best assumptions underlying the analysis of variance include

i.   observations are from normally distributed populations
ii.   observations are from populations with equal variances
iii.   observations are from populations with equal means

a.   i and ii only
b.   i and iii only
c.   ii and iii only
d.   i, ii, and iii

Key: a.   i and ii only   (Ref. Principles Question 15, July 1984)

In ANOVA, we assume that the observations are from normally distributed populations, and

---

[15] *ASQC - CQE Examination*, Quality Progress, October 1974, Principles section Question 39; August 1978, Applications section Question 23, and July 1984 Applications Question 27.

observations are from populations with equal variances. Watch for "iii" where the assumption of equal means is not correct because that is what we have to test for as the null hypothesis.

40.   For a given number of degrees of freedom, as the variability among means (groups, columns) increases relative to the variability within groups:

        a.   the F ratio decreases
        b.   the F ratio increases
        c.   the F ratio is unaffected
        d.   the risk of a Type I error increases
        e.   cannot answer without knowing the number of observations

Key: b.   the F ratio increases   (Ref. Principles Question 20, October 1974)
        The F test is the ratio of the two mean squares, i.e., the ratio of MSB to MSE, and it provides a basis for the F test of significance. Mean square between the groups (MSB) is the ratio of the sum of squares between the groups (SSB) divided by its degrees of freedom (df_b), and it is the unbiased estimate of the population variance. Mean square for error (MSE) is the ratio of the sum of squares for the error term (SSE) divided by its degrees of freedom (df_e). This can be shown as

$$F = \frac{MSB}{MSE} = \frac{SSB / df_b}{SSE / df_e} \; .$$

        As the variability amongst means increases, relative to the variability within groups, SSB increases, i.e., the MSB value also increases. Hence the F ratio increases.

41.   In a single factor analysis of variance the assumption of homogeneity of variance applies to

        a.   the variance within the treatment groups
        b.   the variance of the means associated with the treatment groups
        c.   the total variance
        d.   all of the above
        e.   none of the above

Key: a.   the variance within the treatment groups (Ref. Principles Question 39, October 1974)
        The fundamental assumption in ANOVA is that the variances within the treatment groups are equal. This is a repeat question with slight change from the July 1984 and August 1978 examinations.[16]

42.   If the means of the samples for each of the treatment groups in an experiment were identical the F ratio would be

        a.   1.00
        b.   zero
        c.   a positive number between 0 and 1

---

[16] *ASQC - CQE Examination*, Quality Progress, July 1984, Principles section Question 9 and Applications Question 27 and August 1978, Applications section Question 23.

d.   a negative number
e.   infinite

Key: b.   zero   (Ref. Principles Question 50, October 1974)

Refer to Question 40 above, that explains the F ratio. We have seen that $F = \dfrac{MSB}{MSE} = \dfrac{SSB/df_b}{SSE/df_e}$.
If the means of each treatment group are identical, then SSB will become zero because it is the sum of squared deviations of each column total or row total from its grand mean total. Hence the MSB will be zero, which will result in the F ratio being zero.

43.   In the analysis of variance

a.   the total sum of squares of deviations from the grand mean is equal to the sum of squares of deviations between treatment means and the grand mean minus the sum of squares of deviations within treatments
b.   the total standard deviation is equal to the sum of standard deviations for the treatment effect plus the standard deviation of the random error
c.   the degrees of freedom are additive
d.   a basic population model can be constructed to represent the behavior of the experimentation

Key: c.   the degrees of freedom are additive   (Ref. Principles Question 70, October 1972)
The degrees of freedom (df) are additive means that we add the df of treatments and of error to get total df. Or the df for the error term is the difference of df of the total and df of the treatments, as shown below.

df (total) = df(treatments) + df(error), i.e., df(error) = df(total) − df(treatments)

44.   For a factor A of three levels, the following data (as shown in Table 6-4) are obtained.

Table 6-4 Raw data

A_1	3	4	5	4
A_2	2	4	3	3
A_3	4	6	5	5

The degrees of freedom for treatment, error, and total df are

a.   11, 2, 9 respectively
b.   11, 9, 2 respectively
c.   9, 2, 11 respectively
d.   2, 9, 11 respectively

Key: d.   2, 9, 11 respectively
Given: Raw data of factor A at k = 3 levels, n= 4 samples, and N =3×4=12 total.
Find: Degrees of freedom for treatment, error, and total.

For one-way ANOVA:

df for treatment = $k-1 = 3-1 = 2$

df for error = $k(n-1) = 3(4-1) = 9$ or = df total – df treatment $= 11-9 = 2$

df for total = $kn-1 = N-1 = 12-1 = 11$

45.   In Question 44 above, the SSE, i.e., the sum of squares for the error term, is

   a.   8
   b.   14
   c.   6
   d.   192

Key: c.   6

Given: Raw data Y_i of factor A at $k = 3$ levels, $n = 4$ samples, and N $=3\times4=12$ total.

Find: The sum of squares for the error term, SSE.

This is one-way ANOVA and can be shown as follows in Table 6-5.

Table 6-5 ANOVA data

Machines					Row total R_i	n
A_1	3	4	5	4	16	4
A_2	2	4	3	3	12	4
A_3	4	6	5	5	20	4
					$T=\sum R_i = 48$	$N = 3\times4 = 12$

The correction term $C = \dfrac{T^2}{N} = \dfrac{48^2}{12} = 192$.

$$SSB = \frac{\sum R_i^2}{n} - C = \frac{16^2}{4} + \frac{12^2}{4} + \frac{20^2}{4} - 192 = 200 - 192 = 8.$$

$SST = \sum Y_i^2 - C = (3^2+4^2+5^2+4^2+.... + 5^2) - 192 = 206 - 192 = 14.$

$SSE = SST - SSB = 14 - 8 = 6.$

46.   The F ratio for the data in Question 44 is

   a.   4
   b.   6
   c.   2/3
   d.   8/3

Key: b.   6

Given: Raw data Y_i of factor A at $k = 3$ levels as shown in Table 6-6, $n = 4$ samples and N $=3\times4$ $= 12$ total.

Find: The F ratio.

Refer to Table 6-6 for ANOVA calculations.

Table 6-6 One-way ANOVA table

Source of variation	Sum of squares SS	Degrees of freedom df	Mean squares MS	F ratio
Between treatments	$SSB = \dfrac{\sum Ri^2}{n} - C = 8$ $C = \dfrac{T^2}{n} = \dfrac{T^2}{kn} = 192$	k−1=2	$MSB = \dfrac{SSB}{k-1}$ $= 8/2 = 4$	$F_{cal} = \dfrac{MSB}{MSE}$ $= 4 / 0.67$ $= 6$
Within treatments or error term	$SSE = SST - SSB = 6$	k(n−1)= 9	$MSE = \dfrac{SSE}{k(n-1)}$ $= 6/9 = 0.67$	
total	$SST = \sum Y^2 - C = 14$	kn−1 or N−1 = 11		

47.   For the data of Question 44,

    a.   we reject the null hypothesis that the treatment means are equal at a 5% level of significance
    b.   we accept the null hypothesis that the treatment means are equal
    c. $F_{0.05,\,2,9}$ is 4.26
    d.   both a and c

Key: d.   both a and c
Given: $F_{cal} = 6$.
Find: F_{table} and test of significance.
From the F table, at 2 and 9 df and $\alpha = 0.05$ level of significance, we get $F_{table} = 4.26$.
Hence $F_{cal} > F_{table}$ and hence it is not in the acceptance region. We reject the null hypothesis that the treatment means are equal.

48.   The results of a 2 factor experiments with factor A at 4 levels and B at 5 levels are shown below.

		Factor B				
		B_1	B_2	B_3	B_4	B_5
	A_1	76	67	81	56	51
Factor A	A_2	82	69	96	59	70
	A_3	68	59	67	54	42
	A_4	63	56	64	58	37

The degrees of freedom for factors A, B, error, and total, respectively, are

    a.   3, 12, 4, 19
    b.   3, 4, 12, 19
    c.   4, 3, 12, 19
    d.   3, 4, 19, 12

Key: b.   3, 4, 12, 19
Given: Raw data of Y_i for two factors A at 4 levels, i.e., r = 4, and
         B at 5 levels, i.e., c = 5 columns. Total r×c = 4×5 = 20.
Find: Degrees of freedom for factors A and B, error, and total.
This is a case of a two-way ANOVA as we have two factors, A and B.
df for rows (factor A) $df_A = (r-1) = (4-1) = 3$
df for columns (factor B) $df_B = (c-1) = (5-1) = 4$
df for error $df_e = (r-1)(c-1) = (4-1)(5-1) = 12$
df for total $df_T = r×c - 1 = N-1 = (4×5) - 1 = 19$

49.   In Question 48 above, the SSE, i.e., the sum of squares for the error term, is

   a.   441.3
   b.   1182.95
   c.   394.32
   d.   486.88

Key: a.   441.3
Given: Raw data of Y_i for two factors A at 4 levels as shown in Table 6-7, i.e., r = 4, and B at 5
         levels, i.e., c = 5 columns, total r×c = 4×5 = 20.
Find: The sum of squares for the error term, SSE.

Table 6-7 Two-way ANOVA

Factor B⇒ Factor A⇓	B₁	B₂	B₃	B₄	B₅	Factor A total = R_i r = 4
A₁	76	67	81	56	51	331
A₂	82	69	96	59	70	376
A₃	68	59	67	54	42	290
A₄	63	56	64	58	37	278
Factor A total = C_j c = 5	289	251	308	227	200	$G_T = \sum R_i = \sum C_j = 1275$ $N = r×c = 4×5 = 20$

$$C = \text{Correction term} = \frac{T^2}{N} = \frac{(1275)^2}{20} = 81281.$$

$$\text{For factor A: } SSB_A = \frac{\sum R_i^2}{c} - C = \frac{331^2 + 376^2 + 290^2 + 278^2}{5} - 81281 = 82464 - 81281 = 1183.$$

$$\text{For factor B: } SSB_B = \frac{\sum C_j^2}{r} - C = \frac{289^2 + 251^2 + 308^2 + 227^2 + 200^2}{4} - 81281 = 1948.$$

$$SST = \sum Y_{ij}^2 - C = (76^2 + 67^2 + 81^2 + 56^2 + \ldots + 37^2) - 81281 = 84853 - 81281 = 3572.$$

$$SSE = SST - SSB_A - SSB_B = 3572 - 1183 - 1948 = 441.$$

50.   In Question 48 above, for factor A at a 5% level of significance, which of the following is/are the findings of the analysis?

    i.   We reject the null hypothesis that the treatment means are equal, i.e., the response varies significantly with the change in levels of factor A.
    ii.   We accept the null hypothesis that the treatment means are equal, i.e., the response does not vary significantly with the change in levels of factor A.
    iii.   The $F_{0.05,3,12}$ is 3.49.
    iv.   The $F_{0.05,3,12}$ is 3.26.

    a.   i only
    b.   i and iii both
    c.   i and iv both
    d.   ii and iv both

Key: b.   i and iii both
        Given: Raw data of Y_i for two factors A at 4 levels, i.e., r = 4, and B at 5 levels, i.e., c =5 columns. Total r×c = 4×5 = 20; df_A = 3, df_B = 4, df_e = 12, df_T = 19.
        Find: F_{Atable} and test of significance for factor A.
        Refer to Table 6-8. Factor A: df_A = 3, df_e = 12.

Table 6-8 Two-way ANOVA

Source of variation	Sum of squares SS	Degrees of freedom df	Mean squares MS	F ratio
Between treatments factor A (rows)	$SSB_A = \dfrac{\sum Ri^2}{c} - C$ $= 1183$ $C = \dfrac{T^2}{r \times c} = \dfrac{T^2}{N} = 81281$	$df_A = r-1$ $= 4-1 = 3$	$MSB_A = \dfrac{SSB_A}{df_A}$ $= \dfrac{1183}{3} = 394$	$F_A = \dfrac{MSB_A}{MSE}$ $= \dfrac{394}{37} = 10.65$
Between treatments factor B (columns)	$SSB_B = \dfrac{\sum Cj^2}{r} - C = 1948$	$df_B = c-1$ $= 5-1 = 4$	$MSB_B = \dfrac{SSB_B}{df_B}$ $= \dfrac{1948}{4} = 487$	$F_B = \dfrac{MSB_B}{MSE}$ $= \dfrac{487}{37} = 13.16$
Within treatments or error term	$SSE = SST - SSB_A - SSB_B$ $= 3572 - 1183 - 1948$ $= 441$	$df_e =$ $(r-1)(c-1)$ $= 12$	$MSE = \dfrac{SSE}{df_e}$ $= \dfrac{441}{12} = 37$	
Total	$SST = \sum Y_{ij}^2 - C = 3572$	$(r×c) -1$ $= N-1 = 19$		

From the F tables, the $F_{critical}$ for 3, 12 degrees of freedom at a 5% level of significance, $F_{A,0.05,3,12}$ = 3.49 and F_{Acal} = 10.65. Hence $F_{Acal} > F_{A,0.05,3,12}$. We reject the null hypothesis that the treatment means are equal for factor A. And the response varies significantly with changes in levels of factor A, i.e., factor A is significant.

51.   In Question 48 above, for factor B at a 5% level of significance, which of the following is/are the findings of the analysis?

i.   We reject the null hypothesis that the treatment means are equal, i.e., response varies significantly with change in levels of factor B.
ii.   We accept the null hypothesis that the treatment means are equal i.e. the response does not vary significantly with change in levels of factor B.
iii.   The $F_{0.05,4,12}$ is 3.49.
iv.   The $F_{0.05,4,12}$ is 3.26.

a.   i only
b.   i and iii both
c.   i and iv both
d.   ii and iv both

Key: c.   i and iv both
       Given: Raw data of Y_i for two factors A at 4 levels, i.e., r = 4, and B at 5 levels, i.e., c =5 columns. Total r×c= 4×5 = 20; df_A = 3, df_B = 4, df_e = 12, df_T = 19.
       Find: F_{Btable} and test of significance for factor B.
       From Table 6-8, the ANOVA table of Question 50, F_{Bcal} = 13.16.
       Factor B: df_B = 4, df_e = 12; from the F table, the $F_{critical}$ for 4, 12 degrees of freedom at a 5% level of significance, $F_{B, 0.05,4,12,}$ = 3.26, and F_{Bcal} = 13.16.

       Hence $F_{Bcal} > F_{B, 0.05,4,12}$. We reject the null hypothesis that the treatment means are equal for factor B. And the response varies significantly with changes in levels of factor B, i.e., factor B is significant.

52.   A two-way analysis of variance has r levels for the one variable and c levels for the second variable with two observations per cell. The degrees of freedom for interaction is

a. $2(r \times c)$
b. $(r-1)(c-1)$
c. $rc - 1$
d. $2(r-1)(c-1)$

Key: b. $(r-1)(c-1)$ (Ref. Applications Question 2, July 1984)
       This is the formula for the degrees of freedom of interaction term in two-way ANOVA and does not depend on the number of observations per cell.

53.   The following coded results were obtained from a single factor completely randomized experiment in which the production outputs of three machines (A, B, C) were to be compared.

$$
\begin{array}{lccccc}
\text{A} & 4 & 8 & 5 & 7 & 6 \\
\text{B} & 2 & 0 & 1 & 2 & 4 \\
\text{C} & -3 & 1 & -2 & -1 & 0
\end{array}
$$

What is the sum of the squares for the error term?

a. 170
b. 130
c. 40
d. 14
e. 28.8   (This is ASQC's correction for answer.)

Key: e.   28.8   (Ref. Applications Question 13, July 1984 & ASQC corrected this answer)
Given: The data are one-way ANOVA with the machines as a factor with 3 levels A, B, and C.
Find: The sum of squares of error term SSE.
Refer to Table 6-9 for ANOVA data.

Table 6-9 ANOVA data

Machines						R_i	n
A	4	8	5	7	6	30	5
B	2	0	1	2	4	9	5
C	-3	1	-2	-1	0	-5	5
						$T=\sum R_i=34$	$N=3\times5$ $=15$

The correction term $C = \dfrac{T^2}{N} = \dfrac{34^2}{15} = 77$ and SSB $= \dfrac{\sum R_i^2}{n} - C = \dfrac{30^2 + 9^2 + (-5)^2}{5} - 77 = 124$.

SST $=\sum Y_i^2 - C = [\, 4^2 + 8^2 + 5^2 \ldots\ldots\ldots\ldots + (-5)^2 \,] - 77.1 = 230 - 77 = 153$.
SSE $=$ SST $-$ SSB $= 153 - 124 = 29 \approx 28.8$.

Table 6-10 One-way ANOVA table

Source of variation	Sum of squares SS	Degrees of freedom df	Mean squares MS	F ratio
Between treatments	SSB $= \dfrac{\sum R_i^2}{n} - C = 124$ $C = \dfrac{T^2}{N} = \dfrac{34^2}{15} = 77$	k − 1=2	$MSB = \dfrac{SSB}{k-1}$	$F_{cal} = \dfrac{MSB}{MSE}$
Within treatments or error term	SSE $=$ SST $-$ SSB $= 29$ ≈ 28.8	k(n−1)= 12	$MSE = \dfrac{SSE}{k(n-1)}$	
Total	SST $=\sum Y_i^2 - C = 153$	kn−1= N−1=14		

Choice e is the new corrected answer by ASQC.

54.   Consider the SS and MS columns of an analysis of variance table for a single factor design. The appropriate ratio for testing the null hypothesis of no treatment effect is

    a.   SS treatments divided by SS residual
    b.   MS treatments divided by MS residual
    c.   SS treatments divided by MS residual
    d.   MS treatments divided by SS residual

Key: b.   MS treatments divided by MS residual (Ref. Applications Question 19, July 1984) This is one of the most fundamental concepts for ANOVA. We calculate the F ratio as the ratio of MS treatments and MS residual. We compare the F_{cal} to the $F_{critical}$ value from the F table to determine the null hypothesis that the means are the same, i.e., there is no significant difference in any means of different treatments.

55.   In performing analysis of variance in a single factor experiment, a fundamental assumption which is made is that the

    a.   factor (column) means are equal
    b.   factor (column) means are unequal
    c.   column variances are equal
    d.   column variances are significantly different

Key: c.   column variances are equal   (Ref. Applications Question 23, August 1978) This is the fundamental assumption that the column or treatment variances are equal in a single factor ANOVA. This is a repeat question with slight changes from the July 1984 and October 1974 examinations.[17]

56.   A factorial experiment has been performed to determine the effect of factor A and factor B on the strength of a part. An F test shows a significant interaction effect. This means that

    a.   either factor A or factor B has a significant effect on the strength
    b.   both factor A and factor B affect strength
    c.   the effect of changing factor B can be estimated only if the level of factor A is known
    d.   neither factor A nor factor B affect strength
    e.   strength will increase if factor A is increased while factor B is held at a low level

Key: c.   the effect of changing factor B can be estimated only if the level of factor A is known (Ref. Applications Question 27, August 1978) The key term is "*interaction effect*." In interaction, the change in one factor produces a different change in the response variable at different levels of the other factor. Hence it is necessary to know the level of the factor A to estimate the effect of changing factor B.

57.   You just have conducted a designed experiment at three levels A, B, and C yielding the

---

[17] *ASQC - CQE Examination*, Quality Progress, July 1984, Principles Question 9; Applications Question 27, and October 1974, Principles Question 39.

following coded data

A	B	C
6	5	3
3	9	4
5	1	2
2		

As a major step in your analysis you calculate the degrees of freedom for the error sum of the squares to be

a.   7
b.   9
c.   3
d.   2
e.   10

Key: a.   7   (Ref. Applications Question 33, October 1974)
     Given: Data table for the three treatments, with $N = 10$, $k = 3$ treatments, ***unequal sample sizes***
       for each treatment.
    Find: df for the error term, i.e., for the error sum of squares SSE.
    $N=10$, i.e., df for sum of squares for total $= N-1 = 10 - 1 = 9$.
    df for the sum of squares for the treatments $= k - 1 = 3-1 = 2$.
    Hence df for the sum of squares for the error term $= 9-2 = 7$.

58.   If, in a designed experiment, you obtained an F ratio of 0.68 with 2 and 20 degrees of freedom, you would conclude that

    a.   there were no significant differences among the means
    b.   you had made an error
    c.   the variances were equal
    d.   the null hypothesis was rejected
    e.   all of the above

Key: a.   there were no significant differences among the means
    (Ref. Applications Question 14, October 1974)
    Given: $F_{cal} = 0.68$, $df_1 = n_1 - 1 = 2$ df for numerator, $df_2 = n_2 - 1 = 20$ df for denominator.
      Designed experiment, i.e., test of hypothesis or null hypothesis for treatment means.
    Find: What is your conclusion for the hypothesis?
    Error: Test of the hypothesis requires Type I error α, i.e., the level of significance for the test. However the data does not specify the required level of significance α without which one cannot test the hypothesis. Let us assume $\alpha = 0.05$ or confidence level of 95% and a two tail test.

From the F table, the critical value of F is $F_{0.975,2,20} = 4.46$, i.e., $F_{cal} < F_{0.975,2,20}$. This shows that it is inside the critical region or acceptance region; hence, we accept the null hypothesis that there were no significant differences in the means.

59.   Given the following results obtained from a fixed factor, randomized block designed experiment, in which the production outputs of three machines (A, B, C) were to be compared.

A	4	8	5	7	6
B	2	0	1	−2	4
C	−3	1	−2	−1	0

How many degrees of freedom are used to compute the error variance?

a.   2
b.   3
c.   12
d.   14

Key: c.   12   (Ref. Applications Question 16, October 1972)
       Given: The machine is a single factor (one-way ANOVA) and three machines - A, B, and C
              means there are three levels, k =3 treatments. Each machine has 5 samples, n = 5.
              N = total of all samples = k×n = 3×5 = 15.
       Find: df for the error term
       To get the df for the error term, first find df for the total and df for the treatments.
       df for the total = N −1 = k×n −1 = (3×5) − 1 = 14.
       df for the treatments = k − 1 = 3 − 1 = 2.
       df for the error term = k(n−1) = $df_{total} - df_{treatments}$ = 14−2 = 12.

60.   What is the critical value of F at 0.05 risk for the data in the previous problem?

a.   3.89
b.   4.75
c.   3.49
d.   4.6

Key: a.   3.89   (Ref. Applications Question 17, October 1972)
       Given: Three machines - A, B, C, i.e., the machine is a single factor and has three levels, i.e.,
              k =3 treatments. Each machine has 5 samples, i.e., n = 5; N = total of all samples =
              k×n = 3×5 = 15.
       Find: F at 0.05% risk.
       To obtain $F_{critical}$ at 5% risk, use 2 df of treatments in the numerator and 12 df of error in the
       numerator, i.e., $F_{0.05,2,12}$ = 3.89 for a *one tail test*.
       The question does not clearly indicate the risk to be single sided or two tail until you look at the
       answers. The choices give single value and not the two limits for a total of 5% risk,
       i.e., 2.5% on each side. Also if you refer to the F table for the 97.5% value, you will get 5.1 and
       1/39.41 but none of the choices match with this.

61.   What is the sum of the squares for the error term for the data in the previous problem?

        a.   170
        b.   130
        c.   40
        d.   14

Key: c.   40   (Ref. Applications Question 18, October 1972)
        Given: The data are one-way ANOVA with machine as a factor with 3 levels A, B, and C.
        Find: The sum of squares of the error term SSE.
        First list all formulas for the ANOVA table as shown in Table 6-11.

        Table 6-11 One-way ANOVA raw data

Machines						R_i	n
A	4	8	5	7	6	30	5
B	2	0	1	-2	4	5	5
C	-3	1	-2	-1	0	-5	5
						$T=\sum R_i=30$	

Correction factor $C = \dfrac{T^2}{n} = \dfrac{T^2}{kn} = \dfrac{30^2}{3 \times 5} = 60$

$SSB = \dfrac{\sum Ri^2}{n} - C = \dfrac{30^2 + 5^2 + (-5)^2}{5} - 60 = 190 - 60 = 130$

$SST = \sum Y^2 - C = [\, 4^2 + 8^2 + 5^2 \ldots\ldots\ldots +(-5)^2\,] - 60 = 230 - 60 = 170$

Hence $SSE = SST - SSB = 170 - 130 = 40$

62.   The purpose of such an experiment described in Question 59 is to compare

        a.   the output variances of the three machines
        b.   the variance of the machines against the error
        c.   the output averages of the three machines
        d.   the process capabilities of the tree machines

Key: c.   the output averages of the three machines
        (Ref. Applications Question 19, October 1972)
        One-way ANOVA for one factor machine is used to compare the output averages of three
        machines. The null hypothesis Ho: $\mu_A = \mu_B = \mu_C$ means that there is no significant difference in
        the outputs of the three machines.

63.   Dr. Taguchi defines quality as

        a.   fitness for use
        b.   meeting customer requirements

c.   total loss to society due to its deviation from its target value, i.e., total loss to society due to functional variation and its harmful side effects

d.   the probability of a product performing a specified function without any failure under specified conditions for a given period of time

Key: c.   total loss to society due to its deviation from its target value, i.e., total loss to society due to functional variation and its harmful side effects

This is one of the basic, strong concepts of Taguchi methods. It further defines a *loss function* to determine such loss. Refer to Question 67 below for more details on loss function.

64.   Robust design means making a product insensitive to

a.   raw material variations
b.   manufacturing variation
c.   operating environment
d.   all of the above

Key: d.   all of the above

The robust design is a new, i.e., a contemporary, concept. It requires making a product completely insensitive or forgiving to its design variation or sensitivity, manufacturing variations, and operating environment. This should result in the economical manufacture of high quality products.

65.   In Taguchi robustness concepts, a parameter design means

a.   selection of a system to meet its intended function, i.e., concept selection of the product's overall packaging and architecture
b.   a process of determining the optimum levels of individual control factors to make the design robust
c.   a process to determine optimum values of tolerances or the allowable range of variation of the system
d.   making a list of important product characteristics that affect customer satisfaction

Key: b.   a process of determining the optimum levels of individual control factors to make the design robust

These concepts are based on Taguchi robustness[18] methods, which state that a product design should be done in three important phases.

System design is considered as the primary design. It is a selection of a system to meet its intended function, i.e., concept selection of the product's overall packaging and architecture as seen in choice a.

---

[18] *Introduction to Quality Engineering* by Genichi Taguchi, Asian Productivity Organization, Tokyo, Japan, 1986, pg. 75-79, 97-99; *Quality Engineering* by Yuin Wu and Dr. William Hobbs Moore, American Supplier Institute, Inc., Dearborn, MI, 1985, pg. 24; *Quality Engineering Using Robust Design* by Madhav S. Phadke, Prentice Hall, Englewood Cliffs, NJ, 1989, pg. 31-39.

Parameter design is an optimization method and is considered as a secondary design. It enables selection of optimum levels of the factors without controlling or removing the causes of variation. It makes the design robust against noise factors. It results in reduced cost and improved quality. This means choice b is correct.

Tolerance design is defined as a tertiary design. It is a process to determine optimum values of tolerances or the allowable range of variation of the system. It focuses on the methods to control the causes to balance the level of quality improvement vs. a possible increase in cost. Choice c defines the tolerance design.

These three design phases are also called off-line quality control. The concepts are equally important and applicable for design of production processes.

66.   In the case of Taguchi methods, control factors are defined as

   a.   the factors which affect the response, and their levels can be specified or controlled by the designer or experimenter
   b.   the factors which cannot be controlled by the manufacturer or designer; they are also difficult or expensive to control and may not be intended to be controlled
   c.   the factors that affect the output or the response value, and creates different response values
   d.   the customer requirements

Key: a.   the factors which affect the response, and their levels can be specified or controlled by the designer or experimenter

The parameter design as discussed in Question 66 above, enables the selection of optimum levels of the factors without controlling or removing the causes of variation. Taguchi has defined a method to convert the repetition data in an experiment into one value called "*Signal to noise (S/N) ratio.*" It is defined as follows:

$$\text{Signal to noise (S/N) Ratio} = \frac{\text{Power of signal}}{\text{Power of noise}} = \frac{\text{Power of signal}}{\text{Power of error}}$$

A higher S/N ratio will mean a more desirable result. Hence Taguchi designs recommend a higher value of S/N ratio for optimizing the quality characteristic. The quality characteristic can be influenced by several parameters of factors in the process. All such factors are divided into three main groups.

Signal factors are those factors that affect the output or the response value, and create different response values. They affect the average value of the response. They specify the desired value of the response. They are used to study the measurement systems and to test equipment variability. Choice c defines signal factors.

Control factors are the factors that affect the response. Their levels can be specified or controlled by the designer or experimenter to minimize the sensitivity of the response variable to all noise factors. They help optimize the design. The control factors are set or controlled by the experimenter or manufacturer and the customer cannot control them, specify them, may not want to specify them, or does not know what they are. Choice a defines the control factors.

Noise factors are the factors that cannot be controlled by the manufacturer or designer. They are also difficult or expensive to control and may not be intended to be controlled. Taguchi has divided the noise factors into three types as follows:

1. *Outer noise*: The environmental variations such as temperature, humidity, dirt, vibrations, etc.
2. *Inner noise*: Process shifts, deterioration, wear and tear, changes in the material, shelf life, etc. They reflect the effect of time and function.
3. *Unit-to-unit*: Variability between the products or parts, i.e., part-to-part variation.

The customer requirement (choice d) is the response variable or the quality characteristic that needs to be optimized by selecting the most appropriate control factors and their levels, without trying to control the noise factors.

67.   The quality loss function for a nominal the best characteristic in a single piece case is given as

      a. $L(y) = k(y - m)^2$
      b. $L(y) = k(y)^2$
      c. $L(y) = k(1/y^2)$
      d. $L(y) = k\{\sigma^2 + (\bar{y} - m)^2\}$

Key: a. $L(y) = k(y - m)^2$

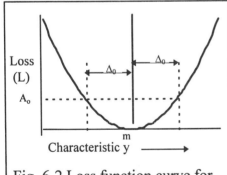

Fig. 6-2 Loss function curve for *nominal the best*

The concept of the quality loss function is introduced by Taguchi.[19] Choice a describes the quality loss function L(y) for *nominal the best case for a single piece* as shown in Fig. 6-2.

Nominal the Best: $L(y) = k(y - m)^2$
      where L(Y) = loss in dollars at a given y
            y = the value of the quality characteristic, e.g., weight, dimension, diameter, etc.
          m = the target value for quality characteristic y
          k = the constant for a given quality characteristic

When the product shows variation from its target m, i.e., the quality characteristic y moves away

[19] *Introduction to Quality Engineering* by Genichi Taguchi, Asian Productivity Organization, Tokyo, Japan, 1986, pg. 13-71; *Quality Engineering* by Yuin Wu and Dr. William Hobbs Moore, American Supplier Institute, Inc., Dearborn, MI, 1985, pg. 27-50; *Quality Engineering Using Robust Design* by Madhav S. Phadke, Prentice Hall, Englewood Cliffs, NJ, pg. 1989, pg. 13-26; *Taguchi Techniques for Quality Engineering* by Phillip J. Ross, McGraw-Hill, New York, pg. 3-21.

from m, it causes loss to the society L(y) as per this equation. Let's assume that y reaches an extreme value of $y = m + \Delta_0$, or $y = m - \Delta_0$ resulting in a loss of A_0, i.e., the customer has to take some countermeasures such as return the product, repair it, throw away or discard the product, etc., costing a total of A_0. If we substitute $y = m + \Delta_0$, the value of L(y) is A_0. The

equation will be: $A_0 = k \ (m + \Delta_0 - m)^2 = k \ \Delta_0^2$.   This gives $k = \dfrac{A_0}{\Delta_0^2}$.

We can now re-write the loss function equation as $L(y) = k(y - m)^2 = \dfrac{A_0}{\Delta_0^2} (y - m)^2$.

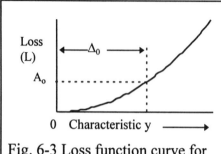

Fig. 6-3 Loss function curve for
smaller the better

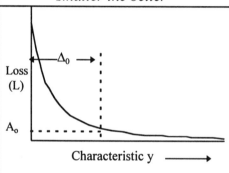

Fig. 6-4 Loss function curve for
larger the better

Choice b describes the quality loss function L(y) for the *smaller (lower) the better case for a single piece.* Refer to Fig. 6-3. *Smaller the better:* $L(y) = ky^2$

Here $y = \Delta_0$. This also gives $k = \dfrac{A_0}{\Delta_0^2}$.

Hence the loss function equation will be $L(y) = \dfrac{A_0}{\Delta_0^2} (y^2)$.

Choice c describes the quality loss function L(y) for the *larger (bigger) the better case for a single piece.* Refer to Fig. 6-4.

Larger the better: $L(y) = k \ (1/ \ y^2)$.
Here $y = \Delta_0$. This also gives $k = A_0 \ \Delta_0^2$.
The loss function equation will be $L(y) = A_0 \ \Delta_0^2 \ (1/ \ y^2)$.

Choice d defines the equation for *the average loss function for the nominal the best characteristic for the more than one piece case.*

The average quality loss L(Y) is given as: $L(y) = k\{\sigma^2 + (\bar{y} - m)^2\} = k \ (MSD)$.

where MSD = Mean standard deviation = $\sigma^2 + (\bar{y} - m)^2$ and σ is the standard deviation of the characteristic y around its mean $\bar{y}$.

This equation has two components.

1.   The deviation of characteristic y from its target value y is given by $k \ (\bar{y} - m)^2$.
2.   The variability around its mean, i.e., squared deviation of y is given by $k\sigma^2$.

The average loss function for the *smaller the better* case is given as $L(y) = k(\sigma^2 + \bar{y}^2)$.

The average loss function for the *larger the better* case is given as $L(y) = k\left[\dfrac{1}{\bar{y}^2}\left(1 + \dfrac{3\sigma^2}{\bar{y}^2}\right)\right]$.

Refer to Table 6-12 which gives a summary of these equations.

Table 6-12 Loss function equations[20]

Characteristic	Constant k	Loss function Single piece L(y)	Mean standard deviation MSD	Average quality loss (more than one piece) L(y)
Nominal the best	$k = \dfrac{A_o}{\Delta_0^2}$	$L(y) = k(y - m)^2$	$MSD = \sigma^2 + (\bar{y} - m)^2$	$L(y) = k(MSD)$ $= k\{\sigma^2 + (\bar{y} - m)^2\}$
Smaller the better	$k = \dfrac{A_o}{\Delta_0^2}$	$L(y) = ky^2$	$MSD = \sigma^2 + \bar{y}^2$	$L(y) = k(MSD)$ $= k(\sigma^2 + \bar{y}^2)$
Larger the better	$k = A_o\,\Delta_0^2$	$L(y) = k\,(1/y^2)$	MSD $= \left[\dfrac{1}{\bar{y}^2}\left(1 + \dfrac{3\sigma^2}{\bar{y}^2}\right)\right]$	$L(y) = k(MSD)$ $= k\left[\dfrac{1}{\bar{y}^2}\left(1 + \dfrac{3\sigma^2}{\bar{y}^2}\right)\right]$

68.   In the case of loss function, the mean standard deviation is defined as

   a. $\sigma^2 + (\bar{y} - m)^2$
   b. $(y - m)^2$
   c. $k(y - m)^2$
   d. ky^2

Key: a. $\sigma^2 + (\bar{y} - m)^2$
   Refer to Table 6-12 in Question 67 above. For the nominal the best characteristic, the mean standard deviation is given as $MSD = (\bar{y} - m)^2$. Be careful with choice b which can mislead you as it looks similar to choice a. The only difference is the use of y instead of $\bar{y}$. Choices c and d define the loss function formula $L(y) = k(y - m)^2$ for the nominal the best case and $L(y) = ky^2$ for the smaller the better case.

69.   The equation $k = \dfrac{A_o}{\Delta_0^2}$ defines

   i.   the constant k for loss function for the nominal the best case
   ii.   the constant k for loss function for the smaller the better case
   iii.   the constant k for loss function for the larger the better case

   a.   i and ii above
   b.   ii and iii above
   c.   iii and i above
   d.   i, ii, and iii above

Key: a.   i and ii above
   Refer to Question 67 and Table 6-12 above which describe the calculation of constant factor k for each case.

---

[20] *Fundamental Concepts of Probability, Statistics, Regression and DOE* by Jagdish Vani, 3rd edition, April 1993, Section 9.

70.   For some characteristics, it is important to achieve the smallest value possible, e.g., the wear of a tool. The loss function used to describe such a case is

        a. $L(y) = \sigma^2 + (\bar{y} - m)^2$
        b. $L(y) = k(y - m)^2$
        c. $L(y) = k\,(1/y^2)$
        d. ky^2

Key: d. ky^2
        This defines the smaller the better case. Refer to Fig. 6-3 and Table 6-12 in Question 67 above.

71.   A signal to noise ratio

        a.   measures the performance of a quality characteristic in the presence of noise factors
        b.   considers both the mean and its variability
        c.   is tied directly to loss function, i.e., cost
        d.   value should be as high a value as possible
        e.   all of the above

Key: e.   all of the above
        Taguchi has defined a method to convert the repetition data in an experiment into one value called the "*Signal to noise (S/N) ratio denoted as* η." It is defined as follows:

$$\text{Signal to noise (S/N) Ratio } \eta = \frac{\text{Power of signal}}{\text{Power of noise}} = \frac{\text{Power of signal}}{\text{Power of error}}$$

The *S/N* ratio, i.e., η, is used to measure the quality of the product. It measures the performance of the quality characteristic in the face of noise factors. As seen in the equation above, we would like to get a good or higher quality of the signal and minimal noise that disturbs the signal. Hence the value of η should be the highest value possible. A high value of η means a more desirable result to optimize the quality characteristic regardless of the nature of the characteristic. Simply stated, η should be the highest value regardless of the nominal the best, smaller the better, or larger the better characteristic.

η takes both the mean and the variability into account. It is tied to loss function. A high value of η indicates a smaller loss value obtained from a corresponding loss function. Refer to Table 6-13 below for a list of formulas for the three different cases.

Table 6-13 Signal to noise (S/N) ratio η and loss function equations[21]

Charact-eristic	Constant k	Mean standard deviation MSD	Average quality loss (more than one piece) L(y)	Signal to noise (S/N) ratio η
Nominal the best	$k = \dfrac{A_o}{\Delta_0^2}$	$MSD = \sigma^2 + (\bar{y} - m)^2$	$L(y) = k(MSD)$ $= k\{\sigma^2 + (\bar{y} - m)^2\}$	$\eta = 10 \log_{10} \left(\dfrac{\mu^2}{\sigma^2} \right)$ $\eta = 10 \log_{10} \left(\dfrac{\bar{y}^2}{s^2} - \dfrac{1}{n} \right)$
Smaller the better	$k = \dfrac{A_o}{\Delta_0^2}$	$MSD = \sigma^2 + \bar{y}^2$	$L(y) = k(MSD)$ $= k(\sigma^2 + \bar{y}^2)$	$\eta = -10 \log_{10} \left(\dfrac{1}{n} \sum_{i=1}^{n} y_i^2 \right)$ $\eta \approx -10 \log_{10} (MSD)$ $\approx -10 \log_{10} (\sigma^2 + \bar{y}^2)$
Larger the better	$k = A_o \Delta_0^2$	$MSD = \left[\dfrac{1}{\bar{y}^2} \left(1 + \dfrac{3\sigma^2}{\bar{y}^2} \right) \right]$	$L(y) = k(MSD)$ $= k \left[\dfrac{1}{\bar{y}^2} \left(1 + \dfrac{3\sigma^2}{\bar{y}^2} \right) \right]$	$\eta = -10 \log_{10} \left(\dfrac{1}{n} \sum_{i=1}^{n} \dfrac{1}{y_i^2} \right)$ $\eta \approx -10 \log_{10} (MSD)$ $\approx -10 \log_{10} \left[\dfrac{1}{\bar{y}^2} \left(1 + \dfrac{3\sigma^2}{\bar{y}^2} \right) \right]$

72.   Which of the following is/are true for the signal to noise (S/N) ratio?

    a.   it should be the smallest value for the nominal the best characteristic
    b.   it should be the smallest value for the smaller the better characteristic
    c.   it should be the smallest value for the larger the better characteristic
    d.   none of the above

Key: d.   none of the above
        The S/N ratio η should be the highest value regardless of the nominal the best, smaller the better, or larger the better characteristic. Refer to Question 71 above for a detailed discussion.

73.   Which of the following is/are true for a signal to noise (S/N) ratio?

    a.   it should be the smallest value for a smaller the better and the highest value for the larger the better characteristic
    b.   it should be the smallest value regardless of the nominal the best, smaller the better, or larger the better characteristic
    c.   it should be the highest value regardless of the nominal the best, smaller the better, or larger the better characteristic
    d.   a and b above
    e.   b and c above

[21] *Fundamental Concepts of Probability, Statistics, Regression and DOE* by Jagdish Vani, 3rd edition, April 1993, Section 9.

Key: c.   it should be the highest value regardless of the nominal the best, smaller the better, or larger the better characteristic
Refer to Question 71 above for a detailed discussion.

74.   A length of a part is an important quality characteristic y for a customer with a desired nominal value of 10 millimeters. The variation in this characteristic y significantly affects the customer and when y varies by ± 0.75 mm, it results in a total loss of $5 per piece to the customer as the customer has to adjust their process to manage this variability. Which of the following gives a correct loss function?

    a. $L(y) = 5 (y - 10)^2$
    b. $L(y) = 0.75 (y - 10)^2$
    c. $L(y) = 8.9 (y - 10)^2$
    d. $L(y) = 8.9 y^2$

Key: c. $L(y) = 8.9 (y - 10)^2$
    Given: y = length, nominal the best case, m = 10 mm, $\Delta_0 = \pm 0.75$ mm, $A_o = \$5$/piece.
    Find: Loss function equation L(y).
    The characteristic y is length which represents the nominal the best case. The quality loss function is given as: $L(y) = k(y - m)^2$. Refer to Question 67 and Table 6-12 above for a detailed discussion and a list of formulas.

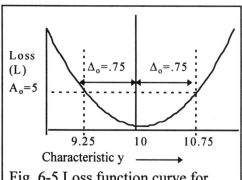

Fig. 6-5 Loss function curve for *nominal the best*

Fig. 6-5 shows the loss function curve for the nominal the best characteristic. When the product shows variation from its target m = 10 mm, and y reaches an extreme value y = 10 ± 0.75, it results in a loss of $A_o = \$5$/piece. First we need to calculate the value of k, the constant for the loss function equation.

$$k = \frac{A_o}{\Delta_0^2} = \frac{5}{0.75^2} = 8.9$$

Hence $L(y) = k(y - m)^2 = 8.9(y - 10)^2$.

75.   Refer to Question 74 above. The following data were collected on length.

9.53	10.65	9.79	10.32	10.18
10.07	9.84	10.91	10.58	10.73
10.39	10.52	10.24	10.81	9.9
10.66	9.6	10.41	9.94	10.89

The mean standard deviation (MSD) is given as

    a.   0.75
    b.   5
    c.   8.9

    d.   0.264

Key: d.   0.264
        Given: Raw data on 20 observations and from Question 74, k = 8.9, L(y) = 8.9(y − 10)^2, and
               the nominal the best case.
        Find: MSD.
        Refer to Question 67 and Table 6-12 above for a detailed discussion and a list of formulas.
        For the nominal the best case, MSD = $\sigma^2 + (\bar{y} - m)^2$. From the above data, you can determine all
        the values to calculate MSD using a scientific calculator.
        $\sigma^2 = (0.417)^2 = 0.174$, $s^2 = (0.428)^2 = 0.183$ and $\bar{y} = 10.30$.
        MSD = $(0.417)^2 + (10.30 - 10.0)^2 = 0.174 + 0.09 = 0.264$.

76.   Refer to Questions 74 and 75 above. The average quality loss is

    a. $5.00/piece
    b. $8.90/piece
    c. $2.35/piece
    d. $0.264/piece

Key: c. $2.35/piece
        Given: Raw data on 20 observations, and from Questions 74 and 75, k = 8.9, and MSD = 0.264.
        Find: Average quality loss.
        Refer to Question 67 and Table 6-12 above for a detailed discussion and a list of formulas.
        For the nominal the best case, average quality loss is given as follows:
        $L(y) = k(MSD) = k\{\sigma^2 + (\bar{y} - m)^2\} = 8.9\,(0.264) = \$2.35/piece$.

77.   Refer to Questions 74, 75, and 76 above. The signal to noise ratio will be

    a.   2
    b.   2.35
    c.   8.9
    d.   27.63

Key: d.   27.63
        Given: Raw data on 20 observations, and from Questions 74 and 75, k = 8.9, $\sigma = 0.417$,
               s = 0.428 and $\bar{y} = 10.30$.
        Find: The signal to noise ratio η.
        Refer to Question 71 and Table 6-13 for a detailed discussion on η and a list of formulas.
        The signal to noise ratio for the nominal the best case is given as $\eta = 10 \log_{10}\left(\dfrac{\bar{y}^2}{s^2} - \dfrac{1}{n}\right)$.

        Hence $\eta = 10 \log_{10}\left(\dfrac{10.3^2}{0.428^2} - \dfrac{1}{20}\right) = 27.63$.

78.   In the case of robust design studies,

        a.   F ratios are calculated to understand and determine the relative importance of the various control factors in relation to the error variance
        b.   we must maximize the signal to noise (S/N) ratio and then adjust the mean of the control factor that has the least or no effect on the S/N ratio
        c.   statistical significance tests are not used to determine if there is a significant difference. Here the best or optimum level of a factor is chosen based on its cost benefit analysis
        d.   all of the above

Key: d.   all of the above
        Phadke[22] provides a sound discussion of the optimization of the product and process design, steps used in robust designs, signal to noise (S/N) ratios, and a comparison of robust design studies to classical statistical experiments. You must refer to additional references for a more detailed understanding of this very powerful concept of robust design.

79.   The following (Fig. 6-6) is an example of what type of response surface?

        a.   rising ridge
        b.   maximum or minimum
        c.   stationary ridge
        d.   minimax

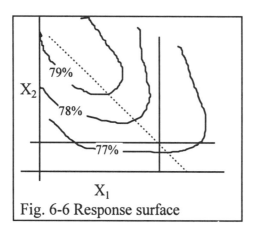

Fig. 6-6 Response surface

Key: a.   rising ridge   (Ref. Principles Question 63, October 1972)

80.   The basic statistical principle in EVOP is the

        a.   ability to find small significant differences through large sample sizes
        b.   operating with low levels of confidence
        c.   making large changes in independent variables
        d.   none of these

---

[22] *Quality Engineering Using Robust Design* by Madhav S. Phadke, Prentice Hall, Englewood Cliffs, NJ, 1989, pg. 32, 67-93, 108-120, 180, 213.

Key: a.   ability to find small significant differences through large sample sizes
(Ref. Principles Question 62, October 1972)
Evolutionary Operation (EVOP) is used to determine the optimum operating conditions for full-scale production processes. It introduces small changes in various levels of factors in the current production process without significantly affecting or disturbing the yield or quality. Hence, there are large numbers of samples available because it is in the current production run without disturbing any production process. As a result, one can detect very small significant differences in the yield.[23]

81.   EVOP should be used

   a.   when there is a manufacturing problem
   b.   when a process is not in statistical control
   c.   when an experimenter first begins working on a new product
   d.   when a process is producing satisfactory material

Key: d.   when a process is producing satisfactory material
(Ref. Applications Question 41, October 1972)
Evolutionary Operation (EVOP) is used to determine the optimum operating conditions for full-scale production processes particularly when the process is producing satisfactory material. It introduces small changes in various levels of factors in the current production process without significantly affecting or disturbing the yield or quality. Hence, there are a large number of samples available because it is in the current production run without disturbing any production process. As a result, one can detect very small significant differences in the yield.[24]

82.   When considering EVOP as a statistical tool

   a.   a change in the means indicates that we are using the wrong model
   b.   an extreme estimate of the experiment error is necessary
   c.   EVOP may be extended beyond the two level factorial case
   d.   we are limited to one response variable at a time. A new EVOP should be run for each response

Key: c.   EVOP may be extended beyond the two level factorial case
(Ref. Applications Question 59, October 1972)
EVOP introduces small changes in various levels of factors in the current production process without significantly affecting or disturbing the yield or quality. Hence, there are a large number of samples available because it is in the current production run without disturbing any production process. As a result, one can detect very small significant differences in the yield.

---

[23] *Juran's Quality Control Handbook* by J. M. Juran, 4th edition, McGraw-Hill, New York, pg. 26.29-36.
[24] *Juran's Quality Control Handbook* by J. M. Juran, 4th edition, McGraw-Hill, New York, pg. 26.29-36.

ASQC-CQE BIBLIOGRAPHY AND OTHER REFERENCES ON DESIGN OF EXPERIMENTS (DOE)

1. ASQC Statistics Division, *Glossary and Tables for Statistical Quality Control*, 2nd ed., Milwaukee, ASQC Quality Press, 1983.
2. Barker, Thomas B., *Engineering Quality by Design*, New York, Marcel Dekker, 1990.
3. Bhote, Keki R., *World Class Quality*, New York, AMACOM, 1991.
4. Box, George E. P., *Statistics for Experimenters*, New York, John Wiley and Sons, 1978.
5. Braverman, Jerome D., *Fundamentals of Statistical Quality Control*, Englewood Cliffs, N. J., Prentice-Hall, 1981.
6. Dovich, Robert A., *Quality Engineering Statistics*, Milwaukee, ASQC Quality Press, 1992.
7. Duncan, A. J., *Quality Control and Industrial Statistics*, Fifth ed., Homewood, IL, Irwin Inc., 1986.
8. Hicks, Charles R., *Fundamental Concepts in the Design of Experiments*, 3rd ed., Fortworth, Holt, Rinehart and Winston, Inc., The Dryden Press, Saunders College Publishing, 1982.
9. Juran, Joseph M., *Juran's Quality Control Handbook*, 4th ed., New York, McGraw-Hill, 1988.
10. Lochner, Robert H. and Joseph E. Matar, *Designing for Quality*, Milwaukee, ASQC Quality Press, 1990.
11. Moen, Ronald D., Thomas W. Nolan, and Lloyd P. Provost, *Improving Quality through Planned Experimentation*, New York, McGraw-Hill, 1991.
12. Montgomery, Douglas C., *Design and Analysis of Experimenters*, 3rd ed., New York, John Wiley and Sons, 1991.
13. Phadke, Madhav S., *Quality Engineering Using Robust Design*, Englewood Cliffs, NJ, Prentice Hall, 1989, pg. 32, 67-93, 108-120, 180, 213.
14. Ross, Phillip J., *Taguchi Techniques for Quality Engineering*, New York, McGraw-Hill, 1988.
15. Taguchi, Genichi, *Introduction to Quality Engineering*, Tokyo, Asian Productivity Organization, 1986 and now available from UniPub, Kraus International /Quality Resources, One Water Street, White Plains, NY, 10601 and American Supplier Institute, Inc., Six Parklane Boulevard, Suite 411, Dearborn, MI, 48126.
16. Taguchi, Genichi, *System of Experimental Design*, White Plains, UniPub, Kraus International Publications, NY, and Dearborn, American Supplier Institute, MI, 1987.
17. Vani, Jagdish, *Fundamental Concepts of Probability, Statistics, Regression and DOE*, 3rd edition, Troy, MI, Quality Quest Inc., 1993.
18. Wu, Yuin and Dr. Willie Hobbs Moore, *Quality Engineering Product and Process Design Optimization*, Dearborn, American Supplier Institute, MI, 1986.

CHAPTER 7

STATISTICAL PROCESS CONTROL

ASQC'S BODY OF KNOWLEDGE FOR THE CQE EXAMINATION

This chapter focuses on the following selected subject areas of BOK from *Section IV, Process and Materials Control.*

Statistical Process Control

1. Basics
   a. Terms and concepts
   b. Objectives and benefits
   c. Common and special causes of variation
2. Types of Control Charts
   a. Variable charts including R, X, s, individual, moving range, and moving average charts
   b. Attribute charts including p, np, c, and u charts
3. Implementation
   a. Variable selection
   b. Control chart selection
   c. Rational subgroup sampling
   d. Control charts interpretation
   e. Rules for determining statistical control
   f. Tampering effects and diagnosis
4. Process Capability Studies and Indices (C_p, C_{pk}, C_{pm})

1.   The Statistical Process Control (SPC) method was developed by

        a.   Dr. W. E. Deming
        b.   Dr. W. A. Shewhart
        c.   Dr. Genichi Taguchi
        d.   Dr. R. A. Fisher

Key: b.   Dr. W. A. Shewhart
        Dr. Walter A. Shewhart applied the statistical techniques for measuring the variation in the processes worked on at Bell Telephone Laboratories in the mid-1920s. He named these methods Statistical Process Control (SPC). This consisted mainly of the widely used SPC control charts. He also used SPC methods, along with acceptance sampling plans, and other problem-solving tools to improve the quality of the processes. He called these methods Statistical Quality Control (SQC) methods. He published the landmark book *Economic Control of Quality of Manufactured Product*.[1]

        Dr. Deming is well known for his legendary role to bring the transformation of the style of American management through application of his well-known "*14 Points*."[2]

        Dr. Taguchi is known for his contribution to the application of experimental designs, called *Taguchi's Design of Experiments (DOE) and Loss Function*.

        Dr. R. A. Fisher is known for his contribution to designed experiments in agricultural fields.

2.   Control charts

        a.   are used to please the management of the company
        b.   are used to show nice charts to the auditors of the customer
        c.   should be done on every quality characteristic
        d.   are used to achieve a state of statistical control and analyze the process capability

Key: d.   are used to achieve a state of statistical control and analyze the process capability
        This is the main purpose of the SPC techniques. It helps identify the special causes and common causes of variation in the process and enables one to determine if the process is in the state of statistical control. Based on the control limits and customer's specification limits, one needs to monitor the long-term performance of the process and analyze the data for process capability.

3.   A useful tool to determine when to investigate excessive variation in a process is

        a.   MIL-STD-105D
        b.   control chart
        c.   Dodge Romig AOQL sampling table
        d.   process capability study

---

[1] *Economic Control of Quality of Manufactured Product* by Walter A. Shewhart, republished in 1980 as the 50th Anniversary edition by the American Society for Quality Control (ASQC) Quality Press.
[2] *Out of the Crisis* by W. E. Deming, Massachusetts Institute of Technology, Center for Advanced Engineering Study, Cambridge, MA, 02139.

Key: b. control chart (Ref. Applications Question 51, October 1972)
A control chart is a very useful tool to study the causes of variation and to control processes. The remaining choices are not tools to study the *process*, but are used to study the quality level or the capability of the *products or parts*.

MIL-STD-105E (latest revision level is E) is a military standard for *sampling procedures and tables for inspection by attributes*. Dodge Romig sampling tables define the acceptance sampling plan and give a minimum total inspection for a product based on a given process average value. The process capability indicates the $\pm 3\sigma$ variation. It provides the magnitude of the variation but not the causes of excessive variation.

4. The prime use of a control chart is to

a. detect assignable causes of variation in the process
b. detect the nonconforming product
c. measure the performance of all quality characteristics of a process
d. detect the presence of random variation in the process

Key: a. detect assignable causes of variation in the process
(Ref. Applications Question 33, July 1984)
The control charts are used mainly to determine the variation because of the assignable or special causes so that we can bring the process under statistical control and reduce the variation economically.

Choice b is not preferable because the control charts are plotted using averages or percent non-conforming and not the individual values. They are not designed to provide an inspection plan to detect the nonconforming product like some of the acceptance sampling plans.

The control chart is used for each quality characteristic separately to determine the capability of the process for that characteristic of interest. But one chart cannot be used to measure the performance of all quality characteristics of the process, and it is not economical to plot separate charts for all quality characteristics. Hence choice c is not very suitable.

Every process has some random variation inherent in the process, called *common cause variation*. A control chart is of little help if there is only random variation in the process, because it can be reduced or improved only by a significant change in the process or system. The process capability can be further improved with such a change in the process or system. The primary purpose of the control chart is not to detect the presence of random variation in the process but to determine whether the process is in a state of statistical control and has no *assignable*, i.e., *special cause variation*, or the process is out of statistical control. Hence choice d is not the best choice.

5. Shewhart $\overline{X}$ control charts are designed with which one of the following objectives?

a. reduce sample size
b. fix risk of accepting poor product
c. decide when to hunt for causes of variation

d.   establish an acceptable quality level

Key: c.   decide when to hunt for causes of variation
        (Ref. Applications Question 27, October 1972). Refer to Question 4 for a similar discussion.

6.   A process in a state of statistical control means

        I.   only common causes are present
        II.   only special causes are present
        III.   the product will always meet its specifications
        IV.   the process is stable and only random or inherent sources of variation are present in the
                process

        a.   I and II above
        b.   II and III above
        c.   III and IV above
        d.   IV and I above

Key: d.   IV and I above
        The common causes mean inherent variation in the process. The process has only random
        causes of variation and no special causes of variation are present in the process. A process can be
        in a state of statistical control but the product may or may not meet its specifications.[3]
        Depending on the consequences of nonconformance to the specifications, it may require more
        analysis and an action plan to meet its specifications.

7.   To secure the state of statistical control, we should

        a.   find the assignable causes of variation and act on them to remove them
        b.   find the special causes of variation and act on them to remove them
        c.   both a and b above
        d.   none of the above

Key: c.   both a and b above
        Any process has two sources of variation. The first is called common or random cause variation
        and it is a variation which is inherent in the process and constant in nature. It can only be reduced
        if the system or the process is changed. It forms a constant system of chance causes.

        The second is called special or assignable cause of variation and occurs because of sudden
        change in the process; it is unpredictable and not constant. It can be found or detected on a
        control chart in the form of a trend, cycle or as a point outside of the control limits. The process
        adjustments should be made to remove these special causes of variation to achieve a state of
        statistical control.

8.   A process can have

        a.   within-piece variation

---

[3] *Juran's Quality Control Handbook* by J. M. Juran, 4th edition, McGraw-Hill, New York, pg. 16.28 and 24.9.

b.   time-to-time variation
c.   piece-to-piece variation
d.   all of the above

Key: d.   all of the above
A process can have mainly three types of variation. *Within-piece variation* is the variation found within an individual part or product, such as paint finish or surface finish. *Time-to-time variation* is the variation caused over a period of time or variation in the products produced at different times, e.g., shift to shift variation in the plant, or tool wear variation. *Piece-to-piece variation* is the variation found in the successive pieces that are produced at the same time.

9.   A large assembly operation plant that receives hundreds of parts from many different suppliers is likely to have

a.   a component-dominant process, which requires aggressive supplier development to control assembly variations
b.   a time-dominant process
c.   a setup-dominant process
d.   an operator-dominant process
e.   any combination of the above dominant processes

Key: e.   any combination of the above dominant processes

10.   The most important step(s) in setting up control charts is(are)

a.   choosing an appropriate type or model of control chart for the situation, e.g., $\overline{X}$ and R charts
b.   selecting proper sample size and frequency of sampling
c.   careful determination of the sample subgroups
d.   all of the above are equally important steps for setting up control charts

Key: d.   all of the above are equally important steps for setting up control charts
You should be familiar with these steps for setting up control chart(s) for your process. Different quality characteristics may require different types of control charts. You should use the above criteria carefully for setting up a control chart for each characteristic. These steps are very important to minimize the improper use or misuse of control charts and to achieve the economic manufacture of quality products.

11.   Control limits are used on control charts to

a.   indicate the condition that warrants immediate action
b.   define the limits for the data to be in the state of statistical control
c.   indicate the 99.73% probability that the population mean is likely to fall within these limits
d.   all of the above

Key: d.   all of the above

12.   A process can

     a.   be in a state of statistical control and able to meet the customer requirements
     b.   be in the state of statistical control and fail to meet the customer requirements
     c.   be out of statistical control and still able to meet the customer requirements
     d.   be out of statistical control and fail to meet the customer requirements
     e.   all of the above

Key: e.   all of the above
     These are the four possible conditions in any process, when SPC methods are used to study the
     variation and control the processes. Table 7-1 indicates the relationship of the state of statistical
     control and customer requirements.

Table 7-1 The relationship of the state of statistical control and customer requirements

Customer Requirements ➔➔➔ State of Statistical Control ⬇⬇⬇	Meets Customer Requirements	Does Not Meet Customer Requirements
In Statistical Control	Best Situation/Case, Strategic Quality Planning, Continuous Improvement	Common Causes of Variation System Change Management Role
Out of Statistical Control	Special Causes of Variation	Worst Case. Both Common and Special Causes of Variation

A process can be in a state of statistical control, and if it is also able to meet the customer
requirements, it is the most preferable situation. One should apply a strategic approach to manage
the dynamic nature of quality. If the quality characteristic is key, critical, or significant to the
customer, i.e., if the variation can significantly affect the customer requirements, then additional
resources should be provided to reduce the variation around the target, continuously improve the
process, and increase the process capability. The quality system requires strategic planning and
it should be designed and implemented throughout all operations such that additional care is
well defined, planned, and implemented for those *vital few* characteristics for which there are
adverse consequences of variation to the customer requirements. If the customer requirements are
not adversely affected by the variation within the specification range, then maintain the state of
statistical control, i.e., ensure that the process is stable and continuously meets the customer
requirements with normal care in day to day operations. This strategic approach to manage
quality is very important to achieve an economic manufacture of quality products in today's
highly competitive market.

A process can be in a state of statistical control but it may not be able to meet the customer
requirements. This means that the process has *common causes of variation* for which significant
system or process changes are required to reduce the inherent variation in the process and make
the process capable to meet the product requirements.

Similarly, a process can be out of statistical control but it can still meet the customer requirements. This means the process has *special causes of variation.* As discussed earlier, depending on the adverse consequences of variation, a root cause analysis of the process parameters should be done to identify and remove the special causes of variation and bring the process in the state of statistical control, i.e., make it stable. This can reduce the variation and improve process capability.

Lastly, a process can be out of statistical control and not be able to meet the customer requirements. It has *both, the common and special causes of variation.* This is the worst case and requires a careful evaluation of the process. First, it requires a containment plan to contain all the nonconforming products to ensure that nonconforming products are properly identified, segregated, and not shipped to the customer. It indicates that either a quality system is not in place or not designed at all. And a strong effort is needed to study the dominant nature of the process. The process characteristics need to be studied and aligned with the product characteristics, and proper methods of control on each characteristic need to be implemented immediately to ensure that the process meets the customer requirements. As discussed earlier, depending on the adverse consequences of variation, process control should be implemented for ongoing control.

Juran[4] provides good discussion on this subject and indicates that a process in a state of statistical control and a process that is meeting customer requirements are two distinct cases. This is one of the reasons, the specification limits are not plotted on the control chart, and they are not the same as control limits on a control chart.

13.   A process is stable means

       I.   it is repeatable
       II.   it is in a state of statistical control
       III.   it is predictable

       a.   I and II only
       b.   II and III only
       c.   III and I only
       d.   I, II, and III above

Key: d.   I, II, and III above
       A stable process is one that is repeatable, in a state of statistical control, and predictable. A process capability study should be done only if the process is stable.

14.   Control limits in an SPC chart can be

       I.   smaller than the specification limits
       II.   bigger than specification limits
       III.   bigger than the ±3S limits of the individual distribution

       a.   I and II only

---

[4] *Juran's Quality Control Handbook* by J. M. Juran, 4th edition, McGraw-Hill, New York, pg. 16.28 and 24.9.

    b.   II and III only
    c.   III and I only

Key: a.   I and II only
The data in item III indicate an impossible situation. The control limits are based on the process average data, and hence form a distribution of sampling means that is smaller than the distribution of individuals.

15.   The rational subgrouping for the control chart means

    a.   a subgroup that is free from the assignable causes as much as possible
    b.   a subgroup that represents the homogeneous conditions as much as possible
    c.   a small group of consecutively produced parts from a production process
    d.   all of the above

Key: d.   all of the above
It is very important that the subgroup size and frequency be designed based on a proper rational subgrouping of samples to minimize the sampling variation or bias and to improve the effectiveness of control charts. The subgroups should represent the population and the normal operations; i.e., they should be random samples to include all types of inherent variations in the process.

16.   To properly select the sample size and sampling frequency, one should

    a.   take smaller size subgroups more frequently, i.e., at short intervals
    b.   take larger size subgroups less frequently, i.e., at less frequent intervals
    c.   take smaller size subgroups less frequently, i.e., at less frequent intervals
    d.   take larger size subgroups more frequently, i.e., at short intervals
    e.   consider the cost of taking different size samples at different intervals or frequencies vs. the cost or risk involved of not catching some process shifts

Key: e.   consider the cost of taking different size samples at different intervals or frequencies vs. the cost or risk involved of not catching some process shifts
There is no fixed rule for deciding the sample size and sampling frequency for a control chart. Let's first discuss the case of *variable data*. If we take a large number of samples at short intervals, i.e., more frequently, it will enable us to study the process shifts more effectively. Also a larger sample size will result in tighter control limits because the *standard error of mean*

$\sigma_x = \dfrac{\sigma}{\sqrt{n}}$ will become smaller as n increases. One can also decide to take smaller size subgroups

more frequently. However, it is important to consider the cost involved in each case and the consequences or risk of not catching the process shifts[5] based on the past history, lessons learned, dominant factors in the process, lot size, etc. An operating characteristic curve can be used to plot the probability of detecting a process change with different subgroup sizes.[6] It plots the probability that a single sample will fall within the control limits for a given true value of a parameter.

[5] *Quality Control and Industrial Statistics* by A. J. Duncan, Fifth edition, Irwin Inc. Chapter 18, Section 5.
[6] *Juran's Quality Control Handbook* by J. M. Juran, 4th edition, McGraw-Hill, New York, pg. 24. 9 and 10.

The selection of proper sample size is even more difficult in the case of attribute data. In the case of a control chart for fraction nonconforming, the sample size depends on its average fraction nonconforming $\bar{p}$ value. In today's high quality driven market, it is necessary that $\bar{p}$ is very small and it requires a very large subgroup size to be able to detect a lack of control on the control chart. Smaller subgroup sizes will not detect the change in the process and it will give wider control limits showing a poor process in control when it is not.

17.   The sampling distribution of means or averages

     a.   has the center of the distribution the same as the center of the distribution of individuals

     b.   tends to be approximately normal even when the distribution of the individuals may or may not be normal

     c.   is narrower than the distribution of the individuals

     d.   has a standard deviation given as the standard error of the mean $\sigma_x = \dfrac{\sigma}{\sqrt{n}}$

     e.   all of the above

Key: e.   all of the above

This describes the central limit theorem discussed in Chapter 4. The control chart such as the $\overline{X}$ and R chart is based on the concept of the sampling distribution of means.

18.   When used together for variable data, which of the following is the most useful pair of quantities in quality control?

     a. $\overline{X}$, R

     b. $\overline{X}$, η

     c.   R, σ

     d. $\bar{p}$, η

     e.   AQL, p'

Key: a. $\overline{X}$, R   (Ref. Principles Question 11, August 1978)

The key phrase is *for variable data*. The two quantities $\overline{X}$ and R are widely used pairs of quantities in *statistical* quality control to plot the $\overline{X}$ and R control charts for the variable data.

Watch for choice c, "R, σ," because both of these are also used for variable data only but both describe the same thing, i.e., only the variability and not the mean or mean shift. Control charts generally indicate both the mean shift and the variability, e.g., $\overline{X}$ and R chart in choice a.

Choices d and e represent the terms AQL, $\bar{p}$, p', and η which are commonly used terms in *attribute* sampling plans and not for variable data.

Note: This is an ambiguous question because it is asking for an opinion to define the most useful pair of quantities in *quality control* and not in *statistical quality control* or in *control charts*. The two quantities $\overline{X}$ and R are widely used pairs of quantities in *statistical quality control,* i.e., for control charts only, but they are not the only terms in quality control. This language is further changed and refined in Question 19 below to read as *the most useful pair of quantities in preparing control charts* from the July 1984 examination with slight changes in answer choices.

19.   When used together for variable data, which of the following pairs of quantities is the most useful in preparing control charts?

    a.   AQL, p
    b.   p, n
    c. $\overline{X}$, R
    d.   R, σ

Key: c. $\overline{X}$, R   (Ref. Principles Question 10, July 1984)

The key phrase is *for variable data*. The two quantities $\overline{X}$ and R are widely used pairs of quantities in *statistical* quality control in preparing the $\overline{X}$ and R control charts for variable data. Refer to Question 18 above for additional discussion, as this is a repeat question.

20.   As a quality engineer, you are given an assignment of setting up control charts. You should

    a.   set up $\overline{X}$ and R charts for every quality characteristic
    b.   set up applicable control charts on product and/or process quality characteristics that have a high impact on customer satisfaction
    c.   set up 100% inspection charts for all product characteristics only
    d.   set up $\overline{X}$ and R charts for all product characteristics

Key: b.   set up applicable control charts on product and/or process quality characteristics that have a high impact on customer satisfaction

An important point here is that you should select a *vital few* quality characteristics in product and processes that have a high impact on customer satisfaction. Review each of these characteristics and where applicable use appropriate control charts. Keep in mind that SPC is only one method of process control, and it may not apply for all product characteristics. Depending on the dominant nature of the process (e.g., operator dominant, setup dominant, time dominant, component dominant, and/or information dominant),[7] other economical methods of process control are equally applicable and should be used.

It is uneconomical to use SPC control charts on every product characteristic. This will result in improper and poor use of SPC. The use of 100% inspection on all product characteristics is expensive and wasteful if used for all characteristics.

21.   You determine that it is sometimes economical to permit X to go out of control when

    a.   the individual R's exceed R
    b.   the cost of inspection is high
    c. 6σ is appreciably less than the difference between specification limits

---

[7] *Juran's Quality Control Handbook* by J. M. Juran, 4th edition, McGraw-Hill, New York, pg. 16.50 and 24.13; and *Advanced Quality Planning and Process Control Plan Methodology Reference Manual*, 1st edition, published jointly by GM/Ford/Chrysler, section 6.

d. the $\overline{X}$ control limits are inside the drawing tolerance limits

e. never

Key: c. 6σ is appreciably less than the difference between specification limits

(Ref. Applications Question 2, August 1978)

This means the process capability is fairly high or very high because 6σ is appreciably less than the difference between the specification limits. However the question refers to variable X and indicates that it is sometimes economical to permit X to go out of control. This seems to be in error because the control chart does not plot variable X, which refers to individual values, but plots the mean $\overline{X}$ and develops the control limits using the standard error of mean.

Refer to Question 12 above for detailed discussion of two distinct cases: *a state of statistical control vs. meeting customer requirements.*

22. If you have a multiposition machine, e.g., a multicavity mold or multispindle machine, you should

a. plot all positions only on one control chart and take subgroups randomly from any position or cavity

b. take one sample from each cavity and put them into one subgroup

c. take all individual samples in a subgroup from one cavity but successive subgroups from different die cavities

d. consider each die cavity as a separate machine and plot a separate control chart for each cavity

Key: d. consider each die cavity as a separate machine and plot a separate control chart for each cavity

Juran[8] provides a good discussion about rational subgrouping to optimize the sensitivity of the chart to understand and capture process changes to control the process. When a plant has a machine with multicavities or spindles, etc., proper implementation of control charts is very critical. If proper care is not taken in preparing rational subgroupings, the chart can be misleading and process changes may not be detected effectively from the control chart.

It is important that each subgroup of a multicavity machine comes from its unique or distinct population alone and samples from any other cavity are not mixed with it. Each successive subgroup is taken from the same cavity only. It means each cavity is treated separately and has its own control chart that enables the operator to study the causes of variation and act on the process.

23. A process has multiple machines producing the same part, e.g., a multicavity molding machine, multiple spindles, etc. Which of the following is not advisable for the different batches produced from each separate machine?

a. All batches should be mixed and samples should be taken at random to monitor the process on a single control chart.

b. Each subgroup in the case of a multicavity machine comes from its unique population of

---

[8] *Juran's Quality Control Handbook* by J. M. Juran, 4th edition, McGraw-Hill, New York, pg. 24. 10.

that cavity alone and all successive subgroups are taken from the same cavity only.
c. Each cavity is treated separately and has its own control chart.
d. All of the above.

Key: a. All batches should be mixed and samples should be taken at random to monitor the process on a single control chart.

The key phrase is *not advisable*. It is not advisable to mix the parts from different batches and take parts at random because the process can have batch-to-batch variation, within-batch variation, and time-to-time variation. Refer to Question 22 above for explanation and additional discussion on multiposition machine situations.

24. When planning for quality functions, which one of the following is most directly related to production of a quality product?

a. process control and process capability
b. suitable blueprints
c. dimensional tolerances
d. product audit

Key: a. process control and process capability (Ref. Applications Question 27, October 1974)
The key phrase is *most directly* related to production.

25. You are monitoring a critical characteristic which is in a state of statistical control for a long period of time. However, the inherent variation or common cause of variation in the process is bigger than the allowable tolerance on the characteristic. The least favorable action that you should take is

a. live with the process as is and a certain level of defectives and implement a containment plan as it is not economical to change the process
b. change the system, i.e., change the current manufacturing process to reduce the inherent variation
c. convince the engineer to open or expand the tolerance and make it realistic based on the data from process capability if there are no adverse consequences to the customer
d. stop monitoring the characteristic as it is not capable

Key: d. stop monitoring the characteristic as it is not capable
Watch out! The key phrase is *the least favorable action* and not a most favorable action.

26. A product characteristic is monitored using control charts, and the quality engineer finds that the process is not in a state of statistical control. Which one of the following actions is not preferable?

a. A root cause analysis of the process parameters should be done to identify and remove the special causes of variation and bring the process in the state of statistical control.
b. Analyze the data of individuals to see if the process meets the tolerance limits even with some special causes present.
c. Do not give a very high priority to quality improvement efforts if the process meets the specifications, and if there are no adverse consequences.

d.   Perform a capability study whether the process is in statistical control or not and predict the capability.

Key: d.   Perform a capability study whether the process is in statistical control or not and predict the capability.

The key phrase is ***not preferable***. Statistically, if the process is unstable, i.e., not in a state of statistical control, one should not do any capability calculations and analysis. Hence choice d is the correct answer.

Refer to Question 12 for detailed discussion of two distinct cases: *a state of statistical control vs. meeting customer requirements*.

27.   A control chart shows that there are seven points in a row on one side of the average, but within the control limits you should interpret this condition as

a.   an out-of-control situation because it shows points beyond the control limits
b.   an out-of-control situation because it shows the presence of a run
c.   an out-of-control condition because it shows the presence of cycles as a nonrandom pattern within the control limits
d.   a process in a state of statistical control

Key: d.   an out-of-control situation because it shows the presence of a run

A run in statistical process control is defined as seven points in a row on one side of the average or seven points in a row that are consistently either decreasing or increasing. This results in a process shift or trend and hence an out-of-control condition.

28.   As a quality engineer, when using the $\overline{X}$ and R control chart, you should

a.   form subgroups in the production sequence
b.   form subgroups by randomly taking samples from the entire production
c.   take subgroups when it is convenient to draw samples
d.   all of the above

Key: a.   form subgroups in the production sequence

The SPC control charts are used to identify causes of variation, achieve a state of statistical control, and analyze process capability. It is important that processes are studied on-line where possible, and data are collected in the production sequence[9] to understand the common and special causes of variation. It is also important for the operator to record process changes such as tool change, setup change, shift change, new operator, new lot or batch of raw material, environment change, etc. as they occur. This will enable the operator to decide whether or not any adjustments are needed in the process. If you take data at random from the entire production, the knowledge of the behavior of the process can be lost and trends, cycles, runs, points outside the control limits, etc., indicating the real out-of-statistical-control conditions may not be captured. It will also be very difficult to identify meaningful causes of variation in the process.

29.   In the case of $\overline{X}$ and R charts,

---

[9] *Juran's Quality Control Handbook* by J. M. Juran, 4th edition, McGraw-Hill, New York, pg. 24.7.

      a.   we plot the cumulative sum of deviations of subgroup averages from some value

      b.   we plot individual values of observations and the range

      c.   we plot subgroup sample average and range

      d.   all of the above

Key: c.   we plot subgroup sample average and range

$\overline{X}$ is the sample average for each subgroup and can be a different value for each sample subgroup. The range is the difference between the high and low values of the samples in a subgroup. The $\overline{X}$ and R control chart is the plot of these two values, i.e., the sample average $\overline{X}$ and range R. Choice a represents mainly a CumSum chart and choice b represents the individuals X and R chart.[10]

30.   The factor D_4 used in $\overline{X}$ and R control charts is

      a.   the distance between the mean and the upper control limit of a range chart

      b.   the number of defects in a second sample

      c.   the constant that corrects the bias in estimating the population standard deviation from the average range of randomly drawn samples

      d.   the probability that $\overline{X}$ is in control

Key: a.   the distance between the mean and the upper control limit of a range chart
(Ref. Principles Question 65, October 1972)

D_4 is a constant used to calculate the upper control limit for a range R chart of $\overline{X}$ and R control charts and is given as: UCL $= D_4\ \overline{R}$, where $\overline{R}$ is the average of range or mean of range.

31.   In statistical process control charts, $D_4\overline{R}$ is used to calculate

      a.   the upper control limit of the $\overline{X}$ chart

      b.   the lower control limit of the $\overline{R}$ chart

      c.   the upper control limit of the $\overline{R}$ chart

      d.   the lower control limit of the $\overline{X}$ chart

Key: c.   the upper control limit of the $\overline{R}$ chart[11]

This is the standard formula to calculate the upper control limit of the range chart in the $\overline{X}$ and R control chart, i.e., $UCL_R = D_4\overline{R}$.

32.   The ratio of the average of all sample standard deviations $\overline{S}$ and estimated population standard deviation σ' in $\overline{X}$ and S charts is called

      a. d_2

      b. A_2

      c.   Coefficient of Variation

---

[10] *Juran's Quality Control Handbook* by J. M. Juran, 4th edition, McGraw-Hill, New York, pg. 24.13.
[11] *Juran's Quality Control Handbook* by J. M. Juran, 4th edition, McGraw-Hill, New York, pg. 24.15.

       d. c_4

Key: d. c_4

c_4 is a factor for the S chart, when you plot $\overline{X}$ and S charts. This factor helps to estimate the σ' and $\overline{S}$ values for a given sample size. It is expressed as $c_4 = \overline{S}/\sigma'$.

33.   The center line on the $\overline{X}$ control chart is

       a.   called $\overline{\overline{X}}$
       b.   calculated as the sum of all sample averages divided by the number of subgroups
       c.   the same as the mean of all the individual observations
       d.   all of the above

Key: d.   all of the above

34.   If a process is out of control, the theoretical probability that four consecutive points on an $\overline{X}$ chart will fall on the same side of the mean is

       a.   unknown
       b. $(1/2)^4$
       c. $2(1/2)^4$
       d. $1/2\,(1/2)^4$

Key: a.   unknown   (Ref. Applications Question 43, October 1972)
The key phrase is *a process is out of control*, i.e., not in a state of statistical control. This means the process has some assignable or special causes, and hence the samples do not show the random variations. The process outcomes are not independent and predictable, and hence it is difficult to calculate the probabilities until the stability is reached.

35.   The factor A_2 used in the $\overline{X}$ and R control charts is used to calculate

       a.   the distance between the mean and the upper control limit of a range chart
       b.   the distance between the mean and the upper and lower control limits in the $\overline{X}$ chart for the averages
       c.   the constant which corrects the bias in estimating the population standard deviation from the average range of randomly drawn samples
       d.   the number of defects in a second sample

Key: b.   the distance between the mean and the upper and lower control limits in the $\overline{X}$ chart for the averages

A_2 is a constant used to calculate the upper and lower control limits for the $\overline{X}$ chart for averages and is given as $UCL_x = \overline{\overline{X}} + A_2\overline{R}$ and $LCL_x = \overline{\overline{X}} - A_2\overline{R}$ where $\overline{R}$ is the average range. The quantity $\pm A_2\overline{R}$ defines the distance between the mean and the upper or lower control limit in the case of an $\overline{X}$ chart for the averages.

36.   Find the upper control limit (UCL$_x$) for the average chart if $\overline{\overline{X}}$ = 25 and the range average is $\overline{R}$ = 5, with n = 5.

      a.   27.9
      b.   22.1
      c.   40
      d.   10

Key: a.   27.9

Given: $\overline{X}$ and R chart, n = 5, $\overline{\overline{X}}$ = 25, $\overline{R}$ = 5.
Find: UCL$_x$
From the table of constant factors for computing control charts lines, we get the following factors for the $\overline{X}$ and R charts for n = 5:
A_2 = 0.577, D_3 = 0, D_4 = 2.114, d_2 = 2.326
and hence UCL$_x$ is given as: UCL$_x$ = $\overline{\overline{X}}$ + $A_2 \overline{R}$ = 25 + 0.577(5) ≈ 279.

37.   If the $\overline{X}$ chart is out of statistical control, but the R chart is in statistical control, the better estimate of the population standard deviation would be

      a. $s = \dfrac{\overline{R}}{d_2}$

      b. $s = \sqrt{\dfrac{\sum(X_i - \overline{X})^2}{n-1}}$

      c. $s = \sqrt{\dfrac{\sum(X_i - \overline{X})^2}{n}}$

      d. $s = \sqrt{\dfrac{\sum(X_i - \overline{X})}{n-1}}$

Key: a. $s = \dfrac{\overline{R}}{d_2}$

This gives the best estimate of standard deviation of the underlying population when we use the $\overline{X}$ and R chart as compared to the square root formula for sample standard deviation in choice b.[12] The $\overline{X}$ chart is out of control indicating that the mean may be shifted to a different value. This may inflate the estimate of standard deviation using the square root formula. The R chart is in statistical control, and hence $s = \dfrac{\overline{R}}{d_2}$ is a better estimate of the population standard deviation. Choice c indicates the population standard deviation as the divider is n and not n − 1. Choice d is an incorrect formula.

38.   A process is in control at $\overline{\overline{X}}$ = 100, $\overline{R}$ = 7.3 with n = 4. If the process level shifts to 101.5 with the same $\overline{R}$, what is the probability that the next $\overline{X}$ point will fall outside the old control limits?

---

[12] *Statistical Quality Control Handbook* by Western Electric Co. Inc, 1986. Section II, Part D, pg. 131.

  a. 0.016
  b. 0.029
  c. 0.122
  d. 0.360

Key: a. 0.016   (Ref. Applications Question 12, July 1984)

Given: $\overline{\overline{X}} = 100$, $\overline{R} = 7.3$, and n = 4, $\overline{\overline{X}}_{new} = 101.5$.

Find: The probability that the next $\overline{X}$ point will fall outside the old control limits.

This is an example of an $\overline{X}$ *and R chart and sampling distribution of means*. First we need to find the UCL and LCL, i.e., the old control limits, for the $\overline{X}$ chart based on the given $\overline{R}$ values as follows: $UCL_x = \overline{\overline{X}} + A_2\overline{R}$ and $LCL_x = \overline{\overline{X}} - A_2\overline{R}$ where A_2 is a constant and a multiplier to $\overline{R}$ to define the ± 3 standard deviation limits above and below the center line $\overline{\overline{X}}$ of the $\overline{X}$ chart. Table 7-2 gives only a partial list of values of constants for different sample sizes to compute the control limits in the table below. Refer to the Appendix for the table of constant factors for computing control charts lines.

Table 7-2 Constants for calculating limits of the $\overline{X}$ and R chart

Sample size n	A_2 factor for control limits for averages chart	d_2 factor for center line for range chart	D_4 factor for control limits for range chart
2	1.880	1.128	3.267
3	1.023	1.693	2.574
4	*0.729*	*2.059*	*2.282*
5	*0.577*	*2.326*	*2.114*
6	0.483	2.534	2.004

For n = 4, we get $A_2 = 0.729$. Hence UCL_x and LCL_x will be

$UCL_x = \overline{\overline{X}} + A_2\overline{R} = 100 + 0.729 \times 7.30 = 105.32$ and

$LCL_x = \overline{\overline{X}} - A_2\overline{R} = 100 - 0.729 \times 7.30 = 94.68$. This is shown in Fig. 7-1.

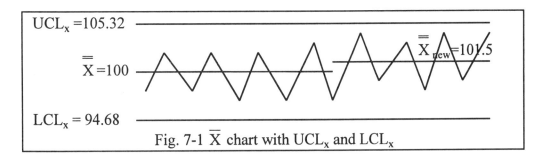

Fig. 7-1 $\overline{X}$ chart with UCL_x and LCL_x

We can calculate the standard deviation S of the process using the average range $\overline{R}$ value and the d_2 factor where d_2 is a constant for the center line of the range chart.

From Table 7-2: $d_2 = 2.059$ and hence $S = \dfrac{\overline{R}}{d_2} = \dfrac{7.3}{2.059} = 3.55$.

The standard error of mean S_x is given as $S_x = \dfrac{S}{\sqrt{n}} = \dfrac{3.55}{\sqrt{4}} = 1.77$.

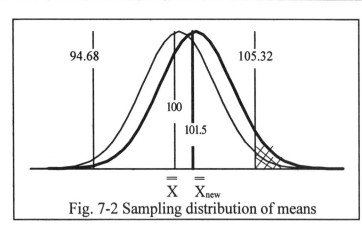

Fig. 7-2 Sampling distribution of means

Here the control limits are the same as the old limits and only the mean $\overline{\overline{X}}$ has shifted from 100.0 to 101.5. The probability that the next point $\overline{X}$ will fall outside the control limits will be more on the UCL side, which is shown in the shaded area in Fig. 7-2. We can calculate the area using the Z table.

$$Z_u = \frac{UCL - \overline{\overline{X}}_{new}}{S/\sqrt{n}} = \frac{105.32 - 101.5}{1.77} = 2.16, \text{ and from the Z table we get:}$$

Probability $P(Z_u \leq 2.16) = 0.9846$, i.e., the area under the curve, or the probability of the next $\overline{X}$ falling within the UCL is 98.46%.

Similarly $Z_l = \dfrac{94.68 - 1015}{1.77} = 3.86$, and from the Z table we get: $P(Z_l = -3.86) \approx 0$.

Hence the probability of finding the next $\overline{X}$ point falling outside the old control limits of 105.32 and 94.68 will be: $P(Z > 2.16) = 1 - P(Z_u \leq 2.16) = 1 - 0.9846 = 0.0154 \approx 0.016$.
Hence choice a is correct.

39. An $\overline{X}$ and R chart was prepared for an operation using 20 samples with five pieces in each sample. $\overline{X}$ was found to be 33.6 and R was 6.2. During production, a sample of five was taken and the pieces were measured 36, 43, 37, 34, and 38. At the time this sample was taken

   a. both average and range were within control limits
   b. neither average nor range were within control limits
   c. only the average was outside control limits
   d. only the range was outside control limits
   e. the information given is not sufficient to construct an $\overline{X}$ and R chart using tables usually available

Key: c. only the average was outside control limits (Ref. Applications Question 18, August 1978)
   Given: $\overline{X}$ = 33.6, R = 6.2. This may be an error in the question, and it should be
        $\overline{\overline{X}}$ = 33.6, $\overline{R}$=6.2, n = 5, and sample data are 36, 43, 37, 34, and 38.
   Find: Determine if the process is in statistical control when 5 pieces were measured.
   Table 7-2 gives: for n = 5, A_2 = 0.577, and D_4 = 2.114

   For $\overline{X}$ chart: $UCL_x = \overline{\overline{X}} + A_2 \overline{R}$ = 33.6 + 0.577 × 6.2 = 37.2
                        $LCL_x = \overline{\overline{X}} - A_2 \overline{R}$ = 33.6 − 0.577 × 6.2 = 30.0
   For R chart: $UCL_R = D_4 \overline{R}$ = 2.114 × 6.2 = 13.1
                        $LCL_R = D_3 \overline{R}$ = 0 × 6.2 = 0
   Sample data: 36, 43, 37, 34, 38 gives $\overline{X}$ = 37.6 and R = 43 − 34 = 9.

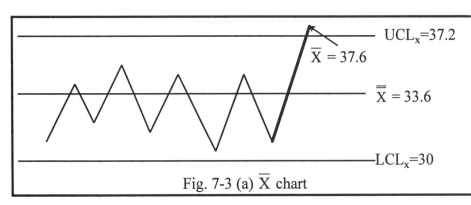

Fig. 7-3(a) shows that the sample average of 37.6 is outside the UCL_x limit.

Fig. 7-3 (a) $\overline{X}$ chart

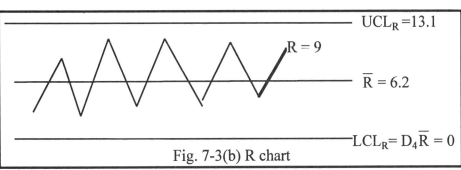

Fig. 7-3(b) shows that the range of the sample is within the control limits.

Fig. 7-3(b) R chart

40.   An $\overline{X}$ and R chart was prepared for an operation using 20 samples with five pieces in each sample. $\overline{X}$ was found to be 33.6 and $\overline{R}$ was 6.20. During production a sample of five was taken and the pieces measured 36, 43, 37, 25, and 38. At the time this sample was taken

        a.   both average and range were within control limits
        b.   neither average nor range were within control limits
        c.   only the average was outside control limits
        d.   only the range was outside control limits

Key: d.   only the range was outside control limits (Ref. Applications Question 15, July 1984)
Refer to Question 39 above for discussion as most of the data are the same except the sample data. This change in the data will give new values of $\overline{X}$ and R as follows.
Sample data: 36, 43, 37, 25, 38, $\overline{X}$ = 35.8,   R = 43 − 25 = 18.
$\overline{X}$ = 35.8 will fall within the control limits of Fig. 7-3(a) but Fig. 7-3(b) indicates that R = 18 will fall outside of UCL_R =13.1.

41.   A process is checked by inspection of random samples of four shafts after a polishing operation, and $\overline{X}$ and R charts are maintained. A person making a spot-check picks out two shafts, measures them accurately, and plots the value of each on the $\overline{X}$ chart. Both points fall outside the control limits. The person advises the department foreman to stop the process. This decision indicates that

        a.   the process level is out of control
        b.   both the levels and dispersion are out of control
        c.   the process level is out of control but not the dispersion
        d.   the person is not using the chart correctly

Key: d.   the person is not using the chart correctly (Ref. Applications Question 26, July 1984)

A few important points. First, the $\overline{X}$ chart is the chart for *averages* and not for *individuals*. Second, the sample size is n = 4 and not 2. Third, the control limits are not for individual points but for averages. Hence, taking 2 shafts is incorrect, plotting these individual values on the $\overline{X}$ chart is incorrect because the person should plot the average of 4 points and not the individual values.

42.   A process is checked at random by inspection of samples of four shafts after a polishing operation and $\overline{X}$ and R charts are maintained. A person making a spot-check measures two shafts accurately, and plots their range on the R chart. The point falls just outside the control limit. He advises the department foreman to stop the process. This decision indicated that

    a.   the process level is out of control
    b.   the process level is out of control but not the dispersion
    c.   the person is misusing the data
    d.   the process dispersion is out of control

Key: d.   the process dispersion is out of control (Ref. Applications Question 86, October 1972)

The range is defined as R = Maximum value – Minimum value, which is plotted in the range chart. Hence if the range of two shafts falls outside the control limit, it indicates that the process dispersion is out of control. Also refer to Question 41, which uses the $\overline{X}$ chart and not the R chart.

43.   You have just returned from a two week vacation and are going over with your QC manager the control charts which have been maintained during your absence. He (she) calls your attention to the fact that one of the X charts shows the last 50 points to be very near the center line. In fact, they all seem to be within about one sigma of the center line. What explanation would you offer him (her)?

    a.   Somebody goofed in the original calculation of the control limits.
    b.   The process standard deviation has decreased during the time the last 50 samples were taken and nobody thought to recompute the control limits.
    c.   This is a terrible situation. I'll get on it right away and see what the trouble is. I hope we haven't produced too much scrap.
    d.   This is fine. The closer the points are to the center line, the better your control.

Key: b.   The process standard deviation has decreased during the time the last 50 samples were taken and nobody thought to recompute the control limits.

(Ref. Applications Question 7, August 1978)

The question uses the terms X charts and 50 points were near the center line. Hence it is not very clear if X charts means the chart for individuals and moving range chart or $\overline{X}$ and R chart and if 50 points means 50 average values, i.e., 50 sample means on the $\overline{X}$ chart. We will assume that the data represent the $\overline{X}$ and R chart.

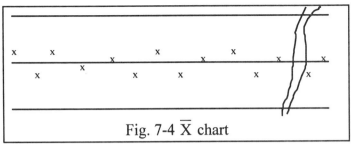

Fig. 7-4 $\overline{X}$ chart

If the last 50 sample means are near the center line, then the points were hugging the center line as shown in Fig. 7-4. This indicates that the process is out of control with respect to the old control limits.

If the last 50 points are near the center line, it means the variability or standard deviation of the process has been significantly reduced during that time period, but it makes the process out of control since too many points are near the center line. Hence one needs to recalculate the control limits.

Be careful of choice d as SPC rules indicate that the process is out of control if there are 15 or more points within the $\pm\sigma_x$ or near, above, or below the center line.[13] This may be a desirable condition but it is out of control, and hence new control limits should be calculated and these points should be reviewed with the new limits. Statistically, only 68.26% (approximately 2/3) of the points fall within $\pm\sigma_x$ and not all of the last 50 points at the same time.[14] This question is repeated in the October 1974 examination.[15]

44.   You look at a process and note that the chart of averages has been in control. If the range suddenly and significantly increases, the mean will

        a.   always increase
        b.   stay the same
        c.   always decrease
        d.   occasionally show out of control of either limit
        e.   none of the above

Key: d.   occasionally show out of control of either limit
        (Ref. Applications Question 26, August 1978)
        Choice d is the most appropriate answer. Choices a, b, and c are strong statements as conclusions for the mean. If the range increases, the mean may remain the same, increase, or decrease, but we are not in a position to conclude any one of these three conditions as the only condition. It is also likely that if the mean increases or decreases, it may occasionally show an out-of-control condition, i.e., be outside of either control limit.

45.   A characteristic in a plant is plotted on an $\overline{X}$ and S chart. The process average is $\overline{\overline{X}} = 60$, and the average of the individual sample subgroup standard deviations is $\overline{S} = 6$ from a sample subgroup size of four each. The lower and upper control limits for the $\overline{X}$ chart will be

        a.   52.2 and 69.8
        b.   55.6 and 64.4

13 *Juran's Quality Control Handbook* by J. M. Juran, 4th edition, McGraw-Hill, New York, pg. 24.18, Fig. 24.8, test 7.
14 *Fundamental SPC Reference Manual*, 1st edition, published jointly by ASQC Automotive Division and AIAG, GM/Ford/ Chrysler, pg. 50, Fig. 17 and pg. 51.
15 *ASQC-CQE Examination*, Quality Progress, October 1974, Applications Question 6.

c. 42 and 78
d. 54 and 66

Key: a. 52.2 and 69.8

Given: $\overline{\overline{X}} = 60$, $\overline{S} = 6$, n = 4.
Find: UCL_x and LCL_x
Refer to any statistical quality control[16] book or reference for commonly used constant factors in the control chart. For n = 4 we get the following factors for the $\overline{X}$ and S charts:
$A_3 = 1.628$, $c_4 = 0.9213$, $B_3 = 0$, and $B_4 = 2.266$.
The control limits for the $\overline{X}$ chart are given as follows:
$UCL_x = \overline{X} + A_3\overline{S} = 60 + 1.628 \times 6 = 69.768$ and $LCL_x = \overline{X} - A_3\overline{S} = 60 - 1.628 \times 6 = 52.232$.

46. In Question 45 above, the lower and upper control limits for the S chart will be

a. 0 and 13.68
b. 0 and 13.6
c. 0 and 18
d. 0 and 6

Key: b. 0 and 13.6

Refer to Question 45 data. We get the following factors for the $\overline{X}$ and S charts for n = 4:
$A_3 = 1.628$, $c_4 = 0.9213$, $B_3 = 0$, and $B_4 = 2.266$.
The control limits for the S chart are given as follows:
$LCL_s = B_3\overline{S} = 0$ because $B_3 = 0$ for n = 4. $\quad UCL_s = B_4\overline{S} = 2.266 \times 6 = 13.596 \approx 13.6$.

47. Using the range method, calculate the machine capability standard deviation to the nearest 0.0001 of the following:

8 am	9 am	10 am	11 am
0.001	0.003	0.001	0.005
−0.001	0.004	− 0.002	0.006
0.003	0.003	− 0.003	0.005
0.002	0.004	0.002	0.005
0.001	0.002	0.000	0.006

a. 0.0024
b. 0.0470
c. 0.0013
d. 0.0030

Key: c. 0.0013 (Ref. Applications Question 69, October 1972)
Given: Data on four time intervals with n = 5 samples each.
Find: Machine capability standard deviation.
The question is not clear because the term *machine capability standard deviation* is not a

---

[16] *Quality Control Handbook* by J. M. Juran, 4th edition, McGraw-Hill, New York, pg. AII-3, Appendix 2, Table A.

universally accepted term. It is not the same as machine capability or process capability, which is given as $\pm 3\sigma$ or a total of 6σ standard deviations. We will assume that we are asked to calculate the standard deviation of the samples using the formula $S = \dfrac{\overline{R}}{d_2}$.

The range for each time data is: $R_1 = 0.004$, $R_2 = 0.002$, $R_3 = 0.005$, and $R_4 = 0.001$.

$$\overline{R} = \frac{0.004 + 0.002 + 0.005 + 0.001}{4} = 0.003; \quad S = \frac{\overline{R}}{d_2} = \frac{0.003}{2.326} = 0.001289 \approx 0.0013.$$

48.   The control chart that is most sensitive to variation in a measurement is the

    a.   p chart
    b.   np chart
    c.   c chart
    d. $\overline{X}$ and R chart

Key: d. $\overline{X}$ and R chart   (Ref. Principles Question 41, October 1972)

The $\overline{X}$ and R charts are based on variable data and hence provide more detailed analysis of the variation and its magnitude. All other charts, such as the p, np, and c charts, are for attributes and hence provide less information about variation.

49.   Pre-Control starts a process specifically centered between

    a.   process shifts
    b.   safety lines
    c.   normal distribution limits
    d.   three sigma control limits
    e.   specification limits

Key: e.   specification limits   (Ref. Applications Question 37, July 1984)

Pre-Control is a method of controlling processes based on tolerances or specifications.[17] Pre-Control can be used for any quality characteristic without concern for the shape, type, and stability of the distribution. Pre-Control is very simple tool, and operators can use it easily to manage their production processes.

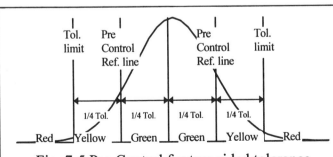

Fig. 7-5 Pre-Control for two sided tolerance

Fig. 7-5 shows Pre-Control for two sided tolerance. Reference lines are placed at 1/4 tolerance range for two sided tolerances. It defines the tolerance zones in three colors: the green area is between the reference lines, the yellow area is between the reference line and its corresponding upper or lower tolerance limit, and the red area is outside the tolerance limit.

---

[17] *Juran's Quality Control Handbook* by J. M. Juran, 4th edition, McGraw-Hill, New York, pg. 24.31.

50.   The control limits in statistical process control charts represent

    a.   ±1S limits
    b.   ±2S limits
    c.   ±3S limits
    d.   ±4S limits
    where S is the standard deviation

Key: c.   ±3S limits

The control limits are ±3S limits and indicate that about 99.73% of the points will be within the control limits. These limits are calculated by using a different formula for each type of control chart.

51.   Recognizing the nature of process variability, the process capability target is usually

    a.   the same as product specifications
    b.   independent of product specifications
    c.   looser than product specifications
    d.   tighter than product specifications

Key: d.   tighter than product specifications   (Ref. Principles Question 56, October 1974)

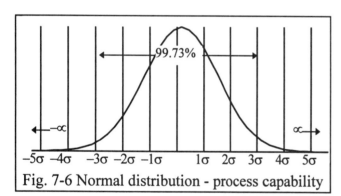

Fig. 7-6 Normal distribution - process capability

The process capability is defined as ±3σ, i.e., ±3 standard deviations, which accounts for 99.73% probability under normally distributed data as shown in Fig. 7-6. If this ±3σ process capability is the same as the product specifications then the product is 99.73% capable, i.e., the process is producing 0.27% or 2700 parts per million outside the specifications.

This may not sound too high at first glance, but in today's competitive customer-driven markets, it is still a very high percentage that does not meet the specification. Depending on the effect on customer satisfaction requirements, there should be more effort to achieve ±4σ, i.e., 60 parts per million out of specifications, ±5σ, i.e., 2 parts per million out of specifications and even ±6σ capabilities instead of merely meeting the specifications with ±3σ capability. Hence the process capability targets should be generally more aggressive and tighter than the product specifications so that the process can be more and more capable. This question is repeated in the October 1972 examination.[18]

52.   A value of 0.9973 refers to the probability that

    a.   the process is in control
    b.   a correct decision will be made as to control or lack of control of the process
    c.   the process is unstable

---

[18] *ASQC-CQE Examination,* Quality Progress, October 1972, Principles section, Question 31.

d. a point will fall inside the three sigma limits for an $\overline{X}$ chart if the process is in control

Key: d. a point will fall inside the three sigma limits for an $\overline{X}$ chart if the process is in control
(Ref. Applications Question 57, October 1972)
The upper and lower control limits (UCL and LCL) of a control chart represent the $\pm 3\sigma_x$ limits. This indicates a confidence level or probability of 0.9973 or 99.73% meaning that there is 0.9973 probability that a point will fall inside the $\pm 3\sigma_x$ limits of the $\overline{X}$ chart if the process is in control.

53. C_p is defined as

a. $C_p = \dfrac{\text{Process variation}}{\text{Tolerance width}} = \dfrac{6\sigma}{\text{USL} - \text{LSL}}$

b. $C_p = \dfrac{X - \text{LSL}}{3\sigma}$

c. $C_p = \dfrac{\text{USL} - \overline{\overline{X}}}{3\sigma}$

d. $C_p = \dfrac{\text{Tolerance width}}{\text{Process variation}} = \dfrac{\text{USL} - \text{LSL}}{6\sigma}$

Key: d. $C_p = \dfrac{\text{Tolerance width}}{\text{Process variation}} = \dfrac{\text{USL} - \text{LSL}}{6\sigma}$

Let's first define some important formulas for process capability, capability ratio, and capability indices.

1. Process Capability = $\pm 3\sigma$ or 6σ and it defines the total process variation.

2. Capability ratio CR = $\dfrac{\text{Process variation}}{\text{Tolerance width}} = \dfrac{6\sigma}{\text{USL} - \text{LSL}}$ and this is generally expressed as a percentage of the total tolerance range used.

3. $C_p = \dfrac{\text{Tolerance width}}{\text{Process variation}} = \dfrac{\text{USL} - \text{LSL}}{6\sigma}$ and it is the inverse of CR, i.e., $C_p = \dfrac{1}{CR}$.

4. $C_{pk} = \dfrac{Z_{min}}{3}$ where Z_{min} is the minimum of $Z_l = \dfrac{\overline{\overline{X}} - \text{LSL}}{\sigma}$ and $Z_u = \dfrac{\text{USL} - \overline{\overline{X}}}{\sigma}$.

Choice a defines the process capability ratio CR and not C_p. Choice b indicates $Z_l/3$ and not C_p. Choice c indicates $Z_u/3$. Hence choice d is the only correct answer.

54. The term *process capability* is

I. defined as 6σ variation of the process
II. the total process variation under stable conditions, i.e., under a state of statistical control
III. the same as the capability ratio
IV. the same as the C_{pk} index

a. I and II

    b.   II and III
    c.   III and IV
    d.   IV and I

Key: a.   I and II
        Process capability is defined as 6σ variation of the process. It defines the total process variation
        under stable conditions, i.e., under a state of statistical control.

        Capability ratio and C_{pk} are the capability indices and they relate the total process variation to
        the product tolerance in the form of a ratio. There are different formulas for different indices. The
        fundamental and industrywide definition of process capability is a total of 6σ variation of the
        process. Please refer to Question 53 above for detail formulas.

55.   Process capability is defined as

        a. 6σ
        b. 3σ
        c. C_p
        d. C_{pk}

Key: a. 6σ
        The question asks for process capability, which is simply defined as 6σ or $\pm 3\sigma$ and not 3σ alone.
        Also the process capability ratio C_p or process capability index C_{pk} are not the same as process
        capability. They indicate if the process is capable to meet the tolerances or customer
        specifications by comparing the tolerances or deviation of the mean from its tolerance limit to
        the process variation. Please refer to Question 53 above for detail formulas.

56.   The spread of individual observations from a normal process capability distribution may be
        expressed numerically as

        a. $6\overline{R} / d_2$
        b. $2A_2 \overline{R}$
        c. $\overline{R} / d_2$
        d. $D_4\overline{R}$

Key: a. $6\overline{R} / d_2$ (Ref. Principles Question 3, July 1984)
        In statistical process control, for $\overline{X}$ and R charts, we take various samples and calculate their
        sample mean $\overline{X}$ and its range average $\overline{R}$.
        The sample standard deviation is given by the formula $\sigma = \overline{R}/d_2$.
        The process capability is defined as $\pm 3S$ or the total of $6\sigma = 6\overline{R} / d_2$.

57.   The following measurements for a sample with dimension X are representative of a process
        known to be in statistical control: 42, 52, 64, 45, 53, 56, 70, 57, 49, 62.
        Which of the following best approximates the upper and lower control limits of the process
        capability? (Use generally accepted sigma limits for the United States.)

a. 81 and 29
b. 59 and 51
c. 64 and 46
d. 70 and 42

Key: a. 81 and 29   (Ref. Applications Question 32, July 1984)

Given: The raw data for dimension X. Process is in statistical control.

Find: The UCL and LCL of the process capability.

The term process capability is defined as 3 standard deviations, i.e., $\pm 3\sigma$.

As this is sample data, we can calculate its sample mean $\overline{X}$ and standard deviation S values.

$\overline{X} = 55$; $S = 8.7$.

$UCL = \overline{X} + 3S = 55 + 3(8.7) = 81$ $LCL = \overline{X} - 3S = 55 - 3(8.7) = 29$.

58.   Machine capability means

a.   a capability study under controlled conditions, i.e., a constant set of conditions, such as best operator, homogeneous raw materials, consistent processing methods, etc.
b.   a study of special causes of variation in the long run
c.   a capability study with normal operating conditions, such as changes in machines, operators, environment, methods, materials, etc., over a long period of time
d.   availability of the machines as a ratio of up time to total time

Key: a.   a capability study under controlled conditions, i.e., a constant set of conditions, such as best operator, homogeneous raw materials, consistent processing methods, etc.

A machine capability study is done to determine the best or maximum capability of the machine under controlled conditions, i.e., a constant set of conditions, such as best operator, homogeneous raw materials, consistent processing methods, etc., where most of the operating parameters are kept constant. This study is done for a short period of time and generally involves a small production run. The data on the capability indicate how capable the machine is, i.e., the inherent variation of the machine, and enables one to decide if the machine can meet the given product requirements under normal production conditions. This type of capability study is often done during buyouts and tryouts of expensive engineering tools, dies, and fixtures. It generally does not account for normal operating conditions such as changes in machines, operators, environment, methods, materials, etc. Hence under normal operating conditions, the process capability is likely to be less than or equal to the machine capability data.

Choice b is incorrect because a process is not studied for special causes of variation alone, but also for common causes of variation to define the state of statistical control. Choice c defines the *process capability study* which is done normally over a long period of time under normal operating conditions and not under controlled conditions. Choice d defines the term *availability* commonly used in reliability applications.

Note: Today, the term machine capability study is treated the same as the process capability study and only the latter term is used in many industries. The automotive industry defines only the term process capability study in its recent publication The Fundamental Statistical Process

Control Reference Manual[19] and does not recognize the term machine capability as a separate concept. The machine is considered as an integral element of the process similar to material, operator, environment, etc., and not an independent item of the process. As the machine capability involves only controlled conditions with smaller samples and gives a snapshot picture of the process, it is less applicable today.

59.   Which one of the following BEST describes machine capability?

    a.   The total variation of all cavities of a mold, cavities of a die cast machine, or spindles of an automatic assembly machine

    b.   The inherent variation of the machine

    c.   The total variation over a shift

    d.   The variation in a short run of consecutively produced parts

Key: b.   The inherent variation of the machine   (Ref. Principles Question 20, July 1984)

Refer to Question 58 above for a discussion. This question is also repeated in the 1974 and 1972 examinations[20] with slight changes in the question.

60.   When introducing the new product to the manufacturing phase of the product's life, the most important justification for a process capability study – after a pilot run for stability but during a controlled operation – is

    a.   it will prove design feasibility

    b.   it will establish machine capability

    c.   it will provide manufacturing engineering with the basis for a preventive maintenance schedule

    d.   it will determine the degree of conformance of tools, materials, and operators with design specifications and economic yield requirements

    e.   none of these

Key: d.   it will determine the degree of conformance of tools, materials, and operators with design specifications and economic yield requirements

(Ref. Principles Question 2, October 1974)

The process capability study is important after the pilot run to revalidate the process with the production level parts that are made from production tools, operations, etc. It helps to determine the maximum or the best process capability and determine if the process is capable to meet the design requirements as it is done under controlled conditions.

The design feasibility study is done during the prototype phases of new product development and the machine capability study should be done during the buyout and tryout of new equipment and machines for a process. The preventive maintenance schedule is developed based on many factors such as tool life, wear and tear of tools, utilization of equipment, equipment manuals, tool manuals, technical bulletins, number of pieces of equipment, number of shifts, etc. A long-term process capability study that reveals some trends of variations and shifts in the control charts can

---

[19] *Fundamental Statistical Process Control Reference Manual,* 1st edition, published jointly by ASQC Automotive Division and AIAG, GM / Ford / Chrysler; Section, pg. 13-15 and 152.

[20] *ASQC-CQE Examination,* Quality Progress, October 1974, Principles section, Question 57 and October 1972, Principles section Question 18.

be a similar indicator for developing preventive maintenance schedules for selected processes only. But this is not the prime objective of a process capability study. Also refer to Question 59 for a discussion on machine capability.

61.   Machine capability studies on four machines yielded the following information:

Machine	Average ($\overline{X}$)	Capability (6σ)
# 1	1.495	0.004"
# 2	1.502	0.006"
# 3	1.500	0.012"
# 4	1.498	0.012"

The tolerance on the particular dimension is $1.5000 \pm 0.005"$. If the average value can be readily shifted by an adjustment to the machine, the BEST machine to use is

    a.   Machine # 1
    b.   Machine # 2
    c.   Machine # 3
    d.   Machine # 4

Key: a.   Machine # 1   (Ref. Principles Question 37, July 1984)
The important comment here is that the average value can be readily shifted by an adjustment to the machine. Each machine shows some mean shift, i.e., the average is different than the ideal mean of 1.500". But this mean shift is not a major concern as it can be adjusted and centered on the desired target.

Machine #1 has the highest mean shift of 1.495" instead of 1.5000" but this is not a concern anymore because we can adjust the machine to the desired mean value. But it has the lowest 6σ variability equal to 0.004". As a result, Machine # 1 is the best machine to use.

62.   The process capability for the attribute data can be defined as

    a.   Capability % = $100(0.5)^{1/N+1}$ where N is the number of samples required
    b. $\overline{p}$, the average percentage of defectives
    c. $\overline{c}$, the average rate of defects
    d.   any of the above, depending on its appropriate application

Key: d.   any of the above, depending on its appropriate application
Choice a is defined by Juran[21] as capability percentages for attribute data. It indicates the number of samples required for different percentages of capability ratios. For attribute data, the process capability is simply defined as the actual value of the average proportion of defectives, or average number of defects, etc. Sometimes it is defined as $1-\overline{p}$, a percentage that meets the requirements.

63.   When an initial study is made of a repetitive industrial process for the purpose of setting up a

---

[21] *Juran's Quality Control Handbook* by J. M. Juran, 4th edition, McGraw-Hill, New York, pg. 16.25; *and Fundamental Statistical Process Control Reference Manual*, 1st edition, published jointly by ASQC Automotive Division and AIAG, GM/Ford/Chrysler, pg. 152.

Shewhart control chart, information on the following process characteristic is sought:

 a. process capability
 b. process performance
 c. process reliability
 d. process conformance
 e. process tolerance

Key: a. process capability (Ref. Applications Question 25, August 1978)
The key term is initial study, which means the short-term process capability study. Process capability indicates the $\pm 3\sigma$ variation of the process, and the data can be used to set up the limits of the Shewhart control chart.

64. In which one of the following is the use of an $\overline{X}$ and R chart liable to be helpful as a tool to control a process?

 a. The machine capability is wider than the specification.
 b. The machine capability is equal to the specification.
 c. The machine capability is somewhat smaller than the specification.
 d. The machine capability is very small compared to the specification.

Key: c. The machine capability is somewhat smaller than the specification.
(Ref. Applications Question 34, October 1972)

65. If you are doing a mini process capability study using a sample size n = 10, the process capability will be approximately

 a. $\pm 1\overline{R}$
 b. $2\overline{R}$
 c. $\pm 3\dfrac{\overline{R}}{3.078}$
 d. all of the above

Key: d. all of the above
Given: n = 10.
Find: Process capability $\pm 3\sigma$ or 6σ.
Be careful here. You may have picked choice c as your answer because it looks like the most obvious answer based on the following formula:

Process capability $= \pm 3\sigma = \pm 3\dfrac{\overline{R}}{d_2} = \pm 3\dfrac{\overline{R}}{3.078}$ where for n = 10, $d_2 = 3.078$.[22] Hence it is a correct choice but other choices are also correct. Let us study each remaining choice now.

Choice a: $\pm 3\sigma = \pm 3\dfrac{\overline{R}}{d_2} = \pm 3\dfrac{\overline{R}}{3.078} \approx \pm 1\overline{R}$. This is a correct choice also.

Choice b: Process capability is defined as $\pm 3\sigma$ or 6σ. We have from choice a $\pm 3\sigma = \pm 1\overline{R}$ and hence $6\sigma = 2\overline{R}$. Hence choice b is correct also.

---

[22] *Quality Control Handbook* by J. M. Juran, 4th edition, McGraw-Hill, New York, pg. AII-3, Appendix 2, Table A.

Hence choice d is the most appropriate choice and not choice a, b, or c alone.

66. A process is under statistical control and has $C_p = 1.5$ and $C_{pk} = 0.75$. This means

    a.   do nothing
    b.   the process is on target and capable of meeting customer requirements or tolerances
    c.   the process center needs to be targeted and variability needs to be reduced
    d.   none of the above

Key: c.   the process center needs to be targeted and variability needs to be reduced
Given: $C_p = 1.5$ and $C_{pk} = 0.75$.
The terms C_p and C_{pk} indicate the process capability indices,[23] and they are used to compare the process variability with the customer tolerances.

C_p is given as the ratio of the tolerance band to process variation, i.e., $C_p = \dfrac{USL - LSL}{6\sigma} = 1.5$, where USL and LSL are upper and lower specification limits, respectively. This means the variability of the process is very low and can comfortably meet the tolerances since it uses only 2/3 of the total tolerance.

C_{pk} is the capability index that takes into consideration the process average mean $\overline{X}$ and its upper or lower specification limit vs. the process variability, i.e.,

$$C_{pk} = \text{min. } (C_{pku} ; C_{pkl}), \text{ i.e., } C_{pk} = \text{min. of } (\dfrac{\overline{X} - LSL}{3\sigma} ; \dfrac{USL - \overline{X}}{3\sigma}) = 0.75$$

The C_{pk} of 0.75 is a comparatively low value as it should be equal to at least 1 or more to be able to meet or exceed customer requirements. The numerator in the formula can suggest that there may be a possible mean shift from its desired nominal, and the denominator may suggest a high variability. Hence the process mean needs to be targeted and variation should be reduced. Also refer to Question 53 for detailed formulas.

67. A process in your plant is unable to meet the tolerances, i.e., its C_{pk} is lower than the customer's targets. You should

    a.   review the sources of variation in the process and try to improve the capability by properly implementing the variation reduction program
    b.   contact the design engineer to review the tolerances, as the part is not likely to meet the customer requirements and tolerances may need to be expanded
    c.   redesign the manufacturing process if necessary and shift the current production job to another piece of equipment that has adequate capability
    d.   any one of the above

Key: d.   any one of the above
The important thing to remember is the possible sequence of steps as a, c, and b above, i.e., first reduce the variability as per choice a, study, then if nothing is doable, shift the part to a different machine or piece of equipment that is capable to meet the requirements. Finally, contact the

---

[23] *Defect Prevention* by Victor Kane, Marcel Dekker, Inc; New York, and ASQC Quality Press, 1989, Part I, Chapter 7; and *Juran's Quality Control Handbook* by J. M. Juran, 4th edition, McGraw-Hill, New York, pg. 16.18 and 20.

design engineer to expand the tolerance.

68.   The p chart is

        I.   a variable chart
        II.   an attribute chart
        III.   a fraction nonconforming chart
        IV.   a number nonconforming chart

        a.   I and II above
        b.   II and III above
        c.   III and IV above
        d.   IV and I above

Key: b.   II and III above
        The p chart is an attribute chart and it represents the fraction nonconforming value commonly
        known as p. Watch out for choice d where a *number nonconforming chart* is indicated as an np
        chart and not a p chart.

69.   A p chart is a type of control chart for

        a.   plotting bar stock lengths from receiving inspection samples
        b.   plotting fraction defective results from shipping inspection samples
        c.   plotting defects per unit from in-process inspection samples
        d.   a, b, and c
        e.   a and c only

Key: b.   plotting fraction defective results from shipping inspection samples
         (Ref. Principles Question 1, August 1978)
        Choice a for bar stock lengths is for a variable chart, and choice c for plotting defects per unit is
        for a u chart. Only choice b reflects the plotting of fraction defectives on the p chart.

70.   A p chart

        a.   can be used for only one type of defect per chart
        b.   plots the number of defects in a sample
        c.   plots either the fraction or percent defective in order of time
        d.   plots variations in dimensions

Key: c.   plots either the fraction or percent defective in order of time
        (Ref. Principles Question 22, October 1972)
        This is a basic concept. You should know such basic concepts.

71.   The sensitivity of a p chart to changes in quality is

        a.   equal to that of a range chart
        b.   equal to that of a chart for averages
        c.   equal to that of a c chart

d.   equal to that of a u chart

e.   none of the above

Key: e.   none of the above   (Ref. Principles Question 2, August 1978)

Choices a and b apply to the $\overline{X}$ and R charts for variable data, and choices c and d apply to attribute charts for nonconformities or a defects chart. Each chart is used for a different application and has a different formula to calculate the control limits. Each chart is based on different probability distribution assumptions. Hence it is not advisable to compare sensitivity of one charting method to another.

72.   A p chart has exhibited statistical control over a period of time. However, the average fraction defective is too high to be satisfactory. Improvement can be obtained by

a.   a change in the basic design of the product
b.   instituting 100% inspection
c.   a change in the production process through substitution of new tooling or machinery
d.   all of the above answers are correct except letter b
e.   all of the above answers are correct except letter c

Key: d.   all of the above answers are correct except letter b
(Ref. Principles Question 3, August 1978)
Because the process is in statistical control over a period of time, it is important to act on the common causes or on the system to bring the desired change in reducing the average fraction defective. Choices a and c are such actions on the system or on the common causes and they can result in a low average fraction defective. When the process is under statistical control, instituting 100% inspection will not result in any improvement in average defectives, as the process is operating under random variation and no special causes are present. Also, it is only a detection. If the process was out of control, one may institute 100% inspection as a short-term corrective action until root causes for the out-of-control conditions have been found.

73.   An electronics firm was experiencing high rejections in their multiple connector manufacturing departments. "P" charts were introduced as part of a program to reduce defectives. Control limits were based on prior history using the formula $P' \pm 3\sqrt{\dfrac{P'(100 - P')}{N}}$, where P' is the historical value of percent defective and N is the number of pieces inspected each week. After six weeks, the following record was accumulated.

Percent Defective

Dept.	P'	Week 1	Week 2	Week 3	Week 4	Week 5	Week 6
101	12	11	11	14	15	10	12
102	17	20	17	21	21	20	13
103	22	18	26	27	17	20	19
104	9	8	11	6	13	12	10
105	16	13	19	20	12	15	17
106	15	18	19	16	11	13	16

600 pieces were inspected each week in each department. Which department(s) exhibited a point

or points out of control during the period?

a.   Dept. 101
b.   Dept. 102
c.   Dept. 103
d.   Dept. 104
e.   Dept. 105

Key: d.   Dept. 104   (Ref. Applications Question 3, August 1978)
      Given: P charts with different values of P for each department; raw data for 6 weeks, N = 600.
      Find: The department(s) having out-of-control points during the six week period.

To find the UCL and LCL, we will use the formula $P' \pm 3\sqrt{\dfrac{P'(100-P')}{N}}$ as shown in Table 7-3.

Department 104 at week 4 has P =13% defectives, which results in a point out of control, i.e., it is outside UCL = 12.5. All other departments are in control during the six week duration. This question is repeated with different data values in the August 1978 examination.[24]

Table 7-3 Calculation of UCL and LCL for P chart

Dept. 101: $P' \pm 3\sqrt{\dfrac{P'(100-P')}{N}} = 2 \pm 3\sqrt{\dfrac{12(100-12)}{600}} = 12 \pm 3.98 = 8.02$ or 15.98
Dept. 102: $P' \pm 3\sqrt{\dfrac{P'(100-P')}{N}} = 7 \pm 3\sqrt{\dfrac{17(100-17)}{600}} = 17 \pm 4.60 = 12.4$ or 21.60
Dept. 103: $P' \pm 3\sqrt{\dfrac{P'(100-P')}{N}} = 22 \pm 3\sqrt{\dfrac{22(100-22)}{600}} = 22 \pm 5.07 = 16.93$ or 27.07
Dept. 104: $P' \pm 3\sqrt{\dfrac{P'(100-P')}{N}} = 9 \pm 3\sqrt{\dfrac{9(100-9)}{600}} = 9 \pm 3.5 = 5.5$ or 12.5
Dept. 105: $P' \pm 3\sqrt{\dfrac{P'(100-P')}{N}} = 6 \pm 3\sqrt{\dfrac{16(100-16)}{600}} = 16 \pm 4.49 = 11.51$ or 20.49
Dept. 106: $P' \pm 3\sqrt{\dfrac{P'(100-P')}{N}} = 5 \pm 3\sqrt{\dfrac{15(100-15)}{600}} = 15 \pm 4.37 = 10.63$ or 19.37

Now we can compare individual weeks' data of each department against these control limits as shown in Table 7-4 and find out if any of the departments have out-of-control situations.

Table 7-4 Comparison of raw data with the calculated UCL and LCL

Dept.	P'	Week 1	Week 2	Week 3	Week 4	Week 5	Week 6	LCL	UCL
101	12	11	11	14	15	10	12	8.02	15.98
102	17	20	17	21	21	20	13	12.4	21.6
103	22	18	26	27	17	20	19	16.93	27.07
104	9	8	11	6	13	12	10	5.5	12.5
105	16	13	19	20	12	15	17	11.51	20.49
106	15	18	19	16	11	13	16	10.63	19.37

74.   An electronics firm was experiencing high rejections in their multiple connector manufacturing departments. "P" charts were introduced as part of a program to reduce defectives. Control

---

[24] *ASQC- CQE Examination*, Quality Progress, August 1978 Applications, Question 3.

limits were based on prior history using the formula $P' \pm 3\sqrt{\dfrac{P'(100-P')}{N}}$, where P' is the historical value of percent defective and N is the number of pieces inspected each week. After six weeks, the following record was accumulated. (The above formula has been corrected by ASQC.)

Dept.	P'	Week 1	Week 2	Week 3	Week 4	Week 5	Week 6
104	9	8	11	6	13	12	10
105	16	13	19	20	12	15	17
106	15	18	19	16	11	13	16

1000 pieces were inspected each week in each department. Which department(s) exhibited a point or points out of control during this period? (Round off calculations to the nearest tenth of a percentage point.)

a.   Dept. 104
b.   Dept. 105
c.   Dept. 106
d.   all of the departments
e.   none of the departments

Key: d.   all of the departments   (Ref. Applications Question 17, July 1984)
         Given: Data on the different values of P for each department; raw data for 6 weeks, N=1000 pcs.
         Find: The department(s) having out-of-control points during the 6 week period.

To find the UCL and LCL, we will use the formula $P' \pm 3\sqrt{\dfrac{P'(100-P')}{N}}$ as shown in Table 7-5.

Table 7-5 Calculation of UCL and LCL for P chart

Dept. 104	$P' \pm 3\sqrt{\dfrac{P'(100-P')}{N}} = 9 \pm 3\sqrt{\dfrac{9(100-9)}{1000}} = 9 \pm 2.56 = 6.44 \text{ or } 11.56$
Dept. 105	$P' \pm 3\sqrt{\dfrac{P'(100-P')}{N}} = 6 \pm 3\sqrt{\dfrac{16(100-16)}{1000}} = 16 \pm 3.48 = 12.52 \text{ or } 19.48$
Dept. 106	$P' \pm 3\sqrt{\dfrac{P'(100-P')}{N}} = 5 \pm 3\sqrt{\dfrac{15(100-15)}{1000}} = 15 \pm 3.39 = 11.61 \text{ or } 18.39$

Now refer to Table 7-6 to compare individual weeks' data of each department against these control limits and find out if any of the departments have out-of-control situations.

Table 7-6 Comparison of raw data with the calculated UCL and LCL

Dept.	P'	Week 1	Week 2	Week 3	Week 4	Week 5	Week 6	LCL	UCL
104	9	8	11	6	13	12	10	6.44	11.56
105	16	13	19	20	12	15	17	12.52	19.48
106	15	18	19	16	11	13	16	11.61	18.39

The shaded area in the above table proves that each department has at least one point out-of-control. Hence choice d, "all of the departments," is the right choice.

75. $\overline{np} \pm 3\sqrt{\overline{np}(1-\overline{p})}$ represents

      a.   the probability mass function for the binomial distribution
      b.   the control limits for the np chart
      c.   the probability mass function for the Poisson distribution
      d.   the control limits for the p chart

Key: b.   the control limits for the np chart
These are the $\pm 3S$ limits for the np chart.

76.   The chart for the number of nonconforming units in a process is called

      a.   c chart
      b.   np chart
      c.   p chart
      d   u chart

Key: b.   np chart
There is a significant difference between an np chart and a p chart. An np chart is used for the *number of nonconforming units* and has a *constant sample size*. A p chart is used for the *proportion of nonconforming units* and can have *varying sample sizes*.

77.   The np chart is advisable to use when

      a.   attribute data are used
      b.   it is more meaningful to report the actual number of nonconforming units, items, or parts rather than reporting the proportion of nonconforming units
      c.   the sample size is the same for each subgroup
      d.   all of the above

Key: d.   all of the above

78.   A process is in control with $\overline{p} = 0.10$ and n = 100. The three sigma limits of the np control chart are

      a.   1 and 19
      b.   9.1 and 10.9
      c.   0.01 and 0.19
      d.   0.07 and 0.13

Key: a.   1 and 19   (Ref. Applications Question 89, October 1972)
Given: $\overline{p} = 0.10$ and n = 100, np control chart.
Find: ± 3 sigma limits, i.e., upper and lower control limits (UCL and LCL).
UCL and LCL = $\overline{np} \pm 3\sqrt{\overline{np}(1-\overline{p})}$.

$$UCL = \overline{np} + 3\sqrt{\overline{np}(1-\overline{p})} = 100(0.1) + 3\sqrt{100(0.1)(1-0.1)} = 19.$$

$$LCL = \overline{np} - 3\sqrt{\overline{np}(1-\overline{p})} = 100(0.01) - 3\sqrt{100(0.1)(1-0.1)} = 1.$$

79.   A nonconformity is

   a.   a specific case of nonconformance to a requirement, a standard, or a specification
   b.   a single part or unit that does not conform to a requirement or specification
   c.   the same as a defective unit
   d.   plotted as a p control chart

Key: a.   a specific case of nonconformance to a requirement, a standard, or a specification
A nonconformity is conventionally defined as a *defect,* i.e., *a case of a single instance of nonconformance to the requirement or standard.*[25] Choice b defines a defective or nonconforming unit and not a nonconformity. Choice c refers to the term *a defective, or* a nonconforming unit, which means that it may contain one or more types of nonconformities. Control charts c and u are used to plot the nonconformities whereas the p chart is used to plot the fraction of nonconforming or proportion of defectives.

80.   In control chart theory, the distribution of the number of defects per unit follows very closely the

   a.   normal distribution
   b.   binomial distribution
   c.   chi-square distribution
   d.   Poisson distribution

Key: d.   Poisson distribution   (Ref. Principles Question 22, August 1978)
A defect or nonconformity is the departure of a characteristic on a product from its requirements or specifications, *and it is a single case of a nonconformance.* A nonconforming or defective item will contain at least one nonconformity or defect. We can develop the c control chart to plot the number of nonconformities. This type of control chart generally assumes that the occurrence of nonconformities in samples of constant sample size is shown by Poisson distribution. The Poisson distribution requires that the number of occurrences of the nonconformities be large and that the probability of occurrence of such nonconformities be constant and small.

81.   The assumed probability distribution for the control chart for the number of defects is the

   a.   binomial distribution
   b.   Poisson distribution
   c.   normal distribution
   d.   Student's t distribution

Key: b.   Poisson distribution   (Ref. Principles Question 43, October 1972)
Refer to Question 80 above.

---

[25] *Juran's Quality Control Handbook* by J. M. Juran, 4th edition, McGraw-Hill, New York, pg. 24.20 and *Fundamental Statistical Process Control Reference Manual*, 1st edition, published by ASQC Automotive Division & AIAG, GM/Ford/Chrysler, pg. 151.

82.   A very useful attribute control chart for plotting the actual number of defects found during an inspection is known as the

       a. $\overline{X}$ and R chart
       b.   np chart
       c.   p chart
       d.   c chart
       e.   u chart

Key: d.   c chart   (Ref. Principles Question 48, October 1974)
       The c chart is an attribute chart where the actual number of defects are plotted when *the sample size is constant*. It is simple to use. The u chart is used for the defects per unit when *the sample size is not constant*. You should know each control chart method and its criteria for use. This is a simple question and should be easy to answer.

83.   The p and u control charts are used

       a.   only if the data are variable
       b.   if the sample size is constant for each subgroup
       c.   when the sample size is not necessarily constant and can vary from subgroup to subgroup
       d.   for the number of nonconforming units and the number of nonconformities in the inspection lot

Key: c.   when the sample size is not necessarily constant and can vary from subgroup to subgroup
       The p chart is the chart for the proportion of units and not the number of nonconforming units, and it is plotted for varying sample sizes. Similarly the u chart is the chart for the number of nonconformities but can have different sample sizes. Hence choices b and d are incorrect. Choice a is incorrect because both the p and u charts are used only for the attribute data, e.g., yes-no, go-no go, pass-fail, etc., and not for the variable data.

84.   A chart for the number of defects is called the

       a.   np chart
       b.   p chart
       c. $\overline{X}$ chart
       d.   c chart

Key: d.   c chart   (Ref. Applications Question 58, October 1972)

85.   The data below indicate the number of defects found in a group of four subassemblies inspected for a product critical characteristic. If a c chart is used for this product characteristic, determine the upper and lower control limits for the c chart.

Data:
23	37	61	53
43	44	67	29
41	58	14	68
81	29	49	75
54	77	40	25

    a.   69.27, 27.53
    b.   26.5, 6.96
    c.   55.36, 41.44
    d.   62.32, 34.48

Key: a.   69.27, 27.53
Given: Number of defects in 20 subgroups of constant sample size of 4 each and use a c chart.
Find: The upper and lower control limits.
The total number of defects $\sum c$ = 968, and hence the average number of defects is given as

$$\bar{c} = \frac{\sum c}{n} = \frac{968}{20} = 48.40.$$

The upper and lower control limits are the 3σ control limits, i.e.,

$$UCL = \bar{c} + 3\sqrt{\bar{c}} = 48.40 + 3\sqrt{48.40} = 69.27 \text{ and } LCL = \bar{c} - 3\sqrt{\bar{c}} = 48.40 - 3\sqrt{48.40} = 27.53.$$

86.   Assuming that each out-of-control limit in the previous data of Question 85 above has a special or assignable cause, the quality engineer decides to drop all such points from the control chart. The revised upper and control limits will be

    a.   69.27, 27.53
    b.   68.87, 27.27
    c.   55.36, 41.44
    d.   62.32, 34.48

Key: b.   68.87, 27.27
Given: From Question 85 above we have the upper and lower control limits as 69.27 and 27.53. Drop the points that are out-of-control limits.
Find: Calculate the revised upper and lower control limits.
Table 7-7 shows 6 points (bold and a strike through the values) that are outside of the old control limits.

Table 7-7 Data for defects

~~23~~	37	61	53
43	44	67	29
41	58	~~14~~	68
~~81~~	29	49	~~75~~
54	~~77~~	40	~~25~~

The average number of defects $\bar{c} = \frac{\sum c}{n} = \frac{673}{14} = 48.07$.

The upper and lower control limits are the 3σ control limits, i.e.,

$$UCL = \bar{c} + 3\sqrt{\bar{c}} = 48.07 + 3\sqrt{48.07} = 68.87 \text{ and } LCL = \bar{c} - 3\sqrt{\bar{c}} = 48.07 - 3\sqrt{48.07} = 27.27.$$

87.   Each value below is the number of defects found in 25 groups of eight subassemblies
        inspected.

77	61	59	22	54
64	49	54	92	22
75	65	41	89	49
93	45	87	55	33
45	77	40	25	20

        Assume that a c chart is to be used for future protection. Calculate the preliminary three sigma
        control limits from the above data.

        a.   65.7, 45.7
        b.   78.2, 33.2
        c.   15.6, 6.6
        d.   82.5, 28.9

Key: b.   78.2, 33.2   (Ref. Applications Question 71, October 1974)
        Given: Number of defects in 25 subgroups of constant sample size of 8 each and use a c chart.
        Find: 3 sigma control limits.

        The average number of defects $\bar{c} = \dfrac{\Sigma c}{n} = \dfrac{1393}{25} = 5.572$.

        The upper and lower control limits are the 3σ control limits, i.e.,

        $UCL = \bar{c} + 3\sqrt{\bar{c}} = 55.72 + 3\sqrt{55.72} = 78.11$ and $LCL = \bar{c} - 3\sqrt{\bar{c}} = 55.72 - 3\sqrt{55.72} = 33.33$.

        This is a repeat question from the October 1972 examination.[26]

88.   Referring to the data in the preceding Question 87, if points are outside of the control limits and
        we wish to set up a control chart for future production

        a.   more data are needed
        b.   discard those points falling outside the control limits, for which you can identify an
                assignable cause, and revise the limits
        c.   check with production to determine the true process capability
        d.   discard those points falling outside the control limits and revise the limits

Key: b.   discard those points falling outside the control limits, for which you can identify an
                assignable cause, and revise the limits (Ref. Applications Question 62, October 1972)
        This is a fundamental concept of statistical process control charts.

89.   Tabular arrays of data and graphs on the same page are especially useful in quality control work
        because

        a.   both are there for those who don't like graphs only
        b.   graphs help spot data transposition or errors
        c.   control limits can be easily applied
        d.   all of the above

---

[26] *ASQC- CQE Examination*, Quality Progress, October 1972, Applications, Question 61.

Key: d.   all of the above   (Ref. Applications Question 80, October 1972)

90.   In the case of process capability analysis, a new measure of process capability called C_{pm} is given as

   a. $\dfrac{USL - LSL}{6\sqrt{\sigma^2 + (\mu - T)^2}}$

   b. $\dfrac{6\sigma}{USL - LSL}$

   c. $\dfrac{USL - LSL}{6\sigma}$

   d.   minimum of $\dfrac{\overline{\overline{X}} - LSL}{3\sigma}$ or $\dfrac{USL - \overline{\overline{X}}}{3\sigma}$

Key: a. $\dfrac{USL - LSL}{6\sqrt{\sigma^2 + (\mu - T)^2}}$

The C_{pm} is a new measure of process capability[27] and it takes into account the departures from the target value and it is given as $C_{pm} = \dfrac{USL - LSL}{6\sqrt{\sigma^2 + (\mu - T)^2}}$. It is an improved indicator of process centering and hence of process capability. When the process mean $\mu = T$, the three process capability indices are equal, i.e., $C_p = C_{pk} = C_{pk}$. The C_{pm} becomes smaller or it decreases as μ shows mean shift, i.e., as it starts deviating away from μ.

The conventionally used process capability indices are described as follows. Also refer to Questions 53 through 56 for a detailed discussion.

1.   Process Capability = $\pm 3\sigma$ or 6σ and it defines the total process variation.

2.   Capability ratio CR = $\dfrac{\text{Process variation}}{\text{Tolerance width}} = \dfrac{6\sigma}{USL - LSL}$ and this is generally expressed as a percentage of the total tolerance range used. Choice b defines CR.

3. $C_p = \dfrac{\text{Tolerance width}}{\text{Process variation}} = \dfrac{USL - LSL}{6\sigma}$ and it is the inverse of CR, i.e., $C_p = \dfrac{1}{CR}$.

The index C_p does not take into consideration the proximity of the measurements to the target value. Choice c defines C_p.

4. $C_{pk} = $ minimum of $C_{pkL} = \dfrac{\overline{\overline{X}} - LSL}{3\sigma}$ or $C_{pkU} = \dfrac{USL - \overline{\overline{X}}}{3\sigma}$. It is also defined as $\dfrac{Z_{min}}{3}$

where Z_{min} is the minimum of $Z_l = \dfrac{\overline{\overline{X}} - LSL}{\sigma}$ and $Z_u = \dfrac{USL - \overline{\overline{X}}}{\sigma}$. Choice d defines C_{pk}. The term C_{pk} takes into account process centering, but it is a misleading indicator in some cases. C_{pk} varies inversely with σ. As σ becomes smaller and approaches zero, C_{pk}

---

[27] *A New Measure of Process Capability, C_{pm}* by Lai K. Chan, Smiley W. Cheng, and Frederick A. Spring, Journal of Quality Technology, ASQC, Volume 20, No. 3, July 1988, pg. 162-175.

becomes large. Hence C_{pk} provides a limited value and an insufficient measure of process centering, i.e., its deviation from its target. A process can have a significantly large mean shift from its target but it may still give a higher value of C_{pk}.

91. A process is monitoring a length dimension as an important product characteristic as the variation in this characteristic can significantly affect customer satisfaction requirements.

Consider the following data.
Length specifications are 10 ± 2 millimeters. The process is operating in a state of statistical control with the process average at 11 mm and a standard deviation of 0.333 mm. The value of the process capability index C_p is

    a.   0.5
    b.   2.0
    c.   1.00
    d.   0.63

Key: b.   2.0
Given: Length specification 10 ± 2, $\mu = 11$ mm, $\sigma = 0.333$ mm.
Find: C_p.
Here USL $= 10 + 2 = 12$ and LSL $= 10 - 2 = 8$ mm.
$C_p = \dfrac{USL - LSL}{6\sigma} = \dfrac{12 - 8}{6 \times 0.333} = 2$. The process mean has shifted to 11 mm, however C_p does not take it into account.

92. Refer to the data given in Question 91 above. The process capability index C_{pk} is

    a.   0.5
    b.   2.0
    c.   1.00
    d.   0.63

Key: c.   1.00
Given: Length specification 10 ± 2, $\mu = 11$ mm, $\sigma = 0.333$ mm.
Find: C_{pk}.

$C_{pk} = \text{minimum of } C_{pkL} = \dfrac{\overline{\overline{X}} - LSL}{3\sigma} \text{ or } C_{pkU} = \dfrac{USL - \overline{\overline{X}}}{3\sigma}$.

$C_{pkL} = \dfrac{\overline{\overline{X}} - LSL}{3\sigma} = \dfrac{11 - 8}{3 \times 0.333} = 3$ and $C_{pkU} = \dfrac{USL - \overline{\overline{X}}}{3\sigma} = \dfrac{12 - 11}{3 \times 0.333} = 1.00$.

Hence $C_{pk} = \text{minimum of } C_{pkL}$ and C_{pkU}, i.e., $C_{pk} = 1.00$.

93. Refer to the data given in Question 91 above. The process capability index C_{pm} is

    a.   0.5
    b.   2.0
    c.   1.00
    d.   0.63

Key: d.   0.63
        Given: Length specification 10 ± 2, $\mu = 11$ mm, $\sigma = 0.333$ mm.
        Find: C_{pm}.

The term $C_{pm} = \dfrac{USL - LSL}{6\sqrt{\sigma^2 + (\mu - T)^2}} = \dfrac{12 - 8}{6\sqrt{0.333^2 + (11 - 10)^2}} = \dfrac{4}{6\sqrt{0.333^2 + (11 - 10)^2}} = 0.6325$.

94.   In the case of a control chart, which of the following is/are possible mistakes and can result in tampering?

        i.   treat the variation as a special cause, when it actually is a common cause variation
        ii.   treat the variation as common cause when it actually is a special cause variation
        iii.   treat the variation as a system cause when it actually is a common cause variation

        a.   i and ii above
        b.   ii and iii above
        c.   i and iii above
        d.   i, ii and iii above

Key: a.   i and ii above
Deming[28] describes two kinds of mistakes because of the confusion between the common cause and special cause variation.

It is a mistake when we treat the variation as a special cause, when it actually is a common cause variation. This results in over adjustment. Similarly, it is wrong to treat the variation as a common cause when it actually is a special cause variation. This can result in lack of serious effort to find any special causes.

Deming warns against both mistakes as it is very possible that one commits one or the other mistake when trying to avoid one mistake. Also the presence of a special cause variation requires completely different types of actions as compared to the presence of a common cause variation.

Item iii is not a mistake. The common cause variation is a chance variation attributable to a system. The control charts are designed to give a statistical signal of the presence of a special cause and/or a common cause variation. If one tries to adjust a process that is in a state of statistical control to take an action for a nonconforming situation, it results in a worse output. The best thing would have been to leave the process alone instead of adjusting it. Deming has described a famous funnel experiment[29] and four rules to explain the effects of tampering with the process. Any over adjustment results in unbelievable losses. It is important to understand the stability of the process using control charts. The process is considered stable, i.e., in a state of statistical control when there is no special cause variation present. You should study this basic concept in more detail. Also refer to Question 12 above for additional discussion.

---

[28] *Out of the Crisis* by W. E. Deming, Massachusetts Institute of Technology, Center for Advanced Engineering Study, Cambridge, MA, 02139, pg. 318-319; 327-329.

[29] *Deming Road to Continual Improvement* by William W. Scherkenbach, SPC Press, Knoxville, TN, 1991, pg. 41-59; *The Deming Library* videotape series, Volume IX, Films Inc., Chicago; *Don't Touch that Funnel* by Thomas J. and Eileen C. Boardman, Quality Progress, ASQC, December 1990, pg. 65-70.

ASQC-CQE BIBLIOGRAPHY AND OTHER REFERENCES ON STATISTICAL PROCESS CONTROL

1. *Advanced Quality Planning and Process Control Plan Methodology Reference Manual*, 1st ed., published jointly by GM/Ford/Chrysler, 1994.

2. *ANSI/ASQC A1-1987 Definitions, Symbols, Formulas, and Tables for Control Charts*, Milwaukee, ASQC Quality Press, 1987.

3. ASQC Statistics Division, *Glossary and Tables for Statistical Quality Control*, 2nd ed., Milwaukee, ASQC Quality Press, 1983.

4. Braverman, Jerome D., *Fundamentals of Statistical Quality Control*, Englewood Cliffs, NJ, Prentice-Hall, 1981.

5. Boardman, Thomas J. and Eileen C. Boardman, *Don't Touch that Funnel*, Quality Progress, Milwaukee, ASQC, December 1990.

6. Deming, W. E., *Out of the Crisis*, Massachusetts Institute of Technology, Center for Advanced Engineering Study, Cambridge, MA, 02139.

7. *The Deming Library* videotape series, Volume IX, Chicago, Films Inc.

8. Dovich, Robert A., *Quality Engineering Statistics*, Milwaukee, ASQC Quality Press, 1992.

9. Duncan, A. J., *Quality Control and Industrial Statistics*, 5th ed., Homewood, IL, Irwin Inc., 1986.

10. *Fundamental SPC Reference Manual*, 1st ed., Southfield, MI, published jointly by ASQC Automotive Division and AIAG, GM/Ford/Chrysler, 1991.

11. Grant, Eugen L. and Richard Leavenworth, *Statistical Quality Control*, 6th ed., New York, McGraw-Hill, 1988.

12. Juran, Joseph M., *Juran's Quality Control Handbook*, 4th ed., New York, McGraw-Hill, 1988.

13. Kane, Victor, *Defect Prevention*, New York, Marcel Dekker, and Milwaukee, WI, ASQC Quality Press, 1989.

14. Keats, J. Bert and Douglas C. Montgomery, *Statistical Process Control in Manufacturing*, New York, Marcel Dekker, 1991.

15. McWilliams, Thomas P., *How to Use Sequential Statistical Methods*, Volume 13, Milwaukee, ASQC, Quality Press, 1989.

16. Scherkenbach, William W., *Deming Road to Continual Improvement*, Knoxville, TN, SPC Press, 1991.

17. Shewhart, W. A., *Economic Control of Quality of Manufactured Product*, Milwaukee, WI, Quality Press, republished as the 50th Anniversary edition by ASQC, 1980.

18. Schooling, Edward G., *Acceptance Sampling in Quality Control.*, New York, Marcel Dekker, 1982.

19. Shapiro, Samuel S., *How to Test Normality and Other Distributional Assumptions*, Volume 3, revised, Milwaukee, ASQC Quality Press, 1990.

20. Stephens, Kenneth S., *How to Perform Continuous Sampling*, Volume 2, Milwaukee, ASQC Quality Press, 1990.

21. Stephens, Kenneth S., *How to Perform Skip Lot and Chain Sampling*, Volume 4, Milwaukee, ASQC Quality Press, 1990.

22. Vani, Jagdish, *Fundamental Concepts of Probability, Statistics, Regression and DOE*, 3rd edition, Troy, MI, Quality Quest, 1993.

23. Western Electric, *Statistical Quality Control Handbook*, Indianapolis, AT&T, 1956.

CHAPTER 8

ACCEPTANCE SAMPLING

ASQC'S <u>BODY OF KNOWLEDGE (BOK)</u> FOR THE CQE EXAMINATION

This chapter focuses on the following selected subject areas of BOK from *Section III, Statistical Principles and Applications.*

Acceptance Sampling

1. Definitions (e.g., AQL, LTPD, AOQ, AOQL)
2. General theory (e.g., operating characteristics curve, producer and consumer risks)
3. Sampling types (e.g., single, double, multiple, sequential)
4. Sampling plans
    a. ANSI/ASQC Z1.4, MIL-STD-105
    b. ANSI/ASQC Z1.9, MIL-STD-414
    c. Dodge Romig

Note: The concepts in acceptance sampling are based on sampling theories in statistics and their applications. Many authors consider these "enumerate studies" which assume the processes are static and hence cannot be used for prediction of process outcomes. There is an increasing emphasis on "analytical studies" which assume processes are dynamic and the prediction of a process outcome is possible if a process is in statistical control. Many industries require statistical process control, and optimization methods such as design of experiments, robust designs, etc., to achieve high process capability.

Some of these applications, e.g., AQL, AOQL, LTPD, and AOQ, etc., are not in wide practice today and hence it is not easy to understand this subject in short overview classes or quick readings. The repetition of questions, definitions, and answers in this chapter is by design, to give you additional practice in understanding the subject, and to prepare you for the examination.

To order the MIL-STD-105E and 414, mail your request to: Standardization Document Order Desk, 700 Robbins Ave., Building 4, Section D, Philadelphia, PA 19111-5094 or call (215) 697-1187 for telephone order or information. Please verify this address in the future.

1.   Consideration(s) to be made prior to the use of any sampling plan is/are

        a.   the consumer's and producer's risks must be specified
        b.   the method of selecting samples must be specified
        c.   the characteristics to be inspected must be specified
        d.   the conditions must be specified (material accumulated in lots or inspected by
                continuous sampling)
        e.   all of the above

Key: e.   all of the above   (Ref. Principles Question 24, August 1978)

2.   The sample size for a product quality audit should be

        a.   based on MIL-STD-105D
        b.   based on the lot size
        c.   a stated percentage of production
        d.   very small

Key: d.   very small (Ref. Applications Question 11, October 1972)
        This question belongs more in a quality audit chapter than in an acceptance sampling chapter.
        However, because it involves MIL-STD-105E as one of the choices, it warrants some discussion
        here.

        The choices given here can be difficult to distinguish. MIL-STD-105E defines the sampling
        procedures and table for inspection by attributes. It is should be used to guide the user in the
        development of an inspection strategy that provides a cost-effective approach to attain
        confidence in a product's compliance with contractual technical requirements. This is generally
        not an audit standard or product assurance standard, but it is an inspection standard to control the
        quality of the product; and hence choice a is incorrect.

        Choices b and c can be effectively covered under choice d. The sample size should be based on
        the lot size and a stated percentage of the production, but should be "very small" to optimize the
        economic impact and hence be more appropriate.

        Product quality audits are not meant to be the process control, but they are used to evaluate a
        product's conformance to requirements. Companies use sample sizes based on the overall
        adverse consequences of too many or too few samples and their economic impact on the overall
        business.

3.   The attribute sampling plans require

        I.   the data in terms of percent defectives or proportion defectives
        II.   the data in terms of defect ratio or actual number of defects
        III.   the data from variable measurements using the mean and standard deviation statistic

a. I and II
b. II and III
c. I and III
d. only I

Key: a.   I and II
The attribute data means either percent or proportion defectives or, in some cases, it can be the number of defects or defects ratio. The OC curves and acceptance sampling plan tables are available for such attribute data.

4.   The attribute acceptance sampling plans are classified as

a.   AOQL acceptance sampling plans
b.   AQL acceptance sampling plans
c.   LTPD acceptance sampling plans
d.   all of the above

Key: d.   all of the above
The terms AOQL, AQL, and LTPD are commonly used terms in attribute acceptance sampling plans. They are defined in military standard MIL-STD-105E.

5.   "A defect that judgment and experience indicate would result in hazardous or unsafe conditions for individuals using, maintaining, or depending upon the product, or a defect that judgment and experience indicate is likely to prevent the performance of the tactical function of a major end item such as a ship, aircraft, tank, missile or space vehicle" is defined in MIL-STD-105E as

a.   Critical Defect
b.   Major Defect
c.   Minor Defect
d.   all of the above

Key: a.   Critical Defect
Refer to MIL-STD-105E[1] Section 3.5, Critical Defect.

6.   An operating characteristic curve (OC) is

a.   a curve indicating the probabilities of acceptance Pa for a sampling plan for a product at all possible levels of percent defectives
b.   the probability of finding at least c defectives from a lot
c.   a curve showing the operator instructions for a given critical characteristic of a product
d.   a scatter plot showing the possible relationship, if any, between two variables

Key: a.   a curve indicating the probabilities of acceptance Pa for a sampling plan for a product at

---

[1] *MIL-STD-105E, Sampling Procedures and Tables for Inspection by Attributes*, Sections 3.19, 3.2, 3.18, and 3.23.

all possible levels of percent defectives

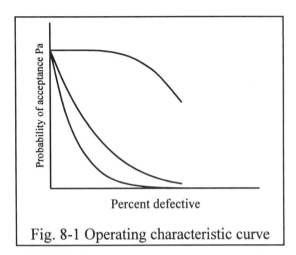

Fig. 8-1 Operating characteristic curve

The OC curve is a graph of percent defectives in a sample vs. its probability of being accepted based on a given sample size n and acceptance number c as shown in Fig. 8-1. It shows the discriminatory power of the sampling plan at a given sample size n and acceptance number c.

Choice b is incorrect because the acceptance criteria apply to the sample taken from a lot but not to the lot.

7.   The operating characteristic curve (OC) of an acceptance sampling plan

        a.   demonstrates the advantages of double sampling over single sampling
        b.   demonstrates how the plan will reject all of the lots worse than AQL
        c.   shows the relative cost of sampling for various levels of quality
        d.   shows the ability of the plan to distinguish between good and bad lots

Key: d.   shows the ability of the plan to distinguish between good and bad lots
        (Ref. Applications Question 57, October 1974, and Applications Question 48, October 1972)
        The OC curve is an important curve in the acceptance sampling plan. It is a plot of the
        probability of accepting a lot (Pa) with a given quality, i.e., a lot with a known (certain %)
        fraction defective p. It shows the protection available to the customer and shows the ability of the
        plan to distinguish between good and bad lots. Also, it can be used to determine the sample size
        n for a given probability of acceptance. OC curve is a widely used term for acceptance sampling
        plans and hypothesis testing, i.e., type II error.

8.   The type A OC curve

        a.   provides the probability of acceptance for an individual lot that comes from finite
                production conditions that cannot be assumed to continue in the future
        b.   provides the probability of acceptance of each lot and assumes that each lot is represent-
                ative of an infinite number of lots produced under similar conditions
        c.   is a more widely applicable OC curve than type B
        d.   all of the above

Key: a.   provides the probability of acceptance for an individual lot that comes from finite
                production conditions that cannot be assumed to continue in the future
        Choice b is incorrect because it defines the type B OC curve. Choice c is incorrect because type
        B is more common than type A.

Choice d, "all of the above," is naturally wrong because choice a defines the type A OC curve only. However, you are likely to pick this as your answer if you did not know the concept. It is an important reminder that many times *all of the above* is not necessarily the correct answer.

9.   An operating characteristic curve shows

     a.   the probability of accepting lots of various quality levels by sampling methods
     b.   the operating characteristics of a machine
     c.   how to operate a machine for best quality results
     d.   the probability that a lot contains a certain number of rejectable parts

Key: a.   the probability of accepting lots of various quality levels by sampling methods
             (Ref. Principles Question 14, July 1984)

The OC curve is an important curve in the acceptance sampling plan. It is a plot of the probability of accepting a lot (Pa) with a given quality, i.e., a lot with a known (certain %) fraction defective p. It shows the protection available to the customer. Also, it can be used to determine the sample size n for a given probability of acceptance.

OC curve is a widely used term for acceptance sampling plans and hypothesis testing, i.e., type II error. It is not a mechanical term referring to operating characteristics of the machine or how to operate a machine for best quality results.

10.   The steeper the OC curve, the

     a.   less protection for both producer and consumer
     b.   more protection for both producer and consumer
     c.   lower the AQL
     d.   smaller the sample size

Key: b.   more protection for both producer and consumer
     (Ref. Principles Question 7, August 1978)
The steeper the slope of the OC curve, the greater the discriminating power of the OC curve. This means the OC curve will be better able to reject all "bad" lots and accept all "good" lots, which will result in more protection for both the consumer and the producer.

11.   An operation requires shipments from a vendor of small lots of fixed size. The attribute sampling plan used for receiving inspection should have its OC curve developed using

     a.   the binomial distribution
     b.   the Gaussian (normal) distribution
     c.   the Poisson distribution
     d.   the hypergeometric distribution

Key: d.   the hypergeometric distribution   (Ref. Principles Question 11, July 1984)

The key phrases are *"**lots of fixed size**,"* i.e., finite lot size and *"**attribute sampling**."* This meets the criteria for the hypergeometric distribution, which is a discrete distribution and requires a finite lot size.

12.   For an operation requiring shipments from a vendor of small lots of fixed size, the sampling plan used for receiving inspection should have its OC curve developed using

   a.   the Poisson distribution
   b.   the hypergeometric distribution
   c.   the binomial distribution
   d.   the log normal distribution
   e.   the Gaussian (normal) distribution

Key: b.   the hypergeometric distribution   (Ref. Principles Question 12, August 1978)
The key words missing here are "using an attribute sampling plan" for receiving inspection. The sampling plan can be either for inspection by attributes or by variables. Hence other distributions for variable data are possible. Refer to Question 11 above where it specifically indicates the use of an attribute sampling plan.

Assuming this has an attribute sampling plan, we use hypergeometric distribution, which is the discrete distribution for finite or fixed lot size. This is a repeat question with slight change from the October 1974 examination.[2]

13.   In the case of acceptance sampling plans, the producer's risk is defined as

   a.   the probability of rejecting a lot when it is a good lot
   b.   the probability of accepting a lot when it is a good lot
   c.   the probability of accepting a lot when it is a bad lot
   d.   the probability of rejecting a lot when it is a bad lot

Key: a.   the probability of rejecting a lot when it is a good lot
The producer's risk (α risk) is defined as the probability of rejecting a lot when it is a good lot. It is also the same as type I error, i.e., rejecting the null hypothesis Ho when Ho is true.[3] Choice b is the probability of accepting a lot when it is a good lot and it is given as $1 - \alpha$, not α. Choice c indicates the consumer's risk (β risk) of accepting the lot when it is a bad lot. It is also the same as type II error, i.e., accepting the null hypothesis when Ho is false. Choice d is the probability of rejecting the lot when it is a bad lot and is expressed as $1 - \beta$, not β.

14.   For a sampling plan, which of the following is true?

   a.   The producer's risk is the probability that a bad lot will be rejected.

---

[2] *ASQC - CQE Examination*, ASQC Quality Progress, Milwaukee, WI, October 1974, Principle section, Question 30.
[3] *Fundamental Concepts of Probability, Statistics, Regression and DOE* by Jagdish Vani, 3rd ed., April 1993, Quality Quest Inc., Troy, MI, Section 4.

b.   The producer's risk is the probability that a good lot will be accepted.
c.   The producer's risk is the probability that a good lot will be rejected.
d.   The producer's risk is the probability that a bad lot will be accepted.

Key: c.   The producer's risk is the probability that a good lot will be rejected.
Choices a and b are wrong because the producer's risk (α) is the probability that a good lot will be rejected by the sampling plan. Choice d is wrong because it defines the consumer's risk and not the producer's risk.

15.   The probability of accepting material produced at an acceptable quality level is defined as

a. α
b. β
c.   AQL
d. $1 - \alpha$
e $1 - \beta$

Key: d. $1 - \alpha$ (Ref. Principles Question 25, August 1978)
The risk of rejecting a lot of AQL quality is known as producer's risk α. Hence $1 - \alpha$ is the probability of accepting the material produced at an acceptable quality level.

16.   In the case of acceptance sampling plans, the consumer's risk is defined as

a.   the probability of rejecting the lot when it is a good lot
b.   the probability of accepting the lot when it is a good lot
c.   the probability of accepting the lot when it is a bad lot
d.   the probability of rejecting the lot when it is a bad lot

Key: c.   the probability of accepting the lot when it is a bad lot
Choice c indicates the consumer's risk (β risk) of accepting the lot when it is a bad lot. It is also the same as type II error, i.e., accepting the null hypothesis when Ho is false. Choice d is the probability of rejecting the lot when it is a bad lot and is expressed as $1 - \beta$, not β.

Choice a defines the producer's risk (α risk) as the probability of rejecting a lot when it is a good lot. It is also the same as type I error, i.e., rejecting the null hypothesis Ho when Ho is true. Choice b is the probability of accepting a lot when it is a good lot, i.e., $1 - \alpha$, not α.

17.   Consumer's risk is defined as

a.   accepting an unsatisfactory lot as satisfactory
b.   passing a satisfactory lot as satisfactory
c.   an alpha risk
d.   a 5% risk of accepting an unsatisfactory lot

Key: a.   accepting an unsatisfactory lot as satisfactory   (Ref. Principles Question 4, August 1978)
Consumer's risk means accepting a bad lot as a good lot. It is also called type II error in hypothesis testing and is denoted as β.

Choice b is wrong because passing a satisfactory lot as satisfactory is the right decision and not an error. Choice c is wrong because alpha means producer's risk. Choice d indicates a single specific value of consumer's risk as 5% but it is not a general rule or a constant condition. Consumer's risk can take different values other than 5%.

18.   Which of the following is true?

    a.   Consumer's risk is the probability that a bad lot will be rejected.
    b.   Consumer's risk is the probability that a good lot will be accepted.
    c.   Consumer's risk is the probability that a good lot will be rejected.
    d.   Consumer's risk is the probability that a bad lot will be accepted.

Key: d.   Consumer's risk is the probability that a bad lot will be accepted.
Choices a and b are wrong because consumer's risk (β) is the probability that a bad lot will be accepted by the sampling plan. Choice c is wrong because it defines the producer's risk and not the consumer's risk.

19.   In acceptance sampling, the probability of accepting a rejectable lot is called

    a.   beta
    b.   AQL
    c.   alpha
    d.   LTPD

Key: a.   beta   (Ref. Applications Question 36, October 1972)
The probability of accepting a rejectable lot is called *consumer's risk* and is denoted as β. The term alpha (α) represents the *producer's risk* of rejecting the lot when it is good. The AQL and LTPD are not the probability of acceptance; they represent the defectives percentage or quality of the lot.

20.   In acceptance sampling, the probability of accepting an undesirable lot is the same as (or may be called)

    a.   alpha
    b.   beta
    c.   AQL
    d.   LTPD
    e.   none of these

Key: b.   beta   (Ref. Principles Question 1, October 1974)

Beta (β) is the consumer's risk, which is the probability of accepting an undesirable lot. In hypothesis testing, this is type II error, i.e., accepting the hypothesis when it is false. Simply stated it is the risk of accepting a bad lot.

Alpha (α) is the producer's risk, which is the probability of rejecting an acceptable lot. In hypothesis testing, this is type I error, i.e., rejecting a hypothesis when it is true. Simply stated, it is the risk of rejecting a good lot.

Acceptable quality level (AQL) is the maximum percent defectives that can be considered satisfactory as a process average. MIL-STD-105E[4] defines AQL as the quality level which, for the purposes of sampling inspection, is the limit of a satisfactory process average. AQL is the maximum percent or proportion of defectives (also called variant units) in a lot or batch that, for the purposes of acceptance sampling, can be considered satisfactory as a process average.

Lot tolerance percent defective (LTPD) is the percentage of defectives that is unsatisfactory and unacceptable and hence should be rejected by the sampling plan. It is the unacceptable quality level, i.e., the rejectable quality level. It should have low probability of being accepted, i.e., low beta (β) risk.

For various definitions of terms, we recommend that you have a good list of references,[5] e.g., MIL-STD-105E and MIL-STD-414.

21.   In the case of acceptance sampling plans, one should

    1.   keep the producer's risk as small as possible
    2.   keep the consumer's risk as small as possible
    3.   keep $(1 - \alpha)$ and $(1 - \beta)$ both as small as possible

    a.   1 and 2
    b.   2 and 3
    c.   3 and 1
    d.   1, 2, and 3

Key: a.   1 and 2
This indicates that we should always try to keep both the producer's risk and consumer's risk as small as possible. Be careful here to not select choice d (1, 2, and 3 above) because item 3 is incorrect. We are trying to keep both α risk and β risk, not $(1 - \alpha)$ and $(1 - \beta)$ as small as possible.

22.   Using a 10% sample of each lot with an acceptance number of zero regardless of lot size

---

[4] *MIL-STD-105E, Sampling Procedures and Tables for Inspection by Attributes*, Sections 3.1, 3.19 and 4.4.
[5] *Glossary and Tables for Statistical Quality Control* prepared by the American Society for Quality Control (ASQC), Quality Press, Milwaukee, WI, Section 5; and *Juran's Quality Control Handbook* by J. M. Juran, 4th ed., McGraw-Hill, New York, pg. 25.9.

a. results in a constant level of protection against a bad product
b. assures a constant producer's risk
c. abdicates the responsibility for predetermining quality requirements
d. provides an AQL of zero and an LTPD of 10%

Key: c. abdicates the responsibility for predetermining quality requirements
(Ref. Applications Question 46, October 1972)
Grant and Leavenworth[6] describe the sampling plans with the same percent samples and its impact on quality protection for the producer as well as for the consumer. Table 8-1 shows the data for the sample size as 10% of the lot size in each case, i.e.,
(i) $N = 40$, $n = 4$, and $A = 0$ and (ii) $N = 400$, $n = 40$, and $A = 0$

Table 8-1 P_a values for sample size as 10% of the lot size

100 p percent defective	np for N = 40, n = 4, A = 0	P_a for N = 40, n = 4, A = 0	np for N = 400, n = 40, A = 0	P_a for N = 400, n = 40, A = 0
0	0	1	0	1
1	0.04	0.961	0.4	0.670
2	0.08	0.923	0.8	0.449
3	0.12	0.887	1.2	0.301
4	0.16	0.853	1.6	0.202
5	0.2	0.819	2.0	0.135
6	0.24	0.787	2.4	0.091
7	0.28	0.756	2.8	0.061
10	0.4	0.67	4.00	0.018

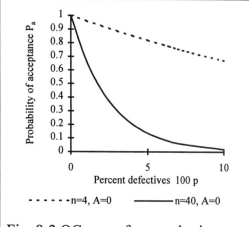

Fig. 8-2 OC curve for sample size as 10% of the lot size

The operating characteristic curves in Fig. 8-2 indicate that each case provides different quality protection. The two curves are not the same.

Hence it is not true to state that the protection given by sampling schemes is constant if the ratio of sample size to lot size is constant for the same acceptance criteria c.

Choice a "results in a constant level of protection against a bad product" and choice b, "assures a constant producer's risk," are incorrect based on the OC curve.

Also they do not provide an AQL of zero and LTPD of 10%. Hence the only choice by default is c, which indicates that it abdicates the responsibility for predetermining quality requirements.

---

[6] *Statistical Quality Control* by E. Grant and R. Leavenworth, 6th ed., McGraw-Hill, New York, pg. 399, Fig. 12-1.

Such thumb rules of 10% of the lot size with c = 0 are misleading and should be discarded or stopped because they do not provide the expected level of protection in most cases.

23.   If a process is running at normally 5% defectives, sample of n = 10, acceptance number c = 1, and the probability of acceptance P_a for these data from the OC curve is 0.9139. The producer's risk will be

   a.   0.9139
   b.   5%
   c.   0.0861
   d.   95%

Key: c.   0.0861
       Given: P_a = 0.9139, n = 10, c = 5, p = 0.05.
       Find: The producer's risk.

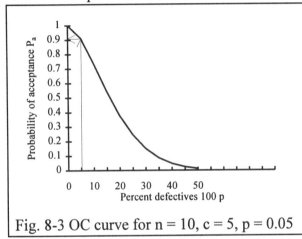

Fig. 8-3 OC curve for n = 10, c = 5, p = 0.05

The producer's risk is defined as the probability of rejecting a lot when it is a good lot, and it is commonly denoted as α risk. Fig. 8-3 shows an OC curve for n = 10, P_a = 0.9139, and c = 5. In the data above, the P_a = 0.9139 is the probability of accepting the lot when it is good, i.e., when it has c = 5 or less defectives. It means 1 − 0.9139 = 0.0861, or 8.61% of the time the lot is likely to be rejected even though it might be of good quality. This 8.61% is called the producer's risk.

24.   The acceptance number commonly denoted as c in acceptance sampling plans is defined as

   a.   the number of good parts required in the sample
   b.   the total number of parts to be inspected
   c.   the largest number of defects or defectives in a given sample which will allow the lot (product) to be still acceptable
   d.   the largest number of defectives that are acceptable

Key: c.   the largest number of defects or defectives in a given sample which will allow the lot (product) to be still acceptable
       In the case of acceptance sampling plans for attributes, an acceptance number denoted as c is established from the beginning as a criterion or a limit. This c means that if a lot or sample of parts contains the maximum number (up to c or less) of defectives or defects in a sample, the lot is still acceptable. If the number of defectives exceeds the value of c, then the lot is rejected.

25.   Two quantities which uniquely determine a single sampling attributes plan are

a.   AQL and LTPD
b.   sample size and rejection number
c.   AQL and producer's risk
d.   LTPD and consumer's risk

Key: b.   sample size and rejection number   (Ref. Principles Question 16, July 1984)
MIL-STD-105E[7] defines the sampling plan as a plan that indicates (1) the number of units of product from each lot or batch that are to be inspected (sample size or series of sample sizes), and (2) the criteria for determining the acceptability of the lot or batch (acceptance and rejection numbers). Hence sample size n and rejection number c are the two important quantities for an attribute sampling plan.

26.   Two quantities which uniquely determine a single sampling attributes plan are

a.   AOQL and LTPD
b.   sample size and rejection number
c.   AQL and producer's risk
d.   LTPD and consumer's risk
e.   AQL and LTPD

Key: b.   sample size and rejection number   (Ref. Principles Question 13, August 1978)
Refer to Question 25 above for discussion.

27.   The two quantities that uniquely determine a single attributes sampling plan are

a.   AQL and LTPD
b.   sample size and rejection number
c.   AQL and producer's risk
d.   LTPD and consumer's risk

Key: b.   sample size and rejection number (Ref. Principles Question 31, October 1974)
Refer to Question 25 above for discussion.

28.   The two factors that have the most to do with determining an attribute sampling plan (assuming a binomial distribution) are

a.   sample size and rejection number
b.   lot size and sample size
c.   lot size and acceptance number
d.   none of the above

Key: a.   sample size and rejection number (Ref. Principles Question 57, October 1972)
Refer to Question 25 above for discussion.

---

[7] *MIL-STD-105E, Sampling Procedures and Tables for Inspection by Attributes*, Section 3.22.

29.   The acronym AQL as used in sampling inspection, means

      a.   that level of lot quality for which there is a small risk of rejecting the lot
      b.   the average quality limit
      c.   the maximum percent defectives that can be considered satisfactory as a process average
      d.   the quality level

Key: c.   the maximum percent defectives that can be considered satisfactory as a process average
(Ref. Principles Question 12, July 1984)
MIL-STD-105E[8] defines AQL as *"the quality level which, for the purposes of sampling inspection, is the limit of a satisfactory process average. AQL is the maximum percent or proportion defectives (also called variant units) in a lot or batch that, for the purposes of acceptance sampling, can be considered satisfactory as a process average."*

AQL alone does not identify the chances of accepting or rejecting the individual lots or batches, but it relates more directly to what might be expected from a series of lots or batches provided the steps in referenced AQL sampling plans are followed. It is necessary to refer to the operating characteristic curve of the plan to determine the relative risks.

30.   The maximum percent defectives that can be considered satisfactory as a process average defines

      a.   the term AOQL, i.e., average outgoing quality limit
      b.   the term average quality limit
      c.   the term AQL (acceptable quality level) as used in sampling inspection
      d.   the quality level

Key: c.   the term AQL (acceptable quality level) as used in sampling inspection
MIL-STD-105E[9] states as follows: *The maximum percent or proportion defectives (also called variant units) in a lot or batch that, for the purposes of acceptance sampling, can be considered satisfactory as a process average is defined as acceptable quality level AQL.* Refer to Question 11 above for additional discussion on AQL.

Be careful of choice b, "average quality limit," because it sounds like the acronym AQL. But it is not the same as acceptable quality level.

31.   The acronym AQL as used in sampling inspection means

      a.   the level of lot quality for which there is a small risk of rejecting the lot
      b.   the same as the limiting quality (LQ) or LTPD
      c.   the same as the rejectable quality level (RQL)
      d.   the maximum percent defective that can be considered satisfactory as a process average
      e.   the average outgoing quality level

---

[8] *MIL-STD-105E, Sampling Procedures and Tables for Inspection by Attributes*, Sections 3.1, 3.19, and 4.4.
[9] *MIL-STD-105E, Sampling Procedures and Tables for Inspection by Attributes*, Sections 3.1, 3.19, and 4.4.

Key: d.   the maximum percent defective that can be considered satisfactory as a process average
                (Ref. Principles Question 13, October 1974)
                Refer to Questions 29 and 30 above for additional discussion on AQL.

32.   The AQL for a given sampling plan is 1.0%. This means that

        a.   the producer takes a small risk of rejecting a product which is 1.0% defective or better
        b.   all accepted lots are 1.0% defective or better
        c.   the average quality limit of the plan is 1.0%
        d.   the average quality level of the plan is 1.0%
        e.   all lots are 1.0% defective or better

Key: a.   the producer takes a small risk of rejecting a product which is 1.0% defective or better
                (Ref. Principles Question 19, August 1978)
                MIL-STD-105E Section 3.1 defines Acceptable Quality Level (AQL) as: *"When a continuous
                series of lots is considered, the AQL is the quality level which for the purposes of sampling
                inspection is the limit of a satisfactory process average."* AQL is a designated value of percent
                defective (or defects per 100 units) for which lots will be accepted most of the time by the
                sampling procedure being used. Hence the risk of rejecting a lot of AQL quality is known as
                producer's risk α.

                In the above question an AQL of 1% means that there is 1% producer's risk, i.e., a lot of AQL of
                1% can be rejected by the sampling plan.

33.   AOQL means

        a.   average outgoing quality level
        b.   average outgoing quality limit
        c.   average outside quality limit
        d.   anticipated optimum quality level

Key: b.   average outgoing quality limit (Ref. Principles Question 29, August 1978)
                As an abbreviation, AOQL means average outgoing quality limit. *AOQL is defined in MIL-STD-
                105E,*[10] *as the maximum average outgoing quality over all possible levels of incoming quality
                for a given acceptance sampling plan.*

34.   AOQL is defined as

        a.   a designated value of percent defective or defects per hundred units, for which lots will
                be accepted most of the time by the sampling procedure being used
        b.   average outgoing quality lot
        c.   the maximum AOQ for a given acceptance sampling plan
        d.   the quality level which, for purposes of sampling inspection, is the limit of a satisfactory

---

[10] *MIL-STD-105E, Sampling Procedures and Tables for Inspection by Attributes*, Sections 3.2, 3.18, 3.19, and 3.23.

process average

Key: c.   the maximum AOQ for a given acceptance sampling plan
MIL-STD-105E[11] Section 3.3, AOQL, defines the average outgoing quality limit as the maximum AOQ for a given acceptance sampling plan.

Choices a and d both define acceptable quality level (AQL). Choice b is a wrong title, because AOQL means average outgoing quality *limit* and not average outgoing quality *lot*.

35.   Under acceptance sampling with screening, average outgoing quality will not be worse in the long run than the

a.   ATI
b.   AQL
c.   AOQL
d.   AOQ

Key: c.   AOQL (Ref. Principles Question 29, July 1984)
Average outgoing quality limit (AOQL) is the *maximum* average outgoing quality (AOQ) for a given acceptance sampling plan. For a particular process, AOQ[12] is the average quality of outgoing product including all accepted lots or batches plus all rejected lots or batches after the rejected lots or batches have been effectively 100% inspected and all defectives replaced by non-defectives.

Acceptable quality level (AQL) is the quality level which, for the purposes of sampling inspection, is the limit of a satisfactory process average. Average total inspection (ATI) is defined as the average number of units inspected per lot. It takes into consideration both sample size for the accepted lots and all the units inspected in unaccepted lots.

36.   The basic concept of MIL-STD-105D (now 105E) sampling tables and procedures is that a

a.   poor product is accepted frequently
b.   good product is accepted rarely
c.   poor product is accepted consistently
d.   good product is accepted most of the time

Key: d.   good product is accepted most of the time (Ref. Applications Question 35, October 1972)
You can eliminate most of the choices quickly here. Choices a and c are incorrect. No poor product, i.e., poor quality product, is accepted frequently or consistently under MIL-STD-105E as it will increase the consumer's risk. Similarly, choice b is incorrect because if the good product is accepted rarely, it will increase the producer's risk. The objective is to be able to discriminate between the good lot and bad lot all the time by minimizing both the risks, i.e., to

---

[11] *MIL-STD-105E, Sampling Procedures and Tables for Inspection by Attributes*, Sections 3.2, 3.18, 3.19, and 3.23.
[12] *MIL-STD-105E, Sampling Procedures and Tables for Inspection by Attributes*, Sections 3.2 and 3.3.

minimize the probability of rejecting the lot when it is good (α) as well as the probability of accepting the lot when it is bad (β).

37.   MIL-STD-105E defines the process average as

    a.   one hundred times the number of defective units of product contained therein divided by the total number of units of product

    b.   the average percent defective or average number of defects per hundred units of product submitted by the supplier for the original inspection

    c.   the thing inspected in order to determine its classification as defective or nondefective or to count the number of defects

    d.   the average quality of outgoing product including all accepted lots or batches, plus all rejected lots or batches after the rejected lots or batches have been effectively 100% inspected and all defectives replaced by nondefectives

Key: b.   the average percent defective or average number of defects per hundred units of product submitted by the supplier for the original inspection
Refer to MIL-STD-105E[13] Section 3.19 for the definition of *process average*. Choice a is defined as *percent defective*, choice c is defined as a *unit of product,* and choice d is defined as *average outgoing quality (AOQ)*.

38.   In MIL-STD-105D, the AQL is always determined at what P_a on the OC curve?

    a.   0.05
    b.   0.10
    c.   0.90
    d.   0.95
    e.   None of the above

Key: e.   None of the above
(Ref. Principles Question 4, July 1984, and Principles Question 5, August 1978)
MIL-STD-105E[14] Table X for each sample size code letter provides the percentage of lots or batches which may be expected to be accepted under the various sampling plans for a given process quality. For each curve shown, it gives the values of AQL for different selected values of P_a and not limiting for a single value of P_a. It calculates the value of P_a for different values of AQL, i.e., different values of percent defectives or defects per hundred units, using Poisson distribution or binomial distribution for different sample sizes.

Attribute sampling plans such as MIL-STD-105E define AQL as a specified quality level for each lot such that the sampling plan will accept a stated percentage of all submitted lots of this given quality level. The operating characteristics curve shows a graph of lot fraction defective vs. the probability that the sampling plan will accept the lot. Hence AQL can be determined at

---

[13] *MIL-STD-105E, Sampling Procedures and Tables for Inspection by Attributes*, Sections 3.2, 3.18, 3.19, and 3.23.
[14] *MIL-STD-105E, Sampling Procedures and Tables for Inspection by Attributes*, Sections 4.4.3 and 4.12.1.

different P_a on the OC curve and not at any one P_a level. Different AQLs may be chosen for groups of defects considered collectively or for individual defects. Refer to Sections 4.4.3, Choosing AQLs, and 4.12.1, Operating Characteristic Curves.

39.   As per MIL-STD-105E, the operating characteristic curves for AQLs greater than 10%, applicable for defects per hundred units, are based on

     a.   Poisson distribution
     b.   binomial distribution
     c.   hypergeometric distribution
     d.   p chart

Key: a.   Poisson distribution
Refer to MIL-STD-105E[15] Section 4.12.1, Operating Characteristic Curves. The AQL curves shown in Table X of this standard for AQL values greater than 10.0 are based on Poisson distribution.

Choice b is incorrect because it uses binomial distribution only for AQLs of 10.0 % or less and sample sizes of 80 or less. Choices c and d are incorrect and not applicable.

40.   One of the major limitations of MIL-STD-105E is that

     a.   it is not possible to use different sample sizes
     b.   the sampling plans are only applicable to an AQL of 0.01% or higher and therefore are not suitable for applications where quality levels in the defective parts per million range can be realized
     c.   the sampling plans can be used for either continuing series of lots or for isolated lots or batches
     d.   it does not require the use of OC curves

Key: b.   the sampling plans are only applicable to an AQL of 0.01% or higher and therefore are not suitable for applications where quality levels in the defective parts per million range can be realized
Refer to MIL-STD-105E[16] Section 1.1, Purpose. The sampling plan for attributes is applicable only for an AQL of 0.01% or higher. This can be a limitation of the acceptance sampling plans where high capability is required, i.e., where the percent defectives from a process is very small, expressed as parts per million and not as percentages.

41.   Lots of 75 parts each are inspected to an AQL of 0.25% using normal inspection, single sampling. A single lower specification limit denoted by L is used. The standard level (Level II in MIL-STD-105D, Level IV in MIL-STD-414) is specified. The sample size for MIL-STD-105D is

[15] *MIL-STD-105E, Sampling Procedures and Tables for Inspection by Attributes*, Sections 3.19, 3.2, 3.18, and 3.23.

[16] *MIL-STD-105E, Sampling Procedures and Tables for Inspection by Attributes*, Sections 3.2, 3.18, 3.19, and 3.23.

a.   13
b.   32
c.   50
d.   75

Key: c.   50   (Ref. Applications Question 7, July 1984)

Given: N = 75 parts, AQL = 0.25%, normal inspection, single sampling, Level II for MIL-STD-105E.

Find: The sample size.

To obtain the sampling plan, we need to use AQL = 0.25%, and the code letter. Refer to MIL-STD-105E[17] for Table I in its entirety. We will show partial tables only for this question.

From Table I below, we get code letter **E** for the lot size of 75 parts. But Table II-A shows that there are no sampling plans available for this combination of AQL = 0.25% and code letter E.

Table I Sample size and code letters for inspection level II

Lot or batch size	Special inspection levels				General inspection levels		
	S1	S2	S3	S4	I	II	III
26 to 50	A	B	B	C	C	D	E
51 to 90	B	B	C	C	C	E	F

Hence follow the arrow symbol ↓, which directs you to the first available sampling plan of Ac = 0 and Re = 1, and a new code letter H which corresponds to a sample size of 50.

Table II-A Single sampling plans for normal inspection (Master table)

Sample size code letter	Sample size	Acceptable quality levels (normal inspection)					
		0.15		0.25		0.40	
		Ac	Re	Ac	Re	Ac	Re
D	8	↓		↓		↓	
E→→	13	↓		↓		↓	
F	20	↓		↓		↓	
G	32	↓		↓		0	1
H	50	↓		0	1	↑	
J	80	0	1	↑		↓	

42.   Using MIL-STD-105E, what sample size should be taken from a lot of 1000 pieces for inspection level II with normal inspection?

a.   32

---

[17] *MIL-STD-105E, Sampling Procedures and Tables for Inspection by Attributes*, Sections 4.9.4 and 4.10.1.2.

b.   50
c.   80
d.   100
e.   125

Key: c.   80   (Ref. Applications Question 22, July 1984)
      Given: N = 1000 parts, normal inspection, single sampling, Level II for MIL-STD-105E.
              AQL is not given here! It may be an error.
      Find: The sample size.
      Refer to MIL-STD-105E for the following complete tables, as they are shown partially here.
      From Table I, we get code letter J for the lot size of 1000 parts. To obtain the sampling plan, we
      need to use the AQL and code letter as per MIL-STD-105E. However, the question does not
      provide the AQL, which seems to be an error. The table indicates sample size = 80 for the letter
      code J, but this can be a wrong sample size depending on the value of AQL.

Table I Sample size and code letters for inspection level II

Lot or batch size	Special inspection levels				General inspection levels		
	S1	S2	S3	S4	I	II	III
281 to 500	B	C	D	E	F	H	J
501 to 1200	C	C	E	F	G	J	K
1201 to 3200	C	D	E	G	H	K	L

Table II-A Single sampling plans for normal inspection (Master table)

Sample size code letter	Sample size	Acceptable quality levels (normal inspection)					
		0.15		0.25		0.40	
		Ac	Re	Ac	Re	Ac	Re
G	32	⬇		⬇		0	1
H	50	⬇		0	1	⬆	
J	80	0	1	⬇		⬇	
K	125	⬇		⬇		1	2
L	200	⬇		1	2	2	3
M	315	1	2	2	3	3	4

Few values of AQL are shown in the example above. You can see, depending on the direction of
the arrow, the table directs you to a value above or below the arrow for different AQLs. It means
the code letter can be any other letter than J, and hence the sample size can be different. For
example, AQL = 0.15% assumed, then sample size = 80 for J. If AQL = 0.25% is assumed, the
⬆ arrow indicates the code letter H and sample size = 50. Hence it is important to know the
AQL.

43.   MIL-STD-105D is to be used to select a single sampling plan for lots of 8000 under normal
      inspection Level II and an AQL of 2.5%. The exact AOQL for the plan is

a.   2.50%
b.   3.00%
c.   3.22%
d.   3.30%
e.   2.60%

Key: c.   3.22% (Ref. Applications Question 4, August 1978)
       Given: MIL-STD-105E, N = 8000, Inspection Level II, AQL = 2.5%
       Find: AOQL
       From Table I below, we can see that the code letter is L for N = 10000. Section 3.3 defines the average outgoing quality limit (AOQL) as the maximum AOQ for a given acceptance sampling plan. Table V-A gives the AOQL values.

Table I Sample size and code letters for inspection level II

Lot or batch size	Special inspection levels				General inspection levels		
	S1	S2	S3	S4	I	II	III
1201 to 3200	C	D	E	G	H	K	L
3201 to 10000	C	D	F	G	J	L	M
10001 to 35000	C	D	F	H	K	M	N

Table V-A Average outgoing quality limit factors for normal inspection (single sampling)

Code letter	Sample size	Acceptable quality levels		
		1.5	2.5	4.0
K	125		3.6	
L	200		3.3	
M	315		3.0	

From the above table, AOQL factor = 3.3. The exact AOQL is multiplied by a factor as follows.

$$AOQL = 3.3 \times \left(1 - \frac{Sample\ size}{Lot\ or\ batch\ size}\right) = 3.3 \times \left(1 - \frac{200}{8000}\right) = 3.3 \times 0.975 = 3.2175 \approx 3.22.$$

Choice c is correct. Be careful to multiply the AOQL factor from the table by (1 − Sample size/lot or batch size) to get the exact AOQL. If you do not do this, you may pick choice d, 3.3 obtained from Table V-A, as your answer, which will be obviously wrong.

44.   On the production floor, parts being produced measure 0.992-1.011. The specification requires the parts to be 0.995-1.005. Which of the following techniques would not be particularly useful in trying to improve and control the process?

       a.   Pre-Control
       b.   MIL-STD-105 charts
       c.   Multi-vari charts

     d. $\overline{X}$ and R charts

     e.   Machine capability analysis

Key: b.   MIL-STD-105 charts (Ref. Applications Question 36, August 1978)
The key term is *not be particularly useful.* MIL-STD-105 is a standard of the sampling procedures and tables for inspection by attributes but they are not any type of control chart. The data above in the question are for *variables, not attributes.* Also, as compared to the remaining choices, MIL-STD-105 tables are not particularly more useful in trying to improve and control the process.

45.   A single sampling plan calls for a sample size of 80 with an acceptance number of 5 and a rejection number of 6. If the quality of the submitted lots is 10% defective, then the percent of lots expected to be accepted in the long run is approximately

     a.   6%

     b.   10%

     c.   30%

     d.   0%

     e.   20%

Key: e.   20%   (Ref. Applications Question 4, October 1974)
     Given: n = 80, Acceptance Number = 5, and p = 0.10, or 10% defective.
     Find: The percent of lots to be accepted, i.e., probability of accepting a lot.
     The data give n = 80 >16 and p = 0.10, which meets the conditions of Poisson distribution.[18]
     For np = 80 × 0.1 = 8 and r = 5 as the acceptance number we will use the Poisson distribution.
     From the Poisson table the probability of accepting a lot is given as $P(r \leq 1) = 0.191$ or 19.1%.
     Only choice e, 20%, is the closest answer. This can also be solved using binomial distribution but it is a lengthy approach.

46.   Select one sampling plan from MIL-STD-105D that meets the following requirements:
lot size = 1000, AQL = 0.65%, inspection level II, tightened inspection.

     a.   Sample size = 125 Ac = 1, Re = 2

     b.   Sample size = 200 Ac = 1, Re = 2

     c.   Sample size = 80 Ac = 1, Re = 2

     d.   Sample size = 50 Ac = 0, Re = 2

     e.   Sample size = 80 Ac = 8, Re = 9

Key: a.   Sample size = 125, Ac = 1, Re = 2 (Ref. Applications Question 25, October 1974)
     Given: N = 1000, AQL = 0.65%, inspection level II Tightened, MIL-STD-105E.
     Find: The sampling plan
     Refer to MIL-STD-105E Table I, partially shown below for N = 1000, to obtain the sampling plan. We need to use AQL = 0.65% and code letter J.

---

[18] *Juran's Quality Control Handbook* by J. M. Juran, 4th ed., McGraw-Hill, New York, pg. 23.29.

Table I Sample size and code letters for inspection level II for N = 1000 parts.

Lot or batch size	Special inspection levels				General inspection levels		
	S1	S2	S3	S4	I	II	III
281 to 500	B	C	D	E	F	H	J
501 to 1200	C	C	E	F	G	J	K
1201 to 3200	C	D	E	G	H	K	L

Table II-B below indicates that n =125, Ac = 1, and Re = 2 are the required sampling plan. Choice a is the correct choice for the sampling plan.

Table II-B Single sampling plans for tightened inspection (Master table)

Sample size code letter	Sample size	Acceptable quality levels (normal inspection)					
		0.40		0.65		1.00	
		Ac	Re	Ac	Re	Ac	Re
G	32	↓		0	1	↓	
H	50	0	1	↓		↓	
J	80	↓		↓		1	2
K	125	↓		1	2	2	3
L	200	1	2	2	3	3	4

47.   The AOQL of the single sampling plan with a sample size of 200, acceptance number of 14, and rejection number of 15, for a lot size of 4000, is approximately

   a.   10.0%
   b.   4.5%
   c.   4.0%
   d.   7.2%

Key: b.   4.5%   (Ref. Applications Question 47, October 1974)
       Given: MIL-STD-105E, N = 4000, n = 200, Ac = 14, Re = 15, and AQL is not given here.
       Find: AOQL

Table I Sample size and code letters for inspection level II for N = 4000

Lot or batch size	Special inspection levels				General inspection levels		
	S1	S2	S3	S4	I	II	III
1201 to 3200	C	D	E	G	H	K	L
3201 to 10000	C	D	F	G	J	L	M
10001 to 35000	C	D	F	H	K	M	N

Refer to MIL-STD-105E for complete tables. Table I is partially shown above, which gives the code letter L for N = 4000.

Table II-A Single sampling plans for normal inspection (Master table)

Sample size code letter	Sample size	Acceptable quality levels (normal inspection)					
		2.5		4.0		6.5	
		Ac	Re	Ac	Re	Ac	Re
K	125	7	8	10	11	14	15
L	200	10	11	14	15	21	22
M	315	14	15	21	22	↑	

For n = 200, Ac = 14, and Re = 15, we get **AQL = 4.0.**
MIL-STD-105E, Section 3.3 defines the average outgoing quality limit (AOQL) as the maximum AOQ for a given acceptance sampling plan. Table V-A gives the AOQL values as follows:

Table V-A Average outgoing quality limit factors for normal inspection (single sampling)

Code letter	Sample size	Acceptable quality levels		
		2.5	4.0	6.5
K	125	3.6	5.2	7.5
L	200	3.3	4.7	7.3
M	315	3.0	4.7	

From Table V-A, AOQL factor = 4.7. Exact AOQL is multiplied by the 4.7 factor as follows:

$$AOQL = 4.7 \times \left(1 - \frac{Sample\ size}{Lot\ or\ batch\ size}\right) = 4.7 \times \left(1 - \frac{200}{4000}\right) = 4.7 \times 0.95 = 4.465 \approx 4.5.$$

Choice b is correct.

48. You have just been put in charge of incoming inspection and have decided to institute a sampling plan on a small gear which your company uses in considerable quantity. The vendor ships them to you in lots of 1000. You have decided to use MIL-STD-105D inspection level II and AQL = 4.0%. Naturally, your inspectors, never having used scientific sampling, are interested in seeing how it works. The first lot is inspected and accepted. One of the inspectors says, "This means that the lot is not more than four percent defective." Assuming the sample was randomly taken and no inspection errors were made, which one of the following would you accept?

    a.   The inspector's statement is correct.
    b.   The probability of accepting the lot is about 0.99.
    c.   You should go to reduced sampling.
    d.   The lot may be 10% defective.
    e.   all of the above

Key: d.   The lot may be 10% defective. (Ref. Applications Question 66, October 1974)
        Given: N = 1000, MIL-STD-105E, inspection level II, AQL = 4%; the first lot is passed.
        Find: The correct choice about the inspector's decision.

Table I Sample size and code letters for inspection level II for N = 1000 parts

Lot or batch size	Special inspection levels				General inspection levels		
	S1	S2	S3	S4	I	II	III
281 to 500	B	C	D	E	F	H	J
501 to 1200	C	C	E	F	G	J	K
1201 to 3200	C	D	E	G	H	K	L

Refer to MIL-STD-105E Table I, partially shown above for N = 1000, to obtain the sampling plan which gives letter J. Table II-A shown partially below indicates that we need to use AQL = 4% and code letter J. This suggests use of n = 80, Ac = 7 and Re = 8 as the required sampling plan.

Table II-A Single sampling plans for normal inspection (Master table)

Sample size code letter	Sample size	Acceptable quality levels (normal inspection)					
		2.5		4.0		6.5	
		Ac	Re	Ac	Re	Ac	Re
H	50	3	4	5	6	7	8
J	80	5	6	7	8	10	11
K	125	7	8	10	11	14	15

Now let's make an operating characteristic curve for n = 80, p = 0.04, or np = 80 × 0.04 = 3.2 using a Poisson table shown below.

100 p percent defective	np for n = 80 A = 7	P_a for n = 80 A = 7	100 p percent defective	np for n = 80 A = 7	P_a for n = 80 A = 7	100 p percent defective	np for n = 80 A = 7	P_a for n = 80 A = 7
0	1	1.00	5	4.0	0.949	10	8.0	0.453
1	0.8		6	4.8	0.887	11	8.8	0.349
2	1.6	1.00	7	5.6	0.797	12	9.6	0.259
3	2.4	0.997	8	6.4	0.687			
4	3.2	0.983	9	7.2	0.569			

Fig. 8-4 shows the operating characteristic curve obtained based on the Poisson probability distribution for n = 80 and acceptance number Ac = 7. The AQL is 4%, for which the probability of acceptance P_a = 0.983 at np = 3.2. which means the producer's risk is 1 − 0.983 = 0.017, or 1.7%.

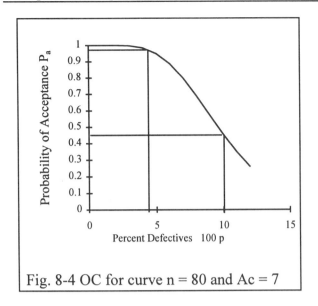

Fig. 8-4 OC for curve n = 80 and Ac = 7

It means that a lot with 4% AQL can be rejected 1.7% of the time even though it may be a good lot. But if the lot is 10% defective, it should be considered as a bad lot and should be rejected because the AQL is 4% and not 10%. However, the OC curve indicates that a lot at a 10% defective level can be accepted 45.3% of the time, i.e., $P_a = 0.453$.

The inspector inspected the lot and accepted it. It does not mean that the lot was good. It may have 10% more or less defectives and still be accepted as seen above. Hence choice d is the most appropriate. You can also eliminate the remaining choices with logic.

Looking at the OC curve above, the lot can be more than 4% defective and still be accepted. Hence choice a, i.e., the inspector's statement about the lot being less than 4% defectives, is incorrect. Choice b is incorrect because, from the Poisson table, the probability of accepting the lot at 4% defectives is 98.3% and not about 99%.

Answers like this one are borderline answers because you can be tempted to round off 98.3% to 99% as the closest answer. Choice c is incorrect because as per MIL-STD-105E,[19] the reduced inspection is instituted when the preceding 10 lots have been on normal inspection and all have been accepted on original inspection. This condition is not met here as the inspector has only inspected the first lot and not 10 lots. Choice e is proved to be incorrect based on the other choices above.

49.   A certain part is produced in lot quantities of 1000. Prior history shows that 90% of the production lots are 1% defective or better, but the remaining 10% range between 5% and 10% defective. A defective part costs $5 to repair at this point but the same defect will average $80 if allowed to be installed in the next higher assembly. Inspection at this part level costs $1.50 per part and rejected lots will be sorted at your expense. What inspection plan would you specify for this part?

   a.   100% inspection
   b.   no inspection
   c.   n = 32, A = 1, R = 2 (single sampling)
   d.   n = 50, A = 0, R = 1 (single sampling)
   e.   n = 5,   A = 1, R = 2 (single sampling)

Key: c.   n = 32, A = 1, R = 2 (single sampling) (Ref. Applications Question 41, July 1984)
       Given: N = 1000, 90% lots are 1% defective or better, 10 % of the lots are 5 to 10% defectives; cost to repair the defective part is $5; cost of assembly if defect passed is $80; and cost of

[19] *MIL-STD-105E, Sampling Procedures and Tables for Inspection by Attributes*, Section 4.7.3.

inspection is $1.50.

Find: The inspection plan.

This question requires a good understanding of many concepts. It also involves significant and lengthy calculations and can be very time consuming from an examination point of view. Be careful and, if necessary, try to solve such a lengthy question at a later time in the examination. First go through the remaining questions, which may be easier or less time consuming.

50.   The inspection should be switched, per MIL-STD-105E, from tightened to normal when

   a.   2 out of 2, 3, 4, or 5 consecutive lots or batches have been rejected on original inspection when normal inspection was in effect
   b.   5 consecutive lots or batches have been considered acceptable on original inspection when tightened inspection was in effect
   c.   when the preceding 10 lots or batches have been on normal inspection and all have been accepted on original inspection
   d.   a lot or batch is rejected when it is under reduced inspection

Key: b.   5 consecutive lots or batches have been considered acceptable on original inspection when tightened inspection was in effect

Refer to MIL-STD-105E[20] Section 4.7.2, which defines the *tightened to normal switching* process as: "*when tightened inspection is in effect, normal inspection shall be instituted when 5 consecutive lots or batches have been considered acceptable on original inspection.*"

51.   According to MIL-STD-105E, which one of the following is not an inspection switching procedure?

   a.   normal to tightened
   b.   tightened to reduced
   c.   tightened to normal
   d.   normal to reduced
   e.   reduced to normal

Key: b.   tightened to reduced

Refer to MIL-STD-105E[21] Section 4.7, which defines the switching procedures for procedures indicated in choices a, c, d, and e.

52.   MIL-STD-105D sampling plans allow reduced inspection when four requirements are met. One of these is

   a.   inspection level I is specified
   b.   10 lots have been on normal inspection and none have been rejected
   c.   the process average is less than the AOQL

---

[20] *MIL-STD-105E, Sampling Procedures and Tables for Inspection by Attributes*, Sections 4.7.2.
[21] *MIL-STD-105E, Sampling Procedures and Tables for Inspection by Attributes*, Sections 4.7.

    d.   the maximum percent defective is less than the AQL
    e.   all of the above

Key: b.   10 lots have been on normal inspection and none have been rejected
(Ref. Principles Question 18, August 1978)
MIL-STD-105E is the latest revision of the standard. This standard in Section 4.7 defines the
switching procedures for *normal to tightened, tightened to normal, and normal to reduced* cases.
Section 4.7.3 defines the normal to reduced switching procedures as follows.

*"When normal inspection is in effect, reduced inspection shall be instituted provided that all of
the following conditions are satisfied.*
    *1. The preceding 10 lots or batches (or more, as indicated by the note to Table VIII of
       this standard) have been on normal inspection and all have been accepted on original
       inspection; and*
    *2. The total number of defectives (or defects) in the samples from the preceding 10 lots or
       batches (or such other number as was used for condition 1 above) is equal to or less
       than the applicable number given in Table VIII. If double or multiple sampling is in
       use, all samples inspected should be included, not 'first' samples only; and*
    3. Production is at a steady rate; and
    4. Reduced inspection is considered desirable."
The above four conditions meet choice b as an answer.

53.   Selection of a sampling plan from the Dodge Romig AOQL sampling tables

    a.   requires an estimate of AOQ
    b.   requires an estimate of the process average
    c.   requires sorting of rejected lots
    d.   requires larger samples than MIL-STD-105E (used to be D) for equivalent quality
          assurance
    e.   requires that we assume the consumer's risk of 0.05

Key: b.   requires an estimate of the process average   (Ref. Principles Question 14, August 1978)
The Dodge Romig AOQL sampling plans (both single sampling and double sampling plans) are
constructed to give minimum total inspection for products of a *given process average,* i.e., they
require an estimate of the process average. These tables are classified according to the average
outgoing quality limit (AOQL) which ranges from 0.10 to 10.0%.

54.   Selection of a sampling plan from the Dodge Romig LTPD sampling tables

    a.   requires knowledge of the AOQ
    b.   requires knowledge of the process average
    c.   requires sorting of rejected lots
    d.   requires larger samples than MIL-STD-105D (now E) for equivalent quality assurance

Key: b. requires knowledge of the process average (Ref. Principles Question 34, October 1974) Refer to Question 53 for discussion.

55. The Dodge Romig tables are classified according to their

    a. AOQL
    b. AQL
    c. LTPD
    d. AOQ

Key: c. LTPD

The Dodge Romig Sampling Inspection Tables are important tables and they use the term LTPD (lot tolerance percent defectives) defined as *allowable percent defective, which has a probability of acceptance of P_a.*

56. To achieve consistent lot-by-lot protection the receiving inspector should

    a. allow no defective product into the shop
    b. return all rejected lots to the vendor
    c. not know how the vendor inspects the product
    d. use a sampling plan based on LTPD

Key: d. use a sampling plan based on LTPD (Ref. Principles Question 17, October 1972)
Lot tolerance percent defective (LTPD) is the percentage of defectives that is unsatisfactory and unacceptable and hence should be rejected by the sampling plan. It is the unacceptable quality level, i.e., the rejectable quality level, and it should have low probability of being accepted. It has low consumer's risk, i.e., beta (β) risk.

If the customer requirements indicate that a lot having 1% defectives should be consistently rejected lot by lot, the plan should use 1% LTPD, i.e., it will have a very low probability of accepting a lot having 1% defectives and it will protect the customer more. Dodge Romig[22] have published tables of sampling plans based on their LTPD, which enables the receiving inspection to ensure that a lot of a particular LTPD has low probability of acceptance.

Choice a means that either the producer or the customer does the 100% inspection of each lot to ensure that no defective product is shipped. This is generally not economical and it is less effective. Choice b is also not the best choice because it describes the containment and disposition of nonconforming or rejected lots. It only protects the customer if the lot of poor quality was caught; however, based on the sampling plans used, there is always some probability of accepting a lot of bad quality, which we would like to minimize. Also, it may require 100% inspection and a sorting operation at the customer's location and the producer's involvement. The producer should use proper sampling plans to minimize both producer's risk and consumer's

[22] *Statistical Quality Control Handbook* by Western Electric Co. Inc., AT&T, IN., pg. 249; and *Juran's Quality Control Handbook* by J. M. Juran, 4th ed., McGraw-Hill, New York, pg. 25.9 and Table 25.15 on pg. 25.50.

risk and should not ship any nonconforming lots. If a customer has to inspect all the lots, identify the rejected lots, and return them to the producer, it is not advisable practice for the producer in the long run and can result in loss of business in today's highly competitive market.

Choice c is also not preferable because the customer should have the assurance that the control plan used by the vendor for process control is adequate to meet the product requirements and specifications consistently from lot to lot. In many cases, the customer's procuring activities require that a control plan be submitted along with the sample parts for approval. This also assures that proper economical control methods are used for the expected level of quality.

57.   The Dodge Romig sampling tables for AOQL protection

   a.   require sorting of rejected lots
   b.   are the same in principle as the MIL-STD-105D tables
   c.   do not depend upon the process average
   d.   require larger samples than MIL-STD-105D for equivalent quality assurances

Key: a.   require sorting of rejected lots (Ref. Applications Question 40, October 1972)
       The AOQL is the maximum average outgoing quality (AOQ) for a given sampling plan. *For a particular process average, AOQ is the average quality of an outgoing product, including all accepted lots or batches, plus all rejected lots or batches after the rejected lots or batches have been effectively 100% inspected and all defectives replaced by nondefectives.*
       The Dodge Romig AOQL sampling plans (both single sampling and double sampling plans) are constructed to give minimum total inspection for products of a *given process average,* i.e., it requires an estimate of the process average. These tables are classified according to the average outgoing quality limit (AOQL) which ranges from 0.10 to 10.0. Hence choice a is the correct answer. As AOQL depends on the process average, choice c is incorrect. Choices b and d are incorrect because MIL-STD-105E provides the sampling plan for a given sample size and acceptance number c. It does not take into consideration the process average and the rejected lots. Also refer to Question 58 below.

58.   The Dodge Romig tables for AOQL protection are designed to provide

   a.   minimum average sampling costs
   b.   maximum protection against poor material
   c.   maximum risk of accepting good lots
   d.   minimum average total inspection for a given process average

Key: d.   minimum average total inspection for a given process average
       (Ref. Applications Question 60, October 1972)
       Refer to Questions 57 and 61 for a detailed explanation.

59.   The Dodge Romig tables are designed to minimize which parameter?

     a.   AOQL
     b.   AQL
     c.   ATI
     d.   AOQ

Key: c.   ATI   (Ref. Principles Question 8, July 1984)

The average total inspection (ATI)[23] is defined as the average number of units inspected per lot. It takes into consideration both the sample size for the accepted lots and all the units inspected in unaccepted lots. The Dodge Romig tables aim at minimizing the ATI, considering the sampling inspection of accepted lots and screening inspection, i.e., 100% inspection of rejected lots.

The aim of minimizing the ATI depends upon the number of rejected lots that must be 100% inspected and the quality level of the submitted products. For a single sampling plan, ATI is expressed as $ATI = nP_a + N(1 - P_a)$ where n is the sample size, N is the lot size, and P_a is the probability of accepting a lot.

60.   You are to construct an OC curve. Which of the following cannot be used as an abscissa value?

     a.   AOQL
     b.   ASN
     c.   AQL
     d.   LTPD
     e.   All of these can be abscissa values.

Key: b.   ASN   (Ref. Applications Question 19, August 1978)

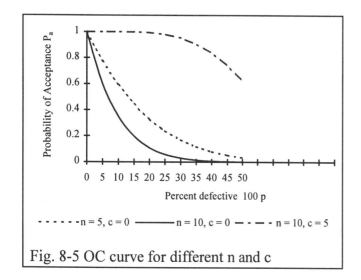

Fig. 8-5 OC curve for different n and c

The OC curve in Fig. 8-5, provides the probability of acceptance on the Y axis (called an ordinate in the Cartesian coordinate system) for different values of defectives p or percent of defectives (100p) on the X axis (called the abscissa) using distributions like Poisson or binomial, etc. Different OC curves can be plotted for different values of sample size n and acceptance number. However, it does not use sample size n as the abscissa value. AOQL, AQL, and LTPD refer to different types of quality levels or defectives, which can be used as the abscissa or X axis on the OC curve.

The ASN is defined as the average number of units inspected per lot in sampling inspection; here

[23] *Juran's Quality Control Handbook* by J. M. Juran, 4th ed., McGraw-Hill, New York, pg. 25.13 - 25.14; *Glossary and Tables for Statistical Quality Control* prepared by ASQC, Quality Press, Milwaukee, WI, 2nd ed., Section 5.10; and *Statistical Quality Control* by E. Grant and R. Leavenworth, 6th ed., McGraw-Hill, New York, pg. 428-430.

100% inspection of any rejected lots is not considered. Fig. 8-6 shows the ASN curve. In the case of the single sampling, the ASN is the same as sample size n. In the case of double sampling, the size of the selected sample depends upon whether or not the second sample is necessary.

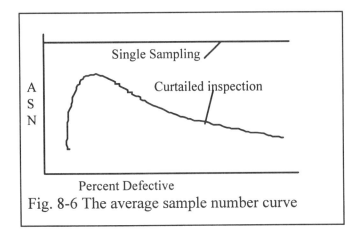

Fig. 8-6 The average sample number curve

The probability of drawing the second sample will vary with the fraction defectives or the quality of the incoming lot.

Hence ASN[24] cannot be an abscissa or X axis legend, as it does not represent the defectives but represents the average sample size only. There are some curves of ASN also available, called ASN curves, which plot percent defectives on the X axis or abscissa, and ASN on the Y axis, or ordinate.

If the inspection of the second sample is terminated and the lot is rejected as soon as the number of observed defectives in the cumulative samples exceed the second acceptance number c_2, it is called the curtailment[25] of the second sample.

61.   A cost estimate associated with average outgoing quality protection is determined from the

       a.   average total inspection
       b.   average outgoing quality
       c.   average sample size
       d.   acceptable quality limit

Key: a.   average total inspection (Ref. Applications Question 45, October 1972)
       The average total inspection (ATI)[26] is defined as the average number of units inspected per lot. It takes into consideration both sample size for the accepted lots and all the units inspected in unaccepted lots. The Dodge Romig tables aim at minimizing the ATI, considering the sampling inspection of accepted lots and screening inspection, i.e., 100% inspection of rejected lots. This helps determine and optimize the cost estimates associated with AOQ protection for inspected lots and sorting of rejected lots. AOQ by itself may not lead to a cost estimate but ATI can make it simple.

       AQL defines the acceptable process level but does not lead directly to a cost estimate for the average outgoing quality. ASN is defined as the average number of units inspected per lot in sampling inspection, and here 100% inspection of any rejected lots is not considered.

[24] *Juran's Quality Control Handbook* by J. M. Juran, 4th ed., McGraw-Hill, New York, pg. 25.12-13.

[25] *Introduction to Statistical Quality Control* by D. C. Montgomery, 2nd ed., John Wiley and Sons, Inc., New York, pg. 574.

[26] *Juran's Quality Control Handbook* by J. M. Juran, 4th ed., McGraw-Hill, New York, pg. 25.13 - 25.14; *Glossary and Tables for Statistical Quality Control* prepared by ASQC, Quality Press, Milwaukee, WI, 2nd ed., Section 5.10; and *Statistical Quality Control* by E. Grant and R. Leavenworth, 5th ed., McGraw-Hill, New York, Chapter 13, pg. 430-432.

The aim of minimizing the ATI depends upon the number of rejected lots that must be 100% inspected and the quality level of the submitted products. For a single sampling plan, ATI is expressed as $ATI = nP_a + N(1- P_a)$ where n is the sample size, and N is the lot size, and P_a is the probability of accepting a lot.

62.   A double sampling plan means

   a.   double the sample size and compare the number of defectives to the acceptance and rejection numbers applicable to the code letter of double sample size for a given AQL

   b.   a tightened inspection when 2 out of 2, 3, 4, or 5 consecutive lots or batches have been rejected on original inspection

   c.   a tightened inspection when 5 consecutive lots or batches have been considered acceptable on original inspection

   d.   if the number of defectives found in the first sample is between the first sample's acceptance and rejection numbers, take a second sample of the same size and inspect the number of defectives as cumulative of both samples against the acceptance and rejection numbers of the second sample

Key: d.   if the number of defectives found in the first sample is between the first sample's acceptance and rejection numbers, take a second sample of the same size and inspect the number of defectives as cumulative of both samples against the acceptance and rejection numbers of the second sample

MIL-STD-105E[27] describes the procedure for determining the acceptability of a lot or batch under percent defectives inspection under Section 4.10.1.2, Double Sampling Plan as follows: *"A number of the sample units equal to the first sample size given by the plan shall be inspected. If the number of defectives found in the first sample is equal to or less than the first acceptance number, the lot or batch shall be considered acceptable. If the number of defectives found in the first sample is equal to or greater than the first rejection number, the lot or batch shall be rejected. If the number of defectives found in the first sample is between the first acceptance and rejection numbers, a second sample of the same size shall be inspected. The number of the defectives found in the first and second sample shall be accumulated. If the cumulative number of defectives is equal to or less than the second acceptance number, the lot or batch shall be considered acceptable. If the cumulative number of defectives is equal to or greater than the second rejection number, the lot or batch shall be rejected."*

63.   Double sampling is better than single sampling because

   a.   it is more economical regardless of lot quality
   b.   it is easier to administer
   c.   it gives the lot a second chance
   d.   if the first sample rejects the lot, the second will accept it
   e.   it involves less inspection when the lots are of very good or very poor quality

---

[27] *MIL-STD-105E, Sampling Procedures and Tables for Inspection by Attributes*, Section 4.10.1.2.

Key: e.   it involves less inspection when the lots are of very good or very poor quality
        (Ref. Principles Question 76, October 1974)
        Refer to MIL-STD-105E[28] Sections 4.9.4, Types of Sampling Plans, and 4.10.1.2, Double
        Sampling Plan, and for complete Table II-A and Table III-A. We will show partial tables only for
        the example below.

    I: Single sampling case, Table II-A (partially shown below) letter code H and AQL = 2.5%, gives
            $n_1 = 50$ (sample size),
            $c_1 = 3$ (acceptance number), i.e., accept the lot if the number of defectives is 3 or less,
            $c_2 = 4$ (rejection number), i.e., reject the sample if the number of defectives is more than
                3, i.e., if the number of defectives is 4 or more.

Table II-A Single sampling plans for normal inspection (Master table)

Sample size code letter	Sample size	Acceptable quality levels (normal inspection) 2.5%	
		Ac	Re
G	32	2	3
H	50	3	4
J	80	5	6

    II: Double sampling case: letter code H, AQL = 2.5%, from Table III-A we get:
    First sample: $n_1 = 32$ sample size, $c_1 = 1$ acceptance number; $R_{e1} = 4$ rejection number.
    Second sample: $n_2 = 32$, $c_2 = 4$, and $R_{e2} = 5$.

    If x_1 = number of defectives found in the *first* sample,
            $x_1 \leq 1$ one or fewer defective, accept the lot
            $x_1 \geq 4$ 4 or more defectives, reject the lot
            $1 < x_1 < 4$ more than 1 but less than 4, take second sample of 32

Table III-A Double sampling plans for normal inspection (Master table)

Sample size code letter	Sample	Sample size	Cumulative sample size	Acceptable quality levels (normal inspection) 2.5%	
				Ac	Re
G	First	20	20	0	3
G	Second	20	40	3	4
H	First	32	32	1	4
H	Second	32	64	4	5
J	First	50	50	2	5
J	Second	50	100	6	7

---

[28] *MIL-STD-105E, Sampling Procedures and Tables for Inspection by Attributes*, Sections 4.9.4 and 4.10.1.2.

If x_2 = cumulative number of defectives in the *first and second* samples,

$x_2 \leq 4$ 4 or fewer defectives as a cumulative, accept the lot

$x_2 \geq 5$ 5 or more defectives as a cumulative, reject the lot

As we can see, if the lot is of very good quality, i.e., contains 1 or fewer defective, we need only $n_1 = 32$ (sample size) in double sampling vs. $n_1 = 50$ in single sampling. Similarly, if the lot is of very bad quality, i.e., it contains 4 or more defectives, we need only $n_1 = 32$ (sample size) in double sampling for a decision, vs. $n_1 = 50$ in single sampling. The above detailed comparison is made to explain to you the concepts of single sampling and double sampling. Duncan[29] provides the OC curves for determining the probability of accepting and probability of rejecting the sample on the first sample in the case of double sampling. These curves show high probability of accepting the lot if the lots are of very good quality and high probability of rejecting the lot if the lots are of very bad quality based on the results of the first sample. Hence this involves fewer samples in inspection. Juran[30] has shown a "Schematic operation of double sampling" in Fig. 25.7 and has discussed *comparative advantages and disadvantages of single, double, and multiple sampling* in Table 25.5.

Choices a and b are incorrect because the double sampling plans are generally not more economical since they require greater administrative cost in training personnel, keeping records, and drawing samples and inspecting them regardless of lot quality. Double sampling plans require an understanding of acceptance criteria based on first and second samples and hence they are difficult to administer.

Choices c and d are incorrect because giving the lot a second chance as per Duncan[31] is only a psychological advantage to a producer. The producers may think that it is unfair that the lot is rejected on the basis of a single sample and that it is possible that the lot would be acceptable if a second sample is taken. However, it is only a psychological myth. If the lots are inspected using the single sampling or double sampling plan, they will be equally fair and discriminating if they have the same OC curve.

64.   Double sampling is better than single sampling because

       a.   it involves less inspection regardless of lot quality
       b.   if the first sample rejects the lot, the second sample will accept it
       c.   it is more economical except when lots are of borderline quality
       d.   it is easier to administer

Key: c.   it is more economical except when lots are of borderline quality
           (Ref. Principles Question 73, October 1972)

---

[29] *Quality Control and Industrial Statistics* by A. J. Duncan, 5th ed., 1986, Irwin, Homewood, IL, Section 1.1, Chapter 8, Fig. 8.1, pg. 185.

[30] *Juran's Quality Control Handbook* by J. M. Juran, 4th ed., McGraw-Hill, New York, pg. 25.28, Fig. 25.7 and pg. 25.22, Table 25.5.

[31] *Quality Control and Industrial Statistics* by A. J. Duncan, 5th ed., 1986, Irwin, Homewood, IL, Section 1.1, Chapter 8, pg. 184-185.

Please refer to Question 63 above for discussion.

65.   In comparison with attributes sampling plans, variables sampling plans

        a.   have the advantage of greater simplicity
        b.   usually require a larger sample size for comparable assurance as to correctness of
                decisions in judging a single quality characteristic
        c.   have the advantage of being applicable to either single or multiple quality characteristics
        d.   provide greater assurance for the same sample size, as to the correctness or decisions in
                judging a single quality characteristic

Key: d.   provide greater assurance for the same sample size, as to the correctness or decisions
                in judging a single quality characteristic (Ref. Principles Question 21, July 1984)
                MIL-STD-414[32] states as follows: *In comparison with attribute sampling plans, variables
                sampling plans have the advantage of usually resulting in considerable savings in sample size
                for comparable assurance as to the correctness of decisions in judging a single quality
                characteristic or for the same sample size, greater assurance is obtained using variable plans.*
                Also refer to Question 66 below for additional discussion.

66.   Your major product cannot be fully inspected without destruction. You have been requested to
        plan the inspection program, including some product testing, in the most cost-effective manner.
        You most probably will recommend that samples selected for product verification be based upon

        a.   MIL-STD-105D latest issue (it is E), attribute sampling
        b.   MIL-STD-414 latest issue, variable sampling
        c.   either answer a or b above will meet your criteria
        d.   neither answer a nor b above will meet your criteria

Key: b.   MIL-STD-414 latest issue, variable sampling
                (Ref. Applications Question 29, August 1978)
                The key word here is *destructive testing* of the product; i.e., the product is destroyed and no
                longer useful after inspection and testing. It means we cannot afford to waste or consume large
                numbers of parts for inspection and testing. From the choices given above, MIL-STD-414 should
                be selected because it requires a smaller number of samples as compared to the MIL-STD-105E
                attributes sampling plans. MIL-STD-414[33] states as follows: *In comparison with attribute
                sampling plans, variables sampling plans have the advantage of usually resulting in
                considerable savings in sample size for comparable assurance as to the correctness of decisions
                in judging a single quality characteristic, or for the same sample size, greater assurance is
                obtained using variable plans.*

                Juran[34] provides a comparison of variables and attributes sample sizes. This comparison

---

[32] *MIL-STD-414, Sampling Procedures and Tables for Inspection by Variables for Percent Defective*, refer to Introduction.
[33] *MIL-STD-414, Sampling Procedures and Tables for Inspection by Variables for Percent Defective*, refer to Introduction.
[34] *Juran's Quality Control Handbook* by J. M. Juran, 4th ed., McGraw-Hill, New York, pg. 25.7, Table 25.2.

indicates that for the case of known sigma the sample size is 19, for unknown sigma it is 52, and for single sampling attributes, the sample size is very large, i.e., 125.

67.   Which of the following is/are the principal disadvantage(s) of the variables sampling plan?

   a.   A separate plan must be employed for each quality characteristic under inspection
   b.   Under the variables sampling plan, a lot will be rejected by the variables criteria, even though the actual sample contains no nonconforming items
   c.   The distribution of the quality characteristic must be of the specified form
   d.   all of the above

Key: d.   all of the above
   Duncan[35] describes the three items in a, b, and c as the principal disadvantages of the variables sampling plans. In Table 25.1, Juran[36] provides a valuable comparison of attributes and variables sampling plans for percent defective along with the strengths and limitations of the variables sampling plans.

68.   A comparison of variable and attribute sampling systems will show that equal protection (as determined by the OC curves) can be obtained

   a.   when the variable and attribute sample sizes are equal
   b.   when the attribute sample is smaller than the variable sample
   c.   when the variable sample is smaller than the attribute sample
   d.   none of these

Key: c.   when the variable sample is smaller than the attribute sample
   (Ref. Principles Question 31, July 1984)
   MIL-STD-414[37] indicates that the variables sampling plans can result in considerable savings in sample size for the same comparable assurance as to the correctness of decisions in judging a single quality characteristic. They can also provide a greater degree of assurance for the same sample size.

   Juran[38] provides a comparison of variables and attributes sample sizes. This comparison indicates that a single sampling attributes plan requires the sample size of 125, but for the same protection the variables plan requires a considerably smaller sample.

   For more detailed explanation refer to Grant and Leavenworth,[39] who describe the OC curve for the single sampling attributes plan for n = 75, c = 2 together with the OC curve for a matched plan using the variables criteria. It indicates that the curve for variables is steeper than that of the

---

[35] *Quality Control and Industrial Statistics* by A. J. Duncan, 5th ed., 1986, Irwin, Homewood, IL, Section 3, Chapter 11, pg. 255-256.
[36] *Juran's Quality Control Handbook* by J. M. Juran, 4th ed., McGraw-Hill, New York, pg. 25.7, Table 25.1.
[37] *MIL-STD-414, Sampling Procedures and Tables for Inspection by Variables for Percent Defective*, refer to Introduction.
[38] *Juran's Quality Control Handbook* by J. M. Juran, 4th ed., McGraw-Hill, New York, pg. 25.7, Table 25.2.
[39] *Statistical Quality Control* by E. Grant and R. Leavenworth, 6th ed., McGraw-Hill, New York, pg. 415, Fig. 12-6 and

single attributes, giving more protection for the same sample size. They further describe a method for computing the OC curve for a *known sigma variables* sampling plan based on the assumption of a normal distribution in Chapter 17, and compare the sample sizes for the variables plan required with that of the attribute sampling plan for similar protection.

Duncan[40] explains that the same OC curve can be obtained with a smaller sample size by using a variables plan rather than an attributes plan, which is the primary advantage of the variables plan.

69.   Why would inspection by variables be superior to inspection by attributes?

   a.   Inspection by variables is easier to administer than inspection by attributes.
   b.   Inspectors like inspection by variables better than inspection by attributes.
   c.   More information is obtained when inspection by variables is utilized.
   d.   Inspection by variables is usually more economical than inspection by attributes.
   e.   Inspection by variables makes more sense than inspection by attributes.

Key: c.   More information is obtained when inspection by variables is utilized.
(Ref. Principles Question 56, August 1978)
Choice d is true in some cases because variables generally require a smaller sample size, which can offset the cost of higher inspection or the clerical cost for measuring all characteristics of a product or part, and hence, in some cases, it is not more economical than the attribute sampling plan. The cost of inspection per item is less by attributes than by variables.[41] However the customer requirements may require variable data and analysis of capability, etc.

70.   Why might inspection by variables be superior to inspection by attributes?

   I.   Inspection by variables is easier to administer than the inspection by attributes
   II.   More information is obtained when inspection by variables is utilized
   III.   Inspection by variables usually requires smaller samples than inspection by attributes

   a.   II and III only
   b.   III only
   c.   I and II only
   d.   I, II, and III only

Key: a.   II and III only (ASQC's correction in answer; Ref. Principles Question 56, July 1984)
Please refer to Question 69 above for discussion.

71.   Lots of 75 parts each are inspected to an AQL of 0.25% using normal inspection, single

---

Chapter 17, pg. 549-550.
[40] *Quality Control and Industrial Statistics* by A. J. Duncan, 5th ed., 1986, Irwin, Homewood, IL, Section 3, Chapter 11, pg. 255-256.
[41] *Statistical Quality Control* by E. Grant and R. Leavenworth, 6th ed., McGraw-Hill, New York, Chapter 17, pg. 537-538.

sampling. A single lower specification limit denoted by L is used. The standard level (Level II in MIL-STD-105D, Level IV in MIL-STD-414) is specified. The sample size for MIL-STD-414, estimating variability by the range method, is

a.   3
b.   7
c.   10
d.   15
e.   20

Key: c.   10   (Ref. Applications Question 8, July 1984)

Given: N = 75 parts, AQL = 0.25%, normal inspection, single sampling, inspection Level IV of MIL-STD-414, single lower specification limit L, range method, variability unknown

Find: The sample size

Refer to MIL-STD-414[42] pg. 4 and pg. 61 for the following complete tables. (Tables shown below are partial tables.) To obtain the sampling plan, we need to use AQL = 0.25%, and the code letter. For a lot size of 66 to 110, the letter code **F** is applicable.

Table A-2 Sample size code letters

Lot sizes	Inspection levels				
	I	II	III	IV	V
41 to 65				E	
66 to 110				F	
111 to 180				G	

Table C-1 Range method - Master table for normal and tightened inspection for plans based on variability unknown (single specification limit form 1)

Sample size code letter	Sample size	Acceptable quality levels (normal inspection)		
		0.15	0.25	0.40
		k	k	k
D	50		↓	
E	80		0.702	
F	125		0.863	

The table above gives the sample size = 10 for applicable letter code F and AQL = 0.25%. (Form 2, Table C-3 on pg. 71 of the standard also gives the same sample size value.)

72.   Lots of 75 parts each are inspected to an AQL of 0.25% using normal inspection, single sampling. A single lower specification limit denoted by L is used. The standard level (Level II in MIL-STD-105D, Level IV in MIL-STD-414) is specified. The acceptance criterion, using MIL-STD-414 and the range method, is: accept the lot if

---

[42] *MIL-STD-414, Sampling Procedures and Tables for Inspection by Variables for Percent Defective*, Section A, Table A-2.

a. $(\overline{X} - L)/R \geq 0.702$

b. $(\overline{X} - L)/R \geq 0.863$

c. $(\overline{X} - L)/R \geq 1.06$

d. $(\overline{X} - L)/R \leq 1.06$

Key: b. $(\overline{X} - L)/R \geq 0.863$ (Ref. Applications Question 9, July 1984)

Given: Using the data of Question 19 above we now have:

$n = 10$, the acceptability constant $k = 0.863$ for AQL = 0.25%, and letter code F.

Find: The acceptability criterion (to accept the lot).

MIL-STD-414, Section C, pg. 61, paragraph C.3, defines lot-by-lot acceptability procedures when Form 1 is used, and C. 3.3 specifically defines the *acceptability criterion* as follows:

Compare $(\overline{X} - L)/R$ with the acceptability constant k obtained from Table C-1 above.

If $(\overline{X} - L)/R \geq k$, then the lot meets the acceptability criterion, i.e., accept the lot.

Hence the acceptability criterion for the data above should be $(\overline{X} - L)/R \geq 0.863$, as $k = 0.863$.

73. A comparison of known sigma and unknown sigma variables plans will show that equal protection is obtained (as determined by the OC curves)

a. when the unknown sigma sample size is smaller than the known sigma sample size

b. when the known sigma sample size is larger than the unknown sigma sample size

c. when the known sigma and unknown sigma sample sizes are equal

d. none of these

Key: d. none of these (Ref. Applications Question 16, July 1984)

An example can explain such concepts. Let the lot size be 500 with an AQL of 1.5%. Table A-2 of MIL-STD-414[43] gives letter code I.

Table A-2 Sample size code letters

Lot sizes	Inspection levels				
	I	II	III	IV	V
181 to 300				H	
301 to 500				I	
501 to 800				J	

Section B describes the "Variability Unknown - Standard Deviation Method - Single Specification Limit" case. Use Table B-1 to get the sample size.

---

[43] *MIL-STD-414, Sampling Procedures and Tables for Inspection by Variables for Percent Defective*, Section A, Table A-2; Section B, Table B-1; Section D, Table D-1.

Table B-1 Standard deviation method - Master table for normal and tightened inspection for plans based on variability unknown (single specification limit, Form 1)

Sample size code letter	Sample size	Acceptable quality levels (normal inspection)		
		1.0	1.5	2.5
		k	k	k
H	20		1.69	
I	25		1.72	
J	30		1.73	

The sample size is n = 25 for *sigma (variability) unknown*. Section D describes the "Variability Known - Standard Deviation Method - Single Specification Limit" case. Use Table D-1 to get the sample size.

This gives the sample size n = 10 for sigma (variability) known. This means *that sigma (variability) known* requires a smaller sample size than the *variability unknown* plan. None of the choices from choices a, b, and c meet this condition.

Table D-1 Standard deviation method - Master table for normal and tightened inspection for plans based on variability known (single specification limit, Form-1)

Sample size code letter	Acceptable quality levels (normal inspection)					
	1.0		1.5		2.5	
	n	k	n	k	n	k
H			8	1.69		
I			10	1.72		

74. Your quality control manager has asked you to make a study of the costs of using variables sampling against attribute sampling for a pipefitting. After searching the literature you find that the following sampling plans will give equal protection over the range of quality levels in which you are interested:

Types of plan	Sample size	Acceptance criterion
Attribute	450	Ac = 10, Re = 11
Variables, sigma unknown	100	k = 2.0
Variables, sigma known	33	k = 2.0

Upon investigating the possible costs involved in each type of sampling with your accounting, production, and inspection departments, you arrive at the following figures.

	Attributes ($)	Sigma known ($)	Sigma unknown ($)
Unit sampling cost	0.05	0.05	0.05
Unit inspection cost	0.05	0.35	0.35
Unit computation cost	0.00	0.02	0.01
Lot overhead cost	6.00	8.00	40.00

Which type of sampling would you advise your quality control manager to use based on the above information?

a.   attribute sampling
b.   since they all give equal protection, it does not make any difference
c.   continuous sampling
d.   variables sampling, sigma known
e.   variables sampling, sigma unknown

Key: d.   variables sampling, sigma known (Ref. Applications Question 20, October 1974)
   Given: Details of sample sizes for each plan and the costs for each plan. Each plan gives equal protection.
   Find: The most appropriate plan.

	Attributes $(n = 450)$	Sigma unknown $(n = 100)$	Sigma known $(n = 33)$
Sampling cost	$0.05 \times 450 = \$22.50$	$0.05 \times 100 = \$5$	$0.05 \times 33 = \$1.65$
Inspection cost	$0.05 \times 450 = \$22.50$	$0.35 \times 100 = \$35$	$0.35 \times 33 = \$11.55$
Computation cost	0.00	$0.02 \times 100 = \$2$	$0.01 \times 33 = \$0.33$
Overhead cost	$6.00	$8.00	$40.00
Total cost	22.50+22.50+6 = $51	5+35+2+8 = $50	1.65+11.55+0.33+40 = $ 53.53

The data results above indicate that each plan costs almost the same and none is significantly better or worse in overall cost point. Also they all provide equal protection. Choice b is given as the correct choice in ASQC's answers. This question is repeated with a slight change in the August 1978 examination.[44]

75.   Multiple sampling means

a.   a sampling plan where more than two samples of a given size are required or permitted; the decision to accept or reject the lot depends on the number of defective items vs. the acceptance number at each stage of the sampling.
b.   a sampling plan where each item or unit is taken as a sample size of one and it is inspected to decide whether to accept, reject, or to continue the sampling.
c.   if the number of defectives found in the first sample is between the first sample's

---

[44] *ASQC - CQE Examination*, ASQC Quality Progress, Milwaukee, WI, August 1978, Application section, Question 8.

acceptance and rejection numbers, take a second sample of the same size and inspect the number of defectives as cumulative of both samples against the acceptance and rejection numbers of the second sample.

d. all of the above

Key: a. a sampling plan where more than two samples of a given size are required or permitted; the decision to accept or reject the lot depends on the number of defective items vs. the acceptance number at each stage of the sampling.

In the case of multiple sampling, more than two samples are taken, each of a given sample size (n_1, n_2, n_3, etc.) and they are inspected to decide the acceptance of the lot. At the end of each sample, the number of defective items are compared with the acceptance number for the cumulative sample size. If the number of defective items is less than the acceptance number for that stage of the sampling, the lot is accepted, otherwise the next sample of the stated size is taken. This process is repeated for up to five stages of sampling. Thereafter, it is recommended that you conduct a 100% inspection of the lot to determine the level of nonconformance and make the disposition decisions if necessary. Juran[45] uses a schematic diagram to show the operation of multiple and sequential sampling. Multiple sampling requires a smaller sample size at each stage of sampling than single and double sampling. However, it is difficult to administer.

Choice b defines sequential sampling. Here, each single unit or item is treated as a sample and inspected to make acceptance decisions. It is called item by item sequential sampling when the sample size equals one item and group sequential sampling when it is more than one item. At each sample, the decision to accept, reject, or to continue further is made. As per Juran sequential sampling can theoretically continue indefinitely and can reach a 100% inspection of the entire lot and hence it is necessary to follow some truncating criteria.

Choice c defines double sampling. MIL-STD-105E[46] describes the procedure for determining the acceptability of a lot or batch under percent defectives inspection as follows:

"A number of the sample units equal to the first sample size given by the plan shall be inspected. If the number of defectives found in the first sample is equal to or less than the first acceptance number, the lot or batch shall be considered acceptable. If the number of defectives found in the first sample is equal to or greater than the first rejection number, the lot or batch shall be rejected. If the number of defectives found in the first sample is between the first acceptance and rejection numbers, a second sample of the same size shall be inspected. The number of the defectives found in the first and second sample shall be accumulated. If the cumulative number of defectives is equal to or less than the second acceptance number, the lot or batch shall be considered acceptable. If the cumulative number of defectives is equal to or greater than the second rejection number, the lot or batch shall be rejected."

Refer to Questions 62, 63, and 64 above for more details.

---

[45] *Juran's Quality Control Handbook* by J. M. Juran, 4th ed., McGraw-Hill, New York, pg. 25.22-23, Table 25.5, and Figure 25-8 for multiple sampling; Fig. 25-9 for sequential sampling.

[46] *MIL-STD-105E, Sampling Procedures and Tables for Inspection by Attributes*, Section 4.10.1.2.

ASQC-CQE BIBLIOGRAPHY AND OTHER REFERENCES ON ACCEPTANCE SAMPLING

1. *ANSI/ASQC A1-1987 Definitions, Symbols, Formulas, and Tables for Control Charts*, Milwaukee, ASQC Quality Press, 1987.

2. *ANSI/ASQC A2-1987, Terms and Symbols for Acceptance Sampling*, Milwaukee, ASQC Quality Press, 1987.

3. *ANSI/ASQC Z1.4-1981, Sampling Procedures and Tables for Inspection by Attributes*, Milwaukee, ASQC Quality Press, 1981.

4. *ANSI/ASQC Z1.9-1980, Sampling Procedures and Tables for Inspection by Variables for Percent Nonconforming* , Milwaukee, ASQC Quality Press, 1980.

5. ASQC Statistics Division, *Glossary and Tables for Statistical Quality Control*, 2nd ed., Milwaukee, ASQC Quality Press, 1983.

6. Duncan, A. J., *Quality Control and Industrial Statistics*, 5th ed., Homewood IL, Irwin Inc., 1986.

7. Grant, Eugen L. and Richard Leavenworth, *Statistical Quality Control*, 6th ed., New York, McGraw-Hill, 1988.

8. Juran, Joseph M., *Juran's Quality Control Handbook*, 4th ed., New York, McGraw-Hill, 1988.

9. Montgomery, Douglas C., *Statistical Quality Control*, 2nd ed., New York, John Wiley and Sons, 1985.

10. *MIL-STD-105E, Sampling Procedures and Tables for Inspection by Attributes*, Standardization Document Order Desk, 700 Robbins Ave., Building 4, Section D, Philadelphia, PA 19111-5094.

11. *MIL-STD-414, Sampling Procedures and Tables for Inspection by Variables* (address same as above).

12. Western Electric, *Statistical Quality Control Handbook*, Indianapolis, AT&T, 1956.

CHAPTER 9

QUALITY PRACTICES AND APPLICATIONS

ASQC'S <u>BODY OF KNOWLEDGE (BOK)</u> FOR THE CQE EXAMINATION

This chapter focuses on the following selected subject areas of BOK from *Section I, General Knowledge, Conduct and Ethics, Section II, Quality Practices and Applications,* and *Section IV, Product, Process and Materials Control.*

General Knowledge and Skills

1. Benefits of quality
2. Domestic or international standards and specifications
3. Quality philosophies (e.g., Juran, Deming, Taguchi, Ishikawa)
4. Communication and presentation skills
5. Project management skills

Professional Conduct and Ethics

1. ASQC Code of Ethics
2. Typical conflict of interest situations for a quality engineer

Quality Planning

1. Pre-production or pre-service planning process
2. Process qualification and validation methods
3. Involvement of customer and supplier in the planning process
4. Data collection and review of customer expectations, needs, requirements, and specifications
5. Procedures for design reviews and qualification

Quality Systems

1. Elements of a quality system
2. Scope and objectives of quality information systems
3. Techniques of assuring data accuracy and integrity
4. Management systems for improving quality (e.g., policy deployment, continuous improvement strategies)
5. Quality documentation systems
6. Problem identification analysis, reporting, and corrective action system

Supplier Management

1. Methodologies
2. Supplier performance evaluation and rating systems
3. Supplier qualification or certification systems

Continuous Improvement Tools

1. Quality Tools
   a. Pareto charts
   b. Cause-and-effect diagrams
   c. Flow charts
   d. Control charts
   e. Check sheets
   f. Scatter diagrams
   g. Histograms
2. Management Tools
   a. Affinity diagrams
   b. Tree diagrams
   c. Process decision program charts (PDPC)
   d. Matrix diagrams
   e. Interrelationship diagrams
   f. Prioritization matrices
   g. Activity network diagrams

Identification of Materials and Status

Lot Traceability

Material Segregation Practices

Materials Review Board Criteria and Procedures

1.   Quality can be defined as

       a.   fitness for use
       b.   meeting the customer requirements
       c.   freedom from deficiencies
       d.   all of the above

Key: d.   all of the above

Quality has been defined as *fitness for use*. It is also defined as meeting the specification or conformance to specifications.[1] Freedom from deficiencies results in less dissatisfied customers; i.e., it results in high quality. Based on today's quality movements, quality is now defined as *meeting (and exceeding) the customer requirements* by focusing on the *voice of the customer* (VOC). It means quality is defined by the customer. Some companies are defining *quality* as *customer delight, customer excitement, and customer enthusiasm.*

2.   Two main parameters of quality are

       a.   normal distribution and C_{pk}
       b.   prevention costs and failure costs
       c.   cost of conformance and cost of nonconformance
       d.   quality of design and quality of conformance

Key: d.   quality of design and quality of conformance

Juran[2] defines quality as customer satisfaction. It requires understanding the following two important parameters or components of quality.

    1.   *Quality of design, i.e., product features, options, etc.* To improve customer satisfaction, the quality of design must be improved to meet the changing needs of the customers and market competition. This may require significant commitments of resources and time to change the existing designs.

    2.   *Quality of conformance, i.e., freedom from deficiencies.* This requires reduction in scrap, customer warranties and complaints, rework, repairs, and other failure costs. The quality improvements to remove deficiencies or nonconformances result in significant reduction in costs.

There are other parameters of fitness for use, e.g., reliability, maintainability, availability, product safety, service, etc.

3.   Two of the most fundamental aspects of product quality are

       a.   appraisal costs and failure costs

---

[1] *Juran's Quality Control Handbook* by J. M. Juran, 4th ed., McGraw-Hill, New York, pg. 2.2-2.5, 2.8; and *Quality Planning and Analysis* by J. M. Juran and F. M. Gryna, 3rd ed., McGraw-Hill, New York, pg. 3, Section 1.3.

[2] *Quality Planning and Analysis* by J. M. Juran and F. M. Gryna, 3rd ed., McGraw-Hill, New York, pg. 4, Section 1.3.

     b.   in-process and finished product quality
     c.   quality of design and quality of conformance
     d.   impact of machines and impact of men
     e.   none of these

Key: c.   quality of design and quality of conformance
(Ref. Principles Question 46, October 1974)
Quality of design and quality of conformance are the two important aspects of product quality to achieve customer satisfaction. Refer to Question 2 above for detailed explanation. There are other parameters of fitness for use, e.g., reliability, maintainability, availability, product safety, service, etc.

4.   There are two basic aspects of product quality

     a.   in-process and finished product quality
     b.   appraisal costs and failure costs
     c.   quality of design and quality of conformance
     d.   impact of machines and impact of men

Key: c.   quality of design and quality of conformance
(Ref. Principles Question 32, October 1972)
This is a repeat question with minor changes in choices. Refer to Question 2 above for detailed explanation.

5.   Which of the following has made a significant contribution to quality and the continuous improvement movement in the industry today?

     a.   Dr. W. E. Deming
     b.   Dr. J. M. Juran
     c.   Dr. A. V. Feigenbaum
     d.   Dr. G. Taguchi
     e.   all of the above

Key: e.   all of the above

6.   Who developed the following concepts/theories or principles in quality?

     i.   Loss function
     ii.   The 14 points for management
     iii.   The control charts
     iv.   The quality trilogy and spiral of progress

     a.   W. E. Deming, G. Taguchi, J. M. Juran, and W. A. Shewhart, respectively

      b.   G. Taguchi, J. M. Juran, W. A. Shewhart, and W. E. Deming, respectively

      c.   G. Taguchi, W. E. Deming, W. A. Shewhart, and J. M. Juran, respectively

      d.   W. A. Shewhart, G. Taguchi, J. M. Juran, and W. E. Deming, respectively

Key: c.   G. Taguchi, W. E. Deming, W. A. Shewhart, and J. M. Juran, respectively

7.   Quality is the responsibility of

      a.   manufacturing engineering and manufacturing operations

      b.   product engineering and marketing

      c.   supplier quality and purchasing

      d.   every person and/or department in the organization

Key: d.   every person and/or department in the organization

Quality is everyone's responsibility and not the quality control department's alone. This is one of the most important concepts known as "Total Quality Control (TQC) or Total Quality Management (TQM)." This also means a paradigm shift from the conventionally defined role of quality control as testing and inspection to the role of quality as a strategic tool for achieving a competitive advantage. Following are some profound thoughts of the leaders who have made a significant impact on industries worldwide.

Feigenbaum[3] defines "Total Quality Control" (TQC) as follows:

Total quality control is an effective system for integrating the quality development, quality maintenance, and quality improvement efforts of the various groups in an organization so as to enable marketing, engineering, production, and service at the most economical levels which allow for full customer satisfaction.

The TQC concept indicates that "every employee of an organization, from top management to the production line worker, will be personally involved in quality control, and it provides a positive motivation for all employees and representatives at every level." He further discusses the TQC's organizationwide impact as "Total Quality Management" (TQM) as follows:

Total quality control's organization wide impact involves the managerial and technical implementation of customer-oriented quality activities as a prime responsibility of general management and of the main-line operations of marketing, engineering, production, industrial relations, finance, and service as well as of the quality control function itself.

Juran[4] defines Quality Function and the "Spiral of Progress" as follows:

The quality function is the entire collection of activities through which we achieve fitness for use, no matter where these activities are performed. A company wide quality function arises from the fact that product quality is the resultant of the work of all departments

---

[3] *Total Quality Control* by A.V. Feigenbaum, 3rd ed., McGraw-Hill, New York, pg. 6, 12-13, Chapter 1, Section 1.7.
[4] *Juran's Quality Control Handbook* by J. M. Juran, 4th ed., McGraw-Hill, New York, pg. 2.2-2.5.

around the Spiral. Each of those specialized departments has not only the responsibility to carry out its special function; it also has the responsibility to do its work correctly–to make its products fit for use. In this way, each department has a quality oriented activity to carry out along with its main function.

Deming[5] has used a flow diagram to view production as a "System" and explains as follows: *The consumer is the most important part of the production line. Quality should be aimed at the needs of the consumer, present and future. Quality begins with the intent which is fixed by management. The intent must be translated by engineers and others into plans, specifications, test, production.*

He has discussed the "Fourteen Points" to bring the transformation of industries. His Point 5 states *"Improve constantly and forever every process for planning, production and service."* Management needs to learn about its responsibilities for improvement at every stage. Deming has explained the importance of continual improvement. The improvement of quality becomes at once, with total commitment, companywide–all plants, management, engineers, production workers, suppliers, everybody–and nationwide.

These are very strong and profound concepts, and it is not easy to describe them in a lot more detail here, but you should study them in more detail to use them effectively.

8.   The term "Total Quality Control" is defined as

   a.   the operational techniques and activities which sustain the quality of a product or service that will satisfy given needs; also use of such activities and techniques
   b.   all those planned or systematic actions necessary to provide adequate confidence that a product or service will satisfy given needs
   c.   an effective system for integrating the quality development, quality maintenance, and quality improvement efforts of the various groups in an organization so as to enable marketing, engineering, production, and service at the most economical levels which allow for full customer satisfaction
   d.   the totality of the features and characteristics of a product or service that bear on its ability to satisfy given needs

Key: c.   an effective system for integrating the quality development, quality maintenance, and quality improvement efforts of the various groups in an organization so as to enable marketing, engineering, production, and service at the most economical levels which allow for full customer satisfaction

Choice c is the definition of "Total Quality Control" according to Feigenbaum.[6] He further has discussed the TQC's organizationwide impact as "Total Quality Management" (TQM) as follows:

---

[5] *Out of Crisis* by W. E. Deming, MIT-CAES, Cambridge, Mass., 02139, 1982, Chapter 1, pg. 4-5.
[6] *Total Quality Control* by A.V. Feigenbaum, 3rd ed., McGraw-Hill, New York, Chapter 1, pg. 6.

Total quality control's organization wide impact involves the managerial and technical implementation of customer-oriented quality activities as a prime responsibility of general management and of the main-line operations of marketing, engineering, production, industrial relations, finance and service as well as of the quality control function itself.

Choice a defines the term "Quality Control"; choice b defines "Quality Assurance"; and choice d defines the term "Quality" according to ASQC.[7]

9.   Which of the following describe(s) the characteristics of a total quality system?

  a. It creates a strong focus on understanding customer requirements and effectively deploying them in the product or service by integrating each individual and all equipments and materials, i.e., the whole organization, so that the customer is satisfied.

  b. It is a well-thought-out identification and documentation of elements of the quality system, and a detailed description of who, what, where, when, why, and how every individual will work to achieve the highest quality.

  c. It is the foundation for quality activities and permits management and employees to focus consistently on customer requirements in each activity.

  d. It is the basis for a systematic engineering of order-of-magnitude improvements throughout the major quality activities of the company.

  e. all of the above

Key: e. all of the above

Feigenbaum[8] has discussed the *system approach to quality*. He has defined the *Total Quality System* as follows:

A total quality system is the agreed company wide and plant wide operating work structure, documented in effective, integrated technical and managerial procedures, for guiding the coordinated actions of the work force, the machines and the information of the company and plant in the best and most practical ways to assure the customer quality satisfaction and economical costs of quality.

He further has explained the characteristics of a total quality system in great detail in Section 5.7, that includes all the choices listed above.

10.   The five (5) key elements of Total Quality Control are

  a. attitude, attention, failure mechanism, skills, and statistics

  b. reliability, vendor control, marketing, geography, and inspection

  c. scope, management, technology, applications, and training

---

[7] *Glossary and Tables for Statistical Quality Control* prepared by the American Society for Quality Control (ASQC), Quality Press, Milwaukee, WI, Sections 1.24, 12.5, and 1.26 (pg. 4-7).

[8] *Total Quality Control* by A.V. Feigenbaum, 3rd ed., McGraw-Hill, New York, Chapter 5, pg. 77-78, 85-86.

d.   none of the above

Key: c.   scope, management, technology, applications, and training
        ASQC-CQT Core Portion,[9] Question 17.

11.   When developing and implementing a modern quality assurance program, the perspective of
        which of the following disciplines is most useful?

        a.   financial management
        b.   production control
        c.   accounting management
        d.   manufacturing engineering
        e.   systems engineering

Key: e.   systems engineering   (Ref. Principles Question 85, October 1974)
        Feigenbaum[10] defines system engineering as *the technological process of creating and
        structuring effective people-machine-information quality systems.* He states that the field of
        system engineering and system management has been widely applied to modern quality control
        activities. The focal point in quality engineering is now to develop and maintain the system
        approach, i.e., an integrated approach of disciplines throughout the company.

12.   The "quality function" of a company is best described as

        a.   the degree to which the company product conforms to a design or specification
        b.   that collection of activities through which "fitness for use" is achieved
        c.   the degree to which a class or category of product possesses satisfaction for people
                generally
        d.   all of the above

Key: b.   that collection of activities through which "fitness for use" is achieved
        (Ref. Principles Question 40, July 1984)
        Juran[11] has discussed "The Quality Function." His spiral of progress in quality depicts a typical
        progression of activities as carried out in industrial companies as follows:
                *The quality function is the entire collection of activities through which we achieve fitness
                for use, no matter where these activities are performed. A company wide quality function
                arises from the fact that product quality is the resultant of the work of all departments
                around the Spiral. Each of those specialized departments has not only the responsibility
                to carry out its special function; it also has the responsibility to do its work correctly–to
                make its products fit for use. In this way, each department has a quality oriented activity
                to carry out along with its main function.*

---

[9] *ASQC - CQT Examination*, ASQC Quality Progress, Milwaukee, WI, August 1982, Core Portion, Question 17.
[10] *Total Quality Control* by A.V. Feigenbaum, 3rd ed., McGraw-Hill, New York, Chapter 5, pg. 84-85.
[11] *Juran's Quality Control Handbook* by J. M. Juran, 4th ed., McGraw-Hill, New York, pg. 2.2-2.5.

For many years, conventionally the focus of quality has been on reducing the warranty claims, customer complaints, i.e., freedom from deficiencies or nonconformities. Today, this is defined as the "Basic Quality" or "Demanded Quality" and it focuses on customer *dissatisfiers* only. It is a survival-based strategy and this approach alone cannot enable a company to be a market leader.

One important reminder is that the definition of quality as "fitness for use" has evolved further and new definitions are more focused to meeting (and exceeding) customer requirements. Quality is defined by the customer and hence includes all those product features and characteristics that meet (and exceed) the customer requirements. It focuses more and more on "Customer Satisfiers" and "Customer Exciters," e.g., a new feature, and on new dimensions of quality.[12] The market leader companies are defining Quality as "Customer Delight, Customer Excitement,[13] and/or Customer Enthusiasm."

13.   Quality engineering is

   a.   a new buzz word
   b.   the same as quality control department activities
   c.   a primary function and responsibility of a Certified Quality Engineer only
   d.   a set of managerial, engineering, and operational activities that an organization uses to ensure that customer requirements are properly deployed and met

Key: d.   a set of managerial, engineering, and operational activities that an organization uses to ensure that customer requirements are properly deployed and met

The important thought here is that quality is everyone's responsibility and no single person or activity alone can achieve customer requirements. It is a team approach and the leadership must define all managerial, engineering, and operational activities to achieve the highest levels of customer satisfaction. Quality engineering is focused to achieve this by providing an integrated approach. Refer to Questions 7, 8, and 12 for additional discussion.

14.   Essential to the success of any Quality Control organization is the receipt of

   a.   adequate and stable resources
   b.   clear and concise project statements
   c.   delegation of authority to accomplish the objective
   d.   all of the above

Key: d.   all of the above   (Ref. Principles Question 37, August 1978)

Always be careful of "all of the above" type questions. The question may contain all choices as

---

[12] *Competing on the Eight Dimensions of Quality* by David A. Garvin, Harvard Business Review, November-December 1987.

[13] *Quality Function Deployment Implementation Manual-Kano Model of Quality*, American Supplier Institute, Inc., Dearborn, MI, 1989.

correct choices. You may be tempted to select any one choice in a rush depending upon your work experience, education, industry, etc. Make sure that you read each choice carefully and evaluate it thoroughly.

15.   The most effective tool for action in any quality control program is

        a.   the effect on profits
        b.   the type and scope of quality reporting
        c.   the dynamic nature of the quality manager
        d.   valid feedback

Key: a.   the effect on profits   (Ref. Principles Question 10, October 1972)

16.   Which of the following functions are normally considered *work elements* of quality-control engineering?

        a.   preproduction planning
        b.   process capability studies
        c.   classification of characteristics
        d.   quality cost analysis
        e.   all of these are *work elements* of quality control engineering

Key: e.   all of these are *work elements* of quality control engineering
        (Ref. Principles Question 24, October 1974)
        Feigenbaum[14] defines the 4 main jobs of quality control as new design control, incoming material control, product control and special process studies.

17.   Which of the following define the jobs of quality control?

        I.   the new design control
        II.   incoming material control
        III.   product control
        IV.   special process studies

        a.   I, II, and III
        b.   II, III, and IV
        c.   III, IV, and I
        d.   I, II, III, and IV

Key: d.   I, II, III, and IV,
        Feigenbaum[15] defines all four jobs as the jobs of *quality control*. He provides a detailed discussion and examples for each of the jobs of quality control which is briefly described here.

---

[14] *Total Quality Control* by A.V. Feigenbaum, 3rd ed., McGraw-Hill, New York, Chapter 4, pg. 64-68.

New design control includes the advance quality engineering efforts during new product selection and development based on customer satisfaction requirements, prototype tests, studies and analyses, development of manufacturing standards, development of product and process design, etc., prior to production.

The function of *incoming material control* requires appraisal methods for acceptance of incoming materials, parts, subassemblies, etc., supplied by suppliers.

Product control involves the process control analysis of process characteristics that has a cause-and-effect (also known as "Fishbone Diagram or Cause and Effect Diagram") relationship with important product quality characteristics. It requires that a process control plan is developed to control and improve the quality of the products at the source of variation, at the root cause level, to avoid the manufacture of nonconforming products. It requires that the product not only meet the specifications when shipped to the customer, but also be reliable, durable, and pleasing to the customer during its expected life cycle in the field and under diverse use and application of the product. It should also include the planning of the quality activities for installation, after-sales service, warranty service, etc.

The *special process study* means the use of statistical tools and methods to perform root cause analysis for chronic problems and implement permanent corrective action. This should lead to the development of robust design of products and processes to eliminate or minimize the adverse effects of variation, and to develop economical methods of error proofing the processes. This should promote continuous improvement of products and result in higher customer satisfaction with the product.

18.   In spite of the Quality Engineer's best efforts, situations may develop in which his(her) decision is overruled. The most appropriate action would be to

   a.   resign his(her) position based upon his(her) convictions
   b.   report his(her) findings to an outside source such as a regulatory agency or the press
   c.   document his(her) findings, report to his(her) superiors, and move on to the next assignment
   d.   discuss his(her) findings with his(her) co-workers in order to gain support, thereby forcing action

Key: c.   document his(her) findings, report to his(her) superiors, and move on to the next assignment   (Ref. Principles Question 42, July 1984)
       Such events are possible in any department. Many times decisions are made or overruled because of several reasons including lack of knowledge. As a quality engineer, you are not only responsible for understanding and implementing quality and continuous improvement methods, but also for assisting the organization in understanding and managing the quality.

---

[15] *Total Quality Control* by A.V. Feigenbaum, 3rd ed., McGraw-Hill, New York, Chapter 4, pg. 64-68.

Hence in such situations, the quality engineer should look at the issue in a broader sense, document it, report it to the supervisors, and move on to the next assignment. Proper documentation of the facts is very important and will help in the future for similar problems or issues, or for a new product or process design. As a lesson learned, it will help solve problems in the future and it will provide a technical memory. Also when you document and report the facts to your supervisors or top management, it makes them responsible and accountable for the actions and decisions taken. It also validates management's commitment to quality and customer satisfaction, as they are primarily responsible not only for defining the company's vision and quality policies but also for implementing them thoroughly and consistently.

19.   A fully developed position description for a Quality Engineer must contain clarification of

        a.   responsibility
        b.   accountability
        c.   authority
        d.   answers a and c above
        e.   answers a, b, and c above

Key: e.   answers a, b, and c above   (Ref. Principles Question 34, August 1978)
        Today, the focus of quality has shifted from conventional quality control practices to quality assurance, "total quality control," and now "total quality management." This has created a need for highly qualified professionals as quality engineers and quality managers who can provide not only operational assistance and direction in improving quality but also strategic decision making. Therefore, for a quality engineer position, it is very important to know or provide clarification about their responsibility, accountability and authority. This will not only improve communication, but also provide clear operating guidelines and an effective measure of performance. This can apply equally well to other positions in the company.

20.   As a quality engineer, which of the following criteria will you use to select appropriate inspection stations in your plant?

        a.   Place the inspection stations where the material is moved between the supplier and customer companies as source inspection, receiving inspection, etc.
        b.   Place the inspection stations at the start of setup dominant processes.
        c.   Place the inspection at points where the product or material is moved from one shop or operation to another, as an in-process inspection.
        d.   Place an inspection at the workstation where the product is finished as a finished-goods inspection.
        e.   All of the above are applicable criteria for selection of the inspection stations.

Key: e.   All of the above are applicable criteria for selection of the inspection stations.
        Juran[16] discusses the criteria for selection of the inspection stations based on the criteria for

---

[16] *Juran's Quality Control Handbook* by J. M. Juran, 4th ed., McGraw-Hill, New York, pg. 18.8.

selection of control stations. These criteria do not cover many complex situations such as complex products that may require mechanical or electrical testing, environmental testing, etc.

21. Which of the following instructions should be given to the inspectors at each of the inspection stations?

    a. which quality characteristics to check
    b. how to determine whether the product conforms to standards or not and how to determine whether a product lot is acceptable or not
    c. what to do with the conforming and nonconforming products
    d. what records to make
    e. all of the above

Key: e. all of the above
Refer to Question 20 above for additional discussion and it provides the instructions needed for each inspection station.

22. Continuous improvement in today's business is very essential because of

    a. rising expectation of customers
    b. increasing awareness of customers regarding quality of products and services
    c. intensive global competition
    d. product liability
    e. all of the above

Key: e. all of the above

23. A quality control program is considered to be

    a. a collection of quality control procedures and guidelines
    b. a step-by-step list of all quality control checkpoints
    c. a summary of company quality control policies
    d. a system of activities to provide quality of products and service

Key: d. a system of activities to provide quality of products and service
(Ref. Principles Question 32, July 1984)
The key term is "quality control program." Watch for subjectivity here in choices a, b, and c. They are individual elements of a quality program, but not a complete description of a quality program. ASQC/ANSI–A3 1978 defines some of the important terms as follows:

Quality Program is the documented plans for implementing the quality system.

Quality Control is the operational techniques and activities which sustain a quality of product or service that will satisfy given needs, also use of such activities and techniques. Quality Assurance is defined as all those planned or systematic actions necessary to provide adequate confidence that a product or service will satisfy given needs.

Hence choice d is the best choice.

24.   Establishing the quality policy for the company is the responsibility of the

      a.   customer
      b.   quality control
      c.   marketing department
      d.   top management

Key: d.   top management   (Ref. Applications Question 37, October 1974)
This is a repeat question with a slight change from the language in the August 1978 and October 1972 examinations.[17]

25.   In the planning of a new major manufacturing program the greatest quality effort should be put logically in

      a.   inspection of the product
      b.   nondestructive testing equipment
      c.   nonconformance to specifications
      d.   prevention of occurrence of substandard quality

Key: d.   prevention of occurrence of substandard quality
(Ref. Applications Question 51, October 1974)

26.   In planning the staffing for your new quality control department, you use which of the following as the best justification for estimating the number of people required?

      a.   a given ratio of production employees to quality personnel, typical of the industry
      b.   a total salary budget as a given percent of sales dollars
      c.   the number of people in the engineering department
      d.   the quality objectives that have been set by top management
      e.   none of the above

Key: d.   the quality objectives that have been set by top management
(Ref. Applications Question 55, October 1974)

27.   A quality program has the best foundation for success when it is initiated by

---

[17] *ASQC - CQE Examination*, ASQC Quality Progress, Milwaukee, WI, August 1978, Principles section, Question 45, and October 1972, Applications section, Question 54.

      a.   a certified quality engineer
      b.   contractual requirements
      c.   a chief executive of the company
      d.   production management
      e.   an experienced quality manager

Key: c.   a chief executive of the company   (Ref. Principles Question 45, August 1978)
The top management of the company should be committed to defining corporate policy including quality policy. This is a repeat question with a slight change in the language from the October 1974 examination.[18]

28.   A thorough analysis of the cause and effect of plant quality problems usually indicates that a major percentage of basic factors effecting poor quality performance are

      a.   operator controllable
      b.   management controllable
      c.   union controllable
      d.   customer controllable
      e.   none of the above

Key: b.   management controllable   (Ref. Principles Question 11, October 1974)
The top management of any company is responsible for setting the company's quality policy integrated with the company's overall policy. It is strongly believed that the management (and not the operator) is largely responsible for most of the plant's or company's problems. It is responsible for providing the means to achieve the established requirements. Leading quality management experts indicate that management is responsible for 70 to 80% of a company's problems. The most common management-controllable problems arise because of the multiple and conflicting standards for cost, productivity, quality, and delivery; programs of the month; failure to "walk like they talk;" lack of long-range planning or strategic planning; inability to solve the chronic problems; and an ongoing vicious cycle of "fire fighting" and detection versus prevention.

Gryna[19] states that management must provide three important criteria to achieve a state of self control: people should know (a) what they are supposed to be doing, (b) what they are actually doing, and (c) the means to regulate the process. If these three criteria are met, then the occurrence of a nonconforming product is "operator controllable." If any of the three criteria are not met, then the occurrence of a nonconforming situation is "management controllable."

Juran[20] defines the three major categories of inspector errors as "technique error, inadvertent error, and conscious errors." The conscious inspector errors initiated by management are

---

[18] *ASQC - CQE Examination*, ASQC Quality Progress, Milwaukee, WI, October 1974, Application section Question 37.
[19] *Juran's Quality Control Handbook* by J. M. Juran, 4th ed., McGraw-Hill, New York, pg. 17.4-17.6, and 22.40-22.61.
[20] *Juran's Quality Control Handbook* by J. M. Juran, 4th ed., McGraw-Hill, New York, pg. 18.84-18.94.

conflicting management priorities, poor enforcement of conformance to standards, management apathy, sometimes management fraud, etc.

29.   In planning for quality, an important consideration at the start is

        a.   the relation of the total cost of quality to the net sales
        b.   the establishment of a company quality policy or objectives
        c.   deciding precisely how much money is to be spent
        d.   the selling of the quality program to the top management

Key: b.   the establishment of a company quality policy or objectives
        (Ref. Applications Question 62, October 1974)
        This question is repeated in the October 1972 examination.[21]

30.   Which of the following indicate the difference between the objectives and policies?

        I.   Objectives cover broad and managerial subject matter, but policies cover a wide range
                of activities.
        II.   Objectives cover a wide range of activities and policies cover broad and managerial
                subject matter.
        III.   Objectives are based on numbers and schedules, whereas policies are narrative.

        a.   I and II
        b.   II and III
        c.   III and I
        d.   all of the above

Key: b.   II and III
        Please refer to Juran[22] for discussion on the comparison of the objectives to policies and
        objectives to standards.

31.   Read the following two statements.

        1.   A statement of those policies which are companywide in their effect and hence binding
                on all company organization units.
        2.   A delegation of authority to subordinate company organization units to establish the
                subsidiary quality policies appropriate to their needs.

        These statements define:

        a.   function quality policy

---

[21] *ASQC - CQE Examination*, ASQC Quality Progress, Milwaukee, WI, October 1972, Applications section, Question 10.
[22] *Juran's Quality Control Handbook* by J. M. Juran, 4th ed., McGraw-Hill, New York, pg. 5.15- 5.17.

      b.   product safety quality policy

      c.   corporate quality policy

      d.   divisional quality policy

Key: c.   corporate quality policy

When a company grows in the market, one quality policy may not fit all divisions. Juran[23] discusses the need for corporate quality policies and suggests creating several levels of quality policies. The two statements above indicate the corporate quality policy elements.

32.   After defining the quality problem, the first step in planning any sound Quality Control organization is to

      a.   prepare QC procedures

      b.   establish the Quality objectives

      c.   choose a QC manager

      d.   perform a Quality survey

      e.   none of the above

Key: b.   establish the Quality objectives

ASQC-CQT Core Portion,[24] Question 15.

33.   In preparing a Product Quality Policy for your company, you should do all of the following except

      a.   specify the means by which quality performance is measured

      b.   develop criteria for identifying risk situations and specify whose approval is required when there are known risks

      c.   include procedural matters and functional responsibilities

      d.   state quality goals

Key: c.   include procedural matters and functional responsibilities

(Ref. Principles Question 43, July 1984)

The company's quality policy is a precise statement of the company's commitment to its quality of products and services. It is a brief declaration and summary statement that summarizes the company's position about its product or service. It should provide specific guidelines for matters important to the company. Juran[25] indicates that the company policy statement should help insiders to understand what is expected of them and outsiders to understand what to expect from the company.

The quality policy may include statements on various subjects, such as importance of quality,

---

[23] *Juran's Quality Control Handbook* by J. M. Juran, 4th ed., McGraw-Hill, New York, pg. 5.3-5.4.

[24] *ASQC - CQT Examination*, ASQC Quality Progress, Milwaukee, WI, August 1982 Core Portion, Question 15.

[25] *Juran's Quality Control Handbook* by J. M. Juran, 4th ed., McGraw-Hill, New York, pg. 5.2-5.4.

customer satisfaction, competitiveness, low cost, delivery, and focus on continuous improvement. These elements form a corporate policy. The divisional quality policies and policies for functions are formed to be consistent with the corporate policy. Written functional policy statements may be included in a comprehensive policy manual or a departmental policy manual. This will in turn drive detailed procedural matters and functional responsibilities. Procedural matters and functional responsibilities are part of the procedures manual, e.g., quality manual or quality plan, design and drafting procedures, testing and validation procedures, etc.

Also refer to Question 34 below from the August 1978 examination, which is repeated with a slight change in some choices.

34.   In preparing a Quality Policy concerning a product line for your company, you should not

   a.   specify the means by which quality performance is measured
   b.   develop criteria for identifying risk situations and specify whose approval is required
          when there are known risks
   c.   load the policy with procedural matters or ordinary functional responsibilities
   d.   identify responsibilities for dispositioning defective hardware
   e.   answers b and d above

Key: c.   load the policy with procedural matters or ordinary functional responsibilities
      (Ref. Principles Question 33, August 1978)
      Refer to Question 33 above which is a repeat question from the July 1984 examination but with
      slightly different choices.

35.   The advantage of a written procedure is

   a.   it provides flexibility in dealing with problems
   b.   unusual conditions are handled better
   c.   it is a perpetual coordination device
   d.   coordination with other departments is not required

Key: c.   it is a perpetual coordination device   (Ref. Principles Question 41, July 1984)
      The written procedure provides a written direction, and a guide for managerial action for all time.
      It continues to provide the consistent direction and standardization of work or operations. It
      establishes authority, accountability, responsibility, method of operation, and legitimacy. It acts
      as a reference standard for internal audits. It also enables demonstration of the conformance to
      customer standards during the conformity audits conducted by the customer. Juran[26] discusses
      the importance of written policies and consistent direction and their advantages and
      disadvantages.

36.   Which of the following is(are) not an advantage(s) of written procedures?

---

[26] *Juran's Quality Control Handbook* by J. M. Juran, 4th ed., McGraw-Hill, New York, pg. 5.2-5.4.

a.   they provide a written guide to both insiders and outsiders for managerial action
b.   they are time-consuming and complex tasks
c.   they force the organization to think about the quality problems in great detail
d.   they establish authority and legitimacy at various levels
e.   all of the above

Key: b.   they are time-consuming and complex tasks
Be careful. The question is asking for the choice that is *not* the advantage of the written procedures, i.e., the disadvantage of the written procedures. Choice b is the disadvantage because developing and writing procedures is a lengthy task. Juran[27] describes several advantages of the written procedures as shown in choices a, c, and d.

37.   The purpose of a written inspection procedure is to

a.   provide answers to inspection questions
b.   let the operator know what the inspector is doing
c.   error-proof the inspection function
d.   standardize methods and procedures of inspectors

Key: d.   standardize methods and procedures of inspectors
(Ref. Applications Question 70, October 1972)
The written procedure provides a written direction and guide for managerial action for all time. It continues to provide the consistent direction and standardization of work or operations. It establishes the authority, accountability, responsibility, and method of operation, and legitimacy. Juran[28] discusses the importance of written polices and consistent direction, and their advantages and disadvantages. Also please refer to Question 30 above.

38.   The purpose of a Quality Manual is to

a.   use it as a basis for every Quality decision
b.   standardize the methods and decisions of a department
c.   optimize company performance in addition to improving the effectiveness of the Quality department
d.   make it possible to handle every situation in exactly the same manner

Key: c.   optimize company performance in addition to improving the effectiveness of the Quality department   (Ref. Principles Question 36, August 1978)
Choice c is the most suitable, because it emphasizes the optimization of company performance. It enables the economical manufacture of quality products. It provides a system view, minimizes departmental suboptimization practices, and focuses on overall performance and its impact on the profitability of the company.

[27] *Juran's Quality Control Handbook* by J. M. Juran, 4th ed., McGraw-Hill, New York, pg. 5.3-5.4.
[28] *Juran's Quality Control Handbook* by J. M. Juran, 4th ed., McGraw-Hill, New York, pg. 5.2-5.4.

39.   A quality manual

    a.   is a static document, best used for Public Relations purposes
    b.   is a benchmark against which current practices may be audited
    c.   is the responsibility of all company departments
    d.   should be approved only by the quality department
    e.   is not needed in most of the organizations

Key: b.   is a benchmark against which current practices may be audited
        (Ref. Principles Question 46, August 1978)
        A quality manual is a technical translation of customer standards into operational requirements
        for the company. It defines the procedures and methods that must be effectively implemented to
        meet customer requirements. The operations must conform to the items in the quality manual as
        standard care or as standard practice. The conformity audit should audit different operations
        against the quality manual.

40.   An adequate quality budget should be

    a.   about ten percent of direct production costs
    b.   estimated from past quality costs
    c.   about two percent of sales
    d.   based on total quality cost trends

Key: d.   based on total quality cost trends   (Ref. Principles Question 68, October 1974)
        The trends provide data over time and hence we can analyze the total quality costs based on long-
        term data and prepare an adequate quality budget.

41.   The most important measure of outgoing quality needed by managers is product performance as
        viewed by

    a.   the customer
    b.   the final inspector
    c.   production
    d.   marketing

Key: a.   the customer   (Ref. Applications Question 38, August 1978)
        "Quality" is defined by the customer. Customer satisfaction is the driver of the quality movement
        today. The *voice of customer (VOC)* and customer feedback on the performance of the current
        product are very important inputs for new product development and design. Also, the VOC can
        be used for analyzing the competitive benchmarking data.

42.   Much managerial decision making is based on comparing actual performance with _____ .

   a.   personnel ratio
   b.   cost of operations
   c.   number of complaints
   d.   standards of performance

Key: d.   standards of performance   (Ref. Applications Question 39, August 1978)
Management should first communicate the standards or requirements. Then it should compare the actual performance to the given standards and develop corrective actions where needed. This is a simple definition for an audit.

43.   When planning a total quality system, one key objective is to provide a means of guaranteeing "the maintenance of product integrity." Which of the following quality system provisions is designed to MOST directly provide such a guarantee?

   a.   drawing and print control
   b.   calibration and maintenance of test equipment
   c.   identification and segregation of nonconforming material
   d.   specification change control

Key: c.   identification and segregation of nonconforming material
(Ref. Principles Question 34, July 1984)
The key phrase here is "guaranteeing the maintenance of product integrity." The product integrity is based on the basic definition of quality–fitness for use. Juran[29] discusses this as knowledge of conformance to specifications and knowledge of fitness for use. Each of the choices are important in a quality system. However choice c "identification and segregation of nonconforming material," ensures that the product is good, i.e., fit for use, and nonconforming products are not shipped with good products. It provides the protection to the customer, preserves the quality and customer satisfaction with the product, and enables creating the atmosphere of law and order. Hence this is an important provision in a quality system to achieve conformance of the product to its specifications and provide a means of guaranteeing the product's fitness for use.

Watch for subjectivity here because each of these items is affecting product quality at a different time. If you are a product engineer, you may be tempted to pick choice a or d, and if you are a manufacturing or quality engineer, you may want to select b. But these do not have direct or immediate impact on the customer, and it will not be sufficient to provide such a product guarantee even if the drawing and print control is good. This is a repeat question with a slight change from the October 1974 examination.[30]

44.   The primary reason that nonconforming material should be identified and segregated is

---

[29] *Juran's Quality Control Handbook* by J. M. Juran, 4th ed., McGraw-Hill, New York, pg. 18.31-32.
[30] *ASQC - CQE Examination*, ASQC Quality Progress, Milwaukee, WI, October 1974, Principles section, Question 27.

a. so that the cause of nonconformity can be determined
b. to provide statistical information for the "zero defect" program
c. so it cannot be used in production without proper authorization
d. to obtain samples of poor workmanship for use in the company's training program
e. so that responsibility can be determined and disciplinary action taken

Key: c. so it cannot be used in production without proper authorization
(Ref. Principles Question 44, August 1978)
It is important to develop and implement the procedures to identify the nonconforming material for incoming, in-process, and finished products, and to segregate it properly. This will prevent further use of nonconforming incoming or in-process material in production without proper authorization. The nonconforming finished products should be segregated so that they do not get mixed with good products and do not get shipped to the customer. The quality manual should include a specific procedure for nonconforming products that describes the specific approval process to use in production, documentation, containment, disposition, and internal or external communication requirements.

45. A system for controlling nonconforming material should have procedures for its

a. identification
b. segregation
c. disposition
d. all of the above
e. none of the above

Key: d. all of the above (Ref. ASQC-CQT Core Portion,[31] Question 24)

46. One of the major hazards in the material review board procedure is the tendency of the board to emphasize only the disposition function and to neglect the _____ function.

a. statistical analysis
b. corrective action
c. material evaluation
d. tolerance review
e. manufacturing methods

Key: b. corrective action (Ref. Applications Question 34, August 1978)
The *material review board* (MRB)[32] is a management team and sometimes it includes the customer representatives. Its responsibility is to (a) evaluate and review all nonconforming material against its standard; (b) make the disposition decision, such as to accept the material for production, if everyone including the customer agrees, or to scrap the material; and (c) to drive

---

[31] *ASQC - CQT Examination*, ASQC Quality Progress, Milwaukee, WI, August 1982, Core Portion, Question 24.
[32] *Juran's Quality Control Handbook* by J. M. Juran, 4th ed., McGraw-Hill, New York, pg. 13-8 - 13.10.

the corrective action to prevent the recurrence of a nonconforming product.

However, in many companies, the MRB may not be a formal committee or may not include the customer representative. If an MRB exists in some companies, its primary function may be solely to evaluate the nonconforming material for its fitness for use, its intended function, or any other substitute use as a by-product. Its scope may not include fact-finding for causes of nonconforming events or driving the corrective actions. This is a possible danger. Hence all such activities must be properly planned and integrated to achieve continuous improvement.

47. The most important activity of a material review board (MRB) would normally be

    a. making sure that corrective action is taken to prevent recurrence of the problem
    b. to provide a bonded or segregated area of holding discrepant material pending disposition
    c. prepare discrepant material reports for management
    d. accept discrepant material when "commercial" decisions dictate
    e. none of these

Key: a. making sure that corrective action is taken to prevent recurrence of the problem
(Ref. Applications Question 38, October 1974.)
Refer to Question 46 above for discussion.

48. The primary reason for evaluating and maintaining surveillance over a supplier's quality program is to

    a. perform product inspection at source
    b. eliminate incoming inspection cost
    c. motivate suppliers to improve quality
    d. make sure the supplier's quality program is functioning effectively

Key: d. make sure the supplier's quality program is functioning effectively
(Ref. Principles Question 35, July 1984)
Supplier surveillance is implemented to ensure that the supplier follows all the activities according to the quality plan and contract requirements. Many companies implement supplier evaluation and surveillance programs, first, to find out if a supplier has a documented quality plan that meets the customer requirements and standards, and, second, to prove that the quality plan is effectively and economically implemented. It enables the company to exercise control over the supplier's activities in order to achieve and maintain conformance to requirements and establish the fitness for use of the product.

Choices a and b are different types of supplier surveillance activities but they are not the reasons for the surveillance. Companies use different forms of supplier surveillance activities such as supplier assessment, quality systems audit, in-process audits or surveillance, initial sample approval programs, and incoming or receiving inspection.

Choice c "motivate suppliers to improve quality," is an important element of supplier development and supplier relations but not generally considered to be supplier surveillance. It requires motivating or stimulating the supplier to improve quality by highlighting chronic problems and discussing the effect of poor quality, i.e., the effect of cost of quality or cost of nonconformance on their operations. Some companies use the competitive data of quality results of other companies. For suppliers whose past performance has been very poor or has recurring problems, some companies use penalizing approaches such as heavy documentation, submission of data, local resident representatives in their plant, rejection and replacement of parts, and loss of business if irreversible corrective actions are not implemented.

This question is repeated in the October 1974 examination[33] with a slight change in the answer. The answer is "to make sure the supplier's quality program is accomplishing its intended functions effectively and economically."

49.   To achieve strong vendor-vendee relationships, we should

      I.   develop mutual respect and cooperation
      II.   have prior contractual understanding
      III.   agree on methods of evaluation
      IV.   exchange of proprietary information

      a.   I, II, and III
      b.   II, III, and IV
      c.   III, IV, and I
      d.   IV, I, and II

Key: a.   I, II, and III
      Item IV is not proper and it would be very difficult to demand proprietary information from a vendor. Juran[34] indicates that a relationship should be based on trust, cooperation, mutual respect, and proper understanding of the requirements and methods of evaluation. This will allow for exchange of essential information from the vendor, but not necessarily proprietary information.

50.   The objectives for supplier quality ratings are

      I.   to obtain an objective, quantified measure of supplier performance
      II.   to make an objective judgment of supplier performance for all categories of the quality standard
      III.   to show the supplier how the product is used

      a.   I and II

---

[33] *ASQC - CQE Examination*, ASQC Quality Progress, Milwaukee, WI, October 1974, Principle section, Question 3.
[34] *Juran's Quality Control Handbook* by J. M. Juran, 4th ed., McGraw-Hill, New York, pg. 15.7.

b.   II and III
c.   III and I
d.   all of the above

Key: a.   I and II above

Juran[35] defines the supplier rating as an overall assessment of supplier quality performance used to assist in making various decisions such as supplier selection, development, and long-term relationships. He provides a brief list of various purposes for supplier quality ratings. Items I and II above are important purposes, but item III is generally not the purpose of the supplier rating process.

51.   Which one of the following is(are) not an inspection action(s)?

a.   interpretation of the specification
b.   measurement of the quality characteristic
c.   supplier rating
d.   judging the conformance

Key: c.   supplier rating

Juran[36] defines inspection as "evaluating the quality of some of the characteristic in relation to its standard." It consists of actions such as:
- interpretation of the specification
- measurement of the quality characteristic
- comparing the measurement data to the specifications
- judging the conformance
- disposition of the conforming and nonconforming areas
- recording the data obtained

The supplier rating is not an action of the inspection process but it is an action of the supplier selection, evaluation, and/or evaluation process.

52.   The communication to the supplier on the nonconformance of predictors must include

I.   the precise description of the symptoms of the defects
II.   providing the samples
III.   a provision for the supplier to visit the plant or site having the trouble or problems

a.   only I and II
b.   only II and III
c.   only III and I
d.   only I, II, and III

---

[35] *Juran's Quality Control Handbook* by J. M. Juran, 4th ed., McGraw-Hill, New York, pg. 15.40-15.42.
[36] *Juran's Quality Control Handbook* by J. M. Juran, 4th ed., McGraw-Hill, New York, pg. 18.4.

Key: d.   only I, II, and III
        Juran[37] discusses the importance of communication with vendors when there is a non-
        conformance. The three choices above create an effective communication with the vendor.
        He also discusses the importance of positive communication in the form of letters of praise,
        supplier awards and recognition, etc.

53.   "Good Housekeeping" is an important quality factor in a supplier's plant because

        a.   it promotes good working conditions
        b.   it minimizes fire hazards
        c.   it enhances safer operations
        d.   it reflects favorably on the efficiency and management of a company
        e.   all of the above

Key: e.   all of the above   (Ref. Principles Question 35, August 1978)
        This is nothing but common sense, and a good practice. The question focuses only on supplier
        plants only for "good housekeeping" which seems to be a narrower focus. It should apply to
        every operation, whether it is a supplier or customer company, an office or service area, a plant,
        or even our homes.

54.   The existence of a quality control manual at your key supplier means

        a.   that a quality system has been developed
        b.   that a quality system has been implemented
        c.   that the firm is quality conscious
        d.   that the firm is a certified supplier
        e.   all of the above

Key: a.   that a quality system has been developed (Ref. Principles Question 16, October 1974)
        A quality manual is a technical translation of customer standards into operational requirements
        for the company. It defines the procedures and methods that must be effectively implemented to
        meet customer requirements. The presence of a quality manual indicates only that a quality
        system is defined at the supplier location. It does not indicate whether a company's quality policy
        and procedures according to the manual are effectively implemented. The conformity audit
        should audit the operations against the quality manual and determine if the operations conform to
        the items in the quality manual as standard care or as standard practice.

55.   The most important step in vendor certification is to

        a.   obtain copies of vendor's handbook
        b.   familiarize vendor with quality requirements
        c.   analyze vendor's first shipment

---

[37] *Juran's Quality Control Handbook* by J. M. Juran, 4th ed., McGraw-Hill, New York, pg. 15. 27.

d.   visit the vendor's plant

Key: b.   familiarize vendor with quality requirements (Ref. Applications Question 29, July 1984)
All the choices above can be important for vendor certification at different stages. However, to implement the vendor certification, a company needs first to provide detailed understanding of its quality requirements to the vendor. This gives the vendor an opportunity to study them and develop proper documentation or a quality manual (choice a) to meet the customer's requirements and expectations.

The customer company can then use this manual to evaluate the suitability of a supplier's quality program. Most companies schedule a pre-award supplier assessment, an audit, or a survey by visiting the supplier plant (choice b). If the supplier is awarded the contract, then the customer company may require evaluation of the supplier's product by incoming inspection of the first shipment (choice c), 100% inspection, sampling inspection, etc. This question is repeated in the August 1978 examination.[38]

56.   A vendor quality control plan has been adopted. Which of the following provisions would you advise top management to be least effective?

a.   product audits
b.   source inspection
c.   certificate of analysis
d.   certificate of compliance
e.   pre-award surveys

Key: d.   certificate of compliance   (Ref. Applications Question 33, August 1978)
The certificate of compliance is a warrant or a document that the supplier provides to certify in writing that the product conforms to all the requirements and specifications. This is the least effective because it is generally a standard letter format stating "to whom it may concern." This certificate may not include any details such as test results, data on dimensions, and sometimes may not include even the part name or part number. It may be given to the customer just to meet the formality of the submission documents for sample approval programs. Hence this is the least effective method of a vendor quality control as compared to the remaining choices. This question is repeated in the October 1974 examination.[39]

57.   The most desirable method of evaluating a supplier is

a.   history evaluation
b.   survey evaluation
c.   questionnaire
d.   discuss with quality manager on phone

---

[38] *ASQC - CQE Examination*, ASQC Quality Progress, Milwaukee, WI, August 1978, Applications section, Question 37.
[39] *ASQC - CQE Examination*, ASQC Quality Progress, Milwaukee, WI, October 1974, Applications section, Question 77.

e.   all of the above

Key: a.   history evaluation   (Ref. Applications Question 35, August 1978)
It is pure common sense to use history information to evaluate a supplier. The history includes the performance, responsiveness, cost and quality of the product, and services provided by the supplier. It includes the details of its capability, quality plan, past performance, or problems faced, and its implementation of short-term and long-term resolutions. History also describes the growth and improvement of a supplier's operations. The buyer (or customer) can use such information as technical memory or lessons learned and this information is more factual and data based than the survey evaluations, questionnaire, and any other discussions with the supplier. It is also less expensive, faster, more reliable, and easier to collect and analyze. It can serve as one of the first steps in beginning a full supplier audit, evaluation, or surveillance program.

58.   When purchasing materials from vendors, it is sometimes advantageous to choose vendors whose prices are higher because

a.   such a statement is basically incorrect, always buy at lowest bid price
b.   such vendors may become obligated to bestow special favors
c.   materials that cost more can be expected to be better, and "you get what you pay for"
d.   the true cost of purchased materials, which should include items such as sorting inspection, contacting vendors, and production delays, may be lower

Key: d.   the true cost of purchased materials, which should include items such as sorting inspection, contacting vendors, and production delays, may be lower
(Ref. Applications Question 19, October 1974)
Juran[40] discusses the concept of "quality and price" based on price and differences. This question is repeated in the October 1972 examination.[41]

59.   The permissible variation in a dimension is the

a.   specification
b.   clearance
c.   tolerance
d.   allowance

Key: c.   tolerance   (Ref. Principles Question 66, October 1974)
Design tolerances or specifications are the limits of maximum permissible design variation. They represent the maximum allowable limits for the process variation. This question is repeated in the October 1972 examination.[42]

---

[40] *Juran's Quality Control Handbook* by J. M. Juran, 4th ed., McGraw-Hill, New York, pg. 3.9-3.11.
[41] *ASQC - CQE Examination*, ASQC Quality Progress, Milwaukee, WI, October 1972, Applications section, Question 32.
[42] *ASQC - CQE Examination*, ASQC Quality Progress, Milwaukee, WI, October 1972, Principles section, Question 87.

60.   Product specifications

     I.   are part of engineering documents and include drawings, engineering specifications, written specifications, and/or product acceptance samples

     II.   describe how to achieve customer requirements, i.e., are the same as the process specifications or written process instructions

     III.   describe what requirements are important to meet the customer requirements

     a.   I and II
     b.   II and III
     c.   III and I
     d.   I, II, and III

Key: c.   III and I

Be careful with item II. It describes the process specifications and not the product specifications. The product specifications generally describe *what* is important in the product, i.e., what end results are important and not how to achieve them. Juran[43] describes the product and process specifications. He suggests that to achieve product specifications, it is necessary to provide unequivocal information, describe critical aspects of the product characteristics, give the rationale (or why the product characteristics are important), and provide clear requirements and standards.

61.   Which one of the following quality management principles would you apply to increase the probability of better quality?

     a.   drawings and specifications should be rigidly set with nominal enforcement
     b.   drawings and specifications should be realistically set with rigid enforcement
     c.   drawings and specifications should be under the direction of quality engineering
     d.   drawings and specifications should be rigidly set and rigidly enforced

Key: b.   drawings and specifications should be realistically set with rigid enforcement
(Ref. Principles Question 69, October 1974)
This is the only choice in which it is recommended to set the drawings and specifications *realistically*, and not rigidly. Also it emphasizes the need for more discipline to enforce these drawings and specifications. Hence choices a, c, and d are not appropriate. Juran[44] states that most companies have a tendency to specify unduly tight tolerances which are not necessarily value added or economical to customer requirements.

To improve quality, the existing tolerances should be selected based on their importance to customer requirements, quality cost studies of internal and external failures, and manufacturing concerns and converted to realistic tolerances. These realistic tolerances should be more

---

[43] *Juran's Quality Control Handbook* by J. M. Juran, 4th ed., McGraw-Hill, New York, pg. 17.6-17.11.
[44] *Juran's Quality Control Handbook* by J. M. Juran, 4th ed., McGraw-Hill, New York, pg. 13.60.

acceptable to all stakeholders and hence will be easy to enforce rigidly. This process should be implemented on all new product development, as it is economical to manage an engineering product design in its concept phases and will not require a large list of late engineering changes on new drawing releases. This will improve new product quality and will create a more positive environment. Slowly the existing designs will phase out and a company will have most of the vital few tolerances as realistic tolerances, rigidly enforced. Also refer to Question 62, which is a repeat question with a slight change in the text.

62.   In comparing the philosophies of "tight tolerances loosely enforced" and "realistic tolerances rigidly enforced," we can conclude that

   a.   the first one is preferred
   b.   the second one is preferred
   c.   neither is really practical
   d.   both have a place in any production operation

Key: b.   the second one is preferred   (Ref. Principles Question 82, October 1972)
       Refer to Question 61, which is a repeat question with a slight change in the text, for a detailed discussion.

63.   In case of conflict between contract specifications and shop practice,

   a.   company procedures normally prevail
   b.   arbitration is necessary
   c.   the customer is always right
   d.   good judgment should be exercised
   e.   contract specifications normally apply

Key: e.   contract specifications normally apply   (Ref. Applications Question 43, July 1984)
       In today's highly competitive industries, customer satisfaction is the primary driver. Contract specifications basically reflect customer requirements and they must be met as a minimum. If the shop practices do not match the contract specifications, i.e., if they are not capable of meeting the contract specifications, it is important that shop practices be changed to meet the contract specifications.

       In some situations, shop practices are based on specifications for process parameters such as temperature, cure time, machine setup, etc., and are not directly in the form of product dimensions or specifications. Hence process specifications may be different than actual product specifications in terms of units and values. However the cause-and-effect relationship between process parameters and product specifications must be established using proper studies such as regression studies, design of experiments, statistical process control studies, error proofing, etc. Such studies must ensure that the process control on process parameters as a shop practice will achieve the product specifications. This will result in a prevention-based approach and bring significant improvement in the product at economical costs.

It is very important that customer service representatives or account representatives are fully aware of their process control methods, and the capability of their shops or plants to meet the contracts before they sign any contracts.

The quality standards ISO 9000, i.e., ANSI/ASQC Q9000-90004, 1994 Series[45] also emphasize that each contract shall be reviewed by the supplier, to ensure that the supplier has the capability to meet contractual requirements. Once the contracts are awarded or signed, the contract specifications must be met.

64. In recent months, several quality problems have resulted from apparent change in the design specifications by engineering, including material substitutions. This has only come to light through Quality Engineering's failure analysis system. You recommend which of the following quality system provisions as the best corrective action:

 a. establishing a formal procedure for initial design review
 b. establishing a formal procedure for process control
 c. establishing a formal procedure for specification change control (sometimes called an ECO or SCO system)
 d. establishing a formal system for drawing and print control
 e. establishing a formal material review board (MRB)

Key: c. establishing a formal procedure for specification change control (sometimes called an ECO or SCO system)   (Ref. Applications Question 30, August 1978)

The question describes quality problems that resulted from apparent change in the *design specifications* by engineering including *material substitutions*. This is a close call between choices c and d. Hence we need to understand the difference between these two choices.

The design specifications are not limited to dimensions, but can include material specifications, engineering specifications for testing and validation, etc. Many companies use separate standards for such specifications, and drawings or prints may or may not include them. Any changes in material, e.g., substitutions, require a formal system of review and change management to ensure that the products meet customer satisfaction requirements, safety, and/or compliance to governmental standards. It will also require agreements and approvals of multidisciplined activities to balance any conflicts or to make tradeoff decisions. Hence a formal procedure for specification change would be more inclusive as an engineering change management procedure than drawing or print control. Quality standards like ISO 9001[46] require the supplier to establish and maintain the procedures for the identification, documentation, appropriate review, and approval of all changes and modifications.

In the case of a plant, as discussed in Question 63 above, specification change control is an

---

[45] *ANSI/ASQC Q9001-1994 Quality Systems - Model for Quality Assurance in Design/Development, Production, Installation, and Servicing,* Section 4.3(c): Contract Review.

[46] *ANSI/ASQC Q9001-1994 Quality Systems - Model for Quality Assurance in Design/Development, Production, Installation and Servicing,* Section 4.4: Design Control.

important element of a quality system because it can include process specifications which are generally not part of any drawing or a print. In some situations, shop practices are based on specifications for process parameters such as temperature, cure time, machine setup, etc., and are not directly in the form of product dimensions or specifications. Hence process specifications may be different than actual product specifications in terms of units and values. Hence choice c is the proper answer.

65. You should encourage the design reviews because they

    a.   will assure that the design will perform successfully during use
    b.   can be manufactured at low cost
    c.   are suitable for prompt, low-cost field maintenance
    d.   all of the above

Key: d.   all of the above
Juran[47] discusses the basic concepts in product development and the importance of design review.

66. Which of the following items should you not do to conduct an effective design review?

    a.   Give more emphasis on constructive feedback rather than criticism to the designers.
    b.   Allow more competition at the technological level to encourage the designers to think that there are others competing for their role.
    c.   Provide realistic schedules.
    d.   Do the adequate planning for the design review meetings.

Key: b.   Allow more competition at the technological level to encourage the designers to think that there are others competing for their role.
Choice b is incorrect because it can create competing designs. Juran[48] has provided valuable discussion on upfront involvement and methods for design review.

67. When planning the specifications for product quality in the so-called *mechanical industries*

    a.   market research helps to establish economic tolerances
    b.   quality control develops products possessing qualities which meet customer needs
    c.   product research issues official product specifications
    d.   product design assumes prime responsibilities for establishing economic tolerances

Key: d.   product design assumes prime responsibilities for establishing economic tolerances
      (Ref. Applications Question 25, October 1972)

---

[47] *Juran's Quality Control Handbook* by J. M. Juran, 4th ed., McGraw-Hill, New York, pg. 3.9-3.11.
[48] *Juran's Quality Control Handbook* by J. M. Juran, 4th ed., McGraw-Hill, New York, pg. 13.7-13.18.

68.   When planning the specifications for product quality in the so-called *mechanical industries*

    a.   market research establishes economic tolerances
    b.   product design assumes prime responsibility for establishing economic tolerances
    c.   product research issues official product specifications
    d.   quality control develops products possessing qualities that meet consumer needs
    e.   all of these

Key: b.   product design assumes prime responsibility for establishing economic tolerances
(Ref. Applications Question 50, October 1974)

69.   In the so-called *process industries*

    a.   quality control has some responsibility in choosing the process
    b.   process development issues process specifications
    c.   quality control may help to establish process tolerances
    d.   all of the above

Key: c.   all of the above   (Ref. Applications Question 59, October 1974)
This question is repeated in the October 1972 examination.[49]

70.   When planning quality control functions, which one of the following is most directly related to production of a quality product?

    a.   process control and process capability
    b.   suitable blueprints
    c.   dimensional tolerances
    d.   product audit

Key: a.   process control and process capability (Ref. Applications Question 27, October 1974)

71.   When a new manufacturing process is contemplated, an important reason for scheduling a trial production lot is

    a.   to prove engineering feasibility
    b.   to prove that the pilot plant results are the same as those in the production shop
    c.   to prove that the tools and processes can produce the product successfully with economic yields
    d.   that it is inexpensive

Key: c.   to prove that the tools and processes can produce the product successfully with economic yields (Ref. Principles Question 14, October 1972)

---

[49] *ASQC - CQE Examination*, ASQC Quality Progress, Milwaukee, WI, October 1972, Applications section Question 26.

72.   Qualification testing means

       a.   an inspection to determine the quality rating of the product
       b.   an inspection to obtain product design information and to determine the product's service
             capability, and it may require more intensive, severe testing
       c.   an inspection used to rate the accuracy of the inspectors
       d.   all of the above

Key: b.   an inspection to obtain product design information and to determine the product's service
             capability, and it may require more intensive, severe testing
       Juran[50] describes different purposes of the inspection. The qualification testing is generally used
       to determine the service capability of the product design to meet the given customer
       requirements.

       Choice a describes quality rating inspection, and choice c is usually called accuracy inspection,
       over inspection, or check inspection.

73.   In the preproduction phase of quality planning, an appropriate activity would be to

       a.   determine responsibility for process control
       b.   determine the technical depth of available labor (manpower)
       c.   establish compatible approaches for accumulation of process data
       d.   conduct the process capability studies to measure process expectations

Key: b.   determine the technical depth of available labor (manpower)
       (Ref. Principles Question 39, October 1972)

74.   To determine the training needs for quality in your company, you should

       a.   contact all the managers who will be sending people to the training program, and ask
             them about what specific courses in quality they require for their people
       b.   contact all the people directly and ask them about what specific courses in quality they
             require
       c.   contact the specialists in quality to decide the tools and techniques that should be selected
             for the training program based on the feedback of managers and/or people.
       d.   all of the above

Key: d.   all of the above
       Refer to Juran[51] for planning a training program. Based on the above data, some companies
       create a detailed matrix of type of personnel to be trained and the training subjects.

---

[50] *Juran's Quality Control Handbook* by J. M. Juran, 4th ed., McGraw-Hill, New York, pg. 18.5.
[51] *Juran's Quality Control Handbook* by J. M. Juran, 4th ed., McGraw-Hill, New York, pg. 115-11.10.

75.   In a visual inspection situation, one of the best ways to minimize deterioration of the quality level is to

        a.   retrain the inspector frequently
        b.   add variety to the task
        c.   have a program of frequent eye examinations
        d.   have frequent breaks
        e.   have a standard to compare against the part of the operation

Key: e.   have a standard to compare against the part of the operation
        (Ref. Applications Question 77, August 1978)
        As a first step to minimize the bias and increase the effectiveness of the visual inspection, we must have or develop a standard to compare against the part of the operation. In any inspection or audit, we must compare the product against its reference standard. The visual standard clearly defines the product requirements and its acceptance criteria. This helps the inspector or the operator to correctly identify the good or acceptable parts and the nonconforming parts.

        The remaining choices, i.e., choices a, b, c, and d, are important to make the inspection more effective and less monotonous. Choice a is important when product requirements change over a period of time, for short production runs, or for products that are extremely sensitive to safety or compliance. Choices b and d are important for proper ergonomics and human factors analysis. Choice c is helpful in special situations, such as color matching. You may need to develop ranking skills for such questions since all the choices look good and seem correct.

76.   If the purpose of the inspection is to determine if the process is approaching the specification limits, it is usually called

        a.   acceptance sampling
        b.   sorting or 100% inspection
        c.   Pre-Control
        d.   quality rating

Key: c.   Pre-Control
        Juran[52] defines various purposes of inspection and their distinguishing features. Pre-Control is a type of inspection used to determine if the process is approaching the specification limits. It primarily uses narrower limits than specifications, and the measurements of the individual unit are compared to the narrowed limits. It helps to determine if the process changes are likely to cause any defective product. Precontrol is a method of controlling a process based on tolerances or specifications. Precontrol can be used for any quality characteristic without concern for the shape, type, and stability of the distribution. Pre-Control is a very simple tool, and operators can use it easily to manage their production processes.

---

[52] *Juran's Quality Control Handbook* by J. M. Juran, 4th ed., McGraw-Hill, New York, pg. 18.5-18.6 and 24.31.

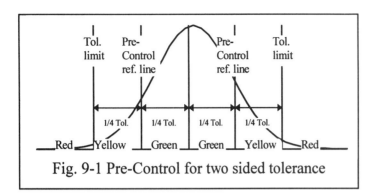
Fig. 9-1 Pre-Control for two sided tolerance

Fig. 9-1 shows precontrol for two sided tolerance. Reference lines are placed at a 1/4 tolerance range for two sided tolerances. It defines the tolerance zones in three colors: the green area is between the reference lines; the yellow area is between the reference line and its corresponding upper or lower tolerance limit; and the red area is outside the tolerance limit.

Montgomery[53] recommends using this technique to detect shifts or upsets resulting from nonconforming parts or units. Pre-Control does not require plotting a control chart to determine if the process is in a state of statistical control. This question is repeated in the July 1984[54] examination and it is discussed in Chapter 7, Statistical Process Control, Question 49.

Acceptance sampling (choice a) means the inspection used to distinguish good lots from bad lots. Sorting and 100% inspection (choice b) means an inspection used to distinguish good pieces from bad pieces. Quality rating (choice d) is used to rate the quality of the product by assigning demerits for various defects in the product.

77.   One of the first questions that should be answered when planning to process quality data is

        a.   will the results of the analysis be used?
        b.   how much will the analysis cost?
        c.   what is the error of measurement (analytical variation)
        d.   is the sample size large enough?

Key: a.   will the results of the analysis be used? (Ref. Principles Question 33, October 1974)
        This is very important but mostly neglected by managers and engineers. What do we do with the results or data? How do *we use data and not opinions* in decision making and managing risk? Will the management understand the data and use them in understanding the magnitude of the issues? If such questions are addressed during the planning stages, significant resources of people, equipment, etc., can be saved, and we will not end up with non-value-added data. All the other choices are important but may be less effective or meaningless if we do not know how to use the results of analysis.

78.   Quality data, which are regularly obtained but not used, should be

        a.   analyzed periodically by an expert statistician to glean as much information as possible
        b.   discontinued to save time and money
        c.   stored until such time as the need arises

---

[53] *Introduction to Statistical Quality Control* by D.C. Montgomery, 2nd ed., John Wiley and Sons, New York, pg. 332-334.
[54] *ASQC - CQE Examination*, ASQC Quality Progress, Milwaukee, WI, July 1984, Applications section Question 37.

    d.   processed by computer and summary reports issued regularly to interested persons

Key: b.   discontinued to save time and money (Ref. Applications Question 77, July 1984)
          This is commonsense. You do not need an expert to say this. However, the fact is that today we
          have high-tech equipment with computers collecting all types of data, but not too many people
          know what to do with it, how to read it, or how to make decisions using the data. Such conditions
          are described as "waste or non-value-added" in the system and should be eliminated.

79.   You have been asked to appraise the new quality data system developed by your statistical
          services group. Which of the following measures need not be considered during your evaluation
          of the effectiveness of that quality data system?

    a.   The information is resulting in effective and timely corrective action.
    b.   The system is being adequately maintained.
    c.   The reports are being distributed monthly.
    d.   Paperwork is held to a minimum.

Key: c.   The reports are being distributed monthly. (Ref. Applications Question 75, October 1974)
          Read the question carefully as it is asking for the measures that need *not* be considered.

80.   Creating a sensor is an important step in defining the control process. This means

    a.   a defined amount of some quality feature which permits evaluation of that feature in
                numbers
    b.   a method or instrument which can carry out the evaluation and state the findings in
                numbers in terms of units of measure
    c.   a regulatory process through which we measure actual quality performance, compare it
                with quality goals, and act on the difference
    d.   all of the above

Key: b.   a method or instrument which can carry out the evaluation and state the findings in
                numbers in terms of units of measure
          Juran[55] defines the sensor as the instrument or equipment used to provide information in terms
          of units of measure. Choice a is a definition of *unit of measure*, and choice c defines quality
          control.

81.   An effective report should have the following characteristics

    a.   the data and information are intermixed within the body of the report
    b.   the report is widely distributed
    c.   charts are never used
    d.   the data are compared with standards of performance which have previously been

[55] *Juran's Quality Control Handbook* by J. M. Juran, 4th ed., McGraw-Hill, New York, pg. 6.31-6.35

established
e.   all of the above

Key: d.   the data are compared with standards of performance which have previously been
                  established   (Ref. Principles Question 81, October 1974)

82.   Which of the following elements is least necessary to a good corrective action feedback report?

        a.   what caused the failure
        b.   who caused the failure
        c.   what correction has been made
        d.   when the correction is effective
        e.   how the corrected product is identified

Key: b.   who caused the failure   (Ref. Principles Question 38, October 1974)
        The emphasis is on the quality system and not on the person. The human element is an integral
        part of the quality system but the system must prevail. So if an operation has failures, instead of
        blaming someone ("who caused failure") it is more important to analyze the system for all the
        root causes of failure, as shown in choices a, c, d, and e.

83.   To minimize the impact of product recall, which one of the following is the most important
        element in a quality system?

        a.   receiving inspection at the plants
        b.   traceability system
        c.   warranty analysis
        d.   all of the above

Key: b.   traceability system
        Juran[56] discusses the importance of a traceability system in the situation of a product recall. A
        product recall is defined as the actions taken due to deficiencies in products that are already
        shipped to customers. This represents quality costs of external failure. The impact of any recall
        can be minimized if the suspect product units can be quickly identified separately from other
        units in production or storage, etc. This means the company should establish a traceability
        system to locate quickly all nonconforming or suspect units in particular and the entire product in
        general.

84.   To study the field performance of your products, you are using the complaints as a tracking
        characteristic. Which one of the following is *not* a good unit of measure for this characteristic?

        a.   cost of claims paid
        b.   total number of complaints

---

[56] *Juran's Quality Control Handbook* by J. M. Juran, 4th ed., McGraw-Hill, New York, pg. 20.32-20.33.

    c.   number of complaints per $1 million of sales

    d.   value of the material under complaint per $100 of sales of the product

Key: a.   cost of claims paid

It is important to design an effective measure of field performance to properly direct the resources for continuous improvement of a product's field performance. Juran[57] describes various types of characteristics, i.e., control subjects using effective units of measure to get meaningful information. Choice a is not a proper unit of measure for evaluating complaints as all complaints are not the same as claims. Some of the complaints are just dissatisfaction or annoyance and may not result in a valid product claim. However, they can damage the company's credibility and reputation with its customers. Hence it is necessary to track and analyze all types of complaints as feedback of a product's field performance.

85.   Which of the following are good factors in setting up a traceability program to manage product recalls?

    I.   unit cost of the product
    II.   product life
    III.   product complexity
    IV.   methods of identification

    a.   I, II, and III
    b.   II, III, IV
    c.   III, IV, and I
    d.   IV, I, and II
    e.   I, II, III, and IV

Key: e.   I, II, III, and IV

ASQC[58] provides several important factors to set up an effective traceability program for effectively locating and identifying the products during a recall. They are, for example, product category, product life (item II), unit cost of the product (item I), recall or repair in the field, product complexity (item III), the rationale for recall, documents, and different methods of identification and coding (item IV).

86.   To minimize product complaints, you should initiate a complaint program, which includes

    a.   a method of resolving the complaint to satisfy the complainant
    b.   a process to identify vital few or serious complaints from many types of complaints
    c.   analysis methods to identify the root causes of different complaints
    d.   long-term corrective actions to prevent the recurrence of the complaints

---

[57] *Juran's Quality Control Handbook* by J. M. Juran, 4th ed., McGraw-Hill, New York, pg. 20.32-20.33.
[58] *Product Recall Planning Guide* by ASQC, 1981; *Juran's Quality Control Handbook* by J. M. Juran, 4th ed., McGraw-Hill, New York, pg. 20.32-20.33.

e.   all of the above

Key: e.   all of the above

Juran[59] indicates that the above items are important action items of any complaint program. However, these are still after-the-fact, detection-based, and very expensive approaches. Companies should start prevention-based upfront approaches of product improvement from the early design phase. The lessons learned from previous products, models or competitive benchmarking, and all other types of voices of customers (VOCs) should be deployed in engineering or technical language using tools such as *quality function deployment (QFD),* a system engineering approach used during the design phase. The design should be evaluated and analyzed for all sources of variation, failure modes, and adverse consequences of variation to customer satisfaction. Also, it should be evaluated for the special or beneficial effects of changes and options in the form of product excitement, customer delight, and customer enthusiasm.

Robust design of product and processes, failure mode and effects analysis (FMEA), process control and capability studies, etc., should be used to make the design less sensitive to product variation, user variation, or user abuse of products. Companies should start implementing commonsense-based, economical methods of errorproofing designs and processes to become low-cost manufacturers of high-quality products. These efforts, in the long term, can result in minimum customer dissatisfaction and increased customer satisfaction. In case of new options, or new product innovations, they can create customer excitement about the product.

87.   In consumer products, the complaint rate is most directly a measure of

a.   product quality
b.   customer satisfaction
c.   market value
d.   rejection rate
e.   specification conformance

Key: b.   customer satisfaction   (Ref. Applications Question 76, July 1984)

This was true a few years ago. Today, the complaint rate is most directly a measure of customer dissatisfaction and not customer satisfaction. It would be a strategic error to consider customer dissatisfaction the same as customer satisfaction. Today, it is not enough to meet the customer requirements to achieve customer satisfaction. To be a market leader, a company needs to do some competitive benchmarking and must try to adopt the best practices to enable it to exceed expectations and excite the customer.

88.   Complaint indices should

a.   recognize the degree of dissatisfaction as viewed by the customer
b.   provide a direct input to corrective action

---

[59] *Juran's Quality Control Handbook* by J. M. Juran, 4th ed., McGraw-Hill, New York, pg. 20.20.

    c.   not necessarily be based on field complaints or dollar values of claims paid or on service calls

    d.   ignore life-cycle costs

Key: a.   recognize the degree of dissatisfaction as viewed by the customer
(Ref. Principles Question 81, July 1984)
A complaint from a customer indicates some mode of failure during its actual use, i.e., an external failure. If failure or breakdown takes place in the customer's hand, or after ownership is transferred to the customer, it results in a high level of dissatisfaction. Every customer demands that the product meet basic quality requirements, expects to receive some additional features or product benefits, and, in some cases, will be excited by them. Failure to meet customer requirements ultimately means more complaints.

Many companies today have well-defined means of tracking such customer dissatisfaction areas in the form of complaint analyses or indices which also are used for benchmarking against the competition. This is the most important area because it results not only in dissatisfied customers, but also in loss of current and prospective customers. It is not easy to quantify such losses.

89.   Analysis of data on all product returns is important because

    a.   failure rates change with length of product usage
    b.   changes in design and in customer use are often well reflected
    c.   immediate feedback and analysis of product performance becomes available
    d.   all of the above
    e.   none of the above

Key: d.   all of the above   (Ref. Principles Question 84, July 1984)
This is self-explanatory. But be careful for such questions that can be answered as "all of the above" or "none of the above."

90.   ANSI/ASQC A3-1987 is a standard for

    a..   Quality Vocabulary
    b.   Quality Systems Terminology
    c.   Generic Guidelines for Auditing of Quality Systems
    d.   Generic Guidelines for Quality Systems

Key: b.   Quality Systems Terminology
ANSI/ASQC A3-1987 is a standard for Quality Systems Terminology. It covers the basic definitions dealing with quality assurance, quality control, quality programs, and quality systems for general use.

Choice a is a standard titled " ISO 8402-1986 Quality -Vocabulary."

Choice c is a standard titled "ANSI/ASQC Q1-1986 Generic Guidelines for Auditing of Quality Systems." Lastly, choice d is a standard titled "ANSI/ASQC Z1.15-1979 Generic Guidelines for Quality Systems."

91.   Which of the following is technically equivalent to the international standard "Quality Management and Quality System Elements - Guidelines?"

       a.   ANSI/ASQC Q1-1986
       b.   ANSI/ASQC Q9000-1994
       c.   ANSI/ASQC Q9004-1994
       d.   ISO 10011

Key: c.   ANSI/ASQC Q9004-1994
       ANSI/ASQC Q9004-1994 - Quality Management and Quality System Elements - Guidelines, is technically equivalent to the ISO 9004 standard. It describes a basic set of elements by which a quality management system can be developed and implemented internally. It incorporates customary American language usage and spelling. Appendices A and B from ANSI/ASQC Z1.15 have been added to this standard but they were not included in the original ISO 9004.

       Choice a is ANSI/ASQC Q1-1986 - Generic Guidelines for Auditing of Quality Systems.
       Choice b is ANSI/ASQC Q9000-1994 - Quality Management and Quality Assurance Standards - Guidelines for Selection and Use.
       Choice d is ISO 10011- Guidelines for Auditing Quality Systems.

92.   ISO 9000-9004 and its U.S. equivalent ANSI/ASQC Q9000-9004 standards are

       a.   a series of Quality Management and Quality Assurance standards
       b.   a series of Supplier Development standards
       c.   a series of Quality Control standards
       d.   a series of Quality Program Requirements.

Key: a.   a series of Quality Management and Quality Assurance standards
       Be careful here as each choice looks somewhat correct. However, these five ISO standards (ISO 9000-9004) and their U.S. equivalent ANSI/ASQC Q9000 through 9004 are a series of Quality Management and Quality Assurance standards.

93.   MIL-Q 9858A is a standard for

       a.   Sampling Procedures and Tables for Inspection by Attributes
       b.   Sampling Procedures and Tables for Inspection by Variables for Percent Defective
       c.   Specifications of General Requirements for a Quality Program
       d.   Quality Program Requirements

Key: d.   Quality Program Requirements
Be careful with choice c which is a ANSI/ASQC Z1.18 - 1971 Specifications of General
Requirements for a Quality Program standard.
Choices a and b are MIL-STD-105E and MIL-STD-414 standards.

94.   AQAP-13-1981 (NATO) is a standard for

a.   Software Quality Assurance Program Requirements
b.   Software Quality Control System Requirements
c.   Advance Quality Assurance Planning
d.   Software Engineering Terminology, Glossary of

Key: b.   Software Quality Control System Requirements
AQAP-13-1981 (NATO) is a standard for Software Quality Control System Requirements. Be
careful with choice c which can be misleading with the abbreviation AQAP. Choice a is ANSI
/IEEE 983-1986, a standard for Software Quality Assurance Program Requirements. Choice d
is ANSI/IEEE 729-1983 Software Engineering Terminology, Glossary of.

95.   Quality Systems - Model for Quality Assurance in Design/Development, Production, Installation,
and Servicing is described by

a.   ANSI/ASQC Q9000-1994
b.   ANSI/ASQC Q9001-1994
c.   ANSI/ASQC Q9002-1994
d.   ANSI/ASQC Q9003-1994
e.   ANSI/ASQC Q9004-1994

Key: b.   ANSI/ASQC Q9001-1994
This question can be reworded different ways as seen in some of the questions above. The
ANSI/ASQC 9000 through 9004 standards are technically equivalent to the ISO 9000-9004
series, but incorporate customary American language usage and spelling. These five ISO
standards are prepared by the Technical Committee ISO/TC 176 on Quality Assurance. They
provide internationally accepted standards in the field of Quality Management and Quality
Assurance. A complete list of these five important standards is given below.

ANSI/ASQC Q9000-1994 describes Quality Management and Quality Assurance Standards -
Guidelines for Selection and Use.
ANSI/ASQC Q9001-1994 describes Quality Systems - Model for Quality Assurance in
Design/Development, Production, Installation, and Servicing.
ANSI/ASQC Q9002-1994 describes Quality Systems - Model for Quality Assurance in
Production, Installation, and Servicing.
ANSI/ASQC Q9003-1994 describes Quality Systems - Model for Quality Assurance in Final
Inspection and Test.

ANSI/ASQC Q9004-1994 describes Quality Management and Quality System Elements - Guidelines.

96.   Which of the following is/are not the purposes of the ANSI/ASQC Q9000 to Q9004 series of standards?

    a.   to clarify the distinctions and interrelationships among the principal quality concepts

    b.   to provide guidelines for the selection and use of a series of standards on quality systems that can be used for internal quality management purposes and for external quality assurance purposes

    c.   to standardize quality systems implemented by organizations

    d.   a and b above

Key: c.   to standardize quality systems implemented by organizations
This is a tricky question. The key word is **"not."** Refer to Section 1.0 Scope and Field of Application in ANSI/ASQC 9000-1994 Quality Management and Quality Assurance Standards - Guidelines for Selection and Use. Choices a and b define the purpose of this American National Standard. The Note in Section 1.0 states: "It is not the purpose of this series of American National Standards (Q9000 to Q9004) to standardize quality systems implemented by organizations."

97.   Which of the standards in the ANSI/ASQC Q9000 to Q9004 series gives guidance to all organizations for quality management purposes?

    a.   ANSI/ASQC Q9000-1994 and ANSI/ASQC Q9001-1994

    b.   ANSI/ASQC Q9001-1994, ANSI/ASQC Q9002-1994, and ANSI/ASQC Q9003-1994

    c.   ANSI/ASQC Q9002-1994 and ANSI/ASQC Q9003-1994

    d.   ANSI/ASQC Q9001-1994 and ANSI/ASQC Q9004-1994

    e.   ANSI/ASQC Q9000-1994 and ANSI/ASQC Q9004-1994

Key: e.   ANSI/ASQC Q9000-1994 and ANSI/ASQC Q9004-1994
Choices a through d are incorrect because ANSI/ASQC Q9001 to Q9003-1994 are used for external quality assurance purposes in contractual situations.[60]

98.   Which of the standards in the ANSI/ASQC Q9000 to Q9004 series are used for external quality assurance purposes in contractual situations?

    a.   ANSI/ASQC Q9000-1994 and ANSI/ASQC Q9001-1994

    b.   ANSI/ASQC Q9001-1994, ANSI/ASQC Q9002-1994, and ANSI/ASQC Q9003-1994

    c.   ANSI/ASQC Q9002-1994 and ANSI/ASQC Q9003-1994

    d.   ANSI/ASQC Q9001-1994 and ANSI/ASQC Q9004-1994

---

[60] *ANSI/ASQC Q9000-1994 Quality Management and Quality Assurance Standards - Guidelines for Selection and Use,* Section 6.0 Types of Standards on Quality Systems.

e.   ANSI/ASQC Q9000-1994 and ANSI/ASQC Q9004-1994

Key: b.   ANSI/ASQC Q9001-1994, ANSI/ASQC Q9002-1994, and ANSI/ASQC Q9003-1994
        Choice e is incorrect because the two standards ANSI/ASQC Q9000 and Q9004 give guidance to
        all organizations for quality management purposes. Refer to Question 97 above for additional
        details.

99.   Which of the following standards should be selected for use when conformance to specified
        requirements is to be assured by the supplier during several stages which may include
        design/development, production, installation, and servicing.

        a.   ANSI/ASQC Q9000-1994
        b.   ANSI/ASQC Q9001-1994
        c.   ANSI/ASQC Q9002-1994
        d.   ANSI/ASQC Q9003-1994
        e.   ANSI/ASQC Q9004-1994

Key: b.   ANSI/ASQC Q9001-1994
        Refer to Question 95 above for a list of the ANSI/ASQC Q9000 to Q9004 series of standards.

100.   An organization should seek which of the following objectives with regard to quality?

        a.   The organization should achieve and sustain the quality of the product or service
                produced so as to meet continually the purchaser's stated or implied needs.
        b.   The organization should provide confidence to its own management that the intended
                quality is being achieved and sustained.
        c.   The organization should provide confidence to the purchaser that the intended quality is
                being, or will be achieved in the delivered product or service provided.
        d.   all of the above

Key: d.   all of the above
        Refer to ANSI/ASQC Q9000-1994[61] which describes the principle concepts. It lists choices a to
        c as the three important objectives with regard to quality.

101.   The responsibility for and commitment to a quality policy belongs to the

        a.   quality engineer
        b.   quality manager
        c.   corporate quality director
        d.   highest level of management

---

[61] *ANSI/ASQC Q9000-1994 Quality Management and Quality Assurance Standards - Guidelines for Selection and Use,*
Section 4.0 Principle Concepts.

Key: d.   highest level of management

ANSI/ASQC Q9004[62] defines the management responsibility. The responsibility for and commitment to a quality policy belongs to the highest level of management. Quality management is part of the overall management function and it determines and implements quality policy. The highest management of a company should develop and state its corporate quality policy. This policy should be consistence with company policies.

102.   Which of the following is/are important element(s) for the quality documentation systems?

        a.   quality policies and procedures
        b.   quality manual
        c.   quality plans
        d.   quality records
        e.   all of the above

Key: e.   all of the above

Management should develop, establish, and implement a quality system to achieve the stated quality policies and quality objectives. To provide the confidence that the system is well understood, and is effectively operational in the company, the company should have adequate quality documentation systems. All the elements, requirements, and provisions adopted by a company to manage its quality goals and objectives should be documented in a systematic manner in the form of formal and written policies and procedures, a quality manual, quality plan, and quality records. Such documentation should be properly identified, distributed, and data and records should be collected. The quality documentation system should have provisions for effective maintenance of all quality documents and records. Refer to the ANSI/ASQC Q9004-1994 standard[63] for more details on quality documentation and records.

103.   To achieve the highest level of customer satisfaction, the quality requirements for a product or service should be defined by

        a.   the quality department
        b.   marketing function
        c.   product engineering
        d.   sales and distribution

Key: b.   marketing function

The definition of quality has evolved from fitness for use to meeting customer requirements and customer satisfaction. Today many companies are even trying to achieve standards of excellence that will not only satisfy the customer but will result in customer excitement, customer

---

[62] *ANSI/ASQC Q9004-1994 Quality Management and Quality System Elements - Guidelines,* Section 4.0 Management Responsibility.

[63] *ANSI/ASQC Q9004-1994 Quality Management and Quality System Elements - Guidelines,* Section 5.3 Documentation of the System and Section 17 Quality Documentation and Records.

enthusiasm, and customer delight.

Marketing should determine the need for the product or service and the market segment. It should estimate the market demand to determine the quantity, market price, and timing to introduce the product or service.

To achieve such standards of excellence, the marketing function should anticipate the customer's future needs, wants, and requirements upfront through market research, market studies, economic trends, buyer profiles, competitive benchmarking, etc. It should assess stated and unstated expectations or customer biases for a particular product or service and should list them in its original form as voice of customer (VOC). The VOC should be provided to the new product development teams to understand and analyze for proper deployment in the technical language of the company. The teams should try to define the system level specifications and target values for the product or service and then deploy them further in major subsystems, subsystems, components, and lastly to processes specifications. This process of systematic translation of the VOC into the technical language of the company is called quality function deployment (QFD).

104.   To effectively meet customer requirements, the marketing function should formally provide a detailed statement of product requirements that includes

    a.   performance, fit and function characteristics (customer usage methods and conditions, environmental conditions, reliability and durability requirements)
    b.   sensory characteristics such as appearance, style, color, smell, taste, feel, etc.
    c.   packaging, installation configuration and restrictions, and serviceability
    d.   requirements that describe the safety and compliance standards or statutory regulations
    e.   all of the above

Key: e.   all of the above

105.   The quality system should provide for a market readiness review that covers

    i.   manufacturability of the design, processing needs, mechanization, and automation
    ii.   evaluation of tolerances and process capabilities
    iii.   availability and adequacy of installation, operation, maintenance, and repair manuals
    iv.   structure of customer service and sales and distribution organizations, and training needs and or records of field personnel

    a.   i and ii above
    b.   ii and iii above
    c.   iii and iv above
    d.   iv and I above

Key: c.   iii and iv above

Items i and ii listed under choice a are the elements of design reviews for the product or service. They are reviewed at the appropriate phase of the design of the product. They should be reviewed upfront in very early phases of the design, as a part of design readiness and not as a part of market readiness. Market readiness generally takes place at later phases in the new product development cycle. Items listed in iii and iv are typical of a market readiness review. Other such items can be review of availability of spare parts, field trial data, certification of compliance, review of labeling, packaging designs, styles, etc.

106.   To ensure quality in specification and design, management should

   a.   clearly assign design responsibilities and ensure that those who contribute to design are aware of their responsibilities to achieve quality
   b.   ensure that the quality aspects of the design are clearly stated, and the important quality characteristics are adequately defined
   c.   ensure that the design activity provides definitive technical data for timely execution of the work and verify that the product and processes conform to the given specifications
   d.   all of the above

Key: d.   all of the above

107.   Which of the following is/are not a part of design reviews?

   a.   review of items pertaining to receiving inspection and controls
   b.   review of items pertaining to customer satisfaction requirements
   c.   review of items pertaining to product specification and service requirements
   d.   review of items pertaining to process specifications and service

Key: a.   review of items pertaining to receiving inspection and controls
        Choices b through d are part of design reviews. Choice a is an important requirement to ensure quality in procurement of products or parts.

108.   Which of the following is not considered as one of the seven basic tools of quality?

   a.   flow chart or flow diagram
   b.   Pareto chart
   c.   Fishbone or cause and effect diagram or Ishikawa diagram
   d.   Process Decision Program Chart (PDPC)

Key: d.   Process Decision Program Chart (PDPC)
        The seven basic tools of quality are as follows:

   1.   Pareto Chart
   2.   Fishbone or Cause and Effect Diagram or Ishikawa Diagram

3.   Flow Chart
4.   Control Chart
5.   Histogram
6.   Scatter Diagram or Scatter Plot
7.   Checksheet

These seven tools are generally considered as the basic tools of quality and are very effective and useful in establishing sound quality improvement processes. Please refer to Quality Progress[64] for a seven part series on "The Tools of Quality." These articles provide a well written and detailed explanation of these tools.

The Society for Quality Control Technique Development in Japan developed the *Seven New QC Tools* in April 1972. Mizuno Shigeru,[65] professor at Tokyo Industrial University, and Kondo Yoshio, professor at Kyoto University, advised the Society on further development of the *Seven New QC Tools*. They formed the Research Society for the Seven New QC Tools and held several meetings. These tools are promoted to encourage more and more use of objective data instead of vague and fuzzy communication. The seven new tools are graphical methods used by management and staff to generate new ideas and to sort the qualitative data. They aid in the timely completion of tasks and they eliminate failures. This results in improved communication and exchange of verbal and technical information in its unfiltered form, and a clear understanding of the problem and/or process.

The new seven management tools (also called M-Tools) for quality are as follows:

1.   Kawakita Jiro (KJ) Method[66] (also called Affinity Diagrams)
2.   Tree Diagrams (also called Systematic Diagram Methods)
3.   Process Decision Program Charts (PDPC)
4.   Matrix Diagrams
5.   Interrelationship digraphs
6.   Prioritization Matrices (also called Matrix Data Analysis Methods)
7.   Activity Network Diagrams (also called Arrow Diagram Methods)

Choice d is a part of the seven new management tools of quality. Process decision program chart (PDPC) is a technique used to determine the best process to be used to obtain desired results. It anticipates various possible outcomes from a process and enables one to develop counter measures. It allows timely process adjustments based on its progress and helps to achieve the best possible solutions.

---

[64] *Tools of Quality* published by ASQC Quality Progress, Milwaukee, WI, June 1990, through December 1990 issues.

[65] *Management for Quality Improvement - The Seven New QC Tools* edited by Shigeru Mizuno, Productivity Press, Cambridge, MA, 1988; *Interrelationship Digraph,* November December 1985a, *Matrix Diagram*, March-April 1986a, and *Program Decision Process Chart (PDPC),* July-August 1986b, published by Growth Opportunity Alliance of Lawrence (G.O.A.L) Newsletter, Boston, MA.

[66] The KJ Method is a trademark registered by the founder of the Kawayoshida Reasearch Center, Japan.

109.   The most widely used tool to group various types of causes within a process into categories such as material, equipment/machine, environment, people, methods, etc., and to identify the most likely causes in the process, is called a

        a.   histogram
        b.   cause and effect or Fishbone diagram
        c.   Pareto chart
        d.   process decision program chart

Key: b.   cause and effect or Fishbone diagram

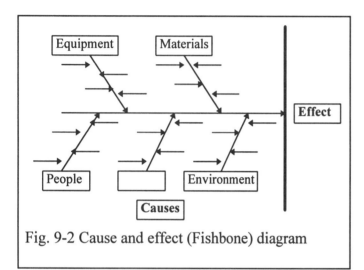

Fig. 9-2 Cause and effect (Fishbone) diagram

Fishbone or cause and effect diagram, as shown in Fig. 9-2, is a simple and basic tool of quality and is very widely used in the industry for understanding the causes of variation, failure modes, and quality problems in the processes. A quality team can identify many possible causes affecting the outcome or the response variable of the process using brainstorming and other idea generation methods. Then all such causes are sorted into major categories such as material, equipment/ machine, environment, people, methods, etc.

This provides a more structured picture of all possible causes and then teams can select the most likely causes from any of these categories for study and evaluation.

Choices a and c are parts of the seven basic tools and choice d is a part of the seven new tools. Refer to Question 108 for an explanation of the PDPC chart.

110.   A basic tool of quality which uses the concept of "*vital few and trivial many*" to categorize the causes of variation or problems and then shows them in the form of vertical bars arranged in descending order from most to least significant is called a

        a.   histogram
        b.   cause and effect or Fishbone diagram
        c.   Pareto chart
        d.   affinity diagram

Key: c.   Pareto chart

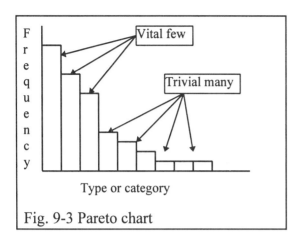

Fig. 9-3 Pareto chart

The Pareto chart is named after an Italian economist Vilfredo Pareto. Dr. Juran introduced this concept as a simple and basic tool for quality improvement. Fig. 9-3 shows a Pareto chart as a bar chart where each bar shows one type of cause, type of issue, or defect, and its height shows the frequency of its occurrence. These bars are arranged in descending order from the most to least significant causes or items. This helps to separate the "vital few" causes from the "significant many."

This is a simple method of prioritization or ranking and actions and resources can be assigned to the *vital few* causes which will bring approximately 75% to 80% improvement at less cost. Choices a and b are part of the seven basic tools of quality.

Choice d is a part of the seven new management tools for quality. An affinity diagram, as shown in Fig. 9-4, provides a creative method of organizing a large set of ideas and qualitative data in subgroups or categories based on the natural relationships between different ideas and items.

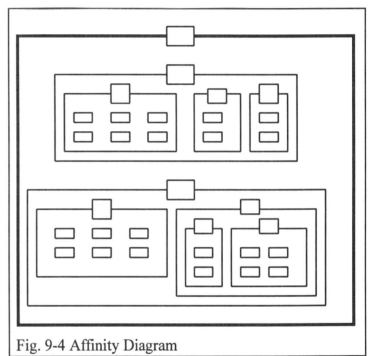

Fig. 9-4 Affinity Diagram

111. Which of the following is/are not a basic tool of quality?

a. Affinity diagram
b. Tree diagram
c. Process decision program chart
d. all of the above

Key: d. all of the above
The key word is "***not***." All of the above are part of the new seven management tools of quality improvement. Refer to Questions 108 through 110 for additional discussion.

112. A management tool used to develop the most optimized schedule for a project involving a large

number of complex activities and tasks and to monitor its completion progress at different events is called a (an)

a.   Affinity Diagram
b.   Activity Network Diagram
b.   Tree Diagram
c.   Process Decision Program Chart

Key: b.   Activity Network Diagram
The activity network diagram (shown in Fig. 9-5) is used to develop plans for defining major events in a project and schedule to complete them, as seen in the critical path method (CPM) and program evaluation review technique (PERT) diagrams.

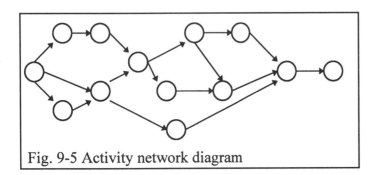

Fig. 9-5 Activity network diagram

As in any quality improvement project, it is very important to develop an itemized list of activities and a schedule of completion. It provides a visible picture of the progress of the quality improvement project and identifies delays and bottlenecks, if any, in a timely manner.

113.   Continuous improvement can be defined as

a.   completing incomplete projects later
b.   fire fighting
c.   corrective actions
d.   achieving a new higher level of performance excellence that is superior to any previous levels

Key: d.   achieving a new higher level of performance excellence that is superior to any previous levels
Juran[67] provides a detailed discussion on quality improvement vs. fire fighting.

114.   To make the most effective communication and presentation to top management, the quality engineer should

a.   use the language of money and the order of magnitude
b.   show a detailed step-by-step breakdown of every activity and process element
c.   provide detailed status on every activity involved in the project
d.   use details of measurement analysis and process capability data

---

[67] *Juran's Quality Control Handbook* by J. M. Juran, 4th ed., McGraw-Hill, New York, pg. 22.2-6.

Key: a.   use the language of money and the order of magnitude
It is important that the quality engineer understands the need to use different types of language for management at different levels. To convince top management that the adverse consequences of the quality problems are severe and a new unconventional approach is needed to attain the quality improvements, the quality manager or engineer should understand and use the language of money to top management. This is particularly very important when the problems are chronic and inherent in the current system, requiring an aggressive action. The quality engineer should convert the size of the problem into the language of money, i.e., dollars saved per quarter or year, etc.

Choices b through d are not correct because they represent the language of middle management, and of lower management's, supervisors and line leaders.

Top management is very familiar with the language of money, i.e., impact on profit, total cost itself, warranty costs, loss of production volume, impact on people resources, productivity, etc. Top management is generally more interested in the strategic impact of the quality problem to their stocks, market image, and overall acceptability of the product.

Lower level management and line supervisors are highly technical people and more involved in day-to-day operational issues and problems. For them, the quality engineer should use the technical language and use tactical approaches and not strategic details. Choices b through d are technical details that top management does not need to know in great detail.

The language for middle management is sometimes the best of both, i.e., one needs to be bilingual. Use the language of money with top management and use the tactical approach and lots of technical details with lower level supervisors.

For effective communication and presentation of information, the quality engineer should understand such distinct approaches.

115.   When making a presentation to top management, the quality engineer should not

      a.   use the language of money and its impact on the company
      b.   provide an inflated picture of the total cost by including open action items, some trivial and nonrelevant items
      c.   promise the top management that once the quality problem is solved, they will reach zero total quality costs
      d.   a and b above
      e.   b and c above

Key: e.   b and c above
The key phrase is *"should not."* Choice a is incorrect, because the language of top management is money and the quality engineer should use it for effective communication of the magnitude of

the problem. Choices b and c represent an important reminder to the quality engineers. The presentation to top management should be factual, simple, and to the point. It should not inflate the anticipated savings. Also one should be careful in making promises of zero total quality costs because failure costs may be reduced significantly but the prevention and appraisal costs may still be needed. Refer to Chapter 10, Quality Cost Analysis, for additional discussion of total quality costs and the optimum point.

116.   The quality engineer should use the Pareto principle to identify the vital few contributors to the total quality costs so that quality improvement efforts can be concentrated effectively. One such approach can be

   a.   Pareto breakdown by organization - plant, division, etc.
   b.   Pareto breakdown by persons - operators
   c.   Pareto breakdown by function - product design, manufacturing, assembly, etc.
   d.   Pareto breakdown by type of defect or problem category
   e.   any of the above

Key: e.   any of the above
Any such breakdown with meaningful and technically correct data is useful and can bring desired quality improvements.

117.   To achieve meaningful results, a quality improvement project should be selected or nominated based on

   a.   Pareto analysis of quality costs
   b.   Pareto analysis of field problems or customer complaints
   c.   the need to study the effect of new processes or product designs and to develop training programs
   d.   the need to resolve technology or design trade off issues
   e.   all of the above

Key: e.   all of the above

118.   A quality improvement project should include details of

   a.   the scope
   b.   the return on investment
   c.   the level of urgency
   d.   the strategic impact to the organization, if any
   e.   all of the above

Key: e.   all of the above

119.   Which of the following is not true to bring significant quality improvements?

    a.   a project should deal mainly with sporadic and not chronic problems.
    b.   a project should be feasible.
    c.   a project should have significant impact on the function, product, or the organization, etc.
    d.   a project can be used to explore new theories and to provide means of training.

Key: a.   a project should deal mainly with sporadic and not chronic problems.
The key phrase is "*is not true*." The chronic problems[68] are inherent and repeat frequently. They can be present in the system for a long time but nobody has solved them. Sporadic problems are the sudden jump in defects or field failures and they result in the fire fighting mode. The important thing in quality improvement is not fire fighting or detection of sporadic problems, but to learn and adapt fire prevention and to remove the chronic problems leading to significant breakthroughs. The projects should focus on various chronic problems as a strategic issue.

120.   Managing a quality improvement project requires understanding of the

    i.   diagnostic journey from symptom to remedy
    ii.   diagnostic journey from symptom to cause
    iii.   remedial journey from cause to remedy
    iv.   remedial journey from symptom to remedy

    a.   i and ii above
    b.   ii and iii above
    c.   iii and iv above
    d.   iv and i above

Key: b.   ii and iii above
Be careful with the confusing combinations here. Juran[69] discusses important journeys for effective completion of quality improvement projects. A diagnostic journey involves a journey from symptom to cause. A remedial journey involves a journey from a cause to a remedy.

121.   As a leader of a quality improvement project team, the quality engineer should not

    a.   lead the team to define the problem based on the analysis of the symptoms
    b.   lead the team to develop possible causes of the problem
    c.   lead the team to develop possible remedial actions
    d.   make the policy changes to implement the remedial actions
    e.   evaluate the effectiveness of the remedial actions to permanently solve the problem

Key: d.   make the policy changes to implement the remedial actions

---

[68] *Juran's Quality Control Handbook* by J. M. Juran, 4th ed., McGraw-Hill, New York, pg. 22.5.
[69] *Juran's Quality Control Handbook* by J. M. Juran, 4th ed., McGraw-Hill, New York, pg. 22.26.

Be careful here. The key phrase is *"should not."* Top management, and not the project team leader, is responsible for and has the authority to make the policy changes to implement the remedial actions. The project team leader should use the language of money to recommend the necessary policy changes to top management for implementing the remedial actions.

122.   Which of the following is true?

        a.   a project team involves members from a single department
        b.   membership in a project team is generally voluntary
        c.   a project team is an adhoc team formed for one of the vital few projects and is disbanded
                after completion of the project
        d.   a project team is the same as a quality circle team

Key: c.   a project team is an adhoc team formed for one of the vital few projects and is disbanded
                after completion of the project
        The key phrase is *"is true."* A project team is a focus team and is formed to solve one of the vital few problems or issues. It is generally a multidisciplined team, as most of the chronic problems are spread out and affect multiple departments. The project team requires a strong dedicated commitment of members and generally membership in a project team is mandatory and not voluntary. Once the project is successfully completed, the project team is disbanded.

        A project team is not the same as a quality circle team. The quality circle team is generally a single department or function activity with voluntary members. They are focusing on many useful smaller issues affecting their function or department. They continue to meet periodically to resolve operational issues of different products or processes in their area.

123.   Policy control (Hoshin Kanri) means

        i.   top management is leading the quality function, promoting it, and establishing the
                company's quality policy and the long term strategic plan to implement total quality, i.e.,
                company wide quality
        ii.   top management is responsible to provide resources, and implement and operationalize
                the quality policy and strategic plan
        iii.   top management is responsible to evaluate and monitor whether the quality policy and
                strategic quality plan are being implemented and operationalized in a timely manner, on
                schedule
        iv.   act on the progress and decide whether corrective actions are needed to fully implement
                quality policy, and identify opportunities for continuous improvement

        a.   i, ii, and iii above
        b.   ii, iii, and iv above
        c.   iii, iv, and i above
        d.   i, ii, iii, and iv above

Key: d.   i, ii, iii, and iv above
        Hoshin Kanri, policy control, is based on Deming's *"plan, do, study (also called check), act"* (PDSA) cycle as shown in Fig. 9-6 below. Hoshin Kanri (policy control) defines the concept of *companywide quality control* (CWQC) and the importance of top management commitment in development of quality policy and policy deployment companywide. This does not mean a so-called "program of the month" but a well-defined and planned activity.

Top management establishes the quality policy, i.e., they establish quality objectives and standards, lead the quality function, and promote it to the entire company. They are responsible for establishing the long term strategic plan for total quality, i.e., companywide quality. This is the *plan* in the PDSA cycle.

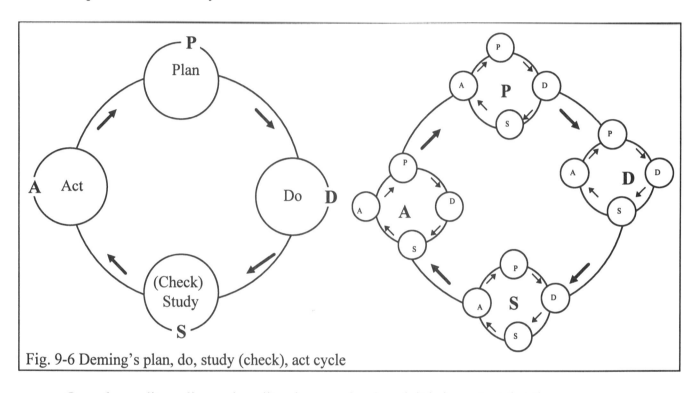

Fig. 9-6 Deming's plan, do, study (check), act cycle

Once the quality policy and quality plans are developed, it is important that they are implemented, i.e., the *do* of the PDSA cycle. Top management is responsible to provide resources, and implement and operationalize the quality policy and strategic plan, i.e., employees are working and doing things that support the strategic plan and quality policy.

As a part of policy control, top management is responsible to evaluate and monitor, i.e., the *study* or check of the PDSA cycle, whether the quality policy and strategic quality plan are being implemented and operationalized as defined, and in a timely manner, i.e., on schedule.

The *act* of the PDSA cycle requires that top management acts on the progress and decides whether corrective actions are needed to fully implement quality policy, and identify opportunities for continuous improvement.

PDSA is an important concept and it is only briefly described here. Hence you should refer to Deming's writing to gain deeper understanding of the PDSA cycle.

124.   The term policy deployment refers to

   a.   developing quality slogans and managing by objectives
   b.   developing policies for problem solving (fire fighting) activities
   c.   distributing policies and procedures to divisions and plants from corporate headquarters
   d.   implementing, operationalizing, and internalizing the quality policies for continuous improvement (KAIZEN) throughout the company, at every level.

Key: d.   implementing, operationalizing, and internalizing the quality policies for continuous improvement (KAIZEN) throughout the company, at every level.

The term policy deployment is based on the spirit of KAIZEN. Policy deployment means implementing, operationalizing, and internalizing the quality policies for continuous improvement (KAIZEN) throughout the company, at every level. Policy indicates both the short and long term goals, objectives, and measures. It requires that information and communications are open from the top down and bottom up before the policies are finalized. It takes into consideration the past performance, current plans for improvement, and lessons learned. It follows the Pareto principle for prioritization of policies. Once the policies are finalized, they must be deployed throughout the company, i.e., at every level in the company. It means the priorities are assigned and operational level measures and action plans, timing schedules, etc., are developed and implemented.

This question requires a strong understanding of KAIZEN. Imai[70] defines KAIZEN *as improvement, i.e., ongoing, continuous improvement that involves everyone, both the management and the operational level work force.* Imai suggests that KAIZEN should become part of our life, a way of life. Every aspect of human life, personal and professional, individual and organizational, needs KAIZEN, i.e., it can and needs to be continuously improved. KAIZEN should be management oriented, group oriented, and individual oriented.

Imai discusses three important prerequisites for policy deployment. First, KAIZEN is only possible if each manager is clear in his or her role to achieve the set goals and targets and to continuously improve the work processes. Second, managers should be clear about the check points (*process oriented-P criterion*) and control points (*result oriented-R criterion*) to achieve the goals. Third, operational procedures and management systems should be in place and be maintained.

The *control points-R criterion* mean the company's goals and actual measures are the check points- R criterion. Policy deployment involves the deployment between the control points and

---

[70] KAIZEN (Ky'zen) - The Key to Japan's Competitive Success by Masaaki Imai, 1st ed., McGraw-Hill, New York, pg. 3, 142-145; KAIZEN is a trademark of the KAIZEN Institute, Ltd.

check points. Every manager must understand the strategic plans and goals to be achieved and must be committed to achieve them. The policy deployment requires that a policy audit is conducted to ensure that the policy and goals are deployed and effectively executed. Policy deployment, KAIZEN, and PDCA are very strong concepts. You should study them in more detail to gain sound understanding. Also refer to Question 123 above for additional discussion.

125. The continuous improvement should be

    a.   management oriented
    b.   group oriented
    c.   individual oriented
    d.   all of the above

Key: d.   all of the above
Refer to Question 124 above for a detailed discussion.

ASQC-CQE BIBLIOGRAPHY AND OTHER REFERENCES ON QUALITY PRACTICES AND APPLICATIONS

1. Aft, Lawrence S., *Fundamentals of Industrial Quality Control*, 2nd ed., Milwaukee, ASQC, Quality Press, 1992.
2. *ANSI/ASQC A1-1987, Definitions, Symbols, Formulas, and Tables for Control Charts*, Milwaukee, ASQC Quality Press, 1987.
3. *ANSI/ASQC A2-1987, Terms and Symbols for Acceptance Sampling*, Milwaukee, ASQC Quality Press, 1987.
4. *ANSI/ASQC A3-1987, Quality Systems Terminology*, Milwaukee, ASQC Quality Press, 1987.
5. *ANSI/ASQC Q90 Series-1987, Quality Management and Quality Assurance Standards*, (Q90-Q94) Milwaukee, ASQC Quality Press, 1987.
6. *ANSI/ASQC C1-1985, Specifications of General Requirements for Quality Program*, Milwaukee, ASQC Quality Press, 1985.
7. ASQC Statistics Division, *Glossary and Tables for Statistical Quality Control*, 2nd ed., Milwaukee, ASQC Quality Press, 1983.
8. Besterfield, Dale H., *Quality Control,* 3rd ed., Prentice Hall, Englewood Cliffs., N.J., 1990.
9. Caplan, Frank, *The Quality System, A Sourcebook for Managers and Engineers*, 2nd ed., Radnor, PA, Chilton Book Co, 1990.
10. Deming, W. Edwards, *Out of Crisis*, Cambridge, MA., MIT Press, 1986.
11. Duncan, A. J., *Quality Control and Industrial Statistics*, 5th ed., Homewood IL, Irwin Inc., 1986.
12. Feigenbaum, A.V., *Total Quality Control*, 3rd ed., Revised, New York, McGraw-Hill, 1991.
13. Grant, Eugen L. and Richard Leavenworth, *Statistical Quality Control*, 6th ed., New York, McGraw-Hill, 1988.
14. Growth Opportunity Alliance of Lawrence (G.O.A.L) Newsletter, *Interrelationship Digraph,* November December 1985a, *Matrix Diagram*, March-April 1986a, and *Program Decision Process*

Chart (PDPC), July-August 1986b, Boston, MA, G.O.A.L./Quality Productivity Competitiveness (QPC) Boston, MA.

15. Hunter, Thomas A., *Engineering Design for Safety*, New York, McGraw-Hill, 1992.

16. Imai, Masaaki, KAIZEN (Ky'zen) - *The Key to Japan's Competitive Success*, New York, McGraw-Hill, 1986. (KAIZEN is a trademark of the KAIZEN Institute, Ltd.)

17. Ishikawa, Kaoru, *Guide to Quality Control*, White Plains, NY, Quality Resources, 1976.

18. Juran, J. M., *Juran's Quality Control Handbook*, 4th ed., New York, McGraw-Hill, 1988.

19. Juran, J. M. and F. M. Gryna, *Quality Planning and Analysis*, 3rd ed., New York, McGraw-Hill, 1993.

20. Mizuno, Shigeru, *Management for Quality Improvement - The Seven New QC Tools,* Cambridge, MA, Productivity Press, 1988.

21. Montgomery, D.C., *Introduction to Statistical Quality Control*, 2nd ed., New York, John Wiley and Sons, 1991.

22. O'Connor, Patrick D.T., *Practical Reliability Engineering*, 3rd ed., New York, John Wiley and Sons.

23. Picard, Lawrence G. Sr., *Fundamentals of Quality Control.*, Milwaukee, 1992.

24. Pyzdek, Thomas and Roger W. Berger, *Quality Engineering Handbook,* Milwaukee, ASQC Quality Press, 1992.

25. Western Electric, *Statistical Quality Control Handbook*, Indianapolis, AT&T, 1956.

CHAPTER 10

QUALITY COST ANALYSIS

ASQC'S <u>BODY OF KNOWLEDGE (BOK)</u> FOR THE CQE EXAMINATION

This chapter focuses on the following selected subject areas of BOK from *Section II, Quality Practices and Applications.*

Cost of Quality

1. Categories
   a. Prevention
   b. Appraisal
   c. Internal failure
   d. External failure
2. Data collection, interpretation, and reporting

1.   Quality costs are defined as

   I.   all those costs that are associated with producing, making, identifying, repairing,
          avoiding, and preventing the nonconforming products
   II.   those costs that are associated with all the activities engaged in designing, implementing,
          and maintaining a quality system to prevent the occurrence of nonconforming products
   III.   those costs that are incurred during the measurement, evaluation, or audit of the products
          to ensure the required level of conformance to given quality requirements
   IV.   the measure of the costs specifically associated with the achievement or nonachievement
          of product or service quality including all product or service requirements established by
          the company and its contracts with customers and society

   a.   I and II only
   b.   II and III only
   c.   III and IV only
   d.   IV and I only

Key: d.   IV and I only
Both IV and I define quality costs. The quality cost definition in IV is as per the ASQC's Quality
Cost Committee. Watch for II, which defines only the prevention cost; and III defines appraisal
cost only. Hence choices a, b, and c are not true.

2.   The total quality cost is defined as the

   a.   sum of internal and external failure costs
   b.   sum of prevention and appraisal costs
   c.   sum of prevention, appraisal, and failure costs
   d.   sum of appraisal, prevention, and external failure costs

Key: c.   sum of prevention, appraisal, and failure costs
Choice c includes all categories of quality costs and as a sum it is called total quality costs.
Hence c is the proper answer. Choice d includes only the external failure costs and not the
internal failure costs. Hence it is not the correct answer. Similarly choice a includes only
failure costs but no prevention of appraisal costs, and choice b does not include the failure
costs.

3.   The total quality cost can be defined as the

   a.   sum of cost of conformance and cost of nonconformance
   b.   sum of prevention, appraisal, and failure costs
   c.   sum of all costs involved for any business
   d.   all of the above
   e.   a and b both

Key: e.   a and b both

These are the major classifications of quality costs and as a sum it is called total quality costs. Choice a defines quality cost as the sum of the cost of conformance and cost of nonconformance, and choice b defines quality costs as the sum of prevention, appraisal, and failure costs.

Watch for choice c, which defines quality costs as the *sum of all costs* involved for any business, which is not true. *All costs* can include all direct and indirect costs, including capital investments, equipment costs, payroll, material costs, etc. In general, it indicates the costs included in the accounting system of any business. Many of these cost elements are not considered quality costs. The main focus here is to find only the costs of poor quality and not all costs that are essential to run a business. Similarly, watch for choice d. This is a very tempting choice for many questions, but not here because choice c is not true.

4.   The basic objective of a quality cost program is to

    a.   identify the source of quality failures
    b.   interface with the accounting department
    c.   improve the profit of your company
    d.   identify quality control department costs

Key: c.   improve the profit of your company (Ref. Principles Question 63, July 1984)
This is the ultimate objective for any company. Be careful here as all choices are good and true to some extent as an objective. However, the basic, prime, or ultimate objective for any company is to become profitable and to continuously improve the profit posture of the company. All quality improvement efforts should result in higher profitability. As a quality engineer, one should always keep the economic impact of all quality improvement programs in mind. Hence c is the best choice. This question is repeated in the October 1974 examination.[1]

5.   The basic objective of a quality cost program is to

    a.   identify the source of quality failures
    b.   determine quality control department responsibilities
    c.   utilize accounting department reports
    d.   improve the profit posture of your company

Key: d.   improve the profit posture of your company
(Ref. Principles Question 80, October 1972) Refer to Question 12 for discussion.

6.   Quality costs are best classified as

    a.   the costs of inspection and test, quality engineering, quality administration, and quality equipment
    b.   direct, indirect, and overhead costs
    c.   costs of prevention, appraisal, and failure
    d.   unnecessary

---

[1] *ASQC - CQE Examination*, ASQC Quality Progress, October 1974, Principles section, Question 83.

e.   none of the above

Key: c.   cost of prevention, appraisal, and failure   (Ref. Principles Question 64, August 1978)
These are three major classifications of quality costs.

7.   Typically, total quality costs include

a.   all costs incurred by the quality department
b.   some costs incurred by production
c.   some costs incurred by production engineering
d.   all of the above

Key: d.   all of the above   (Ref. Applications Question 34, October 1974)
The total quality costs, i.e., prevention, appraisal, internal and external failure, include all the costs indicated above.

8.   The most logical argument for implementing a quality cost program is

a.   to make the boss happy
b.   it is a new accounting practice required by tax laws
c.   because the supplier quality audit manual of your customer requires it
d.   to identify various quality costs and invest properly for prevention and appraisal activities up front to minimize failure costs

Key: d.   to identify various quality costs and invest properly for prevention and appraisal activities up front to minimize failure costs
The goal of a quality cost program is to identify areas of excessive quality costs and implement opportunities for continuous improvement, and this should result in ultimately higher profitability. This requires breakdown of various quality cost categories and their magnitudes. The company must strategically invest more in prevention and appraisal to improve quality of goods produced and thereby to reduce failure costs significantly.

Watch for choice c as subjective thinking. There are many companies which implement SPC, quality cost, and many other tools only to get good or high ratings during quality audits by their customers. Management will approve such programs only if it is required by the customer during its audit and not on its merits or benefits to the company. This, unfortunately, does not help the company in its profitability or in continuous improvement of its products because the implementation is not done with proper rationale or objectives. Such programs are likely to fail in a short time.

9.   In many companies it is possible to discover that

a.   no specific quality costs are known, detected, or tracked
b.   only scrap costs are tracked by quality control and manufacturing

c.   too much money is spent on inspection, sorting, and testing/retesting, but not tracked properly

d.   only some of the appraisal activities such as lab testing or inspection are included as budget items in accounting practices

e.   all of the above

Key: e.   all of the above

Quality cost programs are new for many companies. Some of them have informal systems in place to track only a few activities such as scrap, lab testing, inspection and sorting, warranty charges, etc. They are likely to be spending too much money in "fire fighting" activities under the name of problem solving. This is not a very uncommon situation in companies which are focused on detection-based practices and not on prevention philosophies.

10.   The modern approach to quality cost is to

a.   concentrate on external failures: they are important to the business since they represent customer acceptance

b.   consider the four cost segments and their general trends

c.   budget each cost element, such as amounts for inspection, quality control salaries, scrap, etc.

d.   reduce expenditures on each segment individually

e.   make annual budget cuts where cost elements show major variances

Key: b.   consider the four cost segments and their general trends
       (Ref. Applications Question 41, October 1974)

The four cost segments are prevention, appraisal, and internal failure and external failure costs. Each may follow different trends and will show the proportional magnitude of each of the costs.

11.   It is generally difficult to implement a quality costs program because

a.   people view it as punitive action rather than a continuous improvement opportunity

b.   the accounting department does not have existing means and practices to track quality costs

c.   it requires management commitment and cooperation between all disciplines

d.   all of the above

Key: d.   all of the above

12.   To achieve your top management's commitment and support for implementing quality costs, you should

a.   give them a brief executive overview

b.   give names of your competitors who have implemented quality cost programs

c.   show the magnitude of the current quality costs using available information and indicate the opportunities of saving a significant amount of money

d.   higher a consultant to meet your management and convince them

Key: c.   show the magnitude of the current quality costs using available information and indicate the opportunities of saving a significant amount of money
Choice c is the reason why the management should approve and commit to such an initiative. All other choices are not the preferred approaches to achieve management commitment.

13.   You can fail in implementing a quality cost program successfully if

a.   you place too much emphasis on its accounting rules rather than its importance as a quality improvement tool
b.   you do not have a proper implementation plan
c.   you could not get the top management support and commitment
d.   all the disciplines treat it as another report card
e.   all of the above

Key: e.   all of the above

14.   Market-based cost standards are guided by

a.   what others spend
b.   what we ought to spend
c.   marketing budget
d.   quality analysis forecast

Key: a.   what others spend   (Ref. Applications Question 62, July 1984)
This can be easily described by using the "benchmarking concept." To be competitive, our targets and cost standards should be based on the benchmarking of what others spend or invest. Such competitive benchmarking will enable us to develop effective business strategies. Also, this may mean the spending habits of people.

15.   Look at the Fig. 10-1 below showing the different types of quality costs.

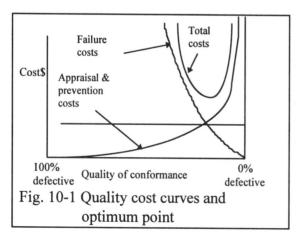

Fig. 10-1 Quality cost curves and optimum point

The optimum point is reached when

a.   prevention costs = appraisal costs
b.   prevention costs = failure costs
c.   prevention costs + appraisal costs = failure costs
d.   appraisal costs − prevention costs = failure costs

Key: c. prevention costs + appraisal costs = failure costs
The quality cost curves[2] shown in Fig. 10-1 above indicate that prevention and appraisal costs are low and failure costs are high when quality is at low levels. As prevention and appraisal costs increase, quality levels increase and failure costs decrease steeply. The optimum point is the one where prevention costs and appraisal costs equal failure costs. After the optimum point, failure costs decrease as quality approaches perfection; but this would require very high efforts or costs in prevention and appraisal.

16. Historic levels of defects, with rare exceptions, have been found to be located at what point with respect to the optimum point in the figure?

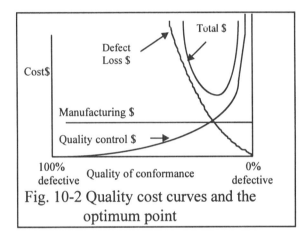

Fig. 10-2 Quality cost curves and the optimum point

a. to the left of the optimum
b. to the right of the optimum
c. at the center of the optimum
d. none of the above

Key: a. to the left of the optimum (Ref. Applications Question 63, July 1984)
The optimum point in Fig. 10-2 is described by the point where the defect loss curve and quality control costs curve intersect each other. The X axis shows the quality of conformance from 100% defects to 0% defects. Hence if we look to the left of the optimum point, we will find the highest levels of defects.

Also if we use the definition of quality costs, we will find that in the beginning, quality control costs, i.e., the prevention and appraisal costs in the figure, are very low, but failure costs are very high in the same period. This results in a high number of defects before we reach the optimum point.

17. The primary reason for collecting and analyzing quality costs is

a. to satisfy requirements of MIL-Q-9858A
b. to see that quality costs are close to industry averages
c. to achieve an optimum balance of prevention, appraisal, and failure costs
d. to identify the source of trouble

Key: c. to achieve an optimum balance of prevention, appraisal, and failure costs
(Ref. Principles Question 89, October 1974)

---

[2] *Juran's Quality Control Handbook* by J. M. Juran, 4th ed., McGraw-Hill, New York, pg. 4.18-19.

These are the main categories of quality costs that need to be reduced. The other choices are not costs of quality.

18.   When one first analyzes quality cost data, he(she) might expect to find that relative to total quality costs

     a.   costs of prevention are high
     b.   costs of appraisal are high
     c.   costs of failure are high
     d.   all of the above

Key: c.   costs of failure are high   (Ref. Principles Question 42, October 1972)
Be careful with such questions. You may tend to think that choice b, "costs of appraisal are high," is the correct choice. Generally most companies do not know the magnitude of the cost of quality because of the internal and external failures which are likely to be very high. And their investment in prevention activities is likely to be very low or almost nothing. This is still an opinion-based question with limited information, but many studies have been conducted which tend to prove this as a fact.[3]

19.   While studying quality costs for most of industry, one will not be surprised to find

     a.   prevention costs < appraisal costs < failure costs
     b.   appraisal costs < failure costs < prevention costs
     c.   failure costs < appraisal costs < prevention costs
     d.   prevention costs = appraisal costs = failure costs

Key: a.   prevention costs < appraisal costs < failure costs
The key word is *not*. Watch for subjectivity here. One can argue that any of the above can be true for different businesses. The important phrase is ***while studying the quality costs*** indicating that a quality cost program may be beginning and/or there may be some understanding and implementation of a quality cost program. Without such a study, it is very likely that most of the companies waste their resources and time in problem solving but do not know its magnitude. This generally results in very high failure costs (both internal and external costs), with some cost for inspection or appraisal. The prevention costs may be a very small proportion. Hence choice a is the best choice. Also refer to Question 20 below for additional discussion.

20.   When analyzing quality cost data gathered during the initial stages of a new management emphasis on quality control and corrective actions as a part of a product improvement program, one normally expects to see

     a.   increased prevention costs and decreased appraisal costs
     b.   increased appraisal costs with little change in prevention costs
     c.   decreased internal failure costs

[3] *Juran's Quality Control Handbook* by J. M. Juran, 4th ed., McGraw-Hill, New York; Section 4, Quality Costs, Ideas and Applications Vol. 1 and Vol. 2, 2nd ed., ASQC Quality Press. 1987.

     d.   decreased total quality costs

     e.   all of the above

Key: b.   increased appraisal costs with little change in prevention costs
            (Ref. Principles Question 63, August 1978)
            This is mainly because of the discovery process that management goes through. When quality cost data are gathered for the first time, high levels of failure costs are likely to be found. Management's initial reaction usually is to implement inspection and evaluation or audits to detect the defects and nonconforming units. Hence appraisal costs can increase rather quickly initially before any prevention activities are planned and implemented. Also refer to Question 19 above for additional discussion.

21.   When analyzing quality cost data during the initial stages of management's emphasis on quality control and corrective action as a part of a product improvement program, one normally expects to see

     a.   increased prevention costs and decreased appraisal costs

     b.   decreased internal failure costs

     c.   increased appraisal costs with little change in prevention costs

     d.   increased external failure costs

     e.   none of these

Key: c.   increased appraisal costs with little change in prevention costs
            (Ref. Principles Question 74, October 1974)
            This is a repeat question with a slight change in one of the choices from Question 20 above.

22.   When operating a quality system, excessive costs can be identified when

     a.   appraisal costs exceed failure costs

     b.   total quality costs exceed 10% of sales

     c.   appraisal and failure costs are equal

     d.   total quality costs exceed 4% of the manufacturing costs

     e.   there is no fixed rule, management experience must be used

Key: e.   there is no fixed rule, management experience must be used
            (Ref. Principles Question 68, August 1978)
            Each choice indicates an arbitrary condition. Be careful before you establish any rule of thumb.

23.   During an initial quality cost study, which of the following will impact top management the most?

     a.   prevention cost

     b.   appraisal cost

     c.   internal failure cost

     d.   total quality cost

     e.   external failure cost

Key: d.   total quality cost

Juran[4] suggests that the total quality costs figure is the figure in the initial quality cost study that has highest impact on top management.

24.   Loss of potential customers is a

     a.   prevention cost
     b.   appraisal cost
     c.   internal failure cost
     d.   external cost
     e.   hidden cost but not easy to quantify as a specific value

Key: e.   hidden cost but not easy to quantify as a specific value

This is not an external failure cost because the potential customers are not the existing customers or users of the products or services. They are prospective or future customers. They have not used the product or service or experienced any failures. They may not be buying or are not interested in buying the product or service because of many factors such as word-of-mouth learning of the product failures, past history or reputation, new technology, late entry in market, poor marketing, poor quality, or not enough inventory. It is not easy to project or quantify this type of loss purely based on market share.

25.   In some instances the ordinary cost balance formula is not valid and cannot be applied because of the presence of vital intangibles. Such an intangible involves

     a.   safety of human beings
     b.   compliance with legislation
     c.   apparatus for collection of revenue
     d.   credit to marketing as new sales for warranty replacements
     e.   none of the above

Key: a.   safety of human beings   (Ref. Principles Question 65, July 1984)

Safety of human beings is one of the major factors in all phases of planning, development, and manufacture of new products. The products are designed with higher safety margins or are overdesigned, and processes are given special attention if the consequences are severe to human safety. Hence the cost of prevention and appraisal may be higher than normal. It is very difficult to quantify the cost of an unsafe product because it may result in a legal recall, liability, and loss of existing and future customers. Some of these losses are intangible and difficult to quantify.

26.   Prevention costs are

     I.   costs incurred during design and/or manufacture to prevent the occurrence of nonconforming products.

---

[4] *Juran's Quality Control Handbook* by J. M. Juran, 4th ed., McGraw-Hill, New York, pg. 4.14-4.15.

      II.   costs incurred to do it right the first time

      III.   costs associated with inspection and testing of all vendor-supplied material

      IV.   costs incurred for measuring, evaluating, or auditing products

      a.   I and II only
      b.   II and III only
      c.   III and IV only
      d.   IV and I only

Key: a.   I and II only

The remaining three choices, b, c, and d are not true because III and IV represent appraisal costs and not prevention costs.

27.   Review of the purchase orders for quality requirements falls into which one of the following quality cost segments?

      a.   prevention
      b.   appraisal
      c.   internal failures
      d.   external failures

Key: a.   prevention   (Ref. Principles Question 59, July 1984)

This is the prevention quality cost. Purchasing should review purchase orders carefully to prevent errors and to ensure that the orders contain clear requirements.

28.   Which of the following cost elements is normally a prevention cost?

      a.   receiving inspection
      b.   outside endorsements or approvals
      c.   design of quality measurement equipment
      d.   all of the above

Key: c.   design of quality measurement equipment (Ref. Principles Question 62, August 1978)

Choice c represents a prevention cost category. Choices a and b are appraisal costs.

29.   Which of the following cost elements is a prevention cost?

      a.   quality planning
      b.   process quality control
      c.   design of quality measurement equipment
      d.   all of the above

Key: d.   all of the above   (Ref. Principles Question 71, October 1974)

Be careful here with choice b, process quality control. It is considered a prevention cost and not an appraisal cost. The process control is done to know the status of the process and not as the criteria for product acceptance. Similarly choice c can mislead you if you do not read it carefully. The choice describes the cost of designing the measuring equipment; the key phrase is ***designing***. The cost of calibrating and maintaining measuring equipment can be part of appraisal, but the cost of designing it is prevention.

30.   Which one of the following is not a prevention cost?

    a.   quality planning
    b.   training
    c.   qualification tests
    d.   new product review

Key: c.   qualification tests
The key word is *not*. Qualification tests are appraisal costs.

31.   If prevention costs are increased to pay for engineering work in quality control and this results in a reduction in the number of product defects, this yields a reduction in

    a.   appraisal costs
    b.   operating costs
    c.   quality costs
    d.   failure costs
    e.   manufacturing costs

Key: d.   failure costs   (Ref. Applications Question 59, July 1984)
The product defects represent both internal and external failure costs. Hence if defects are reduced, this results in low failure cost. This is a repeat question from the August 1978 examination.[5]

32.   The cost of writing instructions and operating procedures for inspection and testing should be charged to

    a.   prevention costs
    b.   appraisal costs
    c.   internal failure costs
    d.   external failure costs

Key: a.   prevention costs   (Ref. Applications Question 64, July 1984)
Writing instructions and/or developing procedures are a part of designing, implementing, and maintaining a quality system. Hence they are prevention costs. This question is repeated in the October 1972 examination.[6]

33.   Included as a prevention quality cost would be

---

[5] *ASQC - CQE Examination*, ASQC Quality Progress, August 1978, Applications section, Question 62.
[6] *ASQC - CQE Examination*, ASQC Quality Progress, October 1972, Applications section, Question 49.

a.   salaries of personnel engaged in the design of measurement and control equipment that is to be purchased

b.   capital equipment purchased

c.   training costs of instructing plant personnel to achieve the production standards

d.   sorting of nonconforming material which will delay or stop production

Key: a.   salaries of personnel engaged in the design of measurement and control equipment that is to be purchased   (Ref. Applications Question 63, October 1972)

34.   Which of the following activities is not normally charged as a preventive cost?

a.   quality training

b.   design and development of quality measurement equipment

c.   quality planning

d.   laboratory acceptance testing

Key: d.   laboratory acceptance testing (Ref. Applications Question 65, July 1984)
The key word is *not*. Choices a, b, and c are all prevention quality costs. Laboratory acceptance testing is an appraisal cost and not a prevention cost.

35.   While studying quality costs, the in-process inspection and tests are

a.   prevention costs

b.   appraisal costs

c.   internal failure costs

d.   external costs

Key: b.   appraisal costs
In-process inspection and tests are the costs incurred to determine the conformance to requirements, and hence classified as appraisal costs. These are the costs incurred to evaluate the product's conformance to customer requirements.

36.   In the case of design activity, the costs incurred to perform qualification tests are

a.   prevention cost

b.   appraisal cost

c.   internal failure cost

d.   external cost

Key: b.   appraisal cost
Qualification test costs are incurred to determine the conformance of a design to requirements, and hence classified as appraisal cost.

37.   Which of the following is the appraisal cost?

     a.   vendor quality surveys
     b.   calibration
     c.   complaints adjustment
     d.   scrap

Key: b.   calibration
Calibration of gages and equipment is an appraisal cost. Vendor quality surveys are prevention costs, complaints adjustments are external failure costs, and scrap is an internal failure cost.

38.   Cost of calibrating the test and inspection equipment would be included in

     a.   prevention cost
     b.   appraisal cost
     c.   failure cost
     d.   material-procurement cost

Key: b.   appraisal cost   (Ref. Principles Question 64, July 1984)
Calibrating the test and inspection equipment is an appraisal cost as it will help to evaluate and determine the degree of conformance of the product to specified requirements.

39.   Of the following, which are typically appraisal costs?

     a.   vendor surveys and vendor faults
     b.   quality planning and quality reports
     c.   drawing control centers and material dispositions
     d.   quality audit and quality final inspection
     e.   none of the above

Key: d.   quality audit and quality final inspection (Ref. Principles Question 61, August 1978)
The key word in this question is *typically*. The quality audit and quality final inspection are appraisal costs.

40.   Outside endorsements or approvals such as Underwriters' Laboratories (UL) fees are usually considered which of the following quality costs?

     a.   external failure
     b.   appraisal
     c.   prevention
     d.   internal failure
     e.   none of the above

Key: b.   appraisal   (Ref. Principles Question 17, October 1974)
UL fees are the costs incurred to determine the degree of conformance to a given standard and hence they are appraisal costs.

41.   Which of the following cost elements is usually considered an appraisal cost?

       a.   screening rejected lots
       b.   receiving inspection
       c.   surveying suppliers
       d.   preparing inspection plans

Key: b.   receiving inspection   (Ref. Applications Question 35, October 1974)
      Choice a is failure cost, and c and d are prevention costs.

42.   Cost incurred in field testing of acceptance at the customer's site, prior to releasing a product
      for customer acceptance, is considered

       a.   prevention cost
       b.   appraisal cost
       c.   failure cost
       d.   none of the above

Key: b.   appraisal cost   (Ref. Applications Question 61, October 1974)
      Field testing at the producer's plant or at the customer's location prior to releasing the product is
      an appraisal cost.

43.   Quality cost analysis has shown that appraisal costs are apparently too high in relation to sales.
      Which of the following actions probably would not be considered in pursuing the problem?

       a.   work sampling in inspection and test areas
       b.   adding inspectors to reduce scrap costs
       c.   Pareto analysis of quality costs
       d.   considering the elimination of some test operations
       e.   comparing appraisal costs to bases other than sales, for example, direct labor, value
          added, etc.

Key: b.   adding inspectors to reduce scrap costs (Ref. Applications Question 53, August 1978)
      The key word is *not*. Inspection is an appraisal cost. The inspectors only find defects, they do not
      create defects. Scrap is created because of process variations and nonconformances. Hence
      adding more inspectors may or may not result in reduction of any scrap. However, the addition
      of inspectors will result in increased appraisal cost instead of decreasing it. The appraisal costs in
      relation to sales will be even higher than before. Hence it will not help solve this problem. This
      question is repeated in the August 1978[7] examination.

44.   When looking for existing sources of internal failure cost data, which of the following are usually
      the best sources available?

       a.   operating budgets

---

[7] *ASQC - CQE Examination*, ASQC Quality Progress, August 1978, Applications section, Question 57.

      b.   salesperson's field reports

      c.   labor and material cost documents

      d.   returned material reports

      e.   purchase orders

Key: c.   labor and material cost documents   (Ref. Principles Question 60, August 1978)

The key phrase in this question is **the best**. Choice c represents the sources to find internal failure cost data. The labor and material costs will indicate the actual magnitude of the internal failure costs. Choices a, b, d, and e are not the internal failure costs. Also refer to Question 45 for additional discussion.

45.   When looking for existing sources of external failure cost data, which of the following is usually the best source available?

      a.   customer corrective action requests

      b.   salesperson's field reports

      c.   accounting reports on "sales of seconds" or "distressed merchandise"

      d.   returned material reports

Key: d.   returned material reports   (Ref. Principles Question 66, July 1984)

The key phrase in this question is **the best**. This is the external failure cost incurred because of receipt and replacement of the returned materials. In this type of question, it is generally easy to rule out all of the remaining three choices. This question is repeated in the October 1974 examination.[8]

46.   Which one of the following is not an internal failure quality cost?

      a.   rework

      b.   warranty charges

      c.   scrap

      d.   retest

Key: b.   warranty charges

The key word is **not**. The internal failure costs are those costs incurred because of the occurrence of product nonconformance *within* the operations of the company, i.e., prior to shipment to the final customer. They are the costs incurred because of unsatisfactory quality within the company. Choices a, c, and d indicate such internal failure costs.

Watch for choice b, "warranty charges," which are the costs of repairing or replacing the product during its warranty period. These are not internal failure costs but are external failure costs, i.e., the cost incurred due to product nonconformance to the customer requirements occurring after the sale to the customer.

47.   Liability costs are

---

[8] *ASQC - CQE Examination*, ASQC Quality Progress, October 1974, Principles section Question 7.

a.   prevention costs
b.   appraisal costs
c.   internal failure costs
d.   external failure costs

Key: d.   external failure costs
Liability costs represent the costs (generally legally required) incurred to resolve product failures
or suspected failures during use by customers. Hence they are considered external failure costs.

48.   Failure costs include costs due to

a.   quality control engineering
b.   inspection setup for tests
c.   certification of special process suppliers
d.   supplier analysis of nonconforming hardware

Key: d.   supplier analysis of nonconforming hardware (Ref. Principles Question 60, July 1984)
This may be internal failure if the supplier finds the nonconforming hardware or products before
they are shipped to the customer. If the customer returns the nonconforming hardware or product,
then the supplier first needs to evaluate and analyze the material, then make the disposition
decision, and finally implement corrective actions. This is hence an external failure.

Choice a is prevention, choice b is appraisal, and choice c is a prevention quality cost.

49.   Which of the following is the least likely to be reported as a failure-related cost?

a.   sorting lots rejected by a sampling procedure
b.   downtime caused by late delivery of a purchased part rejected by the supplier's final
      inspection
c.   repair of field failures
d.   retesting of repaired product

Key: b.   downtime caused by late delivery of a purchased part rejected by the supplier's final
            inspection   (Ref. Principles Question 62, July 1984)
The downtime is not caused because of breakdown or poor maintenance of machines, etc. It is
not caused by internal failures. The receiving inspection may reject a lot from a supplier,
resulting in delay or downtime in the plant. Receiving inspection is an appraisal cost but the
downtime in this case may not be called failure cost. Choices a, c, and d are all obvious failure
costs. You may easily rule out each of the choices as a possible answer.

50.   Rework, quality planning, inspection and test, and warranty charges are

a.   prevention, appraisal, internal failure, and external failure costs, respectively
b.   internal failure, prevention, appraisal, and external failure costs, respectively
c.   internal failure, appraisal, prevention, and external failure costs, respectively

d.   external failure, prevention, appraisal, and internal failure costs, respectively

Key: b.   internal failure, prevention, appraisal, and external failure costs, respectively
Let's first rearrange them in proper order to see their relationship with respective cost categories.

Rework	internal failure
Quality planning	prevention
Inspection and test	appraisal
Warranty charges	external failure

Choice b is the only one that matches the items and categories in proper order. You should be able to eliminate choices a and d immediately by looking at the answers; e.g., the first item, rework, is neither prevention as in choice a nor external failure as in choice d. Similarly for choice c, quality planning is not appraisal; inspection and testing are not prevention and hence it is not true.

51.   Historically, under the sorting inspection type of quality control function,

a.   when failure costs rise, appraisal costs fall
b.   failure and appraisal quality costs trend together
c.   when failure costs fall, appraisal costs rise
d.   failure and appraisal costs generally remain unchanged

Key: b.   failure and appraisal quality costs trend together
(Ref. Principles Question 50, October 1972)

52.   The percentages of total quality costs are described as follows:

Prevention	12%
Appraisal	28%
Internal failure	40%
External failure	20%

We conclude

a.   we should invest more money in prevention
b.   expenditures for failures are excessive
c.   the amount spent for appraisal seems about right
d.   nothing

Key: d.   nothing   (Ref. Applications Question 58, August 1978)
This is subjective and one can argue that each choice seems correct. Prevention is 12% and hence investing more money in prevention seems logical. Expenditures for failures (both internal and external failure costs) are a total of 60%, which does seem excessive. Similarly, the 28% of appraisal cost is neither very high nor very low. Hence each choice seems correct.

However the correct answer is choice d. The only logical rationale is that the data are in percentages only. Whenever you have only percentages, to make any conclusion is difficult because the percentages can be misleading if you do not have the individual numbers or raw data in the question.

53.   The percentages of total quality cost are distributed as follows:

Prevention	10%
Appraisal	25%
Internal failures	40%
External failures	25%

We conclude

a.   we should invest more money in prevention
b.   the amount spent for appraisal seems about right
c.   expenditures for failures are excessive
d.   nothing

Key: d.   nothing   (Ref. Applications Question 76, October 1974)
This is a repeat question with a slight change in the percentage values. Refer to Question 52 above for detailed discussion.

54.   The percentages of total quality cost are distributed as follows:

Prevention	2%
Appraisal	33%
Internal failure	35%
External failure	30%

We can conclude

a.   expenditures for failures are excessive
b.   nothing
c.   we should invest more money in prevention
d.   the amount spent for appraisal seems about right

Key: b.   nothing   (Ref. Applications Question 65, October 1972)
This is a repeat question with a slight change in the percentage values. Refer to Questions 52 and 53 above for detailed discussion.

55.   For a typical month, 900D Manufacturing Company identified and reported the following quality costs:

Inspection wages	$12,000
Quality planning	$4,000
Source inspection	$2,000
In-plant scrap and rework	$88,000
Final product test	$110,000
Retest and troubleshooting	$39,000
Field warranty costs	$205,000
Evaluation and processing of deviation requests	$6,000

What is the total *failure* cost for this month?

a. $244,000
b. $151,000
c. $261,000
d. $205,000
e. $332,000

Key: e. $332,000 (Ref. Applications Question 57, July 1984)

The in-plant scrap and rework, retest, and troubleshooting, and field warranty costs indicate the total failure costs. We can calculate it as follows:

In-plant scrap and rework	$88,000
Retest and troubleshooting	$39,000
Field warranty costs	$205,000
Total failure costs	$332,000

56. Refer to previous question.
One year later, the monthly quality costs reported by 900D Manufacturing Company were as follows:

Inspection wages	$14,000
Quality planning	$8,500
Source inspection	$2,200
In-plant scrap and rework	$51,000
Quality training	$42,000
Audits	$47,000
Final product test	$103,000
Retest and troubleshooting	$19,000
Field warranty costs	$188,000
Evaluation and processing of deviation requests	$4,500

Sales billed have increased 10% from the corresponding month of a year ago. How would you evaluate the effectiveness of the 900D quality improvement program?

a. Quality costs are still to high.

b.   Essentially no change in overall results.
c.   Good improvements.
d.   Still further improvement is unlikely.
e.   Not enough information to evaluate.

Key: c.   Good improvements. (Ref. Applications Question 58, July 1984)
Here we need to compare the effect of quality costs to monthly sales as a measurement base. The total quality costs each year will indicate the effect of proportional increase of quality costs to sales.

Last year:	Total quality costs	(add all costs)	$466, 000
This year:	Total quality costs	(add all costs)	$479, 200

The proportional increase in total quality costs = (479,200 – 466,000)/466,000 = 0.028 or 2.8%. This increase is because of two new items, quality training and audits, as prevention costs. This increase in quality costs is correlated to a sales increase of 10% over the same period, and thus can be considered as positive or good improvement. It is sometimes difficult to establish a direct correlation of quality costs to sales, etc., because they are dependent on many other things in the routine business environment. Hence choice c, good improvements, is the most conservative conclusion compared to all the other choices.

Choice a is not true as we do not know the data about the company's production volume or sales volume. The quality costs may seem to be large, $479, 200, etc., but it may not be high compared to the volume of operations in large companies. Choice b is not correct because the data show two changes, i.e., the sales volume has increased and quality costs also have slightly increased. Choice d is not true because we do not know enough about the quality improvement plan.

57.   Assume that the cost data available to you for a certain period are limited to the following:

Final test	$18,000
Loss on disposition of surplus stock	$15,000
Field warranty costs	$275,000
Scrap	$150,000
Customer returns	$25,000
Planning for inspection	$16,000

The total of the quality costs is

a. $499,000
b. $484,000
c. $468,000
d. $193,000

Key: b. $484,000   (Ref. Applications Question 61, July 1984)

Read the question very carefully. The first line states "assume that the *cost data*" and not assume that the *quality cost data*. This means the items described are not all quality cost categories. We need only to separate quality cost categories to find total quality costs.

In the data above, except "Loss on disposition of surplus stock for $15,000," all categories are quality costs.

Final test	$18,000
Field warranty costs	$275,000
Scrap	$150,000
Customer returns	$25,000
Planning for inspection	$16,000
Total quality costs	$484,000

58.   Analyze the cost data below:

$10,000	Equipment design
$150,000	Scrap
$180,000	Reinspection and retest
$45,000	Loss or disposition of surplus stock
$4,000	Vendor quality surveys
$40,000	Repair

Considering only the quality costs shown above, we might conclude that

a.   prevention costs should be decreased
b.   internal failure costs can be decreased
c.   prevention costs are too low a proportion of the quality costs shown
d.   appraisal costs should be increased
e.   nothing can be concluded

Key: c.   prevention costs are too low a proportion of the quality costs shown
(Ref. Applications Question 54, August 1978)
From the data above all costs except the loss or the disposition of the surplus stock are quality costs.

$10,000	Equipment design
$150,000	Scrap
$180,000	Reinspection and retest
$4,000	Vendor quality surveys
$40,000	Repair
$384,000	Total quality costs

The vendor quality surveys for $4,000 are the only prevention costs in the data. This is apparently a very small proportion of $384,000, the total quality costs.

59.   This month's quality cost data collection shows the following:

Returned material processing	$1,800
Adjustment of customer complaints	$4,500
Rework and repair	$10,700
Quality management salaries	$25,000
Warranty replacement	$54,500
Calibration and testing	$2,500
Inspection and testing	$28,000

For your action report to the top management, you select which of the following as the percentage of external failure to the total quality costs to show the true impact of the field problem?

a.   20%
b.   55%
c.   48%
d.   24%
e.   8%

Key: c.   48%   (Ref. Applications Question 55, August 1978)
The question already indicates that the data show the quality costs. Hence the total quality cost is the straight sum of all the cost figures given, i.e.,

Total quality costs = $1,800 + $4,500 + $10,700 + $25,000 + $54,500 + $2,500 + $28,000
                    = $127,000

The external costs are returned material processing for $1,800, adjustment of the customer complaints for $4,500, and warranty replacement of $54,500; i.e.,
The external quality costs = $1,800 + $4,500 + $54,500 = $60,800 and the ratio in percentages is:
External failure costs/total quality costs = (60,800/127,000) × 100 = 47.8% ≅ 48%.

60.   You have been assigned as a quality engineer to a small company. The quality control manager desires some cost data and the accounting department reported that the following information is available. Cost accounts are production inspection, $14,185; test inspection, $4,264; procurement inspection, $2,198; shop labor, $14,698; shop rework, $1,402; first article, $675; engineering analysis (rework) $845; repair service (warrantee), $298; quality engineering, $2,175; design engineering salaries, $241,451; quality equipment, $18,745; training, $275; receiving laboratories, $385; underwriter laboratories, $1,200; installation service cost, $9,000; scrap, $1,182; and calibration service, $794. What are the prevention costs?

a. $3,727
b. $23,701
c. $23,026
d. $3,295

e. $2,450

Key: e. $2,450   (Ref. Applications Question 56, August 1978)
We need to evaluate each cost element based on the definition of prevention costs. The prevention costs are quality engineering of $2,175 and the training of $275.
The total prevention costs are $2,175 + $275 = $2,450.

61.   In analyzing the cost data below

$20,000   final test
$350,000   field warranty costs
$170,000   reinspection and retest
$4,500   loss or disposition of surplus stock
$4,000   vendor quality surveys
$30,000   rework

we might conclude that

a.   internal failure costs can be decreased
b.   prevention is too low a proportion of the quality costs shown
c.   appraisal costs should be increased
d.   nothing can be concluded

Key: b.   prevention is too low a proportion of the quality costs shown
(Ref. Applications Question 26, October 1974)
Internal failure costs are: reinspection and retest of $170,000 + rework of $30,000 = $200,000.
Prevention costs are vendor quality surveys for $4,000.
Appraisal costs are the final test for $20,000 and the external failure costs for $350,000.
Loss or disposition of surplus stock for $45,000 is not a quality cost.
Hence total quality costs = $20,000 + $350,000 + $170,000 + $4,000 + $30,000 = $574,000.
The prevention costs are only (4,000/574,000) ×100 = 0.70%, which is a very small proportion of the total quality costs. This question is repeated in the October 1972 examination.[9]

62.   This month's quality cost data collection shows the following:

Adjustment of customer complaints	$3,500
Rework and repair	$10,700
Quality management salaries	$25,000
Downgrading expense	$1,800
Warranty replacement	$53,500
Calibration and maintenance of test equipment	$2,500
Inspection and testing	$28,000

[9] *ASQC - CQE Examination*, ASQC Quality Progress, October 1972, Applications section, Question 76.

For your action report to top management you select which one of the following as the percentage of *external failure* to *total quality costs* to show the true impact of field problems?

    a.   24%
    b.   65%
    c.   56%
    d.   46%

Key: d.   46%   (Ref. Applications Question 31, October 1974)
All the costs shown above are quality costs.
External quality costs = $3,500 + $53,500 = $57,000.
Total quality costs   = $3,500 + $10,700 + $25,000 + $1,800 + $53,500 + $2,500 + $28,000
                    = $125,000.
(External failure costs/Total quality costs) $\times 100 = (57,000 / 125,000) \times 100 = 45.6\% \approx 46\%$

63.   Assume that the cost data available to you for a certain period are limited to the following:

$20,000	Final test
$350,000	Field Warranty costs
$170,000	Re inspection and retest
$45,000	Loss on disposition of surplus stock
$4,000	Vendor quality surveys
$30,000	Rework

The total of the quality costs is

    a. $619,000
    b. $574,000
    c. $615,000
    d. $570,000

Key: b. $574,000   (Ref. Applications Question 74, October 1972)
Given: The cost data that include some quality costs and some other costs.
Find: The total quality costs.
The cost of $45,000, loss on disposition of surplus stock is not considered as a cost of quality.
Total quality costs = $20,000 + $350,000 + $170,000 + $4,000 + $30,000 = $574,000.

64.   In the previous problem, the total failure cost is

    a. $550,000
    b. $30,000
    c. $350,000
    d. $380,000

Key: a. $550,000   (Ref. Applications Question 75, October 1972)

Failure costs means both, internal and external failure costs.

Total failure costs = $350,000 warranty + $170,000 reinspection /retest + $30,000 rework
= $550,000.

65.   In analyzing the cost data in Question 64, we can conclude that

a.   prevention cost is too low a proportion of total quality cost
b.   the total of the quality costs is excessive
c.   internal failure costs can be decreased
d.   appraisal costs should be decreased

Key: a.   prevention cost is too low a proportion of total quality cost
(Ref. Applications Question 76, October 1972)
The data indicate that the vendor quality survey at $4,000 is the only prevention cost among
the other costs. The prevention cost to total quality cost ratio = (4000/574,000)×100 = 0.7%,
which means it is a very low proportion of the total quality costs. This is a repeat question in the
October 1974 examination.[10]

66.   Quality cost data

a.   must be maintained when the end product is for the government
b.   must be mailed to the contacting officer on request
c.   is often an effective means of identifying quality problem areas
d.   all of the above

Key: c.   is often an effective means of identifying quality problem areas
(Ref. Principles Question 66, August 1978)
This is an obvious answer. Choice a is incorrect, and hence choice d, all of the above, is not
possible. Similarly, choice b is not the main purpose of quality costs.

67.   A good quality cost reporting system will

a.   lead to operating at the lowest possible costs
b.   supplement the company's financial reporting system
c.   get the best product quality possible
d.   indicate areas of excessive costs
e.   none of these

Key: d.   indicate areas of excessive costs (Ref. Principles Question 45, October 1974)
This is one of the prime objectives of the quality costs reporting system. It highlights or shows
the magnitude of current costs and where they are excessive. Also it indicates the opportunities
for improvement in excessive quality costs.

Choice a is likely to mislead you. It reads the *lowest possible costs* and *not the lowest possible*

---

[10] *ASQC - CQE Examination*, ASQC Quality Progress, October 1974, Applications section, Question 26.

quality costs. A good quality cost reporting program can result in optimizing the quality costs but it may or may not result in lowest (total) costs because the costs include other costs such as direct labor, fixed and variable costs, material costs, etc.

Similarly be careful with choice c. The question is focusing on the *"reporting system"* and not on the *"quality system."* The ultimate goal of the program is to identify opportunities for improvement and to result in better product quality at economical costs. This should be an integral part of the quality system and of the overall implementation process, and not part of the quality cost reporting system.

68.   A goal of a quality cost report should be to

    a.   get the best product quality possible
    b.   be able to satisfy MIL-Q-9858A
    c.   integrate two financial reporting techniques
    d.   indicate areas of excessive costs

Key: d.   indicate areas of excessive costs   (Ref. Principles Question 12, October 1972)
This is one of the prime objectives of a quality cost reporting system. It highlights or shows the magnitude of current costs and where they are excessive. Also, it indicates opportunities for improvements in excessive quality costs.

Choice a is likely to mislead you. It says that the goal of a quality cost *"report"* is to get the "best product quality possible." This requires a good quality cost program and not merely a quality cost report. A report only summarizes the findings and results of a quality cost program.

Choices b and c are not appropriate as the goals of a quality cost report.

69.   When analyzing quality costs, a helpful method for singling out the highest-cost contributors is

    a.   a series of interviews with the line foreman
    b.   the application of the Pareto theory
    c.   an audit of budget variances
    d.   the application of breakeven and profit volume analysis

Key: b.   the application of the Pareto theory   (Ref. Applications Question 38, October 1972)
The Pareto principle identifies the "vital few" areas that can bring 70% to 80% improvement at less effort and indicates the "trivial many" areas for which normal attention is required. It can identify a few major areas of failure costs which should first be attacked aggressively.

70.   One of the best analytical methods for identifying those failure costs that should be attacked first for the greatest return on the invested prevention dollar is to

    a.   perform an internal financial audit
    b.   study the budget-variance report

      c.   apply the Gompertz curve technique

      d.   apply the Pareto principle

      e.   perform a breakeven analysis

Key: d.   apply the Pareto principle   (Ref. Applications Question 46, October 1974)
Refer to Question 69 above for detailed discussion.

71.   As a quality manager, if you would like to study the quality costs in your company with a new approach rather than using the current accounting system, you should

      I.   prepare definitions of various quality cost categories and collect the data on your own

      II.   review accounting department data on scrap, rework, and some other categories and present the currently available data to top management

      III.   recommend that a detailed study should be made using a multidiscipline team approach of accounting, quality, and other departments

      a.   I and II

      b.   II and III

      c.   III and I

      d.   All of the above

Key: b.   II and III
Juran[11] discusses the approach described in II and III as more appropriate for making the initial quality cost study.

72.   Which of the following methods should be used to collect quality costs data to make the initial cost study?

      I.   Estimating the data as a practical approach

      II.   Expanding the current accounting system as an elaborate and extensive approach.

      III.   Do not collect the data as management may not understand the language of money.

      a.   I only

      b.   II only

      c.   I and II only

      d.   I, II, and III only

Key: c.   I and II only
Juran[12] indicates that to make an initial quality costs study, it may be difficult to obtain the quality cost data. The data can be collected as estimates within a few days or weeks. In some cases, the data can be collected by expanding current accounting systems, which can be a time consuming and expensive approach. The statement in III is not correct because the language of the top management is money. The available data on costs of poor quality should be presented to

---

[11] *Juran's Quality Control Handbook* by J. M. Juran, 4th ed., McGraw-Hill, New York, pg. 4.12.
[12] *Juran's Quality Control Handbook* by J. M. Juran, 4th ed., McGraw-Hill, New York, pg. 4.12-4.13.

show the magnitude of the quality costs.

73.   When analyzing monthly quality cost trends on failure reports of many types of consumer goods, you must be most alert to the effects of

    a.   changes in marketing management personnel
    b.   secular trends in the data
    c.   seasonal variations in the data
    d.   cyclical variations within the data
    e.   changes in prevailing labor rates

Key: c.   seasonal variations in the data   (Ref. Principles Question 72, October 1974)
Consumer goods are more sensitive to seasonal variations and can create unexpected product failures in the field. This is mainly true for products with shelf life, such as perishable food products, environment-dominant products, etc. This type of data should be separated from other actual failures in the field to properly evaluate it.

74.   Quality costs should not be reported against which one of the following measurement bases?

    a.   direct labor
    b.   sales
    c.   net profit
    d.   unit volume of production

Key: c.   net profit   (Ref. Principles Question 46, October 1972)
The key word in the question is *not*. Quality costs as a percentage of net profit is not advisable because net profit is difficult to quantify for most companies. It involves many accounting short-term and long-term adjustments for tax benefits and future planning. Hence to use it as a basis sometimes is misleading. In many small- and medium-scale companies, net profit is not an easily available figure. According to Juran,[13] sometimes its magnitude with respect to net profit is so high that it is shocking to most of the top management. In some cases the quality costs exceed the company's profit, and hence it is less practical to use as a measurement basis.

75.   Which of the following quality cost indices is likely to have greatest appeal to top management as an indicator of relative cost?

    a.   Quality cost per unit of product
    b.   Quality cost per hour of direct production labor
    c.   Quality cost per unit of processing cost
    d.   Quality cost per unit of sales
    e.   Quality cost per dollar of direct production labor

Key: d.   Quality cost per unit of sales (Ref. Principles Question 58, July 1984)
The key phrase in the question is *greatest appeal*. The language of top management is *money*.

---

[13] *Juran's Quality Control Handbook* by J. M. Juran, 4th ed., McGraw-Hill, New York, pg. 4.15.

The measurement basis such as the ratio of quality cost per unit of sales will catch top management's attention first. This can help top management develop a sound strategic plan to minimize the quality costs, mainly the failure costs and its impact on the final buyer or on sales. All other choices are the measurement basis that are not necessarily strategic in nature but are more tactical. Middle management, operations management, or plant management can directly and easily understand such measurement basis as they provide technical details and data. Top management may not easily understand the impact of technical details on the overall business.

76.   In selecting a base for measuring quality costs, which of the following should be considered?

        a.   Is it sensitive to increase and decrease in production schedules?
        b.   Is it affected by mechanization and resulting lower direct labor costs?
        c.   Is it affected by seasonal product sales?
        d.   Is it oversensitive to material price fluctuations?
        e.   all of the above

Key: e.   all of the above   (Ref. Applications Question 56, July 1984)
        The magnitude of quality costs should be described by using appropriate measurement bases. For top management, the most important language is the language of money. All of the above measurement bases reflect the importance of quality costs to top management and are proper to use.

77.   Analysis of quality costs consists of

        a.   reviewing labor (manpower) utilization against standards
        b.   evaluating seasonal productivity
        c.   establishing management tools to determine net worth
        d.   examining each cost element in relation to other elements and the total
        e.   providing an accounting mechanism to spread costs over service areas

Key: d.   examining each cost element in relation to other elements and the total
        (Ref. Applications Question 60, July 1984)
        The objective of a quality cost program is only reflected by choice d. All the remaining choices are parts of financial analysis or production standards analysis, but it is not proper to include them as a part of quality costs.

78.   Quality cost trend analysis is facilitated by comparing quality costs to

        a.   manufacturing costs over the same time period
        b.   cash flow reports
        c.   appropriate measurement basis
        d.   QC department budget

Key: c.   appropriate measurement basis   (Ref. Principles Question 61, July 1984)
        Quality costs should relate to some appropriate measurement basis, i.e., quality costs as a

percentage of sales, cost of goods sold, manufacturing cost, etc. The measurement basis will create significant impact on top management and will indicate the major opportunities for improvement. These bases can be used to establish some trend analysis over a long period of time. This question is repeated in the October 1972 examination.[14]

79.   Which of the following bases of performance measurement (denominators) when related to operating quality costs (numerators) would provide a reliable indicator(s) to quality management for overall evaluation of the effectiveness of the company's quality program? Quality costs per

      a.   total manufacturing costs
      b.   units produced
      c.   total direct labor dollars
      d.   only one of the above
      e.   any two of the above

Key: e.   any two of the above   (Ref. Principles Question 65, August 1978)
       The language of top management is money. We can use various types of measurement bases to report the magnitude and consequences of quality costs to top management. The measurement bases listed in the choices above are meaningful and effective, and any two, choice e, can be used to report quality costs.

80.   Operating quality costs can be related to different volume bases. An example of volume base that could be used would be

      a.   direct labor cost
      b.   standard manufacturing cost
      c.   processing costs
      d.   sales
      e.   all of the above

Key: e.   all of the above   (Ref. Principles Question 67, August 1978)
       Each item above represents a possible measurement base to report the operating quality costs.

81.   One method to control inspection costs even without a budget is by comparing _____ as a ratio to productive machine time to produce the product.

      a.   product cost
      b.   company profit
      c.   inspection hours
      d.   scrap material

Key: c.   inspection hours   (Ref. Applications Question 60, August 1978)
       Inspection cost depends on the inspection hours. Hence the ratio of inspection hours to productive time is a good indicator to control inspection costs. All other choices, i.e., the ratio of

---

[14] *ASQC - CQE Examination*, ASQC Quality Progress, October 1972, Principles section, Question 60.

product costs or company profit or scrap material to the productive time to produce the product, are not directly indicators to control the inspection costs.

82. Management requests that you analyze the quality costs in department A which produces an average of one large complex product every six months. After reviewing the alternatives, you select which of the following indexes as the most valid and reliable indicator for cost trends?

    a.   quality costs per net sales billed
    b.   quality costs per unit produced
    c.   quality costs per direct labor dollar
    d.   quality costs per total manufacturing costs
    e.   any of the above

Key: b.   quality costs per unit produced   (Ref. Applications Question 67, October 1974)
Department A produces an average of one large complex product every six months, not a mass production. Hence it will be easier to use the index of quality costs per unit produced.

83. A complete quality cost reporting system would include which of the following as part of the quality cost?

    a.   test time costs associated with installing the product at the customer's facility prior to turning the product over to the customer
    b.   the salary of a product designer preparing a deviation authorization for material produced outside of design specifications
    c.   cost of scrap
    d.   all of the above
    e.   none of the above

Key: d.   all of the above   (Ref. Applications Question 61, August 1978)
Choice a is the appraisal cost; b and c are the failure costs. Hence the quality cost reporting system should include all three items.

84. Quality cost data would not normally be obtained from which of the following?

    a.   labor reports
    b.   capital expenditure reports
    c.   salary budget reports
    d.   scrap reports
    e.   any of these

Key: b.   capital expenditure reports   (Ref. Principles Question 90, October 1974)
Capital expenditure expenses are not considered as quality costs but operating costs. Choices a, c and d can provide meaningful data for quality costs.

85. Sources of quality cost data do not normally include

      a.   scrap reports

      b.   labor reports

      c.   salary budget reports

      d.   capital expenditure reports

Key: d.   capital expenditure reports   (Ref. Principles Question 16, October 1972)
Capital expenditure expense are not considered as quality costs but as operating costs. Choices a, b, and c can provide meaningful data for quality costs.

86.   The concept of quality cost budgeting

      a.   involves budgeting the individual elements

      b.   replaces the traditional profit and loss statement

      c.   does not consider total quality costs

      d.   considers the four categories of quality costs and their general trends

Key: d.   considers the four categories of quality costs and their general trends
(Ref. Principles Question 13, October 1972)
The question refers to *quality cost budgeting* and not *cost budgeting*. Hence choices a and b can be eliminated as they are not related to quality costs directly. Choice c is incorrect because the quality cost budgeting should or must consider the total quality costs. Hence choice d is the obvious choice.

87.   The modern concept of budgeting quality costs is to

      a.   budget each of the four segments: prevention, appraisal, and internal failure and external failure

      b.   concentrate on external failures; they are important to the business since they represent customer acceptance

      c.   establish a budget for reducing the total of the quality costs

      d.   reduce the expenditures on each segment

Key: c.   establish a budget for reducing the total of the quality costs
(Ref. Applications Question 64, October 1972)
The question represents difficult choices. Each choice seems correct. However only choice c focuses on reducing the total quality costs. Choice a indicates budgeting for each segment, not reducing. Choice b indicates concentrating only on external failures, which is suboptimizing. Efforts should be made to reduce quality costs as a total and analyze each segment to concentrate resources effectively.

88.   Quality cost systems provide for defect prevention. Which of the following elements is primary to defect prevention?

      a.   corrective action

      b.   data collection

   c.   cost analysis
   d.   training

Key: a.   corrective action   (Ref. Principles Question 69, August 1978)
The key term is "defect prevention" and not the *prevention cost* of quality. If defects occur, corrective actions as short-term and long-term irreversible reactions are developed and implemented. They are reactionary in nature. This means the quality system has significant nonconforming units or parts. Hence ASQC's answer to this question was given as choice a.

89.   One of the following is not a factor to consider in establishing quality information equipment cost:

   a.   debugging cost
   b.   amortization period
   c.   design cost
   d.   replacement cost
   e.   book cost

Key: e.   book cost   (Ref. Applications Question 59, August 1978)
The quality information equipment (QIE)[15] is defined as the device used to measure product and/ or process, analyze the information, and provide the feedback loop for continuous improvement. Choices a through d are the costs associated with QIE but not choice e.

---

[15] *Juran's Quality Control Handbook* by J. M. Juran, 4th ed., McGraw-Hill, New York, pg. 16.52.

ASQC-CQE BIBLIOGRAPHY AND OTHER REFERENCES ON QUALITY COSTS

1. *ANSI/ASQC A3-1987, Quality Systems Terminology*, Milwaukee, ASQC Quality Press, 1987.

2. *ANSI/ASQC Q90 Series-1987, Quality Management and Quality Assurance Standards*, (Q90-Q94) Milwaukee, ASQC Quality Press, 1987.

3. *ANSI/ASQC C1-1985, Specifications of General Requirements for Quality Program*, Milwaukee, ASQC Quality Press, 1985.

4. ASQC Quality Costs Committee, *Principles of Quality Costs,* edited by Jack Campernella, 2nd ed., Milwaukee, ASQC Quality Press, 1990.

5. ASQC Statistics Division, *Glossary and Tables for Statistical Quality Control*, 2nd ed., Milwaukee, ASQC Quality Press, 1983.

6. Besterfield, Dale H., *Quality Control,* 3rd ed., Prentice Hall, Englewood Cliffs., N.J., 1990.

7. Caplan, Frank, *The Quality System, A Sourcebook for Managers and Engineers*, 2nd ed., Radnor, PA, Chilton Book Co, 1990.

8. Deming, W. Edwards, *Out of Crisis*, Cambridge, MA, MIT Press, 1986.

9. Duncan, A. J., *Quality Control and Industrial Statistics*, 5th ed., Homewood, IL, Irwin Inc., 1986.

10. Feigenbaum, A.V., *Total Quality Control*, 3rd ed., Revised, New York, McGraw-Hill, 1991.

11. Ishikawa, Kaoru, *Guide to Quality Control*, White Plains, NY, Quality Resources, 1976.

12. Juran, J. M., *Juran's Quality Control Handbook*, 4th ed., New York, McGraw-Hill, 1988.

13. Juran, J. M. and F. M. Gryna, *Quality Planning and Analysis*, 3rd ed., New York, McGraw-Hill, 1993.

14. Montgomery, D.C., *Introduction to Statistical Quality Control*, 2nd ed., New York, John Wiley and Sons, 1991.

15. Picard, Lawrence G., Sr., *Fundamentals of Quality Control*, Milwaukee, 1992.

16. Pyzdek, Thomas and Roger W. Berger, *Quality Engineering Handbook,* Milwaukee, ASQC Quality Press, 1992.

17. *Quality Costs, Ideas and Applications* edited by Andrew G. Grimm, Volume 1 and 2, 2nd ed., Milwaukee, ASQC Quality Press. 1987.

CHAPTER 11

QUALITY AUDITING

ASQC'S BODY OF KNOWLEDGE (BOK) FOR THE CQE EXAMINATION

This chapter focuses on the following selected subject areas of BOK from *Section II, Quality Practices and Applications.*

Quality Audit

1.   Types of quality audits
2.   Auditor and auditee responsibilities
3.   Quality audit planning and preparation
4.   Steps in conducting an audit
5.   Audit reporting process
6.   Post-audit activities (e.g., corrective action, verification)

Supplier Management

1.   Methodologies
2.   Supplier performance evaluation and rating systems
3.   Supplier qualification or certification systems

1.   A quality system audit

        a.   verifies that applicable quality system elements have been developed
        b.   verifies that applicable quality system elements are appropriate and have been developed
        c.   verifies that the quality system is effectively maintained
        d.   does not evaluate the quality system's effectiveness, only compliance
        e.   validates an auditee's qualifications

Key: b.   verifies that applicable quality system elements are appropriate and have been developed
        (Ref. CQA examination application brochure of ASQC)
        American National Standards Institute ANSI/ASQC Q1-1986, Generic Guidelines for Auditing
        Quality Systems, defines a "Quality System Audit" as follows:
                *Quality System Audit is a documented activity performed to verify, by examination and
                evaluations of objective evidence, that applicable elements of the quality system are
                appropriate and have been developed, documented and effectively implemented in
                accordance and in conjunction with specified requirements.*

        American National Standards Institute ANSI/ASQC A3-1987, Quality Systems Terminology,
        defines "Quality System Audit" as follows:
                *Quality System Audit is a documented activity performed to verify, by examination and
                evaluation of objective evidence, that applicable elements of the quality system are
                suitable and have been developed, documented, and effectively implemented in
                accordance with specified requirements.*

        Feigenbaum[1] indicates that the quality system audit assesses the effectiveness of the
        implementation of a quality system and enables to determine which objectives are achieved
        effectively.

2.   A quality audit program should begin with

        a.   a study of the quality documentation system
        b.   an evaluation of the work being performed
        c.   a report listing findings, the action taken, and recommendations
        d.   a charter of policy, objectives, and procedures
        e.   a follow-up check on the manager's response to recommendations

Key: d.   a charter of policy, objectives, and procedures (Ref. Applications Question 66, July 1984)

3.   What is the purpose of a "Quality Audit Program"?

        a.   to provide a spy system for management
        b.   to catch defects missed by inspection
        c.   to make people follow procedure
        d.   to provide a super control system

---

[1] *Total Quality Control* by A.V. Feigenbaum, 3rd ed., McGraw-Hill, New York, pg. 295-296.

    e.   to measure and report the effectiveness of the control functions

Key: e.   to measure and report the effectiveness of the control functions (Ref. CQA examination application brochure of ASQC)

Juran[2] defines the quality audit or assurance as an activity that provides evidence that the quality function is performed effectively. Mills[3] discusses "why do quality audits" in detail. He states that a quality audit program provides objective evidence to the management of the organization being audited and of the organization requesting the audit about the suitability, conformity to requirements, and effectiveness of the various elements of the quality system.

4.   A quality audit can be used to

    a.   measure the effectiveness of a quality program
    b.   verify product quality
    c.   determine inspection inefficiency
    d.   any of the above

Key: d.   any of the above   (Ref. Applications Question 29, October 1974)

The term "quality audit" can refer to the appraisal of the quality system of an entire plant, company, one product, or one major quality activity. Depending upon the scope of the audit, it can be a system audit for evaluating the effectiveness of the entire quality program of the company, a product audit to verify the product quality audit, or an in-process audit to determine the inspection efficiency (or inefficiency).

5.   What items should be included by management when establishing a quality audit function within its organization?

    a.   proper positioning of the audit function within the quality organization
    b.   a planned audit approach, efficient and timely audit reporting, and a method for obtaining effective corrective action
    c.   selection of capable audit personnel
    d.   management objectivity toward the quality program audit concept
    e.   all of the above

Key: e.   all of the above (Ref. Principles Question 72, August 1978)

6.   Auditing of a quality program is most effective on a

    a.   quarterly basis, auditing all characteristics on the checklist
    b.   periodic unscheduled basis, auditing some procedures
    c.   monthly basis, auditing randomly selected procedures
    d.   continuing basis, auditing randomly selected procedures

---

[2] *Juran's Quality Control Handbook* by J. M. Juran, 4th ed., McGraw-Hill, New York, pg. 9.2-9.4.
[3] *The Quality Audit* by Charles A. Mills, McGraw-Hill, New York, pg. 7.

e.   continually specified time period basis, frequently adjustable, auditing randomly selected procedures

Key: e.   continually specified time period basis, frequently adjustable, auditing randomly selected procedures   (Ref. Applications Question 67, July 1984)

Choice e is broader and is not restricted to one condition to determine the frequency of an audit. The question however does not distinguish between the external and internal audits. All the choices above can be very expensive and time consuming for an external audit. Choice e is more applicable for an internal audit of the quality program.[4] It also depends on the type of audit, i.e., product quality audit, process quality audit, service quality audit, customer service audit,[5] etc.

7.   There are several types of quality assurance audits. Which of the following is not a type of quality assurance audit?

a.   product audit, in-line
b.   product audit, end-item
c.   primary audit
d.   process audit
e.   software audit

Key: c.   primary audit   (Ref. CQA examination application brochure of ASQC)

The term *primary audit* is not a commonly used term in quality assurance. Juran[6] discusses three forms of quality assurance: *quality audits*, *quality surveys,* and *product audits*. The in-line and end-item product audits, process audits, and software audits are different types of quality assurance audits.

8.   End-item product audits will directly measure

a.   outgoing product quality
b.   adequacy of inspection methods
c.   quality of capability of production
d.   adequate level of worker motivation

Key: a.   outgoing product quality   (Ref. CQT examination application brochure of ASQC)

The term end-item means the end-of-the-line or finished products audit, or final audit which is carried out to ensure that the outgoing product quality conforms to customer requirements. It is generally done as a second level of control in addition to other in-line or in-process methods of process control.

9.   A shipping line product audit will directly measure

a.   the outgoing product quality

---

[4] *The Quality Audit* by Charles A. Mills, McGraw-Hill, New York, Chapter 6, pg. 75-76.
[5] *The Quality Audit* by Charles A. Mills, McGraw-Hill, New York, Chapter 3, pg. 32-32.
[6] *Juran's Quality Control Handbook* by J. M. Juran, 4th ed., McGraw-Hill, New York, New York, pg. 9.2.

b.   the quality capability of production
c.   the adequacy of inspection methods
d.   the motivational level of the operators

Key: a.   the outgoing product quality (Ref. Applications Question 40, October 1974)
The term shipping line audit or end-item audit means an end-of-the-line, finished-product audit or final audit. Its purpose is to ensure that the outgoing product quality meets customer requirements. It is generally done as a second level of control in addition to other in-line or in-process methods of process control.

10.   Complete examination of a small sample of a finished product is characteristic of

a.   final inspection
b.   work sampling
c.   process audit
d.   product audit

Key: d.   product audit   (Ref. Principles Question 84, October 1974)

11.   Which of the following best describes the "specific activity" type of audit?

a.   customer-oriented sampling of finished goods
b.   evaluation for contractual compliance of a quality system
c.   assessment or survey of a potential vendor
d.   inspection performance audit
e.   none of the above

Key: d.   inspection performance audit (Ref. Principles Question 75, August 1978)
Choices a, b, and c are broader and generic in nature. They are not an evaluation of a specific activity, but cover all products or all elements of a quality system. Choice d is a very specific activity as it describes specifically the audit of the inspection performance.

12.   An example of a situation where an unscheduled (surprise) audit could be used is a(n)

a.   investigative audit of financial transactions
b.   quality systems audit
c.   vendor quality audit
d.   process quality audit

Key: a.   investigative audit of financial transactions
(Ref. CQA examination application brochure of ASQC)

13.   The quality assurance function is comparable to which of the following other business functions in concept?

a.   general accounting
b.   cost accounting
c.   audit accounting
d.   all of the above

Key: c.   audit accounting   (Ref. Principles Question 67, July 1984)
Audit accounting is the independent verification that the accounting system meets tax laws and is effectively implemented. Quality assurance focuses on all systems and activities so that customer requirements are properly deployed in all functions and the system meets customer requirements. Hence it is more comparable to audit accounting than general or cost accounting. Assurance is important to ensure that the quality function is effective and the quality system is implemented; similarly, audit is important to ensure that the accounting function is effective and the accounting system is implemented consistently. Assurance bears the same relation to the quality function that audit does to the accounting function.

14.   Assurance bears the same relation to the quality function that _____ does to the accounting function.

a.   vacation
b.   audit
c.   variable overhead
d.   control

Key: b.   audit   (Ref. Principles Question 73, August 1978)
Refer to Question 13 above for an explanation.

15.   The term *quality audit* can refer to the appraisal of the quality system of

a.   an entire plant or company
b.   one product
c.   one major quality activity
d.   any of the above

Key: d.   any of the above   (Ref. Principles Question 68, July 1984)
The scope of the quality audit can include any of the items listed above and hence it has to be clearly defined before beginning the audit.

16.   In order to be effective, the quality audit function should ideally be

a.   an independent organizational segment in the quality control function
b.   an independent organizational segment in the production control function
c.   an independent organizational segment in the manufacturing operation function
d.   all of the above

Key: a.   an independent organizational segment in the quality control function

(Ref. Principles Question 70, July 1984)
Audit is an *independent* and systematic evaluation to determine that a quality system is effectively designed and implemented based on the agreed upon requirements. If the quality audit function is a part of the production control function (b) or a part of the manufacturing operations function (d), then its objective as an independent function will be questionable. Juran[7] considers the term *independent* used in the definition of the audit to be very critical and recommends that neither the auditor should be responsible for the performance under review nor his or her immediate supervisor, and the auditor should be completely independent and unbiased. Hence the audit function should be an independent organizational segment in the quality control function.

17.   In organizing an audit group, it is most important

       a.   that the group be independent of the operating functions
       b.   that it be compatible with the accounting audit group
       c.   for it to cover all company functions
       d.   for it to report to top management only

Key: a.   that the group be independent of the operating functions
       (Ref. Principles Question 23, October 1974)
       This is the fundamental concept of an audit. Audit is defined as a systematic and *independent* examination to determine whether the quality activities and related results comply with the planned arrangements, and whether these arrangements are implemented effectively and are suitable to achieve these objectives. Hence the group must be independent of the operating functions to conduct the audit.

18.   A basic requirement of an audit organization is that it report to

       a.   the president of the company
       b.   the quality control department
       c.   the quality assurance department
       d.   someone outside the organization element being audited

Key: d.   someone outside the organization element being audited
       (Ref. CQA examination application brochure of ASQC)
       Refer to Question 17 above for explanation.

19.   Audit inspectors should report to someone who is independent from

       a.   middle management
       b.   marketing
       c.   inspection supervision
       d.   production staff

---

[7] *Juran's Quality Control Handbook* by J. M. Juran, 4th ed., McGraw-Hill, New York, pg. 9.4.

Key: c.   inspection supervision   (Ref. Applications Question 70, July 1984)
        The key word is *independent*, i.e., the auditor should not be part of the function being audited.
        Hence audit inspectors should not be part of inspection supervision.

20.   You are requested by top management to establish an audit program of the quality system in each
       branch plant of your firm. Which of the following schemes would you use in selecting the audit
       team to optimize continuity, direction, availability, and technology transfer?

       a.   full-time audit staff
       b.   all-volunteer audit staff
       c.   the boss's son and son-in-law
       d.   hybrid audit staff (a proportion of answers a and b above)
       e.   any of the above will make an effective audit team

Key: d.   hybrid audit staff (a proportion of answers a and b above)
        (Ref. Applications Question 66, August 1978)
        As a quality auditor you should remember and follow the ethical and moral requirements for the
        audit, the conflict of interest, the independent nature of the audit, and the qualification of the
        auditors. Mills[8] provides detailed discussion on the aptitudes and qualifications of the quality
        auditor.

21.   Qualifications for a lead auditor must include

       a.   the ability to field antagonistic responses
       b.   the ability to differentiate "the vital few from the trivial many"
       c.   technical expertise in the engineering field that will be audited
       d.   answers a and b only
       e.   answers a, b, and c

Key: d.   answers a and b only (Ref. CQA examination application brochure of ASQC)

22.   Which of the following is potentially the most costly part of an audit?

       a.   the auditor's time spent on the audit
       b.   the auditee's time spent being audited
       c.   overhead of the auditing organization
       d.   the cost of processing nonconformance reports
       e.   costs generated by using untrained or unsuitable auditors

Key: e.   costs generated by using untrained or unsuitable auditors
        (Ref. CQA examination application brochure of ASQC)

23.   Upon completion of a branch plant or division quality systems audit, an "exit briefing" of
       concerned personnel should be conducted by the audit team. Which of the following is usually a

---

[8] *The Quality Audit* by Charles A. Mills, McGraw-Hill, New York, Chapter 6, pg. 81-96.

violation of quality audit integrity?

    a.   identifying major quality system deficiencies found during the last audit
    b.   comparing audit results with the branch plant/division last audited
    c.   obtaining corrective actions commitments
    d.   highlighting key areas of improvements since the last audit
    e.   all of the above are good audit practices

Key: b.   comparing audit results with the branch plant/division last audited
(Ref. Principles Question 37, October 1974)
The audit must be an independent evaluation of conformance to requirements. If the audit team compares the audit results with the branch plant or division last audited, it is detrimental to the purpose of an audit and can add some biases in auditing. This can make the audit team less independent and sometimes create a negative atmosphere between two plants. Also it may not be an equal comparison of circumstances and can mislead the client or the plant. In some cases, it can be viewed as providing proprietary or confidential information to other plant management. It may result in conflict of interest and can violate the audit integrity if you directly or indirectly share the results of the last audit of a plant.

24.   Which of the following is not a legitimate audit function?

    a.   identify the function responsible for primary control and corrective action
    b.   provide no surprises
    c.   provide data on worker performance to supervision for punitive action
    d.   contribute to a reduction in quality cost
    e.   none of the above

Key: c.   provide data on worker performance to supervision for punitive action
(Ref. Principles Question 70, August 1978)
The purpose of an audit is to identify the opportunities for continuous improvement by conducting an independent evaluation to find evidence of conformance to an agreed standard. It can highlight the areas of nonconformance and requires a plan for corrective action.

Audits are not intended to be performance appraisals for operators and should not be used for punitive action. They are intended to verify that the quality system is in place and its practices and procedures are effectively implemented. Juran[9] discusses the importance of human relations during the audit and avoiding an atmosphere of blame. The purpose of the audit is to create an atmosphere of improvement and not of blame. Blaming people and not the system causes resentment and affects the cooperation in future audits. Hence the audit findings and conclusion reports should be fact-based and system-oriented or problem-oriented and not person-oriented, i.e., they should not focus on "who."

25.   Which of the following is the poorest reason for a quality audit?

---

[9] *Juran's Quality Control Handbook* by J. M. Juran, 4th ed., McGraw-Hill, New York, pg. 9-11.

    a.   product quality evaluation
    b.   to start disciplinary action
    c.   to initiate corrective action
    d.   identification of hardware deficiency

Key: b.   to start disciplinary action   (Ref. Principles Question 52, October 1974)
    Refer to Question 24 above for an explanation.

26.   The following are reasons why an independent audit of actual practice vs. procedures should be performed periodically.

    I.   Pressures may force the supervisors to deviate from approved procedures.
    II.   The supervisor may not have time for organized follow-up or adherence to procedures.
    III.   Supervisors are not responsible for implementing procedures.

    a.   I and II only
    b.   II and III only
    c.   I and III only
    d.   I, II, and III

Key: a.   I and II only   (Ref. Principles Question 72, July 1984)
    These two choices together form or define the conformity audit; i.e., procedures or quality systems are effectively implemented as an actual practice at all times and are operationalized. The periodic audits, mainly internal audits, are very effective in ensuring that actual practices meet the procedures, and restrict supervisors and their top management from deviating from quality practices. The supervisors generally are busy in meeting the production and quality standards but may not be able periodically to evaluate each procedure in their operations. Also if a supervisor conducts the evaluation of his or her conformance to procedures, the results may be biased and not independent.

    Item III is incorrect because supervisors are responsible for understanding and implementing each quality requirement or procedure effectively to ensure that the operations meet or exceed customer requirements.

27.   Which of the following quality system provisions is of the greatest concern when preparing an audit checklist for a quality system audit?

    a.   Drawing and print control
    b.   Make up of the MRB (Material Review Board)
    c.   Training level of inspectors
    d.   Optimization of production processes
    e.   Calibration of test equipment

Key: e.   Calibration of test equipment   (Ref. Principles Question 71, July 1984)
    Calibration of test equipment as a part of the measurement system analysis is very important.

The ability to meet customer requirements effectively depends on an effective measurement system and so it is the correct answer, as per ASQC.

This can be viewed as a subjective answer since choice a, "drawing and print control" and choice c, "training level of inspectors," are also important items for an audit. Most of the quality system standards require the existence of a group such as an MRB to review material that does not conform to requirements. However, there are no specific rules for the exact makeup of the MRB as it can be a multidisciplined team or small committee. Hence choice b is not a proper answer.

28.   Which of the following quality system provisions is of the least concern when preparing an audit checklist for the upcoming branch operation quality system audit?

        a.   drawing and print control
        b.   makeup of the MRB (material review board)
        c.   control of nonconforming materials
        d.   control of special processes
        e.   calibration of test equipment

Key: b.   makeup of the MRB (material review board)
        (Ref. Principles Question 53, October 1974)
        It is important to know if the company or the branch has procedures for identification, segregation, and disposition of nonconforming materials, and if an MRB is in place to perform this function. But the makeup of the MRB is the least concern as per ASQC's answer.

        This can be a subjective answer because, for some operations, the makeup of the MRB is important depending on its roles,[10] particularly operations or products dealing with safety and compliance to regulations. Thus it can be a part of the quality system requirements. This is a repeat question with slight changes from the August 1978 examination.[11]

29.   In many programs, what is generally the weakest link in quality auditing programs?

        a.   lack of adequate audit checklists
        b.   scheduling of audits (frequency)
        c.   audit reporting
        d.   follow-up of corrective action implementation

Key: d.   follow-up of corrective action implementation
        (Ref. Principles Question 71, August 1978)
        Choices a, b, and c are not generally the weakest links in quality auditing. The audit is not fully complete and closed unless corrective actions are followed up properly and implemented.

30.   Follow-up and close-out of audit-initiated corrective actions should be performed by

---

[10] *Juran's Quality Control Handbook* by J. M. Juran, 4th ed., McGraw-Hill, New York, pg. 18.32-33.
[11] *ASQC - CQE Examination*, ASQC Quality Progress, August 1978, Applications section, Question 65.

a.   the corrective action board (where one exists) with the audit function's participation
b.   the audit function
c.   quality engineering with the audit function's participation
d.   an authority defined by company policy

Key: b.   the audit function (Ref. CQA examination application brochure of ASQC)
       Refer to Question 29 above.

31.   Consider the statement "even if corrective action is taken immediately for a finding during the audit, all significant deficiencies should be detailed in the written report." This statement is

a.   true, because the auditor is responsible for an accurate report of all findings
b.   false, because the audit report should include only unresolved deficiencies
c.   false, because the corrective action can be verified during the audit
d.   true, because the auditor must account for time spent
e.   true, because a follow-up audit will need to be made on all findings

Key: a.   true, because the auditor is responsible for an accurate report of all findings
       (Ref. CQA examination application brochure of ASQC)

32.   An audit will be viewed as a constructive service to the function which is audited when it

a.   is conducted by nontechnical auditors
b.   proposes corrective action for each item covered
c.   furnishes enough detailed facts so the necessary actions can be determined
d.   is general enough to permit managerial intervention

Key: c.   furnishes enough detailed facts so the necessary actions can be determined
       (Ref. Applications Question 67, August 1978)
       The remaining choices are easily ruled out. Be careful with choice b about making recommendations for corrective actions. Many leading authors in quality auditing advise that one not make recommendations for each item covered because it makes the auditor a part of the auditee's system and affects the independence of the audit. Also, making recommendations requires exceptional subject matter expertise on the part of the auditor, which may not exist in some teams for each product/process. Sometimes the recommendations may result in a conflict of interest if they are based on knowledge or information gained (sometimes proprietary in nature) during similar audits at competitor companies. You must review such sensitive issues up-front with your client to avoid such conflicts.

       Another important point is that corrective actions are not for every item covered but are required for every discrepancy, nonconformance, or noncompliance to a given standard.

33.   Which of the following is not a responsibility of the auditor?

a.   prepare a plan and checklist

b. report results to those responsible
c. investigate deficiencies for a cause and define the corrective actions that must be taken
d. follow-up to see if the corrective action was taken
e. none of the above

Key: c. investigate deficiencies for a cause and define the corrective actions that must be taken
(Ref. Applications Question 68, August 1978)
The audit should provide details of each observation or finding so that the auditee can find the root cause for each deficiency or nonconformity found. Making recommendations during the audit is generally not advisable in order to maintain the independence of the audit. Also, refer to the comments made in the answer to Question 32 above.

34. The primary responsibility for follow-up on corrective action commitments after an audit report usually rests with

a. production management
b. quality engineering
c. the function being audited
d. the audit group

Key: d. the audit group (Ref. Applications Question 72, October 1974)
The audit is not fully complete and closed unless the follow-up on the corrective actions is done in a timely manner. The follow-up for the corrective actions implementation is one of the weakest links in the quality auditing program. The client needs to define the scope of the follow-up audit.

35. To insure the success of a quality audit program, the most important activity for a quality supervisor is

a. setting up audit frequency
b. maintenance of a checking procedure to see that all required audits are performed
c. getting corrective action as a result of audit findings
d. checking that the audit procedure is adequate and complete

Key: c. getting corrective action as a result of audit findings
(Ref. Applications Question 6, October 1972)

36. The auditor should always let the auditee know about significant deficiencies promptly so that the auditee has the chance to take corrective action before the post audit conference (if possible). Which of the following is not a rationale for doing this?

a. It gives the auditee the chance to show a genuine concern for quality improvement.
b. It saves a re-audit or follow-up and therefore saves time and money.
c. It allows the auditor to omit the deficiencies during the post-audit conference.
d. It shows that the audit can get results.

Key: c.   It allows the auditor to omit the deficiencies during the post audit conference.
            (Ref. CQA examination application brochure of ASQC)

37.   After auditors report deficiencies that have not yet been corrected, their role should be to

         a.   assure that corrective action is done right
         b.   leave all further action up to the auditee
         c.   evaluate corrective action after it is taken
         d.   inform the auditee's top management that they should monitor the corrective action

Key: c.   evaluate corrective action after it is taken
            (Ref. CQA examination application brochure of ASQC)

38.   A well prepared checklist for a quality audit is a vital tool to provide

         a.   assurance that areas having major deficiencies during past audits are reviewed
         b.   a training method for developing new auditors
         c.   a means of obtaining relatively uniform audits
         d.   all of the above
         e.   none of the above

Key: d.   all of the above   (Ref. Principles Question 28, October 1974)

39.   The most important reason for a checklist in a process control audit is to

         a.   assure that the auditor is qualified
         b.   minimize the time required for audit
         c.   obtain relatively uniform audits
         d.   notify the audited function prior to audit

Key: c.   obtain relatively uniform audits   (Ref. Principles Question 69, October 1972)
            A checklist is a written instruction sheet for the auditor. It creates consistent criteria for audits
            and uniform application of audit standard requirements.

40.   Which of the following is not a benefit of using checklists in conducting an audit?

         a.   The checklist is a helpful memory aid.
         b.   The checklist provides uniformity to the auditing process.
         c.   The checklist will help identify who has the responsibility for deficiencies.
         d.   The checklist is a useful training aid.

Key: c.   The checklist will help identify who has the responsibility for deficiencies.
            (Ref. CQA examination application brochure of ASQC)
            A checklist is a written instruction sheet for the auditor. It creates consistent criteria for audits
            and uniform application of audit standard requirements. It is a good guide for organizing notes.

41.   The primary purpose of audit working papers is to provide

        a.   evidence of the analysis of internal control
        b.   support for the audit report
        c.   a basis for evaluating audit personnel
        d.   a guide for subsequent audits of the same area
        e.   identification of personnel causing problems

Key: b.   support for the audit report   (Ref. CQA examination application brochure of ASQC)
        Refer to Questions 38, 39, and 40 above of this chapter for similar questions. The working papers
        or checklists used during an audit will assure that all audits are relatively uniform, and the areas
        having major deficiencies during the previous audits are reviewed. They provide the support to
        the audit report as they systematically review each operation and then document the areas having
        deficiencies. They help in organizing the audit program.

42.   Which one of the following activities best reflects the fact that the systematic management of
        quality audits includes planning and control functions?

        a.   verifying the implementation of an inspection system
        b.   establishing an audit schedule and preparing an appropriate checklist
        c.   reviewing the audit procedures and instructions
        d.   determining the traceability within a change-control system
        e.   certifying auditors on the basis of experience and an examination

Key: b.   establishing an audit schedule and preparing an appropriate checklist
        (Ref. CQA examination application brochure of ASQC)
        The key words are "systematic management of quality audits," i.e., planning and conducting and
        reporting/closing the audit. To effectively manage the audit, we need to develop a well-balanced
        audit schedule that includes managing the work loads, assigning the personnel, and other
        activities. It also reduces stress and frustration on the part of the auditee when audits are well
        planned and scheduled in advance except for some surprise audits. The audit schedule should
        include all important elements of a quality standard such as choices a, c, and d above.

        The checklists, often called the working papers, are the documents required to effectively
        execute the audit. They describe the format of the audit function, and the scope and approach of
        the audit. Checklists provide a means of attaining uniform audits, give assurance that the areas
        having some major deficiencies have been reviewed, and can be used as training tools for new
        auditors.

43.   Audits should be scheduled with regard to

        a.   the availability of objective evidence
        b.   obtaining an unbiased sample of evidence
        c.   the demand pattern for end items
        d.   the convenience of the audit team

e.   answers a and b only

Key: e.   answers a and b only (Ref. CQA examination application brochure of ASQC)
        It is simple to rule out choices c and d above.

44.   Management has been receiving complaints from the field about the performance of its product.
        Although the quality system being used does require a final inspection for lot acceptance, it also
        has been decided to do an end-item (product) quality audit. Which sampling procedure would
        you recommend to your quality control manager?

        a.   ten percent of production
        b.   a fixed quantity per time period
        c.   a plan selected from MIL-STD-105D (it is now 105E)
        d.   a small sample
        e.   any of the above

Key: e.   any of the above   (Ref. Applications Question 17, October 1974)
        The choices above indicate different possible ways of setting up an audit plan and its frequency.
        Feigenbaum[12] discusses the various criteria for frequency of audits. It should be based on
        production changes in the volume, new product introductions, new applications, and operator
        rotations or absenteeism. Juran[13] indicates that the sample size for audits will generally be
        arbitrary, and be based on economical approaches to balance the cost, or based on the cost of
        reducing the internal failure of quality costs on the current production. The sample size of
        different groups should be based on the concepts of variability and practical approaches in
        statistics. Mills[14] has developed tables for binomial limiting quality level sampling plans and
        Poisson limiting quality level sampling plans for determining the sample size for a quality audit
        based on acceptable performance levels and confidence levels, etc.

45.   When selecting an audit sample size, which of the following rules should govern your choice?

        a.   Since quality may change over time, we should look at a fixed quantity each time period
                  for audit purposes.
        b.   We need only a very small sample for audit purposes, as long as it is chosen at random.
        c.   Any size sample if randomly selected can be suitable for audit purposes, since we are not
                  directly performing lot acceptance or rejection.
        d.   MIL-STD-105E is a scientific sampling procedure, and we need scientific sampling for
                  audit purposes.
        e.   In general, ten percent is a good sample size to use. Also it is easy to remember.

Key: c.   Any size sample if randomly selected can be suitable for audit purposes, since we are
                  not directly performing lot acceptance or rejection.
        (Ref. Applications Question 24, October 1974) Refer to Question 44 above for a discussion.

---

[12] *Total Quality Control* by A.V. Feigenbaum, 3rd ed., McGraw-Hill, New York, pg. 294.
[13] *Juran's Quality Control Handbook* by J. M. Juran, 4th ed., McGraw-Hill, New York, pg. 9.24.
[14] *The Quality Audit* by Charles A. Mills, McGraw-Hill, New York, Chapter 6, pg. 174-177.

46.   Attribute sampling should be used when

        a.   the population contains attributes
        b.   a yes-or-no decision is to be made
        c.   the population has variability
        d.   a multi-stage sampling plan is needed
        e.   the population has no variability

Key: b.   a yes-or-no decision is to be made
        (Ref. CQA examination application brochure of ASQC)
        In any audit, an auditor is evaluating every situation and operation step-by-step to find if they are
        either satisfactory or not satisfactory. Hence an auditor is more often dealing with attribute
        sampling plans than variable sampling plans. Mills[15] has developed tables for binomial limiting
        quality level sampling plans and Poisson limiting quality level sampling plans for determining
        the sample size for a quality audit based on acceptable performance levels and confidence levels,
        etc. This question is repeated with similar choices in Questions 45 and 46 above from the
        October 1974 examination.

47.   You would normally *not* include data from which of the following investigations in quality
        auditing?

        a.   examination of all items produced
        b.   examination of customer needs and the adequacy of design specifications in reflecting
                these needs
        c.   examination of vendor product specifications and monitoring procedures
        d.   examination of customer quality complaints and adequacy of corrective action

Key: a.   examination of all items produced   (Ref. Principles Question 69, July 1984)
        It is generally impossible to perform examination or inspection of all items produced during the
        audit. During an audit, a sampling plan, with a sample size based on the level of confidence, is
        used instead of 100% inspection of all the items produced. Choices b, c, and d are part of
        auditing, and the data or results of these areas should be included in the audit analysis. This is a
        repeat question with a slight change from the October 1974 examination.[16]

48.   An inspection performance audit is made up of eight inspectors in an area of complex assembly,
        all doing similar work. Seven inspectors have an average monthly acceptance rate of 86 to 92%;
        one inspector has an average rate of 72% with approximately four times the daily variation as
        the others. As inspection supervisor you should, based on this audit,

        a.   promote the 72% inspector as he is very conscientious
        b.   discipline the 72% inspector as he is creating needless rework and wasted time
        c.   initiate a special investigation of inspection and manufacturing performance
        d.   discipline the other seven inspectors as they are not "cracking down"

---

[15] *The Quality Audit* by Charles A. Mills, McGraw-Hill, New York, Chapter 6, pg. 174-177.
[16] *ASQC - CQE Examination*, ASQC Quality Progress, October 1974, Principles section, Question 36.

Key: c.   initiate a special investigation of inspection and manufacturing performance
       (Ref. Applications Question 68, July 1984)
       The data show a high degree of inconsistency in the inspection capability. The high or low
       acceptance rate of the inspector does not mean that he or she is also accurate and efficient. Hence
       choices a, b, and d are not correct. Juran[17] describes the methods and formula to calculate
       inspector accuracy.

49.   In the "trace forward" method of auditing, the auditor begins with sales, selects the order(s) of
       interest, and follows them through the various departments. Which of the following is not an
       advantage of trace forward auditing?

       a.   It shows the processing flow through the company.
       b.   It provides a useful method for training auditors.
       c.   It is practical for partial audits.
       d.   It permits quick detection of deficiencies at the front end.

Key: c.   It is practical for partial audits. (Ref. CQA examination application brochure of ASQC)

50.   When you are performing a branch plant quality system audit, it is most necessary that you

       a.   report every deficiency identified
       b.   obtain corroboration by management of any system deficiency reported
       c.   complete every item on the audit checklist
       d.   take corrective action on each deficiency identified
       e.   all of the above

Key: b.   obtain corroboration by management of any system deficiency reported
       (Ref. Applications Question 15, October 1974)
       The term quality audit can refer to the appraisal of the quality system of an entire plant or
       company, one product, or one major quality activity. The quality system audit determines the
       effectiveness of implementation of the quality system. The audit report should be formally
       documented and reported to all key individuals and the top management. It should identify all
       areas of system implementation weaknesses thoroughly. The areas where the quality system has
       deficiencies should be identified and thoroughly discussed with the appropriate management. Its
       prompt attention and support should be obtained to ensure that required corrective actions are
       identified promptly and given top priority. They should also be verified by scheduled follow-up
       audits since they are branch audits.

51.   The quality audit could be used to judge all of the following except

       a.   a prospective vendor's capability for meeting quality standards
       b.   the adequacy of a current vendor's system for controlling quality
       c.   the application of a specification to a unique situation
       d.   the adequacy of a company's own system for controlling quality

---

[17] *Juran's Quality Control Handbook* by J. M. Juran, 4th ed., McGraw-Hill, New York, pg. 18.94-18.97.

Key: c.   the application of a specification to a unique situation
        (Ref. Applications Question 69, July 1984)
        Choice c describes the term "specification" and not the standard. Audit can be generally used
        to evaluate the application of a standard and not a specification to a unique situation. Choices a,
        b, and d are the appropriate reasons or objectives for a quality audit.

52.   Which of the following techniques would not be used in a quality audit?

        a.   select samples only from completed work
        b.   examine samples from viewpoint of critical customer
        c.   audit only those items which have caused customer complaints
        d.   use audit information in future design planning
        e.   frequency of audit to depend on economic and quality requirements

Key: c.   audit only those items which have caused customer complaints
        (Ref. Applications Question 63, August 1978)
        This is very dangerous but often directed by top management. The audit of only those items that
        have caused customer complaints reflects very narrow focus in a quality audit. The quality audit
        should include those items and review a company's policies and procedures for handling
        customer complaints, but should not be limited to those items. The quality audit should be
        based on the applicable reference standard. It should be performed to verify by examination and
        evaluation of objective evidence that applicable elements of the quality system are suitable and
        have been developed, documented, and effectively implemented in accordance with specified
        requirements.

53.   You have been asked to appraise the new quality data system developed by your statistical
        services group. Which of the following measures need not be considered during your evaluation
        of the effectiveness of that quality data system?

        a.   The information is resulting in effective and timely corrective action.
        b.   The system is being adequately maintained.
        c.   The reports are being distributed monthly.
        d.   Paperwork is held to a minimum.

Key: c.   The reports are being distributed monthly. (Ref. Applications Question 75, October 1974)
        Choices b and a are very important because they tie in strongly with the effective maintenance
        of the system, resulting in effective and timely corrective action. Choice d is important to
        minimize the paperwork. However choice c is of no direct value as generally it does not add any
        value to the customer.

54.   It is generally considered desirable that quality audit reports be

        a.   stated in terms different from those of the function being audited
        b.   simple but complete
        c.   sent to the general manager in all cases

d.   quantitative in all cases

Key: b.   simple but complete   (Ref. Applications Question 53, October 1972)
       Choices a, c, and d are obviously incorrect.

55.   The audit report is an important information source for the client of the auditor. Many auditors
       may be employed in auditing organizations or departments. The audit supervisor should

       a.   avoid interfering with the audit once the auditor has been assigned to conduct an audit
                and write the report
       b.   review and approve the report before submitting it to the client
       c.   decide on the distribution of the report
       d.   send the entire report to the auditor in charge of the follow-up audit
       e.   keep close contact with the auditee during all stages of the audit report preparation

Key: b.   review and approve the report before submitting it to the client
       (Ref. CQA examination application brochure of ASQC)

56.   When can an audit be discontinued?

       a.   when the audit objectives appear to have become unattainable
       b.   when the auditee disputes important observations
       c.   as soon as it appears that everything is in order
       d.   once started, it must be completed

Key: a.   when the audit objectives appear to have become unattainable
       (Ref. CQA examination application brochure of ASQC)

57.   One of the best analytical methods to identify failure costs that represent the greatest return on
       the invested prevention dollar is to

       a.   perform an internal financial audit
       b.   study the budget variance report
       c.   apply the Gompertz curve technique
       d.   apply the Pareto principle
       e.   perform a break-even analysis

Key: d.   apply the Pareto principle   (Ref. CQA examination application brochure of ASQC)

58.   The primary reason for evaluating and maintaining surveillance over a supplier's quality program
       is to

       a.   perform product inspection at the source
       b.   eliminate incoming inspection cost
       c.   motivate suppliers to improve quality

      d.   make sure the supplier's quality program is functioning effectively

Key: d.   make sure the supplier's quality program is functioning effectively
(Ref. Principles Question 35, July 1984)
The supplier audit or evaluation is generally conducted to determine that the quality activities and related results comply with the customer standards or requirements and to verify that these activities are effectively implemented. This enables the customer to ensure that the supplier has developed a written quality plan for improving and maintaining quality and is effectively following the plan.

Surveillance is exercised over the activities of the supplier to continuously verify that the supplier follows the previously agreed quality plan and activities and the supplier is capable of meeting customer requirements. This question is repeated with a slight change in the October 1974 examination.[18]

59.   A vendor quality survey

      a.   is used to predict whether a potential vendor can meet quality requirements
      b.   is an audit of a vendor's product for a designated period of time
      c.   is always conducted by quality control personnel only
      d.   reduces cost by eliminating the need for receiving inspection of the surveyed vendor's product

Key: a.   is used to predict whether a potential vendor can meet quality requirements
(Ref. Principles Question 73, July 1984)
The key word is "survey" and not audit. A vendor quality survey is a vendor appraisal technique which is used to evaluate the ability of the potential supplier to provide a particular product or service before awarding business. The survey should cover areas such as product design, manufacturing, assembly, subsuppliers, quality, shipping, etc., to ensure that a quality system is developed that meets customer requirements and is effectively implemented. Hence a is the best choice. The vendor quality survey should not be conducted by quality control personnel only but by a team of experts from different areas. Hence choice c is a poor choice.

Choices b and d are not part of the vendor quality survey but are part of the vendor surveillance, i.e., the ongoing observation or audit of products and activities to ensure that the product meets the specified requirements. The survey is not an inspection of a particular product but it is generally meant for the evaluation of the quality system. The product audit conducted at the supplier location by the customer or the supplier itself (as self-certification) can minimize subsequent measurements or inspections at the customer's receiving location.

60.   A preaward survey of a potential supplier is best described as a (an) _____ audit.

      a.   compliance
      b.   assessment

---

[18] *ASQC - CQE Examination*, ASQC Quality Progress, October 1974, Principles section, Question 3.

c.   quantitative
d.   all of these
e.   none of these

Key: b.   assessment   (Ref. Principles Question 74, August 1978)
Suppliers normally undergo an assessment for business as a preaward survey.

61.   The existence of a quality control manual at your key supplier means

a.   that a quality system has been developed
b.   that a quality system has been implemented
c.   that the firm is quality conscious
d.   that the firm is a certified supplier
e.   all of the above

Key: a.   that a quality system has been developed
(Ref. Principles Question 16, October 1974)
A quality manual is a technical translation of customer standards into operational requirements
for the company. It defines the procedures and methods that must be effectively implemented to
meet customer requirements. The presence of a quality manual indicates only that a quality
system is defined at the supplier location. It does not indicate whether the company's quality
policy and procedures per the manual are effectively implemented. The operations must conform
to the items in the quality manual as standard practice. The conformity audit will audit the
operations against the quality manual.

62.   Vendor audits are usually arranged and coordinated by the

a.   quality assurance department
b.   manufacturing department
c.   engineering department
d.   purchasing department

Key: d.   purchasing department (Ref. CQA examination application brochure of ASQC)

63.   A vendor quality survey report should describe

a.   the quality status of products examined
b.   discrepant conditions causing or contributing to inferior quality
c.   recommendations for actions necessary to correct discrepancies
d.   all of the above

Key: d.   all of the above   (Ref. CQT examination questions of ASQC)

64.   The most important step in vendor certification is to

a. obtain copies of the vendor's handbook
b. familiarize the vendor with quality requirements
c. analyze the vendor's first shipment
d. visit the vendor's plant

Key: b. familiarize the vendor with quality requirements
(Ref. Applications Question 29, July 1984)
The vendor certification, development, or audit requires that you first provide the vendor with a complete set of documents for the quality requirements. This gives the vendor an opportunity to study it and evaluate its capability to meet them. The vendor can then develop a quality plan or manual to include all the elements of the customer requirements. This will result in the vendor's commitment to meet your quality requirements.

65. The most important step in vendor certification is to

a. obtain copies of vendor's handbook
b. familiarize the vendor with quality requirements
c. analyze vendor's first shipment
d. visit the vendor's plant

Key: b. familiarize the vendor with quality requirements
(Ref. Applications Question 37, August 1978)
This is the first step among the four choices. Once the vendor is familiar with your quality requirements, she or he can prepare a quality manual or vendor handbook to meet the expectations as per choice a. Then, if necessary, the customer can plan to visit the vendor's plant as a simple visit, an assessment, or a preaward audit. If the customer is satisfied with the quality manual and the plant visit or audit, the result may be to award the vendor business. Then the last one is the start of business activity, i.e., shipment of goods. The customer may choose to analyze the first shipment, its inspection, lab test data, etc.

66. A vendor quality control plan has been adopted. Which of the following provisions would you advise top management to be least effective?

a. product audits
b. source inspection
c. certificate of analysis
d. certificate of compliance
e. preaward surveys

Key: d. certificate of compliance (Ref. Applications Question 33, August 1978)
The *certificate of compliance* is a warrant or a document that the supplier provides to certify in writing that the product conforms to all the requirements/specifications. But the supplier is responsible anyway, even by law, to ensure that the product conforms to all requirements or specifications. Hence this does not provide any added assurance, other than the formality to the

customer for a given shipment. Therefore it is the least effective among all the choices. This question is repeated in the October 1974 examination.[19]

67.   The most desirable method of evaluating a supplier is

        a.   history evaluation
        b.   survey evaluation
        c.   questionnaire
        d.   discuss with quality manager on phone
        e.   all of the above

Key: a.   history evaluation   (Ref. Applications Question 35, August 1978)
        It is pure common sense to use the history information of a supplier to evaluate it. This history includes mainly the supplier's performance and responsiveness, and the cost and the quality of the product and services provided by the supplier. It also includes the details of its capability, quality plan, past performance or problems faced, and their short-term and long-term resolutions. History also defines the growth and improvement of a supplier's operations. The buyer (or customer) can use such information as technical memory or lessons learned, and this information is more factual and data based than the survey evaluations, questionnaire, and any other discussions with the supplier. It is also less expensive, faster, more reliable, and easier to collect or analyze. It is one of the first steps in beginning a full supplier audit, evaluation, or surveillance program.

68.   During the preaward survey at a potential key supplier, you discover the existence of a quality control manual, this means

        a.   that a quality system has been developed
        b.   that a quality system has been implemented
        c.   that a firm is quality conscious
        d.   that the firm has a quality manager
        e.   all of the above

Key: a.   that a quality system has been developed
        (Ref. Applications Question 64, August 1978)
        Presence of a quality manual indicates that the supplier has developed a definition of the company's quality system and quality plans. The quality manual may or may not reflect the customer standard. First the customer needs to do a complete "Systems Audit" to evaluate the company's quality system in relation to the customer standard. Then a conformity audit should be conducted to decide if each quality procedure is effectively implemented. Hence choice b is not true. Similarly choices c and d are very preliminary and do not carry much weight.

69.   When purchasing materials from vendors, it is sometimes advantageous to choose vendors whose prices are higher because

---

[19] *ASQC - CQE Examination*, ASQC Quality Progress, October 1974, Applications section, Question 77.

a. such a statement is basically incorrect; always buy at lowest bid price
b. such vendors may become obligated to bestow special favors
c. materials that cost more can be expected to be better, and "you get what you pay for"
d. the true cost of purchased materials, which should include items such as sorting, inspection, contacting vendors, and production delays, may be lower

Key: d. the true cost of purchased materials, which should include items such as sorting, inspection, contacting vendors, and production delays, may be lower
(Ref. Applications Question 19, October 1974)

ASQC-CQE BIBLIOGRAPHY AND OTHER REFERENCES ON QUALITY AUDITING

1. *ANSI/ASQC A2-1987, Terms and Symbols for Acceptance Sampling*, Milwaukee, ASQC Quality Press, 1987.
2. *ANSI/ASQC A3-1987, Quality Systems Terminology*, Milwaukee, ASQC Quality Press, 1987.
3. *ANSI/ASQC Q90 Series-1987, Quality Management and Quality Assurance Standards*, (Q90-Q94) Milwaukee, ASQC Quality Press, 1987.
4. *ANSI/ASQC C1-1985, Specifications of General Requirements for Quality Program*, Milwaukee, ASQC Quality Press, 1985.
5. ASQC Statistics Division, *Glossary and Tables for Statistical Quality Control*, 2nd ed., Milwaukee, ASQC Quality Press, 1983.
6. Besterfield, Dale H., *Quality Control,* 3rd ed., Prentice Hall, Englewood Cliffs., NJ, 1990.
7. Caplan, Frank, *The Quality System, A Sourcebook for Managers and Engineers*, 2nd ed., Radnor, PA, Chilton Book Co, 1990.
8. Deming, W. Edwards, *Out of Crisis*, Cambridge, MA, MIT Press, 1986.
9. Feigenbaum, A.V., *Total Quality Control*, 3rd ed., Revised, New York, McGraw-Hill, 1991.
10. Ishikawa, Kaoru, *Guide to Quality Control*, White Plains, NY, Quality Resources, 1976.
11. Juran, J. M., *Juran's Quality Control Handbook*, 4th ed., New York, McGraw-Hill, 1988.
12. Juran, J. M. and F. M. Gryna, *Quality Planning and Analysis*, 3rd ed., New York, McGraw-Hill, 1993.

CHAPTER 12

PRODUCT AND MATERIALS CONTROL AND MEASUREMENT SYSTEMS

ASQC'S BODY OF KNOWLEDGE (BOK) FOR THE CQE EXAMINATION

This chapter focuses on the following selected subject areas of BOK from *Section I, General Knowledge, Conduct and Ethics, Section IV, Product, Process and Materials Control,* and *Section V, Measurement Systems.*

Work Instructions

Classification of Characteristics and Defects

Identification of Materials and Status

Lot Traceability

Material Segregation Practices

Materials Review Board Criteria and Procedures

Sample Integrity and Control

Measurement Systems - Terms and Definitions (e.g., precision, accuracy, bias, reproducibility)

Metrology

1. Traceability to standards
2. Measurement error
3. Calibration systems
4. Control of standard integrity

Repeatability and Reproducibility Studies

Destructive and Nondestructive Testing Concepts

General Knowledge and Skills

1. Interpretation of diagrams, schematics, drawings, or blue prints

Professional Conduct and Ethics

1.   ASQC Code of Ethics
2.   Typical conflict of interest situations for a quality engineer

1.   The terms critical, major, minor, or incidental may be used in planning for

      a.   classification of defects
      b.   classification of characteristics
      c.   acceptance sampling
      d.   all of the above
      e.   none of the above

Key: d.   all of the above   (Ref. Principles Question 15, October 1974)

Today many companies classify product features as key, significant, or important based on their relative importance to the customer requirements, which is a new customer-driven approach. The characteristics are classified based on adverse consequences of a product's variation to customer satisfaction and customer excitement. They classify these features as important quality characteristics using the terms critical, major, and minor; critical and significant; fit-function and safety/compliance characteristics; etc. This applies to both variable and attribute type characteristics. Based on such a classification of characteristics, the process characteristics, variable or attribute in nature, can be developed to align the process strength to the product. A process control plan for both the process and product characteristics should be developed that includes the type and level of control, sample size, and frequency for every process or operation. Currently such classifications are being standardized under ISO standards.

Some companies use classification of characteristics as their priority system for classification, but others only focus on negatives of quality, i.e., on customer dissatisfaction, and not on customer satisfaction, excitement, delight, and enthusiasm. An important reminder is that customer satisfaction is not the same as no customer dissatisfaction, i.e., *customer satisfaction ≠ no customer dissatisfaction.*

Some companies have used the same system of classification such as critical, major and minor, for defects, particularly when the characteristics are attribute type. They follow MIL-STD-105E, the acceptance sampling plans for attributes. This is a repeat question with a slight change from the August 1978 examination.[1]

2.   Product characteristics should be classified (critical, major etc.) so that

      a.   a more meaningful assessment of quality can be made
      b.   emphasis can be placed on important characteristics
      c.   action with the responsible individuals can be taken
      d.   a quality audit would be more meaningful
      e.   none of these

Key: b.   emphasis can be placed on important characteristics
(Ref. Principles Question 77, October 1974)

Today, quality is defined in the form of *customer satisfaction, customer excitement, customer delight,* and/or *customer enthusiasm.* Hence it is necessary to understand customer satisfaction

---

[1] *ASQC - CQE Examination*, ASQC Quality Progress, August 1978, Applications section, Question 40.

requirements and deploy them to the product level in the form of critical or key product quality characteristics. Some companies use the *quality function deployment* (QFD) method to understand the voice of customer (VOC), and then to translate the VOC into new product design. Multi-disciplined teams are formed to identify important characteristics that have high impact on customer satisfaction. The VOC is then deployed from the finished product level to its subsystems, components, and to operations. A higher level of attention or care is implemented for these characteristics by developing the process control plans and implementing ongoing control for these critical or key characteristics. The process control plans are used as a living document, and based on the capability analysis of each quality characteristic, the level of care or control is changed to achieve economical manufacture of quality products.

Choice a is not the main objective of classification as classification itself cannot give an assessment of the quality of products. Classification is meant to be a priority system. Once characteristics are classified or prioritized, they should be validated, monitored, measured, and evaluated against specifications or standards. Depending on the level of capability, an assessment of quality of product or service should be made to determine its effect on customer satisfaction.

Choice c is incorrect because the focus should be not on *who* but on the system or the process as a whole. The actions should be taken on the product in the design review to make it *robust* or less sensitive to variation and on the process to make the process easier to work, error-proof, and simple. Considering the main elements of the Ishikawa cause and effect diagram, people are only one cause or a variable that affects the output, but there are other important variables, such as equipment, method, material, and environment, which affect the product and hence they need to be studied.

Choice d is less applicable. The quality audit is generally designed not only for important product quality characteristics but for all elements of the product or of a quality system. Quality audit assesses the suitability and conformity of various operations to the given reference standard.

Note: *Be careful in such subjective areas. The selection of the answer is based on the given choices. Many or all choices may seem to be correct to some extent. However, the choice that is the best, most appropriate, or suitable, should be selected as an answer. Such questions can have a different answer if the wording or details of some choices are changed or new choices are added. Refer to Question 3 below which has different choices.*

3.   Characteristics are often classified (critical, major, etc.) so that

     a.   equal emphasis can be placed on each characteristic
     b.   punitive action against the responsible individuals can be equitably distributed
     c.   an assessment of quality can be made
     d.   a quality audit is compatible with management desires

Key: c.   an assessment of quality can be made (Ref. Principles Question 29, October 1972)
         Refer to Question 2 above for discussion. The major difference is in the type of the choices

given here. It has one choice changed and hence the answer is changed.

Choice a is incorrect because it indicates that *equal emphasis* can be placed on *each characteristic*. However, the objective of the classification is to provide a priority system and place the emphasis only on important characteristics and not on each characteristic.

4.   A technique whereby various product features are graded as to relative importance is called

   a.   classification of defects
   b.   quality engineering
   c.   classification of characteristics
   d.   feature grading

Key: c.   classification of characteristics   (Ref. Applications Question 38, July 1984)
       Refer to Questions 1 and 2 above for additional discussion.

5.   A technique whereby various product features are graded and varying degrees of quality control are applied is called

   a.   zero defects
   b.   quality engineering
   c.   classification of characteristics
   d.   feature grading
   e.   nonsense - you cannot do it

Key: c.   classification of characteristics   (Ref. Applications Question 40, August 1978)
       Refer to Questions 1 to 4 above. Please note that here some of the choices are slightly changed.

6.   Classification of characteristics

   a.   is the same as classification of defects
   b.   can only be performed after the product is produced
   c.   must have tolerances associated with it
   d.   is independent of defects

Key: d.   is independent of defects   (Ref. Principles Question 2, October 1972)
       Choice a is incorrect because classification of characteristics is based on the adverse consequences of product variation to customer satisfaction. It applies to both the variable product dimensions and attribute characteristics. The classification of defects focuses mainly on attribute characteristics and the acceptance sampling plans for attributes are used.

       The classification of characteristics shows the level of sensitivity or criticality to customer requirements and may require a higher level of control or monitoring to achieve or to exceed customer requirements. It is independent of defects because defects can occur due to manufacturing problems, poor process design, or planning. It may result in high scrap but customers may not be affected directly by it.

Classification of characteristics should be done early in the design stage of product development and not during the production stage. Product designs should be evaluated for all possible failure modes and design robustness, which can enable a company to achieve quality by design and not by traditional methods of quality control. Hence choice b is a highly uneconomical condition in today's competitive and faster market conditions. Once the product is produced, it is too late and costly to make significant product or process design changes to improve the quality. It is a *detection*-based approach that only focuses on operational problems or warranty type field failures, and thereby minimizes only customer dissatisfaction. This, however, may not focus on many characteristics that can result in higher customer satisfaction and excitement.

Choice c applies to all characteristics, but more important are the optimum targets that result in customer satisfaction and excitement. The tolerances then should be assigned to these characteristics based on their process capability and of processes and adverse consequences of variation to customer satisfaction.

7.   A classification of characteristics makes it possible to

     a.   separate the "vital few"' from the "trivial many" kinds of defects
     b.   direct the greatest inspection efforts to the most important quality characteristics
     c.   establish inspection tolerances
     d.   allow the inspector to choose what to inspect and what not to inspect

Key: b.   direct the greatest inspection efforts to the most important quality characteristics
     (Ref. Principles Question 51, October 1972)
     This is a repeat question with a slight change in the text. Refer to Questions 1 to 6 above for discussion.

8.   Which of the following does not generate product quality characteristics?

     a.   designer
     b.   inspector
     c.   machinist
     d.   equipment engineer

Key: b.   inspector (Ref. Principles Question 30, July 1984)
     Product quality characteristics are features or aspects of the product, i.e., a dimension, test, material property, chemistry, finish, appearance, etc., and they generally affect the product and its quality. Such product quality characteristics are developed during the product and process design stages. The design function, product design engineer, or equipment engineer is responsible for defining the product quality characteristics and their specifications or tolerances. The inspector does not generate it but he/she monitors and controls the product characteristics by choosing the appropriate method of process control. The machinist works on the product and

hence indirectly can be responsible for developing or creating a sensitive product quality characteristic.

9. Classification of defects is most essential as a prior step to a valid establishment of

   a. design characteristics to be inspected
   b. vendor specification of crucial parts
   c. process control points
   d. economical sampling inspection
   e. a product audit check sheet

Key: d. economical sampling inspection   (Ref. Principles Question 39, August 1978)
Some companies use classifications such as critical, major, and minor for defects, particularly when the product characteristics are attribute type and not variable. Then the acceptance sampling plans for attributes, such as MIL-STD-105E, can be used to develop an economical sampling inspection plan. Process control points or process characteristics are established to control the process as prevention.

The design characteristics to be inspected are established first during the product design phase and not after the classification of defects. A product audit check sheet is a working paper for product quality audits that outlines the functions or activities to be audited based on a given reference standard. It is also not a correct choice. This question is repeated in the October 1974 examination.[2]

10. A major defect is a defect, other than critical, that is likely to result in

   a. proper decisions
   b. acceptance of the unit of product
   c. reducing the usability of the unit of product
   d. hazardous or unsafe conditions
   e. none of the above

Key: c. reducing the usability of the unit of product
(Ref. ASQC - CQT Examination Core Portion Question 21)
MIL-STD-105E[3] defines the "*Major Defect*" as follows: "*A major defect is a defect, other than critical, that is likely to result in failure or to reduce materially the usability of the unit of product for its intended purpose.*"

11. Products should be subjected to tests which are designed to

   a. demonstrate advertised performance
   b. demonstrate basic function at minimum testing cost
   c. approximate the conditions to be experienced in the customer's application

---

[2] *ASQC - CQE Examination*, ASQC Quality Progress, October 1974, Principles section, Question 58.
[3] MIL-STD-105E, *Sampling Procedures and Tables for Inspection by Attributes*, Section 3.14.

    d.   assure that specifications are met under laboratory conditions

    e.   assure performance under severe environmental conditions

Key: c.   approximate the conditions to be experienced in the customer's application
(Ref. Principles Question 46, July 1984)
Quality is defined as meeting and exceeding the customer's requirements. Hence the product testing and validation should approximate or simulate the conditions to be expected in the customer's application. Other choices are not appropriate because they may or may not reflect the voice of the customer and customer requirements. To be the market leader, it is necessary to be customer driven and to focus on the products that best meet those requirements.

12.   In planning process controls

    a.   deciding whether the process runs or not is determined by whether the resulting product conforms or not

    b.   the basic approach follows the servomechanism cycle so common in engineering

    c.   collection of information goes hand-in-hand with decision making

    d.   meeting process specification tolerances is the same as meeting product tolerances

Key: b.   the basic approach follows the servomechanism cycle so common in engineering
(Ref. Principles Question 67, October 1972)
This question requires evaluation of each choice individually.

Choice a is less applicable because during the planning stage, whether the product conforms or not is not known, and no actual data are available about the resulting product. Some predictions may be made about the resulting product as the process is only in the planning mode.

Choice c is somewhat vague as we do not know what type of information is being collected and if the information is meaningful or not. In most cases decisions are made without data or information.

Choice d is not correct because the process specifications are generally based on manufacturing tolerances and not on product tolerances. Product tolerances may be affected by different variables and their interactions in the process, which can be quantified in some cases using regression or designed experiments. Hence meeting tolerances of the process may or may not be sufficient to determine the product's conformance to its tolerances. Depending on the consequences of product variation to customer satisfaction, the product tolerances or product characteristics may need to be monitored at some frequency in addition to the process characteristics.

Choice b is the only correct choice, but you need to know and understand the term "servo-mechanism." Servomechanism in the electrical/mechanical sense is an automatic device for controlling large amounts of power by means of small amounts of power and has an automatic or built-in feedback mechanism that corrects the performance of the equipment. Process planning is based on such a servomechanism cycle or feedback concept to align the process strength with the product requirements. Controlling the process parameters is less expensive than controlling the product characteristics. Also, the data on process should act as a quick feedback to the operation to make real-time-based, on line, adjustments in the process to improve the performance.

13.   The primary reason for first piece inspection is to

    a.   approve a setup for further production
    b.   accept a lot prior to completion of the lot
    c.   try out a new inspection method
    d.   eliminate need for further inspection

Key: a.   approve a setup for further production (Ref. Principles Question 36, July 1984)
Different processes have different dominant parameters. For a setup-dominant process, the control system should emphasize the verification of the setup before production begins. Once the setup is verified and approved, it will provide high reproducibility, repeatability, and a stable process output for the entire run, provided setups are followed, and not changed arbitrarily.

14.   Incoming inspection is based most directly on

    a.   design requirements
    b.   purchase order requirements
    c.   manufacturing requirements
    d.   customer use of the end product

Key: b.   purchase order requirements (Ref. Principles Question 39, July 1984)
Incoming inspection is intended mainly to ensure that all the requirements of the product as per the contract or purchase order are met as a minimum. Choice b is incorrect because the design requirements are on the final product, whereas the incoming inspection is for the raw material or components of an assembly purchased from a subcontractor. Similarly choice c is incorrect because the manufacturing requirements are for the process that manufactures the end product. The incoming inspection checks the conformance of incoming raw material to the purchase order requirements before it is allowed to be further processed in manufacturing. Choice d is also incorrect because the incoming inspection is not directly tied to the end user or the customer of the end product.

15.   Source inspection should be employed when

    a.   purchasing placed the order late and you want to help
    b.   manufacturing is screaming for the material and you want to help
    c.   you don't have the appropriate gates and management won't buy them
    d.   source is more costly than receiving inspection but it reduces backlog in receiving
    e.   none of the above

Key: c.   you don't have the appropriate gates and management won't buy them
(Ref. Applications Question 32, August 1978)

There may be a typographical error in choice c because when we read it, it does not make sense. If we change or correct the choice to read the word gates as *gages* instead, it may be more meaningful. Choice c with this correction is the appropriate choice. Other choices are obviously not the correct choices.

16.   In the area for receiving inspection, which of the following items would not be in the inspection package?

       a.   purchase order
       b.   drawings to the latest revisions
       c.   drawings to the revisions of the purchase order
       d.   detailed inspection instructions

Key: b.   drawings to the latest revisions   (Ref. Applications Question 45, August 1978)
       In the receiving area, the drawings to the latest revisions are of very little use unless the purchase order is revised or amended to include the latest revisions. Then only the material received against this revision can be inspected accordingly. Hence the receiving department should have the drawings to the revisions of the purchase order and the copy of the inspection instructions but not necessarily the latest revisions.

17.   The inspection plan for a new product line may include

       a.   a detailed production schedule
       b.   sampling procedures and techniques
       c.   internal techniques for control and segregation of conforming or nonconforming products
       d.   answers a and b
       e.   answers a, b, and c

Key: e.   answers a, b, and c   (Ref. Principles Question 38, August 1978)

18.   When giving instructions to those who will perform a task, the communications process is completed

       a.   when the worker goes to his or her workstation to do the task
       b.   when the person giving the instruction has finished talking
       c.   when the worker acknowledges these instructions by describing how he or she will perform the task
       d.   when the worker says that he or she understands the instructions

Key: c.   when the worker acknowledges these instructions by describing how he or she will perform the task   (Ref. Principles Question 42, August 1978)
       This results in a better operational definition of the task. When the worker repeats the instructions, it removes the confusion in the task, if any, and ensures proper communication and understanding of the requirements. It also removes the variation in interpretation of the requirements. Choices a, b, and d reflect an incomplete communication because they assume that

the worker has understood the instructions; however, it may or may not be the true intent of the instruction.

19.   Some product specifications contain a section called "Quality assurance" which contains the design engineer's requirements for acceptance testing. The relationship between the acceptance test procedure for a product and the acceptance test portion of the quality assurance section of the specification for that product is

    a.   the test procedure must require testing for the characteristics listed in the acceptance test portion of the specifications, and the quality engineer can add additional tests he or she believes necessary

    b.   the test procedure must require testing for the characteristics selected from the acceptance test portion of the specification, but does not have to require testing for all such characteristics

    c.   the test procedure must require testing for those and only those characteristics listed in the acceptance test portion of the specifications

    d.   the acceptance test portion of the specification is a good general guide to the test procedure writer and the test procedure reviewer, but is not mandatory anyway

Key: a.   the test procedure must require testing for the characteristics listed in the acceptance test portion of the specifications and the quality engineer can add additional tests he or she believes necessary   (Ref. Principles Question 43, August 1978)

20.   A qualification test is used to determine that design and selected production methods will yield a product that conforms to specification. An acceptance test is used to determine that a completed product conforms to design. On this basis, a destructive test can be used for

    a.   qualification only
    b.   qualification or acceptance
    c.   acceptance only
    d.   neither qualification nor acceptance

Key: b.   qualification or acceptance   (Ref. Principles Question 48, August 1978)
The destructive test can be used in earlier phases of new product development for qualification tests. As the product approaches launch as a final product, the acceptance tests of final validation tests determine that the product meets the design requirements.

21.   Criteria for a comprehensive acceptance inspection system include which of the following?

    a.   It should encourage and assist the supplier to improve the quality of his or her product.
    b.   It should be easy to administer and economical in cost.
    c.   It should enable the purchaser to accept all conforming items and to reject all nonconforming items.
    d.   all of the above

Key: d. all of the above (Ref. Principles Question 53, August 1978)
Each choice is very important in developing the acceptance inspection system or supplier submission system.

22. The major purpose of test and inspection is to

   a. remove all defects to prevent shipments of substandard product
   b. find which operations are problems
   c. identify the poor operators
   d. develop information to enable corrective action
   e. keep costs down by finding defects early in the cycle

Key: d. develop information to enable corrective action
(Ref. Principles Question 54, August 1978)
Choices a, b, c, and e are more focused on detection than prevention and also on operators. Choice d focuses on the corrective actions. It forces root-cause analysis and long-term corrective actions to prevent recurrence of the issue. Choice a may not guarantee the economical manufacture of quality products since it is focusing on detection only.

23. It has been found that the more complex the inspection task, the less accurate inspection becomes. This can be partially overcome by

   a. using several inspectors in a team approach
   b. reducing the inspection task to a scanning operation
   c. providing inspectors with an unlimited amount of inspection time
   d. restricting inspection time in order to encourage increased concentration on the part of the inspector

Key: a. using several inspectors in a team approach (Ref. Principles Question 71, October 1972)
This type of question can be answered easily by screening each choice. Choice b is incorrect because the inspection type and level or frequency depends on the adverse consequences of variation to customer satisfaction. Choice c is not economical and may not still guarantee the inspection accuracy and quality of the product. Choice d is also incorrect. The inspection time should be optimized to minimize inspector-initiated errors and increase inspector accuracy.

24. Process acceptance involves decision making with regard to

   a. the type of equipment or machinery used to process items during manufacture
   b. items not yet made, that is, approval of "first piece" and periodic checks during the production run
   c. items already made regardless of the technique used to control quality during processing
   d. acceptance sampling using MIL-STD-105D

Key: b. items not yet made, that is, approval of "first piece" and periodic checks during the production run (Ref. Principles Question 40, October 1972)

The key words are *process acceptance,* and not product inspection. Choice b defines the normal operating procedure for process setup and process acceptance during in-process inspection.

Choice a focuses only on equipment or machinery and not on the entire process, i.e., methods, operators, environment, and materials. Process acceptance after the items are made is reactionary and it is a detection-based approach. The goal should be to act upfront and not after the fact. Hence choice c is incorrect. The last choice, d, is incorrect because MIL-STD-105E is the standard for a product acceptance sampling plan, not a process acceptance standard.

25.   Station control is

    a.   a technique to implement quality plans in the shop
    b.   applied to assure that planned quality performance is consistently and economically maintained
    c.   a technique which emphasizes control of input
    d.   all of the above

Key: d.   all of the above   (Ref. Principles Question 51, July 1984)

26.   The primary visual consideration in designing an inspection workplace is

    a.   the environmental color decor because of its psychological effect
    b.   the size and shape of the inspection table or bench
    c.   the illumination and how it is provided
    d.   the traffic flow in or near the inspection station

Key: c.   the illumination and how it is provided   (Ref. Principles Question 77, October 1972)
    The key words are *visual consideration* and hence choice c is correct.

27.   Methods of inspection and process monitoring shall be corrected when

    a.   the inspector wants a change
    b.   manufacturing wants a change
    c.   their unsuitability is demonstrated
    d.   their acceptance is demonstrated
    e.   none of the above

Key: c.   their unsuitability is demonstrated
    (Ref. ASQC - CQT Examination Core Portion Question 20)

28.   If physical inspection of processed material is impossible or disadvantageous, an acceptable substitute is to

    a.   accept material as is when presented to inspection
    b.   inspect the treatment of the material while being processed for conformance to

specifications

   c.   monitor the rejects from the end use of the material

   d.   none of the above

Key: b.   inspect the treatment of the material while being processed for conformance to specifications (Ref. ASQC - CQT Examination Core Portion Question 22)

29.   Sample selection of parts for inspection must be selected at random to ensure

   a.   a maximum sample size

   b.   a minimum sample size

   c.   the probability of not rejecting the lot

   d.   the probability of accepting the lot

   e.   finding typical characteristics of the lot

Key: e.   finding typical characteristics of the lot
(Ref. ASQC - CMI Examination brochure Question 24)

30.   Controls on raw material are maintained to prevent

   a.   use of the wrong material by manufacturing

   b.   storerooms from issuing the wrong material

   c.   use of material failing test

   d.   a, b, and c above

   e.   a and c above

Key: d.   a, b, and c above   (Ref. ASQC-CMI Examination brochure Question 25)

31.   In deciding whether sampling inspection of parts would be more economical than 100% inspection, you need to determine all of the following except

   a.   cost of inspecting parts

   b.   cost of correcting the defective parts

   c.   cost of not finding defective parts

   d.   cost of improving the production process

Key: d.   cost of improving the production process (Ref. Applications Question 36, July 1984) Choices a, b, and c are more important factors in deciding whether sampling inspection or 100% inspection would be more economical. Choice d, cost of improving the production process is an important consideration overall but not a direct consideration in sampling plans. Sampling plans are selected to decide optimum sample size required to economically and effectively evaluate the quality level of the parts.

The cost of improving the production process should be thoroughly evaluated during the production planning stage based on the current processes, equipment, and available alternatives, and not during actual production. The planning stage should consider all the potential failure modes in the process and determine the cost of removing or reducing their impact by proper process design or redesign of the process if necessary. During actual production, to improve the production process economically is very difficult and has many givens or constraints as "common cause" no matter what sampling plan is selected. The sampling plans can help identify the amount of variation and the causes in some cases. The production process can be improved by trying to reduce the variation where possible, depending on the sources of variation.

32.   100 percent inspection

      a.   is used to sort items
      b.   at best is only 60% effective
      c.   assures a satisfactory outgoing quality level
      d.   is theoretically unsound but is an excellent practice

Key: a.   used to sort items   (Ref. Principles Question 61, October 1972)

33.   In linear measurement, what overriding consideration should guide the quality control engineer in specifying the measuring instrument to be used?

      a.   the ability of the instrument to be read to one decimal place beyond that of the base dimension to be measured
      b.   the ability of the instrument to meet the error rule of thumb
      c.   the ability of the instrument-inspector system to obtain the necessary accurate data at a minimum overall cost
      d.   the combination of base dimension and tolerance in relation to measurement error
      e.   the ability of the inspector to use the measuring instrument

Key: c.   the ability of the instrument-inspector system to obtain the necessary accurate data at a minimum overall cost   (Ref. Principles Question 5, October 1974)
Choice c is important because it considers both the elements, i.e., the measuring instrument and the inspector, to specify the measuring instrument. In designing any procedure or process, one can never overlook the human interaction with the equipment, material, environment, and method (commonly known elements of a *cause and effect diagram*) and their overall effect on the final outcome. In the case of a measuring instrument and inspector, the final outcome is to have an accurate and precise measurement with the least number of errors possible.

34.   In linear measurement, what overriding consideration should guide the quality control engineer in specifying the measuring instrument to be used?

      a.   The ability of the instrument to be read to one decimal place beyond the places in the base dimension or tolerance.
      b.   The ability of the instrument to meet an error design goal of 10%.
      c.   The combination of base dimension and tolerance as they relate to measurement error.

    d.   The ability of the instrument-inspector system to obtain the necessary correct information at minimum overall cost.

Key: d.   The ability of the instrument-inspector system to obtain the necessary correct information at minimum overall cost.   (Ref. Principles Question 72, October 1972)
Refer to Question 33 above for discussion.

35.   Who has the initial responsibility for manufactured product quality?

    a.   the inspector
    b.   the vice president
    c.   the operator
    d.   the quality manager

Key: c.   the operator   (Ref. Applications Question 14, October 1972)
The initial responsibility of the manufactured product quality lies with the operator first. The operator is the first level of control or primary person responsible for ensuring that the manufactured product conforms to product specifications. The inspection responsibility is not delegated to a separate inspection department. Juran[4] describes this concept as "Self Inspection."

36.   Characteristics of a good incoming inspection department are

    a.   written and visual quality standards
    b.   proper inspection equipment and gages
    c.   inspector knowledge of sampling techniques
    d.   all of the above

Key: d.   all of the above   (Ref. Applications Question 8, October 1972)

37.   When planning the quality aspects of packing and shipping, it is not usual that the

    a.   product design department specify packaging and shipping procedures
    b.   shipping department conduct packing and shipping operations
    c.   inspection department determine packing specifications
    d.   inspection department check the adequacy of packing and shipping operations

Key: c.   inspection department determine packing specifications
(Ref. Applications Question 30, October 1972)
The inspection department is generally not involved or responsible for the packing and shipping specifications. It is generally done by the product design department. The inspection department should provide input in terms of material-handling damage, etc., affecting the product quality and the adequacy of packing and shipping.

---

[4] *Juran's Quality Control Handbook* by J. M. Juran, 4th ed., McGraw-Hill, New York, pg. 17.23.

38.   If the distribution of defectives among various lots is found to follow the laws of chance, we can conclude that

      a.   the product was well mixed before dividing into lots
      b.   the manufacturing process is not predictable
      c.   all lots should be accepted
      d.   none of the above is true

Key: a.   the product was well mixed before dividing into lots
(Ref. Applications Question 31, October 1972)
If the product is well mixed before dividing into lots, each product in the lot has equal probability of being selected. Hence the probability of finding good or bad parts can follow a specific distribution based on the theory of probability or chance.

Choice b is incorrect because whether the process is predictable or not depends on the stability of the process over a long period of time. Choice c is incorrect because the lot acceptance decision is based on the sampling plan and the acceptance criteria.

39.   When setting up a sorting operation for a visual defect, which one of the following is most important?

      a.   the importance of the defect
      b.   whether the operator or inspector does the job
      c.   the percent defective estimated to be in the lot
      d.   the quality standard

Key: a.   the quality standard   (Ref. Applications Question 22, October 1972)
The most important step in designing the sorting inspection is the quality standard of what is acceptable and what is not acceptable.

40.   One method to control inspection costs even without a budget is by comparing _____ as a ratio to productive machine time to produce the product.

      a.   product cost
      b.   company profit
      c.   inspection hours
      d.   scrap material

Key: c.   inspection hours   (Ref. Applications Question 60, August 1978)
Inspection cost depends on the inspection hours. Hence the ratio of inspection hours to productive time to produce the product is a good indicator in controlling the inspection costs. All other choices, i.e., the ratio of product costs, or company profit, or scrap material to the productive time to produce the product, are not directly indicators to control the inspection costs.

41.   "Determine the flux meter reading of the part per specification." This inspection instruction

violates which of the following guiding principles?

I: The inspection method should be stated in operational terms.
II: A specific objective should be established for each instruction.

a.   I only
b.   II only
c.   I and II only
d.   Neither I nor II

Key: a.   I only   (Ref. Applications Question 34, July 1984)
Processes are getting very complex in today's industries. It is hence very important that the operator instructions be prepared and written in very simple form and operational language and not in engineering or management language. They should operationally define the steps in proper detail, giving visual control where necessary, details of which equipment to use for measuring, where to record the information, what to do with the information, i.e., what actions are required, etc.

42.   "Determine the flux meter reading of the part per specification." This inspection instruction violates which of the following guiding principles?

a.   A specific objective should be established for each instruction
b.   Only necessary words should be used
c.   The correct inspection method should be stated in operational terms
d.   all of the above

Key: c.   The correct inspection method should be stated in operational terms
(Ref. Applications Question 56, October 1972) Refer to Question 41 above.

43.   Where inspector efficiency is defined as the ratio of correct decisions to total decisions regarding individual items, most inspection operations performed by human inspectors are approximately

a.   40-55% efficient
b.   55-70% efficient
c.   70-95% efficient
d.   95-100% efficient

Key: c.   70-95% efficient   (Ref. Principles Question 54, July 1984)
This percent efficiency is not a specific accurate number. That is why they are shown as a range of 70 to 95%. Based on the studies conducted for inspector error or inspector efficiency, it has been found that inspectors find about 80% of the defects actually present in the product and miss the remaining 20%.[5]

44.   The inspector accuracy is defined as

[5] *Juran's Quality Control Handbook* by J. M. Juran, 4th ed., McGraw-Hill, New York, pg. 18.84.

   a.   the largest number of defects found from a given lot
   b.   the smallest number of defects found from a given lot
   c.   the ratio of the number of true defects found by the inspector to the true defects that are originally in the product, which should have been found by the inspector
   d.   all of the above

Key: c.   the ratio of the number of true defects found by the inspector to the true defects that are originally in the product, which should have been found by the inspector

There are various purposes of inspection, such as to identify good lots from bad lots, to determine if a product conforms to specification, and to evaluate the accuracy of inspectors. In order to determine the accuracy of inspectors in finding defects, Juran[6] compares two items as the ratio, i.e.,

$$\text{Inspector accuracy} = \frac{\text{Number of true defects found by inspector}}{\text{Total number of true defects originally in the product}}$$

Choices a and b are incorrect because the purpose of the inspection is not to find too many or too few defects, but to find the true number of defects that are originally in the product.

45.   Normally occurring inspector errors are

   a.   accepting defective units or products as good
   b.   rejecting good units or products as bad
   c.   using incorrect instruments to inspect or measure the products
   d.   inspecting without a specification or against incorrect specifications or requirements
   e.   all of the above

Key: e.   all of the above

All of the above are normally occurring errors. In addition, inspectors may be using noncalibrated instruments; they may not properly tag or correctly identify defective parts; they may document defects, categories, or data incorrectly; they may do incomplete paperwork; etc. These errors are expensive and hence it is necessary that companies conduct periodic inspection checks to determine the accuracy of inspectors.

This becomes even more critical from the training point. Today many companies are defining the production operator as the primary person responsible for quality, inspection, and acceptance of the product. In some complex assembly operations, workstations have job rotation requirements for the operators, from ergonomic concerns. This makes the issue of inspector accuracy even more important but also very difficult to manage. Hence the manufacturing engineers responsible for process design have a bigger responsibility of making the operations more robust and less or nonsensitive to operator errors. Training, error proofing, automation, visual controls, proper floor layout, minimum handling, etc., are required to minimize operator dominance in the operation.

---

[6] *Juran's Quality Control Handbook* by J. M. Juran, 4th ed., McGraw-Hill, New York, pg. 18.6 and 18.94-95.

46.   In a *scanning* type of inspection task, inspection accuracy is likely to be greater if

    a.   the product moves toward the inspector rather than laterally past him or her
    b.   the inspector scans each item for all types of defects rather than an entire lot for one type of defect at a time
    c.   the magnification is increased
    d.   the product is inspected while it is stationary rather than while it is moving

Key: d.   the product is inspected while it is stationary rather than while it is moving
(Ref. Applications Question 44, October 1974)
This is a repeat question in the October 1972 examination.[7]

47.   If test data do not support a quality engineer's expectations, the best thing to do is

    a.   adjust the data to support expectations if it is only slightly off
    b.   draw the expected conclusion omitting that data not supporting it
    c.   reevaluate the expectations of the test based upon the data
    d.   report the data and expected conclusion with no reference to one another

Key: c.   reevaluate the expectations of the test based upon the data
(Ref. Applications Question 35, July 1984)
Choices a, b, and d are not acceptable, morally, ethically, and professionally.

48.   The laboratory has notified the quality engineer of an incoming product which has changed from acceptable to marginal over a period of six months. Which of the following actions should be taken?

    I.   Notify the laboratory to check their analysis and send a sample to an outside laboratory to verify the results.
    II.   Notify the supplier of your observations and concern about the acceptability of his or her product.
    III.   Notify receiving to reject the product based on the product's trend towards unacceptability.

    a.   I and II only
    b.   I and II only
    c.   II and III only
    d.   I, II, and III

Key: a.   I and II only   (Ref. Applications Question 39, July 1984)
Item III is not proper as an immediate action, because the product is marginal but still meets the requirements or specifications.

49.   Which of the following may be considered a justification for reinspection by the contractor of a

---

[7] *ASQC - CQE Examination*, ASQC Quality Progress, October 1972, Applications section, Question 33.

lot which has been verified as nonconforming by the inspector?

    a.   Belief by the contractor that the random samples did not constitute a true picture of the lot.

    b.   The fact that the contractor had not produced to these specifications before.

    c.   Discovery that the scales used for inspection were out of adjustment.

    d.   None of the above.

Key: c.   Discovery that the scales used for inspection were out of adjustment.
(Ref. Applications Question 45, July 1984)
This represents a measurement error caused by an out-of-adjustment scale. It is a sound justification for reinspection by the contractor.

50.   An inspection performance audit is made of eight inspectors in an area of complex assembly, all doing similar work. Seven inspectors have an average monthly acceptance rate of 86 to 92%; one inspector has an average rate of 72% with approximately four times the daily variation as the others. As inspection supervisor you should, based on this audit,

    a.   promote the 72% inspector as he or she is very conscientious

    b.   discipline the 72% inspector as he or she is creating needless rework and wasted time

    c.   initiate a special investigation of inspection and manufacturing performance

    d.   discipline the other seven inspectors as they are not cracking down

Key: c.   initiate a special investigation of inspection and manufacturing performance
(Ref. Applications Question 68, July 1984)
The question describes only the percentage acceptance rates of inspectors but that does not indicate the percentage of inspection accuracy. We cannot decide which inspectors are more effective and accurate unless we have more information about the parts that are inspected, i.e., the number of parts accepted as good, number of parts that are wrongly accepted as good when they are bad, and number of parts that are wrongly identified as bad when they are good out of total parts. It requires proper investigation of both the inspection and manufacturing performance. Choices a, b and d are not proper in classifying the inspectors as good or bad.

51.   Primary personal characteristics for reliable inspector performance evaluation are

    a.   experience and amount of time of observed performance

    b.   relevancy, consistency, and lack of bias

    c.   personal appearance, mental alertness, and ability to communicate

    d.   seniority, age, and good health

    e.   all of the above

Key: b.   relevancy, consistency, and lack of bias (Ref. Applications Question 78, July 1984)
This is naturally an obvious choice.

52.   A method of dealing with an inspector found to be falsifying the results of inspection of a

borderline product is to

   a.   criticize the inspector on the basis that the pattern of reading does not follow the laws of chance
   b.   review the procedure for evaluating and reporting a borderline product
   c.   review the inspector's results against the expected results calculated from a normal curve
   d.   criticize the inspector for not knowing how to read the inspection equipment

Key: b.   review the procedure for evaluating and reporting a borderline product
(Ref. Applications Question 80, July 1984)
The question shows pure lack of concern for understanding the procedure and following it in any situation. Hence instead of criticizing the inspector or reviewing the sorted or biased results against any probability distribution, it is very important to review the procedure for evaluation, inspection, and reporting of borderline products and make the inspection department understand, accept, and follow it.

Juran[8] defines the tendency of inspectors to falsify the results of inspection of borderline products as *flinching*. He also recommends that a positive environment and atmosphere of respect for pure facts in inspection departments be created, and ethical spirit be encouraged in inspectors. Juran also warns against use of rules of chance or the normal curve because such arbitrary criticism of inspectors may focus only on symptoms (unnatural patterns) and not on the disease (of falsifying the inspection results). The inspector may try to make the results fit the curve, but this may not remove the habit of falsifying the results.

53.   Much managerial decision making is based on comparing actual performance with _____ .

   a.   personnel ratio
   b.   cost of operations
   c.   number of complaints
   d.   standards of performance

Key: d.   standards of performance   (Ref. Applications Question 39, August 1978)
Management should first communicate the standards or requirements. Then it should compare the actual performance to the given standards and develop corrective actions where needed. This is a simple definition for an audit.

54.   When planning a total quality system, one key objective is to provide a means of guaranteeing "the maintenance of product integrity." Which of the following quality system provisions is designed to MOST directly provide such a guarantee?

   a.   drawing and print control
   b.   calibration and maintenance of test equipment
   c.   identification and segregation of nonconforming material
   d.   specification change control

---

[8] *Juran's Quality Control Handbook* by J. M. Juran, 4th ed., McGraw-Hill, New York, pg. 18.92.

Key: c. identification and segregation of nonconforming material
(Ref. Principles Question 34, July 1984)
The key phrase here is "guaranteeing the maintenance of product integrity." The product integrity is based on the basic definition of quality–fitness for use. Juran[9] discusses this as knowledge of conformance to specifications and knowledge of fitness for use. Each of the choices are important in a quality system. However choice c "identification and segregation of nonconforming material," ensures that the product is good, i.e., fit for use, and nonconforming products are not shipped with good products. It provides the protection to the customer, preserves the quality and customer satisfaction with the product, and enables creating the atmosphere of law and order. Hence this is an important provision in a quality system to achieve conformance of the product to its specifications and provide a means of guaranteeing the product's fitness for use.

Watch for subjectivity here because each of these items is affecting product quality at a different time. If you are a product engineer, you may be tempted to pick choice a or d, and if you are a manufacturing or quality engineer, you may want to select b. But these do not have direct or immediate impact on the customer, and it will not be sufficient to provide such a product guarantee even if the drawing and print control is good. This is a repeat question with a slight change from the October 1974 examination.[10]

55. The primary reason that nonconforming material should be identified and segregated is

   a. so that the cause of nonconformity can be determined
   b. to provide statistical information for the "zero defect" program
   c. so it cannot be used in production without proper authorization
   d. to obtain samples of poor workmanship for use in the company's training program
   e. so that responsibility can be determined and disciplinary action taken

Key: c. so it cannot be used in production without proper authorization
(Ref. Principles Question 44, August 1978)
It is important to develop and implement the procedures to identify the nonconforming material for incoming, in-process, and finished products, and to segregate it properly. This will prevent further use of nonconforming incoming or in-process material in production without proper authorization. The nonconforming finished products should be segregated so that they do not get mixed with good products and do not get shipped to the customer. The quality manual should include a specific procedure for nonconforming products that describes the specific approval process to use in production, documentation, containment, disposition, and internal or external communication requirements.

56. A system for controlling nonconforming material should have procedures for its

   a. identification
   b. segregation

---

[9] *Juran's Quality Control Handbook* by J. M. Juran, 4th ed., McGraw-Hill, New York, pg. 18.31-32.
[10] *ASQC - CQE Examination*, ASQC Quality Progress, Milwaukee, WI, October 1974, Principles section, Question 27.

    c.   disposition
    d.   all of the above
    e.   none of the above

Key: d.   all of the above (Ref. ASQC-CQT Core Portion,[11] Question 24)

57.   Quality cost systems provide for defect prevention. Which of the following elements is primary to defect prevention?

    a.   corrective action
    b.   data collection
    c.   cost analysis
    d.   training

Key: a.   corrective action   (Ref. Principles Question 69, August 1978)
The key term is "defect prevention" and not the *prevention cost* of quality. If defects occur, corrective actions as short-term and long-term irreversible reactions are developed and implemented. They are reactionary in nature. This means the quality system has significant nonconforming units or parts. Hence ASQC's answer to this question was given as choice a.

58.   One of the major hazards in the material review board procedure is the tendency of the board to emphasize only the disposition function and to neglect the _____ function.

    a.   statistical analysis
    b.   corrective action
    c.   material evaluation
    d.   tolerance review
    e.   manufacturing methods

Key: b.   corrective action   (Ref. Applications Question 34, August 1978)
The *material review board* (MRB)[12] is a management team and sometimes it includes the customer representatives. Its responsibility is to (a) evaluate and review all nonconforming material against its standard; (b) make the disposition decision, such as to accept the material for production, if everyone including the customer agrees, or to scrap the material; and (c) to drive the corrective action to prevent the recurrence of a nonconforming product.

However, in many companies, the MRB may not be a formal committee or may not include the customer representative. If an MRB exists in some companies, its primary function may be solely to evaluate the nonconforming material for its fitness for use, its intended function, or any other substitute use as a by-product. Its scope may not include fact-finding for causes of nonconforming events or driving the corrective actions. This is a possible danger. Hence all such activities must be properly planned and integrated to achieve continuous improvement.

---

[11] *ASQC - CQT Examination*, ASQC Quality Progress, Milwaukee, WI, August 1982, Core Portion, Question 24.
[12] *Juran's Quality Control Handbook* by J. M. Juran, 4th ed., McGraw-Hill, New York, pg. 13.8-10.

59.   One of the major hazards in material review board (MRB) procedures is the tendency of the board to emphasize only the disposition function and to neglect the _____ function.

   a.   statistical analysis
   b.   corrective action
   c.   material evaluation
   d.   tolerance review
   e.   manufacturing methods

Key: b.   corrective action   (Ref. Applications Question 40, July 1984)
   Corrective actions are very important to resolve nonconforming situations and to implement proper actions to prevent their reoccurrence. The MRB generally ends up resolving the containment issues, i.e., what to do with nonconforming products, how to communicate to the customer and how to dispose of them, etc. Very seldom the MRB focuses on the root causes for the nonconformances and proper corrective actions to prevent its reoccurrence in the future.

60.   The most important activity of a material review board (MRB) would normally be

   a.   making sure that corrective action is taken to prevent recurrence of the problem
   b.   to provide a bonded or segregated area of holding discrepant material pending disposition
   c.   prepare discrepant material reports for management
   d.   accept discrepant material when "commercial" decisions dictate
   e.   none of these

Key: a.   making sure that corrective action is taken to prevent recurrence of the problem
   (Ref. Applications Question 38, October 1974.)
   Refer to Questions 59 and 60 above for discussion.

61.   Which of the following quality system provisions is of the least concern when preparing an audit checklist for the upcoming branch operation quality system audit?

   a.   drawing and print control
   b.   makeup of the MRB (material review board)
   c.   control of nonconforming materials
   d.   control of special processes
   e.   calibration of test equipment

Key: b.   makeup of the MRB (material review board)
   (Ref. Principles Question 53, October 1974)
   It is important to know if the company or the branch has procedures for identification, segregation, and disposition of nonconforming materials, and if an MRB is in place to perform this function. But the makeup of the MRB is the least concern as per ASQC's answer.

   This can be a subjective answer because, for some operations, the makeup of the MRB is important depending on its roles,[13] particularly operations or products dealing with safety and compliance to regulations. Thus it can be a part of the quality system requirements. This is a repeat question with slight changes from the August 1978 examination.[14]

62.   Which of the following elements is least necessary to a good corrective action feedback report?

    a.   what caused the failure
    b.   who caused the failure
    c.   what correction has been made
    d.   when the correction is effective
    e.   how the corrected product is identified

Key: b.   who caused the failure   (Ref. Principles Question 38, October 1974)
The emphasis is on the quality system and not on the person. The human element is an integral part of the quality system but the system must prevail. So if an operation has failures, instead of blaming someone ("who caused failure") it is more important to analyze the system for all the root causes of failure, as shown in choices a, c, d, and e.

63.   To minimize the impact of product recall, which one of the following is the most important element in a quality system?

    a.   receiving inspection at the plants
    b.   traceability system
    c.   warranty analysis
    d.   all of the above

Key: b.   traceability system
Juran[15] discusses the importance of a traceability system in the situation of a product recall. A product recall is defined as the actions taken due to deficiencies in products that are already shipped to customers. This represents quality costs of external failure. The impact of any recall can be minimized if the suspect product units can be quickly identified separately from other units in production or storage, etc. This means the company should establish a traceability system to locate quickly all nonconforming or suspect units in particular and the entire product in general.

64.   Which of the following are good factors in setting up a traceability program to manage product recalls?

    I.   unit cost of the product
    II.   product life
    III.   product complexity
    IV.   methods of identification

---

[13] *Juran's Quality Control Handbook* by J. M. Juran, 4th ed., McGraw-Hill, New York, pg. 18.32-33.
[14] *ASQC - CQE Examination*, ASQC Quality Progress, August 1978, Applications section, Question 65.
[15] *Juran's Quality Control Handbook* by J. M. Juran, 4th ed., McGraw-Hill, New York, pg. 20.32-33.

a.   I, II, and III
b.   II, III, IV
c.   III, IV, and I
d.   IV, I, and II
e.   I, II, III, and IV

Key: e.   I, II, III, and IV

ASQC[16] provides several important factors to set up an effective traceability program for effectively locating and identifying the products during a recall. They are, for example, product category, product life (item II), unit cost of the product (item I), recall or repair in the field, product complexity (item III), the rationale for recall, documents, and different methods of identification and coding (item IV).

65.   To minimize product complaints, you should initiate a complaint program, which includes

a.   a method of resolving the complaint to satisfy the complainant
b.   a process to identify vital few or serious complaints from many types of complaints
c.   analysis methods to identify the root causes of different complaints
d.   long-term corrective actions to prevent the recurrence of the complaints
e.   all of the above

Key: e.   all of the above

Juran[17] indicates that the above items are important action items of any complaint program. However, these are still after-the-fact, detection-based, and very expensive approaches. Companies should start prevention-based upfront approaches of product improvement from the early design phase. The lessons learned from previous products, models or competitive benchmarking, and all other types of voices of customers (VOCs) should be deployed in engineering or technical language using tools such as *quality function deployment (QFD),* a system engineering approach used during the design phase. The design should be evaluated and analyzed for all sources of variation, failure modes, and adverse consequences of variation to customer satisfaction. Also, it should be evaluated for the special or beneficial effects of changes and options in the form of product excitement, customer delight, and customer enthusiasm.

Robust design of product and processes, failure mode and effects analysis (FMEA), process control and capability studies, etc., should be used to make the design less sensitive to product variation, user variation, or user abuse of products. Companies should start implementing commonsense-based, economical methods of errorproofing designs and processes to become low-cost manufacturers of high-quality products. These efforts, in the long term, can result in minimum customer dissatisfaction and increased customer satisfaction. In case of new options, or new product innovations, they can create customer excitement about the product.

66.   Metrology is defined as

---

[16] *Product Recall Planning Guide* by ASQC, 1981; *Juran's Quality Control Handbook* by J. M. Juran, 4th ed., McGraw-Hill, New York, pg. 20.32-33.
[17] *Juran's Quality Control Handbook* by J. M. Juran, 4th ed., McGraw-Hill, New York, pg. 20.20.

      a.   the science of measurement
      b.   the same as meteorology
      c.   the same as metallurgy
      d.   a department responsible for measurement

Key: a.   the science of measurement
Metrology[18] is a Greek word consisting of "metro" meaning *measure* and "logy" meaning the *science of*. It is also defined as the science of weights and measures. Meteorology is the science that deals with the atmosphere, its phenomena, and weather forecasting. Metallurgy means the science and technology of metals.

67.   A measurement can be

      a.   inaccurate but precise
      b.   accurate and precise
      c.   accurate and imprecise
      d.   inaccurate and imprecise
      e.   all of the above

Key: e.   all of the above
The key phrase is *can be* which means any one of the above conditions can occur when a measurement is made.

68.   A measurement should be

      a.   inaccurate but precise
      b.   accurate and precise
      c.   accurate and imprecise
      d.   inaccurate and imprecise

Key: b.   accurate and precise
The key phrase is *should be*, i.e., a measuring instrument should be both accurate and precise. It has no error and it is repeatable.

69.   Specification can be

      a.   bilateral with equal value above and below the target value
      b.   unilateral
      c.   bilateral with unequal value above and below the target value
      d.   any one of the above

Key: d.   any one of the above
Specification is an important aspect for product quality and one should develop the inspection around the specification value to achieve the fitness for use and maximize customer satisfaction.

---

[18] *Webster's Ninth New Collegiate Dictionary*, Merriam Webster, Inc., Springfield, Mass., 1988.

Some specifications are bilateral with equal value above and below the nominal, e.g., diameter of 10 ± 1 mm. A specification can be unilateral, i.e., *smaller the better*, e.g., no gap allowed; or it can be *larger the better* type, e.g., minimum tensile strength. In some special situations, a specification can be bilateral with unequal tolerances, e.g., 10 + 1/–0 mm.

70.   Specifying a tolerance by +0.000/–0.0001 is known as

     a.   limit dimensioning
     b.   manufacturing limits
     c.   unilateral tolerancing
     d.   bilateral tolerancing

Key: c.   unilateral tolerancing   (Ref. Applications Question 21, October 1974)
Unilateral tolerance means tolerance for one side of the specification only. This question is repeated in the October 1972 examination.[19]

71.   A variable measurement of a dimension should include

     a.   an estimate of the accuracy of the measurement process
     b.   a controlled measurement procedure
     c.   a numerical value for the parameter being measured
     d.   an estimate of the precision of the measurement process
     e.   all of the above

Key: e.   all of the above   (Ref. Principles Question 59, August 1978)

72.   Accuracy is

     a.   getting consistent results repeatedly
     b.   reading to four decimals
     c.   using the best measuring device available
     d.   getting an unbiased true value

Key: d.   getting an unbiased true value   (Ref. Principles Question 1, October 1972)
The term *accuracy* is defined as the level of agreement between the average of the observed data or measurement with its true value. The objective for every measuring instrument is to get an unbiased or error-free value in the measurement; i.e., the measured value should be as close as possible to the true value and the bias or error should be minimum.

The term *error* means the difference between the average value of the data and the true value, and it can be positive or negative depending on the usage, application, and wear and tear. It is the extent to which the instrument is out of control and shows the extent of the *correction* needed in the test instrument.

---

[19] *ASQC CQE Examination*, Quality Progress, October 1972, Applications section, Question 66.

Fig. 12-1b shows the variation in the individual measurements from the center, i.e., less precise, but the average of the data is very close to the target value and hence has "good"

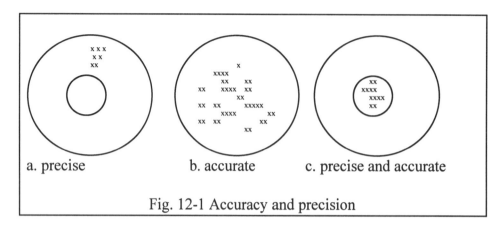

Fig. 12-1 Accuracy and precision

accuracy. Fig. 12-1a shows high precision but its average has shifted, i.e., low accuracy. Fig. 12-1c shows high accuracy and high precision, because the average of the data is close to the center or the target value and it is repeatable, i.e., precise.

73. Accuracy is

    a.   getting consistent results
    b.   reading to four decimal places
    c.   using the best measuring device available
    d.   getting an unbiased true value
    e.   the difference between the average of multiple measurements and the true value

Key: e.   the difference between the average of multiple measurements and the true value
(Ref. ASQC - CMI Examination Brochure Question 12)
Refer to Question 72 above for discussion.

74. Precision is

    a.   getting consistent results repeatedly
    b.   reading to four or more decimals
    c.   distinguishing small deviations from the standard value
    d.   extreme care in the analysis of data

Key: a.   getting consistent results repeatedly (Ref. Principles Question 6, October 1972)
The term *precision* is defined as the degree to which the measurement values are repeatable and consistent. It is the ability of the measuring instrument to repeat or reproduce its own previous set of readings. See Fig. 12-1a and c in Question 72.

Choice b is incorrect because the number of decimals has little to do with precision, but it may be important in defining the measurement error caused by rounding off. The number of decimals depends on the sensitivity of the measurement and type of measuring instrument. Some instruments are designed to provide readings up to varying numbers of decimals.

Choice c defines accuracy and not precision. Choice d indicates the extreme care in analysis of data, which has little meaning. Extreme care is required during the measurement process, i.e., data collection; use, handling, and storage of gage; handling the parts; recording; etc. Analysis is generally done now using computers or calculators, and hence calculation errors are less likely to occur.

75.   When making measurements with test instruments, precision and accuracy mean

    a.   the same
    b.   the opposite
    c.   consistency and correctness, respectively
    d.   exactness and traceability, respectively
    e.   none of the above

Key: c.   consistency and correctness, respectively (Ref. Applications Question 49, July 1984)
        Refer to Fig. 12-1 in Question 72. Precision is the ability of the test instrument to reproduce its own measurements. It shows how *consistent* the test instrument is in reproducing its own readings.

        Accuracy means the difference between the observed average of measurements and the true value. It is the extent to which the instrument is out of control. It means also the measurement error and shows the extent of the *correction* needed in the test instrument.

76.   Measurement error

    a.   is the fault of the inspector
    b.   can be determined
    c.   is usually of no consequences
    d.   can be eliminated by frequent calibrations of the measuring device

Key: b.   can be determined   (Ref. Principles Question 5, October 1972)
        Choice b is the best choice. The measurement error can occur for various reasons but it can be determined by using appropriate methods. Automotive industry's Measurement Systems Analysis Reference Manual[20] and Wheeler and Lyday[21] describe various methods to quantify the measurement error.

        Choice a is only partially true because inspector variation is called operator error variation but it is not the only source of measurement error. The measurement error can be because of gage, operator, and part-to-part variability. Choice c is obviously incorrect as the measurement error

---

[20] *Measurement Systems Analysis Reference Manual*, AIAG 1990 (jointly developed by ASQC Automotive Division, AIAG, and GM/Ford/Chrysler Motor Company), Southfield, MI, 1990.

[21] *Evaluating the Measurement Process (EMP)* by Donald J. Wheeler and Richard W. Lyday, 2nd edition, SPC Press, Inc., TN, 1984.

can have significant consequences depending on the magnitude of error and the application of the product. Choice d is partially correct also because calibration can only reduce the gage errors but not by the operator variation or part-to-part variability.

77.   In measurement systems, bias is defined as

    a.   persistent tendency of the measurements as a group to be too large or too small
    b.   the difference between a measurement and its average value
    c.   an agreed upon permissible departure from specification
    d.   the extent of agreement between the average value of the measurements and its true value

Key: a.   persistent tendency of the measurements as a group to be too large or too small
Bias defines the amount of constant error that can be too large or too small and can occur over the full range of the measurements. It can be reduced or removed normally by calibration. Choice b defines the term *deviation* for a single measurement from its mean. Choice c defines *tolerance* and choice d defines *accuracy*.

78.   The difference in the accuracy values of a measuring instrument (gage) over its normal operating range is defined as

    a.   gage stability
    b.   gage linearity
    c.   gage accuracy
    d.   gage repeatability

Key: b.   gage linearity
The terms above describe different types of measurement system variations.[22]
Choice a, *gage stability,* is defined as stability of the gage in measuring the same master standard over a long period of time. Choice c, *accuracy,* is defined as the extent of agreement between the average value of the measurements and its true value. Choice d, *gage repeatability,* defines the measurement variation caused by the gage, i.e., the measuring equipment when used by only one operator repeatedly. It is also called *equipment variation*[23] (EV) in calculation of a *gage repeatability and reproducibility (Gage R&R) study.*

79.   Gage reproducibility is defined as

    a.   the measurement variation caused by the gage, i.e., the measuring equipment, when used by only one operator repeatedly
    b.   stability of the gage in measuring the same master standard over a long period of time
    c.   the difference in the accuracy values of a measuring instrument (gage) over its normal

---

[22] *Measurement Systems Analysis Reference Manual,* AIAG 1990 (jointly developed by ASQC Automotive Division, AIAG, and GM/Ford/Chrysler Motor Company), Southfield, MI, 1990, pg. 15-17.
[23] *Measurement Systems Analysis Reference Manual,* AIAG 1990 (jointly developed by ASQC Automotive Division, AIAG, and GM/Ford/Chrysler Motor Company), Southfield, MI, 1990, pg. 38-46.

operating range

    d.   the measurement variation caused by different operators by using the same gage

Key: d.   the measurement variation caused by different operators by using the same gage
This is also called "appraiser variation[24] (AV)" in the calculation of a gage repeatability and reproducibility (Gage R&R) study. Choice a defines *gage repeatability*, b defines *gage stability*, and c defines *gage linearity*.

80.   Calibration is defined as

    a.   a process of comparing the instrument or equipment against a standard instrument of known accuracy

    b.   a process of inspecting the instrument and adjusting it to bring it within its tolerances for accuracy

    c.   a process of standardizing the measuring instrument by determining the deviation from a standard to assess the accuracy

    d.   all of the above

Key: d.   all of the above

81.   Adjusting an instrument or device to a standard is called

    a.   correction
    b.   angulation
    c.   correlation
    d.   calibration
    e.   standardization

Key: d.   calibration   (Ref. ASQC-CMI Examination Brochure Question 9)
Refer to Question 80 above for different definitions of calibration.

82.   The basis for establishing calibration intervals is

    a.   stability
    b.   purpose
    c.   degree of usage
    d.   MIL-STD-45662 intervals must be used
    e.   a, b, and c only

Key: e.   a, b, and c only   (Ref. ASQC-CMI Examination Brochure Question 10)
The calibration schedule or interval depends upon the stability of the measuring device, its purpose, and the degree of usage. Juran[25] indicates that calibration schedules are established by the class of the equipment and are defined to reflect the precision, nature, and extent of use as

---

[24] *Measurement Systems Analysis Reference Manual*, AIAG 1990 (jointly developed by ASQC Automotive Division, AIAG, and GM/Ford/Chrysler Motor Company), Southfield, MI, 1990, pg. 38-46.

well as other factors.

83.   To assure continued accuracy, inspection devices must be periodically

    a.   polished
    b.   corrected
    c.   calibrated
    d.   rust-proofed
    e.   all of the above

Key: c.   calibrated   (Ref. ASQC-CMI Examination Brochure Question 11)

84.   Which of the following is most important when calibrating a piece of equipment?

    a.   calibration sticker
    b.   maintenance history card
    c.   standard used
    d.   calibration interval

Key: c.   standard used (Ref. Principles Question 44, July 1984)
The key words are *when calibrating,* i.e., a specific incident of calibrating a measuring instrument. It does not mean the entire system of calibration control.

Calibration is defined as a process of comparing the instrument against a standard instrument of known accuracy. It can also be defined as a process of standardizing the measuring instrument by determining the deviation from a standard to assess the accuracy. Therefore the most important step during calibration is the standard used. The calibration standards can be national standards e.g., National Bureau of Standards (NBS), metrology standards (reference standards), or working standards. This question is repeated with a slight change in the October 1974 examination.[26]

Calibration sticker, maintenance history, and calibration interval are also important factors after the gage or measuring instrument is properly calibrated using the appropriate standard. Refer to Question 85 below, which discusses the important element of the calibration control system.

85.   A basic requirement of most gage calibration system specifications is

    a.   all inspection equipment must be calibrated with master gage blocks
    b.   gages must be color-coded for identification
    c.   equipment shall be labeled or coded to indicate the date calibrated, by whom, and date due for next calibration
    d.   gages must be identified with a tool number
    e.   all of the above

---

[25] *Juran's Quality Control Handbook* by J. M. Juran, 4th ed., McGraw-Hill, New York, pg. 18.78.
[26] *ASQC - CQE Examination*, ASQC Quality Progress, October 1974, Principles section, Question 55.

Key: c.   equipment shall be labeled or coded to indicate date calibrated, by whom, and date due
                 for next calibration   (Ref. Principles Question 57, August 1978)
        The key words are *calibration system,* which means that the gage calibration control system is
        effectively designed and implemented. The calibration schedules are designed based on the type
        and class of equipment, precision required, nature and extent of the use of the equipment, etc.
        Juran[27] indicates that adherence to the calibration schedule is the most important and vital
        element of the entire system of calibration control.

        Juran discusses that the calibration standards are generally scattered over numerous locations,
        and are under the control and custody of several supervisors and workers. Hence, it is difficult to
        ensure compliance to calibration schedules. Shop people often have lack of knowledge of when
        the recalibration is due and who is supposed to do it. They need to be reminded of which piece of
        equipment is due on what day. Also they often cannot easily recall the date of the last calibration
        for several types of equipment all over the shop. Therefore, for effective and timely implementa-
        tion of the calibration, the measuring equipment should be labeled or coded to indicate the date
        calibrated, by whom, and date due for next calibration.

        This question focuses on the elements of a calibration control system and not on a particular
        instance of calibrating a piece of measuring equipment as shown in Question 84.

86.   When specifying the "10:1 calibration principle" we are referring to what?

        a.   the ratio of operators to inspectors
        b.   the ratio of quality engineers to metrology personnel
        c.   the ratio of main scale to vernier scale calibration
        d.   the ratio of calibration standard accuracy to calibrated instrument accuracy
        e.   none of the above

Key: d.   the ratio of calibration standard accuracy to calibrated instrument accuracy
                 (Ref. Principles Question 47, August 1978)
        Juran[28] discusses composite errors using the relationship $\sigma_{obs}^2 = \sigma_{prod}^2 + \sigma_{meas}^2$. If the instrument
        variation σ_{meas} is less than one tenth of σ_{obs}, then its effect on σ_{prod} will be less than 1 percent.
        Hence the measuring instrument should be able to divide the tolerance into about 10 parts. This
        will also provide assurance that the measuring instrument error does not significantly inflate the
        variation of the part or the measurement errors are at a minimum.

87.   Measuring and test equipment are calibrated to

        a.   comply with federal regulations
        b.   assure their precision
        c.   determine and/or assure their accuracy
        d.   check the validity of reference standards

---

[27] *Juran's Quality Control Handbook* by J. M. Juran, 4th ed., McGraw-Hill, New York, pg. 18.78-79.
[28] *Juran's Quality Control Handbook* by J. M. Juran, 4th ed., McGraw-Hill, New York, pg. 18.66-67.

e.   accomplish all of the above

Key: c.   determine and/or assure their accuracy (Ref. Principles Question 55, August 1978)
The measurement instruments or standards used deteriorate in accuracy during their operation and in storage. Calibration control systems are hence necessary to determine and maintain the accuracy of measuring equipment.

88.   What four functions are necessary to have an acceptable calibration system covering measuring and test equipment in a written procedure?

a.   calibration sources, calibration intervals, environmental conditions, and sensitivity required for use
b.   calibration sources, calibration intervals, humidity control, and utilization of published standards
c.   calibration sources, calibration intervals, environmental conditions under which equipment is calibrated, and controls for unsuitable equipment
d.   list of standards, identification report, certificate number, and recall records
e.   all of the above

Key: c.   calibration sources, calibration intervals, environmental conditions under which equipment is calibrated, and controls for unsuitable equipment
(Ref. Principles Question 58, August 1978)
Choice c provides a clear and specific description of four functions in a written procedure for an acceptable calibration system. Choices a, b, and d are too broad and somewhat unclear.

89.   Calibration intervals should be adjusted when

a.   no defective product is reported as acceptable due to measurement errors
b.   few instruments are scrapped during calibration
c.   the results of previous calibrations reflect few "out of tolerance" conditions during calibration
d.   a particular characteristic on the gage is consistently found out of tolerance

Key: d.   a particular characteristic on the gage is consistently found out of tolerance
(Ref. Applications Question 55, July 1984)
The calibration intervals are based on the required precision, nature, and extent of use of the gage. They are adjusted to detect the deterioration beyond tolerable levels of accuracy, caused by the amount of the usage and the length of time. This question is repeated with a slight change in the August 1978 examination.[29]

90.   Which of the following need not appear on the calibration label on a unit of measuring and test equipment?

a.   The date that the unit is due for calibration.

---

[29] *ASQC - CQE Examination*, ASQC Quality Progress, August 1978, Applications section, Question 47.

    b.   The procedure by which the unit was calibrated.

    c.   Identification of the person who performed the calibration.

    d.   Identification of the calibrating organization.

    e.   Instrument error found during the calibration.

Key: b.   The procedure by which the unit was calibrated.
           (Ref. ASQC - CQE Examination brochure, 1993 revision; Question 24)

91.   Test and measurement equipment found out of tolerance at the end of a calibration cycle could indicate several problems. The best course of action to be taken under these conditions is to

    a.   disregard, since the product may have been already shipped

    b.   disregard, since this does not happen very often

    c.   review for possible effect on product already inspected by the equipment

    d.   calibrate the equipment with no further actions

    e.   recall all products and reinspect after calibration

Key: c.   review for possible effect on product already inspected by the equipment
           (Ref. ASQC - CQT Examination Core Portion Question 25)

92.   Test and inspection equipment should be

    a.   replaced periodically

    b.   covered when not in use

    c.   calibrated periodically

    d.   as sophisticated as possible

Key: c.   calibrated periodically   (Ref. Applications Question 88, October 1972)
           The most important item here is calibration at a defined interval to minimize any gage error.

93.   The accuracy of measuring equipment is linked to U.S. National Standards by

    a.   standardization

    b.   capability

    c.   traceability

    d.   confirmation

    e.   metrology

Key: c.   traceability (Ref. ASQC - CQT Examination Core Portion Question 31)

94.   The reliability of the measuring instrument is linked to the U.S. national standards by

    a.   traceability

    b.   confirmation

    c.   unification

d.   capability

Key: a.   traceability   (Ref. Applications Question 69, October 1974)
Traceability means the ability of the system to identify and preserve the information on the measuring equipment, its origin, and its reference standard for calibration. Every measuring instrument should be calibrated to U.S. national standards for traceability and validity of the measuring instrument. There should be documented proof that the reference standards used to calibrate a gage are inspected, approved, and certified by the National Bureau of Standards (NBS).

95.   Characteristics for which 100% inspection may be practicable include all of the following except

a.   dimensions subject to measurements or go no-go gaging
b.   performance characteristics subject to nondestructive testing
c.   characteristics observable by visual inspection
d.   ultimate physical properties (tensile strength, viscosity)

Key: d.   ultimate physical properties (tensile strength, viscosity)
(Ref. Principles Question 48, July 1984)
100% inspection is only possible if the inspection does not involve destructive testing. Some of the ultimate physical properties are destructive in nature and hence 100% inspection is not possible. Choices a, b, and c are all examples of nondestructive testing.

96.   Holography is a nondestructive test technique which is used to

a.   measure the hole locations with an optical device
b.   measure the depth of the "halos" around drilled holes in printed wiring boards
c.   measure the continuity of plated-through holes in printed wiring boards
d.   measure surface displacements by recording interference patterns
e.   measure flaws using acoustic vibration

Key: d.   measure surface displacements by recording interference patterns
(Ref. Principles Question 47, July 1984)
Juran[30] discusses various potential applications for automated inspection and the computers. Holography is applicable in dimensional gaging, automatic stress, strain, displacement, and image processing.

97.   Which material listed below can be usefully tested by the magnetic particle method?

a.   carbon steel
b.   aluminum
c.   magnesium
d.   lead
e.   none of the above

---

[30] *Juran's Quality Control Handbook* by J. M. Juran, 4th ed., McGraw-Hill, New York, pg. 27.18-22, Table 27.8.

Key: a.   carbon steel   (Ref. Principles Question 53, July 1984)
Magnetic particle testing is a nondestructive testing (NDT) method and it is used for detecting surface defects or subsurface flaws such as cracks, seams, fractures, holes, porosity, etc., in ferromagnetic materials. It is a simple, flexible, and economical method. Carbon steel is the only one that is a ferromagnetic material in the choices above.

The magnetic particle method is based on electromagnetic principles. It sets up an intense magnetic field in the part under inspection. If there is any crack or discontinuity in the part, sudden disruptions will occur in the magnetic field. Some of the magnetic flux will get crowded outside the surface of the part. The ferromagnetic particles are dusted on the part's surface as a *dry method* or suspended in a suitable liquid as a *wet method*. This will show the exact size and shape of the crack or other discontinuity. Refer to Question 98 below which is also a similar question.

98.   Which of the following nondestructive testing methods is best for rapid inspection of 1/2 in diameter carbon steel rod one foot long for surface cracks?

       a.   radiography
       b.   ultrasonic
       c.   magnetic particle
       d.   liquid penetrant

Key: c.   magnetic particle   (Ref. Applications Question 12, October 1972)
Please refer to Question 97 above for discussion.

99.   If not specifically required by the product drawings or specification, nondestructive test (NDT) may be required during production and/or during acceptance at the discretion of the quality engineer responsible for the inspection planning. This statement is

       a.   false, because testing is limited to that specified by the design engineer
       b.   true, because NDT is a form of inspection (with enhanced senses), not a functional test
       c.   false, QE may impose NDT as he or she believes necessary, but cannot delete it without design engineering's permission
       d.   true, because all acceptance testing and inspection requirements are up to quality engineering

Key: b.   true, because NDT is a form of inspection (with enhanced senses), not a functional test
(Ref. Principles Question 41, August 1978)
NDT is a method of testing or inspection done without affecting or impairing the subsequent usefulness of the product. It is like any other inspection plan used to detect defects in materials or components so that a failure may be prevented or to define the sampling location on a failed part, and to test physical properties such as dimensions, hardness, etc. NDT can be used to detect cracking or defects so that a failure may be prevented or to define the sampling location on a failed part. Visual inspection can be considered one of the most widely used methods of NDT.

100. X-rays and gamma rays are both commonly used in industrial radiography for detecting flaws in materials. Which of the following statements most correctly describes the differences between these two types of radiation?

    a.   X-rays have wavelengths of 10^{-6} to 10^{-10} cm, whereas gamma rays have wavelengths 10^{-9} to 10^{-12} cm.

    b.   Both originate from the nucleus of an atom.

    c.   X-rays are lower energy than gamma rays.

    d.   They are similar, both being electromagnetic radiation, however differing in origin.

Key: d.   They are similar, both being electromagnetic radiation, however differing in origin. (Ref. Principles Question 52, August 1978)

X-rays are created using an X-ray tube consisting of a cathode and anode. When the cathode filament is heated in the vacuum, it emits X-rays. X-rays and gamma rays are very commonly used as an NDT method for inspecting cracks, discontinuities, weld defects, slag, etc. X-ray inspection is based on short wavelength radiation's ability to penetrate any opaque material. The X-ray film shows the cracks or defects.

Gamma rays are similar to X-rays but their wavelengths are shorter. The source of gamma rays is the atomic disintegration of radioisotopes such as cobalt 60 or iridium 192. Gamma rays are easier to use because they are portable. They require longer exposure time than X-rays and may lose some sharpness in resolution. This question is repeated in the August 1978 examination.[31]

101. In dry magnetic particle testing, best results are obtained when the magnetic field from prods is applied

    a.   along the length of the discontinuity

    b.   in a direction crosswise to the direction in which the discontinuity lies

    c.   so that the magnetic field parallels the direction of the discontinuity

    d.   none of the above

Key: b.   in a direction crosswise to the direction in which the discontinuity lies (Ref. Principles Question 86, October 1974)

The magnetic particle method is based on electromagnetic principles. It sets up an intense magnetic field in the part under inspection. If there is any crack or discontinuity in the part, sudden disruptions will occur in the magnetic field. Some of the magnetic flux will get crowded outside the surface of the part. The ferromagnetic particles are dusted on the part's surface as a dry method (or suspended in a suitable liquid as a wet method). This will show the exact size and shape of the crack or other discontinuity.

Juran[32] discusses the limitations of magnetic particle testing. It is limited to ferromagnetic materials only. It does not provide any indications of cracks parallel to the magnetic field, hence,

---

[31] *ASQC - CQE Examination*, ASQC Quality Progress, August 1978, Applications section, Question 44.

[32] *Juran's Quality Control Handbook* by J. M. Juran, 4th ed., McGraw-Hill, New York, pg. 18.71-73.

it requires magnetism in two directions to find all discontinuities. Therefore the field should be applied in the direction crosswise to the direction in which the discontinuity lies.

102.   The strength of a magnetic field is known as

    a.   flux density
    b.   ferromagnetic force
    c.   magnetic density
    d.   coercive force

Key: a.   flux density   (Ref. Principles Question 49, July 1984)
Magnetic field is defined as the region of space in which there is an appreciable magnetic force. Flux density is defined in physics as the quantity of a fluid or energy emitted per unit of time through a unit of surface area.

103.   Which of the following tests is nondestructive?

    a.   Charpy impact
    b.   electrical conductivity
    c.   shear strength
    d.   stress corrosion
    e.   peal strength

Key: b.   electrical conductivity
(Ref. ASQC - CQE Examination brochure 1993 revision; Principles section Question 8)
Choice a, Charpy impact test,[33] is an impact test used to determine the ductility of a metal. The test uses a pendulum that swings freely. It is released to strike and break a notched specimen that is laid loosely on a support. The positions of the pendulum before the impact and after the impact, i.e., after breaking the specimen, are measured and recorded.

Choice b, electrical conductivity, is defined as the ratio of the electric current density to the electric field in a material, and it is NDT. Choice c, shear strength, means the maximum shear stress that a material can withstand without rupture. Choice d, stress corrosion, means the corrosion caused and accelerated because of the stress in the material. Choice e, peal strength, means a loud sound or succcssion of sounds. If it is spelled "peel test," it means a test to ascertain the adhesive strength of bonded strips of metals or decals by peeling the strips and recording the bond values.

104.   A substance discontinuity in some purchased steel bar stock is a suspected cause for the high failure rate in your parts fabrication area. All of the following nondestructive test (NDT) methods could be used to screen the bar stock except

    a.   magnetic particle testing
    b.   radiographic testing

---

[33] *Dictionary of Scientific and Technical Terms* edited by S. P. Parker, 4th ed., McGraw-Hill, New York, 1989, pg. 333.

    c.   liquid penetrant testing
    d.   eddy current testing
    e.   ultrasonic testing

Key: c.   liquid penetrant testing   (Ref. Applications Question 51, July 1984)
The liquid penetrant testing is a nondestructive testing method used on nonmagnetic parts. It is used to inspect for porosity, cracks, and other types of surface defects for nonmagnetic parts. A penetrant dye is sprayed or applied and it makes any defects on the surface visible.

The remaining methods are NDT methods used for magnetic or ferromagnetic parts. This question is repeated in the October 1974 examination.[34]

105.   In attempting to replace human evaluation of foods in order to achieve objectivity, we must use as an ultimate criterion of accuracy

    a.   gas chromatography
    b.   shear press
    c.   viscosimeter
    d.   none of the above

Key: d.   none of the above   (Ref. Applications Question 52, July 1984)

106.   Generally, the best ultrasonic testing method for detecting discontinuities oriented along the fusion zone in a welded plate is

    a.   an angle beam contact method employing surface waves
    b.   a contact test using a straight longitudinal wave
    c.   an immersion test using surface waves
    d.   an angle beam method using shear waves

Key: d.   an angle beam method using shear waves (Ref. Applications Question 53, July 1984)

107.   When considering whether to use radiography or ultrasonic inspection to examine critical welds in thick materials, which of the following criteria is the best reason for this selection?

    a.   ultrasonic; since greater thicknesses can be prevented
    b.   radiography; since ultrasonic is less sensitive to porosity and inclusions
    c.   both; since the methods complement rather than supplant one another
    d.   both; since each is equally effective, the chance of missing a serious flaw is reduced

Key: c.   both, since the methods complement rather than supplant one another
(Ref. Applications Question 44, August 1978)
Ultrasonic inspection is used to detect types of flaws in welds and castings. The ultrasonic instrument generates the high-frequency waves in the transducer that are directed on the part

---

[34] *ASQC - CQE Examination*, Quality Progress, October 1974, Applications section, Question 64.

being measured in cycles as high as 1000 times per second. The waves are reflected back to the transducer and displayed on an oscilloscope. Ultrasonic equipment is calibrated by using reference plates to show any deterioration in electronic components. Standard reference plates are available from the American Society of Mechanical Engineers (ASME) and the American Society for Testing Materials (ASTM). X-rays are created by using an X-ray tube consisting of a cathode and anode. When the cathode filament is heated in the vacuum, it emits X-rays. X-rays and gamma rays are very commonly used as NDT methods for inspecting cracks, discontinuities, weld defects, slag, etc. X-ray inspection is based on the ability of short wavelength radiation to penetrate any opaque material. X-ray film shows the cracks or defects.

Gamma rays are similar to X-rays, but are shorter in wavelength. The source of gamma rays is the atomic disintegration of radioisotopes such as cobalt 60 or iridium 192. The gamma rays are easier to use because they are portable, but require longer exposure time compared to X-rays and some loss of sharpness in resolution may occur.

108.   One of the practical limits on the application of ultrasonic testing method is

   a.   lack of portability
   b.   poor penetration capability
   c.   reference standards are required
   d.   inability to record results permanently

Key: c.   reference standards are required   (Ref. Applications Question 54, July 1984)
Ultrasonic testing[35] is a nondestructive testing method that employs high-frequency mechanical vibration energy to detect and locate structural discontinuities or differences. Ultrasonic equipment is calibrated by using the reference plates to show any deterioration in the electronic components. Standard reference plates are available from the American Society of Mechanical Engineers (ASME) and the American Society for Testing Materials (ASTM).

109.   Ultrasonic flaw detection instruments are calibrated using which of the following types of standards?

   a.   NBS traceable time voltage standards
   b.   natural flaws in the material being inspected
   c.   not calibrated since NBS traceable standards are not available
   d.   distance amplitude reference blocks
   e.   artificial flaw transfer standards

Key: d.   distance amplitude reference blocks (Ref. Applications Question 41, August 1978)
Ultrasonic inspection is used to detect the types of flaws in welds and castings. The instrument generates high-frequency waves in the transducer that are directed on the part being measured in cycles as high as 1000 times per second. The waves are reflected back to the transducer and displayed on an oscilloscope. Ultrasonic equipment is calibrated by using the reference plates to show any deterioration in its electronic components. Standard reference plates are available from

---

[35] *Dictionary of Scientific and Technical Terms*, edited by S. P. Parker, 4th ed., McGraw-Hill, New York, 1989, pg. 1991.

the American Society of Mechanical Engineers (ASME) and the American Society for Testing Materials (ASTM).

110. The primary advantage of the use of radioisotopes, such as cobalt 60, as compared to an X-ray generator, such as betatron, is

   a. duration of radiation can be controlled by turning off the source
   b. portability
   c. the energy given off is heterogeneous, covering a wide range of wavelengths
   d. the energy given off by the source stays constant with time

Key: b. portability (Ref. Applications Question 49, August 1978)

111. The gradual loss of sonic energy as ultrasonic vibrations travel through the material is referred to as

   a. refraction
   b. reproducibility
   c. reflection
   d. attenuation
   e. diffraction

Key: d. attenuation (Ref. Applications Question 50, August 1978)
Attenuation[36] means a reduction in the level of the intensity of the wave or amplitude of an electric signal traveling along a very long uniform transmitting line.

Diffraction means modification of the waves caused by the presence of an object in the form of a change in the amplitude and/or the phase of the waves. In light waves, it is the modification or redistribution light waves when they undergo in passing by the edges of opaque objects or narrow slits. It can create parallel light and dark bands. It is found in all types of wave phenomena.

Reflection means the return of light or sound waves from a surface.

Refraction means a change or deflection in the path of light or energy wave in passing from one medium into another medium.

Reproducibility is the term used in measurement systems analysis for gage repeatability and reproducibility (Gage R&R). It means the extent of the variation caused by the operators or technicians commonly called *appraiser variation*. Please refer to Question 79 above for the definition of gage reproducibility.

112. Which of these testing methods is destructive?

---

[36] *Dictionary of Scientific and Technical Terms*, edited by S. P. Parker, 4th ed., McGraw-Hill, New York, 1989, pg. 144.

    a.   radiographic
    b.   spectrographic
    c.   ultrasonic
    d.   liquid penetrant

Key: b.   spectrographic   (Ref. ASQC - CQT Examination Core Portion, Question 36)
Choice a, radiographic,[37] means a technique of a photographic image of an opaque specimen by transmitting a beam of X-rays or gamma rays through the specimen onto an adjacent photographic film. The image results from variations in thickness, density, and chemical composition of the specimen.

Choice b, spectrographic, means the use of photography to record the electromagnetic spectrum displayed in a spectroscope. Choice c, ultrasonic, means pertaining to signals, equipment, or phenomena involving frequencies just above the range of human hearing, i.e., above 20,000 Hz. Choice d, liquid penetrant test, is a method of nondestructive testing used to locate defects open to the surface of nonferrous materials. It uses a penetrant liquid that is applied to the surface, and after test time the surface is cleaned of any excess liquid. A developer liquid is applied to identify surface defects, their location, shape, and size.

113.   True testing variability can be obtained in a destructive testing situation under one of these conditions

    a.   enough samples have been tested
    b.   it cannot be obtained
    c.   all samples are taken closely together
    d.   the same person and instrument are used

Key: b.   it cannot be obtained   (Ref. Principles Question 30, October 1972)
Destructive testing is a difficult situation to obtain true testing variability because the product or unit is destroyed and hence is not available for further measurement.

114.   The vernier makes measurement readings as fine as thousandths of an inch possible by

    a.   magnifying the graduations
    b.   providing more widely spaced graduations
    c.   visually subdividing the smallest divisions on a scale
    d.   providing more closely spaced graduations

Key: c.   visually subdividing the smallest divisions on a scale
(Ref. Principles Question 21, October 1974)
The vernier instrument has two scales: a main scale and a vernier scale. The main scale length unit is represented as inches with 40 divisions, i.e., the smallest division on the main scale is 1/40 or 0.025 inch or 25 mil. The vernier scale has 25 divisions for an equivalent of 24 divisions of

---

[37] *Dictionary of Scientific and Technical Terms* edited by S. P. Parker, 4th ed., McGraw-Hill, New York, 1989, pg. 1554, 1786, 1990, 1090.

the main scale, i.e., the vernier division is 1/25th of the main scale division or 0.001 inch (1 mil), also called the *least count* of the vernier gage. When a vernier instrument is used, the main scale reading value is added to 0.001 inch of the vernier scale.

As a quality engineer or a professional, you should already be familiar with the operating principles of such basic, commonly used measurement tools in the industry.

115.   What type of gaging instrument would you use to determine the fractional part of an inch that can be read by multiplying the denominator of the finest subdivision on the scale by the total number of divisions on the second scale?

a.   vernier
b.   micrometer
c.   comparator
d.   demonimeter

Key: a.   vernier   (Ref. Applications Question 15, October 1972)
The vernier instrument has two scales: a main scale and a vernier scale. The main scale has length unit represented as inches with 40 divisions, i.e., the smallest division on the main scale is 1/40 or 0.025 in (25 mil). The vernier scale has 25 divisions for an equivalent of 24 divisions of the main scale, i.e., the vernier division is 1/25th of the main scale division or 0.001 in (1 mil), also called the *least count* of the vernier gage. When a vernier instrument is used, the main-scale reading value is added to the 0.001 in or thousandths of the values of the vernier scale.

116.   The finest reading possible with a vernier micrometer in inches is

a.   hundred-thousandths
b.   ten-thousandths
c.   micro lengths
d.   thousandths

Key: b.   ten-thousandths   (Ref. Applications Question 73, October 1974)
The quality level of the micrometer depends on the basis of the least increment of the indicated measurement. Some micrometers are of "thousandths" grade where the micrometer has 40 threads per inch and 25 graduations on the thimble circumference. Every turn of the micrometer will result in 0.025 inch advancement as the micrometer has 40 threads per inch and the 25 graduations on the thimble circumference will allow the reading of 0.001 or "thousandths" of an inch grade.

In some cases, the single mark on the sleeve may have a vernier scale instead of a single reference mark which can result in further subdivision of the thimble graduation to 10 more graduations. This can make the micrometer "ten-thousandths" grade.

117.   When using an inside or outside caliper, care must be taken to get proper

    a.   slip
    b.   depth
    c.   grip
    d.   feel

Key: d.   feel   (Ref. Applications Question 11, October 1974)

118.   Which of the following is in the class of caliper tools?

    a.   micrometer
    b.   depth gauge
    c.   height gauge
    d.   sine bar

Key: a.   micrometer   (Ref. ASQC- CMI Examination brochure Question 13)
A caliper is a measuring instrument, e.g., a micrometer, with two jaws that are adjustable to measure the dimensions.

119.   A standard two-inch micrometer has how many threads per inch?

    a.   25
    b.   50
    c.   40
    d.   80
    e.   20

Key: c.   40   (Ref. ASQC - CMI Examination brochure Question 15)

120.   The smallest size a 3 in. micrometer can measure is

    a.   3 in.
    b.   2 in.
    c.   1 in.
    d.   2.5 in.

Key: b.   2 in.   (Ref. Applications Question 71, October 1972)

121.   Which is not a limit gage?

    a.   ring gage
    b.   radius gage
    c.   vernier height gage
    d.   gage blocks

Key: c.   vernier height gage   (Ref. Principles Question 50, August 1978)

Limit gages are gages that are made to sizes identical to the design limit sizes of the dimension to be inspected. A limit gage can be a *go or a no-go gage*.

The vernier height gage is not a limit gage. The primary use of the vernier height gage is in the field of surface plate work as a layout tool. It is used to mark off vertical distances and to measure the differences between steps at various heights.

122.   A gage that checks a single dimension (and tolerance) is a

      a.   micrometer
      b.   vernier
      c.   varigage
      d.   plug gage

Key: d.   plug gage   (Ref. Principles Question 70, October 1974)
Plug gages are commonly made for a single size and called *single ended plug gages*. They are also referred to as single dimension gages or dedicated gages[38] and are used to measure the same characteristic in a high-volume production operation. They can be cylindrical limit plug gages, indicating snap gages, air gages, and electronic plug gages. Some may be indicator plug gages with expanding segments and expanding blades. Air gages or pneumatic gages have the advantage of noncontact measurement over electronic gages.

123.   Fixed gages

      a.   measure one or more dimensions
      b.   measure only one dimension
      c.   are all made of tool steel
      d.   are a fast method of checking parts

Key: d.   are a fast method of checking parts   (Ref. Applications Question 65, October 1974)
Fixed gages are attribute gages that are very simple to use and a faster method of checking the parts. They can be used to represent the part's nominal dimension as a " master gage." Some fixed gages are made to measure the reverse replica of the dimension to be measured and can be used as an "inspection gage." Such gages are normally called "Limit Gages."

Farago[39] describes many advantages of fixed gages. They are consistent and free from errors, provide attribute-type "yes-no", or "go-no-go" type information, are easy to carry and portable, can be used to measure various combinations of dimensions, and in general are very economical to use.

124.   Gages that tell how much a dimension varies from specification are called

[38] *Handbook of Dimensional Measurement* by Francis T. Farago, 2nd edition, Industrial Press, New York, 1982, pg. 35, 91; and *Quality Management Handbook* edited by L. Walsh, R. Wurster, and R. J. Kimber, Marcel Dekker, and ASQC Quality Press, 1986, pg. 541.
[39] *Handbook of Dimensional Measurement* by Francis T. Farago, 2nd ed., Industrial Press, New York, 1982, pg. 27.

a.   accurators
b.   depth gages
c.   indicating gages
d.   tolerators

Key: c.   indicating gages   (Ref. Applications Question 70, October 1974)
Indicating gages are the mechanical indicators used to measure specific dimensions and display the readings on a dial or a graduated scale. The dial indicator generally amplifies the measurement value on the dial. They are used for various types of measurements, e.g., comparative measurement of length, bore size, and distance of a surface from some datum plane.

125.   Wear allowances in a "go plug gage" result in gages that are

a.   on the low limit of the specification
b.   slightly larger diameter than the high limit of the specification
c.   slightly smaller diameter than the low limit of the specification
d.   slightly larger diameter than the low limit of the specification
e.   on the high limit of the specification

Key: d.   slightly larger diameter than the low limit of the specification
(Ref. Applications Question 42, August 1978)
Every gage or measuring instrument wears every time it is used. Hence the gage specifications reflect the impact of wear on the gage every time it is used. A *wear allowance* is allowed in the standardized gage specifications.

A *go plug gage* is a gage that is used to measure hole diameters. The go plug gage enters the hole every time it is used to measure the part. The diameter of the go plug gage is at the minimum allowable tolerance limit, i.e., it is at the lowest specification of the hole; it will wear out every time it is used to measure the hole. Slowly the diameter of the go plug gage shows wear, which means the go plug gage becomes even smaller than the smallest specification and can pass or accept some undersized parts. To avoid such error, the wear allowance is used on the go plug gage, and the go plug gage has slightly larger diameter than the low limit of the specification.

A *no-go plug* gage is not able to and should not enter a hole in a part. This is a repeat question in the October 1972 examination.[40]

126.   The method whereby several sizes of gage blocks can be conveniently combined to total a desired dimension is called

a.   magnetism
b.   interlocking
c.   wringing
d.   stacking

---

[40] *ASQC - CQE Examination*, ASQC Quality Progress, October 1972, Applications section, Question 5.

Key: c.   wringing   (Ref. Applications Question 79, October 1974)
Wringing is defined as the process of bringing a stack of gage blocks together as one unit for a desired dimension. The gage block's flat and smooth surfaces will adhere to each other.

127.   Measurement gaging is preferable to go-no-go gaging in a quality characteristic because

    a.   it is more scientific
    b.   it provides the most information per piece inspected
    c.   it requires greater skills
    d.   it requires a larger sample than gaging does

Key: b.   it provides the most information per piece inspected
(Ref. Applications Question 7, October 1972)
The attribute gage provides only "yes-no" or "go-no go" type information and no specific information about the dimension of a product feature is available. Hence measurement gaging that provides variable data on the product characteristic is more meaningful. It provides information about variation of the part from its nominal and enables one to make decisions about the process's performance with respect to given product requirements.

128.   Pneumatic gaging has one major advantage over electronic gaging and that is

    a.   cost
    b.   higher amplification
    c.   the elimination of metal to metal contact
    d.   increased accuracy

Key: c.   the elimination of metal to metal contact (Ref. Principles Question 88, October 1974)
Pneumatic gaging is also called air gaging and used as a plug gage to measure a particular characteristic, e.g., the inside diameter. They are dedicated to measuring a single dimension and are easier to use, faster, convenient, and more accurate than any other gaging method. They are noncontact because the operator just has to insert the air plug in the hole and read the dial or meter. They are widely used to measure soft, highly polished, thin-walled, delicate materials as in Walsh.[41] The electronic gage uses mechanical contacts to measure dimensions.

129.   The various grades of gauge blocks indicate

    a.   different base metals
    b.   different coefficients of expansion
    c.   different tolerance ranges
    d.   different number of blocks per set

Key: c.   different tolerance ranges   (Ref. ASQC - CMI Examination brochure Question 18)

---

[41] *Quality Management Handbook* edited by L. Walsh, R. Wurster, and R. J. Kimber; Marcel Dekker, Inc. 1986 and ASQC Quality Press, Chapter 29, pg. 541.

130. A master or reference gage is used for the purpose of checking

    a. the finished product
    b. the gage for accuracy prior to measuring the product
    c. the gage after measuring the part to see that part and measurements are correct
    d. the gage for accuracy after measuring a given number of parts

Key: b. the gage for accuracy prior to measuring the product
(Ref. ASQC- CQT Examination Core Portion Question 34)

131. While using electronic surface gauging, an inspector decides to "switch" to a different scale on the amplifier. The _____ of the instrument has changed.

    a. sensitivity
    b. precision
    c. accuracy
    d. all of the above

Key: a. sensitivity   (ASQC - CMI Examination brochure Question 14)

132. All measuring instruments used on a surface plate have a common feature, which is

    a. an accurately finished base
    b. sliding jaws
    c. scales reading to 0.0001"
    d. graduated thimbles

Key: a. an accurately finished base   (Ref. ASQC - CMI Examination brochure Question 19)

133. A surface plate is always

    a. used as a reference surface
    b. granite
    c. magnetic
    d. square

Key: a. used as a reference surface   (Ref. ASQC-CMI Examination brochure Question 20)

134. A tracer type surface finish instrument, such as a profilometer, can be used to measure all of the following except

    a. roughness on gear teeth
    b. depth of the scratches on a metal surface
    c. roughness on a mild steel plate
    d. surface quality of a tapered hole

Key: b.   depth of the scratches on a metal surface (Ref. Principles Question 52, July 1984)
A profilometer[42] is an instrument for measuring the roughness of a surface by means of a diamond-pointed tracer arm attached to a coil in an electric field. The surface measurement is made based on the movement of the arm across the surface. This question is repeated in the October 1974 examination.[43]

135.   Dial indicator inaccuracies are stated in terms of

   a.   percentage of full scale range
   b.   dial indicator divisions
   c.   percent reliability
   d.   thousands of full scale range
   e.   none of these

Key: a.   percentage of full scale range   (Ref. Principles Question 40, October 1974)
Dial indicator is an instrument used to measure distance or mechanical displacement. It generally has a long measuring range and permits a reasonable amount of over travel.[44] The American Gage Design standard defines the calibration accuracy as the linearity of indicators as follows, "the dial indicator should be accurate within one graduation, at any point plus or minus, from the approximate 10 o'clock position to the final two o'clock position (2 1/3 turns)." It uses the percentage of the full scale range to define inaccuracy. This question is repeated in the CQT Examination.[45]

136.   Dial indicators are adaptable for use with

   a.   height gauges
   b.   bore gauges
   c.   snap gauges
   d.   measuring calipers
   e.   all of the above

Key: e.   all of the above   (Ref. ASQC - CMI Examination brochure Question 16)

137.   A typical use for the optical comparator would be to measure

   a.   surface finish
   b.   contours
   c.   depth of holes
   d.   diameters of interval grooves
   e.   all of the above

---

[42] *Dictionary of Scientific and Technical Terms*, edited by S. P. Parker, 4th edition, McGraw-Hill, New York, 1989, pg. 1501.
[43] *ASQC - CQE Examination*, ASQC Quality Progress, October 1974, Principles section, Question 73.
[44] *Handbook of Dimensional Measurement* by Francis T. Farago, 2nd ed., Industrial Press, New York, 1982, pg. 68-71.
[45] *ASQC - CQT Examination*, Core Portion, Question 32.

Key: b.   contours   (Ref. Applications Question 48, August 1978)
        The optical comparators are used to magnify the image on a large screen. They project the profile
        or image of a precision part onto a large screen that has a precision magnification of the actual
        part. The optical comparator is used to measure the difficult-to-measure parts. The optical
        comparator called "contour projector" is widely used in the stamping/metal forming industry.

138.   The distinguishing feature of the optical comparator is that adjustments for measurements are
        observed on a

        a.   screen
        b.   reticle coordinator
        c.   dial indicator
        d.   rotating stage

Key: a.   screen   (Ref. Applications Question 22, October 1974)
        Refer to Question 137 above.

139.   A dial indicator nib must be perpendicular to measurement to avoid

        a.   cosine error
        b.   axis error
        c.   profile error
        d.   configuration error

Key: a.   cosine error   (Ref. Applications Question 43, August 1978)
        The cosine error is caused because of the misalignment of the axis of the indicator with the line
        of measurement of the part. To avoid cosine error, the dial nib indicator must be perpendicular to
        the part.

140.   Terminal-based linearity, as applied to the linearity accuracy of voltage or resistance division of
        slide wires, potentiometers, step dividers, etc., is defined as

        a.   the maximum deviation from an arc of 180°, based on the effective electrical travel
        b.   the maximum deviation from a straight line which passes through the zero and 100%
                points, based on the effective electric travel
        c.   the algebraic difference of the end-scale values
        d.   the percent of the end-scale value of an instrument that corresponds to the end-scale
                indication
        e.   none of the above

Key: b.   the maximum deviation from a straight line which passes through the zero and 100%
                points, based on the effective electric travel (Ref. Principles Question 55, July 1984)

141.   Sensory testing is used in a number of industries to evaluate their products. Which of the
        following is not a sensory test?

a. ferritic annial test
b. triangle test
c. duo-trio test
d. ranking test
e. paired comparison test

Key: a. ferritic annial test (Ref. Principles Question 51, August 1978)
Sensory quality characteristics are those for which the senses of human beings are used as measurement equipment when no specific technology is available. Various tests are designed to measure sensory characteristics. Many of the tests are similar to those used in market research and advertising copy development. These tests can be used to measure similarities or differences. All the tests except the ferritic annial test are commonly used sensory tests.[46]

142. "Beauty Defects" can best be described for inspection acceptance purposes by

a. simply stating such defects are unacceptable
b. verbally describing rejection criteria
c. leaving them up to the inspector
d. establishing visual standards and or samples describing the defects
e. establishing written standards describing the defects

Key: d. establishing visual standards and or samples describing the defects
(Ref. Applications Question 51, August 1978)
Beauty defects are part of sensory characteristics and are a visual form of inspections. Visual standards and or the samples describing the types and size of defects should be developed and provided to the operators or inspectors as an inspection acceptance critera.

143. The principal use of V blocks is, holding in fixed relation the surface plate

a. angular pieces
b. cylindrical pieces
c. spherical parts
d. measuring tools

Key: b. cylindrical pieces (Ref. Principles Question 14, October 1974)
V block is used for roundness measurements of round objects and is a very reliable method for roundness measurement of cylindrical pieces. The V block has flat walls or flanks which are symmetrical to the vertical axis and are at a defined angle (like alphabet V). The object is held in the V block by gravity as well as by the gaging pressure of the indicator in the direction of gravity. The roundness inspection is done by means of an indicator dial or instrument.[47]

144. Several types of food instruments are usually equipped with a mirror behind the dial pointer to reduce which of the following measurement errors?

---

[46] *Juran's Quality Control Handbook* by J. M. Juran, 4th ed., McGraw-Hill, New York, pg. 18.54-55.
[47] *Handbook of Dimensional Measurement* by Francis T. Farago, 2nd ed., Industrial Press, New York, 1982, pg. 346.

        a.   interpolation rounding
        b.   parallax
        c.   nonlinearity in lower scale regions
        d.   miniscus
        e.   wrong scale reading

Key: b.   parallax   (Ref. Principles Question 78, October 1974)
Parallax is generally defined in food instruments as the difference in the apparent position of the dial pointer and its image in the mirror. The mirror helps reduce such visual errors because a person has to look in a straight perpendicular direction to the mirror to avoid any parallax.

145.   A flow meter (in air gaging) is used for the purpose of

        a.   measurement of hydraulic pressure
        b.   measurement of hydraulic temperature
        c.   measurement of hydraulic oil viscosity
        d.   none of the above

Key: d.   none of the above (Ref. ASQC - CQT Examination Core Portion Question 33)

146.   The maximum stress to which a material may be subjected without any permanent deformation remaining upon complete release of stress is its

        a.   ultimate yield
        b.   fatigue life
        c.   elastic limit
        d.   elastic hysteresis

Key: c.   elastic limit   (Ref. Applications Question 50, July 1984)
This is the basic definition of elastic limit. Choice d, elastic hysteresis, is a material property of some solids in which deformation of the solid depends not only on the stress applied to the solid but also on the previous history of such stress.

147.   When conducting an inspection for surface cleanliness, a simple and effective means for detecting the presence of oils, grease, or waxes is

        a.   stereomicroscopic inspection
        b.   the Aqueous Conductivity test
        c.   the Liebermann Storch test
        d.   the Water Break test

Key: d.   the Water Break test   (Ref. Applications Question 46, July 1984)
The Water Break test indicates a break in the continuity of the film of water on the surface of a metal withdrawn from an aqueous bath. This enables the detection of the presence of oils, grease, or waxes on the surface with which water does not mix well.

148.   Creep is defined as that deformation occurring over a period of time with material subjected to

    a.   fluctuating stress and fluctuating strap
    b.   constant temperature and a fluctuating stress
    c.   constant temperature with no stress
    d.   constant stress at constant temperature

Key: d.   constant stress at constant temperature (Ref. Applications Question 47, July 1984)
Creep is defined as the permanent change in the shape from prolonged stress or exposure to constant or high temperatures.

149.   When there is a bank of dials to be read on a monitoring panel, it helps to orient them in which one of the following arrangements?

    a.   a random unpatterned display for the normal indicating positions to reduce boredom
    b.   half in a patterned group for the normal position at the 12 o'clock position and half in a patterned group at the 6 o'clock position to minimize eye fatigue
    c.   all normal indication positions in a pattern so that normal readings are in the 9 o'clock or 12 o'clock positions
    d.   each with the normal indicating position in a new position varying in a clockwise pattern
    e.   any of the above

Key: c.   all normal indication positions in a pattern so that normal readings are in the 9 o'clock or 12 o'clock positions   (Ref. Applications Question 36, October 1974)

150.   A device used to measure viscosity or consistency is

    a.   Viscosimeter
    b.   Farinograph
    c.   Consistometer
    d.   all of the above

Key: d.   all of the above   (Ref. Applications Question 23, October 1972)

151.   Color can be described as

    a.   photometric
    b.   two dimensional
    c.   one dimensional
    d.   three dimensional

Key: d.   three dimensional   (Ref. Applications Question 39, October 1974)
The colors of any surface can be described by three attributes. A. H. Munsell, in 1905 developed the method for defining color in his book, "Color Notation."[48] The first attribute is "Hue," i.e.,

---

[48] *Quality Management Handbook* edited by L. Walsh, R. Wurster, and R. J. Kimber, Marcel Dekker, Inc., 1986, and ASQC

red, yellow, green, blue, or purple; second, is "Value," i.e., light or dark; and the third attribute is "Chroma," i.e., the difference from gray. This question is repeated in the October 1972 examination.[49]

152. There is a potential saving by using optical scanning to

   a. have less data to process
   b. reduce written information
   c. eliminate key punching
   d. reduce card sorting

Key: c. eliminate key punching (Ref. Applications Question 1, October 1974)
     Optical scanning is used in television films, electronic writing, and character recognition. A moving spot of light or a laser beam (generally computerized or computer controlled) scans the image field on the subject. The scanner picks up the light reflected from or transmitted by the image field and generates electronic signals. This minimizes the data entry time and efforts. This is a very popular technology today in publishing, data collection, and analysis activities. Quality engineering requires proper use of such technology to enhance and expedite quality improvement efforts.

153. The provisions of the FDA regulations for thermally processed, low-acid foods, packaged in hermetically sealed containers, require all of the following except

   a. copies of all production and laboratory records be kept for six (6) months then reviewed and destroyed by an authorized person
   b. incoming raw material, ingredients, and packaging components should be inspected upon receipt to ensure that they are suitable for processing
   c. scheduled processes for low-acid foods shall be established by qualified persons having expert knowledge of thermal processing
   d. it is either destroyed or evaluated by a component processing authority to detect any hazard to public health

Key: a. copies of all production and laboratory records be kept for six (6) months then reviewed and destroyed by an authorized person (Ref. Applications Question 44, July 1984)
     Choices b, c, and d, are correct choices. Choice a is incorrect because the records may be required for periods longer than 6 months based on the shelf life of the sealed food containers.

154. The metric system

   a. is based upon the circumference of the earth's equator
   b. originated in England
   c. is better than the inch-pound system
   d. is legal in the United States

Quality Press, Chapter 30, pg. 557.
[49] *ASQC CQE Examination*, ASQC Quality Progress, October 1972, Applications section, Question 4.

Key: d.   is legal in the United States   (Ref. Applications Question 90, October 1972)
        This requires elimination of the choices. Choices c and d are difficult to analyze in order to
        select one of the two.

155.   The ultimate standard for U.S. units of measurement used to verify all masters is

        a.   the official meter
        b.   the imperial yard
        c.   the length of light wave
        d.   the Geiger counter

Key: c.   the length of light wave   (Ref. Principles Question 76, October 1972)
        The question is missing the type or the name of the physical quantity such as length, mass, or
        time. To evaluate the choices properly, the question should read: "The ultimate standard for U.S.
        units of measurement *for length*, used to verify all masters is the ...." We can then evaluate each
        choice as a candidate for the ultimate standard unit of measure for length.

        As the choices reflect the different systems of measurement of length as a physical quantity, we
        will define the ultimate standard for U.S. units of measurement used to verify all masters based
        on the SI (System International d'Unites) units as internationally agreed upon standard units.

        Recently (in 1983), the fundamental unit of *meter* for measuring length was defined[50] as the
        "length of path traveled by light in an interval of 1/299,792,458 seconds."

156.   How should measurement standards be controlled?

        I.   Develop a listing of measurement standards with nomenclature and a number for control.
        II.   Determine calibration intervals and calibration sources for measurement standards.
        III.   Maintain proper environmental conditions and traceability of accuracy to the National
                Bureau of Standards.

        a.   I and II only
        b.   I and III only
        c.   II and III only
        d.   I, II, and III

Key: d.   I, II, and III   (Ref. Applications Question 48, July 1984)
        This is self-explanatory. A measurement control program or gage control program should include
        the steps as shown in I, II, and III.

157. 9.192631770×10^9 cycles of radiation from vaporized cesium 133 (an accuracy of 1 in 10^{12} or 1
        second in 36,000 years) defines the fundamental unit of measure of

---

[50] *Measurement and Calibration for Quality Assurance* by Alan S. Morris, Prentice Hall International (UK), Ltd., 1991,
Chapter 1, pg. 12.

    a.   time in seconds
    b.   length in meters
    c.   mass in kilograms
    d.   temperature in Kelvin

Key: b.   length in meters

158.   The mass of a platinum-iridium cylinder kept in the International Bureau of Weights and Measures, in Sevres, France, defines[51] the fundamental unit of measure of

    a   pound
    b.   liter
    c.   kilogram
    d.   ton

Key: c.   Kilogram

159.   Candela (cd) is defined as

    a.   the current flowing through two infinitely long parallel conductors of negligible cross section placed 1 meter apart in a vacuum and producing a force of 2×10^{-7} Newtons per meter length of conductor
    b.   the luminous intensity in a given direction from a source emitting monochromatic radiation at a frequency of 540 terahertz (10^{12} Hz) and with a radiant density in that direction of 1.4641 mW/steradian
    c.   the number of atoms in a 0.012 kg mass of carbon 12
    d. $9.192631770 \times 10^{9}$ cycles of radiation from vaporized cesium 133 (an accuracy of 1 in 10^{12} or 1 second in 36,000 years)

Key: b.   the luminous intensity in a given direction from a source emitting monochromatic radiation at a frequency of 540 terahertz (10^{12} Hz) and with a radiant density in that direction of 1.4641 mW/steradian

    Choice b[52] defines the Candela (cd).
    Choice a is the definition of an ampere for current.
    Choice c is the definition of mole for matter.
    Choice d is the definition of second for time.

160.   The basic (primary) standard for time (seconds) in SI units (International System of Units) adopted by the U.S. is based on

---

[51] *Measurement and Calibration for Quality Assurance* by Alan S. Morris, Prentice Hall International (UK), Ltd., 1991, Chapter 1, pg. 12.

[52] *Measurement and Calibration for Quality Assurance* by Alan S. Morris, Prentice Hall International (UK), Ltd., 1991, Chapter 1, pg. 12.

a.   the transition between two radiation levels of krypton 86
b.   the time it takes an SI cylinder of platinum-iridium alloy to fall 1 meter
c.   the transition between two radiation levels of the ground state of cesium 133
d.   the time it takes to plate 1 millimeter of silver on an SI cylinder with 1 ampere of current

Key: c.   the transition between two radiation levels of the ground state of cesium -133
(Ref. Principles Question 59, October 1974)
The standard unit of measurement for the physical characteristic such as time is second.[53] It is defined as 9.192631770×10^9 cycles of radiation from vaporized cesium 133 (an accuracy of 1 in 10^{12} or 1 second in 36,000 years).

161.   Which of the following pairs measure the same type of characteristics?

A. Pounds-Kelvin   D. PSI-Grams
B. BTU-Kelvin   E. Fahrenheit-Hectre
C. Pound Force-Newton   F. Acre-grams

a.   A, B, D, and F
b.   A, C, and E
c.   B and C
d.   B, D, and F
e.   A, C, E, and F

Key: c.   B and C   (Ref. Applications Question 46, August 1978)

162.   Which of the following is the symbol for surface finish requirements?

a. λ
b.   M
c. $\sqrt{}$
d.   M/S

e.

Key: c. $\sqrt{}$ (Ref. Applications Question 52, August 1978)

163.   In geometric dimensioning and tolerancing the symbol M means

a.   maximum material condition
b.   use a micrometer to check
c.   machined surface
d.   measure at this point

---

[53] *Measurement and Calibration for Quality Assurance* by Alan S. Morris, Prentice Hall International (UK), Ltd., 1991, Chapter 1, pg. 12 and *Juran's Quality Control Handbook* by J. M. Juran, 4th ed., McGraw-Hill, New York, pg. 18.61.

Key: a. maximum material condition (Ref. Principles Question 49, August 1978)
In geometric dimensioning and tolerancing (GD&T), the symbol "M" means *maximum material condition* or MMC[54] and is defined as the condition where the feature of size contains the maximum amount of material within the stated limits of size. MMC refers to the feature when it is at its worst or most material size. MMC designation, when applied to a given feature such as a hole, thread, etc., indicates that the dimension results in a maximum amount of material within the allowed dimension limits or tolerances. For a hole, the MMC is when the hole diameter is at its smallest specified size. For a thread or bolt, the MMC is when the outside diameter is at its maximum specified size. This means, MMC for an internal dimension is its minimum limit, and for an external dimension, it is the maximum limit.

164. In the drawing tolerance

| θ | 0.005 | Ⓜ | A | B | C |

"C" is the

a. primary datum
b. tertiary datum
c. basic datum
d. largest datum

Key: b. tertiary datum (Ref. Principles Question 50, July 1984)
This is the language of geometric dimensioning and tolerancing (GD&T), a system used to define the dimensions and tolerances for geometric shapes of surfaces and hole locations based on their functions. It uses various symbols with respect to their actual functions to define various dimensions for a part on a drawing. In the question above, you can see the use of various symbols. We will define a few terms here first based on ANSI Y14.5-1982,[55] Dimensioning Standard.

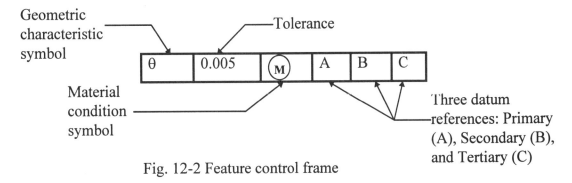

Fig. 12-2 Feature control frame

---

[54] *Dimensioning and Tolerancing*, American National Standard, ANSI Y14.5M -1982, published by American Society of Mechanical Engineers, United Engineering Center, New York, Section 1.2, Definitions, pg. 2.

[55] *Dimensioning and Tolerancing*, American National Standard, ANSI Y14.5M -1982, by American Society of Mechanical Engineers, United Engineering Center, New York, Section 1.2, Definitions, pg. 2, 29-34.

Feature Control Frame: A geometric tolerance for an individual feature is specified by means of a feature control frame divided into compartments containing the geometric characteristic symbol followed by the tolerance. Refer to Fig. 12-2 above, where the long rectangular box is called the *feature control frame*, consisting of four main elements. First, on the left, is a *symbol* that describes the type of control for the dimension. The second item is the *tolerance*, i.e., the tolerance zone for the feature. The third box indicates the *material condition symbol*. The fourth, i.e., the last portion of the frame, is *the reference letter for Datum(s),* and it may contain one letter reference, e.g., letter A, which indicates the *primary datum*. It may contain two compartments with two letter references for datums, e.g., letter A indicates the primary datum A and B indicates the secondary datum B. The question above shows three compartments with letters A, B, and C, which indicates that letter A is the primary datum, B is the secondary datum, and C is the tertiary datum.

Datum: Datum is the surface from which one can start to measure. It is the theoretically exact or perfect plane, line or point. It is the origin from which one can establish the location, dimensions, or other geometric characteristics of a feature on a part. A datum feature is an actual feature on a part from which a datum is established. Datum features on a particular part are real and never imaginary.

165.   The intentional difference in the sizes of mating parts is the

   a.   specification
   b.   clearance
   c.   natural tolerance
   d.   satisfactory functioning

Key: b.   clearance   (Ref. Principles Question 75, October 1972)

166.   Which trigonometric function finds the most use in ordinary angular measurement?

   a.   sine
   b.   cosine
   c.   tangent
   d.   cotangent

Key: a.   sine   (Ref. Principles Question 38, October 1972)

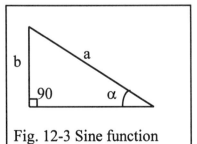

Fig. 12-3 Sine function

The trigonometric sine function of an angle is defined as the ratio of the vertical side opposite the angle, to the hypotenuse, i.e., sine $\alpha = b/a$; as shown in Fig. 12-3.

Angular measurements are convenient to perform using the sine function, which consists of a beam or a "sine bar" of fixed length as dimension a and the gage blocks of different sizes b and a flat plate.

The gage block stack height can be varied to measure the desired angle α. This makes it convenient to measure the angle.

167. To measure an angle on a work piece, the most accurate method would involve use of

    a. a sine bar
    b. a set of plastic triangles
    c. a bevel protractor
    d. none of the above

Key: a. a sine bar   (Ref. Applications Question 16, October 1974)
    See Question 166 above.

168. To measure an angle on a work piece the most accurate method would involve use of

    a. a sine bar
    b. a set of plastic triangles
    c. a bevel protractor
    d. none of the above

Key: a. a sine bar   (Ref. Applications Question 16, October 1974)
    The trigonometric sine function of an angle is defined as the ratio of the vertical side to the hypotenuse, i.e., sine α = b/a, as shown in Fig. 12-3 of Question 166 above.
    Angular measurements are convenient using the sine function, which consists of a beam or a sine bar of fixed length as dimension a, gage blocks of different sizes b, and a flat plate. The gage block stack height can be varied to measure the desired angle α. This makes it convenient to measure the angle. This question is repeated in the October 1972 examination[56] in both the *Principles and Applications sections*.

169. A title block on a drawing does not include which of the following?

    a. information about a part, i.e., part name, part number
    b. product engineer name, designer name, draftsperson name
    c. date released, company logo, and scale of the drawing
    d. footnotes and general notes

Key: d. footnotes and general notes
    Footnotes and general notes are part of a drawing but are not generally part of a title block.

170. Phantom lines are used on a drawing to

    a. show an existing structure that needs some modification or an alternate position of some object

---

[56] *ASQC - CQE Examination*, ASQC Quality Progress, October 1972, Principles section, Question 38, and Applications section, Question 13.

      b.   point or lead from a dimension to the feature or the surface to show where that dimension applies

      c.   show the surface of the part that has been cut as a section

      d.   show the center of an object

Key: a.   show an existing structure that needs some modification or an alternate position of some object

The phantom lines are generally shown as one long and two short dash lines.	—— · · · —— · · · ——
Choice b defines a leader line which looks like a pointer or an arrow.	
Choice c defines section lines which are generally solid lines at a 45 degree angle	
Choice d defines a centerline which is shown as long and short dashes	

171.   Which of the following is true?

      a.   The maximum material condition (MMC) is the largest pin and the largest hole diameter.

      b.   The maximum material condition (MMC) is the largest pin and the smallest hole diameter.

      c.   The maximum material condition (MMC) is the smallest pin and the smallest hole diameter.

      d.   The maximum material condition (MMC) is the smallest pin and the largest hole diameter.

Key: b.   The maximum material condition (MMC) is the largest pin and the smallest hole diameter.
ANSI Y14.5-1982[57] defines the maximum material condition (MMC) as *"a condition in which a feature of the size contains the maximum amount of material within stated limits of size,"* for example, the largest pin and the smallest hole diameter. Here the feature is at its worst or maximum material size and most of the material that is permissible remains there.

172.   Which of the following is true?

      a.   The least material condition (LMC) is the largest pin and the largest hole diameter.

      b.   The least material condition (LMC) is the largest pin and the smallest hole diameter.

      c.   The least material condition (LMC) is the smallest pin and the smallest hole diameter.

      d.   The least material condition (LMC) is the smallest pin and the largest hole diameter.

Key: d.   The least material condition (LMC) is the smallest pin and the largest hole diameter.

---

[57] *Dimensioning and Tolerancing*, American National Standard, ANSI Y14.5M -1982, by American Society of Mechanical Engineers, United Engineering Center, New York, Section 1.3.12.

ANSI Y14.5-1982[58] defines the least material condition (LMC) as *"the condition in which a feature of size contains the least amount of material within the stated limits of size,"* for example, the smallest pin and largest hole diameter. Here the feature is at its least material size and most of the material allowed to be removed is removed.

173. An auxiliary view in a blue print is

a. a view used to show angled or inclined surfaces of a part that cannot be clearly shown in any of the principal views
b. a view that shows every detail of a part when viewed from a particular side
c. a view used to show specific information about a limited area of a part
d. a sectional view that is drawn to identify, isolate, and enlarge special internal details that are not clearly visible in a principal view or another sectional view

Key: a. a view used to show angled or inclined surfaces of a part that cannot be clearly shown in any of the principal views
Choice b defines the complete view, choice c defines the partial view and choice d defines the sectional detail view.

174. Allowance is defined as

a. a numerical value used to describe the theoretically exact size, profile, orientation, or location of a feature or datum target
b. the minimum intentional difference in the size between two mating parts
c. a tolerance that shows the high and low limits of a dimension
d. a tolerance that varies in both directions from a specified dimension

Key: b. the minimum intentional difference in the size between two mating parts
An allowance is used to define the relationship between two mating parts. There are two types of allowances.

1. If two mating parts such as a shaft (male) and a hole (female) can be assembled easily and have some air space between them, it is called a *positive allowance*. Here the male part is smaller than the female part and results in a *clearance fit*.
2. If two mating parts are assembled by using an intentional force and are forced together, it results in a *negative allowance* or *an interference fit*. Here the male part is larger than the female part.

Choice a is a definition of *basic dimension*, as per ANSI Y14.5M-1982.[59] A basic dimension is a numerical value used to describe the theoretically exact size, profile, orientation, or location of a feature or datum target. It is the basis from which permissible variations are established by

---

[58] *Dimensioning and Tolerancing*, American National Standard, ANSI Y14.5M -1982, by American Society of Mechanical Engineers, United Engineering Center, New York, Section 1.3.12.
[59] *Dimensioning and Tolerancing*, American National Standard, ANSI Y14.5M -1982, by American Society of Mechanical Engineers, United Engineering Center, New York, Sections 1.3.2, 1.3.18 and 2.2.

tolerances on other dimensions, in notes or in feature control frames.

ANSI Y14.5M-1982 establishes the practices for general tolerancing. Choice c defines *limit tolerance*. Here the high limit (maximum value) is placed above the low limit (minimum value). Choice d defines *bilateral tolerance*.

175.   A parallax error is

    a.   the difference between the average of multiple measurements and the true value
    b.   getting consistent results repeatedly
    c.   an error in reading a scale on an instrument and the pointer position because of the viewer's eye position or alignment with the pointer
    d.   a direct distance between two lines on a scale

Key: c.   an error in reading a scale on an instrument and the pointer position because of the viewer's eye position or alignment with the pointer
The parallax error occurs when the observer is looking at an angle and is not perpendicular to the the plane of the scale.

Choice a defines accuracy and choice b defines precision. Refer to Questions 72, 73, and 74 above for a detailed discussion.

Choice d defines the discrimination of the measuring equipment. It helps to understand the capability of the measuring equipment to detect the smallest variation in a measured dimension.

ASQC-CQE BIBLIOGRAPHY AND OTHER REFERENCES ON PRODUCT AND MATERIALS CONTROL AND MEASUREMENT SYSTEMS

1. ANSI Y14.5M-1982, *Dimensioning and Tolerancing*, New York, American Society of Mechanical Engineers (ASME), 1982.
2. Besterfield, Dale H., *Quality Control*, 3rd ed., Englewood Cliffs, NJ, Prentice Hall, 1992.
3. Busch, Ted, *Fundamentals of Dimensional Metrology*, 3rd ed., New York, Delmar Publishers, Inc., 1966.
4. Calvin, Thomas W., *How and When to Perform Bayesian Acceptance Sampling*, Volume 7, Milwaukee, ASQC Quality Press, 1990.
5. Feigenbaum, A. V., *Total Quality Control*, 3rd ed. Revised, New York, McGraw-Hill, 1991.
6. Farago, Francis T., *Handbook of Dimensional Measurement,* Englewood Cliffs, NJ, Prentice Hall, 1982.
7. Griffith, Gary, *Quality Technician's Handbook*, New York, John Wiley and Sons, 1986.
8. Juran, Joseph M., *Juran's Quality Control Handbook*, 4th ed., New York, McGraw-Hill, 1988.
9. Juran, J. M. and Frank M. Gryna, *Quality Planning and Analysis*, 3rd ed., New York, McGraw-Hill, 1993.
10. *Measurement Systems Analysis Reference Manual*, published jointly by AIAG/ASQC and GM, Ford and Chrysler Motor Corporation, Southfield, MI, 1990.
11. Morris, Alan S., *Measurement and Calibration for Quality Assurance,* Englewood Cliffs, NJ, Prentice Hall, 1991.
12. Pennella, Robert C., *Managing the Metrology System*, Milwaukee, ASQC Quality Press, 1992.
13. Pyzdek, Thomas and Roger W. Berger, eds., *Quality Engineering Handbook.*, Milwaukee, ASQC Quality Press, 1992.
14. Suntag, Charles, *Inspection and Inspection Management*, Milwaukee, ASQC Quality Press, 1993.
15. Walsh, Wurster and R. J. Kimber, *Quality Management Handbook*, New York, Marcel Dekker and ASQC Quality Press, Milwaukee, 1986.
16. Wheeler, Donald J. and Richard W. Lyday, *Evaluating the Measurement Process*, 2nd ed., Knoxville, TN, SPC Press Inc., 1989.

CHAPTER 13

RELIABILITY, MAINTAINABILITY, AND PRODUCT SAFETY

ASQC'S BODY OF KNOWLEDGE (BOK) FOR THE CQE EXAMINATION

This chapter focuses on the following selected subject areas of BOK from *Section VI, Safety and Reliability.*

Terms and Definitions

Types of Reliability Systems

1. Series
2. Parallel
3. Redundant

Reliability Life Characteristics Concepts (e.g., "bathtub" curve)

Risk Assessment Tools (e.g., FMECA, FMEA, FTA) and Risk Prevention

Product Traceability Systems and Recall Procedures

1.   The term reliability is defined as

   a.   the probability of a product performing a specified function without any failure under specified conditions for a given period of time
   b.   the process of estimating performance
   c.   the probability of a system being restored to functional operation within a given period of time
   d.   all of the above

Key: a.   the probability of a product performing a specified function without any failure under specified conditions for a given period of time

Choices a and c may seem to be similar and you may have to decide which is either true or the better choice. Choice c is incorrect as it defines the term *maintainability* and not reliability. Choice b is incorrect because it does not include the probability, performance, time, and specific conditions.

Note: Questions regarding definitions like the one above are bonus questions. You should focus strongly on the basic definitions of important concepts. You should be able to answer quickly if you have read the definition thoroughly, and understood the meaning, merits, and purpose of the concept(s). You should also be able to understand the language of the definition as it may be reworded, broken into individual statements in different choices, or stated differently than your text reference. When in doubt, you should be able to refer to your reference material quickly and select the true or most appropriate answer.

2.   Product reliability is the probability of a product performing its intended function under the operating conditions encountered. A significant element in this concept includes

   a.   probability
   b.   performance
   c.   time
   d.   environment
   e.   all of the above

Key: e.   all of the above   (Ref. Principles Question 78, August 1978)

Juran[1] defines the term reliability and four key elements as follows.
   I.   a statement about probability as an expression for reliability
   II.   a statement that defines the performance of the product
   III.   a statement of the required operating time between the failures
   IV.   a definition of the environmental conditions in which the system is required to operate

3.   From the definition of reliability, it follows that in any reliability program there must be

   a.   a quantification of reliability in terms of probability
   b.   a clear statement defining successful performance

---

[1] *Juran's Quality Control Handbook* by J. M. Juran, 4th ed., McGraw-Hill, New York, pg. 13.18.

c.   a definition of the environment in which the equipment must operate
d.   a statement of the required operating times between failures
e.   all of the above

Key: e.   all of the above   (Ref. CRE Question 129, February 1976)
      Refer to Questions 1 and 2 above for discussion.

4.   The best way to set an overall reliability goal is to

a.   write a specification calling for a product to have high reliability and incorporate it into a contract
b.   put down specific numerical requirements for reliability with confidence levels and statements of operating environments along with a definition of successful product performance
c.   insist that the goal be expressed in terms of mean time between failures
d.   indicate who is to blame if the desired reliability is not obtained

Key: b.   put down specific numerical requirements for reliability with confidence levels and statements of operating environments along with a definition of successful product performance   (Ref. CRE Question 134, February 1976)
      This choice includes all the important elements for defining reliability as discussed in Questions 2 and 3 above.

5.   Which of the following does not enter into the definition of reliability?

a.   mission time
b.   stress level
c.   age
d.   conditional probability
e.   all of the above are essential

Key: e.   all of the above are essential   (Ref. CRE Question 2, September 1980)

6.   When evaluating parts for high-reliability applications, which of the following is considered to be important?

a.   functional performance requirements
b.   environmental requirements
c.   part usage
d.   all of the above

Key: d.   all of the above   (Ref. CRE Question 10, February 1976)

7.   Reliability is affected by

     a.   design
     b.   production
     c.   fuel service
     d.   user
     e.   all of the above

Key: e.   all of the above   (Ref. CRE Question 16, September 1980)

8.   According to the definition of reliability, performance over the expected or intended life is one criterion. In order to obtain a measurement for reliability, the actual life (t) must be compared to which of the following?

     a.   sampling of components
     b.   test cycles (T)
     c.   required life (T)
     d.   MTBF
     e.   probability of failures (P_t)

Key: c.   required life (T)   (Ref. Applications Question 71, August 1978)
Reliability is defined as the probability that an item will perform a required function under stated conditions for a stated period of time. Hence actual life (t) should be compared to its intended or required life (T) to determine reliability.

9.   "The probability that a failed system will be restored to operable conditions within a specific repair time" is a definition of

     a.   reliability
     b.   maintainability
     c.   availability
     d.   none of the above
     e.   serviceability

Key: d.   none of the above   (Ref. CRE Question 83, September 1980)
Omdahl[2] defines the term *reparability as a probability that a failed system will be restored to operating conditions within a specific repair time*. He also indicates that for overall system effectiveness, maintenance has to be performed per a given schedule. The term reparability is not listed above as a choice.

The key words are "a failed system," which is not a commonly used term in defining either reliability, maintainability, or availability, which are defined below for a repeat study.

10.   Reliability testing of parts is performed to yield which of the following type of information?

---

[2] *Reliability, Availability and Maintainability (RAM) Dictionary* edited by Tracy P. Omdahl, ASQC Quality Press, Milwaukee, WI, 1987, pg. 279.

a. application suitability
b. environmental capability
c. measurement of life characteristics
d. all of the above
e. none of the above

Key: d. all of the above (Ref. Applications Question 69, August 1978)
Reliability is defined as the probability that an item will perform a required function under stated conditions for a stated period of time. Choice a, application suitability, focuses on product performance. Environmental capability in choice b reflects the environmental conditions in which the product has to operate. Measurement of life characteristics in choice c reflects the required operating time between failures. Refer to several questions in the Principles section for the basic concepts.

Reliability is defined as the probability of a product performing a specified function without any failure under specified conditions for a given period of time.

Maintainability is defined as the probability of a system being restored to functional operation within a given period of time.

Availability is defined as the ratio of uptime to total time where total time includes both the uptime and downtime.

11. Inherent or intrinsic reliability

a. is that reliability which can be improved only by design change
b. can be improved only by an improvement in the state of the art
c. is that reliability estimated over a stated period of time by a stated measurement technique
d. is not an estimated reliability

Key: a. is that reliability which can be improved only by design change
(Ref. Principles Question 76, July 1984)
Omdahl[3] defines *inherent reliability as the potential reliability of an item or the potential in its design under realistic and/or stated conditions of use and operation.* Intrinsic reliability means something is inherent in the system. This inherent reliability can only be improved if you change the design or redesign it. Choice c defines the term reliability, but not as intrinsic reliability and b and d are poor choices. This question is repeated in the October 1974 examination.[4]

12. Inherent reliability can be increased by

a. design change

---

[3] *Reliability, Availability and Maintainability (RAM) Dictionary* edited by Tracy P. Omdahl, ASQC Quality Press, Milwaukee, WI, 1987, pg. 157.
[4] *ASQC - CQE Examination*, ASQC Quality Progress, October 1974, Principles section, Question 60.

      b.   training in the manufacturing area

      c.   inspection

      d.   all of the above

Key: a.   design change   (Ref. CRE Question 26, April 1980)
Refer to Question 11 above for discussion.

13.   Reliability prediction is

      a.   the process of estimating performance

      b.   the process of estimating the probability that a product will perform its intended function for a stated time

      c.   the process of telling "how you can get there from here"

      d.   all of the above

Key: b.   the process of estimating the probability that a product will perform its intended function for a stated time   (Ref. Principles Question 77, July 1984)
Reliability prediction is a process of estimating or predicting the reliability in advance of producing the product, and it is applied from the early design phase to the final production stage. The prediction is based on the number of components, past failure data, field performance data, etc. The term reliability prediction hence requires probability, the performance of intended function, and also the time factor or effect of time over some period.

14.   Reliability prediction and measurement is primarily useful in

      a.   evaluating feasibility

      b.   establishing reliability goals

      c.   evaluating overall areas

      d.   defining problem areas

      e.   all of the above

Key: e.   all of the above   (Ref. CRE Question 149, February 1976)
Reliability estimation, prediction, and growth plans are important for each stage of the life cycle of any product. O'Connor[5] states that the reliability prediction for a new product is very important to know before starting actual production. It is not generally possible to make an exact prediction of reliability of any product, but reliability predictions can provide a base for forecasting and evaluating the new product, its costs, failure rates, warranty costs, etc. It can highlight the potential problem areas and critical parts of the design in some failure modes.

The reliability engineer needs to use the information obtained from various tests, field data, etc., on the reliability of components, parts, or materials to estimate the reliability that can be obtained from a given design. It is also necessary to predict the reliability if changes are made in the

---

[5] *Practical Reliability Engineering* by Patrick D.T. O'Connor, 3rd ed., John Wiley and Sons, New York, pg. 110-117.

design or system. The reliability prediction and the data on reliability help in failure rate predictions, system reliability, and availability predictions. Various MIL-Standards[6] define the basic methods of reliability prediction. Ireson and Coombs[7] describe various statistical techniques useful in reliability prediction.

15. Reliability prediction is

    a.   a one-shot estimation process
    b.   a continuous process starting with paper predictions
    c.   a process to be viewed as an end in itself in fulfillment of a contract
    d.   none of the above

Key: b.   a continuous process starting with paper predictions
(Ref. CRE Question 147, February 1976)
Refer to Questions 13 and 14 above for discussion.

16. Defining the product, establishing the reliability model, assigning applicable failure rates to the equipment involved, and computing the reliability for each function and for the product are the principal part of the process for

    a.   predicting reliability
    b.   design review
    c.   defining the program plan
    d.   demonstrating reliability

Key: a.   predicting reliability   (Ref. CRE Question 73, February 1976)
Refer to Questions 13 and 14 above for discussion.

17. Which of the following are not reliability activities?

    a.   design review
    b.   vendor control
    c.   failure reporting
    d.   probabilistic design analysis
    e.   all of the above are reliability activities

Key: e.   all of the above are reliability activities (Ref. CRE Question 24, September 1980)

18. The ratio of probability density function f(t) to reliability R(t) is called

    a.   useful life

---

[6] MIL-HDBK-217, *Reliability Prediction of Electronic Equipment*, MIL-STD-756B, *Reliability Modeling and Prediction*, Department of Defense, Washington, D.C., 1981.

[7] *Handbook of Reliability Engineering and Management* by W. Grant Ireson and Clyde F. Coombs, Jr., McGraw-Hill, New York, 1988, pg. 1.11, 7.19, 10.19-21.

    b.   failure rate

    c.   MTBF

    d.   median

Key: b.   failure rate   (Ref. Principles Question 20, October 1972)

The failure rate is defined as number of failures per unit of time and is denoted as λ. For an exponential distribution, the probability density function is given as $f(t) = \lambda e^{-\lambda t}$ and the reliability R(t) is given as $R(t) = e^{-\lambda t}$. Hence the ratio $\dfrac{f(t)}{R(t)} = \dfrac{\lambda e^{-\lambda t}}{e^{-\lambda t}} = \lambda$.

Ireson and Coombs[8] define the failure rate as *hazard rate* also, and it is the rate at which the items or components in the population will fail at time $t + \Delta t$, if they have survived up to any point in time t.

19.   Failure rate is calculated as a

    a.   probability of survival

    b.   average of secondary failures

    c.   reciprocal of MTTF

    d.   reciprocal of maintainability

Key: c.   reciprocal of MTTF   (Ref. CRE Question 102, February 1976)

The failure rate is defined as number of failures per unit of time and is denoted as λ. It is also denoted as the reciprocal of mean time between failures (MTBF) μ, i.e.,

Failure rate $\lambda = \dfrac{1}{\text{MTBF}} = \dfrac{1}{\mu}$. For detailed reading, refer to Juran.[9]

20.   The ratio of total operating time to total number of failures is

    a.   maintenance action rate

    b.   maintainability

    c.   failure rate

    d.   mean time to failure

    e.   availability

Key: d.   mean time to failure   (Ref. CRE Question 107, February 1976)

MTBF is defined as the mean or the average time between successive failures of a product, assuming that the product is repairable, and is denoted as μ. It is also denoted as the reciprocal of the failure rate λ, i.e., $\mu = 1/\lambda$.

21.   Availability is defined as

---

[8] *Handbook of Reliability Engineering and Management* by W. Grant Ireson and Clyde F. Coombs, Jr., McGraw-Hill, New York, 1988, pg. 19.9-10.

[9] *Juran's Quality Control Handbook* by J. M. Juran, 4th ed., McGraw-Hill, New York, pg. 23.81-87.

a. $\dfrac{\text{Uptime}}{\text{Uptime} + \text{Downtime}}$

b. $\dfrac{\text{MTBF}}{\text{MTBF} + \text{Mean Time To Repair}}$

c. uptime only

d. a and b

e. a, b, and c

Key: d. a and b

Availability is a term that generally depends on time. If a product is in an operative state, then we can use that product when we need it. Juran[10] defines the availability as the two ratios in choices a and b above. In other words, *it is the ratio of the operating time to operating time plus downtime.*

Omdahl[11] defines *availability as the percentage of time or number of occurrences for which a product will operate properly when required.* O'Connor[12] discusses the close relationship between reliability and maintainability and their effect on availability and cost. If the process is in steady state, i.e., it is settled down, and if scheduled maintenance is carried out at a regular rate, availability can be defined as

$$\text{Availability} = \dfrac{\text{MTBF}}{\text{MTBF} + \text{MTTR} + \text{Mean Preventive Maintenance Time}}$$

where MTBF is mean time between failures and MTTR means mean time to repair.

For all repairable systems, Lewis[13] defines system availability as the probability that the system will be operational when needed. He has defined two types of availability: "point availability" is the probability that the system is performing satisfactorily at time t; and "interval availability" is the point availability averaged over some interval of time T.

22. What is the expression for operational availability?

a. operate time/operate time and total downtime

b. active downtime/operate time

c. operated time/total downtime

d. off time/operate time

Key: a. operate time/operate time and total downtime (Ref. CRE Question 90, September 1980)
Refer to Question 21 above for discussion.

23. Availability is always

---

[10] *Juran's Quality Control Handbook* by J. M. Juran, 4th ed., McGraw-Hill, New York, pg. 2.9, 13.41.

[11] *Reliability, Availability and Maintainability (RAM) Dictionary* edited by Tracy P. Omdahl, ASQC Quality Press, Milwaukee, WI, 1987, pg. 19.

[12] *Practical Reliability Engineering* by Patrick D.T. O'Connor, 3rd edition, John Wiley and Sons, New York, pg. 322-323.

[13] *Introduction to Reliability Engineering* by E.E. Lewis, John Wiley and Sons, New York, 1987, pg. 250-252, 265.

     a.   a percentage
     b.   related to operate time
     c.   neither of the above
     d.   both a and b above

Key: d.   both a and b above   (Ref. CRE Question 85, September 1980)
Refer to Questions 21 and 22 above for discussion. As availability is expressed as a ratio, it can be expressed as a percentage.

24.   Uptime can be defined as

     a.   the total time in operative state
     b.   the sum of time spent in active state and in standby state
     c.   the total time in operative and nonoperative states
     d.   a and b
     e.   a, b, and c

Key: d.   a and b
Juran[14] defines *uptime as the total time in operative state, i.e., sum of the time spent in active state and time spent in standby state*. This time is measured from the completion of a repair or recovery action until the next failure.

25.   Specifically, uptime ratio is a measure of

     a.   maintenance action rate
     b.   hazard rate
     c.   maintainability
     d.   availability

Key: d.   availability   (Ref. CRE Question 86, September 1980)

The uptime ratio is expressed as $\dfrac{uptime}{uptime + downtime}$ *and it also defines the term availability.*

Refer to Questions 21, 22, and 24 above for additional discussion.

26.   Downtime can be defined as

     a.   the total time in operative and nonoperative states
     b.   the total time in nonoperative state
     c.   the sum of time spent while waiting for the part and the time under active repair
     d.   a and c both
     e.   b and c both

Key: e.   b and c both
Downtime is defined by Juran[15] as *the total time in nonoperative state* (choice b)*, and the sum of*

---

[14] *Juran's Quality Control Handbook* by J. M. Juran, 4th ed., McGraw-Hill, New York, pg. 2.9, 13.41.

time spent while waiting for the part and the time under active repair (choice c). Omdahl[16] defines *downtime* as *the time the system or the equipment is not available to the user for useful work.* It is the amount of time during which the system or the equipment is not in an operable condition to perform its intended function. Downtime results in a reduced level of availability.

27.   Preliminary hazard analysis

    a.   is a review of safety problems prior to production
    b.   is normally done at a time when there is little design detail
    c.   can be used to identify principal hazards when the product is first conceived
    d.   all of the above

Key: d.   all of the above   (Ref. Principles Question 75, July 1984)
The important word is "preliminary," which means initial, i.e., prior to production, as in choice a. For choice b, it means little design detail or early design stage. Choice c describes "preliminary" as when the product is first conceived.

28.   Maintainability is

    a.   the probability of a system being restored to functional operation within a given period of time
    b.   performing adequate maintenance on a system
    c.   the probability of survival of a system for a given period of time
    d.   maintaining a machine in satisfactory working condition
    e.   none of the above

Key: a.   the probability of a system being restored to functional operation within a given period of
          time   (Ref. Principles Question 78, July 1984)
This is the fundamental definition of "maintainability." ANSI/ASQC Standard A3 (ANSI, 1978) defines *maintainability as the ability of the items under stated conditions to be retained in, or restored to, within a given period of time, a specified state in which it can perform its required functions, when maintenance is performed.* It is also defined as the probability that a system will be restored to operable condition within a specified total downtime. It is a characteristic of design and installation and it contributes to fast and easy maintenance at the lowest life-cycle cost. This is a repeat question with a slight change from the August 1978 examination.[17]

29.   A maintainability group is primarily concerned with

    a.   determining the probability of survival of a system for a given period of time
    b.   establishing the probability of a system being restored to functional operation within a
       given period of time

---

[15] *Juran's Quality Control Handbook* by J. M. Juran, 4th ed., McGraw-Hill, New York, pg. 2.9, 13.41.
[16] *Reliability, Availability and Maintainability (RAM) Dictionary* edited by Tracy P. Omdahl, ASQC Quality Press, Milwaukee, WI, 1987, pg. 79.
[17] *ASQC - CQE Examination*, ASQC Quality Progress, August 1978, Principles section, Question 76.

    c.   performing adequate maintenance on a system

    d.   administration of maintenance supplies inventories

    e.   none of these

Key: b.   establishing the probability of a system being restored to functional operation within a given period of time   (Ref. Principles Question 35, October 1974)
Refer to Question 28 above for discussion.

30.   "Maintainability" is

    a.   the probability that a system will not fail

    b.   the process by which a system is restored to operation after failure

    c.   a characteristic of design and installation

    d.   the time required to restore a system to operation after failure

Key: c.   a characteristic of design and installation (Ref. Principles Question 23, October 1972)
Choice a is incorrect because *maintainability is the probability that a system will be restored to operable condition within a specified total downtime* and not "the probability that a system will not fail." Choice b defines a process and d defines the time, but they do not define the probability. Refer to Questions 28 and 29 above for additional discussion.

31.   Maintainability of equipment may be measured in terms of

    a.   maintenance labor hours

    b.   repair time

    c.   maintenance dollar cost

    d.   all of the above

Key: d.   all of the above   (Ref. Applications Question 18, October 1974)
This question is a repeat question in the October 1972 examination.[18]

32.   The results of a maintainability analysis should include

    a.   depth and frequency of maintenance requirements at each level

    b.   facilities required

    c.   support equipment and tools required

    d.   skill levels and tools required

    e.   all of the above

Key: e.   all of the above   (Ref. CRE Question 84, September 1980)
Refer to Questions 28 to 30, which indicate that maintainability is a characteristic of design and installation. The analysis should include a sound planning for maintainability so that the preventive and corrective actions on the product or equipment can be achieved in a specified time. It requires a careful consideration of magnitude of the maintenance; the facility; tools and

---

[18] *ASQC - CQE Examination*, ASQC Quality Progress, October 1972, Applications section, Question 73.

equipment; and the skills required.

33. Quality assurance plans for computer software packages should include all of the following elements except

    a.   accurate and complete documentation of programs
    b.   test criteria and test procedures
    c.   provision of alternate packages
    d.   testing under real life conditions

Key: c.   provision of alternate packages   (Ref. Principles Question 79, July 1984)
      Choices a, b, and d are important elements of quality assurance plans or quality systems but c is not.

34. Basic sources of reliability data are

    I.   in-plant testing
    II.   field testing
    III.   operation by user

    a.   I and II
    b.   II and III
    c.   I and III
    d.   I, II, and III

Key: d.   I, II, and III   (Ref. Principles Question 80, July 1984)
      All three are important sources for reliability data. Hence choice d is correct.

35. In some reliability models redundancy may take the form of standby elements. What is the major disadvantage of such a model as regards its reliability?

    a.   more costly
    b.   Reliability may be reduced by failure of sensing devices.
    c.   Failure rates are generally high.
    d.   The system is too complex.
    e.   none of these

Key: b.   Reliability may be reduced by failure of sensing devices.
      (Ref. Principles Question 77, August 1978)
      Standby redundancy is defined as a reliability model in which one unit is used as a standby and that unit does not operate continuously. The standby unit is used only when the primary unit fails or is inoperable. If the standby element has not been maintained and monitored, it can reduce standby system reliability significantly.

36. In the failure model rate model shown below, the part of the curve identified as A represents

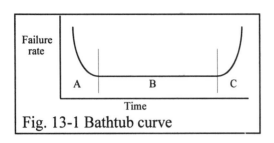

Fig. 13-1 Bathtub curve

a.   the "bathtub" curve
b.   random and independent failures fitting a
      Poisson model
c.   the debugging period for complex equipment
d.   the wearout period

Key: c.   the debugging period for complex equipment
       (Ref. Principles Question 8, October 1972)
       In the case of the *bathtub* curve (Juran[19]), there is a decreasing failure rate for the early burn-in
       period as shown in area A of Fig. 13-1. This represents the debugging period for most complex
       equipment.

37.   Parts in use during the random failure or normal portion of the part life-cycle curve will exhibit

       a.   a constant failure rate
       b.   a decreasing failure rate
       c.   a low failure rate
       d.   an increasing failure rate

Key: a.   a constant failure rate   (Ref. Principles Question 32, October 1974)

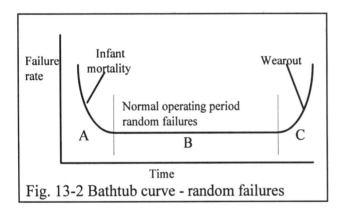

Fig. 13-2 Bathtub curve - random failures

Juran[20] explains the concept of a bathtub
curve and the part life cycle. *Portion B in
Fig. 13-2 describes the normal use or
random failure portion which has a
constant failure rate.* Part A describes the
infant mortality failures with decreasing
failure rate. Part C describes the wearout
failures with increasing failure rate.

38.   Parts in use during the wearout portion of the part life-cycle curve will exhibit

       a.   a constant failure rate
       b.   a decreasing failure rate
       c.   a low failure rate
       d.   an increasing failure rate

Key: d.   an increasing failure rate   (Ref. Principles Question 79, August 1978)
       The wearout portion is shown as portion C in Fig. 13-2, where the product failure rate is an
       increasing rate but not a constant rate. Portion C shows that the failures are due to the product

[19] *Juran's Quality Control Handbook* by J. M. Juran, 4th ed., McGraw-Hill, New York, pg. 23.81-83.
[20] *Juran's Quality Control Handbook* by J. M. Juran, 4th ed., McGraw-Hill, New York, pg. 23.81-83.

wearing out. Juran[21] discusses the bathtub curve and the three zones as infant mortality rate, constant failure rate, and wearout zone.

39.   The failure rate model shown in Fig. 13-3 is used to show a typical relationship of many parts between their failure rate and the time in service. The reliability function for period B is best represented by

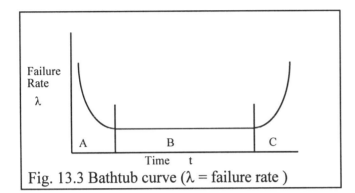

Fig. 13.3 Bathtub curve (λ = failure rate)

a. $R = e^{\lambda t}$
b. $\lambda = at^2 + bt + R$
c. $R(t) = e^{\lambda to}$
d. $R(t) = e^{-\lambda t}$

Key: d. $R(t) = e^{-\lambda t}$ (Ref. Principles Question 54, October 1974)
Juran[22] explains the concept of bathtub curve and the part life cycle. Part B in Fig. 13-3 describes the normal use or random failure portion, which has a constant failure rate and is expressed by $R(t) = e^{-\lambda t}$. Part A describes the infant mortality failures with decreasing failure rate. Part C describes the wearout failures with increasing failure rate.

40.   Unless repair or maintenance action is taken, the probability of failure of a device which has progressed to the point of wearout will

a.   decrease
b.   increase
c.   not change

Key: b.   increase   (Ref. CRE Question 94, February 1976)
Refer to Question 38 above for discussion.

41.   In order to use the exponential reliability function, several conditions must be met. Which one of the following is *not* one of those conditions?

a.   The failure rate is constant.
b.   Occurrence of failures is not affected by failure history.
c.   Failure rate follows the familiar bathtub curve.
d.   Number of failures in a given interval follows a Poisson distribution.

Key: c.   Failure rate follows the familiar bathtub curve. (Ref. CRE Question 18, September 1980)

---

[21] *Juran's Quality Control Handbook* by J. M. Juran, 4th ed., McGraw-Hill, New York, pg. 23.81-83.
[22] *Juran's Quality Control Handbook* by J. M. Juran, 4th ed., McGraw-Hill, New York, pg. 23.81-83.

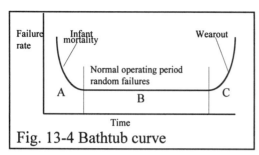

Fig. 13-4 Bathtub curve

Juran[23] explains the concept of the bathtub curve and the part life cycle. Part B in Fig. 13-4 describes the normal use or random failure portion which has a constant failure rate. Part A describes the infant mortality failures with decreasing failure rate. Part C describes the wearout failures with increasing failure rate.

The bathtub curve is discussed in Questions 36 to 39 for a constant failure rate and normal operating period where the failures are random. In the exponential distribution case, the failure rate is assumed to be constant and not varying at different times in the life cycle. All other choices except c are correct for an exponential reliability function.

42. For a high compression aircraft air conditioning system, the MTBF is 100 h. This mean life is allocated to four serial units comprising the total system. The unit failure rates are then weighted as follows:

$W_1 = 0.1250$, $W_3 = 0.1875$, $W_2 = 0.2500$, $W_4 = 0.4375$.

Based upon the above data, indicate which of the following is the correct calculation for one of the units

   a. $\lambda_3 = 0.0018750$
   b. $\lambda_4 = 0.0435700$
   c. $\lambda_1 = 0.0125000$
   d. $\lambda_3 = 0.0001875$
   e. $\lambda_2 = 0.0025100$

Key: a. $\lambda_3 = 0.0018750$ (Ref. Applications Question 72, July 1984)
   Given: MTBF = 100 h, 4 units in series, 4 individual unit failure rates are weighted
   Find: Correct failure rate for one of the units.
   For the system, we have MTBF = 100 h, i.e., $\lambda_s = 1/\text{MTBF} = 1/100 = 0.01$.
   Hence corrected individual failure rates will be as follows:
   $\lambda_1 = W_1 \times \lambda_s = 0.1250 \times 0.01 = 0.001250$; $\lambda_2 = W_2 \times \lambda_s = 0.2500 \times 0.01 = 0.002500$;
   $\boldsymbol{\lambda_3 = W_3 \times \lambda_s = 0.1875 \times 0.01 = 0.001875}$; $\lambda_4 = W_4 \times \lambda_s = 0.4375 \times 0.01 = 0.004375$.
   Hence only choice a is the correct answer. This question has been repeated in the August 1978 examination.[24]

43. What is the reliability of the system at 850 h if the average usage on the system was 400 h for 1650 items and the total number of failures was 145? Assume an exponential distribution.

   a.   0%
   b.   36%

[23] *Juran's Quality Control Handbook* by J. M. Juran, 4th ed., McGraw-Hill, New York, pg. 23.81-83.
[24] *ASQC - CQE Examination*, ASQC Quality Progress, August 1978, Applications section, Question 72.

       c.   18%

       d.   83%

Key: d.   83%   (Ref. Applications Question 73, July 1984)

       Given: Average usage time $\overline{T}$ = 400 h, N = 1650 items, number of failures = 145, exponential
distribution.

       Find: The reliability of the system at t = 850 h, i.e., R(t = 850) = ?

       The failure rate can be calculated as follows: λ = number of failures/total number of failures,
λ = 145/400 ×1650 = 2.19696×10^{-4}

       Hence the reliability at 850 h for an exponential distribution is

       R(t = 850) = $e^{-\lambda t}$ = $e^{-2.19696 \times 10{-4} \times 850}$ = 0.8296 = 0.83 or 83%. Hence choice d is the answer.

       This question is repeated in the CRE September 1980 examination.[25]

44.   For the exponential model, the reliability at mean time to failure is about

       a.   37%

       b.   50%

       c.   63%

       d.   73%

Key: a.   37%   (Ref. Principles Question 21, October 1972)

       Given: Exponential model, t = mean time between failures (MTBF) or μ.

       Find: Reliability at t = MTBF, i.e., R(t = MTBF) = ?

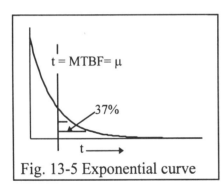

Fig. 13-5 Exponential curve

Method 1: Reliability is given as R(t) = $e^{-t/\mu}$.

If t = MTBF = μ,

R(t = μ) = $e^{-t/\mu}$ = $e^{-\mu/\mu}$. = e^{-1} = 0.3678 = 0.37 = 37%.

This means the exponential reliability model as shown in Fig. 13-5 has 37% of the population above the mean value and 63% below the mean.

Method 2: Refer to the exponential table in the Appendix for t/μ = 1 because t = MTBF = μ.
The table gives area as 0.3678 ≈ 37%.

45.   For the exponential model, the reliability at mean time to fail is about:

       a.   73%

       b.   67%

       c.   50%

       d.   37%

---

[25] *ASQC - CRE Examination*, ASQC Quality Progress, September 1980, Question 49.

Key: d.   37%   (Ref. CRE Question 41, February 1976)
       Given: Exponential model, t = mean time between failures (MTBF) = μ.
       Find: Reliability at t = MTBF, i.e., R(t = MTBF) = ?
       Method 1: Reliability is given as $R(t) = e^{-t/\mu}$.

       At t = MTBF = μ, $R(t = \mu) = e^{-t/\mu} = e^{-1} = 0.3678 \approx 0.37$.
       The exponential reliability model as shown in Fig. 13-5 has 37% of the population above the
       mean value and 63% below the mean.

       Method 2: Refer to the exponential table for t/μ = 1 because t = MTBF = μ. The table gives area
       as 0.3678 $\approx$ 37%.

       Also refer to Question 44 above.

46.   If the mean time between failures is 200 h, what is the probability of surviving for 200 h?

       a.   0.20
       b.   0.90
       c.   0.10
       d.   0.63
       e.   0.37

Key: e.   0.37   (Ref. CRE Question 49, February 1976)
       Refer to Questions 44 to 45 above. The only difference here is that we know the value of t = μ =
       200 h. As seen above, the reliability of surviving for 200 h is 37%, i.e., there is a 37%
       probability that the system/item will survive for 200 h at least, or it will not fail before 200 h.

47.   The MTBF of an equipment is 5000 h. Assuming a constant failure rate, its chance to fail in
       5000 h of operation is

       a.   63%
       b.   37%
       c.   100%
       d.   50%

Key: a.   63%   (Ref. CRE Question 54, September 1980)
       Refer to Questions 44 to 46 above. The only difference here is that we know the value of t = μ =
       5000 h. As seen above, the reliability of the equipment is R(t) = 37% at t = 5000 h. But we are
       looking for the probability that the system will fail in 5000 h; i.e., it will not last up to 5000 h is
       given as F(t) = 1 – R(t) = 1 – 0.37 = 0.63.

48.   A certain component has a constant failure rate, i.e., is exponentially distributed with a mean of
       26 hours. What is the probability of a particular component having a life of less than 26 hours?

       a.   0.5000

    b.   0.6320

    c.   0.3680

    d.   0.6065

    e.   0.3935

Key: b.   0.6320

Refer to Questions 44 to 46 above. The only difference here is that we know the value of $t = \mu = 26$ hrs. As seen above, the reliability of the equipment is $R(t) = 37\%$ at $t = 26$ hrs. But we are looking for the probability that the system will fail in 26 hours, i.e., it will not last up to 26 hours or it has life less than 26 hours is given as $F(t) = 1 - R(t) = 1 - 0.37 = 0.63$.

49.   If the mean time between failures is 200 h, what is the probability of surviving for 2000 h?

    a.   0.20

    b.   0.90

    c.   0.10

    d.   less than 0.01 percent

    e.   0.36

Key: d.   less than 0.01 percent   (Ref. CRE Question 50, February 1976)

Given: MTBF $= \mu = 2000$ h, i.e., $\lambda = 1/200$; $t = 2000$ h, assume *exponential distribution for a constant failure rate.*

Find: Probability of surviving, i.e., $R(t = 2000)$?

For an exponential reliability distribution, $R(t) = e^{-\lambda t}$ and substituting the values

$R(t) = R(t) = e^{-\lambda t} = e^{-(1/200)(2000)} = 4.54 \times 10^{-5}$ or 0.0045%, which is less than 0.01%.

The answer in the ASQC set is choice c as 0.10, which is likely to be a typographical error.

50.   Given mean time to failure for three components as $m_1 = 100$ h, $m_2 = 500$ h, $m_3 = 1000$ h, what is the mean time to failure of the system if the three components are in series?

    a.   1600 h

    b.   100 h

    c.   77 h

    d.   0.013 h

    e.   1000 h

Key: c.   77 h   (Ref. CRE Question 59, February 1976)

Given: $m_1 = 100$ h, $m_2 = 500$ h, $m_3 = 1000$ h, three components in series.

Find: MTBF for system.

Assumption: Assume exponential distribution as MTBF is constant for each component.

$m_1 = 100$ h   the failure rate $\lambda_1 = 1/100 = 0.01$

$m_2 = 500$ h   the failure rate $\lambda_2 = 1/500 = 0.002$

$m_3 = 1000$ h   the failure rate $\lambda_3 = 1/1000 = 0.001$

For three components in series, the failure rate for the system will be

$\lambda_{sys} = \lambda_1 + \lambda_2 + \lambda_3 = 0.01 + 0.002 + 0.001 = 0.013$.
Hence the system MTBF will be $MTBF_{sys} = 1/\lambda_{sys} = 1/0.013 \approx 77$ h.

51.   The lives of a certain component are normally distributed with mean 26 h and standard deviation of 2 h. What is the probability of a particular component having a life of less than 21 h?

   a.   0.994
   b.   0.988
   c.   0.006
   d.   0.012

Key: c.   0.006   (Ref. CRE Question 123, September 1980)

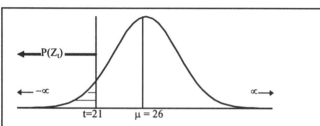

Fig. 13-6 Area under the normal distribution for t > 21

Given: $t = 21$ h, $\mu = 26$ h, and $\sigma = 2$ h,
Find: $P(t < 21$ h$)$.
Refer to Fig. 13-6.
Reliability $R(t) = P(t < 21$ h$)$ can be found as $P(Z_t)$ using the Z table values.

Calculate Z: $Z_t = \dfrac{t - \mu}{\sigma} = \dfrac{21 - 26}{2} = -2.5$.
From the Z table: $P(Z_t < -2.5) = 0.0062$.

52.   If a test is run for 500 h and five failures are observed during this period, what is the mean time between failures?

   a.   500 h
   b.   5 h
   c.   0.02 h
   d.   2500 h
   e.   100 h

Key: e.   100 h   (Ref. CRE Question 62, February 1976)
        Given: 5 failures, 500 h.
        Find: MTBF
        MTBF = Total time/number of failures = 500/5 = 100 h.

53.   Assuming an exponential failure distribution, the probability of surviving an operating time equal to twice the MTBF is

   a.   practically zero
   b.   about 14 percent
   c.   about 36 percent
   d.   none of the above

Key: b.   about 14 percent   (Ref. CRE Question 119, February 1976)

Given: MTBF $= \mu$ hrs, i.e., $\lambda = 1/\mu$; time $t = 2\mu$ hrs exponential distribution for a constant failure rate.

Find: Probability of surviving, i.e., $R(t = 2\mu)$?

Method 1: For an exponential reliability distribution, $R(t) = e^{-\lambda t}$ and $\lambda = 1/\mu$, and substituting values, $R(t) = e^{-\lambda t} = e^{-(1/\mu)(2\mu)} = 0.135 \approx 0.14$ or about 14%.

Method 2: From the exponential table, for $t/\mu = 2$, we get $R(t) = 0.1353$ as the reliability of surviving an operating time equal to twice the MTBF.

54.   If the reliability of a component to survive for 200 h is 95%, what is its mean time between failures? Assume exponential distribution.

    a.   200 h
    b.   2000 h
    c.   400 h
    d.   4000 h

Key: d.   4000 h.

Given: $R(t = 200 \text{ h}) = 0.95$, $t = 200$ h.

Find: MTBF or μ.

Method 1:   Using the exponential table: $R(t) = 0.95$ occurs at $t/\mu = 0.05$ approximately. And $t = 200$ h, substituting we get: $200/\mu = 0.05$, then, $\mu = 200/0.05 = 4000$ h.

Method 2:   Using the equation for reliability: $R(t) = e^{-t/\mu}$ and substituting values we get $0.95 = e^{-t/\mu} = e^{-200/\mu}$.
Now take natural log on both sides: $-0.051 = -200/\mu$
and solve for μ, i.e., $\mu = 3899$ or approximately 4000 h.

55.   Failure rates in the exponential case

    a.   are multiplied together for independent events
    b.   are summed to combine independent series elements in reliability analysis
    c.   continually decrease
    d.   increase to the mean value and then decrease
    e.   are used to evaluate goodness-of-fit

Key: b.   are summed to combine independent series elements in reliability analysis
(Ref. CRE Question 22, September 1980)
If a system has n independent components or parts in series and each part follows the exponential distribution, then the system reliability R_s is given as

$$R_s = R_1 \times R_2 \times R_3 \times \ldots \times R_n = e^{-\lambda_1 t_1} \times e^{-\lambda_2 t_2} \times e^{-\lambda_3 t_3} \ldots \times e^{-\lambda_n t_n}.$$
$$= e^{-(\lambda_1 t_1 + \lambda_2 t_2 + \lambda_3 t_3 + \ldots + \lambda_n t_n)}.$$

If the time t is same for each part, then we can rewrite the above equation as

$$R_s = e^{-t(\lambda_1 + \lambda_2 + \lambda_3 + \ldots + \lambda_n)} = e^{-t \Sigma \lambda_I}.$$

Hence when the failure rate λ_i is constant for each component, and they follow an exponential distribution, then the reliability prediction of the system can be made by adding the individual failure rates of the components.

56.   In order to attain a high order of series reliability,

     a.   the number of parts must be kept to a minimum
     b.   the number of parts must be increased
     c.   the number of parts must be squared and the standard deviation computed
     d.   the number of parts is insignificant if each part has a reliability of 95 percent or more

Key: a.   the number of parts must be kept to a minimum
(Ref. CRE Question 27, February 1976)
If n parts are in a series, then the system reliability R_s is the product of the individual reliabilities of n parts within the system, i.e., $R_s = R_1 \times R_2 \times R_3 \times \ldots \times R_n$.

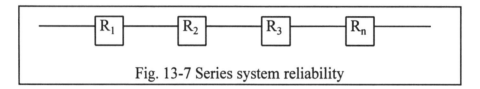

Fig. 13-7 Series system reliability

In a series type of system, as shown in Fig. 13-7, if any one part fails, the whole system will fail and the overall system reliability R_s will be lower than the individual component reliabilities. Hence the system should have a minimum number of parts to achieve overall high reliability in case of series reliability.

Juran[26] discusses the economics of reliability improvements and actions required to improve the design. The reliability engineer should develop alternatives for improving the reliability and should eliminate the parts that are not reliable or not required for meeting the user needs.

57.   Availability of a system is roughly the

     a.   product of the individual subsystem availabilities
     b.   sum of the individual system availabilities
     c.   difference of the individual subsystem availabilities
     d.   quotient of the individual subsystem availabilities

Key: a.   product of the individual subsystem availabilities
(Ref. CRE Question 87, September 1980)
This is true mainly when the individual components are in series. If n parts are in series, then the system availability (or reliability) R_s is the product of the individual reliabilities of n parts within the system, i.e., $R_s = R_1 \times R_2 \times R_3 \times \ldots \times R_n$. Hence no other choices except choice a are applicable.

[26] *Juran's Quality Control Handbook* by J. M. Juran, 4th ed., McGraw-Hill, New York, pg. 13.38-40; 23.90-91.

58.   An expression for three components in series with component reliability R is

        a. R^3
        b. $3R$
        c. $3R - 3R^2 + R^3$
        d. $[1 - (1 - R)^2] \times R$
        e. $(1 - R)^3$

Key: a. R^3 (Ref. CRE Question 60, February 1976)
        If three parts are in a series, as shown in Fig. 13-8 below, the system reliability R_s is the product
        of the individual reliabilities of three parts within the system, i.e.,

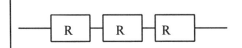

Fig. 13-8 Series reliability for three components	$R_s = R_1 \times R_2 \times R_3 = R \times R \times R = R^3.$

59.   A reliability expression for three independent components in series with component reliability R
        is

        a. $3R$
        b. $3R - 3R^2 + R^3$
        c. $[1 - (1 - R)^2] + 2$
        d. $(1 - R)^3$
        e.   none of the above

Key: e.   none of the above   (Ref. CRE Question 41, September 1980)
        Refer to Question 58 above, where the system reliability R_s is given as $R_s = R^3$, which is not
        listed above.

60.   Component 1 has an exponential failure rate of 3×10^{-4} failures per hour. Component 2 is
        normally distributed with a mean of 600 hours and standard deviation of 200 hours. Refer to Fig.
        13-9 below. Assuming independence, calculate the reliability of the system after 200 hours.

        Fig. 13-9 Two components in series

        a.   0.878
        b.   0.918
        c.   0.940
        d.   0.977

Key: b.   0.918   (Ref. Applications Question 67, October 1972)
        Given: Component 1: exponentially distributed with $\lambda = 3 \times 10^{-4}$ failures per hour.

Component 2: normally distributed with μ = 600 hours and σ = 200 h.

Find: R_{sys} at t = 200 h.

First draw the pictures for exponential and normal distribution for the required probability at t = 200 h as shown in Fig. 13-10 a and b.

Reliability for component 1 will be $R_1 = e^{-\lambda t} = e^{-(3 \times 10^{-4} \times 200)} = 0.94176$.

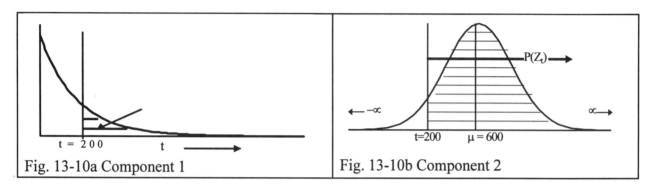

| Fig. 13-10a Component 1 | Fig. 13-10b Component 2 |

Reliability for component 2 = P(t > 200) = 1 − P(t ≤ 200).

$$Z_t = \frac{t - \mu}{\sigma} = \frac{200 - 600}{200} = -2 .$$

From the Z table you get P($Z_t \le -2$) = 0.0228.   The area P($Z_t > -2$) = 1 − 0.0228 = 0.9772.

$R_{sys} = R_1 \times R_2 = 0.94176 \times 0.9772 = 0.9202$

61.   Given components with the following reliabilities, R_1 = 0.99, R_2 = 0.98, R_3 = 0.97, determine the following system reliability as shown in Fig. 13-11.

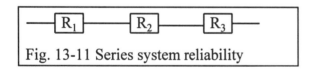

Fig. 13-11 Series system reliability

        a. R_s = 0.96
        b. R_s = 0.97
        c. R_s = 0.94
        d. R_s = 0.999994
        e. R_s = 0.000006

Key: c. R_s = 0.94   (Ref. CRE Question 51, February 1976)
       Given: R_1 = 0.99, R_2 = 0.98, R_3 = 0.97 for a series system.
       Find: R_s
       $R_s = R_1 \times R_2 \times R_3 = 0.99 \times 0.98 \times 0.97 = 0.94$.

62.   If a system reliability of 0.998 is required, what reliability of two components in series is required?

        a. R_c = 0.99
        b. R_c = 0.999

    c. $R_c = 0.98$
    d. $R_c = 0.9999$
    e. $R_c = 0.998$

Key: b. $R_c = 0.999$ (Ref. CRE Question 56, February 1976)
        Given: Two components in series; $R_s = 0.998$.
        Find: Reliability of components.
        Assumption: We have to assume that *both the components have equal reliability R.*
        For two components in series, the product rule states $R_s = R \times R = R^2$.
        We have $R^2 = 0.998$ and taking the square root, the component reliability will be $R = 0.999$.

63.   An expression for three components in parallel with component reliability R is

        a. R^3
        b. $3R$
        c. $3R - 3R^2 + R^3$
        d. $[1 - (1 - R)^2] \times R$
        e. $(1 - R)^3$

Key: c. $3R - 3R^2 + R^3$ (Ref. CRE Question 61, February 1976)

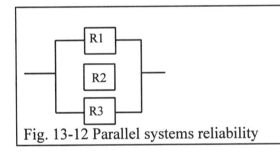

Fig. 13-12 Parallel systems reliability

Fig. 13-12 shows three components in parallel. The system reliability R_s is given as:
$R_s = 1 - (1 - R_1)(1 - R_2)(1 - R_3)$.
The reliability of each component is R. Hence
$R_s = 1 - (1 - R)(1 - R)(1 - R)$
$= 1 - [1 - 3R + 3R^2 - R^3]$
$= 3R - 3R^2 + R^3$.

The parallel system increases the system reliability by introducing the *redundancy,* and here the system operates if at least one of its components is operating. This question is also repeated in the September 1980 CRE examination.[27]

64.   Given components with the following reliabilities, $R_1 = 0.99$, $R_2 = 0.98$, determine the following system reliability as shown in Fig. 13-13.

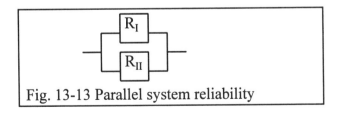

Fig. 13-13 Parallel system reliability

        a. $R_s = 0.97$
        b. $R_s = 0.9998$
        c. $R_s = 0.03$
        d. $R_s = $ less than 0.01 percent
        e. $R_s = 0.99$

Key: b. $R_s = 0.9998$ (Ref. CRE Question 52, February 1976)

---

[27] *ASQC - CRE Examination,* ASQC Quality Progress, September 1980, Question 44.

Given: $R_1 = 0.99$, $R_2 = 0.98$, for a parallel system.
Find: R_s
For a parallel system, $R_s = 1 - [(1 - R_1)(1 - R_2)] = 1 - [(1 - 0.99)(1 - 0.98)] = 0.9998$.

65.   The probability of an accident for the head event H shown in Fig. 13-14 below is

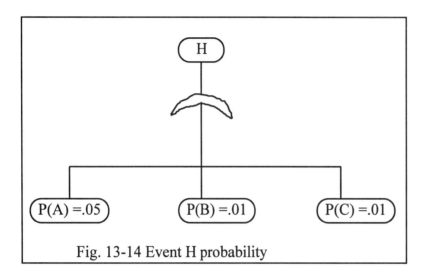

a.   0.1125
b.   0.0689
c.   0.1100
d.   none of the above

Fig. 13-14 Event H probability

Key: b.   0.0689   (Ref. Applications Question 74, July 1984)
        Given: $P(A) = 0.05$, $P(B) = 0.01$, and $P(C) = 0.01$ three units in parallel.
        Find: $P(H)$ for the whole system.
        The reliability of the parallel system having 3 units is given as
        $R_s = P(H) = 1 - [\{1 - R_A\}\{1 - R_B\}\{1 - R_C\}]$
        $\qquad\qquad = 1 - [\{1 - P(A)\}\{1 - P(B)\}\{1 - P(C)\}]$
        $\qquad\qquad = 1 - [\{1 - 0.05\}\{1 - 0.01\}\{1 - 0.01\}] = 0.0689$.

66.   Find the predicted system reliability for the three parts shown if the individual part reliability is
        90% each for a specified mission time and mission conditions:

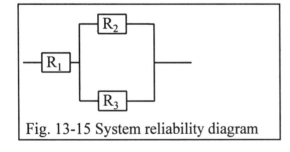

a.   72.9%
b.   70%
c.   99.9%
d.   89.1%
e.   90%

Fig. 13-15 System reliability diagram

Key: d.   89.1%   (Ref. Applications Question 68, October 1974)
        Given: Three parts block diagram, each with reliability of $R_1 = R_2 = R_3 = 0.90$.
                Parts P_2 and P_3 are in parallel and part P_1 in series with P_2 and P_3.
        Find: System reliability $R_{sys} = R_{123}$?
        Refer to Fig. 13-15 above. First calculate R_{23} = reliability for P_2 and P_3 in parallel.

R_{23} $= 1 - [(1 - R_2)(1 - R_3)] = 1 - [(1 - 0.9)(1 - 0.9)]$
$= 1 - 0.01 = 0.99.$

Now R_1 and R_{23} are series reliability given as
$R_{123} = R_1 \times R_{23} = 0.9 \times 0.99 = 0.891 = 89.1\%.$

67.   The reliability of the circuit in Fig. 13-16 is:

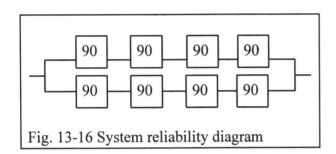

Fig. 13-16 System reliability diagram

a.   19 percent approximately
b.   0.8029
c.   0.4439
d.   0.8817

Key: d.   0.8817   (Ref. CRE Question 26, February 1976)

Given: A circuit diagram consisting of two parallel circuits of four components in series, component reliability for each component = 90, i.e., 90% or 0.90.

Find: System reliability R_s for the whole circuit.

Each component has R = 0.90. Fig. 13-17a and b shows the breakdown of two series I and II and their parallel relationship.

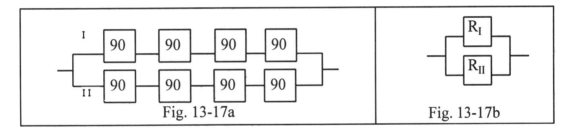

Fig. 13-17a   Fig. 13-17b

Using the product rule for series systems
$R_I = R_1 \times R_2 \times R_3 \times R_4 = 0.9 \times 0.9 \times 0.9 \times 0.9 = 0.6561$
$R_{II} = R_5 \times R_6 \times R_7 \times R_8 = 0.9 \times 0.9 \times 0.9 \times 0.9 = 0.6561$
And for parallel systems between I and II,
$R_s = 1 - [(1 - R_I)(1 - R_{II})] = 1 - [(1 - 0.6561)(1 - 0.6561)] = 1 - (0.3439)^2 = 0.8817.$

68.   Given components with the following reliabilities, $R_1 = 0.99$, $R_2 = 0.98$, $R_3 = 0.97$, determine the following system reliability as shown in Fig. 13-18.

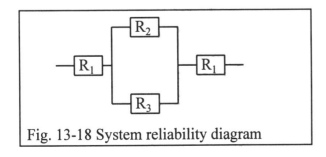

Fig. 13-18 System reliability diagram

a. $R_s = 0.97$
b. $R_s = 0.90$
c. $R_s = 0.93$
d. $R_s = 0.98$
e. $R_s = 0.99$

Key: d. $R_s = 0.98$ (Ref. CRE Question 53, February 1976)
        Given: $R_1 = 0.99$, $R_2 = 0.98$, $R_3 = 0.97$ for a series-parallel-series system.
        Find: R_s
        $R_s = R_1 \times [1 - (1 - R_2)(1 - R_3)] \times R_1 = 0.99 \times [1 - (1 - 0.98)(1 - 0.97)] \times 0.99$
        $$= 0.99 \times 0.9994 \times 0.99 = 0.9795 \approx 0.98.$$

69.   Given components with the following reliabilities, $R_1 = 0.99$, $R_2 = 0.98$, $R_3 = 0.97$, determine the following system reliability as shown in Fig. 13-19.

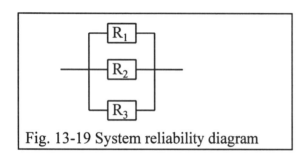

Fig. 13-19 System reliability diagram

a. $R_s = 0.99$
b. $R_s = 0.94$
c. $R_s = 0.9994$
d. $R_s = 0.999994$
e. $R_s = 0.99994$

Key: d. $R_s = 0.999994$ (Ref. CRE Question 54, February 1976)
        Given: $R_1 = 0.99$, $R_2 = 0.98$, $R_3 = 0.97$ for a parallel system.
        Find: R_s
        $R_s = 1 - [(1 - R_1)(1 - R_2)(1 - R_3)] = 1 - [(1 - 0.99)(1 - 0.98)(1 - 0.97)] = 0.999994.$

70.   Given components with the following reliabilities, $R_1 = 0.99$, $R_2 = 0.98$, $R_3 = 0.97$, determine the following system reliability as shown in Fig. 13-20.

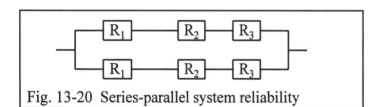

Fig. 13-20 Series-parallel system reliability

a. $R_s = 0.94$
b. $R_s = 0.999994$
c. $R_s = 0.9964$
d. $R_s = 0.8836$
e. $R_s = 0.999964$

Key: c. $R_s = 0.9964$ (Ref. CRE Question 55, February 1976)
        Given: $R_1 = 0.99$, $R_2 = 0.98$, $R_3 = 0.97$ for a series-parallel system.
        Find: R_s
        $R_s = 1 - [(1 - R_1 R_2 R_3)(1 - R_1 R_2 R_3)]$
        $= 1 - [(1 - 0.99 \times 0.98 \times 0.97)(1 - 0.99 \times 0.98 \times 0.97)] = 0.9965.$

71.   The greatest contribution of a reliability effort is made in the

    a.   design area
    b.   manufacturing area
    c.   shipping area
    d.   field service area

Key: a.   design area   (Ref. Principles Question 74, July 1984)

This is prevention. Also, it is most economical to evaluate the design thoroughly in its early stages of the development for quality and reliability. An early design failure mode and effects analysis (DFMEA) can highlight the design failure modes and design weaknesses or sensitivity to customer requirements. It can force the redesign of the part if necessary based on the adverse consequences of failure.

Choices b, c, and d are obviously poor choices and can be easily ruled out. The main reason is that each of them indicates a reactionary approach based on *detection* instead of *prevention*. The effectiveness of the contribution of reliability decreases in manufacturing, shipping, and field service since it is difficult to make major changes in design economically. This question is repeated in the CRE examination.[28]

72.   Reliability, maintainability, and product safety improvements are most often economically accomplished during the _____ phase of a program.

    a.   design and development
    b.   prototype test
    c.   production
    d.   field operation
    e.   redesign and retrofit

Key: a.   design and development   (Ref. Principles Question 80, August 1978)
    The design and development phases are generally the earliest phases of a product program. The product design must consider the reliability, maintainability, and product safety improvement areas along with the cost, time, and other program objectives. The product design function needs to account for and evaluate each failure mode and try to design the failures out, i.e., make designs *robust or nonsensitive* to field uses, abuses, and failures. This will result in the economical manufacture of a quality product. Juran[29] discusses in detail the design phase, prototype phase, and concept of design reviews during product development as a part of quality planning.

73.   Design reviews should be held

    a.   during the design phase
    b.   at each critical design program milestone
    c.   at least once per year
    d.   after the design is completed

Key: b.   at each critical design program milestone (Ref. CRE Question 77, September 1980)
    Refer to Questions 71 and 72 for discussion.

74.   Of the following, which is the most important reliability principle?

    a.   Use only proven designs.

---

[28] *ASQC - CRE Examination*, ASQC Quality Progress, February 1976, Question 131.
[29] *Juran's Quality Control Handbook* by J. M. Juran, 4th ed., McGraw-Hill, New York, pg. 13.4-8.

     b.   Specify only high reliability components.
     c.   Consider reliability early in the design phase.
     d.   Use redundancy throughout the design.
     e.   Have an adequate reliability staff.

Key: c.   Consider reliability early in the design phase.
        (Ref. Principles Question 96, September 1980)
        Refer to Questions 71 to 73 above for discussion.

75.   Design reviews are made to assure that the design can be fabricated at the lowest possible cost and perform successfully under end-use conditions. Good design reviews require

     a.   exclusion of personnel external to the company
     b.   exclusion of engineers who had no connection with the proposed design
     c.   exclusion of manufacturing and quality control personnel who had nothing to do with the design
     d.   documentation

Key: d.   documentation   (Ref. CRE Question 150, February 1976)
        This can be answered easily by eliminating each choice except choice d.

76.   It is of primary importance that the choice of the time-to-failure distribution to represent a particular reliability situation should be based on

     a.   convenience
     b.   simplicity of use
     c.   empirical grounds
     d.   good representation of the underlying physical failure mechanism, if known

Key: d.   good representation of the underlying physical failure mechanism, if known
        (Ref. CRE Question 90, February 1976)
        The question is describing the time-to-failure distribution, i.e., a distribution of a possible failure mode and its probability of occurrence. Choice d is the only choice that includes a study of the physical failure mechanism, and not the convenience or simplicity to use alone, or the mere reliance on empirical grounds, i.e., on observations or experiences.

77.   A reliability test conducted during the preproduction stage is called a(n)

     a.   demonstration test
     b.   acceptance test
     c.   significance test
     d.   qualification test

Key: d.   qualification test   (Ref. Applications Question 84, October 1972)

Juran[30] defines the reliability *qualification test* as the test conducted on the product during the earlier phases of new product development or during preproduction, and it represents the production intent designs. The qualification test provides a degree of assurance that the product will meet customer requirements during its production. Ireson and Coombs[31] define two types of qualification testing as follows:

(a) *Margin tests to assure that the failures extent and threshold are beyond the specified conditions for the product use.*

(b) *Life tests to find patterns of failures which may not be detectable during pre-production as the probability of occurrence may not be too frequent.*

78. Specifications are written on parts to

    a.   enable procurement to buy parts
    b.   establish mechanical, functional, environmental, and reliability requirements
    c.   provide inspection criteria
    d.   serve as a communication to the part supplier

Key: b.   establish mechanical, functional, environmental, and reliability requirements
      (Ref. CRE Question 14, February 1976, and CRE Question 67, September 1980)
      The specifications communicate the "*whats*" of the product, i.e., the requirements of the product in terms of mechanical, dimensional, functional, environmental, and reliability requirements. Hence choice b is the most appropriate, as compared to the other choices above.

79. Which of the following may be uncovered as a result of failure analysis during the development phase of a program?

    a.   mechanical design weaknesses
    b.   part application or circuit design problems
    c.   assembly or workmanship problems
    d.   all of the above

Key: d.   all of the above   (Ref. CRE Question 8, February 1976)
      Failure mode and effects analysis is likely to uncover the failure modes in both the product design as well as the manufacturing process design. It may force the product engineer to explore ways to make the current design as insensitive to adverse consequences of the failure modes as possible or to consider a redesign to develop a robust design of the product. Similarly, the process or manufacturing engineer needs to evaluate the possible failure modes of the process and explore ways of error-proofing and simplifying the processing methods in order to minimize the adverse consequences of variation during manufacturing operations. This can make the manufacturing process robust. For additional reading, you can refer to Juran[32] which will also be

---

[30] *Juran's Quality Control Handbook* by J. M. Juran, 4th ed., McGraw-Hill, New York, pg. 13.34-35.

[31] *Handbook of Reliability Engineering and Management* by W. Grant Ireson and Clyde F. Coombs, Jr., McGraw-Hill, NewYork, 1988, pg. 9.14-16.

[32] *Juran's Quality Control Handbook* by J. M. Juran, 4th ed., McGraw-Hill, New York, pg. 13.28-30.

helpful for many similar questions in this chapter.

80.   A first step in the FMECA is to

       a.   define the system requirements
       b.   compile a critical items list
       c.   identify failure modes
       d.   establish ground rules to which the FMEA is performed

Key: a.   define the system requirements (Ref. CRE Question 46, February 1976)
       This is the first step similar to the design of experiments or any problem-solving tool. In such
       tools we first need to define the purpose, the objective, or the definition of the problem, the
       response variable, and the system requirements.

81.   Failure mode analysis is a good technique to achieve

       a.   a constant failure rate
       b.   only wearout failures
       c.   a minimum of failures
       d.   a reduction in test time

Key: c.   a minimum of failures   (Ref. CRE Question 120, February 1976)
       The failure mode analysis evaluates all possible potential failure modes in a system, their
       probability of occurrence, degree of severity, and likelihood of detection. It leads to exploring
       ways to minimize the number of failures or its occurrence and improving the likelihood of
       detection by taking appropriate design actions.

82.   A Failure Modes and Effects Analysis

       a.   can best be conducted with a digital computer
       b.   requires a knowledge of Boolean algebra
       c.   is a qualitative technique
       d.   is a quantitative technique

Key: c.   is a qualitative technique   (Ref. CRE Question 60, September 1980)
       Choice c is more appropriate because it generally involves a multidisciplinary team to evaluate
       the possible failure modes, and its probability of occurrence based on the past data on warranty,
       scrap, field reports, or failures, etc., and reliability estimation or prediction of the available
       design. Many industries and books[33] try to quantify these elements of analysis on a scale of 1-10
       and define the overall Risk Priority Number (RPN) which may sound like a quantitative

---

[33] *Juran's Quality Control Handbook* by J. M. Juran, 4th ed., McGraw-Hill, New York, pg. 13.28-30; *Practical
Reliability Engineering* by Patrick D.T. O'Conner; 3rd edition, John Wiley and Sons, New York, pg. 146-152; *Handbook
of Reliability Engineering and Management* by W. Grant Ireson and Clyde F. Coombs, Jr., McGraw Hill, New York,
1988, pg. 10.12-10.16; and *Potential FMEA Reference Manual* by AIAG/ASQC, GM/Ford/Chrysler as an automotive
industry standard.

analysis but it is largely qualitative in nature. Refer to Questions 79 to 81 above for discussion.

83.   Failure modes

   a.   are very consistent among components of a given product class, i.e., pumps, transformers, integrated circuits
   b.   are well documented in military and industry handbooks
   c.   can vary dramatically due to changes in use applications
   d.   are easy to determine for any product class
   e.   are difficult to determine for any product class

Key: c.   can vary dramatically due to changes in use applications
(Ref. CRE Question 59, September 1980)
The user variation and, in some cases, a possible abuse of the product have to be evaluated as sources of failure mode. Refer to Questions 79 to 82 above for discussion.

84.   FMECA is

   a.   an organization referred to as the fraternal members of engineering and associates
   b.   a formal technique for review of failure potentials during design
   c.   a technique to assure that design performance guidelines are fulfilled
   d.   primarily useful for space-government projects

Key: b.   a formal technique for review of failure potentials during design
(Ref. CRE Principles Question 125, February 1976)
FMECA means failure mode, effect, and criticality analysis. Refer to Questions 79 to 83 above for discussion.

85.   Analysis of the specific causes of failure is called

   a.   mathematical model building
   b.   mean time between failures
   c.   failure mode analysis
   d.   apportionment analysis

Key: c.   failure mode analysis   (Ref. CRE Question 40, February 1976)
Refer to Questions 79 to 83 above for discussion.

86.   A comprehensive failure analysis and corrective action feedback loop must determine

   a.   what failed
   b.   how it failed
   c.   why it failed
   d.   all of the above

Key: d.   all of the above   (Ref. CRE Question 44, February 1976)
      Refer to Questions 79 to 83 above for discussion.

87.   Failure modes and effects analysis involves what activity?

       a.   the determination of the probability of failure in a specified period of time
       b.   the expected number of failures in a given time interval
       c.   the study of the physics of failure to determine exactly how a product fails and what
              causes the failure
       d.   a study of the probability of success in a given time period
       e.   none of the above

Key: c.   the study of the physics of failure to determine exactly how a product fails and what
              causes the failure   (Ref. CRE Question 62, September 1980)
      Refer to Questions 79 to 83 above for discussion.

88.   Failure modes and effects analysis is a good technique to achieve

       a.   a constant failure rate
       b.   only wearout failures
       c.   a minimum of failures
       d.   reduction in test time

Key: c.   a minimum of failures   (Ref. CRE Question 63, September 1980)
      Refer to Questions 79 through 83 above for discussion.

89.   The criticality analysis

       a.   is part of the FMECA
       b.   identifies critical hardware items
       c.   identifies safety problem areas
       d.   all of the above

Key: d.   all of the above   (Ref. CRE Question 64, September 1980)
      Refer to Questions 79 through 83 above for discussion.

90.   The failure data collection, analysis, and corrective action system

       a.   should include failures due to equipment failure and those due to human error in
              designing, manufacturing, and operating the equipment
       b.   should include elapsed operating time (or cycles) prior to failure
       c.   should include all failures from initial development through acceptance testing
       d.   all of the above

Key: d.   all of the above

Refer to Questions 79 through 83 above for discussion.

91.   Failure mode effect and criticality analysis (FMECA) is primarily for the purpose of

    a.   learning as much about the item as possible after qualification test
    b.   determining the way an item will most likely fail to help obtain design and procedural safeguards against such failures
    c.   determining by extensive analysis, the reliability of an item
    d.   determining the cause of a failure, by dissecting the item, to help obtain corrective action

Key: b.   determining the way an item will most likely fail to help obtain design and procedural safeguards against such failures   (Ref. Applications Question 70, August 1978)
    This is the basic definition for FMECA. Refer to Questions 79 through 83 above. This question is repeated in the October 1974 examination.[34]

92.   Which of the following quantitative methods does not apply to the assessment of actual system or component reliability?

    a.   statistical analysis of field test data
    b.   statistical allocation of reliability goals
    c.   evaluation of laboratory test data
    d.   analysis of results of reliability demonstration tests
    e.   analysis of failure data

Key: b.   statistical allocation of reliability goals   (Ref. Principles Question 26, October 1974)
    The key phrase is "assessment of actual system or component reliability." All the choices except choice b provide actual data on assessment of reliability from laboratory tests, field tests, demonstration tests, and failure tests. Juran[35] provides detailed discussions on analysis as an important phase in quantification of reliability, different analysis techniques, and methods of evaluating designs by using a well-defined test program. Statistical allocation of reliability goals enables deployment of the allocated reliability requirements in design of the system and components, but it does not provide any information on the assessment of the actual system or component reliability. This question is repeated in the February 1976 examination.[36]

93.   The design function that assigns probability of failure among components or subsystems is called

    a.   confidence
    b.   qualification
    c.   significance
    d.   apportionment

---

[34] *ASQC - CQE Examination*, ASQC Quality Progress, October 1974, Applications section, Question 56.
[35] *Juran's Quality Control Handbook* by J. M. Juran, 4th ed., McGraw-Hill, New York, pg. 13.19-21, 31, 34.
[36] *ASQC - CRE Examination*, ASQC Quality Progress, February 1976, Question 6.

Key: d.   apportionment   (Ref. Applications Question 3, October 1974)
Reliability apportionment is defined as the process of assigning the overall system reliability requirements to the individual subsystem or component reliabilities. It requires significant knowledge of the subsystems, their interrelationships, past experiences, and their degree of severity. It requires a reliability block diagram of the system to show the system and its subsystem structures.

94.   The design function which assigns probability of failures between components or subsystems is called

   a.   apportionment
   b.   significance
   c.   confidence
   d.   qualification

Key: a.   apportionment (Ref. Applications Question 77, October 1972)

95.   A reliability data system usually implies collecting data on

   a.   process machine downtime
   b.   product failures and operating time
   c.   maintenance costs
   d.   repair times

Key: b.   product failures and operating time   (Ref. Applications Question 75, July 1984)
This is the most appropriate choice. Reliability systems are mainly used to determine the effect of failure rates on total reliability or the effect of operating time on reliability. Process machine downtime or repair times are used to calculate the availability of the system or machine.

96.   When testing to establish failure rate data and prediction, which of the following is not normally a feasible acceleration factor with respect to rated conditions?

   a.   longer time
   b.   greater humidity
   c.   higher temperature
   d.   higher voltage

Key: a.   longer time   (Ref. Applications Question 7, October 1974)
The key words are feasible acceleration factor, which means shorter times, not longer times.

97.   Methods for predicting human reliability in production processes

   a.   are represented by the many motivation programs in effect
   b.   are inevitably correlated with monetary rewards
   c.   are still in the developmental stages

d.   are based on the complexity of the process

Key: c.   are still in the developmental stages   (Ref. Applications Question 30, October 1974)
        This question is a repeat question in the October 1972 examination.[37]

98.   The Monte Carlo method refers to a technique for

        a.   the simulation of operations when random variations are an essential consideration
        b.   programming roulette for maximum return
        c.   random sampling from a homogeneous population
        d.   establishing quantitative values to unknown restrictive variables in linear programming

Key: a.   the simulation of operations when random variations are an essential consideration
        (Ref. Principles Question 90, October 1972)
        The Monte Carlo method is a simulation technique which can be used for an assembly made at
        random from many components. The computer is used to generate random numbers to select
        values at random from the assumed distribution of each component. An assembly value is
        calculated using an assumed mathematical model or equation by combining at random these
        values of individual component distribution. One can repeat this simulation several hundreds to
        thousands of times and create a computer simulation for these assemblies under different
        variability of components. Many computer programs today create a capability analysis for such
        assemblies in very early phases of design and try to predict or estimate the assembly variation
        and its sensitivity to customer satisfaction.

99.   Monte Carlo simulation to evaluate performance of a system from component information can
        be advantageously used even in situations where

        a.   the system is complex
        b.   the components are interrelated
        c.   a small estimating error is required
        d.   all of the above conditions are present

Key: d.   all of the above conditions are present
        (Ref. CRE Question 89, February 1976, and Question 112, September 1980)

100.   In life-cycle costing, the term life refers to whose viewpoint?

        a.   producer's
        b.   user's
        c.   contractor's
        d.   quality control

Key: b.   user's   (Ref. Principles Question 57, July 1984)
        The life cycle of a product is the time, e.g., total number of years, a product is effectively used by

---

[37] *ASQC - CQE Examination*, ASQC Quality Progress, October 1972, Applications section, Question 9.

the user. Hence life refers to the user's viewpoint. It is used to determine the actual cost of use of the product over its life to the customer. To optimize the life-cycle cost, a company should identify in specific detail all the phases and activities that the product will go through. For each of these activities, then identify the associated cost to the user in detail. The ultimate objective of determining the life-cycle cost is to find the optimum cost for both the customer and its supplier (i.e., company or manufacturer). Thus, the product or service will meet the customer's requirements at the optimum cost.

101.   The concept of accelerated cycling or a burn-in program of all devices for six months under normal operating conditions would

    a.   reduce premature failures in use
    b.   improve constant failure rate probability
    c.   be of little use
    d.   assure acceptable quality to the customer

Key: a.   reduce premature failures in use   (Ref. Principles Question 7, October 1972)

102.   When requesting worst case design analysis, you expect the reliability group to

    a.   analyze the worst rejects
    b.   analyze only those products failing to meet specification requirements
    c.   determine whether product requirements can be met with subassemblies assumed at their worst combination of tolerances
    d.   assume all subassembly tolerances are at their maximum limit

Key: c.   determine whether product requirements can be met with subassemblies assumed at their worst combination of tolerances (Ref. Applications Question 71, July 1984)

103.   To minimize the impact of product recall, which one of the following is the most important element in a quality system?

    a.   receiving inspection at the plants
    b.   traceability system
    c.   warranty analysis
    d.   all of the above

Key: b.   traceability system
        Juran[38] discusses the importance of a traceability system in the situation of a product recall. A product recall is defined as the actions taken due to deficiencies in products that are already shipped to customers. This represents quality costs of external failure. The impact of any recall can be minimized if the suspect product units can be quickly identified separately from other units in production or storage, etc. This means the company should establish a traceability system to locate quickly all nonconforming or suspect units in particular and the entire product in

---

[38] *Juran's Quality Control Handbook* by J. M. Juran, 4th ed., McGraw-Hill, New York, pg. 20.32-33.

general.

104. Which of the following are good factors in setting up a traceability program to manage product recalls?

    I.   unit cost of the product
    II.   product life
    III.   product complexity
    IV.   methods of identification

    a.   I, II, and III
    b.   II, III, IV
    c.   III, IV, and I
    d.   IV, I, and II
    e.   I, II, III, and IV

Key: e.   I, II, III, and IV

ASQC[39] provides several important factors to set up an effective traceability program for effectively locating and identifying the products during a recall. They are, for example, product category, product life (item II), unit cost of the product (item I), recall or repair in the field, product complexity (item III), the rationale for recall, documents, and different methods of identification and coding (item IV).

105. To minimize product complaints, you should initiate a complaint program, which includes

    a.   a method of resolving the complaint to satisfy the complainant
    b.   a process to identify vital few or serious complaints from many types of complaints
    c.   analysis methods to identify the root causes of different complaints
    d.   long-term corrective actions to prevent the recurrence of the complaints
    e.   all of the above

Key: e.   all of the above

Juran[40] indicates that the above items are important action items of any complaint program. However, these are still after-the-fact, detection-based, and very expensive approaches. Companies should start prevention-based upfront approaches of product improvement from the early design phase. The lessons learned from previous products, models or competitive benchmarking, and all other types of voices of customers (VOCs) should be deployed in engineering or technical language using tools such as *quality function deployment (QFD),* a system engineering approach used during the design phase. The design should be evaluated and analyzed for all sources of variation, failure modes, and adverse consequences of variation to customer satisfaction. Also, it should be evaluated for the special or beneficial effects of changes and options in the form of product excitement, customer delight, and customer enthusiasm.

---

[39] *Product Recall Planning Guide* by ASQC, 1981; *Juran's Quality Control Handbook* by J. M. Juran, 4th ed., McGraw-Hill, New York, pg. 20.32-33.
[40] *Juran's Quality Control Handbook* by J. M. Juran, 4th ed., McGraw-Hill, New York, pg. 20.20.

Robust design of product and processes, failure mode and effects analysis (FMEA), process control and capability studies, etc., should be used to make the design less sensitive to product variation, user variation, or user abuse of products. Companies should start implementing commonsense-based, economical methods of errorproofing designs and processes to become low-cost manufacturers of high-quality products. These efforts, in the long term, can result in minimum customer dissatisfaction and increased customer satisfaction. In case of new options, or new product innovations, they can create customer excitement about the product.

106.   The term "strict product liability" means

   I.   manufacturer or sellers are likely to have liability primarily when they are unreasonably careless or negligent in what they have produced or how they have produced it
   II.   a strong "product paternity responsibility" in the law for both manufacturer and merchandiser, requiring immediate responsiveness to unsatisfactory quality through product service or replacement
   III.   a full, completely accurate, and truthful product life, safety, and quality reporting in advertising

   a.   I and II
   b.   II and III
   c.   III and I
   d.   only I

Key: b.   II and III
        Feigenbaum[41] discusses the concept of product or service liability and provides a list of some of the landmark cases in product liability. Item I was based on the case of *MacPherson vs Buick Motor Co. tried before the New York Court of Appeals in 1916. Justice Kellog ruled that the manufacturer had a "product liability" obligation to the consumer, even though the sales contract was between the buyer and the dealer and not between the manufacturer and the buyer directly.* Manufacturers are liable when they are unreasonably careless or negligent in what and how they have produced a product or service. This ruling removed the "privity of contract" shield as a defense where *negligence* was the primary factor.

        The concept of product liability has been further changed, and courts have put more stringent rules called "strict product liability" as discussed in items II and III above.

        Item II, "product paternity responsibility" of the manufacturer, extends beyond the time of manufacture and store shelf-life, all the way to its useful life. The manufacturer is responsible for the product in use, for its performance, safety, effects on the environment, and compliance to applicable laws, standards, etc. Item III requires that all types of advertising of the product include valid company data and test or analysis results to support the advertisements. Juran[42] provides additional discussion on the concepts of product safety and liability, strict liability, personal liability, and criminal liability.

---

[41] *Total Quality Control* by A.V. Feigenbaum, 3rd ed., McGraw-Hill, New York, Chapter 2, pg. 34-37.
[42] *Juran's Quality Control Handbook* by J. M. Juran, 4th ed., McGraw-Hill, New York, pg. 34.19-21.

107. A milestone in product quality liability was accomplished in 1963 as a result of *"Greenmail vs Yuba Power Products Inc."* The court stated that "the costs of injuries resulting from defective products are borne by the manufacturers that put such products on the market rather than by the injured persons who are powerless to protect themselves." This ruling caused a phase-out of which of the following concepts?

   a. Implied warranty
   b. Caveat Emptor
   c. Privity of contract
   d. Res ipsa loquitur

Key: c.   Privity of contract   (Ref. Principles Question 33, July 1984)
     Feigenbaum[43] discusses the concept of product or service liability and provides a list of some of the landmark cases in product liability.

     This has put more stringent responsibility on the producer about product safety and liability. Juran[44] provides the explanation of the term *"Privity of Contract,"* meaning that the plaintiff had to establish the contract relationship between the user and the manufacturer. The plaintiff had to establish the "privity," i.e., that he or she was a party to the contract.

     Hunter[45] discusses various important cases in product liability and how the law gradually switched from *privity of contract* to, *strict liability* from 1916 to 1963. He discusses that as the marketing of products became more complex, from a *producer-to-buyer system* to a *producer-wholesaler-dealer(retailer)-to user* system, the privity of contract provided very little protection to the user. The privity of contract existed between two immediate parties in the contract in this long chain, i.e., the wholesaler had the privity of contract with the manufacturer, the dealer or retailer had the privity of contract with the wholesaler, and the ultimate buyer had the privity of contract with the retailer or dealer. This means the buyer had no direct contractual relationship, i.e., the privity of contract, with the producer, and hence the producer was insulated or protected from the product liability actions in law.

     The *MacPherson vs Buick Motor Co.* case tried before the New York Court of Appeals in 1916 ruled that manufacturers are liable when they are unreasonably careless or negligent in what and how they have produced the product or service. This ruling removed the *privity of contract* shield as a defense where *negligence* was the primary factor.

     In 1961, in an automobile case by Ms. Henningsen, the court found that the implied warranty went with the product and accomplished it through each party involved in the distribution and sale channel. The producer was liable for any injury or damage resulting from the breach of the *implied warranty*, in spite of the fact that there was no direct privity of contract with the buyer. This wiped out the privity shield as a defense against the breach of warranty. This means the producer owed a duty to the ultimate buyer not to cause the wrongful harm or injury by placing a

---

[43] *Total Quality Control* by A.V. Feigenbaum, 3rd ed., McGraw-Hill, New York, Chapter 2, pp. 34-37.
[44] *Juran's Quality Control Handbook* by J. M. Juran, 4th ed., McGraw-Hill, New York, pp. 34.19.
[45] *Engineering Design for Safety* by Thomas A. Hunter, McGraw-Hill, New York, 1992, pg. 181-182.

dangerously defective product on the market. This resulted in laws of *Torts* for such acts as *civil wrongs* rather than contract violation.

Greenman vs Yuba Power Products Inc. (1963) is the landmark case, as the grounds for the suit were both negligence and breach of implied warranty. The court ruled that the producer had committed a wrongful act, a *tort,* to the buyer, and was held liable for the consequences. It ruled that a manufacturer is responsible when he(she) sells a product that proves to have a defect that causes injury. The need of privity was abolished by the court when it stated that *there is an implied "representation" that the product is safe and this implication follows the product around, irrespective of who the user is.*

Choice a, *implied warranty,* means warranties that are not spelled out in detail but are part of the contract by implication. The term *warranty* means a guarantee or an assurance, explicit or implied, of something having to do with a contract, as of sale, i.e., it is the seller's assurance to the purchaser that the goods or services are or shall be as represented.[46] Warranty constitutes a part of the contract and must be fulfilled to keep the contract in force. The concept of privity did apply when it was claimed that a breach of warranty was responsible for the injury or damage to property or a wrongful act.

Choice b, c*aveat emptor* is defined as *let the buyer beware*, i.e., *what you see is what you get*. This means that the buyers were responsible to evaluate the condition of the product that they wanted to purchase, including any hazard or undiscovered characteristics of the purchase. The liability for any injury or damage was only limited by the privity of contract.

108.   In product liability, the proper legal term for statements regarding the reliability of a product is known as

      a.   advertisements
      b.   warranties
      c.   contracts
      d.   representations
      e.   obligations

Key: d.   representations   (Ref. Applications Question 42, July 1984)
Webster's dictionary[47] defines the term "representation" as *a statement or implication of fact, oral or written, as made by one party to induce another to enter into a contract.* The term representation in the case of product liability implies that the product is safe regardless of who the customer or user is.[48]

Another term that may attract your response is choice b, "warranties." But the term warranty means a guarantee or an assurance, explicit or implied, of something having to do with a contract, e.g., in a sale, it is the seller's assurance to the purchaser that the goods or services are

---

[46] *Webster's New World Dictionary*, 2nd College edition, Prentice Hall, Englewood Cliffs, N.J.
[47] *Webster's New World Dictionary*, 2nd College edition, Prentice Hall, Englewood Cliffs, N.J.
[48] *Juran's Quality Control Handbook* by J. M. Juran, 4th ed., McGraw-Hill, New York, pg. 34.19-21.

or shall be as represented.[49] Warranty constitutes a part of the contract and must be fulfilled to keep the contract in force. Hence choice d, "representation" is a more applicable term than choice b, "warranties."

109. The provisions of the FDA regulations for thermally processed, low acid foods, packaged in hermetically sealed containers, require all of the following except

    a.   copies of all production and laboratory records be kept for six (6) months then reviewed and destroyed by an authorized person

    b.   incoming raw material, ingredients, and packaging components should be inspected upon receipt to ensure that they are suitable for processing

    c.   scheduled processes for low-acid foods shall be established by qualified persons having expert knowledge of thermal processing

    d.   it is either destroyed or evaluated by a component processing authority to detect any hazard to public health

Key: a.   copies of all production and laboratory records be kept for six (6) months then reviewed and destroyed by an authorized person (Ref. Applications Question 44, July 1984)

110. Which of the following is not applicable for software reliability?

    a.   Software failures are due to wearout.
    b.   Software failures are due to design errors.
    c.   The external environment does not affect software reliability generally.
    d.   Reliability cannot be improved by redundancy.

Key: a.   Software failures are due to wearout.
Software reliability is an important concept today and is focused on minimizing software errors, by using proper methods of programming, testing, and validation. In the case of software, wearout does not take place. Software failures occur without any prior warning. Software does not degrade over time and it is possible to restore software to its original standard. O'Connor[50] discusses the differences between software and hardware reliability.

111. Software errors can arise from all of the following except

    a.   specification errors
    b.   firmware failures
    c.   software system design
    d.   software code generation errors

Key: b.   firmware failures
Firmware is a class of equipment that includes memory devices of all types and indicates their interface status. System failures can be caused by any type of memory devices, whether optical

---

[49] *Webster's New World Dictionary*, 2nd college ed., Prentice Hall, Englewood Cliffs, N.J.
[50] *Practical Reliability Engineering* by Patrick D.T. O'Connor, 3rd ed., John Wiley and Sons, New York, pg. 233-234.

or magnetic media or semiconductor type, and can appear to be due to software errors. Firmware failures can only occur under certain operating conditions and can lead to system failures.

The remaining choices can cause software errors. O'Connor[51] states that more than half the errors are caused due to specification errors during software development. The software specifications must be clear, nonambiguous and consistent, and must describe the software program requirements accurately. If there is any misunderstanding of the requirements of the program, serious software errors can result and will be difficult to catch. This can result in a rework situation, i.e., rewriting and reprogramming the whole program or part thereof.

Accurate and clear specifications enable proper software system design. The system design is generally in the form of a logical flow diagram which defines the structure, inputs, outputs, test conditions, feedback loops, etc.

Software code generation can cause errors because of the large number of code statements in the program. There may be typographical errors, incorrect numerical values, incorrect symbols, and incorrect equations or expressions.

112.   A software development project requires several important elements except

    a.   analysis of effect of environmental factors
    b.   clear and complete requirements
    c.   a design of the structured program and details of each module
    d.   evaluation of the written program thoroughly for errors
    e.   a list of all tests, developmental notes, checks, and program changes

Key: a.   analysis of effect of environmental factors
The key term is "except." The software reliability is generally not affected by external environmental factors and does not have a wearout factor. O'Connor[52] provides details on hardware and software reliability and lists the essential elements for developing software effectively.

---

[51] *Practical Reliability Engineering* by Patrick D.T. O'Connor, 3rd ed., John Wiley and Sons, New York, pg. 235-237.
[52] *Practical Reliability Engineering* by Patrick D.T. O'Connor, 3rd ed., John Wiley and Sons Ltd. pg. 234 and 251.

ASQC-CQE BIBLIOGRAPHY AND OTHER REFERENCES ON RELIABILITY, MAINTAINABILITY, AND PRODUCT SAFETY

1. ASQC Statistics Division, *Glossary and Tables for Statistical Quality Control*, 2nd ed., Milwaukee, ASQC Quality Press, 1983.
2. Dovich, Robert A., *Quality Engineering Statistics,* Milwaukee, ASQC Quality Press, 1992.
3. Dovich, Robert A., *Reliability Statistics,* ASQC Quality Press, Milwaukee, 1990.
4. Duncan, A. J., *Quality Control and Industrial Statistics,* 5th ed., Homewood IL, Irwin Inc., 1986.
5. Grant, Eugen L. and Richard Leavenworth, *Statistical Quality Control,* 6th ed., New York, McGraw-Hill, 1988.
6. Ireson, William G. and Clyde F. Coombs Jr., *Handbook of Reliability Engineering and Management,* New York, McGraw-Hill, 1989.
7. Juran, Joseph M., *Juran's Quality Control Handbook*, 4th ed., New York, McGraw-Hill, 1988.
8. Krishnamoorthi, K.S., *Reliability Methods for Engineers,* Milwaukee, ASQC Quality Press, 1990.
9. Lewis, E. E., *Introduction to Reliability Engineering,* New York, John Wiley and Sons, 1987.
10. Lloyd, David K. and Myron Lipow, *Reliability, Management Methods and Mathematics,* 2nd ed., Milwaukee, ASQC Quality Press, 1984.
11. MIL-HDBK-217, *Reliability Prediction of Electronic Equipment,* Washington, D.C., Department of Defense, 1981.
12. MIL-STD-756B, *Reliability Modeling and Prediction*, Washington D.C., Department of Defense, 1981.
13. Nelson, Wayne, *How to Analyze Data with Simple Plots,* Volume 1, Milwaukee, ASQC Quality Press, 1979.
14. Nelson, Wayne, *How to Analyze Reliability Data,* Volume 6, Milwaukee, ASQC Quality Press, 1979.
15. O'Connor, Patrick D.T., *Practical Reliability Engineering,* 3rd ed., New York, John Wiley and Sons, 1991.
16. Omdahl, Tracy P., *Reliability, Availability and Maintainability (RAM) Dictionary,* Milwaukee, ASQC Quality Press, 1987.
17. Vani, Jagdish, *Fundamental Concepts of Probability, Statistics, Regression and DOE*, 3rd ed., Troy, MI, Quality Quest Inc., 1993.
18. Western Electric, *Statistical Quality Control Handbook*, Indianapolis, AT&T, 1956.

CHAPTER 14

QUALITY INFORMATION SYSTEMS

ASQC'S <u>BODY OF KNOWLEDGE (BOK)</u> FOR THE CQE EXAMINATION

This chapter focuses on the following selected subject areas of BOK from *Section II, Quality Practices and Applications.*

Quality Planning

1.   Data collection and review of customer expectations, needs, requirements, and specifications

Quality Systems

1.   Scope and objectives of quality information systems
2.   Techniques for assuring data accuracy and integrity
3.   Problem identification, analysis, reporting, and corrective action system

1.   Computer information processing can become available to any quality engineer through the use
      of

      a.   a terminal and time-sharing agreement
      b.   a batch processing system in which data are brought to a central area for processing
      c.   an in-house system with applicable software
      d.   all of the above

Key: d.   all of the above   (Ref. Applications Question 76, August 1978)
      Today, personal computers are easily accessible and commonly used.

2.   When designing a quality reporting system to insure a tight feedback loop, care must be taken
      to be sure that the information produced is

      a.   timely
      b.   reliable
      c.   accurate
      d.   valid
      e.   all of the above

Key: e.   all of the above   (Ref. Principles Question 82, October 1974)

3.   The basic steps in any data-processing system using computers are generally arranged in which
      of the following orders?

      a.   data input, storage and retrieval, processing and output
      b.   collection, analysis, input and output
      c.   evaluation, keypunch, processing and output
      d.   recording, input, calculation and output
      e.   keypunch, FORTRAN programming, output

Key: a.   data input, storage and retrieval, processing and output
      (Ref. Applications Question 73, August 1978)
      Data input is naturally a first step in any data-processing system. Refer to Juran[1] for steps in
      software development and software quality.

4.   When planning a system for processing quality data or for keeping inspection and other quality
      records, the first step should be to

      a.   depict the system in a flowchart
      b.   hire a statistician
      c.   investigate applicable data-processing equipment
      d.   determine the cost of operating the system
      e.   start coding your input data

---

[1] *Juran's Quality Control Handbook* by J. M. Juran, 4th ed., McGraw-Hill, New York, pg. 14.6-14.24, 27.7-27.11.

Key: a.   depict the system in a flowchart   (Ref. Applications Question 74, August 1978)
        This is one of the fundamental steps in any process design. Know your process, i.e., the current
        as is and what it should be in the future for continuous improvement.

5.   Management is constantly seeking new ways to make profitable use of its expensive computers.
        Which of the following computer applications promises to be the most beneficial from
        management's standpoint?

        a.   decision-making help in combination with simulation techniques
        b.   wider use as an accounting machine
        c.   high-density information storage and rapid retrieval rates
        d.   solution of complex mathematical formulas

Key: a.   decision-making help in combination with simulation techniques
        (Ref. Principles Question 81, October 1972)

6.   Management is consistently seeking new ways to make profitable use of its expensive computers.
        Which of the following computer applications promises to be the most beneficial from
        management's standpoint?

        a.   information storage and retrieval
        b.   decision-making help in combination with simulation techniques
        c.   wider use as an accounting machine
        d.   solution of complex mathematical formulas

Key: b.   decision-making help in combination with simulation techniques
        (Ref. Applications Question 12, October 1974)

7.   The quality needs for historical information in the areas of specifications, performance, reporting,
        complaint analysis, or run records would fall into which of the following computer application
        categories?

        a.   data accumulation
        b.   data reduction analysis and reporting
        c.   rcal-timc process control
        d.   statistical analysis
        e.   information retrieval

Key: e.   information retrieval   (Ref. Principles Question 83, August 1978)
        The key phrases are *"needs for historical information"* and *"run records,"* which means we
        need to retrieve historical information. Other choices, a, b, and d, are also important categories
        for computer application. However, if it is historical information, information retrieval is very
        important. Choice c is not correct because the question is focusing on historical information, not
        on real-time process control data.

8.   All quality information reports should be audited periodically to

    a.   determine their continued validity
    b.   reappraise the routing or copy list
    c.   determine their current effectiveness
    d.   all of the above
    e.   none of the above

Key: d.   all of the above   (Ref. Principles Question 85, August 1978)

9.   Effective automated data processing is

    a.   a process which uses punch cards to sort, compile, and analyze data
    b.   a process in which computers are used to analyze data
    c.   a process, largely self-regulating, in which information is handled with a minimum of human effort and intervention
    d.   a process in which records are classified, sorted, computed, summarized, transmitted, and stored
    e.   none of the above

Key: c.   a process, largely self-regulating, in which information is handled with a minimum of human effort and intervention (Ref. Principles Question 82, July 1984)
       The key phrases are *"**automated,**"* i.e., self-regulating, and *"**minimum of human effort.**"*

10.   A computer program is

    a.   the overall computer project for an entire company
    b.   a set of instructions to accomplish a given set of calculations
    c.   subsets of instructions later patched into a larger project
    d.   instructions written only in basic computer language

Key: b.   a set of instructions to accomplish a given set of calculations
              (Ref. Principles Question 47, October 1972)
       Juran[2] defines a computer program as a sequence of instructions given to the computer to perform specific functions or tasks. He has also briefly described different types of software and high-level programming languages.

11.   Defining the required data output should be

    a.   performed next after the use of a computer is economically justified
    b.   performed next after input preparation
    c.   done in such a way as to optimize computing formulas
    d.   the first step in computer planning

---

[2] *Juran's Quality Control Handbook* by J. M. Juran, 4th ed., McGraw-Hill, New York, pg. 27.3-27.4.

Key: d.   the first step in computer planning   (Ref. Principles Question 59, October 1972)
Juran[3] discusses the requirements for managing computer projects. Defining the quality requirements in terms of scope and objectives (outputs) is the starting point for computer project planning.

12.   Which of the following elements is least necessary to a good corrective action feedback report?

       a.   what caused the failure
       b.   who caused the failure
       c.   what correction has been made
       d.   when the correction is effective
       e.   what system deficiency allowed the error to occur

Key: b.   who caused the failure
       (Ref. ASQC-CQE Examination brochure, 1993 revision, Principles section, Question 15)

13.   In establishing a quality reporting and information feedback system, primary consideration must be given to

       a.   the number of inspection stations
       b.   management approval
       c.   timely feedback and corrective action
       d.   historical preservation of data
       e.   routing copy list

Key: c.   timely feedback and corrective action (Ref. Principles Question 84, August 1978)

14.   Good forms design and layout are essential in both manual and electronic data processing because

       a.   they are easier to read, check data, use, and file
       b.   they are cheaper (faster) to use although initial cost is higher than quickly made forms
       c.   they help to avoid typographical errors
       d.   all of the above

Key: d.   all of the above   (Ref. Principles Question 83, October 1972)

15.   An important aid to the quality supervisor in the area of record-keeping and data processing is

       a.   adaptability of records to computer processing
       b.   using well-designed forms and records
       c.   getting sufficient copies of records and reports distributed to key personnel
       d.   training inspectors to follow inspection instructions and procedures

---

[3] *Juran's Quality Control Handbook* by J. M. Juran, 4th ed., McGraw-Hill, New York, pg. 27.7-27.9.

Key: b.   using well-designed forms and records   (Ref. Applications Question 78, October 1972)

16.   The management team is establishing priorities to attack a serious quality problem. You are requested to establish a data-collection system to direct this attack. You use which of these general management rules to support your recommendations as to the quantity of data required?

   a.   You have compared the incremental cost of additional data to the value of the information obtained and stopped when they are equal.
   b.   Your decision corresponds to the rules applicable to management decisions for other factors of production.
   c.   Your decision is based upon the relationship between value and cost.
   d.   all of the above.

Key: d.   all of the above   (Ref. Applications Question 75, August 1978)
        This question is repeated in the October 1974 examination.[4]

17.   Quality information equipment

   a.   is used only by the quality control function
   b.   is used only for the purpose of accepting or rejecting products
   c.   makes measurements of either products or processes and feeds the resulting data back for decision making
   d.   includes automatic electronic instruments but not go-nogo gages

Key: c.   makes measurements of either products or processes and feeds the resulting data back for decision making   (Ref. Principles Question 81, August 1978)
        The term quality information equipment (QIE) is widely used in manufacturing planning and during product evaluation. Juran[5] defines the term QIE as "*a physical apparatus which makes the measurements of products and processes and feeds the information back for decision making.*" It focuses on faster feedback of the observations and decisions made during product evaluation to production for current items and to product designs for future programs as lessons learned. Feigenbaum[6] states that the quality information may be thought of as the "intelligence" of the total quality control program and defines the term *QIE engineering* as "*the body of knowledge relating to techniques and equipment which measure quality characteristics and which process the resulting information for use in analysis and control.*"

18.   The best reason for investment in quality information equipment (QIE) is that it will improve the total quality system by

   a.   providing better data collection
   b.   reducing the timespan in the corrective action feedback loop
   c.   providing better information retrieval

---

[4] *ASQC - CQE Examination*, ASQC Quality Progress, October 1974, Applications section, Question 2.
[5] *Juran's Quality Control Handbook* by J. M. Juran, 4th ed., McGraw-Hill, New York, pg. 16.52.
[6] *Total Quality Control* by A. V. Feigenbaum, 3rd ed., McGraw-Hill, New York, pg. 260-261, 302-303.

        d.   reducing the paperwork load of the QC department

Key: b.   reducing the timespan in the corrective action feedback loop
            (Ref. Principles Question 49, October 1974)
            Refer to Question 17 above for discussion.

19.   In establishing a quality reporting and information feedback system, primary consideration must be given to

        a.   the number of inspection stations
        b.   management approval
        c.   timely feedback and corrective action
        d.   historical preservation of data
        e.   routing copy list

Key: c.   timely feedback and corrective action
            See Question 17 above for discussion.

20.   In planning for quality information equipment, an appropriate activity would be to

        a.   establish training plans as required for the operation of the equipment
        b.   review present process capabilities to permit correlation with newer processes
        c.   establish the calibration frequency
        d.   evaluate process cost relative to performance

Key: a.   establish training plans as required for the operation of the equipment
            (Ref. Principles Question 80, October 1974)
            Juran[7] applies the term QIE to physical equipment that measures either products or processes and feeds the resulting data back for decision making. Hence during the planning for QIE, it is important to establish training plans to learn the operating methods for the equipment. Other choices represent elements of manufacturing and process control planning, but not QIE planning. Refer to Question 17 above for discussion. This question is also repeated in the October 1972 examination.[8]

21.   What results can you expect from QIE in the area of quality costs?

        a.   lowered equipment utilization factors
        b.   reduced percents defective for both scrap and rework
        c.   less extensive and complicated equipment maintenance
        d.   decreased quality control direct and indirect labor

Key: d.   decreased quality control direct and indirect labor
            (Ref. Principles Question 9, October 1972)

---

[7] *Juran's Quality Control Handbook* by J. M. Juran, 4th ed., McGraw-Hill, New York, pg. 16.52-53.
[8] *ASQC - CQE Examination*, ASQC Quality Progress, October 1972, Principles section, Question 68.

Quality information equipment (QIE) has contributed to the evolution of automated processes, which has resulted in reduced quality control direct and indirect labor. Refer to Question 17 above for discussion.

22.   Quality information equipment (QIE) is the physical apparatus that is concerned with

     a.   data collection and analysis
     b.   data collection, storage, and retrieval
     c.   data collection and storage
     d.   data collection, analysis, and feedback

Key: d.   data collection, analysis, and feedback (Ref. Principles Question 27, October 1972)
Refer to Question 17 above for discussion.

23.   What conditions are now developing which require the installation of QIE (quality information equipment) for continued quality control effectiveness?

     a.   need for better vendor-vendee relations
     b.   mechanization and automation of manufacturing operations
     c.   automation and mechanization of data processing activities
     d.   new and more accurate measurement methods

Key: b.   mechanization and automation of manufacturing operations
(Ref. Principles Question 55, October 1972)
Refer to Question 17 above for discussion. Feigenbaum[9] indicates that there is an increased need for the faster and easier-to-operate quality information equipment that can meet the rapid growth of modern manufacturing processes that are highly computerized and automated. He describes QIE as the basic factor in productivity, mechanization, and electronicization, i.e., automation. QIE affects the advance quality and manufacturing process planning.

24.   In today's world, quality information documentation is called

     a.   end-item hardware
     b.   hardware
     c.   data pack
     d.   software
     e.   warrantee

Key: d.   software   (Ref. Principles Question 82, August 1978)
Refer to Juran[10] for a discussion on the role of computers and software in quality information equipment (QIE), software types, software quality, and issues in software development. Also refer to Feigenbaum[11] for a discussion on QIE engineering technology.

---

[9] *Total Quality Control* by A. V. Feigenbaum, 3rd ed., McGraw-Hill, New York, pg. 300-301, 338-339.

[10] *Juran's Quality Control Handbook* by J. M. Juran, 4th ed., McGraw-Hill, New York, pg. 16.52 and Chapters 14 and 27.

[11] *Total Quality Control* by A. V. Feigenbaum, 3rd ed., McGraw-Hill, New York, pg. 338-339.

25.   The principal reason for a quality control department using EDP (effective automated data processing) is

       a.   the planning forces reexamination of the value of storing quality data
       b.   it's cheap
       c.   the data are available for analyses faster than by any other method
       d.   analyses can be standardized

Key: c.   the data are available for analyses faster than by any other method
       (Ref. Principles Question 41, October 1974)
       Refer to Question 9 above.

26.   In planning EDP (effective automated data processing) applications, which element is necessary to reduce computing costs?

       a.   selecting quality control applications having little input and output but extensive calculations
       b.   selecting applications with high-volume input and output but simple calculations
       c.   a limited number of highly repetitive jobs
       d.   a group of jobs where the output of one determines the input of another

Key: c.   a limited number of highly repetitive jobs   (Ref. Principles Question 3, October 1972)

27.   What piece of data processing equipment can facilitate the handling of common quality control calculations on EDP equipment?

       a.   Boolean algebra calculator
       b.   collator
       c.   matrix converter
       d.   tensor analyzer

Key: b.   collator   (Ref. Applications Question 79, October 1972)
       Collating means combining two or more similarly ordered sets of values in one set or pile, or to assemble all papers, sheets, etc., in proper sequence. A collator is an electromechanical device capable of assembling different types of data, sheets, or documents into one proper set or sequence.

28.   The term random access identifies information stored

       a.   outside a computer, so it has to be sought by humans rather than electronically
       b.   some place inside a computer, whose address only the computer's scanning device can locate
       c.   where all parts of it are designed to be equally accessible when needed
       d.   in the special part of the processing unit for temporary storage only

Key: c.   where all parts of it are designed to be equally accessible when needed
                 (Ref. Applications Question 8, October 1974)
                 This question is repeated in the October 1972 examination.[12]

29.   The sequence of punched fields for punched cards generally should be the same as

       a.   the data from previous reports with similar source data
       b.   the data to be punched from the original documents
       c.   prescribed form the output report
       d.   no generally accepted practice can be prescribed

Key: b.   the data to be punched from the original documents
                 (Ref. Applications Question 58, October 1974)
                 This question is repeated in the October 1972 examination.[13] The punch cards are obsolete
                 today.

30.   What is the major drawback to using punch cards in a sophisticated information retrieval
       system?

       a.   They answer only one question in a complete pass of the file.
       b.   They do not store sufficient information.
       c.   They take up too much space.
       d.   They are not as fast as magnetic tape.

Key: d.   They are not as fast as magnetic tape.
                 (Ref. Applications Question 82, October 1972). The punch cards are obsolete today.

31.   For complex electronic equipment, the major contributor to repair time is generally

       a.   diagnosis
       b.   disassembly/reassembly
       c.   remove/replace
       d.   final checkout

Key: a.   diagnosis   (Ref. Applications Question 81, October 1972)

---

[12] *ASQC - CQE Examination*, ASQC Quality Progress, October 1972, Applications section, Question 20.
[13] *ASQC - CQE Examination*, ASQC Quality Progress, October 1974, Applications section, Question 83.

ASQC-CQE BIBLIOGRAPHY AND OTHER REFERENCES ON QUALITY INFORMATION SYSTEMS

1. Besterfield, Dale H. *Quality Control,* 3rd ed., Prentice Hall, Englewood Cliffs, N.J., 1990.
2. Caplan, Frank, *The Quality System, A Source book for Managers and Engineers*, 2nd ed., Radnor, PA, Chilton Book Co., 1990.
3. Crosby, Philip B., *Quality is Free,* McGraw-Hill Publishing Co., New York, 1979.
4. Deming, W. Edwards, *Out of Crisis*, Cambridge, MA, MIT Press, 1986.
5. Feigenbaum A. V., *Total Quality Control*, 3rd ed., New York, McGraw-Hill, 1991.
6. Ishikawa, Kaoru, *Guide to Quality Control*, White Plains, NY, Quality Resources, 1976.
7. Juran, J. M., *Juran's Quality Control Handbook*, 4th ed., New York, McGraw-Hill, 1988.
8. Juran, J. M. and F. M. Gryna, *Quality Planning and Analysis*, 3rd ed., New York, McGraw-Hill, 1993.
9. Walsh, Wurster and R. J. Kimber, *Quality Management Handbook*, New York, Marcel Dekker, 1986.

CHAPTER 15

MOTIVATION AND HUMAN FACTORS

ASQC'S <u>BODY OF KNOWLEDGE (BOK)</u> FOR THE CQE EXAMINATION

This chapter focuses on the following selected subject areas of BOK from *Section II, Quality Practices and Applications.*

Human Resource Management

1. Motivation theories and principles
2. Barriers to the implementation or success of quality improvement efforts
3. Organization and implementation of various types of quality teams
4. Principles of team leadership and facilitation
5. Team dynamics management, including conflict resolution

1.   The famous Hawthorne study provided the following clinical evidence regarding the factors
      that can increase work group productivity:

      a.   attention and recognition are more important than working conditions
      b.   productivity did not change significantly under any of the test conditions
      c.   informal group pressures set a production "goal"
      d.   people with higher capabilities are bored with routine jobs
      e.   workstation layout is critical to higher productivity

Key: a.   attention and recognition are more important than working conditions
      (Ref. Principles Question 86, July 1984)
      You should be familiar with various theories of management organizational behavior and how
      humans are motivated. Then you will be able to answer questions on topics such as the
      Hawthorne study, Abraham Maslow's hierarchy of needs, Theory X and Theory Y, etc.

      Hawthorne studies were conducted in 1927-32 at Western Electric's Hawthorne plant near
      Chicago. They studied the effects of different lighting conditions on productivity. This
      experiment suggested that productivity might increase simply because workers in the study
      group were singled out, got special attention or treatment, and felt more valued. The change in
      lighting conditions did not make any significant difference in productivity.

      The second study included a piecework incentive program, i.e., if you produce more, you get
      paid more. They found that this effort did not motivate people, but the group themselves
      established new targets and an acceptable level of output. The team then concluded that the
      human element in the workplace is more important than the working conditions alone. This is
      a repeat question in the August 1978 examination.[1]

2.   Which one of these human management approaches has led to the practice of job enrichment?

      a.   Skinner
      b.   Maslow
      c.   Herzberg's "Hygiene Theory"
      d.   McGregor

Key: c.   Herzberg's "Hygiene Theory" (Ref. Principles Question 88, July 1984)
      All these choices reflect major work of these four people in defining different theories of
      motivation.

      Frederick Herzberg (1959) had developed a "two-factor theory" in the late 1950s to early 1960s.
      He concluded that the traditional model of satisfaction and motivation was incorrect. In other
      words, traditionally, job satisfaction was considered one dimensional, i.e., ranged from
      satisfaction to *dissatisfaction*. This is shown in the traditional approach to motivation as follows:

---

[1] *ASQC - CQE Examination*, ASQC Quality Progress, August 1978, Applications section, Question 80.

SATISFIED	DISSATISFIED

His research found that there are two different sets of factors or dimensions involved here. He concluded that there is one dimension from "dissatisfaction to no dissatisfaction" and another from "satisfaction to no satisfaction" as shown below.

DISSATISFIED	NOT DISSATISFIED
SATISFACTION	NO SATISFACTION

Herzberg stated that employees could be either dissatisfied or not dissatisfied but at the same time they might be satisfied or not satisfied. Based on these two dimensions, he suggested two sets of factors to motivate employees, "motivation factors" and "hygiene factors."

Hygiene factors are not motivators but are *dissatisfiers*. If these factors are absent or inadequate, they can cause high dissatisfaction. But if they are present and are considered acceptable, the employees may not be dissatisfied. However, their presence does not mean that the employees will be satisfied. Examples of hygiene factors are working conditions and environment, supervision, interpersonal relationships, wages and job security, company policies, etc.

Motivation factors are job related and if they are present in the job, they can cause satisfaction and motivation. If these factors are absent, the employees will feel no satisfaction as opposed to feeling dissatisfaction. Examples of motivation factors are responsibility, the job or work itself, achievement, recognition, advancement, growth, etc.

For proper motivation, managers should first work on hygiene factors and eliminate all causes for dissatisfaction. Then they should work on the motivation factors of recognition, growth, etc., and these factors can create job enrichment which makes employees feel satisfied and motivated.

We will briefly describe the main concepts only. Such theories on motivation and organizational behavior are discussed in detail in many reference books.[2] As a quality engineer or manager, it is important to know and understand human factors in quality improvement, team dynamics, and the factors or methods to motivate them effectively.

Choice a, Skinner, is known for the *operant conditioning or instrumental conditioning* model for learning. It explains the learning process by defining a *conditioned stimulus* (S) to a *conditioned response* (R) connection. It focuses on the reinforcement or the reward of desired behaviors. As a motivation model, it is concerned with the arousal, direction, maintenance, and changes in behavior in organizations. If the people are properly reinforced, the desired behavior can be increased and undesired behavior can be reduced.

---

[2] *Juran's Quality Control Handbook* by J. M. Juran, 4th ed., McGraw-Hill, New York, pg. 10.2-10.7; *One More Time, How Do You Motivate Employees?* by Frederick Herzberg, January-February 1968, Harvard Business Review; *The Motivation to Work* by Frederick Herzberg, Bernard Mausner, and Barbara Snyderman, Wiley & Sons, New York, 1959; and *Management Tasks, Responsibilities and Practices* by Peter F. Drucker, 1973.

Choice b, Abraham Maslow (1954), is known for the *hierarchy of needs*. He ranked the needs according to their apparent importance, i.e., *physiological needs, security needs, belongingness needs, self-esteem needs, and self-actualization needs.*[3]

Choice d, Douglas McGregor (1960), has contributed to the human relations movement by defining *Theory X and Theory Y*. His Theory X defines the traditional approach to managing and is characterized by a lack of trust from management and a high level of external control on the employees. Theory Y is based on the concepts of trust and delegation of the responsibility, and it relies on self-control of employees.

Hence choices a, b, and d are not the correct choices for this question.

3.   Select the nonhygienic motivator, as defined by Maslow,

      a.   salary increases
      b.   longer vacations
      c.   improved medical plan
      d.   sales bonuses
      e.   performance recognition

Key: e.   performance recognition   (Ref. Principles Question 90, July 1984)
Maslow (1954) is known for his *hierarchy of needs*. He ranked needs according to their apparent importance. He indicated that people have different levels of needs and they will work to satisfy these needs in a hierarchical order, starting with the lower-level needs to slowly higher levels of needs. He described different types of needs[4] as follows.

Physiological needs:	basic needs, i.e., need for food, shelter, and survival
Security needs:	long-term employment security
Social needs:	belongingness to a group and group acceptance needs
Self-esteem needs:	self-respect, respect of peers, superiors, and other fellow employees; also called ego needs
Self-actualization needs:	need for self-fulfillment, creativity

Choices a, b, c, and d are all hygiene factors. Only choice e is the one which is not a hygiene factor but is based on the usual type of quality motivation.

4.   When considering human motivation in solving quality problems, it is most important to recognize that

      a.   individuals have *wants*
      b.   individual motivation is of little concern in quality problem solving
      c.   individuals have different levels of needs
      d.   individuals have basic needs

---

[3] *Juran's Quality Control Handbook* by J. M. Juran, 4th ed., McGraw-Hill, New York, pg. 10.2-10.7.
[4] *Juran's Quality Control Handbook* by J. M. Juran, 4th ed., McGraw-Hill, New York, pg. 10.2-10.7.

Key: c.   individuals have different levels of needs
        (Ref. Principles Question 18, October 1974)
        Refer to Question 2 above.

5.   McGregor's Theory X manager is typified as one who operates from the following basic
        assumption about people working for him or her (select the best answer).

        a.   Performance can be improved through tolerance and trust.
        b.   People have a basic need to produce.
        c.   Status is more important than money.
        d.   Self-actualization is the highest order of human need.
        e.   People are lazy and are motivated by reward and punishment.

Key: e.   People are lazy and are motivated by reward and punishment.
        (Ref. Principles Question 86, August 1978)
        Theory X represents the traditional approach to managing and is based on the following
        assumptions. People dislike work and will avoid it if possible. Hence people must be corrected,
        controlled, directed, threatened, and punished to motivate them to achieve the company's
        objectives. They are motivated and influenced by monetary rewards for meeting the standards
        and by penalties for failures. This also represents the "carrot and stick" approach discussed in
        Question 6 below.

6.   One human management approach, often called the "carrot and stick" approach, is best typified
        by which of the following theories?

        a.   Herzberg's "Hygiene Theory"
        b.   Maslow's "Hierarchy of Motivation"
        c.   Skinner's "Reinforcement of Behavior Theory"
        d.   McGregor's "Theory X"

Key: d.   McGregor's "Theory X"   (Ref. Principles Question 87, October 1974)
        Refer to Questions 2 and 5 above for detailed discussion.

7.   Extensive research on the results of quality motivation has shown that

        a.   the supervisor's attitude towards his or her people is of little long term consequence
        b.   motivation is too nebulous to be correlated with results
        c.   motivation is increased when employees set their own goals
        d.   motivation is increased when management sets challenging goals slightly beyond the
                attainment of the better employees

Key: c.   motivation is increased when employees set their own goals
        (Ref. Principles Question 89, July 1984)
        Here it is not difficult to rule out choices a and b. Choice d is not a good choice because it is not
        realistic to set goals that are higher or more difficult to achieve even by the better employees.

8.   Which of the following does not describe Deming's 14 points for management?

        a.   create constancy of purpose toward improvement of product and service, with the aim to
                become competitive
        b.   institute training on the job
        c.   the measure of quality is the price of nonconformance
        d.   drive out fear

Key: c.   the measure of quality is the price of nonconformance
        Choice c indicates Crosby's[5] one of the four *absolutes of quality management* described below.
                1. Quality is defined as conformance to requirements.
                2. Quality is caused by prevention.
                3. Zero defects should be the performance standard.
                4. The measure of the quality is the price of nonconformance.

        Choice a represents Deming's point 1, choice b represents point 6, and choice d represents point
        8. Deming's 14 Points[6] for management are the basis for the transformation of U.S. industries
        and they are described briefly as follows.

        1.   Create constancy of the purpose for improvement of product and service.
        2.   Adopt the new philosophy.
        3.   Cease dependence on inspection to achieve quality.
        *4.   End the practice of awarding business on the basis of the price tag alone. Instead,
                minimize total cost by working with a single supplier.*
        5.   Improve constantly and forever every process for planning, production and service.
        6.   Institute training on the job.
        7.   Adopt and institute the leadership.
        8.   Drive out the fear.
        9.   Break down barriers between the staff areas.
        10.   Eliminate the slogans, exhortations and targets for the work force.
        11.   Eliminate numerical quotas for the work force and numerical goals for management.
        *12.   Remove the barriers that rob people of the pride of workmanship. Eliminate the annual
                rating or merit system.*
        13.   Institute a vigorous program of education and self-improvement of everyone.
        14.   Put everybody in the company to work to accomplish the transformation.

        For detailed discussion, please refer to, read, and try to understand Deming's philosophy in his
        legendary book, *Out of Crisis,* and other books on the subject.

9.   A successful quality circle program should produce all of the following benefits except

        a.   improved worker morale

---

[5] *Quality is Free* by Philip B. Crosby, McGraw-Hill, New York.
[6] *Out Of Crisis* by W. E. Deming, Massachusetts Institute of Technology, Center for Advanced Engineering Study (CAES),
   Cambridge, Mass., 1982.

  b.　　　decreased need for management efforts to maintain quality
  c.　　　improved communication between managers and quality circle members
  d.　　　cost savings from participative problem solving

Key:　b.　　　decreased need for management efforts to maintain quality
(Ref. Principles Question 85, July 1984)
A *quality circle* is a group of employees that acts as a quality improvement and self-improvement study group. Lack of management commitment is one of the reasons why quality circles did not become successful. Management considered the quality circle or employee involvement and empowerment a magic tool that will improve quality by itself without management effort. Quality circles can achieve choices a, c, and d, but they require top management's strong commitment and efforts to implement all the suggestions of the quality circle team in a timely manner. Juran[7] discusses quality circles and its application in Japan.

Feigenbaum[8] discusses 10 important principles of participation that contribute to commitment to quality. The first principle states that successful employee involvement programs (such as quality circles) require genuine, not superficial, management commitment.

10.　　An essential element of a quality motivation program is

  a.　　　the establishment of attainable goals
  b.　　　the establishment of failure costs
  c.　　　a stable environment
  d.　　　the generation of a minimum level of defects

Key:　a.　　　the establishment of attainable goals (Ref. Applications Question 42, October 1974)
A good-quality motivation program should define the goal of the company in terms of the product or service and its importance to customer satisfaction. The goal should be attainable, i.e., it should be possible for people to meet with reasonable effort. It should give meaning to efforts of people. The goals and targets should be visible and enable the employees to know what they are supposed to know.[9] The goals should be set many times by an intensive quality improvement drive or campaign to get a "breakthrough." This requires setting the goals jointly, at local worker levels and management levels, based on the analysis of what is achievable at each level.

11.　　Which of the following is not a true benefit of a well-defined quality objective?

  a.　　　it promotes strong teamwork in all concerned
  b.　　　it creates positive motivation
  c.　　　it promotes prevention-based planning rather than reaction-based actions
  d.　　　it permits very little comparison of performance to objectives

---

[7] *Juran's Quality Control Handbook* by J. M. Juran, 4th ed., McGraw-Hill, New York, pg. 10.9-10.12, 10.45-10.48.
[8] *Total Quality Control* by A.V. Feigenbaum, 3rd ed., McGraw-Hill, New York, pg. 208-212.
[9] *Juran's Quality Control Handbook* by J. M. Juran, 4th ed., McGraw-Hill, New York, pg. 5.17, 10.18, 10.28, 10.51.

Key: d.   it permits very little comparison of performance to objectives
        Juran[10] defines the quality objective as *an aimed at target,* and it is an achievement toward which
        efforts should be directed. Quality objectives form the basis for planning. A well-defined quality
        objective provides all the benefits except choice d. The true benefit will be that it permits a
        subsequent comparison of performance to objectives.

12.   A quality objective should be

        a.   measurable
        b.   legitimate
        c.   understandable
        d.   attainable
        e.   all of the above

Key: e.   all of the above
        Juran[11] defines various criteria to be followed for setting any quality objectives. Objectives
        should be measurable in numbers. They should not promote any suboptimization of departmental
        performances, should cover all activities, and should result in more economical benefits. They
        should have legitimate and official status for people to follow. They should be easy to
        understand, i.e., stated in operational language, and achievable with reasonable effort for the
        people who have to meet these objectives.

13.   In the long run, important steps to enhance quality motivation are to

        I.   establish quality objectives
        II.   provide a *zero defect* program
        III.   communicate quality objectives

        a.   I and II
        b.   I and III
        c.   II and III

Key: b.   I and III   (Ref. ASQC-CQT Core Portion Question 19)

14.   Which of the following should you consider as bases for establishing effective quality
        objectives?

        I.   the market data on field performance on current products, competitive products, and
                market research for future products
        II.   the historical information on performance, scrap, etc.
        III.   engineering study and analysis of data from technical or scientific studies

        a.   I and II

---

[10] *Juran's Quality Control Handbook* by J. M. Juran, 4th ed., McGraw-Hill, New York, pg. 5.15-5.18.
[11] *Juran's Quality Control Handbook* by J. M. Juran, 4th ed., McGraw-Hill, New York, pg. 5.17-5.18.

b.   II and III
c.   III and I
d.   I, II and III

Key: d.   I, II and III
        Juran[12] discusses all of the above three bases in detail.

15.   Quality motivation in industry should be directed at

        a.   manufacturing management
        b.   procurement and engineering
        c.   the quality assurance staff
        d.   the working force
        e.   all of the above

Key: e.   all of the above   (Ref. Principles Question 89, August 1978)

16.   In order to instill the quality control employee with the desire to perform to his or her utmost and
        optimum ability, which of the following recognitions for sustaining motivation has been found
        effective for most people?

        a.   recognition by issuance of monetary award
        b.   verbal recognition policy
        c.   private verbal recognition
        d.   public recognition plus nonmonetary award
        e.   no recognition, salary he or she obtains is sufficient motivation

Key: d.   public recognition plus nonmonetary award
        Ref. Principles Question 90, August 1978)
        Recognition is an important motivation factor and more effective than monetary rewards and
        gains. Juran[13] defines the term *recognition* as *a ceremonial action to publicize good performance*
        and it is generally nonmonetary in nature.

17.   The reason(s) that people succeed or fail to produce quality products depends (depend) upon

        a.   the capability of the system in which they operate
        b.   the extent to which they are given self-control
        c.   what happens to them from the results of their performance
        d.   all of the above
        e.   only a and b

Key: d.   all of the above
        Juran[14] indicates the importance of diagnosing the people's performance. He defines *the*

---

[12] *Juran's Quality Control Handbook* by J. M. Juran, 4th ed., McGraw-Hill, New York, pg. 5.18-5.19.
[13] *Juran's Quality Control Handbook* by J. M. Juran, 4th ed., McGraw-Hill, New York, pg. 8.6.

execution deficiencies and the motivation (consequences) deficiencies. The execution deficiencies place limits on how well an individual *can* perform, whereas consequences deficiencies place limits on how well an individual *will* perform.

18.   Which of the following is a potential error in launching a quality campaign?

    a.   The quality campaign should be initiated by the top executive(s) of the company.

    b.   A quality campaign should be aimed at changing the management system to enable the people to produce consistently high levels of quality.

    c.   The campaign should emphasize and convince the workers to take greater care and pride in their work without providing clear directions or methods to improve.

    d.   The quality campaign should be viewed as an improvement opportunity to try newer approaches and to bring the intended changes faster.

Key: c.   The campaign should emphasize and convince the workers to take greater care and pride in their work without providing clear directions or methods to improve.

Juran[15] indicates that the top executives sometimes launch intensive quality drives or campaigns to bring quick improvements in quality. Choice c is a potential error and the workers or line people are left on their own to implement some elements of campaigns without being provided any clear direction or methods. This results in suboptimization, low morale, and lower confidence in the campaign. Workers consider such programs as management hype or *programs of the month.*

19.   When installing a new system for collecting failure data in a manufacturing plant, the following approach is recommended.

    a.   Issue a procedure written by a quality engineer without help from other departments to prevent a biased input from production test technicians.

    b.   Have production write their own procedure.

    c.   Use a procedure from another company.

    d.   Enlist the collaboration of all affected departments in drafting and approving the procedure.

    e.   None of the above.

Key: d.   Enlist the collaboration of all affected departments in drafting and approving the procedure.   (Ref. Principles Question 87, August 1978)

Choices a, b, and c are obviously not the best choices because any new system generally requires strong teamwork and a simultaneous engineering approach.

20.   Which of the following is true?

    a.   The execution deficiencies occur when people lack performance resources such as required skills, knowledge, ability, and information, etc., to achieve the performance

[14] *Juran's Quality Control Handbook* by J. M. Juran, 4th ed., McGraw-Hill, New York, pg. 10.31-10.32.
[15] *Juran's Quality Control Handbook* by J. M. Juran, 4th ed., McGraw-Hill, New York, pg. 10.48-10.55.

goals.

b.   Execution deficiencies are correctable by workers.
c.   Execution deficiencies occur because people have little or no motivation to do things the right way, or they knowingly try to avoid doing things right, even though the process may be technically capable to meet the requirements.
d.   Execution deficiencies place limits on how well an individual will perform.

Key: a.   The execution deficiencies occur when people lack performance resources such as required skills, knowledge, ability, and information, etc., to achieve the performance goals.
Refer to Question 17 for additional details which discusses the importance of diagnosing the performance of people. You should be able to understand the execution deficiencies and motivation (consequences) deficiencies.

Choice a is the definition of "execution deficiency." Choice b is wrong because execution deficiencies are correctable by the top management by providing a better system of selection, training, information, equipment, etc. Choices c and d are wrong because they define "motivation (consequences) deficiencies."

21.   Which of the following is true?

a.   Motivational deficiencies occur when people lack performance resources such as required skills, knowledge, abilities, information, etc., to achieve the performance goals.
b.   Motivational deficiencies are correctable by workers.
c.   Consequences deficiencies occur because people have little or no motivation to do things the right way, or they knowingly try to avoid doing things right, even though the process may be technically capable to meet the requirements.
d.   Execution deficiencies place limits on how well an individual will perform.

Key: c.   Consequences deficiencies occur because people have little or no motivation to do things the right way, or they knowingly try to avoid doing things right, even though the process may be technically capable to meet the requirements.
Refer to Questions 17 and 20 for additional details which discuss the importance of diagnosing the performance of people. You should be able to understand the execution deficiencies and motivation (consequences) deficiencies.

Choice a is wrong because it defines execution deficiencies; choice b is incorrect because motivational deficiencies are not correctable by workers but by the top management. The top management is responsible to motivate and inspire people to achieve the quality objectives. Choice d is incorrect because execution deficiencies place limits on how well an individual can perform whereas consequences deficiencies place limits on how well an individual will perform.

22.   Which of the following is not true?

a.   Executional deficiencies occur when people lack performance resources such as required skills, knowledge, abilities, information, etc., to achieve the performance goals.

b.   Consequences deficiencies occur because people have little or no motivation to do things the right way, or they knowingly try to avoid doing things right, even though the process may be technically capable to meet the requirements.

c.   Execution deficiencies place limits on how well an individual can perform.

d.   Execution deficiencies place limits on how well an individual will perform.

Key.   d.   Execution deficiencies place limits on how well an individual will perform.
Refer to Questions 17, 20, and 21, for additional details which discuss the importance of diagnosing the performance of people. You should be able to understand the execution deficiencies and motivation (consequences) deficiencies.

23.   Which of the following is not a management-initiated error?

a.   the imposition of conflicting priorities

b.   the lack of operator capacity

c.   management indifference or apathy

d.   conflicting quality specifications

e.   work space, equipment, and environment

Key: b.   the lack of operator capacity   (Ref. Principles Question 87, July 1984)
Let's take an easy approach, i.e., rule out all the incorrect possibilities first. Choices a, c, d, and e are clearly the management-initiated errors and management is responsible for such errors. Hence choice b is the only choice left, which does not really seem like management-initiated or -controlled error. The term *operator capacity* is a little vague and ambiguous because it is not clear what it means. The term *capability* may seem more appropriate than the term capacity.

24.   Human factors engineering concepts introduced to your final inspection area

a.   are not valuable until the test equipment has been set up and is operating

b.   should be incorporated during the design and planning stage of the area

c.   will result in schedule slippage wherever incorporated

d.   are most costly when introduced during the design and planning stage of the area

e.   will result in reduced efficiency of your inspectors, but greater accuracy

Key: b.   should be incorporated during the design and planning stage of the area
(Ref. Principles Question 61, October 1974)
Human factors engineering or *ergonomics* is getting more emphasis in the industry. It is defined as the process of assuring the compatibility and harmony of people with the machines, operations, environment, and products. It requires an extremely well-thought-out system where both people and machines interact with each other in harmony and most effectively.

Juran[16] considers the interaction between the person and the product very important to achieve fitness for use. The design should be evaluated for its effect on the ease with which the person,

---

[16] *Juran's Quality Control Handbook* by J. M. Juran, 4th ed., McGraw-Hill, New York, pg. 13.55.

i.e., the customer or the user, can install, operate, and maintain the product. It should be error-proofed early during the product and process design phases to avoid any human error or operator error during its use and life cycle. The design should also identify why human errors are made and reduce the impact of an operator-dominant process on the output. It should be evaluated for each possible failure mode and its effect on users and on the whole system. It should be *robust, i.e., less sensitive or nonsensitive to variation and abuse of the user if any.*

25.   The application of human factors in a plant production environment

      a.   identifies the reasons why errors are made
      b.   is a practical example of using psychological techniques on workers
      c.   is identified with a formal quality motivation program
      d.   relates attitudes and prejudices among plant personnel

Key: a.   identifies the reasons why errors are made (Ref. Principles Question 11, October 1972) Refer to Question 24 above for detailed discussion on human factors engineering or ergonomics.

26.   The quality engineer should be concerned with the human factors of a new piece of in-house manufacturing equipment as well as its operational effects because it

      a.   may speed the line to the point where a visual operator inspection is impossible
      b.   may require the operator's undivided attention at the controls so the product cannot be fully seen
      c.   may remove an operator formerly devoting some portion of time to inspection
      d.   all of the above

Key: d.   all of the above   (Ref. Applications Question 79, August 1978) This defines the importance of the term *human factors* or *ergonomics. Human factors engineering* or *ergonomics* is getting more emphasis in the industry. It is defined as the process of assuring the compatibility and harmony of people with the machines, operations, environment, and products. It requires an extremely well-thought-out system where both people and machines interact with each other in harmony and most effectively.

Juran[17] considers the interaction between the person and the product very important to achieve fitness for use. The design should be evaluated for its effect on the ease with which the person, i.e., the customer or the user, can install, operate, and maintain the product. It should be error-proofed early during the product and process design phases to avoid any human error or operator error during its use and life cycle. The design should also identify why human errors are made and reduce the impact of an operator-dominant process on the output. It should be evaluated for each possible failure mode and its effect on users and on the whole system. It should be *robust, i.e., less sensitive or nonsensitive to variation and abuse of the user if any.*

Refer to Questions 24, 25, and 28.

---

[17] *Juran's Quality Control Handbook* by J. M. Juran, 4th ed., McGraw-Hill, New York, pg. 13.55.

27.   During the design review stage for new equipment, you recommend that a human factors use
      test be performed under one of the following conditions

      a.   on a production model if possible
      b.   not combined with engineering test on the same equipment
      c.   it demonstrates the capability of personnel to perform the required functions using the
            equipment
      d.   all of the above

Key: c.   it demonstrates the capability of personnel to perform the required functions using the
            equipment   (Ref. Applications Question 52, October 1974)
      Refer to Questions 24, 25, and 28.

28.   Having designed a test fixture to performance requirements, the design should be carefully
      evaluated by the quality engineer to insure that it has included

      a.   low cost components
      b.   printout capability
      c.   human motor coordination factors
      d.   mass production methods
      e.   computer inputs

Key: c.   human motor coordination factors   (Ref. Principles Question 88, August 1978)
      Refer to Questions 24 and 25 above for detailed discussion on human factors engineering or
      ergonomics.

29.   An effective supervisor

      a.   sometimes does a job him or herself because he or she can do it better than others
      b.   sees part of his or her role as one of creating worker satisfaction
      c.   has objectives of growth and increased profit by working through other people
      d.   all of the above

Key: d.   all of the above   (Ref. Principles Question 63, October 1974)
      This may sound very simple and self-explanatory, but it is not as simple as it seems in real life.
      This is the tough part for today's management and requires sound understanding of many
      motivational and organizational behavior theories.

30.   The effective supervisor

      a.   sees his or her role primarily as one of making people happy
      b.   sometimes does a job him or herself because he or she can do it better than others
      c.   has objectives of growth and increased profit by working through other people
      d.   assumes the functions of planning, decision making, and monitoring performance, but
            leaves personnel development to the personnel department

Key: c.   has objectives of growth and increased profit by working through other people
        (Ref. Principles Question 15, October 1972)
        Choice c is the most appropriate choice. It may sound very simple and self-explanatory, but it is
        not as simple as it seems in real life. It is a very difficult task for today's management since it
        requires sound understanding of many motivational and organizational behavior theories.
        Choices a and b are important but c is most appropriate. Choice d is incorrect.

31.   When a quality engineer wants parts removed from a line which is operating for tolerance
        checking, he or she should

        a.   request the operator and/or supervisor to get them while he or she is observing
        b.   request the operator and/or supervisor to sample the line and bring them to his or her
                office
        c.   get the samples him- or herself without notifying either the operator and/or supervisor
        d.   go out to the line, stop it him- or herself, take the part, start it, and leave as quickly as
                possible

Key: a.   request the operator and or supervisor to get them while he or she is observing
        (Ref. Applications Question 31, August 1978)
        Choices b, c, and d are not proper because each can cause a feeling of authority, and can result in
        interruption and/or distraction for the operator and supervisor. Also they may result in poor team-
        work. It is necessary to follow formal protocols and use interpersonal skills in such situations
        that can create more motivation on the floor. If you observe the sampling process, you are likely
        to get an unbiased sample that represents the population.

32.   In a visual inspection situation, one of the best ways to minimize deterioration of the quality
        level is to

        a.   retrain the inspector frequently
        b.   add variety to the task
        c.   have a program of frequent eye examinations
        d.   have frequent breaks
        e.   have a standard to compare against the part of the operation

Key: e.   have a standard to compare against the part of the operation
        (Ref. Applications Question 77, August 1978)
        As a first step to minimize the bias and increase the effectiveness of the visual inspection, we
        must have or develop a standard to compare against the part of the operation. In any inspection
        or audit, we must compare the product against its reference standard. The visual standard clearly
        defines the product requirements and its acceptance criteria. This helps the inspector or the
        operator to correctly identify the good or acceptable parts and the nonconforming parts.

        The remaining choices, a, b, c, and d, are important to make the inspection more effective and
        less monotonous. Choice a is important when the product requirements change over a period of
        time, for short production runs, or for products that are extremely sensitive for safety or

compliance. Choices b and d are important for proper ergonomics and human factors analysis. Choice c is helpful in special situations such as color matching, etc. You may need to develop the ranking skills in such questions when all choices look good and seem correct.

33.   Which of the following methods used to improve employee efficiency and promote an atmosphere conducive to quality and profit is the most effective in the long run?

     a.   offering incentives such as bonus, praise, profit sharing, etc.
     b.   strict discipline to reduce mistakes, idleness, and sloppiness
     c.   combination of incentive and discipline to provide both reward for excellence and punishment for inferior performance
     d.   building constructive attitudes through development of realistic quality goals relating to both company and employee success
     e.   all of the above, provided emphasis is placed on attitude motivation, with incentive and discipline used with utmost caution

Key: e.   all of the above, provided emphasis is placed on attitude motivation, with incentive and discipline used with utmost caution   (Ref. Applications Question 78, August 1978)

34.   Which one of the following tasks has been shown to have the most incentive or motivational value to the quality engineer?

     a.   attend defect control meetings
     b.   document action taken on special problems
     c.   investigate product quality problems
     d.   initiate corrective actions to solve nonroutine problems

Key: c.   investigate product quality problems   (Ref. Applications Question 24, October 1972)

35.   Studies have shown that the most effective communications method for transferring information is

     a.   oral only
     b.   written only
     c.   combined written and oral
     d.   bulletin board

Key: c.   combined written and oral   (Ref. Applications Question 72, October 1972)

36.   An essential technique in making training programs effective is to

     a.   set group goals
     b.   have training classes which teach skills and knowledge required
     c.   feedback to the employee meaningful measures of his or her performance
     d.   post results of performance before and after the training program

e.   set individual goals instead of group goals

Key: c.   feedback to the employee meaningful measures of his or her performance
(Ref. Applications Question 79, July 1984)
The key term is *feedback*. If meaningful measures of performance are defined upfront for an employee, then the training needs can be addressed for the weaker areas. The training efforts should be focused on those people who actually need it, based on their measures of performance. This requires setting goals or targets that are attainable and visible. The employees should know what they are supposed to know. They should also know what they are doing, i.e., the output is measurable in a simple and very timely manner with immediate feedback. The training should clearly define and explain the goal of the company, the output, and the method of measuring the output. The training should enable the employee to perform the task and achieve the attainable goal.

Choices a and e are contradictory and improper. The training program does not set the goals, it explains the company's or department goals. Choice b is important, but without feedback of the performance, the effectiveness of training cannot be determined.

37.   One of the most important techniques in making a training program effective is to

a.   concentrate only on developing knowledge and skills needed to do a good job
b.   transmit all of the information that is even remotely related to the function
c.   set individual goals instead of group goals
d.   give people meaningful measures of performance

Key: d.   give people meaningful measures of performance
(Ref. Applications Question 43, October 1974)
Refer to Question 36 above for a detailed discussion. Choice a is important but without feedback of the performance, the effectiveness of training can-not be determined. Choice b is improper because training should transmit only the relevant information, not just any information. Choice c is improper because the training program does not set the goals, it explains the company's or department's goals. This question is repeated in the 1972 examination.[18]

38.   To build an effective quality training program, which of the following should you consider?

a.   The training should be simple and centered upon real company quality problems.
b.   The scope and the content of the training material should be jointly developed by the training staff, the quality engineer, and the personnel from the line organization.
c.   It should be based upon the fact that quality is dynamic and hence the nature of quality problems and training programs will change over time.
d.   The training programs should include personnel from all levels, both management and operators.
e.   all of the above

---

[18] *ASQC - CQE Examination*, ASQC Quality Progress, October 1972, Applications section, Question 39.

Key: e. all of the above

Feigenbaum[19] discusses formalized training in quality control. He discusses all of the above choices as fundamental principles for developing any training program in quality control. He emphasizes that the training programs should be simple, down to earth, and quality-problem-centered rather than quality-theory-centered.

39. You should develop training programs that are tailored to the needs of your company instead of using the generic training programs because of

   I. the unique quality problems and challenges faced by your company
   II. the level of knowledge and skills possessed by the people in the company
   III. the environment and morale of people for training

   a. I and II
   b. II and III
   c. III and I
   d. I, II and III

Key: d. I, II and III

Juran[20] discusses the subject of training for quality and some major issues to be considered for developing any training program.

40. Which of the following will not provide a basis for setting the quality objectives for a breakthrough that will bring unprecedented levels of performance?

   a. To attain and maintain the quality and market leadership position.
   b. The company is loosing the market share rapidly because of lack of competitiveness.
   c. There are too many field problems.
   d. Present performance is competitive.

Key: d. Present performance is competitive.

Juran[21] provides a detailed explanation for setting the quality objectives for a breakthrough that can lead the company to unprecedented levels of performance vs. quality objectives for control to hold the status quo. Choice d is a reason for holding the status quo as a quality objective for control and not for breakthrough.

41. A team can be

   a. a top level management team or a council that promotes, supports, and oversees many functional teams
   b. a project team
   c. a quality circle team

---

[19] *Total Quality Control* by A.V. Feigenbaum, 3rd ed., McGraw-Hill, New York, pg. 214-218.
[20] *Juran's Quality Control Handbook* by J. M. Juran, 4th ed., McGraw-Hill, New York, pg. 11.4-11.5.
[21] *Juran's Quality Control Handbook* by J. M. Juran, 4th ed., McGraw-Hill, New York, pg. 5.20-5.21.

      d.   a problem solving team

      e.   all of the above

Key: e.   all of the above

42.   A quality engineer can be

      a.   an active member of a product development team

      b.   a team leader

      c.   a consultant, i.e., a subject matter expert on quality tools and methods

      d.   a facilitator

      e.   any of the above depending on the objective of the team

Key: e.   any of the above depending on the objective of the team

43.   As a team leader, which of the following is not advisable?

      a.   act as a facilitator for the meeting and follow the agenda properly

      b.   arrange the schedule, logistics, record keeping, publishing of minutes, etc.

      c.   ensure that every team member understands the objective or the goal of the team and create an environment to resolve conflicts

      d.   ask the team members to leave if they disagree with the team leader

Key: d.   ask the team members to leave if they disagree with the team leader

The key word is *not*. Every team is likely to have some disagreements and conflicts. As a team leader, one should not be too personal, but act as a professional. A team leader should keep the team focused on the objectives of the project or problem at hand and act on resolving conflicts. It is possible that some members disagree with some other members, etc. However, such disagreements should be reviewed with the available data. A team leader can use the basic tools of quality such as flow diagram, Pareto diagram, etc., to prioritize the disagreements and assign action items to the proper persons in the team to resolve those items.

It is demoralizing to team members if they are asked to leave the team because of their disagreements.

44.   To make meetings more effective, you as a team leader should

      a.   set clear objectives for the team

      b.   be well prepared

      c.   act as a facilitator, keeping the focus on the agenda

      d.   steer the team to reach a decision and/or a consensus

      e.   all of the above

Key: e.   all of the above

45.   As a member of a quality improvement team, you should

      a.   give only positive feedback
      b.   give only negative feedback
      c.   give constructive feedback
      d.   give feedback to outsmart other team members, or to get back at other people

Key: c.   give constructive feedback

You should be able to give both positive or negative feedback in a constructive manner and not a destructive manner. The feedback should be given at the right time in the team process and should be within the context of the objectives of the team. It should not be at a personal level or should not be focused on personalities but on the objectives and the goals of the team. The feedback giver and receiver should have open minds and understand the context of the feedback. The feedback should identify the weakness in the process, not in the people, and the opportunities for continuous improvement. The feedback should be clear and based on some data or facts and not on judgement. It should not exaggerate the situation.

46.   A conflict can be

      i.   intrapersonal
      ii.   interpersonal
      iii.   between groups or teams

      a.   i and ii above
      b.   ii and iii above
      c.   i and iii above
      d.   i, ii, and iii above

Key: d.   i, ii, and iii above

A conflict means a difference or a disagreement between two people, teams, or parties. There are three main types of conflicts.

Intrapersonal conflict can be simply defined as personal conflict. This type of conflict occurs at a personal level because of differences in the form of beliefs, values, opinions, work processes, methods used, etc. An individual is frustrated personally and/or professionally because of the limitations faced. It also depends on the type of personality, i.e., an introvert or an extrovert, etc.

Interpersonal conflict is a conflict between two or more individuals. This can occur because of a hidden agenda, conflicting goals, competition between two individuals, disagreement in mangement style, a project's progress, roles and/or responsibilities.

Intergroup conflict means conflict between two teams, departments, organizations, parties, etc. This can happen if the project definition is unclear and two different teams are working on the same or similar projects, but sponsored by two different sponsors. Many companies face this largely because the departmental goals and business plans are not in compliance and support of the company's strategic plan, resulting in different plans, priorities, and directions. As a result, people in the respective departments can face conflicts frequently. The willing workers are trying to optimize their departmental goals but actually this can result in a suboptimization of goals locally. Such conflicts actually affect project completion schedules, cost, resources, and ultimately the success of the project. This requires a strong deployment and understanding of a company's vision and strategic plan by all levels in the company.

47.   A conflict in a team activity

        i.   can be positive, resulting in an increased challenge to find new opportunities and
                solutions to a given situation
        ii.   is negative, i.e., it creates a destructive and/or unproductive atmosphere
        iii.   is negative, i.e., it causes stress and also a loss of personal status, i.e., a winner-loser
                situation

        a.   i and ii above
        b.   ii and iii above
        c.   i and iii above
        d.   i, ii, and iii above

Key: d.   i, ii, and iii above
        A conflict means a difference or a disagreement between two parties, in the form of beliefs, values, opinions, work processes, methods used, etc. The effects of the conflict can be both positive and negative. Normally the positive effects of a conflict are not well understood by teams. A good team leader should anticipate conflicts during the course of the team project and anticipate some of them in very early stages of the project. If taken positively, the conflict can identify a weakness, a missing link or a misunderstanding in the goal, objectives, roles and responsibilities, etc. The team leader should address this as a positive situation. He or she should welcome such a conflict as an opportunity and not as a problem and immediately discuss the solution or change in the team's objective, project plan, etc. as a value added input. This can be a proactive approach.

        Conflict is known to have more negative effects. Any difference between two people or activities generally creates both personal and emotional imbalance. This can result in stress and frustration. This can cause a personal feeling of loss of status, position, and/or power. This can result in a winner and a loser. It creates a destructive and/or unproductive atmosphere on the team. The team leader should try to create win-win opportunities for all members by treating it positively and objectively resolving the conflict.

48.   As a team leader, you should try to avoid or resolve conflicts on your team. Which of the
        following action(s) is/are advisable?

        i.   try to explain the goal of the team clearly, so that none of the team members have a
                different goal, outcome, or a hidden agenda.

ii.   try to avoid those members whose ideas, feelings, and/or attitudes are different and incompatible with you and other team members

iii.   try to avoid or manage situations in which the behavior of any member becomes unacceptable to team norms or to other team members

a.   i and ii above
b.   ii and iii above
c.   i and iii above
d.   i, ii, and iii above

Key: c.   i and iii above

Refer to item ii above carefully. As a team leader, you should understand the personality, personal likes and dislikes, and beliefs and values of the team members. It is very likely that some members may have different ideas, attitudes, or feelings that are incompatible with you and other team members. You should not try to avoid them, but respect them and create a positive environment so that they understand the goal of the team and work towards achieving it as a team. As a team leader, you should create an environment of cooperativeness and assertiveness. This will result in a higher level of trust and agreement within the team and also help resolve a conflict.

49.   As a team leader, you can attempt a conflict resolution by being

a.   unassertive and uncooperative
b.   unassertive and cooperative
c.   assertive and uncooperative
d.   assertive and cooperative
e.   all of the above

Key: e.   all of the above

Be careful here. You may be tempted here to select choice d, i.e., being assertive and cooperative. However the correct choice is e.

Conflict resolution is an important but difficult element in many teams and organizations. There is no right method or approach to resolve a conflict and depending on the situation and nature of the conflict, different models of conflict resolution can be appropriate.

Thomas[22] has developed a model using two dimensions - assertiveness (concern for one's own views) and cooperativeness (concern for others' views). Depending on which level of assertiveness and cooperativeness, Thomas has defined five possible conflict resolving modes. They are as follows:

1. *Unassertive and uncooperative* means one's own concerns and others' concerns are not respected, or are neglected. This results in an "*avoiding*" mode of conflict resolution.

---

[22] "Conflict and Conflict Management" by Kenneth Thomas, in M.D. Dunnette (ed.), *Handbook of Industrial and Organizational Psychology*, Rand McNally College Publishing Company, Chicago, 1976.

2. *Unassertive and cooperative* means other members can be satisfied or addressed but one's own concerns can be neglected. This mode is called "*accommodating.*"

3. *Assertive and uncooperative* means addressing one's own concerns at the sake or expense of others. This is called a "*competing*" mode of conflict resolution.

4. *Assertive and cooperative* means addressing one's own and others' concerns at the same time. This results in a "*collaborating*" mode of conflict resolution.

5. A *neutral or mid level* situation where you are somewhat assertive and cooperative (a happy median), means you are giving partial consideration or attention to your own as well as to others' concerns. Here you are trying to reach a common ground. This is called a "*compromising*" mode of conflict resolution.

As a manager, or a team leader, you can choose any of the above conflict resolution modes depending on many factors, e.g., the nature of the conflict, goal of the team, composition of the team, position of the organization, type of team, type and magnitude of the decision and power, etc.

The main purpose of conflict resolution is to bring a high degree of agreement and trust among members of the team or employees of any organization. One should try to minimize the feeling of being adversaries and opponents.

50.   As a manager, you should be able to minimize and resolve conflicts successfully. Which of the following strategies is(are) the most appropriate?

   a.   disregard the conflict or the hostile situation and pay no attention
   b.   physically separate the two parties or groups
   c.   buy more time
   d.   try to improve communication and understanding between the two groups for some period of time

Key: d.   try to improve communication and understanding between the two groups for some period of time

The key word is the "*most.*" Choice a indicates that you are trying to "avoid" a conflict. However, it can be less effective because the sources of conflict are not identified. Choice b is less effective because it may be difficult to separate the two parties, or more resources are required to create and monitor the physical separation. Choice c helps to resolve minor conflicts or it is useful when the conflict is not very crucial or important in nature. Compromising is a win-win situation, i.e., one should try to improve communication and understanding between the two groups for some period of time. Refer to Question 49 above for a detailed discussion on five different conflict resolution modes.

51.   An organization can be

   a.   horizontal
   b.   vertical
   c.   line

      d.   staff

      e.   any one of the above

Key: e.   any one of the above

52.   A quality improvement team may be called a

      a.   quality circle
      b.   project team
      c.   self directed work team
      d.   cross functional/multi disciplined work group
      e.   any one of the above

Key: e.   any one of the above

53.   For effective quality improvements, which of the following item(s) should be considered before selecting a project?

      a.   there is a need to meet the voice of customer, i.e., effect on meeting the customer requirements and/or improving the capability to meet the customer requirements
      b.   there is a need to focus on a key business initiative or issue
      c.   the project is unique in nature and no other project teams are working on it at the same time
      d.   the management at all levels agree and sponsor it is an opportunity for improving the product or process and it will benefit the business plan
      e.   all of the above

Key: e.   all of the above

54.   Which of the following is not a commonly used project management technique?

      a.   a milestone chart
      b.   Gantt chart
      c.   quality function deployment (QFD) matrix
      d.   critical path method (CPM)
      e.   program evaluation and review technique (PERT)

Key: c.   quality function deployment matrix
         The key word is *"not."* The QFD is a matrix used to translate the voice of customer into technical or organizational language and then further deploy it to subsytems, components, and to processes on the floor. It is a strong planning tool for quality and provides an enhanced understanding of voice of customer and the role of every activity in meeting it. It is not generally or commonly used as a project management tool.

A milestone chart is a timing chart or process model that shows a summary of major activities and reviews, decision points, etc., for timely completion of the project.

The Gantt chart is a schedule chart in a bar form. It lists activities and the time required to complete them as bars against different weeks or months, etc. It sometimes has two bars for each activity, showing the estimated completion time and actual completion time to manage the project's progress.

The critical path method and program evaluation and review technique are widely used tools in project management. They list all activities, and the allowable time, and develop a list of critical activities in a graphical form to properly schedule, manage, and act. Refer to Chapter 9, Question 111 Fig. 9-5 for additional discussion.

ASQC-CQE BIBLIOGRAPHY AND OTHER REFERENCES ON MOTIVATION AND HUMAN FACTORS

1. Besterfield, Dale H., *Quality Control,* 3rd ed., Prentice Hall, Englewood Cliffs., N.J., 1990.
2. Caplan, Frank, *The Quality System, A Source book for Managers and Engineers*, 2nd ed., Radnor, PA, Chilton Book Co., 1990.
3. Crosby, Philip B., *Quality is Free*, McGraw-Hill Publishing Co., New York, 1979.
4. Deming, W. Edwards, *Out of Crisis*, Cambridge, MA, MIT Press, 1986.
5. Feigenbaum A.V., *Total Quality Control*, 3rd ed., New York, McGraw-Hill, 1991.
6. Ishikawa, Kaoru, *Guide to Quality Control*, White Plains, NY, Quality Resources, 1976.
7. Juran, J. M., *Juran's Quality Control Handbook*, 4th ed., New York, McGraw-Hill, 1988.
8. Juran, J. M. and F. M. Gryna, *Quality Planning and Analysis*, 3rd ed., New York, McGraw-Hill, 1993.
9. Walsh, Wurster and R. J. Kimber, *Quality Management Handbook*, New York, Marcel Dekker, 1986.

CHAPTER 16

ASQC-CQE EXAMINATION, QUALITY PROGRESS, JULY 1984

PRINCIPLES

Note: *The old examination sets used numbers, e.g., 1, 2, 3, 4, and 5, for various choices for each question. Hence the following questions use the numerical choices in its original format.*

Recent examinations and the study guides published in ASQC's recent certification brochures use letters, e.g., a, b, c, d, and e, for choices to a question in place of numbers. Hence letters are used in all individual subject matter chapters 3 through 15. Readers are advised to note this difference while referring to solutions in respective chapters.

1. A null hypothesis assumes that a process is producing no more than the maximum allowable rate of defective items. The Type II error is to conclude that the process

    1. is producing too many defectives when it actually isn't
    2. is not producing too many defectives when it actually is
    3. is not producing too many defectives when it is not
    4. is producing too many defectives when it is

    Refer to Question 50 in Chapter 4, Statistical Inference and Hypothesis Testing.

2. A number derived from sample data which describes the data in some useful way is called a

    1. constant
    2. statistic
    3. parameter
    4. critical value

    Refer to Question 3 in Chapter 3, Fundamental Concepts of Probability and Statistics.

3. The spread of individual observations from a normal process capability distribution may be expressed numerically as

    1. $6\overline{R}/d_2$
    2. $2 \times A_2\overline{R}$
    3. $\overline{R} / d_2$
    4. $D_4\overline{R}$

    Refer to Question 56 in Chapter 7, Statistical Process Control.

4.   In MIL-STD-105D, the AQL is always determined at what P_a on the OC curve?

      1.   0.05
      2.   0.10
      3.   0.90
      4.   0.95
      5.   none of the above

      Refer to Question 38 in Chapter 8, Acceptance Sampling.

5.   For the normal distribution the relationships among the median, mean and mode are that

      1.   they are all equal to the same value
      2.   the mean and mode have the same value but the median is different
      3.   each has a value different from the other two
      4.   the mean and median are the same but the mode is different

      Refer to Question 88 in Chapter 3, Fundamental Concepts of Probability and Statistics.

6.   The test used for testing significance in an analysis of variance table is

      1.   the Z test
      2.   the t test
      3.   the F test
      4.   the chi-square test

      Refer to Question 37 in Chapter 6, Design of Experiments.

7.   A sample of n observations has a mean $\overline{X}$ and standard deviation $s_x > 0$. If a single observation which equals the value of the sample mean $\overline{X}$ is removed from the sample, which of the following is true?

      1. $\overline{X}$ and s_x both change.
      2. $\overline{X}$ and s_x remain the same.
      3. $\overline{X}$ remains the same but s_x increases.
      4. $\overline{X}$ remains the same but s_x decreases.

      Refer to Question 109 in Chapter 3, Fundamental Concepts of Probability and Statistics.

8.   The Dodge Romig tables are designed to minimize which parameter?

      1.   AOQL
      2.   AQL
      3.   ATI
      4.   AOQ

Refer to Question 59 in Chapter 8, Acceptance Sampling.

9.   In a single factor analysis of variance, the assumption of homogeneity of variance applies to

        1.   the variance within the treatment groups
        2.   the variance of the treatment means
        3.   the total variance
        4.   all of the above

Refer to Questions 38, 39, and 41 in Chapter 6, Design of Experiments. This question is repeated with slight changes in the October 1974 and August 1978 examinations.[1]

10.   When used together for variable data, which of the following pair of quantities is the most useful in preparing control charts?

        1.   AQL, p
        2.   p, n
        3. $\overline{X}$, R
        4.   R, σ

Refer to Question 19 in Chapter 7, Statistical Process Control.

11.   An operation requires shipments from your vendor of small lots of fixed size. The attribute sampling plan used for receiving inspection should have its OC curve developed using

        1.   the Binomial distribution
        2.   the Gaussian (Normal) distribution
        3.   the Poisson distribution
        4.   the Hypergeometric distribution

Refer to Question 11 in Chapter 8, Acceptance Sampling.

12.   The acronym "AQL" as used in sampling inspection means

        1.   that level of lot quality for which there is a small risk of rejecting the lot
        2.   the Average Quality Limit
        3.   the maximum percent defective that can be considered satisfactory as a process average
        4.   the quality level

Refer to Question 29 in Chapter 8, Acceptance Sampling. This question is repeated in the October 1974 examination.[2]

---

[1] *ASQC - CQE Examination*, Quality Progress, October 1974, Principles section, Question 39, and August 1978, Applications section, Question 23.
[2] *ASQC - CQE Examination*, Quality Progress, October 1974, Principles section, Question 13.

13. A 3^2 experiment means that we are considering

    1. two levels of three factors
    2. two dependent variables and three independent variables
    3. two go/nogo variables and three continuous variables
    4. three levels of two factors

Refer to Question 29 in Chapter 6, Design of Experiments.

14. An operating characteristic curve shows

    1. the probability of accepting lots of various quality levels by sampling methods
    2. the operating characteristics of a machine
    3. how to operate a machine for best quality results
    4. the probability that a lot contains a certain number of rejectable parts

Refer to Question 9 in Chapter 8, Acceptance Sampling.

15. Best assumptions underlying the Analysis of Variance include

    A. observations are from normally distributed populations
    B. observations are from populations with equal variances
    C. observations are from populations with equal means

    1. A and B only
    2. A and C only
    3. B and C only
    4. A, B, and C

Refer to Questions 38, 39, and 41 in Chapter 6, Design of Experiments.

16. Two quantities which uniquely determine a single sampling attribute plan are

    1. AQL and LTPD
    2. sample size and rejection number
    3. AQL and producer's risk
    4. LTPD and consumer's risk

Refer to Questions 25 through 28 in Chapter 8, Acceptance Sampling.

17. All of the following statements are true except

    1. in multiple regression, extrapolation beyond the region of observation can lead to erroneous predications
    2. at least three variables are involved in multiple regression
    3. multiple regression involves one independent and two or more dependent variables

Refer to Question 18 in Chapter 5, Regression and Correlation Analysis.

18.   The primary advantage of the Latin square design compared to the factorial design is that

       1.   it requires less data
       2.   it eliminates the need for interactions
       3.   it allows higher significance levels
       4.   it does not require homogeneity of variance

       Refer to Question 33 in Chapter 6, Design of Experiments.

19.   For two events, A and B, one of the following is a true probability statement

       1. $P(A \text{ or } B) = P(A) + P(B)$ if A and B are independent
       2. $P(A \text{ or } B) = P(A) + P(B)$ if A and B are mutually exclusive
       3. $P(A \text{ and } B) = P(A) \times P(B)$ if A and B are mutually exclusive
       4. $P(A \text{ or } B) = P(A) \times P(B)$ if A and B are independent

       Refer to Question 38 in Chapter 3, Fundamental Concepts of Probability and Statistics.

20.   Which one of the following best describes machine capability?

       1.   the total variation of all cavities of a mold, cavities of a die cast machine of spindles of an automatic assembly machine
       2.   the inherent variation of the machine
       3.   the total variation over a shift
       4.   the variation in a short run of consecutively produced parts

       Refer to Question 59 in Chapter 7, Statistical Process Control.

21.   In comparison with attributes sampling plans, variables sampling plans

       1.   have the advantage of greater simplicity
       2.   usually require a larger sample size for comparable assurance as to correctness of decisions in judging a single quality characteristic
       3.   have the advantage of being applicable to either single or multiple quality characteristics
       4.   provide greater assurance for the same sample size, as to the correctness or decisions in judging a single quality characteristic

       Refer to Question 65 in Chapter 8, Acceptance Sampling.

22.   To state that a model in an experimental design is fixed indicates that

       1.   the levels used for each factor are the only ones of interest
       2.   the levels were chosen from a fixed population
       3.   the equipment from which the data are collected must not be moved
       4.   the factors under consideration are qualitative

Refer to Question 9 in Chapter 6, Design of Experiments.

23.   Which of the following cannot be a null hypothesis?

        1.   The population means are equal.
        2.   p' = 0.5.
        3.   The sample means are equal.
        4.   The difference in the population means is 3.85".

Refer to Question 45 in Chapter 4, Statistical Inference and Hypothesis Testing.

24.   You have been doing precision testing on a special-order micrometer delivered by a vendor.
        The sample size in your test was 25 readings. The acceptance specification requires a precision
        sigma of 0.003 inch. Your observed precision sigma was 0.0033 inch. Although the observed
        precision did not meet the requirements, you are reluctant to reject it because you need it badly.
        You should

        1.   accept it because it is close enough
        2.   reject it because it did not meet the criteria
        3.   apply the chi-square test to see if the micrometer should be accepted
        4.   apply the F test to see if the micrometer should be accepted
        5.   send the micrometer to the gage lab for adjustment

Refer to Question 73 in Chapter 4, Statistical Inference and Hypothesis Testing.

25.   If in a t test alpha is 0.05,

        1.   5% of the time we will say that there is no real difference but in reality there is a
                difference
        2.   5% of the time we will make a correct inference
        3.   5% of the time we will say that there is a real difference when there really is not a
                difference
        4.   95% of the time we will make an incorrect inference
        5.   95% of the time the null hypothesis will be correct

Refer to Question 53 in Chapter 4, Statistical Inference and Hypothesis Testing.

26.   The expression $P(x) = \dfrac{\mu^x e^{-\mu}}{x!}$ is the general term for

        1.   Poisson distribution
        2.   Pascal distribution
        3.   Hypergeometric distribution
        4.   Binomial distribution

Refer to Question 171 in Chapter 3, Fundamental Concepts of Probability and Statistics.

27.   An experiment with two factors, in which all levels of one variable are run at each level of the
        second variable, is called a

        1.   one way experiment
        2.   Latin square experiment
        3.   factorial experiment
        4.   fractional factorial experiment

        Refer to Question 26 in Chapter 6, Design of Experiments.

28.   How many outcomes are possible when performing a single trial of a binomial experiment?

        1.   One
        2.   Two
        3.   Three

        Refer to Question 152 in Chapter 3, Fundamental Concepts of Probability and Statistics.

29.   Under acceptance sampling, with screening, average outgoing quality will not be worse
        in the long run than the

        1.   ATI
        2.   AQL
        3.   AOQL
        4.   AOQ

        Refer to Question 35 in Chapter 8, Acceptance Sampling.

30.   Which of the following does not generate product quality characteristics?

        1.   Designer
        2.   Inspector
        3.   Machinist
        4.   Equipment engineer

        Refer to Question 8 in Chapter 12, Product and Materials Control and Measurement Systems.

31.   A comparison of variable and attribute sampling systems will show that equal protection (as
        determined by the OC curves) can be obtained

        1.   when the variable and attribute sample sizes are equal
        2.   when the attribute sample is smaller than the variable sample
        3.   when the variable sample is smaller than the attribute sample
        4.   none of these

        Refer to Question 68 in Chapter 8, Acceptance Sampling.

32. A quality control program is considered to be

    1. a collection of quality control procedures and guidelines
    2. a step-by-step list of all quality control checkpoints
    3. a summary of company quality control policies
    4. a system of activities to provide quality of products and service

    Refer to Question 23 in Chapter 9, Quality Practices and Applications.

33. A milestone in product quality liability was accomplished in 1963 as a result of Greenman vs. Yuba Power Products Inc. The court stated that the costs of injuries resulting from defective products are borne by the manufacturers that put such products on the market rather than by the injured persons who are powerless to protect themselves. This ruling caused a phase-out of which of the following concepts?

    1. Implied warranty
    2. Caveat Emptor
    3. Privity of contract
    4. Res ipsa loquitur

    Refer to Question 107 in Chapter 13, Reliability, Maintainability, and Product Safety.

34. When planning a total quality system, one key objective is to provide a means of guaranteeing "the maintenance of product integrity." Which of the following quality system provisions is designed to MOST directly provide such a guarantee?

    1. Drawing and print control.
    2. Calibration and maintenance of test equipment.
    3. Identification and segregation of nonconforming material.
    4. Specification change control.

    Refer to Question 43 in Chapter 9, Quality Practices and Applications and Question 54 in Chapter 12, Product and Materials Control and Measurement Systems. This question is repeated with a slight change in the October 1974 examination.[3]

35. The primary reason for evaluating and maintaining surveillance over a supplier's quality program is to

    1. perform product inspection at source
    2. eliminate incoming inspection cost
    3. motivate suppliers to improve quality
    4. make sure the supplier's quality program is functioning effectively

    Refer to Question 48 in Chapter 9, Quality Practices and Applications and Question 58 in Chapter 11, Quality Auditing.

---

[3] *ASQC - CQE Examination*, Quality Progress, October 1974, Principles section, Question 27.

36.   The primary reason for first piece inspection is to

       1.   approve a setup for further production
       2.   accept a lot prior to completion of the lot
       3.   try out a new inspection method
       4.   eliminate need for further inspection

       Refer to Question 13 in Chapter 12, Product and Materials Control and Measurement Systems.

37.   Machine capabilities studies on four machines yielded the following information:

Machine	Average ($\overline{X}$)	Capability (6σ)
#1	1.495	0.004"
#2	1.502	0.006"
#3	1.500	0.012"
#4	1.498	0.012"

       The tolerance on the particular dimension is 1.5000 ± 0.005". If the average value can be readily shifted by adjustment to the machine, the best machine to use is

       1.   Machine #1
       2.   Machine #2
       3.   Machine #3
       4.   Machine #4

       Refer to Question 61 in Chapter 7, Statistical Process Control.

38.   Based on the information given in the above question, if the average value cannot be readily shifted by adjustment to the machine and no rework or repair is possible then the best machine to use is

       1.   Machine #1
       2.   Machine #2
       3.   Machine #3
       4.   Machine #4

       Note: ASQC's correction: *delete this question.*

39.   Incoming inspection is based most directly on

       1.   design requirements
       2.   purchase order requirements
       3.   manufacturing requirements
       4.   customer use of the end product

       Refer to Question 14 in Chapter 12, Product and Materials Control and Measurement Systems.

40. The "quality function" of a company is best described as

    1. the degree to which the company product conforms to a design or specification
    2. that collection of activities through which "fitness for use" is achieved
    3. the degree to which a class or category of product possesses satisfaction for people generally
    4. all of the above

    Refer to Question 12 in Chapter 9, Quality Practices and Applications.

41. The advantage of a written procedure is

    1. it provides flexibility in dealing with problems
    2. unusual conditions are handled better
    3. it is a perpetual coordination device
    4. coordination with other departments is not required

    Refer to Question 35 in Chapter 9, Quality Practices and Applications.

42. In spite of the quality engineer's best efforts, situations may develop in which his or her decision is overruled. The most appropriate action would be to

    1. resign his or her position based upon his (or her) convictions
    2. report his or her findings to an outside source such as a regulatory agency or the press
    3. document his or her findings, report to his (or her) superiors, and move on to the next assignment
    4. discuss his or her findings with co-workers in order to gain support, thereby forcing action

    Refer to Question 18 in Chapter 9, Quality Practices and Applications.

43. In preparing a product quality policy for your company, you should do all of the following except

    1. specify the means by which quality performance is measured
    2. develop criteria for identifying risk situations and specify whose approval is required when there are known risks
    3. include procedural matters and functional responsibilities
    4. state quality goals

    Refer to Question 33 in Chapter 9, Quality Practices and Applications.

44. Which of the following is the most important when calibrating a piece of the equipment?

    1. Calibration sticker
    2. Maintenance history card
    3. Standard used

4.   Calibration interval

Refer to Question 84 in Chapter 12, Product and Materials Control and Measurement Systems.

45.   A "negative" specification on an attribute (such as Salmonella) of a food product generally means

1.   that gram negative organisms are permissible
2.   that given the state or the technology, none can be detected
3.   that levels above one part per billion are to be rejected
4.   none of the above

46.   Products should be subjected to tests which are designed to

1.   demonstrate advertised performance
2.   demonstrate basic function at minimum testing cost
3.   approximate the conditions to be experienced in customer's application
4.   assure that specifications are met under laboratory conditions
5.   assure performance under severe environmental conditions

Refer to Question 11 in Chapter 12, Product and Materials Control and Measurement Systems.

47.   Holography is a nondestructive test technique which is used to

1.   measure hole locations with an optical device
2.   measure the depth of the halos around drilled holes in printed wiring boards
3.   measure the continuity of plated-through holes in printed wiring boards
4.   measure surface displacements by recording interference patterns
5.   measure flaws using acoustic vibration

Refer to Question 96 in Chapter 12, Product and Materials Control and Measurement Systems.

48.   Characteristics for which 100% inspection may be practicable include all of the following except

1.   dimensions subject to measurements or go/nogo gaging
2.   performance characteristics subject to nondestructive testing
3.   characteristics observable by visual inspection
4.   ultimate physical properties (tensile strength, viscosity)

Refer to Question 95 in Chapter 12, Product and Materials Control and Measurement Systems.

49.   The strength of a magnetic field is known as

1.   flux density
2.   ferromagnetic force
3.   magnetic density
4.   coercive force

Refer to Question 102 in Chapter 12, Product and Materials Control and Measurement Systems.

50.   In the drawing tolerance

| θ | 0.005 | (M) | A | B | C |

"C" is the

1.   primary datum
2.   tertiary datum
3.   basic datum
4.   largest datum

Refer to Question 164 in Chapter 12, Product and Materials Control and Measurement Systems.

51.   Station control is

1.   a technique to implement quality plans in the shop
2.   applied to assure that planned quality performance is consistently and economically maintained
3.   a technique which emphasizes control of input
4.   all of the above

Refer to Question 25 in Chapter 12, Product and Materials Control and Measurement Systems.

52.   A tracer-type surface finish instrument, such as a profilometer, can be used to measure all of the following except

1.   roughness on gear teeth
2.   depth of the scratches on a metal surface
3.   roughness on mild steel plate
4.   surface quality of tapered hole

Refer to Question 134 in Chapter 12, Product and Materials Control and Measurement Systems.

53.   Which material listed below can be usefully tested by the magnetic particle method?

1.   Carbon steel
2.   Aluminum
3.   Magnesium
4.   Lead
5.   None of the above

Refer to Question 97 in Chapter 12, Product and Materials Control and Measurement Systems.

54.   Where inspector efficiency is defined as the ratio of correct decisions to the total decisions

regarding individual items, most inspection operations performed by human inspectors are approximately

1.   40-55% efficient
2.   55-70% efficient
3.   70-95% efficient
4.   95-100% efficient

Refer to Question 43 in Chapter 12, Product and Materials Control and Measurement Systems.

55.   Terminal-based linearity, as applied to the linearity accuracy of voltage or resistance division of slide wires, potentiometers, step dividers, etc., is defined as

1.   the maximum deviation from an arc of 180°, based on the effective electrical travel
2.   the maximum deviation from a straight line which passes through the zero and 100% points, based on the effective electric travel
3.   the algebraic difference of the end-scale values
4.   the percent of the end-scale value of an instrument that corresponds to the end-scale indication
5.   none of the above

Refer to Question 140 in Chapter 12, Product and Materials Control and Measurement Systems.

56.   Why would inspection by variables be superior to inspection by attributes?

A.   Inspection by variables is easier to administer than inspection by attributes.
B.   More information is obtained when inspection by variables is utilized.
C.   Inspection by variables usually requires smaller samples than inspection by attributes.

1.   B and C only
2.   C only
3.   A and B only
4.   A, B, and C only

Refer to Questions 69 and 70 in Chapter 8, Acceptance Sampling.

57.   In life cycle costing, the term "life" refers to whose viewpoint?

1.   Producer's
2.   User's
3.   Contractor's
4.   Quality control

Refer to Question 100 in Chapter 13, Reliability, Maintainability, and Product Safety.

58.   Which of the following quality cost indices is likely to have greatest appeal to top management as an indicator of relative cost?

1.   Quality cost per unit of product
2.   Quality cost per hour of direct production labor
3.   Quality cost per unit of processing cost
4.   Quality cost per unit of sales
5.   Quality cost per dollar of direct production labor

Refer to Question 75 in Chapter 10, Quality Cost Analysis.

59.   Review of the purchase orders for quality requirements falls into which one of the following quality cost segments?

1.   Prevention
2.   Appraisal
3.   Internal failures
4.   External failures

Refer to Question 27 in Chapter 10, Quality Cost Analysis.

60.   Failure costs include costs due to

1.   quality control engineering
2.   inspection setup for tests
3.   certification of special process suppliers
4.   supplier analysis of nonconforming hardware

Refer to Question 48 in Chapter 10, Quality Cost Analysis.

61.   Quality cost trend analysis is facilitated by comparing quality costs to

1.   manufacturing costs over the same time period
2.   cash flow reports
3.   appropriate measurement basis
4.   QC department budget

Refer to Question 78 in Chapter 10, Quality Cost Analysis.

62.   Which of the following is the least likely to be reported as a failure-related cost?

1.   Sorting lots rejected by a sampling procedure
2.   Downtime caused by late delivery of a purchased part rejected by the supplier's final inspection
3.   Repair of field failures
4.   Retesting of repaired product

Refer to Question 49 in Chapter 10, Quality Cost Analysis.

63.   The basic objective of a quality cost program is to

       1.   identify the source of quality failures
       2.   interface with the accounting department
       3.   improve the profit of your company
       4.   identify quality control department costs

       Refer to Question 4 in Chapter 10, Quality Cost Analysis.

64.   Cost of calibrating the test and inspection equipment would be included in

       1.   prevention cost
       2.   appraisal cost
       3.   failure cost
       4.   material-procurement cost

       Refer to Question 38 in Chapter 10, Quality Cost Analysis.

65.   In some instances the ordinary cost balance formula is not valid and cannot be applied because of the presence of vital intangibles. Such an intangible involves

       1.   safety of human beings
       2.   compliance with legislation
       3.   apparatus for collection of revenue
       4.   credit to marketing as new sales for warranty replacements
       5.   none of the above

       Refer to Question 25 in Chapter 10, Quality Cost Analysis.

66.   When looking for existing sources of external failure cost data, which of the following is usually the best source available?

       1.   Customer corrective action requests
       2.   Salesmen's field reports
       3.   Accounting reports on "salcs of seconds" or "distressed merchandise"
       4.   Returned material reports

       Refer to Question 45 in Chapter 10, Quality Cost Analysis.

67.   The quality assurance function is comparable to which of the following other business functions in concept?

       1.   General accounting
       2.   Cost accounting
       3.   Audit accounting
       4.   All of the above

Refer to Question 13 in Chapter 11, Quality Auditing.

68. The term "quality audit" can refer to the appraisal of the quality system of

1. an entire plant or company
2. one product
3. one major quality activity
4. any of the above

Refer to Question 15 in Chapter 11, Quality Auditing.

69. You would normally NOT include data from which of the following investigations in quality auditing?

1. Examination of all items produced
2. Examination of customer needs and the adequacy of design specifications in reflecting these needs
3. Examination of vendor product specifications and monitoring procedures
4. Examination of customer quality complaints and adequacy of corrective action

Refer to Question 47 in Chapter 11, Quality Auditing. This question is repeated with a slight change in the October 1974 examination.[4]

70. In order to be effective, the Quality Audit function should ideally be

1. an independent organizational segment in the Quality Control function
2. an independent organizational segment in the Production control function
3. an independent organizational segment in the Manufacturing operations function
4. all of the above

Refer to Question 16 in Chapter 11, Quality Auditing.

71. Which of the following quality system provisions is of the greatest concern when preparing an audit checklist for a quality system audit?

1. Drawing and print control
2. Make-up of the MRB (Material Review Board)
3. Training level of inspectors
4. Optimization of production processes
5. Calibration of test equipment

Refer to Question 27 in Chapter 11, Quality Auditing. This question is repeated with a slight change in the question, i.e., greatest concern vs. least concern, in the October 1974 examination.[5]

---

[4] *ASQC - CQE Examination*, Quality Progress, October 1974, Principles section, Question 36.
[5] *ASQC - CQE Examination*, Quality Progress, October 1974, Principles section, Question 53.

72. The following are reasons why an independent audit of actual practice vs. procedures should be performed periodically.

   A. Pressures may force the supervisors to deviate from approved procedures.
   B. The supervisor may not have time for organized follow-up or adherence to procedures.
   C. Supervisors are not responsible for implementing procedures.

   1. A and B only
   2. B and C only
   3. A and C only
   4. A, B, and C

   Refer to Question 26 in Chapter 11, Quality Auditing.

73. A Vendor Quality Survey

   1. is used to predict whether a potential vendor can meet quality requirements
   2. is an audit of a vendor's product for a designated period of time
   3. is always conducted by Quality Control personnel only
   4. reduces cost by eliminating the need for receiving inspection of the surveyed vendor's product

   Refer to Question 59 in Chapter 11, Quality Auditing.

74. The greatest contribution of a reliability effort is made in the

   1. design area
   2. manufacturing area
   3. shipping area
   4. field service area

   Refer to Question 71 in Chapter 13, Reliability, Maintainability, and Product Safety

75. Preliminary hazard analysis

   1. is a review of safety problems prior to production
   2. is normally done at a time when there is little design detail
   3. can be used to identify the principal hazards when the product is first conceived
   4. all of the above

   Refer to Question 27 in Chapter 13, Reliability, Maintainability, and Product Safety.

76. Inherent or intrinsic reliability

   1. is that reliability which can be improved only by design change
   2. can be improved only by an improvement in the state of the art

3. is that reliability estimated over a stated period of time by a stated measurement technique

4. is not an estimated reliability

Refer to Question 11 in Chapter 13, Reliability, Maintainability, and Product Safety.

77. Reliability prediction is

1. the process of estimating performance
2. the process of estimating the probability that a product will perform its intended function for a stated time
3. the process of telling "how you can get there from here"
4. all of the above

Refer to Question 13 in Chapter 13, Reliability, Maintainability, and Product Safety.

78. Maintainability is

1. the probability of a system being restored to functional operation within a given period of time
2. performing adequate maintenance on a system
3. the probability of survival of a system for a given period of time
4. maintaining a machine in satisfactory working condition
5. none of the above

Refer to Question 28 in Chapter 13, Reliability, Maintainability, and Product Safety. This question is repeated with a slight change in the October 1974 examination.[6]

79. Quality assurance plans for computer software packages should include all of the following elements except

1. accurate and complete documentation of programs
2. test criteria and test procedures
3. provision of alternate packages
4. testing under real life conditions

Refer to Question 33 in Chapter 13, Reliability, Maintainability, and Product Safety.

80. Basic sources of reliability data are

A. In-plant testing
B. Field testing
C. Operation by user

1. A and B

---

[6] *ASQC - CQE Examination, Quality Progress*, October 1974, Principles section, Question 35.

2.   B and C only
3.   A and C only
4.   A, B, and C

Refer to Question 34 in Chapter 13, Reliability, Maintainability, and Product Safety.

81.   Complaint indices should

1.   recognize the degree of dissatisfaction as viewed by the customer
2.   provide a direct input to corrective action
3.   not necessarily be based on field complaints or dollar values of claims paid or on service calls
4.   ignore life-cycle costs

Refer to Question 88 in Chapter 9, Quality Practices and Applications.

82.   Effective Automated Data Processing is

1.   a process which uses punch cards to sort, compile, and analyze data
2.   a process in which computers are used to analyze data
3.   a process, largely self-regulating, in which information is handled with a minimum of human effort and intervention
4.   a process in which records are classified, sorted, computed, summarized, transmitted, and stored
5.   none of the above

Refer to Question 9 in Chapter 14, Quality Information Systems.

83.   When using a hand-held programmable calculator to compute the adjusted sum of squares for a variable, the formula $[\sum(X^2) - (\overline{X})(\sum X)]$ is preferred to $[\sum(X^2) - (\sum X)^2/N]$ because

1. $\overline{X}$ has already been calculated
2.   the preferred formula is significantly easier to compute
3.   there is less chance of underflow or overflow
4.   division by N may produce a rounding error

Refer to Question 119 in Chapter 3, Fundamental Concepts of Probability and Statistics.

84.   Analysis of data on all product return is important because

1.   failure rates change with length of product usage
2.   changes in design and in customer use are often well reflected
3.   immediate feedback and analysis of product performance becomes available
4.   all of the above
5.   none of the above

Refer to Question 89 in Chapter 9, Quality Practices and Applications.

85.   A successful quality circle program should produce all of the following benefits except

    1.   improved worker morale
    2.   decreased need for management efforts to maintain quality
    3.   improved communication between managers and quality circle members
    4.   cost savings from participative problem solving

Refer to Question 9 in Chapter 15, Motivation and Human Factors.

86.   The famous Hawthorne study provided the following clinical evidence regarding the factors that can increase work group productivity.

    1.   Attention and recognition are more important than working conditions.
    2.   Productivity did not change significantly under any of the test conditions.
    3.   Informal group pressures set a production "goal".
    4.   People with higher capabilities are bored with routine jobs.
    5.   Workstation layout is critical to higher productivity.

Refer to Question 1 in Chapter 15, Motivation and Human Factors. This question is repeated in the August 1978 examination.[7]

87.   Which of the following is NOT a management-initiated error?

    1.   The imposition of conflicting priorities
    2.   The lack of operator capacity
    3.   Management indifference or apathy
    4.   Conflicting quality specifications
    5.   Work space, equipment, and environment

Refer to Question 23 in Chapter 15, Motivation and Human Factors.

88.   Which one of these human management approaches has led to the practice of job enrichment?

    1.   Skinner
    2.   Maslow
    3.   Herzberg's "Hygiene Theory"
    4.   McGregor

Refer to Question 2 in Chapter 15, Motivation and Human Factors.

89.   Extensive research into the results of quality motivation has shown that

    1.   the supervisor's attitude towards his (or her) people is of little long term consequence

---

[7] *ASQC - CQE Examination*, Quality Progress, August 1978, Applications section, Question 80.

2.   motivation is too nebulous to be correlated with results
3.   motivation is increased when employees set their own goals
4.   motivation is increased when management sets challenging goals slightly beyond the attainment of the better employees

Refer to Question 7 in Chapter 15, Motivation and Human Factors.

90.   Select the nonhygienic motivator as defined by Maslow

1.   Salary increases
2.   Longer vacations
3.   Improved medical plan
4.   Sales bonuses
5.   Performance recognition

Refer to Question 3 in Chapter 15, Motivation and Human Factors.

APPLICATIONS

1. A study was conducted on the relationship between the speed of different cars and their gasoline mileage. The correlation coefficient was found to be 0.35. Later it was discovered that there was a defect in the speedometers and they had all been set 5 miles per hour too fast. The correlation coefficient was computed using the corrected scores. Its new value will be

    1. 0.30
    2. 0.35
    3. 0.40
    4. −0.35

    Refer to Question 35 in Chapter 5, Regression and Correlation Analysis.

2. A two-way Analysis of Variance has r levels for one variable and c levels for the second variable with two observations per cell. The degrees of freedom for interaction is

    1. $2(r \times c)$
    2. $(r - 1)(c - 1)$
    3. $rc - 1$
    4. $2(r - 1)(c - 1)$

    Refer to Question 52 in Chapter 6, Design of Experiments.

3. For a certain make of car, the factory-installed brake linings have a mean lifetime of 40,000 miles with a 5000 mile standard deviation. A sample of 100 cars has been selected for testing. Assuming that the finite population correction may be ignored, the standard error of $\overline{X}$ is

    1. 50 miles
    2. 500 miles
    3. 400 miles
    4. 4000 miles

    Refer to Question 12 in Chapter 4, Statistical Inference and Hypothesis Testing.

4. You have been asked to sample a lot of 500 (this is ASQC's correction in this question) units from a vendor whose past quality has been about 2% defective. A sample of 40 pieces have been drawn from the lot and you have been told to reject the lot if you find two or more parts defective. What is the probability of finding two or more parts defective?

    1. 0.953
    2. 0.809
    3. 0.191
    4. 0.047

Refer to Question 174 in Chapter 3, Fundamental Concepts of Probability and Statistics.

5.   What is the probability of finding no defective items in a random sample of 100 items taken from the output of a continuous process which averages 0.70% defective items?

    1.   0.49
    2.   1.74
    3.   0.10
    4.   0.74
    5.   0.33

Refer to Question 175 in Chapter 3, Fundamental Concepts of Probability and Statistics.

6.   What is the standard deviation of the following sample:
3.2, 3.1, 3.3, 3.3, 3.17? (The answer was corrected by ASQC.)

    1.   3.2
    2.   0.0894
    3.   0.10
    4.   0.0498
    5.   0.20

Refer to Question 98 in Chapter 3, Fundamental Concepts of Probability and Statistics.

Note: *Please refer to the dialogue below for the following three (3) questions.*

Lots of 75 parts each are inspected to an AQL of 0.25% using normal inspection, single sampling. A single lower specification limit denoted by L is used. The standard level (Level II in MIL-STD-105D, Level IV in MIL-STD-414) is specified.

7.   The sample size for MIL-STD-105D is

    1.   13
    2.   32
    3.   50
    4.   75

Refer to Question 41 in Chapter 8, Acceptance Sampling.

8.   The sample size for MIL-STD-414, estimating variability by the range method, is
    1.   3
    2.   7
    3.   10
    4.   15
    5.   20

Refer to Question 71 in Chapter 8, Acceptance Sampling.

9.   The acceptance criterion, using MIL-STD-414 and the range method, is: Accept the lot if

     1. $(\overline{X} - L)/R \geq 0.702$
     2. $(\overline{X} - L)/R \geq 0.863$
     3. $(\overline{X} - L)/R \geq 1.06$
     4. $(\overline{X} - L)/R \leq 1.06$

     Refer to Question 72 in Chapter 8, Acceptance Sampling.

10.   A process is producing material which is 30% defective. Five pieces are selected at random for the inspection. What is the probability of exactly two good pieces being found in the sample?

     1.   0.868
     2.   0.309
     3.   0.436
     4.   0.132

     Refer to Question 160 in Chapter 3, Fundamental Concepts of Probability and Statistics.

11.   An inspection plan is set up to randomly sample 3 ft² of a 1000 ft² carpet and to accept the carpet only if no flaws are found in the 3 ft² sample. What is the probability that a roll of carpet with an average of one flaw per square foot will be rejected by the plan?

     1.   0.05
     2.   0.72
     3.   0.90
     4.   0.95

     Refer to Question 176 in Chapter 3, Fundamental Concepts of Probability and Statistics.

12.   A process is in control at $\overline{\overline{X}} = 100$, $\overline{R} = 7.3$ with n = 4. If the process level shifts to 101.5 with the same $\overline{R}$, what is the probability that the next $\overline{X}$ point will fall outside the old control limits?

     1.   0.016
     2.   0.029
     3.   0.122
     4.   0.360

     Refer to Question 144 in Chapter 3, Fundamental Concepts of Probability and Statistics, and Question 38 in Chapter 7, Statistical Process Control.

13.   The following coded results were obtained from a single factor completely randomized experiment, in which the production outputs of three machines (A, B, C) were to be compared.

A	4	8	5	7	6
B	2	0	1	2	4
C	−3	1	−2	−1	0

What is the sum of the squares for the error term?

1.   170
2.   130
3.   40
4.   14
5.   28.8   (This is ASQC's correction for this answer.)

Refer to Question 53 in Chapter 6, Design of Experiments.

14.   What value in the Z table has 5% of the area in the tail beyond it?

1.   1.960
2.   1.645
3.   2.576
4.   1.282

Refer to Question 131 in Chapter 3, Fundamental Concepts of Probability and Statistics.

15.   An $\overline{X}$ and R chart was prepared for an operation using twenty samples with five pieces in each sample. $\overline{X}$ was found to be 33.6 and $\overline{R}$ was 6.20. During production a sample of five was taken, and the pieces measured 36, 43, 37, 25, and 38. At the time this sample was taken

1.   both average and range were within control limits
2.   neither average nor range were within control limits
3.   only the average was outside control limits
4.   only the range was outside control limits

Refer to Question 40 in Chapter 7, Statistical Process Control.

16.   A comparison of known sigma and unknown sigma variables plans will show that equal protection is obtained (as determined by the OC curves)

1.   when the unknown sigma sample size is smaller than the known sigma sample size
2.   when the known sigma sample size is larger than the unknown sigma sample size
3.   when the known sigma and unknown sigma sample sizes are equal
4.   none of these

Refer to Question 73 in Chapter 8, Acceptance Sampling.

17.   An electronics firm was experiencing high rejections in their multiple connector manufacturing departments. P charts were introduced as part of a program to reduce defectives. Control limits

were based on prior history using the formula $P' \pm 3\sqrt{\dfrac{P'(100-P')}{N}}$, where P' is the historical value of percent defectives and N is the number of pieces inspected each week. After six weeks, the following record was accumulated. (The above formula has been corrected by ASQC.)

Dept.	P'	Week 1	Week 2	Week 3	Week 4	Week 5	Week 6
104	9	8	11	6	13	12	10
105	16	13	19	20	12	15	17
106	15	18	19	16	11	13	16

1000 pieces were inspected each week in each department. Which department(s) exhibited a point or points out of control during this period? (Round off calculations to the nearest tenth of a percentage point.)

1. Department 104
2. Department 105
3. Department 106
4. All of the departments
5. None of the departments

Refer to Question 74 in Chapter 7, Statistical Process Control.

18. A large lot of parts is rejected by your customer and found upon screening to be 20% defective. What is the probability that the lot would have been accepted by the following sampling plan: sample size =10; accept if no defectives, reject if one or more defectives?

1. .89
2. .20
3. .80
4. .11
5. none of the above

Refer to Question 162 in Chapter 3, Fundamental Concepts of Probability and Statistics.

19. Consider the SS and MS columns of an Analysis of Variance table for a single-factor design. The appropriate ratio for testing the null hypothesis of no treatment effect is

1. SS treatments divided by SS residual
2. MS treatments divided by MS residual
3. SS treatments divided by MS residual
4. MS treatments divided by SS residual

Refer to Question 54 in Chapter 6, Design of Experiments.

20. Which table should be used to determine a confidence interval on the mean when σ is not known and the sample size is 10?

1.   z
2.   t
3.   F
4. χ^2

Refer to Question 35 in Chapter 4, Statistical Inference and Hypothesis Testing.

21.   The results of a designed experiment are to be analyzed using a chi-square test. There are five treatments under consideration and each observation falls into one of the two categories (success or failure). The calculated value of chi-square is compared to the tabulated chi-square with how many degrees of freedom?

1.   10
2.   9
3.   5
4.   4

Refer to Question 75 in Chapter 4, Statistical Inference and Hypothesis Testing.

22.   Using MIL-STD-105D, what sample size should be taken from a lot of 1000 pieces for inspection level II with normal inspection?

1.   32
2.   50
3.   80
4.   100
5.   125

Refer to Question 42 in Chapter 8, Acceptance Sampling.

Mini Case Study

A certain equipment manufacturer offers a warranty on a product for a period of one year after installation. The manufacturer's investigation revealed the following additional information.

	Mean	Std. Dev.
Time lag from date of production to date of sale (to dealer or distributor)	10 weeks	3 weeks
Time lag from date of sale to date of installation	14 weeks	3.5 weeks
Time lag from date of installation to date of processing warranty claim	30 weeks	10 weeks

Each of these time lags is normally distributed and each is independent of the other. (For example, time to failure is independent of equipment age at time of installation.)

In February of last year, this manufacturer produced 4000 units of a particular model. Through December of the same year (45 weeks), a total of 23 warranty claims had been processed on these 4000 units.

Please refer to the above dialogue for the following three (3) questions. Carry all calculations to three places.

23.   The standard deviation of total time from date of production to date of processing claims is

    1.   ten (10) weeks
    2.   eleven (11) weeks
    3.   thirteen and one half (13.5) weeks
    4.   sixteen and one half (16.5) weeks

24.   What proportion of the likely total (eventual) number of warranty claims on February's production has been processed through December?

    1.   0.186
    2.   0.207
    3.   0.468
    4.   0.532
    5.   0.793

Note: ASQC's correction - *delete this question.*

25.   How many of these units are likely to eventually result in warranty claims?

    1.   28
    2.   55
    3.   88
    4.   111
    5.   152

26.   A process is checked by inspection of random samples of four shafts after a polishing operation and $\overline{X}$ and R chart are maintained. A person making a spotcheck picks out two shafts, measures them accurately, and plots the value of each on the $\overline{X}$ chart. Both points fall outside the control limits. He or she advises the department supervisor or foreman to stop the process. This decision indicates that

    1.   the process level is out of control
    2.   both the levels and dispersion are out of control
    3.   the process level is out of control but not the dispersion
    4.   the person is not using the chart correctly

Refer to Question 41 in Chapter 7, Statistical Process Control.

27.   In performing an Analysis of Variance, for a single-factor experiment, a fundamental assumption is made that the factor

   1.   means are equal
   2.   means are unequal
   3.   variances are equal
   4.   variances are unequal

   Refer to Questions 38, 39, and 41 in Chapter 6, Design of Experiments.

28.   A purchaser wants to determine whether or not there is any difference between the means of the convolute paperboard cans supplied by two different vendors, A and B. A random sample of 100 cans is selected from the output of each vendor. The sample from A yielded a mean of 13.59 with a standard deviation of 5.94. The sample from B yielded a mean of 14.43 with a standard deviation of 5.61. Which of the following would be a suitable null hypothesis to test?

   1. $\mu_A = \mu_B$
   2. $\mu_A > \mu_B$
   3. $\mu_A < \mu_B$
   4. $\mu_A \neq \mu_B$

   Refer to Question 62 in Chapter 4, Statistical Inference and Hypothesis Testing.

29.   The most important step in vendor certification is to

   1.   obtain copies of vendor's handbook
   2.   familiarize the vendor with quality requirements
   3.   analyze vendor's first shipment
   4.   visit the vendor's plant

   Refer to Question 55 in Chapter 9, Quality Practices and Applications and Question 64 in Chapter 11, Quality Auditing.

30.   Which of the following purposes are served by replicating an experiment?

   A.   Provide a means for estimating the experimental error.
   B.   Increase the number of treatments included in the experiment.
   C.   Improve the precision of estimates of treatment effects.

   1.   A and B only
   2.   A and C only
   3.   B and C only
   4.   A, B, and C

   Refer to Question 4 in Chapter 6, Design of Experiments.

31.   Three trainees were given the same lots of 50 pieces and asked to classify them as defective or nondefective with the following results.

	Trainee #1	Trainee #2	Trainee #3	Total
Defective	17	30	25	72
Non defective	33	20	25	78
Total	50	50	50	150

In determining whether or not there is a difference in the ability of the three trainees to properly classify the parts

1.   the value of chi-square is about 6.9 (This is ASQC's correction.)
2.   using a level of significance of 0.05, the critical value of chi-square is 5.99
3.   since the obtained chi-square is greater than 5.99, we reject the null hypothesis
4.   all of the above
5.   none of the above

Refer to Question 76 in Chapter 4, Statistical Inference and Hypothesis Testing.

32.   The following measurements for a sample with dimension X are representative of a process known to be in statistical control: 42, 52, 64, 45, 53, 56, 70, 57, 49, 62. Which of the following best approximates the upper and lower control limits of the process capability?

1.   81 and 29
2.   59 and 51
3.   64 and 46
4.   70 and 42

Refer to Question 57 in Chapter 7, Statistical Process Control.

33.   The prime use of a control chart is to

1.   detect assignable causes of variation in the process
2.   detect the nonconforming product
3.   measure the performance of all quality characteristics of a process
4.   detect the presence of random variation in the process

Refer to Question 4 in Chapter 7, Statistical Process Control.

34.   "Determine the flux meter reading of the part per specification." This inspection instruction violates which of the following guiding principles?

A.   The inspection method should be stated in operational terms.
B.   A specific objective should be established for each instruction.

1.   A only

2.   B only
3.   A and B only
4.   neither A nor B

Refer to Question 41 in Chapter 12, Product and Materials Control and Measurement Systems.

35.   If a test data does not support a quality engineer's expectations, the best thing to do is

1.   adjust the data to support expectations if it is only slightly off
2.   draw the expected conclusion omitting that data not supporting it
3.   reevaluate the expectations of the test based upon the data
4.   report the data and expected conclusion with no reference to one another

Refer to Question 47 in Chapter 12, Product and Materials Control and Measurement Systems.

36.   In deciding whether a sampling inspection of parts would be more economical than 100% inspection, you need to determine all of the following except

1.   cost of inspecting parts
2.   cost of correcting the defective parts
3.   cost of not finding defective parts
4.   cost of improving the production process

Refer to Question 31 in Chapter 12, Product and Materials Control and Measurement Systems.

37.   Pre-Control starts a process specifically centered between

1.   process shifts
2.   safety lines
3.   normal distribution limits
4.   three sigma control limits
5.   specification limits

Refer to Question 49 in Chapter 7, Statistical Process Control.

38.   A technique whereby various product features are graded as to relative importance is called

1.   classification of defects
2.   quality engineering
3.   classification of characteristics
4.   feature grading

Refer to Question 5 in Chapter 12, Product and Materials Control and Measurement Systems.

39.   The laboratory has notified the quality engineer of an incoming product which has changed from acceptable to marginal over a period of six months. Which of the following actions should be taken?

A.   Notify the laboratory to check their analysis and send a sample to an outside laboratory to verify the results.

B.   Notify the supplier of your observations and concern about the acceptability of his product.

C.   Notify receiving to reject the product based on the product's trend towards unacceptability.

1.   A and B only
2.   A and C only
3.   B and C only
4.   A, B, and C

Refer to Question 48 in Chapter 12, Product and Materials Control and Measurement Systems.

40.   One of the major hazards in the Material Review Board procedures is the tendency of the board to emphasize only the disposition function and to neglect the _____ function.

1.   statistical analysis
2.   corrective action
3.   material evaluation
4.   tolerance review
5.   manufacturing methods

Refer to Question 59 in Chapter 12, Product and Materials Control and Measurement Systems.

41.   A certain part is produced in lot quantities of 1000. Prior history shows that 90% of the production lots are 1% defective or better, but the remaining 10% range between 5% and 10% defective. A defective part costs $5 to repair at this point but the same defect will average $80 if allowed to be installed in the next higher assembly. Inspection at this part level costs $1.50 per part and rejected lots will be sorted at your expense. What inspection plan would you specify for this part?

1.   100% inspection
2.   no inspection
3.   n = 32, A = 1, R = 2 (single sampling)
4.   n = 50, A = 0, R = 1 (single sampling)
5.   n = 5, A = 1, R = 2 (single sampling)

Refer to Question 49 in Chapter 8, Acceptance Sampling.

42.   In product liability, the proper legal term for statements regarding the reliability of a product are known as

1.   advertisements
2.   warranties
3.   contracts
4.   representations

5.   obligations

Refer to Question 108 in Chapter 13, Reliability, Maintainability, and Product Safety.

43.   In case of conflict between contract specifications and shop practice,

1.   company procedures normally prevail
2.   arbitration is necessary
3.   the customer is always right
4.   good judgment should be exercised
5.   contract specifications normally apply

Refer to Question 63 in Chapter 9, Quality Practices and Applications.

44.   The provisions of the FDA Regulations for thermally processed, low-acid foods packaged in hermetically sealed containers require all of the following except

1.   copies of all production and laboratory records be kept for six (6) months then reviewed and destroyed by an authorized person
2.   incoming raw material, ingredients, and packaging components should be inspected upon receipt to ensure that they are suitable for processing
3.   scheduled processes for low-acid foods shall be established by qualified persons having expert knowledge of thermal processing
4.   it is either destroyed or evaluated by a component processing authority to detect any hazard to public health

Refer to Question 109 in Chapter 13, Reliability, Maintainability, and Product Safety, and Question 153 in Chapter 12, Product and Materials Control and Measurement Systems.

45.   Which of the following may be considered a justification for reinspection by the contractor of a lot which has been verified as nonconforming by the inspector?

1.   Belief by the contractor that the random samples did not constitute a true picture of the lot.
2.   The fact that the contractor had not produced to these specifications before.
3.   Discovery that the scales used for inspection were out of adjustment.
4.   None of the above.

Refer to Question 49 in Chapter 12, Product and Materials Control and Measurement Systems.

46.   When conducting an inspection for surface cleanliness, a simple and effective means for detecting the presence of oils, grease, or waxes is

1.   stereo microscopic inspection
2.   the Aqueous Conductivity test
3.   the Liebermann Storch test
4.   the Water Break Test

Refer to Question 147 in Chapter 12, Product and Materials Control and Measurement Systems.

47.   Creep is defined as that deformation occurring over a period of time with material subjected to

       1.   fluctuating stress and fluctuating strap
       2.   constant temperature and a fluctuating stress
       3.   constant temperature with no stress
       4.   constant stress at constant temperature

Refer to Question 148 in Chapter 12, Product and Materials Control and Measurement Systems.

48.   How should measurement standards be controlled?

       A.   Develop a listing of measurement standards with nomenclature and number for control.
       B.   Determine calibration intervals and calibration sources for measurement standards.
       C.   Maintain proper environmental conditions and traceability of accuracy to the National
             Bureau of Standards.

       1.   A and B only
       2.   A and C only
       3.   B and C only
       4.   A, B, and C

Refer to Question 156 in Chapter 12, Product and Materials Control and Measurement Systems.

49.   When making measurements with test instruments, precision and accuracy mean

       1.   the same
       2.   the opposite
       3.   consistency and correctness, respectively
       4.   exactness and traceability, respectively
       5.   none of the above

Refer to Question 75 in Chapter 12, Product and Materials Control and Measurement Systems.

50.   The maximum stress to which a material may be subjected without any permanent deformation
       remaining upon complete release of stress is its

       1.   ultimate yield
       2.   fatigue life
       3.   elastic limit
       4.   elastic hysteresis

Refer to Question 146 in Chapter 12, Product and Materials Control and Measurement Systems.

51.   A substance discontinuity in some purchased steel bar stock is a suspected cause for the high
       failure rate in your parts fabrication area. All of the following nondestructive test (NDT)

methods could be used to screen the bar stock except

1. magnetic particle testing
2. radiographic testing
3. liquid penetrant testing
4. eddy current testing
5. ultrasonic testing

Refer to Question 104 in Chapter 12, Product and Materials Control and Measurement Systems.

52. In attempting to replace human evaluation of foods in order to achieve objectivity, we must use as an ultimate criterion of accuracy

1. gas chromatography
2. shear press
3. viscosimeter
4. none of the above

Refer to Question 105 in Chapter 12, Product and Materials Control and Measurement Systems.

53. Generally, the best ultrasonic testing method for detecting discontinuities oriented along the fusion zone in a welded plate is

1. an angle beam contact method employing surface waves
2. a contact test using a straight longitudinal wave
3. an immersion test using surface waves
4. an angle beam method using shear waves

Refer to Question 106 in Chapter 12, Product and Materials Control and Measurement Systems.

54. One of the practical limits on the application of the ultrasonic testing method is

1. lack of portability
2. poor penetration capability
3. reference standards are required
4. inability to record results permanently

Refer to Question 108 in Chapter 12, Product and Materials Control and Measurement Systems.

55. Calibration intervals should be adjusted when

1. no defective product is reported as acceptable due to measurement errors
2. few instruments are scrapped during calibration
3. the results of previous calibrations reflect few "out of tolerance" conditions during calibration
4. a particular characteristic on the gage is consistently found out of tolerance

Refer to Question 89 in Chapter 12, Product and Materials Control and Measurement Systems.

56.   In selecting a base for measuring quality costs, which of the following should be considered?

1.   Is it sensitive to increase and decrease in production schedules?
2.   Is it affected by mechanization and resulting lower direct labor costs?
3.   Is it affected by seasonal product sales?
4.   Is it oversensitive to material price fluctuations?
5.   All of the above.

Refer to Question 76 in Chapter 10, Quality Costs Analysis.

57.   For a typical month, 900D Manufacturing Company identified and reported the following quality costs:

Inspection wages	$ 12,000
Quality planning	$ 4,000
Source inspection	$ 2,000
In-plant scrap and rework	$ 88,000
Final product test	$ 110,000
Retest and troubleshooting	$ 39,000
Field warranty costs	$ 205,000
Evaluation and processing of deviation requests	$ 6,000

What is the total *failure* cost for this month?

1. $244,000
2. $151,000
3. $261,000
4. $205,000
5. $332,000

Refer to Question 55 in Chapter 10, Quality Costs Analysis.

58.   Refer to the previous question. One year later, the monthly quality costs reported by 900D Manufacturing Company were as follows:

Inspection wages	$ 14,000
Quality planning	$ 8,500
Source inspection	$ 2,200
In-plant scrap and rework	$ 51,000
Quality training	$ 42,000
Audits	$ 47.000
Final product test	$ 103,000
Retest and troubleshooting	$ 19,000
Field warranty costs	$ 188,000
Evaluation and processing of deviation requests	$ 4,500

Sales billed have increased 10% from the corresponding month of a year ago. How would you evaluate the effectiveness of the 900D quality improvement program?

1. Quality costs are still too high.
2. Essentially no change in overall results.
3. Good improvements.
4. Still further improvement is unlikely.
5. Not enough information to evaluate.

Refer to Question 56 in Chapter 10, Quality Costs Analysis.

59. If prevention costs are increased to pay for engineering work in quality control, and this results in a reduction in the number of product defects, this yields a reduction in

1. appraisal costs
2. operating costs
3. quality costs
4. failure costs
5. manufacturing costs

Refer to Question 31 in Chapter 10, Quality Costs Analysis.

60. Analysis of quality costs consists of

1. reviewing manpower utilization against a standard
2. evaluating seasonal productivity
3. establishing management tools to determine net worth
4. examining each cost element in relation to other elements and the total
5. providing an accounting mechanism to spread costs over service areas

Refer to Question 77 in Chapter 10, Quality Costs Analysis.

61. Assume that the cost data available to you for a certain period are limited to the following:

Final test	$ 18,000
Loss on disposition of surplus stock	$ 15,000
Field warranty costs	$ 275,000
Scrap	$ 150,000
Customer returns	$ 25,000
Planning for inspection	$ 16,000

The total of the quality costs is

1. $ 499,000
2. $ 484,000
3. $ 468,000
4. $ 193,000

Refer to Question 57 in Chapter 10, Quality Costs Analysis.

62.   Market-based cost standards are guided by

        1.   what others spend
        2.   what we ought to spend
        3.   marketing budget
        4.   quality analysis forecast

        Refer to Question 14 in Chapter 10, Quality Costs Analysis.

63.   Historic levels of defects, with rare exceptions, have been found to be located at what point with respect to the optimum point in Fig. 16-1?

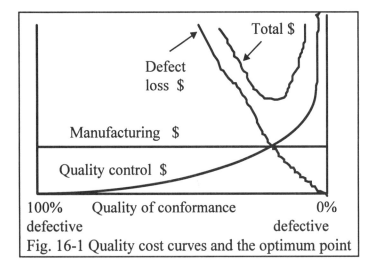

Fig. 16-1 Quality cost curves and the optimum point

a.   to the left of the optimum
b.   to the right of the optimum
c.   at the center of the optimum
d.   none of the above

        Refer to Question 16 in Chapter 10, Quality Costs Analysis.

64.   The cost of writing instructions and operating procedures for inspection and testing should be charged to

        1.   prevention costs
        2.   appraisal costs
        3.   internal failure costs
        4.   external failure costs

        Refer to Question 32 in Chapter 10, Quality Costs Analysis.

65.   Which of the following activities is not normally charged as a preventive cost?

        1.   Quality training.
        2.   Design and development of quality measurement equipment.
        3.   Quality planning.
        4.   Laboratory acceptance testing.

Refer to Question 34 in Chapter 10, Quality Costs Analysis.

66.   A quality audit program should begin with

    1.   a study of the quality documentation system
    2.   an evaluation of the work being performed
    3.   a report listing findings, the action taken, and recommendations
    4.   a charter of policy, objectives, and procedures
    5.   a followup check on the manager's response to recommendations

Refer to Question 2 in Chapter 11, Quality Auditing.

67.   Auditing of a quality program is most effective on a

    1.   quarterly basis, auditing all characteristics on the checklist
    2.   periodic unscheduled basis, auditing some of the procedures
    3.   monthly basis, auditing randomly selected procedures
    4.   continuing basis, auditing randomly selected procedures
    5.   continually specified time period basis, frequently adjustable, auditing randomly selected procedures

Refer to Question 6 in Chapter 11, Quality Auditing.

68.   An inspection performance audit is made of eight inspectors in an area of complex assembly, all doing similar work. Seven inspectors have an average monthly acceptance rate of 86 to 92%; one inspector has an average rate of 72% with approximately four times the daily variation as the others. As inspection supervisor you should, based on this audit,

    1.   promote the 72% inspector as he or she is very conscientious
    2.   discipline the 72% inspector as he or she is creating needless rework and wasted time
    3.   initiate a special investigation of inspection and manufacturing performance
    4.   discipline the other seven inspectors as they are not "cracking down."

Refer to Question 48 in Chapter 11, Quality Auditing, and Question 50 in Chapter 12, Product and Materials Control and Measurement Systems.

69.   The quality audit could be used to judge all of the following except

    1.   a prospective vendor's capability for meeting quality standards
    2.   the adequacy of a current vendor's system for controlling quality
    3.   the application of a specification to a unique situation
    4.   the adequacy of a company's own system for controlling quality

Refer to Question 51 in Chapter 11, Quality Auditing.

70.   Audit inspectors should report to someone who is independent from

1. middle management
2. marketing
3. inspection supervision
4. production staff

Refer to Question 19 in Chapter 11, Quality Auditing.

71. When requesting "worst case" design analysis, you expect the reliability group to

1. analyze the worst rejects
2. analyze only those products failing to meet specification requirements
3. determine whether product requirements can be met with subassemblies assumed at their worst combination of tolerances
4. assume all subassembly tolerances at their maximum limit

Refer to Question 102 in Chapter 13, Reliability, Maintainability, and Product Safety.

72. For a high compression aircraft air conditioning system, the MTBF is 100 hours. This mean life is allocated to four serial units comprising the total system. The unit failure rates are then weighted as follows: $W_1 = 0.1250$ $W_3 = 0.1875$ $W_2 = 0.2500$ $W_4 = 0.4375$

Based upon the above data, indicate which of the following is the correct calculation for one of the units.

1. $\lambda_3 = 0.0018750$
2. $\lambda_4 = 0.0435700$
3. $\lambda_1 = 0.0125000$
4. $\lambda_3 = 0.0001875$
5. $\lambda_2 = 0.0025100$

Refer to Question 42 in Chapter 13, Reliability, Maintainability, and Product Safety. This question is repeated in the August 1978 examination.[8]

73. What is the reliability of the system at 850 hours if the average usage on the system was 400 hours for 1650 items and the total number of failures was 145? Assume an exponential distribution.

1. 0%
2. 36%
3. 18%
4. 83%

Refer to Question 43 in Chapter 13, Reliability, Maintainability, and Product Safety.

74. The probability of an accident for the head event H given below is

---

[8] *ASQC - CQE Examination*, Quality Progress, August 1978, Applications section, Question 72.

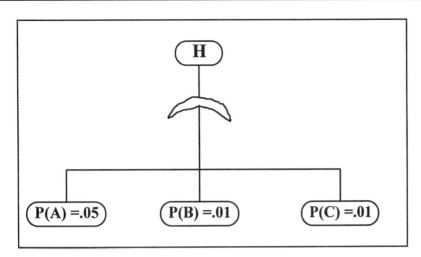

1.   0.1125
2.   0.0689
3.   0.1100
4.   none of the above

Refer to Question 65 in Chapter 13, Reliability, Maintainability, and Product Safety.

75.   A reliability data system usually implies collecting data on

    1.   process machine downtime
    2.   product failures and operating time
    3.   maintenance costs
    4.   repair times

Refer to Question 95 in Chapter 13, Reliability, Maintainability, and Product Safety.

76.   In consumer products, the complaint rate is most directly a measure of

    1.   product quality
    2.   customer satisfaction
    3.   market value
    4.   rejection rate
    5.   specification conformance

Refer to Question 87 in Chapter 9, Quality Practices and Applications.

77.   Quality data which are regularly obtained but not used, should be

    1.   analyzed periodically by an expert statistician to glean as much information as possible
    2.   discontinued to save time and money
    3.   stored until such time as the need arises
    4.   processed by computer and summary reports issued regularly to interested persons

Refer to Question 78 in Chapter 9, Quality Practices and Applications.

78.   Primary personal characteristics for reliable inspector performance evaluation are

    1.   experience and amount of time of observed performance
    2.   relevancy, consistency, and lack of bias

3.   personal appearance, mental alertness, and ability to communicate
4.   seniority, age, and good health
5.   all of the above

Refer to Question 51 in Chapter 12, Product and Materials Control and Measurement Systems.

79.   An essential technique in making training programs effective is to

1.   set group goals
2.   have training classes which teach skills and knowledge required
3.   feedback to the employee on meaningful measures of his or her performance
4.   post results of performance before and after the training program
5.   set individual goals instead of group goals

Refer to Question 36 in Chapter 15, Motivation and Human Factors.

80.   A method of dealing with an inspector found to be falsifying the results of inspection of a borderline product is to

1.   criticize the inspector on the basis that the pattern of reading does not follow the laws of chance
2.   review the procedure for evaluating and reporting a borderline product
3.   review the inspector's results against the expected results calculated from a normal curve
4.   criticize the inspector for not knowing how to read the inspection equipment

Refer to Question 52 in Chapter 12, Product and Materials Control and Measurement Systems.

ANSWERS FOR JULY 1984 EXAMINATION

PRINCIPLES

Q	A
1.	2
2.	2
3.	1
4.	5
5.	1
6.	3
7.	3
8.	3
9.	1
10.	3
11.	4
12.	3
13.	4
14.	1
15.	1
16.	2
17.	3
18.	1
19.	2
20.	2

Q	A
21.	4
22.	1
23.	3
24.	3
25.	3
26.	1
27.	3
28.	2
29.	3
30.	2
31.	3
32.	4
33.	3
34.	3
35.	4
36.	1
37.	1
38.	2
39.	2
40.	2

Q	A
41.	3
42.	3
43.	3
44.	3
45.	2
46.	3
47.	4
48.	4
49.	1
50.	2
51.	4
52.	2
53.	1
54.	3
55.	2
56.	1
57.	2
58.	4
59.	1
60.	4

Q	A
61.	3
62.	2
63.	3
64.	2
65.	1
66.	4
67.	3
68.	4
69.	1
70.	1
71.	5
72.	1
73.	1
74.	1
75.	4
76.	1
77.	2
78.	1
79.	3
80.	4

Q	A
81.	1
82.	3
83.	3
84.	4
85.	2
86.	1
87.	2
88.	3
89.	3
90.	5

COMMENTS / NOTES:

ANSWERS FOR JULY 1984 EXAMINATION

APPLICATIONS

Q	A
1.	2
2.	2
3.	2
4.	3
5.	1
6.	2*
7.	3
8.	3
9.	2
10.	4
11.	4
12.	1
13.	5*
14.	2
15.	4
16.	4
17.	4
18.	4
19.	2
20.	2

Q	A
21.	4
22.	3
23.	2
24.	2
25.	4
26.	4
27.	3
28.	1
29.	2
30.	2
31.	4
32.	1
33.	1
34.	1
35.	3
36.	4
37.	5
38.	3
39.	1
40.	2

Q	A
41.	3
42.	4
43.	5
44.	1
45.	3
46.	4
47.	4
48.	4
49.	3
50.	3
51.	3
52.	4
53.	4
54.	3
55.	4
56.	5
57.	5
58.	3
59.	4
60.	4

Q	A
61.	2
62.	1
63.	1
64.	1
65.	4
66.	4
67.	5
68.	3
69.	3
70.	3
71.	3
72.	1
73.	4
74.	2
75.	2
76.	2
77.	2
78.	2
79.	3
80.	2

COMMENTS / NOTES:

* ASQC's correction to these questions.

CHAPTER 17

ASQC-CQE EXAMINATION, QUALITY PROGRESS, AUGUST 1978

PRINCIPLES

Note: *The old examination sets used numbers, e.g., 1, 2, 3, 4, and 5, for various choices for each question. Hence the following questions use the numerical choices in its original format.*

Recent examinations and the study guides published in ASQC's recent certification brochures use letters, e.g., a, b, c, d, and e, for choices to a question in place of numbers. Hence letters are used in all individual subject matter chapters 3 through 15. Readers are advised to note this difference while referring to solutions in respective chapters.

1. A p-chart is a type of control chart for

    1. plotting bar stock lengths from receiving inspection samples
    2. plotting fraction defective results from shipping inspection samples
    3. plotting defects per unit from in-process inspection samples
    4. answers 1, 2, and 3 above
    5. answers 1 and 3 only

    Refer to Question 69 in Chapter 7, Statistical Process Control.

2. The sensitivity of a p-chart to changes in quality is

    1. equal to that of a range chart
    2. equal to that of a chart for averages
    3. equal to that of a c-chart
    4. equal to that of a u-chart
    5. none of the above

    Refer to Question 71 in Chapter 7, Statistical Process Control.

3. A p-chart has exhibited statistical control over a period of time. However the average fraction defective is too high to be satisfactory. Improvement can be obtained by

    1. a change in the basic design of the product
    2. instituting 100% inspection
    3. a change in the production process through substitution of new tooling or machinery
    4. all of the above answers are correct except number 2
    5. all of the above answers are correct except number 3

Refer to Question 72 in Chapter 7, Statistical Process Control.

4.   Consumer's risk is defined as

     1.   accepting an unsatisfactory lot as satisfactory
     2.   passing a satisfactory lot as satisfactory
     3.   an alpha risk
     4.   a 5% risk of accepting an unsatisfactory lot

Refer to Question 17 in Chapter 8, Acceptance Sampling.

5.   In MIL-STD-105D, the AQL is always determined at what P on the OC curve?

     1.   0.05
     2.   0.10
     3.   0.90
     4.   0.95
     5.   none of the above

Refer to Question 38 in Chapter 8, Acceptance Sampling. This question is repeated in the July 1984 examinations.[1]

6.   If a distribution is skewed to the left, the median will always be

     1.   less than the mean
     2.   between the mean and mode
     3.   greater than the mode
     4.   equal to the mean
     5.   none of the above

Refer to Question 84 in Chapter 3, Fundamental Concepts of Probability and Statistics.

7.   The steeper the OC curve, the

     1.   less protection for both producer and consumer
     2.   more protection for both producer and consumer
     3.   lower the AQL
     4.   smaller the sample size

Refer to Question 10 in Chapter 8, Acceptance Sampling.

8.   The sum of the squared deviations of a group of measurements from their mean divided by the number of the measurements equals

     1. σ

---

[1] *ASQC - CQE Examination*, Quality Progress, July 1984, Principles section, Question 4.

2. σ^2
3.   zero
4.   X
5.   the mean deviation

Refer to Question 103 in Chapter 3, Fundamental Concepts of Probability and Statistics.

9.   In determining a process average fraction defective using inductive or inferential statistics, we use _____ computed from _____ to make the inferences about _____ .

   1.   statistics, samples, populations
   2.   populations, samples, populations
   3.   samples, statistics, populations
   4.   samples, populations, samples
   5.   statistics, populations, statistics

Refer to Question 13 in Chapter 3, Fundamental Concepts of Probability and Statistics.

10.   Which of the following statistical measures of variability is not dependent on the exact value of every measurement?

   1.   interquartile range
   2.   variance
   3.   range
   4.   coefficient of variation
   5.   none of the above

Refer to Question 107 in Chapter 3, Fundamental Concepts of Probability and Statistics.

11.   When used together for variable data, which of the following is the most useful pair of quantities in quality control?

   1. $\overline{X}$, R
   2. $\overline{X}$, η
   3.   R, σ
   4. $\overline{p}$, η
   5.   AQL, p'

Refer to Question 18 in Chapter 7, Statistical Process Control.

12.   For an operation requiring shipments from your vendor of small lots of fixed size, the sampling plan used for receiving inspection should have its OC curve developed using

   1.   the Poisson distribution
   2.   the Hypergeometric distribution
   3.   the Binomial distribution

4.   the Log Normal distribution
5.   the Gaussian (normal) distribution

Refer to Question 12 in Chapter 8, Acceptance Sampling.

13.   Two quantities which uniquely determine a single sampling attributes plan are

1.   AOQL and LTPD
2.   sample size and rejection number
3.   AQL and producer's risk
4.   LTPD and consumer's risk
5.   AQL and LTPD

Refer to Questions 25, 26, 27, and 28 in Chapter 8, Acceptance Sampling.

14.   Selection of a sampling plan from the Dodge Romig AOQL sampling tables

1.   requires an estimate of AOQ
2.   requires an estimate of the process average
3.   requires sorting of rejected lots
4.   requires larger samples than MIL-STD-105D (now 105E) for equivalent quality
       assurance
5.   requires that we assume the consumer's risk of 0.05

Refer to Question 53 in Chapter 8, Acceptance Sampling.

15.   The expression $\dfrac{v^x e^{-\mu}}{x!}$ is the general term for the

1.   Hypergeometric distribution
2.   Pascal distribution
3.   Poisson distribution
4.   Binomial distribution
5.   none of the above

Refer to Question 172 in Chapter 3, Fundamental Concepts of Probability and Statistics.

16.   If in a t test alpha is 0.01,

1.   1% of the time we will say that there is a real difference, when there really is not a
       difference
2.   1% of the time we will make the correct inference
3.   1% of the time we will say that there is no real difference, but in reality there is a
       difference
4.   99% of the time we will make an incorrect inference
5.   99% of the time the null hypothesis will be correct

Refer to Question 54 in Chapter 4, Statistical Inference and Hypothesis Testing.

17.   Suppose that given X = 50 and Z = ±1.96, we established 95% confidence limits for μ of 30 and 70. This means that

    1.   the probability that μ = 50 is 0.05
    2.   the probability that μ = 50 is 0.95
    3.   the probability that the interval contains μ is 0.05
    4.   the probability that the interval contains μ is 0.95
    5.   none of the above

Refer to Question 21 in Chapter 4, Statistical Inference and Hypothesis Testing.

18.   MIL-STD-105D sampling plans allow reduced inspection when four requirements are met. One of these is

    1.   inspection level I is specified
    2.   10 lots have been on normal inspection and none have been rejected
    3.   the process average is less than the AOQL
    4.   the maximum percent defective is less than the AQL
    5.   all of the above

Refer to Question 52 in Chapter 8, Acceptance Sampling.

19.   The AQL for a given sampling plan is 1.0%. This means that

    1.   the producer takes a small risk of rejecting a product which is 1.0% defective or better
    2.   all accepted lots are 1.0% defective or better
    3.   the average quality limit of the plan is 1.0%
    4.   the average quality level of the plan is 1.0%
    5.   all lots are 1.0% defective or better

Refer to Question 32 in Chapter 8, Acceptance Sampling.

20.   If X and Y are distributed normally and independently, the variance of X-Y is equal to

    1. $\sigma^2_x + \sigma^2_y$
    2. $\sigma^2_x - \sigma^2_y$
    3. $\sqrt{\sigma^2_x + \sigma^2_y}$
    4. $\sqrt{\sigma^2_x - \sigma^2_y}$

Refer to Question 114 in Chapter 3, Fundamental Concepts of Probability and Statistics.

21.   The mean of either a discrete or a continuous distribution can always be visualized as

    1.   the point where 50% of the values are to the left side and 50% are to the right side

2.   its center of gravity
3.   the point where the most values in the distribution occur
4.   all of the above

Refer to Question 86 in Chapter 3, Fundamental Concepts of Probability and Statistics.

22.   In control chart theory, the distribution of the number of the defects per unit follows very closely the

   1.   normal distribution
   2.   binomial distribution
   3.   chi-square distribution
   4.   Poisson distribution

Refer to Question 80 in Chapter 7, Statistical Process Control.

23.   A Latin square design is noted for its straightforward analysis of the interaction effects. The above statement is

   1.   true in every case
   2.   true sometimes, depending on the size of the square
   3.   true only for Greco-Latin squares
   4.   false in every case
   5.   false except for Greco-Latin squares

Refer to Question 35 in Chapter 6, Design of Experiments.

24.   Considerations to be made prior to the use of any sampling plan is (are)

   1.   the consumer's and producer's risks must be specified
   2.   the method of selecting samples must be specified
   3.   the characteristics to be inspected must be specified
   4.   the conditions must be specified (material accumulated in lots or inspected by continuous sampling)
   5.   all of the above

Refer to Question 1 in Chapter 8, Acceptance Sampling.

25.   The probability of accepting material produced at an acceptable quality level is defined as

   1. α
   2. β
   3.   AQL
   4. $1 - \alpha$
   5. $1 - \beta$

Refer to Question 15 in Chapter 8, Acceptance Sampling.

26.   A null hypothesis requires several assumptions, a basic one of which is

       1.   that the variables are dependent
       2.   that the variables are independent
       3.   that the sample size is adequate
       4.   that the confidence interval is ±2 standard deviations
       5.   that the correlation coefficient is −0.95

       Refer to Question 44 in Chapter 4, Statistical Inference and Hypothesis Testing.

27.   One use of the Student t test is to determine whether or not differences exist in

       1.   variability
       2.   quality costs
       3.   correlation coefficients
       4.   averages
       5.   none of the above

       Refer to Question 41 in Chapter 4, Statistical Inference and Hypothesis Testing.

28.   The least squares method is used in

       1.   the central limit theorem
       2.   calculating σ^2
       3.   calculating σ^2 from σ^2
       4.   calculating a best fit regression line
       5.   inspecting hole locations

       Refer to Question 25 in Chapter 5, Regression and Correlation Analysis.

29.   AOQL means

       1.   average outgoing quality level
       2.   average outgoing quality limit
       3.   average outside quality limit
       4.   anticipated optimum quality level

       Refer to Question 33 in Chapter 8, Acceptance Sampling.

30.   In nonparametric statistics

       1.   no assumptions are made concerning the distribution from which the samples are taken
       2.   the parameters of the distribution must have no parameters in common
       3.   the sample and the distribution must have no parameters in common
       4.   none of the above

       Refer to Question 60 in Chapter 3, Fundamental Concepts of Probability and Statistics.

31.   Given 6 books, how many sets can be arranged in lots of 3 but always in the different order?

      1.   18 sets
      2.   54 sets
      3.   108 sets
      4.   120 sets

Refer to Question 56 in Chapter 3, Fundamental Concepts of Probability and Statistics.

32.   The probability of observing at least one defective in a random sample of size ten, drawn from a population that has been producing on the average ten percent defective units is:

      1. $(0.10)^{10}$
      2. $(0.90)^{10}$
      3. $1 - (0.10)^{10}$
      4. $1 - (0.90)^{10}$
      5. $(0.10)(0.90)^{9}$

Refer to Question 153 in Chapter 3, Fundamental Concepts of Probability and Statistics.

33.   In preparing a Quality Policy concerning a product line for your company, you should not

      1.   specify the means by which quality performance is measured
      2.   develop criteria for identifying risk situations and specify whose approval is required when there are known risks
      3.   load the policy with procedural matters or ordinary functional responsibilities
      4.   identify responsibilities for dispositioning defective hardware
      5.   answers 2 and 4 above

Refer to Question 34 in Chapter 9, Quality Practices and Applications.

34.   A fully developed position description for a Quality Engineer must contain clarification of

      1.   responsibility
      2.   accountability
      3.   authority
      4.   answers 1 and 3 above
      5.   answers 1, 2, and 3 above

Refer to Question 19 in Chapter 9, Quality Practices and Applications.

35.   "Good Housekeeping" is an important quality factor in a supplier's plant because

      1.   it promotes good working conditions
      2.   it minimizes fire hazards
      3.   it enhances safer operations
      4.   it reflects favorably on the efficiency and management of a company

5.   all of the above

Refer to Question 53 in Chapter 9, Quality Practices and Applications.

36.   The purpose of a Quality Manual is to

1.   use it as a basis for every Quality decision
2.   standardize the methods and decisions of a department
3.   optimize company performance in addition to improving effectiveness of the Quality department
4.   make it possible to handle every situation in exactly the same manner

Refer to Question 38 in Chapter 9, Quality Practices and Applications.

37.   Essential to the success of any Quality Control organization is the receipt of

1.   adequate and stable resources
2.   clear and concise project statements
3.   delegation of authority to accomplish the objective
4.   all of the above

Refer to Question 14 in Chapter 9, Quality Practices and Applications.

38.   The inspection plan for a new product line may include

1.   detailed production schedule
2.   sampling procedures and techniques
3.   internal techniques for control and segregation of conforming or nonconforming product
4.   answers 1 and 2 above
5.   answers 1, 2, and 3 above

Refer to Question 17 in Chapter 12, Product and Materials Control and Measurement Systems.

39.   Classification of defects is most essential as a prior step to a valid establishment of

1.   design characteristics to be inspected
2.   vendor specification of crucial parts
3.   process control points
4.   economical sampling inspection
5.   a product audit check sheet

Refer to Question 9 in Chapter 12, Product and Materials Control and Measurement Systems. This question is repeated with a slight change in the October 1974 and October 1972 examinations.[2]

---

[2] *ASQC - CQE Examination*, Quality Progress, October 1974, Principles section, Question 15, 65, and 77; also October 1972 Principles section, Question 2.

40.   The first step and most important in establishing a good corporate quality plan is

     1.   determining customer requirements
     2.   determining manufacturing process capabilities
     3.   evaluating the vendor quality system
     4.   ensuring quality participation in design review

Refer to Question 90 in Chapter 9, Quality Practices and Applications.

41.   If not specifically required by the product drawings or specification, nondestructive test (NDT) may be required during production and/or during acceptance at the discretion of the quality engineer responsible for the inspection planning. This statement is

     1.   false, because testing is limited to that specified by the design engineer
     2.   true, because NDT is a form of inspection (with enhanced senses), not a functional test
     3.   false, the QE may impose NDT as he or she believes necessary, but cannot delete it without design engineering permission
     4.   true, because all acceptance testing and inspection requirements are up to quality engineering

Refer to Question 99 in Chapter 12, Product and Materials Control and Measurement Systems.

42.   When giving instructions to those who will perform a task, the communications process is completed

     1.   when the worker goes to his or her workstation to do the task
     2.   when the person giving the instruction has finished talking
     3.   when the worker acknowledges these instructions by describing how he or she will perform the task
     4.   when the worker says that he or she understands the instructions

Refer to Question 18 in Chapter 12, Product and Materials Control and Measurement Systems.

43.   Some product specifications contain a section called "Quality assurance" which contains the design engineer's requirements for acceptance testing. The relationship between the acceptance test procedure for a product and the acceptance test portion of the quality assurance section of the specification for that product is

     1.   test procedure must require testing for the characteristics listed in the acceptance test portion of the specifications and the quality engineer can add additional tests he or she believes necessary
     2.   test procedure must require testing for the characteristics selected from the acceptance test portion of the specification but does not have to require testing for all such characteristics
     3.   test procedure must require testing for those and only those characteristics listed in the acceptance test portion of the specifications

4.   the acceptance test portion of the specification is a good general guide to the test
        procedure writer and the test procedure reviewer but is not mandatory anyway

Refer to Question 19 in Chapter 12, Product and Materials Control and Measurement Systems.

44.   The primary reason that non conforming material should be identified and segregated is

    1.   so that the cause of non conforming can be determined
    2.   to provide statistical information for the zero defect program
    3.   so it cannot be used in production without proper authorization
    4.   to obtain samples of poor workmanship for use in the company's training program
    5.   so that responsibility can be determined and disciplinary action taken

Refer to Question 44 in Chapter 9, Quality Practices and Applications and Question 55 in
Chapter 12, Product and Materials Control and Measurement Systems.

45.   A quality program has the best foundation for success when it is initiated by

    1.   a certified quality engineer
    2.   contractual requirements
    3.   chief executive of the company
    4.   production management
    5.   an experienced quality manager

Refer to Question 27 in Chapter 9, Quality Practices and Applications.

46.   A quality manual

    1.   is a static document, best used for Public Relations purposes
    2.   is a benchmark against which current practices may be audited
    3.   is the responsibility of all company departments
    4.   should be approved only by the quality department
    5.   is not needed in most organizations

Refer to Question 39 in Chapter 9, Quality Practices and Applications. This question is repeated
with a slight change in the October 1974 Examination.[3]

47.   When specifying the "10:1 calibration principle" we are referring to what?

    1.   the ratio of operators to inspectors
    2.   the ratio of quality engineers to metrology personnel
    3.   the ratio of main scale to vernier scale calibration
    4.   the ratio of calibration standard accuracy to calibrated instrument accuracy
    5.   none of the above

---

[3] *ASQC - CQE Examination*, Quality Progress, October 1974, Principles section, Question 16.

Refer to Question 86 in Chapter 12, Product and Materials Control and Measurement Systems.

48.   A qualification test is used to determine that design and selected production methods will yield a product that conforms to specification. An acceptance test is used to determine that a completed product conforms to design. On this basis, a destructive test can be used for

1.   qualification only
2.   qualification or acceptance
3.   acceptance only
4.   neither qualification nor acceptance

Refer to Question 20 in Chapter 12, Product and Materials Control and Measurement Systems.

49.   In geometric dimensioning and tolerancing the symbol M means

1.   maximum material condition
2.   use a micrometer to check
3.   machined surface
4.   measure at this point

Refer to Question 163 in Chapter 12, Product and Materials Control and Measurement Systems.

50.   Which is not a limit gage?

1.   ring gage
2.   radius gage
3.   vernier height gage
4.   gage blocks

Refer to Question 121 in Chapter 12, Product and Materials Control and Measurement Systems.

51.   Sensory testing is used in a number of industries to evaluate their products. Which of the following is not a sensory test?

1.   ferritic annial test
2.   triangle test
3.   duo-trio test
4.   ranking test
5.   paired comparison test

Refer to Question 141 in Chapter 12, Product and Materials Control and Measurement Systems.

52.   X-rays and gamma rays are both commonly used in industrial radiography for detecting flaws in materials. Which of the following statements most correctly describes the differences between these two types of radiation?

1.   X-rays have wavelengths 10^{-6} to 10^{-10} cm whereas gamma rays have wavelengths 10^{-9} to

10^{-12} cm.
2. Both originate from the nucleus of an atom.
3. X-rays are lower energy than gamma rays.
4. They are similar, both being electromagnetic radiation, however differing in origin.

Refer to Question 100 in Chapter 12, Product and Materials Control and Measurement Systems.

53. Criteria for a comprehensive acceptance inspection system include which of the following?

1. It should encourage and assist the supplier to improve the quality of his or her product.
2. It should be easy to administer and economical in cost.
3. It should enable the purchaser to accept all conforming items and to reject all non-conforming items.
4. all of the above

Refer to Question 21 in Chapter 12, Product and Materials Control and Measurement Systems.

54. The major purpose of test and inspection is to

1. remove all defects to prevent shipments of substandard product
2. find which operations are problems
3. identify the poor operators
4. develop information to enable corrective action
5. keep costs down by finding defects early in the cycle

Refer to Question 22 in Chapter 12, Product and Materials Control and Measurement Systems.

55. Measuring and test equipment are calibrated to

1. comply with federal regulations
2. assure their precision
3. determine and/or assure their accuracy
4. check the validity of reference standards
5. accomplish all of the above

Refer to Question 87 in Chapter 12, Product and Materials Control and Measurement Systems.

56. Why would inspection by variables be superior to inspection by attributes?

1. Inspection by variables is easier to administer than inspection by attributes.
2. Inspectors like inspection by variables better than inspection by attributes.
3. More information is obtained when inspection by variables is utilized.
4. Inspection by variables is usually more economical than inspection by attributes.
5. Inspection by variables makes more sense than inspection by attributes.

Refer to Questions 69 and 70 in Chapter 8, Acceptance Sampling.

57.   A basic requirement of most gage calibration system specifications is

       1.   all inspection equipment must be calibrated with master gage blocks
       2.   gages must be color coded for identification
       3.   equipment shall be labeled or coded to indicate date calibrated, by whom, and date due
             for next calibration
       4.   gages must be identified with a tool number
       5.   all of the above

       Refer to Question 85 in Chapter 12, Product and Materials Control and Measurement Systems.

58.   What four functions are necessary to have an acceptable calibration system covering measuring
       and test equipment in a written procedure?

       1.   calibration sources, calibration intervals, environmental conditions, and sensitivity
             required for use
       2.   calibration sources, calibration intervals, humidity control, and utilization of published
             standards
       3.   calibration sources, calibration intervals, environmental conditions under which
             equipment is calibrated, and controls for unsuitable equipment
       4.   list of standards, identification report, certificate number, and recall records
       5.   all of the above

       Refer to Question 88 in Chapter 12, Product and Materials Control and Measurement Systems.

59.   A variable measurement of a dimension should include

       1.   an estimate of the accuracy of the measurement process
       2.   a controlled measurement procedure
       3.   a numerical value for the parameter being measured
       4.   an estimate of the precision of the measurement process
       5.   all of the above

       Refer to Question 71 in Chapter 12, Product and Materials Control and Measurement Systems.

60.   When looking for existing sources of internal failure cost data, which of the following is usually
       the best source available?

       1.   operating budgets
       2.   salesperson's field reports
       3.   labor and material cost documents
       4.   returned material reports
       5.   purchase orders

       Refer to Question 44 in Chapter 10, Quality Cost Analysis.

61.   Of the following, which are typically appraisal costs?

1.   vendor surveys and vendor faults
2.   quality planning and quality reports
3.   drawing control centers and material dispositions
4.   quality audit and quality final inspection
5.   none of the above

Refer to Question 39 in Chapter 10, Quality Cost Analysis.

62.   Which of the following cost elements is normally a prevention cost?

1.   receiving inspection
2.   outside endorsements or approvals
3.   design of quality measurement equipment
4.   all of the above

Refer to Question 28 in Chapter 10, Quality Cost Analysis.

63.   When analyzing quality cost data gathered during the initial stages of a new management emphasis on quality control and corrective actions as a part of a product improvement program, one normally expects to see

1.   increased prevention costs and decreased appraisal costs
2.   increased appraisal costs with little change in prevention costs
3.   decreased internal failure costs
4.   decreased total quality costs
5.   all of the above

Refer to Question 20 in Chapter 10, Quality Cost Analysis.

64.   Quality costs are best classified as

1.   cost of inspection and test, cost of quality engineering, cost of quality administration, and cost of quality equipment
2.   direct, indirect, and overhead
3.   cost of prevention, cost of appraisal, and cost of failure
4.   unnecessary
5.   none of the above

Refer to Question 6 in Chapter 10, Quality Cost Analysis.

65.   Which of the following bases of performance measurement (denominators) when related to operating quality costs (numerator), would provide reliable indicator(s) to quality management for overall evaluation of the effectiveness of the company's quality program? Quality costs per:

1.   total manufacturing costs
2.   unit produced
3.   total direct labor dollars

4.   only one of the above
5.   any two of the above

Refer to Question 79 in Chapter 10, Quality Cost Analysis.

66.   Quality cost data

1.   must be maintained when the end product is for the government
2.   must be mailed to the contacting officer on request
3.   is often an effective means of identifying quality problem areas
4.   all of the above

Refer to Question 66 in Chapter 10, Quality Cost Analysis.

67.   Operating quality costs can be related to different volume bases. An example of a volume base that could be used would be

1.   direct labor cost
2.   standard manufacturing cost
3.   processing costs
4.   sales
5.   all of the above

Refer to Question 80 in Chapter 10, Quality Cost Analysis.

68.   When operating a quality system, excessive costs can be identified when

1.   appraisal costs exceed failure costs
2.   total quality costs exceed 10% of sales
3.   appraisal and failure costs are equal
4.   total quality costs exceed 4% of the manufacturing costs
5.   there is no fixed rule - management experience must bc used

Refer to Question 22 in Chapter 10, Quality Cost Analysis.

69.   Quality cost systems provide for defect prevention. Which of the following elements is primary to defect prevention?

1.   corrective action
2.   data collection
3.   cost analysis
4.   training

Refer to Question 88 in Chapter 10, Quality Cost Analysis and Question 57 in Chapter 12, Product and Materials Control and Measurement Systems.

70.   Which of the following is not a legitimate audit function?

1.   identify function responsible for primary control and corrective action
2.   provide no surprises
3.   provide data on worker performance to supervision for punitive action
4.   contribute to a reduction in quality cost
5.   none of the above

Refer to Question 24 in Chapter 11, Quality Auditing.

71.   In many programs, what is generally the weakest link in the quality auditing programs?

1.   lack of adequate audit checklists
2.   scheduling of audits (frequency)
3.   audit reporting
4.   follow-up of corrective action implementation

Refer to Question 29 in Chapter 11, Quality Auditing.

72.   What items should be included by management when establishing a quality audit function within their organization?

1.   proper positioning of the audit function within the quality organization
2.   a planned audit approach, efficient and timely audit reporting, and a method for obtaining effective corrective action
3.   selection of capable audit personnel
4.   management objectivity toward the quality program audit concept
5.   all of the above

Refer to Question 5 in Chapter 11, Quality Auditing.

73.   Assurance bears the same relation to the quality function that _____ does to the accounting function.

1.   vacation
2.   audit
3.   variable overhead
4.   control

Refer to Question 14 in Chapter 11, Quality Auditing.

74.   A preaward survey of a potential supplier is best described as a _____ audit.

1.   compliance
2.   assessment
3.   quantitative
4.   all of these
5.   none of these

Refer to Question 60 in Chapter 11, Quality Auditing.

75. Which of the following best describes the "specific activity" type of audit?

    1. customer-oriented sampling of finished goods
    2. evaluation for contractual compliance of quality system
    3. assessment or survey of a potential vendor
    4. an inspection performance audit
    5. none of the above

Refer to Question 11 in Chapter 11, Quality Auditing.

76. Maintainability is

    1. the probability of a system being restored to functional operation within a given period of time
    2. performing adequate maintenance on a system
    3. probability of survival of a system for a given period of time
    4. maintaining a machine in satisfactory working condition
    5. none of the above

Refer to Question 28 in Chapter 13, Reliability, Maintainability, and Product Safety.

77. In some reliability models redundancy may take the form of standby elements. What is the major disadvantage of such a model as regards its reliability?

    1. more costly
    2. reliability may be reduced by failure of sensing devices
    3. failure rates are generally high
    4. the system is too complex
    5. none of these

Refer to Question 35 in Chapter 13, Reliability, Maintainability, and Product Safety.

78. Product reliability is the probability of a product performing its intended function and under the operating conditions encountered. A significant element in this concept includes

    1. probability
    2. performance
    3. time
    4. environment
    5. all of the above

Refer to Question 2 in Chapter 13, Reliability, Maintainability, and Product Safety.

79. Parts in use during the "wear out" portion of the part life-cycle curve will exhibit

1.   a constant failure rate
2.   a decreasing failure rate
3.   a low failure rate
4.   an increasing failure rate

Refer to Question 38 in Chapter 13, Reliability, Maintainability, and Product Safety.

80.   Reliability, maintainability, and product safety improvements are most often economically accomplished during the _____ phase of a program.

1.   design and development
2.   prototype test
3.   production
4.   field operation
5.   redesign and retrofit

Refer to Question 72 in Chapter 13, Reliability, Maintainability, and Product Safety.

81.   Quality information equipment

1.   is used only by the Quality Control function
2.   is used only for the purpose of accepting or rejecting products
3.   makes measurements of either products or processes and feeds the resulting data back for decision making
4.   includes automatic electronic instruments but not go/nogo gages

Refer to Question 17 in Chapter 14, Quality Information Systems.

82.   In today's world, quality information documentation is called

1.   end-item hardware
2.   hardware
3.   data pack
4.   software
5.   warranty

Refer to Question 24 in Chapter 14, Quality Information Systems.

83.   The quality needs for historical information in the areas of specifications, performance, reporting, complaint analysis, or run records would fall into which of the following computer application categories?

1.   data accumulation
2.   data reduction analysis and reporting
3.   real-time process control
4.   statistical analysis
5.   information retrieval

Refer to Question 7 in Chapter 14, Quality Information Systems.

84.   In establishing a quality reporting and information feedback system primary consideration must
       be given to

       1.   number of inspection stations
       2.   management approval
       3.   timely feedback and corrective action
       4.   historical preservation of data
       5.   routing copy list

       Refer to Question 13 in Chapter 14, Quality Information Systems.

85.   All quality information reports should be audited periodically to

       1.   determine their continued validity
       2.   reappraise the routing or copy list
       3.   determine their current effectiveness
       4.   all of the above
       5.   none of the above

       Refer to Question 8 in Chapter 14, Quality Information Systems.

86.   McGregor's Theory X manager is typified as one who operates from the following basic
       assumption about people working for him or her (select the best answer).

       1.   Performance can be improved through tolerance and trust.
       2.   People have a basic need to produce.
       3.   Status is more important than money.
       4.   Self-actualization is the highest order of human need.
       5.   People are lazy and are motivated by reward and punishment.

       Refer to Question 5 in Chapter 15, Motivation and Human Factors.

87.   When installing a new system for collecting failure data in a manufacturing plant, the following
       approach is recommended.

       1.   Issue a procedure written by a quality engineer without help from other departments to
             prevent a biased input from production test technicians.
       2.   Have production write their own procedure.
       3.   Use a procedure from another company.
       4.   Enlist the collaboration of all affected departments in drafting and approving the
             procedure.
       5.   None of the above.

       Refer to Question 19 in Chapter 15, Motivation and Human Factors.

88. Having designed a test fixture to performance requirements, the design should be carefully evaluated by the quality engineer to insure that it has included

  1. low-cost components
  2. printout capability
  3. human motor coordination factors
  4. mass production methods
  5. computer inputs

  Refer to Question 28 in Chapter 15, Motivation and Human Factors.

89. Quality motivation in industry should be directed at

  1. manufacturing management
  2. procurement and engineering
  3. the quality assurance staff
  4. the working force
  5. all of the above

  Refer to Question 15 in Chapter 15, Motivation and Human Factors.

90. In order to instill the quality control employee with the desire to perform to his or her utmost and optimum ability, which of the following recognitions for sustaining motivation has been found effective for most people?

  1. recognition by issuance of monetary award
  2. verbal recognition policy
  3. private verbal recognition
  4. public recognition plus nonmonetary award
  5. no recognition, salary he obtains is sufficient motivation

  Refer to Question 16 in Chapter 15, Motivation and Human Factors.

APPLICATIONS

1.   Determine the coefficient of the variation for the last 500 pilot plant test runs of high-temperature film having a mean of 900° Kelvin with a standard deviation of 54°.

    1.   6%

    2.   16.7%

    3.   0.06%

    4.   31%

    5.   the reciprocal of the relative standard deviation

Refer to Question 113 in Chapter 3, Fundamental Concepts of Probability and Statistics.

2.   You determine that it is sometimes economical to permit X to go out of control when

    1.   the individual R's exceed R

    2.   the cost of inspection is high

    3. 6σ is appreciably less than the difference between specification limits

    4.   the $\overline{X}$ control limits are inside the drawing tolerance limits

    5.   never

Refer to Question 21 in Chapter 7, Statistical Process Control.

3.   An electronics firm was experiencing high rejections in their multiple connector manufacturing departments. P charts were introduced as part of a program to reduce defectives. Control limits were based on prior history using the formula $P' \pm 3\sqrt{\dfrac{P'(100 - P')}{N}}$ where P' is the historical value of percent defective and N is the number of pieces inspected each week. After six weeks, the following record was accumulated.

Percent Defective

Dept.	P'	Week 1	Week 2	Week 3	Week 4	Week 5	Week 6
101	12	11	11	14	15	10	12
102	17	20	17	21	21	20	13
103	22	18	26	27	17	20	19
104	9	8	11	6	13	12	10
105	16	13	19	20	12	15	17
106	15	18	19	16	11	13	16

600 pieces were inspected each week in each department. Which department(s) exhibited a point or points out of control during the period?

1.   dept. 101
2.   dept. 102
3.   dept. 103
4.   dept. 104
5.   dept. 105

Refer to Question 73 in Chapter 7, Statistical Process Control.

4.   MIL-STD-105D is to be used to select a single sampling plan for lots of 8000 under normal inspection Level II, and an AQL of 2.5%. The exact AOQL for the plan is

1.   2.50%
2.   3.00%
3.   3.22%
4.   3.30%
5.   2.60%

Refer to Question 43 in Chapter 8, Acceptance Sampling.

5.   A lot of 50 pieces contains 5 defectives. A sample of two is drawn without replacement. The probability that both will be defective is approximately

1.   0.4000
2.   0.1000
3.   0.0010
4.   0.0082
5.   0.0093

Refer to Question 184 in Chapter 3, Fundamental Concepts of Probability and Statistics.

6.   Large panes of plate glass contain on the average 0.25 flaw per pane. The standard deviation of the distribution of the flaws is

1.   .25
2.   .05
3.   .50
4.   .75
5.   none of the above

Refer to Question 179 in Chapter 3, Fundamental Concepts of Probability and Statistics.

7.   You have just returned from a two week vacation and are going over with your QC manager the control charts which have been maintained during your absence. He or she calls your attention to the fact that one of the X-charts shows the last 50 points to be very near the centerline. In fact, they all seem to be within about one sigma of the centerline. What explanation would you offer him or her?

    1.   Somebody "goofed" in the original calculation of the control limits.

    2.   The process standard deviation has decreased during the time the last 50 samples were taken and nobody thought to recompute the control limits.

    3.   This is a terrible situation. I'll get on it right away and see what the trouble is. I hope we haven't produced too much scrap.

    4.   This is fine. The closer the points are to the centerline, the better your control.

Refer to Question 43 in Chapter 7, Statistical Process Control.

8.   Your quality control manger has asked you to make a study of the costs of using variables sampling as against attributes sampling for a pipeline fitting. After searching the literature you find that the following sampling plan will give you equal protection over the range of quality levels in which you are interested.

Type of Plan	Sample Size	Acceptance Criterion
Attributes	450	Ac = 10, Re = 11
Variables, sigma unknown	100	k = 2.0
Variables, sigma known	33	k = 2.0

Upon investigating the possible costs involved in each type of sampling with your accounting, production, and inspection departments, you arrive at the following figures.

	Attributes	Sigma Unknown	Sigma Known
Unit Sampling Cost	$0.05	0.05	0.05
Unit Inspection Cost	0.05	0.35	0.35
Unit Computation Cost	0.00	0.02	0.01
Lot Overhead Cost	6.00	18.00	40.00

Based on the above information, which sampling plan would you advise your inspector to use?

    1.   Since they all give equal protection, it does not make any difference.

    2.   Use attribute sampling.

    3.   Use continuous sampling.

    4.   Use variable sampling, sigma unknown.

    5.   Use variable sampling, sigma known.

Refer to Question 74 in Chapter 8, Acceptance Sampling.

9.   Suppose that 5 bad electron tubes get mixed up with 8 good tubes. If 2 tubes are drawn simultaneously, what is the probability that both are good?

    1.   8/13

    2.   14/39

    3.   7/12

    4.   7/13

    5.   36/91

Refer to Question 49 in Chapter 3, Fundamental Concepts of Probability and Statistics.

10.   The lengths of a certain bushing are normally distributed with a mean $\overline{X}$. How many standard deviation units symmetrical about the $\overline{X}$ will include 80% of the lengths?

   1.   ± 1.04
   2.   ± 0.52
   3.   ± 1.28
   4.   ± 0.84

Refer to Question 134 in Chapter 3, Fundamental Concepts of Probability and Statistics.

11.   Three trainees were given the same lots of 50 pieces and asked to classify them as defective or nondefective with the following results.

	Trainee #1	Trainee #2	Trainee #3	Total
Defective	17	30	25	72
Nondefective	33	20	25	78
Total	50	50	50	150

In determining whether or not there is a difference in the ability of the three trainees to properly classify the parts

   1.   the value of chi-square is about 6.90 (This is ASQC's correction.)
   2.   using a level of significance of 0.05, the critical value of chi-square is 5.99
   3.   since the obtained chi-square is greater than 5.99, we reject the null hypothesis
   4.   all of the above
   5.   none of the above

Refer to Question 76 in Chapter 4, Statistical Inference and Hypothesis Testing.

12.   A process is producing material which is 40% defective. Four pieces are selected at random for inspection. What is the probability of exactly one good piece being found in the sample?

   1.   0.875
   2.   0.575
   3.   0.346
   4.   0.130
   5.   0.154

Refer to Question 161 in Chapter 3, Fundamental Concepts of Probability and Statistics.

13.   An inspection plan is set up to randomly sample 3' of a 100' cable and accept if no flaws are found in the 3' length. What is the probability that a cable with an average of 1 flaw per foot will be rejected by the plan?

1.   0.05
2.   0.95
3.   0.72
4.   0.03
5.   0.10

Refer to Question 177 in Chapter 3, Fundamental Concepts of Probability and Statistics.

14.   A process is turning out end items which have defects of type A or type B in them. If the probability of a type A defect is 0.10 and of a type B defect is 0.20, the probability that an end item will have no defect is

1.   .02
2.   .28
3.   .30
4.   .72
5.   .68

Refer to Question 44 in Chapter 3, Fundamental Concepts of Probability and Statistics.

15.   A bin contains 40 pills with a weight of 3.1 gms each, 30 pills weighing 3.2 gms and 10 pills weighing 3.3 gms. The weight of an average pill is found from

1. $\dfrac{3.1 + 3.2 + 3.3}{3}$

2. $\dfrac{3.1(40) + 3.2(30) + 3.3(10)}{3}$

3. $\dfrac{(3.1 + 3.2 + 3.3)(10 + 30 + 40)}{80}$

4. $\overline{X} = \dfrac{3.1(40) + 3.2(30) + 3.3(10)}{80}$

Refer to Question 91 in Chapter 3, Fundamental Concepts of Probability and Statistics.

16.   If it was known that a population of 30,000 parts had a standard deviation of 0.05 second, what size sample would be required to maintain an error no greater than 0.01 second with a confidence level of 95%?

1.   235
2.   487
3.   123
4.   96
5.   78

Refer to Question 32 in Chapter 4, Statistical Inference and Hypothesis Testing.

17.   When you perform "one experiment" with "forty-nine repetitions," what are the fifty experiments called?

        1.   randomization
        2.   replications
        3.   planned grouping
        4.   experimental pattern
        5.   sequential

        Refer to Question 5 in Chapter 6, Design of Experiments.

18.   An $\overline{X}$ and R chart was prepared for an operation using twenty samples with five pieces in each sample. $\overline{X}$ was found to be 33.6 and R was 6.2. During production, a sample of five was taken and the pieces were measured 36, 43, 37, 34, and 38. At the time this sample was taken

        1.   both average and range were within control limits
        2.   neither average nor range was within control limits
        3.   only the average was outside control limits
        4.   only the range was outside control limits
        5.   the information given is not sufficient to construct an $\overline{X}$ and R chart using tables usually available

        Refer to Question 39 in Chapter 7, Statistical Process Control.

19.   You are to construct an OC curve. Which of the following cannot be used as an abscissa value?

        1.   AOQL
        2.   ASN
        3.   AQL
        4.   LTPD
        5.   All of these can be abscissa values.

        Refer to Question 60 in Chapter 8, Acceptance Sampling.

20.   Determine whether the following two types of rockets have significant different variances at the 5% level.

        Rocket 1   Rocket 2
        61 readings   31 readings
        1346.89 miles²   2237.29 miles²

        1.   significant difference because $F_{calc} < F_{table}$
        2.   no significant difference because $F_{calc} < F_{table}$
        3.   significant difference because $F_{calc} > F_{table}$
        4.   no significant difference because $F_{calc} < F_{table}$

        Refer to Question 70 in Chapter 4, Statistical Inference and Hypothesis Testing.

21.   When small samples are used to estimate the standard deviation through use of the range statistic, sample subgroup sizes larger than 20 should not be used because

      1.   the number 20 causes calculation difficulties
      2.   the efficiency of the range as an estimator of the standard deviation falls to 70%
      3.   the distribution for $n = 20$ is skewed
      4. $n = 20$ adversely affects the location of the mean
      5.   the variance is a biased estimate

Refer to Question 117 in Chapter 3, Fundamental Concepts of Probability and Statistics.

22.   A large lot of parts is rejected by your customer and found to be 20% defective. What is the probability that the lot would have been accepted by the plan: sample size = 10; accept if no defectives and reject if one or more defectives?

      1.   0.89
      2.   0.63
      3.   0.01
      4.   0.80
      5.   0.11

Refer to Question 163 in Chapter 3, Fundamental Concepts of Probability and Statistics.

23.   In performing analysis of variance in a single factor experiment, a fundamental assumption which is made is that the

      1.   factor (column) means are equal
      2.   factor (column) means are unequal
      3.   column variances are equal
      4.   column variances are significantly different

Refer to Question 55 in Chapter 6, Design of Experiments.

24.   The distribution of a characteristic is negatively skewed. The sampling distribution of the mean for large samples is

      1.   negatively skewed
      2.   approximately normal
      3.   positively skewed
      4.   bimodal
      5.   Poisson

Refer to Question 9 in Chapter 4, Statistical Inference and Hypothesis Testing.

25.   When an initial study is made of a repetitive industrial process for the purpose of setting up a Shewhart control chart, information on the following process characteristics is sought.

1. process capability
2. process performance
3. process reliability
4. process conformance
5. process tolerance

Refer to Question 63 in Chapter 7, Statistical Process Control.

26. You look at a process and note that the chart of averages has been in control. If the range suddenly and significantly increases, the mean will

1. always increase
2. stay the same
3. always decrease
4. occasionally show out of control of either limit
5. none of the above

Refer to Question 44 in Chapter 7, Statistical Process Control.

27. A factorial experiment has been performed to determine the effect of a factor A and factor B on the strength of a part. An F-test shows a significant interaction effect. This means that

1. either factor A or factor B has a significant effect on the strength
2. both factor A and factor B effect strength
3. the effect of changing factor B can be estimated only if the level of factor A is known
4. neither factor A nor factor B effect strength
5. that strength will increase if factor A is increased while factor B is held at a low level

Refer to Question 56 in Chapter 6, Design of Experiments.

28. When using a Poisson as an approximation to the binomial, the following conditions apply for the best approximation:

1. Larger sample size and larger fraction defective
2. Larger sample size and smaller fraction defective
3. Smaller sample size and larger fraction defective
4. Smaller sample size and smaller fraction defective

Refer to Question 180 in Chapter 3, Fundamental Concepts of Probability and Statistics.

29. Your major product cannot be fully inspected without destruction. You have been requested to plan the inspection program, including some product testing, in the most cost-effective manner. You most probably will recommend that samples selected for the product verification be based upon

1. MIL-STD-105D, latest issue (it is E), attribute sampling
2. MIL-STD-414 latest issue, variable sampling

3.   either answer 1 or 2 above will meet your criteria
4.   neither answer 1 nor 2 above will meet your criteria

Refer to Question 66 in Chapter 8, Acceptance Sampling.

30.   In recent months several quality problems resulted from apparent change in the design specifications by engineering including material substitutions. This has only come to light throughout quality engineering's failure analysis system. You recommend which of the following quality system provisions as the best corrective action?

1.   establishing a formal procedure for initial design review
2.   establishing a formal procedure for process control
3.   establishing a formal procedure for specification change control (sometimes called an ECO or SCO system)
4.   establishing a formal system for drawing and print control
5.   establishing a formal material review board (MRB)

Refer to Question 64 in Chapter 9, Quality Practices and Applications.

31.   When a Quality Engineer wants parts removed from a line which is operating for tolerance checking, he or she should

1.   request the operator and/or supervisor to get them while he or she is observing
2.   request the operator and/or supervisor to sample the line and bring them to his or her office
3.   get the samples him or herself without notifying either the operator and/or supervisor
4.   go out to the line, stop it him or herself, take the part, start it, and leave as quickly as possible

Refer to Question 31 in Chapter 15, Motivation and Human Factors.

32.   Source inspection should be employed when

1.   purchasing placed the order late and you want to help
2.   manufacturing is screaming for the material and you want to help
3.   you don't have the appropriate gates and management won't buy them
4.   source is more costly than receiving inspection but it reduces backlog in receiving
5.   none of the above

Refer to Question 15 in Chapter 12, Product and Materials Control and Measurement Systems.

33.   A vendor quality control plan has been adopted. Which of the following provisions would you advise top management to be least effective?

1.   product audits
2.   source inspection
3.   certificate of analysis

4.   certificate of compliance
5.   preaward surveys

Refer to Question 56 in Chapter 9, Quality Practices and Applications, and Question 66 in Chapter 11, Quality Auditing.

34.   One of the major hazards in the material review board procedure is the tendency of the board to emphasize only the disposition function and to neglect the _____ function.

1.   statistical analysis
2.   corrective action
3.   material evaluation
4.   tolerance review
5.   manufacturing methods

Refer to Question 46 in Chapter 9, Quality Practices and Applications, and Question 58 in Chapter 12, Product and Materials Control and Measurement Systems.

35.   The most desirable method of evaluating a supplier is

1.   history evaluation
2.   survey evaluation
3.   questionnaire
4.   discuss with quality manager on phone
5.   all of the above

Refer to Question 57 in Chapter 9, Quality Practices and Applications, and Question 67 in Chapter 11, Quality Auditing.

36.   On the production floor, parts being produced that measure 0.992-1.011. The specification requires the parts to be 0.995-1.005. Which of the following techniques would not be particularly useful in trying to improve and control the process?

1.   Pre-Control
2.   MIL-STD-105 charts
3.   Multi vari charts
4. $\overline{X}$ and R charts
5.   machine capability analysis

Refer to Question 44 in Chapter 8, Acceptance Sampling.

37.   The most important step in vendor certification is to

1.   obtain copies of vendor's handbook
2.   familiarize the vendor with quality requirements
3.   analyze vendor's first shipment

4.   visit the vendor's plant

Refer to Question 55 in Chapter 9, Quality Practices and Applications, and Question 65 in Chapter 11, Quality Auditing.

38.   The most important measure of outgoing quality needed by managers is product performance as viewed by

1.   the customer
2.   the final inspector
3.   production
4.   marketing

Refer to Question 41 in Chapter 9, Quality Practices and Applications.

39.   Much managerial decision making is based on comparing actual performance with _____ .

1.   personnel ratio
2.   cost of operations
3.   number of complaints
4.   standards of performance

Refer to Question 42 in Chapter 9, Quality Practices and Applications, and Question 53 in Chapter 12, Product and Materials Control and Measurement Systems.

40.   A technique whereby various product features are graded and varying degrees of quality control applied is called

1.   zero defects
2.   quality engineering
3.   classification of characteristics
4.   feature grading
5.   nonsense - you cannot do it

Refer to Questions 1 to 4 in Chapter 12, Product and Materials Control and Measurement Systems.

41.   Ultrasonic flaw detection instruments are calibrated using which of the following types of standards?

1.   NBS traceable time voltage standards
2.   natural flaws in the material being inspected
3.   not calibrated since NBS traceable standards are not available
4.   distance amplitude reference blocks
5.   artificial flaw transfer standards

Refer to Question 109 in Chapter 12, Product and Materials Control and Measurement Systems.

42.   Wear allowances in a go plug gage results in gages that are

1.   on the low limit of the specification
2.   slightly larger diameter than the hi-limit of the specification
3.   slightly smaller diameter than the low limit of the specification
4.   slightly larger diameter than the low limit of the specification
5.   on the high limit of the specification

Refer to Question 125 in Chapter 12, Product and Materials Control and Measurement Systems.

43.   A dial indicator nib must be perpendicular to measurement to avoid

1.   cosine error
2.   axis error
3.   profile error
4.   configuration error

Refer to Question 139 in Chapter 12, Product and Materials Control and Measurement Systems.

44.   When considering whether to use radiography or ultrasonic inspection to examine critical welds in thick materials, which of the following criteria is the best reason for this selection?

1.   ultrasonic, since greater thicknesses can be prevented
2.   radiography, since ultrasonic is less sensitive to porosity and inclusions
3.   both, since the methods complement rather than supplant one another
4.   both, since each is equally effective, the chance of missing a serious flaw is reduced

Refer to Question 107 in Chapter 12, Product and Materials Control and Measurement Systems.

45.   In the area for receiving inspection, which of the following items would not be in the inspection package?

1.   purchase order
2.   drawings to the latest revisions
3.   drawings to the revisions of the purchase order
4.   detailed inspection instructions

Refer to Question 16 in Chapter 12, Product and Materials Control and Measurement Systems.

46.   Which of the following pairs measure the same type of characteristics?

A) Pounds-Kelvin   D) PSI-Grams
B) BTU-Kelvin   E) Fahrenheit-Hectare
C) Pound Force-Newton   F) Acre-grams

1.   A, B, D, and F
2.   A, C, and E

3.   B and C
4.   B, D, and F
5.   A, C, E, and F

Refer to Question 161 in Chapter 12, Product and Materials Control and Measurement Systems.

47.   Calibration intervals should be adjusted when

1.   no defective product is reported as being erroneously accepted as a result of measurement errors
2.   few instruments are scrapped out during calibration
3.   the results of previous calibrations reflect few out of tolerance conditions during calibration
4.   a particular characteristic on a gage is consistently found out of tolerance

Refer to Question 89 in Chapter 12, Product and Materials Control and Measurement Systems.

48.   A typical use for the optical comparator would be to measure

1.   surface finish
2.   contours
3.   depth of holes
4.   diameters of interval grooves
5.   all of the above

Refer to Question 137 in Chapter 12, Product and Materials Control and Measurement Systems.

49.   The primary advantage of the use of radio-isotopes, such as cobalt 60 as compared to an X-ray generator, such as a betatron, is

1.   duration of radiation can be controlled by turning off the source
2.   portability
3.   the energy given off is heterogeneous, covering a wide range of wavelengths
4.   the energy given off by the source stays constant with time

Refer to Question 110 in Chapter 12, Product and Materials Control and Measurement Systems.

50.   The gradual loss of sonic energy as ultrasonic vibrations travel through the material is referred to as

1.   refraction
2.   reproducibility
3.   reflection
4.   attenuation
5.   diffraction

Refer to Question 111 in Chapter 12, Product and Materials Control and Measurement Systems.

51.   "'Beauty Defects'" can best be described for inspection acceptance purposes by

       1.   simply stating such defects are unacceptable
       2.   verbally describing rejection criteria
       3.   leaving them up to the inspector
       4.   establishing visual standards and or samples describing the defects
       5.   establishing written standards describing the defects

       Refer to Question 142 in Chapter 12, Product and Materials Control and Measurement Systems.

52.   Which of the following is the symbol for surface finish requirements?

       1.   λ
       2.   M
       3.   √⎯⎯⎯
       4.   M/S

       5.   △ T 100

       Refer to Question 162 in Chapter 12, Product and Materials Control and Measurement Systems.

53.   Quality cost analysis has shown that appraisal costs are apparently too high in relation to sales.
       Which of the following actions probably would *not* be considered in pursuing the problem?

       1.   work sampling in inspection and test areas
       2.   adding inspectors to reduce scrap costs
       3.   Pareto analysis of quality costs
       4.   considering elimination of some test operations
       5.   comparing appraisal costs to bases other than sales, for example, direct labor, value
             added, etc.

       Refer to Question 43 in Chapter 10, Quality Cost Analysis. Also refer to Question 57 in this
       section.

54.   Analyze the cost data below

       $10,000   equipment design
       150,000   scrap
       180,000   reinspection and retest
        45,000   loss or disposition of surplus stock
         4,000   vendor quality surveys
        40,000   repair

       Considering only the Quality Costs shown above, we might conclude that

       1.   prevention costs should be decreased

2.　　internal failure costs can be decreased
3.　　prevention costs are too low a proportion of the quality costs shown
4.　　appraisal costs should be increased
5.　　nothing can be concluded

Refer to Question 58 in Chapter 10, Quality Cost Analysis.

55.　This month's quality cost data collection shows the following:

Returned material processing	$1,800
Adjustment of customer complaints	4,500
Rework and repair	10,700
Quality management salaries	25,000
Warranty replacement	54,500
Calibration and testing	2,500
Inspection and testing	28,000

For your action report to top management, you select which of the following as the percentage of "External Failure" to the "Total Quality Costs" to show the true impact of the field problems?

1.　20%
2.　55%
3.　48%
4.　24%
5.　8%

Refer to Question 59 in Chapter 10, Quality Cost Analysis.

56.　You have been assigned as a quality engineer to a small company. The quality control manager desires some cost data and the accounting department reported that the following information is available. Cost accounts are production inspection, $14,185; test-inspection, $4264; procurement inspection, $2198; shop labor, $14,698; shop rework, $1402; first article, $675; engineering analysis (rework), $845; repair service (warrantee), $298; quality engineering, $2175; design engineering salaries, $241,451; quality equipment, $18,745; training, $275; receiving laboratories, $385; underwriter laboratories, $1200; installation service cost, $9000; scrap, $1182; and calibration service, $794.

What are the prevention costs?

1.　　$3,727
2.　　$23,701
3.　　$23,026
4.　　$3,295
5.　　$2,450

Refer to Question 60 in Chapter 10, Quality Cost Analysis.

57. Quality cost analysis has shown that appraisal costs are apparently too high in relation to sales. Which of the following actions probably would not be considered in pursuing this problem?

1. work sampling in inspection and test areas
2. adding inspectors to reduce scrap costs
3. Pareto analysis of quality costs
4. considering elimination of some test operations
5. comparing appraisal costs to bases other than sales, for example, direct labor, value added, etc.

Refer to Question 43 in Chapter 10, Quality Cost Analysis. Also refer to Question 53 above in this section.

58. The percentages of total quality costs are described as follows:

Prevention	12%
Appraisal	28%
Internal failure	40%
External failure	20%

We conclude

1. We should invest more money in prevention
2. Expenditures for failures are excessive
3. The amount spent for appraisal seems about right
4. nothing

Refer to Question 52 in Chapter 10, Quality Cost Analysis.

59. One of the following is not a factor to consider in establishing quality information equipment cost

1. debugging cost
2. amortization period
3. design cost
4. replacement cost
5. book cost

Refer to Question 89 in Chapter 10, Quality Cost Analysis.

60. One method to control inspection costs even without a budget is by comparing _____ as a ratio to productive machine time to produce the product.

1. product cost
2. company profit
3. inspection hours
4. scrap material

Refer to Question 40 in Chapter 12, Product and Materials Control and Measurement Systems, and Question 81 in Chapter 10, Quality Cost Analysis.

61.   A complete Quality Cost Reporting System would include which of the following as part of the quality cost?

    1.   test time costs associated with installing the product at the customer's facility prior to turning the product over to the customer
    2.   the salary of a product designer preparing a deviation authorization for material produced outside of design specifications
    3.   cost of scrap
    4.   all of the above
    5.   none of the above

Refer to Question 83 in Chapter 10, Quality Cost Analysis.

62.   When prevention costs are increased, to pay for the right kind of engineering work in quality control, a reduction in the number of product defect occurs. This defect reduction means a substantial reduction in _____.

    1.   appraisal costs
    2.   operating costs
    3.   prevention costs
    4.   failure costs
    5.   manufacturing costs

Refer to Question 31 in Chapter 10, Quality Cost Analysis.

63.   Which of the following techniques would not be used in a quality audit?

    1.   select samples only from completed work
    2.   examine samples from viewpoint of critical customer
    3.   audit only those items which have caused customer complaints
    4.   use audit information in future design planning
    5.   frequency of audit to depend on economic and quality requirements

Refer to Question 52 in Chapter 11, Quality Auditing.

64.   During the pre-award survey at a potential key supplier, you discover the existence of a Quality Control Manual, this means

    1.   that a quality system has been developed
    2.   that a quality system has been implemented
    3.   that a firm is quality conscious
    4.   that the firm has a quality manager
    5.   all of the above

Refer to Question 68 in Chapter 11, Quality Auditing.

65.   Which of the following quality system provisions is of the least concern when preparing an audit checklist for the upcoming branch operation quality system audit:

    1.   drawing and print control
    2.   makeup of the MRB (material review board)
    3.   engineering design change control
    4.   control of special processes
    5.   all of the above

Refer to Questions 27 and 28 in Chapter 11, Quality Auditing.

66.   You are requested by the top management to establish an audit program of the quality system in each branch plant of your firm. Which of the following schemes would you use in selecting the audit team to optimize continuity, direction, availability, and technology transfer?

    1.   full-time audit staff
    2.   all-volunteer audit staff
    3.   the boss's son and son-in-law
    4.   hybrid audit staff (a proportion of answers 1 and 2 above)
    5.   any of the above will make an effective audit team

Refer to Question 20 in Chapter 11, Quality Auditing.

67.   An audit will be viewed as a constructive service to the function which is audited when it

    1.   is conducted by nontechnical auditors
    2.   proposes corrective action for each item covered
    3.   furnishes enough detailed facts so the necessary actions can be determined
    4.   is general enough to permit managerial intervention

Refer to Question 32 in Chapter 11, Quality Auditing.

68.   Which of the following is not a responsibility of the auditor?

    1.   prepare a plan and checklist
    2.   report results to those responsible
    3.   investigate deficiencies for a cause and define the corrective actions that must be taken
    4.   follow up to see if the corrective action was taken
    5.   is general enough to permit managerial intervention

Refer to Question 33 in Chapter 11, Quality Auditing.

69.   Reliability testing of parts is performed to yield which of the following type of information?

    1.   application suitability

    2.   environmental capability
    3.   measurement of the life characteristics
    4.   all of the above
    5.   none of the above

Refer to Question 10 in Chapter 13, Reliability, Maintainability, and Product Safety.

70.   Failure mode effect and criticality analysis (FMECA) is primarily for the purpose of

    1.   learning as much about the item as possible after qualification test
    2.   determining the way an item will most likely fail to help obtain design and procedural safeguards against such failures
    3.   determining by extensive analysis the reliability of an item
    4.   determining the cause of a failure by dissecting the item to help obtain corrective action

Refer to Question 91 in Chapter 13, Reliability, Maintainability, and Product Safety.

71.   According to the definition of reliability, performance over the expected or intended life is one criterion. In order to obtain a measurement for reliability, the actual life (t) must be compared to which of the following?

    1.   sampling of components
    2.   Test cycles (T)
    3.   Required life (T)
    4.   MTBF
    5.   probability of failures (P_t)

Refer to Question 8 in Chapter 13, Reliability, Maintainability, and Product Safety.

72.   For a high compression aircraft air conditioning system, the MTBF is 100 hours. This mean life is allocated to four serial units comprising the total system. The unit failure rates are then weighted as follows: $w_1 = 0.1250$ $w_3 = 0.1875$ $w_2 = 0.2500$ $w_4 = 0.4375$

Based upon the above data, indicate which of the following is the correct calculation for one of the units.

    1. $\lambda_3 = 0.001875$
    2. $\lambda_4 = 0.043570$
    3. $\lambda_1 = 0.012500$
    4. $\lambda_3 = 0.0001875$
    5. $\lambda_2 = 0.002510$

Refer to Question 42 in Chapter 13, Reliability, Maintainability, and Product Safety. This question is repeated in the July 1984 examination.[4]

---

[4] *ASQC - CQE Examination*, Quality Progress, July 1984, Applications section, Question 72.

73.   The basic steps in any data processing system using computers generally are arranged in which of the following orders?

    1.   data input, storage and retrieval, processing and output
    2.   collection, analysis, input and output
    3.   evaluation, keypunch, processing and output
    4.   recording, input, calculation and output
    5.   keypunch, Fortran programming, output

Refer to Question 3 in Chapter 14, Quality Information Systems.

74.   When planning a system for processing quality data, or for keeping inspection and other quality records, the first step should be to

    1.   depict the system in a flowchart
    2.   hire a statistician
    3.   investigate applicable data processing equipment
    4.   determine the cost of operating the system
    5.   start coding your input data

Refer to Question 4 in Chapter 14, Quality Information Systems.

75.   The management team is establishing priorities to attack a serious quality problem. You are requested to establish a data collection system to direct this attack. You use which of these general management rules to support your recommendations as to the quantity of data required:

    1.   You have compared the incremental cost of additional data with the value of the information obtained and stopped when they are equal.
    2.   Your decision corresponds to the rules applicable to management decisions for other factors of production.
    3.   Your decision is based upon the relationship between value and cost.
    4.   all of the above

Refer to Question 16 in Chapter 14, Quality Information Systems.

76.   Computer information processing can become available to any Quality Engineer through the use of

    1.   a terminal and time sharing agreement
    2.   a batch processing system in which data are brought to a central area for processing
    3.   an in-house system with applicable software
    4.   all of the above

Refer to Question 1 in Chapter 14, Quality Information Systems.

77.   In a visual inspection situation, one of the best ways to minimize deterioration of the quality level is to

1.   retrain the inspector frequently
2.   add variety to the task
3.   have a program of frequent eye examinations
4.   have frequent breaks
5.   have a standard to compare against the part of the operation

Refer to Question 75 in Chapter 9, Quality Practices and Applications, and Question 32 in Chapter 15, Motivation and Human Factors.

78.   Which of the following methods used to improve employee efficiency and promote an atmosphere conducive to quality and profit is the most effective in the long run?

1.   offering incentives such as bonus, praise, profit sharing, etc.
2.   strict discipline to reduce mistakes, idleness, and sloppiness
3.   combination of incentive and discipline to provide both reward for excellence and punishment for inferior performance
4.   building constructive attitudes through development of realistic quality goals relating to both company and employee success
5.   all of the above, provided emphasis is placed on attitude motivation, with incentive and discipline used with utmost caution

Refer to Question 33 in Chapter 15, Motivation and Human Factors.

79.   The Quality Engineer should be concerned with the human factors of a new piece of in-house manufacturing equipment as well as its operational effects because it

1.   may speed the line to the point where a visual operator inspection is impossible
2.   may require the operator's undivided attention at the controls so the product cannot be fully seen
3.   may remove an operator formerly devoting some portion of time to inspection
4.   all of the above

Refer to Question 26 in Chapter 15, Motivation and Human Factors.

80.   The famous Hawthorne study provided which of the following clinical evidence regarding the factors that can increase workgroup productivity?

1.   Attention and recognition are more important than working conditions.
2.   Productivity did not change significantly under any of the test conditions.
3.   Informal group pressures set a production goal.
4.   People with higher capabilities are bored with routine jobs.
5.   Workstation layout is critical to higher productivity.

Refer to Question 1 in Chapter 15, Motivation and Human Factors. This question is repeated in the July 1984 examination.[5]

ANSWERS FOR AUGUST 1978 EXAMINATION

PRINCIPLES

Q	A	Q	A	Q	A	Q	A	Q	A
1.	2	21.	2	41.	2	61.	4	81.	3
2.	5	22.	4	42.	3	62.	3	82.	4
3.	4	23.	4	43.	1	63.	2	83.	5
4.	1	24.	5	44.	3	64.	3	84.	3
5.	5	25.	4	45.	3	65.	5	85.	4
6.	2	26.	2	46.	2	66.	3	86.	5
7.	2	27.	4	47.	4	67.	5	87.	4
8.	2	28.	4	48.	2	68.	5	88.	3
9.	1	29.	2	49.	1	69.	1	89.	5
10.	3	30.	1	50.	3	70.	3	90.	4
11.	1	31.	4	51.	1	71.	4		
12.	2	32.	4	52.	4	72.	5		
13.	2	33.	3	53.	4	73.	2		
14.	2	34.	5	54.	4	74.	2		
15.	3	35.	5	55.	3	75.	4		
16.	1	36.	3	56.	3	76.	1		
17.	4	37.	4	57.	3	77.	2		
18.	2	38.	5	58.	3	78.	5		
19.	1	39.	4	59.	5	79.	4		
20.	1	40.	1	60.	3	80.	1		

COMMENTS / NOTES:

---

[5] *ASQC - CQE Examination*, Quality Progress, July 1984, Principles section, Question 86.

ANSWERS FOR AUGUST 1978 EXAMINATION

APPLICATIONS

Q	A	Q	A	Q	A	Q	A
1.	1	21.	2	41.	4	61.	4
2.	3	22.	5	42.	4	62.	4
3.	4	23.	3	43.	1	63.	3
4.	3	24.	2	44.	3	64.	1
5.	4	25.	1	45.	2	65.	2
6.	3	26.	4	46.	3	66.	4
7.	2	27.	3	47.	4	67.	3
8.	2	28.	2	48.	2	68.	3
9.	2	29.	2	49.	2	69.	4
10.	3	30.	3	50.	4	70.	2
11.	4	31.	1	51.	4	71.	3
12.	5	32.	3	52.	3	72.	1
13.	2	33.	4	53.	2	73.	1
14.	4	34.	2	54.	3	74.	1
15.	4	35.	1	55.	3	75.	4
16.	4	36.	2	56.	5	76.	4
17.	2	37.	2	57.	2	77.	5
18.	3	38.	1	58.	4	78.	5
19.	2	39.	4	59.	5	79.	4
20.	2	40.	3	60.	3	80.	1

COMMENTS / NOTES:

CHAPTER 18

ASQC-CQE EXAMINATION, QUALITY PROGRESS, OCTOBER 1974

PRINCIPLES

Note: *The old examination sets used numbers, e.g., 1, 2, 3, 4, and 5, for various choices for each question. Hence the following questions use the numerical choices in its original format.*

Recent examinations and the study guides published in ASQC's recent certification brochures use letters, e.g., a, b, c, d, and e, for choices to a question in place of numbers. Hence letters are used in all individual subject matter chapters 3 through 15. Readers are advised to note this difference while referring to solutions in respective chapters.

1. In acceptance sampling, the probability of accepting an undesirable lot is the same as (or may be called)

    1. alpha
    2. beta
    3. AQL
    4. LTPD
    5. none of these

    Refer to Question 20 in Chapter 8, Acceptance Sampling.

2. When introducing the new product to the manufacturing phase of the product's life, the most important justification for a process capability study after a pilot run for stability but during a controlled operation is

    1. it will prove design feasibility
    2. it will establish machine capability
    3. it will provide manufacturing engineering with the basis for a preventive maintenance schedule
    4. it will determine the degree of conformance of tools, materials, and operators with design specifications and economic yield requirements
    5. none of these

    Refer to Question 60 in Chapter 7, Statistical Process Control.

3. The primary reason for evaluating and maintaining surveillance over a supplier's quality program is to

    1. perform product inspection at source
    2. eliminate incoming inspection costs

3. improve human and customer relations and motivate suppliers in improving quality
4. make sure the supplier's quality program is accomplishing its intended functions effectively and economically

Refer to Question 58 in Chapter 11, Quality Auditing.

4. In determining a process average fraction defective using inductive or inferential statistics, we are making inferences about _____ based on _____ taken from the _____ .

1. statistics, samples, populations
2. populations, samples, populations
3. samples, statistics, populations
4. samples, populations, samples
5. statistics, populations, statistics

Refer to Question 12 in Chapter 3, Fundamental Concepts of Probability and Statistics.

5. In linear measurement, what overriding consideration should guide the quality control engineer in specifying the measuring instrument to be used?

1. the ability of the instrument to be read to one decimal place beyond that of the base dimension to be measured
2. the ability of the instrument to meet the error rule of thumb
3. the ability of the instrument-inspector system to obtain the necessary accurate data at a minimum overall cost
4. the combination of base dimension and tolerance in relation to measurement error
5. the ability of the inspector to use the measuring instrument

Refer to Question 33 in Chapter 12, Product and Materials Control and Measurement Systems.

6. When we arrange a set of measurements in order of magnitude and indicate the frequency associated with each measurement, we have constructed

1. a grouped frequency distribution
2. a cumulative frequency distribution
3. an ungrouped frequency distribution
4. a bar graph
5. a histogram

Refer to Question 62 in Chapter 3, Fundamental Concepts of Probability and Statistics.

7. When looking for existing sources of external failure cost data, which of the following is usually the best source available:

1. customer corrective action requests
2. salesperson's field reports
3. accounting reports on sales of "seconds" or "distressed merchandise"

4.   returned material reports
5.   purchase orders

Refer to Questions 44 and 45 in Chapter 10, Quality Cost Analysis.

8.   For a two-factor experiment with n observations per cell run as a completely randomized design

1.   the degrees of freedom cannot be determined because of the interaction term in the mathematical model
2.   if both factors are fixed, all tests of significance are made using the error mean square
3.   the interaction term cannot be calculated by subtracting the main effects sum of squares from the cell sum of squares
4.   when the interactions effect is significant, it becomes obvious that one of the main effects is also significant
5.   all of the above

Refer to Question 21 in Chapter 6, Design of Experiments.

9.   Sensitivity in experimentation is

1.   getting the true result
2.   extreme care in data analysis
3.   using the best measuring device
4.   ability to distinguish differences in the response variables

Refer to Question 16 in Chapter 6, Design of Experiments.

10.   If we draw a large number of samples from a controlled process, we would not be surprised to discover

1.   some differences among the values of the sample means
2.   a distribution of sample means around some central value
3.   that many sample means differ from the process average
4.   all of the above
5.   none of the above

Refer to Question 116 in Chapter 3, Fundamental Concepts of Probability and Statistics.

11.   A thorough analysis of the cause and effect of plant quality problems usually indicates that a major percentage of basic factors effecting poor quality performance are

1.   operator controllable
2.   management controllable
3.   union controllable
4.   customer controllable
5.   none of the above

Refer to Question 28 in Chapter 9, Quality Practices and Applications.

12.   Quality control has been labeled as the science and art of identifying and controlling variability. One measure of variability as used in this context is

    1.   the arithmetic mean
    2.   the size of a lot
    3.   the mode
    4.   the variance
    5.   the geometric mean

Refer to Question 102 in Chapter 3, Fundamental Concepts of Probability and Statistics.

13.   The acronym AQL as used in sampling inspection means

    1.   the level of lot quality for which there is a small risk of rejecting the lot
    2.   the same as the limiting quality (LQ) or LTPD
    3.   the same as the rejectable quality level (RQL)
    4.   the maximum percent defective that can be considered satisfactory as a process average
    5.   the average outgoing quality level

Refer to Question 31 in Chapter 8, Acceptance Sampling.

14.   The principal use of V blocks is holding in fixed relation the surface plate

    1.   angular pieces
    2.   cylindrical pieces
    3.   spherical parts
    4.   measuring tools

Refer to Question 143 in Chapter 12, Product and Materials Control and Measurement Systems.

15.   The terms *critical, major, minor,* or *incidental* may be used in planning for

    1.   classification of defects
    2.   classification of characteristics
    3.   acceptance sampling
    4.   all of the above
    5.   none of the above

Refer to Question 1 in Chapter 12, Product and Materials Control and Measurement Systems.

16.   The existence of a quality control manual at your key supplier means

    1.   that a quality system has been developed
    2.   that a quality system has been implemented
    3.   that the firm is quality conscious

4.   that the firm is a certified supplier

5.   all of the above

Refer to Question 54 in Chapter 9, Quality Practices and Applications and Question 61 in Chapter 11, Quality Auditing. This question is repeated with a slight change in the August 1978 examination.[1]

17.   Outside endorsements or approvals such as Underwriters Laboratories fees are usually considered which of following quality costs:

1.   external failure

2.   appraisal

3.   prevention

4.   internal failure

5.   none of the above

Refer to Question 40 in Chapter 10, Quality Cost Analysis.

18.   When considering human motivation in solving quality problems, it is most important to recognize that

1.   individuals have *wants*

2.   individual motivation is of little concern in quality problem solving

3.   individuals have different levels of needs

4.   individuals have basic needs

Refer to Question 4 in Chapter 15, Motivation and Human Factors.
Also refer to the July 1984 examination for a similar question on Maslow's theory of needs.[2]

19.   Which of the following measures of variability is *not* dependent on the exact value of every measurement?

1.   mean deviation

2.   variance

3.   range

4.   standard deviation

5.   none of the above

Refer to Question 108 in Chapter 3, Fundamental Concepts of Probability and Statistics.

20.   For a given number of degrees of freedom, as the variability amongst means (groups, columns) increases relative to the variability within groups

1.   the F ratio decreases

---

[1] *ASQC - CQE Examination*, Quality Progress, August 1978, Principles section, Question 46.
[2] *ASQC - CQE Examination*, Quality Progress, July 1984, Principles section, Question 90.

2.   the F ratio increases
3.   the F ratio is unaffected
4.   the risk of a Type I error increases
5.   cannot answer without knowing the number of observations

Refer to Question 40 in Chapter 6, Design of Experiments.

21.   The vernier makes measurement readings as fine as thousandths of an inch possible by

1.   magnifying the graduations
2.   providing more widely spaced graduations
3.   visually subdividing the smallest divisions on a scale
4.   providing more closely spaced graduations

Refer to Question 114 in Chapter 12, Product and Materials Control and Measurement Systems.

22.   The Y axis of a cumulative probability function shows:

1.   the incremental probability of events
2.   the probability of an event for a given X
3.   the relative frequency of events
4.   the relative frequency of events equal to or less than a given X
5.   all of the above

Refer to Question 68 in Chapter 3, Fundamental Concepts of Probability and Statistics.

23.   In organizing an audit group, it is most important

1.   that the group be independent of the operating functions
2.   that it be compatible with the accounting audit group
3.   for it to cover all company functions
4.   for it to report to top management only

Refer to Question 17 in Chapter 11, Quality Auditing.

24.   Which of the following functions are normally considered "work elements" of quality control engineering?

1.   preproduction planning
2.   process capability studies
3.   classification of characteristics
4.   quality cost analysis
5.   all of these are work elements of quality control engineering

Refer to Question 16 in Chapter 9, Quality Practices and Applications.

25.   A process calls for the mean value of a dimension to be 2.02". Which of the following should

be used as the null hypothesis to test whether or not the process is achieving this mean?

1. the mean of the population is 2.02"
2. the mean of the sample is 2.02"
3. the mean of the population is not 2.02"
4. the mean of the sample is not 2.02"
5. all of the above are acceptable null hypotheses

Refer to Question 52 in Chapter 4, Statistical Inference and Hypothesis Testing.

26. Which of the following quantitative methods does not apply to the assessment of actual system or component reliability?

   1. statistical analysis of field test data
   2. statistical allocation of reliability goals
   3. evaluation of laboratory test data
   4. analysis of results of reliability demonstration tests
   5. analysis of failure data

Refer to Question 92 in Chapter 13, Reliability, Maintainability, and Product Safety.

27. When planning a total quality system, one key objective is to provide a means of guaranteeing "the maintenance of product integrity." Which of the following quality system provisions is designed to most directly provide such a guarantee?

   1. drawing and print control
   2. special process control
   3. calibration and maintenance of test equipment
   4. identification and segregation of nonconforming material
   5. specification change control

Refer to Question 43 in Chapter 9, Quality Practices and Applications. This question is repeated with a slight change in the July 1984 examination.[3]

28. A well-prepared checklist for a quality audit is a vital tool to provide

   1. assurance that areas having major deficiencies during past audits are reviewed
   2. a training method for developing new auditors
   3. a means of obtaining relatively uniform audits
   4. all of the above
   5. none of the above

Refer to Question 38 in Chapter 11, Quality Auditing.

29. Which of the following cannot be a null hypothesis?

---

[3] *ASQC - CQE Examination*, Quality Progress, July 1984, Principles section, Question 34.

1.   The population means are equal.
2. $p' = 0.5$
3. $p' = 0.25$
4.   The sample means are equal.
5.   The differences in the population means from which the samples were drawn is 3.85."

Refer to Question 46 in Chapter 4, Statistical Inference and Hypothesis Testing.

30.   Your operation requires infrequent vendor shipments of a relatively small number of parts for a critical assembly. Desiring the best protection for the lowest cost, you advise the chief inspector that the most appropriate sampling plan for receiving inspection should be one developed from

1.   the Poisson distribution
2.   the hypergeometric distribution
3.   the binomial distribution
4.   the log-normal distribution
5.   the Gaussian (normal) distribution

Refer to Questions 11 and 12 in Chapter 8, Acceptance Sampling.

31.   The two quantities that uniquely determine a single attributes sampling plan are

1.   AQL and LTPD
2.   sample size and rejection number
3.   AQL and producer's risk
4.   LTPD and consumer's risk

Refer to Questions 25 through 28 in Chapter 8, Acceptance Sampling.

32.   Parts in use during the random failure or normal portion of the part life-cycle curve will exhibit

1.   a constant failure rate
2.   a decreasing failure rate
3.   a low failure rate
4.   an increasing failure rate

Refer to Question 37 in Chapter 13, Reliability, Maintainability, and Product Safety.
Refer to Question 54 in this section for additional practice. This question is also repeated in the August 1978 examination.[4]

33.   One of the first questions that should be answered when planning to process quality data is:

1.   Will the results of the analysis be used?
2.   How much will the analysis cost?

---

[4] *ASQC - CQE Examination*, Quality Progress, August 1978, Principles section, Question 79.

3.   What is the error of measurement (analytical variation)?
4.   Is the sample size large enough?

Refer to Question 77 in Chapter 9, Quality Practices and Applications.

34.   Selection of a sampling plan from the Dodge-Romig LTPD sampling tables

1.   requires knowledge of the AOQ
2.   requires knowledge of the process average
3.   requires sorting of rejected lots
4.   requires larger samples than MIL-STD-105D (now E) for equivalent quality assurance

Refer to Question 54 in Chapter 8, Acceptance Sampling.

35.   A maintainability group is primarily concerned with

1.   determining the probability of survival of a system for a given period of time
2.   establishing the probability of a system being restored to functional operation within a given period of time
3.   performing adequate maintenance on a system
4.   administration of maintenance supplies inventories
5.   none of these

Refer to Question 29 in Chapter 13, Reliability, Maintainability, and Product Safety.
This question is repeated with a slight change in the July 1984 examination.[5]

36.   Data from which of the following investigations would normally not be included in auditing a complete quality system:

1.   examination of all items produced
2.   examination of customer need and the adequacy of design specifications in reflecting these needs
3.   examination of vendor product specifications and monitoring procedures
4.   examination of customer quality complaints and adequacy for corrective actions

Refer to Question 47 in Chapter 11, Quality Auditing.

37.   Upon completion of a branch plant or division quality systems audit, an "exit briefing" of concerned personnel should be conducted by the audit team. Which of the following is usually a violation of quality audit integrity?

1.   identifying major quality system deficiencies found during the last audit
2.   comparing audit results with the branch plant/division last audited
3.   obtaining corrective actions commitments
4.   highlighting key areas of improvements since the last audit

---

[5] *ASQC - CQE Examination*, Quality Progress, July 1984, Principles section, Question 78.

5.   all of the above are good audit practices

Refer to Question 23 in Chapter 11, Quality Auditing.

38.   Which of the following elements is least necessary to a good corrective action feedback report?

1.   what caused failure
2.   who caused failure
3.   what correction has been made
4.   when the correction is effective
5.   how the corrected product is identified

Refer to Question 82 in Chapter 9, Quality Practices and Applications and Question 62 in Chapter 12, Product and Materials Control and Measurement Systems.

39.   In a single-factor analysis of variance, the assumption of homogeneity of variance applies to

1.   the variance within the treatment groups
2.   the variance of the means associated with the treatment groups
3.   the total variance
4.   all of the above
5.   none of the above

Refer to Question 41 in Chapter 6, Design of Experiments.

40.   Dial indicator inaccuracies are stated in terms of

1.   percentage of full-scale range
2.   dial indicator divisions
3.   percent reliability
4.   thousands of full-scale range
5.   none of these

Refer to Question 135 in Chapter 12, Product and Materials Control and Measurement Systems.

41.   The principal reason for a quality control department using EDP is

1.   the planning forces reexamination of the value of storing quality data
2.   it's cheap
3.   the data are available for analyses faster than by any other method
4.   analyses can be standardized

Refer to Question 25 in Chapter 14, Quality Information Systems.

42.   Which of the following statements concerning the coefficient of simple linear correlation r is *not* true?

        1.   r = 0.00 represents the absence of relationship.
        2.   The relationship between the two variables must be nonlinear.
        3.   r = 0.76 has the same predictive power as r = − 0.76.
        4.   r = 1.00 represents a perfect relationship.

Refer to Question 9 in Chapter 5, Regression and Correlation Analysis.

43.   The expression $\dfrac{x!}{x!(x-n)!} p'^x (1-p')^{n-x}$ is the general term for the

        1.   Poisson distribution
        2.   Pascal distribution
        3.   Hypergeometric distribution
        4.   Binomial distribution
        5.   none of the above

Refer to Question 154 in Chapter 3, Fundamental Concepts of Probability and Statistics.

44.   The appropriate mathematical model for describing the sampling distribution of the fraction defective in samples from a controlled process in which p' = 0.05 is

        1.   the normal curve
        2.   the binomial distribution in which p' = 0.05
        3.   the binomial distribution in which p' = 0.95
        4.   the alpha level

Refer to Question 56 in Chapter 4, Statistical Inference and Hypothesis Testing.

45.   A good quality cost reporting system will

        1.   lead to operating at the lowest possible costs
        2.   supplement the company's financial reporting system
        3.   get the best product quality possible
        4.   indicate areas of excessive costs
        5.   none of these

Refer to Question 67 in Chapter 10, Quality Cost Analysis.

46.   Two of the most fundamental aspects of product quality are

        1.   appraisal costs and failure costs
        2.   in-process and finished product quality
        3.   quality of design and quality of conformance
        4.   impact of machines and impact of men
        5.   none of these

Refer to Question 3 in Chapter 9, Quality Practices and Applications.

47. A number resulting from the manipulation of some raw data according to certain specified procedures is called

   1. a sample
   2. a population
   3. a constant
   4. a statistic
   5. a parameter

Refer to Question 4 in Chapter 3, Fundamental Concepts of Probability and Statistics.

48. A very useful attribute control chart for plotting the actual number of defects found during an inspection is known as the

   1. $\overline{X}$ and R chart
   2. np chart
   3. p chart
   4. c chart
   5. u chart

Refer to Question 82 in Chapter 7, Statistical Process Control.

49. The best reason for investment in quality information equipment (QIE) is that it will improve the total quality system by

   1. providing better data collection
   2. reducing the time span in the corrective action feedback loop
   3. providing better information retrieval
   4. reducing the paperwork load of the QC department

Refer to Question 18 in Chapter 14, Quality Information Systems.

50. If the means of the samples for each of the treatment groups in an experiment were identical, the F ratio would be

   1. 1.00
   2. zero
   3. a positive number between 0 and 1
   4. a negative number
   5. infinite

Refer to Question 42 in Chapter 6, Design of Experiments.

51. If in a t test, alpha is 0.05,

1. 5% of the time we will say that there is no real difference but in reality there is a difference
2. 5% of the time we will make a correct inference
3. 5% of the time we will say that there is a real difference when there really is not a difference
4. 95% of the time we will make an incorrect inference
5. 95% of the time the null hypothesis will be correct

Refer to Question 53 in Chapter 4, Statistical Inference and Hypothesis Testing.

52. Which of the following is the poorest reason for a quality audit?

1. product quality evaluation
2. to start disciplinary action
3. to initiate corrective action
4. identification of hardware deficiency

Refer to Question 25 in Chapter 11, Quality Auditing.

53. Which of the following quality system provisions is of the least concern when preparing an audit checklist for the upcoming branch operation quality system audit?

1. drawing and print control
2. makeup of the MRB (material review board)
3. control of nonconforming materials
4. control of special processes
5. calibration of test equipment

Refer to Question 28 in Chapter 11, Quality Auditing and Questions 60 and 61 in Chapter 12, Product and Materials Control and Measurement Systems. This question is repeated with a slight change in the question, i.e., *least concern* vs. *greatest concern,* in the July 1984 examination.[6]

54. The failure rate model shown in Fig. 18-1 is used to show a typical relationship of many parts between their failure rate and the time in service. The reliability function for period B is best represented by

1. $R = e^{\lambda t}$
2. $\lambda = at^2 + bt + R$
3. $R(t) = e^{\lambda t_0}$
4. $R(t) = e^{-\lambda t}$
5. none of these

Refer to Question 39 in Chapter 13, Reliability, Maintainability, and Product Safety.

---

[6] *ASQC - CQE Examination*, Quality Progress, July 1984, Principles section, Question 71.

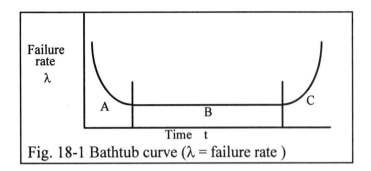
Fig. 18-1 Bathtub curve (λ = failure rate)

55.   Which of the following is most important to consider when calibrating a piece of equipment?

1.   calibration sticker
2.   maintenance history data
3.   wheatstone bridge
4.   standard used
5.   calibration interval

Refer to Question 84 in Chapter 12, Metrology, Inspection, and Testing.

56.   Recognizing the nature of process variability, the process capability target is usually

1.   the same as product specifications
2.   independent of product specifications
3.   looser than product specifications
4.   tighter than product specifications

Refer to Question 146 in Chapter 3, Fundamental Concepts of Probability and Statistics, and Question 51 in Chapter 7, Statistical Process Control.

57.   Which one of the following statements best describes machine capability?

1.   the total variation of all cavities of a mold, cavities of a die cast machine, or spindles of an automatic assembly machine
2.   the inherent variation of the machine
3.   the total variation over a shift
4.   the variation in a short run of consecutively produced parts
5.   none of these

Refer to Question 59 in Chapter 7, Statistical Process Control.

58.   Suppose that given $\overline{X} = 35$ and $Z_{0.01} = \pm 2.58$, we established confidence limits for μ of 30 and 40. This means that

1.   the probability that $\mu = 35$ is 0.01
2.   the probability that $\mu = 35$ is 0.99
3.   the probability that the interval contains μ is 0.01

4.   the probability that the interval contains μ is 0.99
5.   none of the above

Refer to Questions 21 and 22 in Chapter 4, Statistical Inference and Hypothesis Testing.

59.   The basic (primary) standard for time (the seconds) in SI units (International System of Units) adopted by the U.S. is based on

1.   the transition between two radiation levels of krypton 86
2.   the time it takes an SI cylinder of platinum-iridium alloy to fall one meter
3.   the transition between two radiation levels of the ground state of cesium −133
4.   the time it takes to plate one millimeter of silver on an SI cylinder with one ampere of current

Refer to Question 160 in Chapter 12, Product and Materials Control and Measurement Systems.

60.   Inherent or intrinsic reliability

1.   is that reliability which can be improved only by design change
2.   can be improved only by an improvement in the state the art
3.   is that reliability estimated over stated period of time by a stated measurement technique
4.   is not an estimated reliability

Refer to Question 11 in Chapter 13, Reliability, Maintainability, and Product Safety.

61.   Human factors engineering concepts introduced to your final inspection area

1.   are not valuable until the test equipment has been set up and operating
2.   should be incorporated during the design and planning stage of the area
3.   will result in schedule slippage wherever incorporated
4.   are most costly when introduced during the design and planning stage of the area
5.   will result in reduced efficiency of your inspectors, but greater accuracy

Refer to Question 24 in Chapter 15, Motivation and Human Factors.

62.   In statistical quality control, a parameter is

1.   a random variable
2.   a sample value
3.   a population value
4.   the solution to a statistical problem

Refer Question 7 in Chapter 3, Fundamental Concepts of Probability and Statistics.

63.   An effective supervisor

1.   sometimes does a job himself because he can do it better than others

2.   sees part of his role as one of creating worker satisfaction
3.   has objectives of growth and increased profit by working through other people
4.   all of the above

Refer to Questions 29 and 30 in Chapter 15, Motivation and Human Factors.

64.   The difference between setting alpha equal to 0.05 and alpha equal to 0.01 in hypothesis testing is

1.   with alpha equal to 0.05 we are more willing to risk a Type I error
2.   with alpha equal to 0.05 we are more willing to risk a Type II error
3.   alpha equal to 0.05 is a more "conservative" test of the null hypothesis (Ho)
4.   with alpha equal to 0.05 we are less willing to risk a Type I error
5.   none of the above

Refer to Question 55 in Chapter 4, Statistical Inference and Hypothesis Testing.

65.   Classification of defects is most essential as a prior step to a valid establishment of

1.   design characteristics
2.   vendor specifications of critical parts
3.   process control charts
4.   economical sampling inspection
5.   a product audit checklist

Refer to Question 9 in Chapter 12, Product and Materials Control and Measurement Systems.

66.   The permissible variation in a dimension is the

1.   specification
2.   clearance
3.   tolerance
4.   allowance

Refer to Question 59 in Chapter 9, Quality Practices and Applications.

67.   Data are

1.   coded test/inspection measurements
2.   computer prepared summaries
3.   collected raw facts
4.   the output after processing that management wishes to know

Refer to Question 5 in Chapter 3, Fundamental Concepts of Probability and Statistics.

68.   An adequate quality budget should be

1.   about ten percent of direct production costs
2.   estimated from past quality costs
3.   about two percent of sales
4.   based on total quality cost trends

Refer to Question 40 in Chapter 9, Quality Practices and Applications.

69.   Which one of the following quality management principles would you apply to increase the probability of better quality?

1.   Drawings and specifications should be rigidly set with nominal enforcement.
2.   Drawings and specifications should be realistically set with rigid enforcement.
3.   Drawings and specifications should be under the direction of quality engineering.
4.   Drawings and specifications should be rigidly set and rigidly enforced.

Refer to Question 61 in Chapter 9, Quality Practices and Applications. This question is repeated with a slight change in the text in the October 1972 examination.[7]

70.   A gage that checks a single dimension (and tolerance) is

1.   a micrometer
2.   a vernier
3.   a varigage
4.   a plug gage

Refer to Question 122 in Chapter 12, Product and Materials Control and Measurement Systems.

71.   Which of the following cost elements is a prevention cost?

1.   quality planning
2.   process quality control
3.   design of quality measurement equipment
4.   all of the above

Refer to Question 29 in Chapter 10, Quality Cost Analysis.

72.   When analyzing monthly quality cost trends on failure reports of many types of consumer goods, you must be most alert to the effects of

1.   changes in marketing management personnel
2.   secular trends in the data
3.   seasonal variations in the data
4.   cyclical variations within the data
5.   changes in prevailing labor rates

---

[7] *ASQC - CQE Examination*, Quality Progress, October 1972, Principles section, Question 82.

Refer to Question 73 in Chapter 10, Quality Cost Analysis.

73.   A tracer type surface finish instrument, such as a profilometer, should not be used to measure

      1.   roughness measurement on gear teeth
      2.   depth of scratches on a metal surface
      3.   roughness measurement on a mild steel plate
      4.   surface condition of a tapered hole

Refer to Question 134 in Chapter 12, Product and Materials Control and Measurement Systems.

74.   When analyzing quality cost data during the initial stages of management's emphasis on quality control and corrective action as a part of a product improvement program, one normally expects to see

      1.   increased prevention costs and decreased appraisal costs
      2.   decreased internal failure costs
      3.   increased appraisal costs with little change in prevention costs
      4.   increased external failure costs
      5.   none of these

Refer to Question 21 in Chapter 10, Quality Cost Analysis.

75.   Which of the following statements is correct?

      1.   The higher the correlation, the better the regression equation estimate.
      2.   The lower the correlation, the better the regression estimate.
      3.   Regression estimates are better made with positive than with negative correlation.
      4.   The lower the correlation, the greater is the likelihood that homoscedasticity exists with respect to the predicted variable.
      5.   The better the regression estimate, the greater is the likelihood that homoscedasticity exists with respect to the predicted variable.

Refer to Question 7 in Chapter 5, Regression and Correlation Analysis.

76.   Double sampling is better than single sampling because

      1.   it is more economical regardless of lot quality
      2.   it is easier to administer
      3.   it gives the lot a second chance
      4.   if the first sample rejects the lot, the second will accept it
      5.   it involves less inspection when the lots are of very good or very poor quality

Refer to Questions 63 and 64 in Chapter 8, Acceptance Sampling.

77.   Product characteristics should be classified (critical, major, etc.) so that

1.   a more meaningful assessment of quality can be made
2.   emphasis can be placed on important characteristics
3.   action with the responsible individuals can be taken
4.   a quality audit would be more meaningful
5.   none of these

Refer to Question 2 in Chapter 12, Product and Materials Control and Measurement Systems.

78.   Several types of food instruments are usually equipped with a mirror behind the dial pointer to reduce which of the following measurement errors:

1.   interpolation rounding
2.   parallax
3.   nonlinearity in lower scale regions
4.   miniscus
5.   wrong scale reading

Refer to Question 144 in Chapter 12, Product and Materials Control and Measurement Systems.

79.   A test of significance using a given value of α is performed on the yield data from a process using a standard material and a proposed substitute. Which of the following conclusions is not possible from this test?

1.   The standard material is better than the substitute material.
2.   We have an interaction between the two materials.
3.   The probability of Type I error is α.
4.   The sample size is too small to detect the difference necessary to justify a material change.
5.   The proposed material is better than standard parts/material.

Refer to Question 30 in Chapter 6, Design of Experiments.

80.   In planning for quality information equipment, an appropriate activity would be to

1.   establish training plans as required for the operation of the equipment
2.   review present process capabilities to permit correlation with newer processes
3.   establish the calibration frequency
4.   evaluate process cost relative to performance

Refer to Question 20 in Chapter 14, Quality Information Systems.

81.   An effective report should have the following characteristics

1.   the data and information are intermixed within the body of the report
2.   the report is widely distributed
3.   charts are never used

4.   the data are compared with standards of performance which have previously been established

5.   all of the above

Refer to Question 81 in Chapter 9, Quality Practices and Applications.

82.   When designing a quality reporting system to insure a tight feedback loop, care must be taken to be sure that the information produced is

1.   timely
2.   reliable
3.   accurate
4.   valid
5.   all of the above

Refer to Question 2 in Chapter 14, Quality Information Systems.

83.   The basic objective of a quality cost program is to

1.   improve the profit posture of your company
2.   interface with the accounting department
3.   identify the source of quality failures
4.   identify quality control department costs

Refer to Questions 4 and 5 in Chapter 10, Quality Cost Analysis.

84.   Complete examination of a small sample of finished product is characteristic of

1.   final inspection
2.   work sampling
3.   process audit
4.   product audit

Refer to Question 10 in Chapter 11, Quality Auditing.

85.   When developing and implementing a modern quality assurance program, the perspective of which of the following disciplines is most useful?

1.   financial management
2.   production control
3.   accounting management
4.   manufacturing engineering
5.   systems engineering

Refer to Question 11 in Chapter 9, Quality Practices and Applications.

86.   In dry magnetic particle testing, best results are obtained when the magnetic field from prods is applied

       1.   along the length of the discontinuity
       2.   in a direction crosswise to the direction in which the discontinuity lies
       3.   so that the magnetic field parallels the direction of the discontinuity
       4.   none of the above

       Refer to Question 101 in Chapter 12, Product and Materials Control and Measurement Systems.

87.   One human management approach, often called the "carrot and stick" approach, is best typified by which of the following theories?

       1.   Herzberg's "Hygiene Theory"
       2.   Maslow's "Hierarchy of Motivation"
       3.   Skinner's "Reinforcement of Behavior Theory"
       4.   McGregor's Theory X

       Refer to Question 6 in Chapter 15, Motivation and Human Factors.

88.   Pneumatic gaging has one major advantage over electronic gaging and that is

       1.   cost
       2.   higher amplification
       3.   the elimination of metal to metal contact
       4.   increased accuracy

       Refer to Question 128 in Chapter 12, Product and Materials Control and Measurement Systems.

89.   The primary reason for collecting and analyzing quality costs is

       1.   to satisfy requirements of MIL-Q-9858A
       2.   to see that quality costs are close to the industry averages
       3.   to achieve an optimum balance of prevention, appraisal, and failure costs
       4.   to identify the source of trouble

       Refer to Question 17 in Chapter 10, Quality Cost Analysis.

90.   Quality cost data would not normally be obtained from which of the following?

       1.   labor reports
       2.   capital expenditure reports
       3.   salary budget reports
       4.   scrap reports
       5.   any of these

       Refer to Question 84 in Chapter 10, Quality Cost Analysis.

APPLICATIONS

1.   There is a potential saving by using optical scanning to

    1.   have less data to process
    2.   reduce written information
    3.   eliminate key punching
    4.   reduce card sorting

    Refer to Question 152 in Chapter 12, Product and Materials Control and Measurement Systems.

2.   The management team is establishing priorities to attack a serious quality problem. You are requested to establish a data collection system to direct this attack. You use which of these general management rules to support your recommendations as to the quality of the data required?

    1.   You have compared the incremental cost of additional data with the value of the information obtained and stopped when they are equal.
    2.   Your decision corresponds to the rules applicable to the other factors of production.
    3.   Your decision is based upon the relationship between value and cost.
    4.   all of the above

    Refer to Question 16 in Chapter 14, Quality Information Systems.

3.   The design function that assigns probability of failure among components or subsystems is called

    1.   confidence
    2.   qualification
    3.   significance
    4.   apportionment

    Refer to Question 93 in Chapter 13, Reliability, Maintainability, and Product Safety.

4.   A single sampling plan calls for a sample size of 80 with an acceptance number of 5 and rejection number of 6. If the quality of the submitted lots is ten percent defective, then the percent of lots expected to be accepted in the long run is approximately

    1.   6%
    2.   10%
    3.   30%
    4.   0%
    5.   20%

    Refer to Question 45 in Chapter 8, Acceptance Sampling.

5. If the probability of the success on a single trial is 0.30 and two trials are performed what is the probability of at least one success?

    1. 0.910
    2. 0.410
    3. 0.510
    4. 0.490
    5. 0.030

Refer to Question 164 in Chapter 3, Fundamental Concepts of Probability and Statistics.

6. You have returned from a two week vacation and are going over the control charts that have been maintained during your absence with your quality control manager. He calls your attention to the fact that one of the $\overline{X}$ charts shows the last 50 points to be very near the centerline. In fact, they all seem to be within about one sigma of the centerline. What explanation would you offer him?

    1. Somebody "goofed" in the original calculation of the control limits.
    2. The process standard deviation has decreased during the time the last 40 samples were taken and nobody thought to recompute the control limits.
    3. This is a terrible situation. I'll get on it right away and see what the trouble is. I hope we have not produced too much scrap.
    4. This is fine. The closer the points are to the centerline the better our control.

Refer to Question 43 in Chapter 7, Statistical Process Control.

7. When testing to establish failure rate data and prediction, which of the following is not normally a feasible acceleration factor with respect to rated conditions?

    1. longer time
    2. greater humidity
    3. higher temperature
    4. higher voltage

Refer to Question 96 in Chapter 13, Reliability, Maintainability, and Product Safety.

8. The term "random access" identifies information stored

    1. outside a computer, so it has to be sought by humans rather than electronically
    2. someplace inside a computer, whose address only the computer's scanning device can locate
    3. where all parts of it are designed to be equally accessible when needed
    4. in the special part of the processing unit for temporary storage only

Refer to Question 28 in Chapter 14, Quality Information Systems.

9.   Select the incorrect statement from among the following:
      The IDs of a certain piece of the tubing are normally distributed with a mean 1.00". The portion
      of the tubing with IDs less than 0.90" is

      1.   less than the proportion with IDs greater than 0.90"
      2.   less than 50%
      3.   less than the proportion with IDs greater than 1.10"
      4.   less than the proportion with IDs greater than 1.00"

      Refer to Question 140 in Chapter 3, Fundamental Concepts of Probability and Statistics.

10.   Suppliers A and B each have sent us samples of 50 items to examine for us to choose between
      them toward contract. The samples have the same mean and range. However the standard
      deviation of A's product is 15 and B's is 5. We may conclude that

      1.   A's product is grouped closer to the mean than B's
      2.   B's product is grouped closer to the mean than A's
      3.   there are three times as many measurements from −1 standard deviation to +1 standard
            deviation in A's product as in B's
      4.   there are one third as many measurements from −1 standard deviation to +1 standard
            deviation in A's product as in B's
      5.   cannot say anything unless we know the value of the common mean

      Refer to Question 142 in Chapter 3, Fundamental Concepts of Probability and Statistics.

11.   When using an inside or outside caliper, care must be taken to get proper

      1.   slip
      2.   depth
      3.   grip
      4.   feel

      Refer to Question 117 in Chapter 12, Product and Materials Control and Measurement Systems.

12.   Management is consistently seeking new ways to make profitable use of their expensive
      computers. Which of the following computer applications promises to be the most beneficial
      from management's standpoint?

      1.   information storage and retrieval
      2.   decision-making help in combination with simulation techniques
      3.   wider use as an accounting machine
      4.   solution of complex mathematical formulas

      Refer to Question 6 in Chapter 14, Quality Information Systems.

13.   In an experiment designed to compare two different ways of measuring a given quantity, it
      was desired to test the null hypothesis that the means were equal at the 0.05 level of

significance. A sample of five parts was measured by method I and a sample of seven parts with method II. A t ratio of 2.179 was obtained. We should

1.   reject the null hypothesis
2.   fail to reject the null hypothesis
3.   assert that there is no difference between the two methods
4.   conclude that $\overline{X}_1$ is significantly greater than $\overline{X}_2$
5.   conclude that we must know the sample means in order to answer the question

Refer to Question 65 in Chapter 4, Statistical Inference and Hypothesis Testing.

14.   If, in a designed experiment, you obtained an F-ratio of 0.68 with 2 and 20 degrees of freedom, you would conclude that

1.   there were no significant differences among the means
2.   you had made an error
3.   the variances were equal
4.   the null hypothesis was rejected
5.   all of the above

Refer to Question 71 in Chapter 4, Statistical Inference and Hypothesis Testing, and Question 58 in Chapter 6, Design of Experiments.

15.   When you are performing a branch plant quality system audit, it is most necessary that you

1.   report every deficiency identified
2.   obtain corroboration by management of any system deficiency reported
3.   complete every item on the audit checklist
4.   take corrective action on each deficiency identified
5.   all of the above

Refer to Question 50 in Chapter 11, Quality Auditing.

16.   To measure an angle on a work piece, the most accurate method would involve use of

1.   sine bar
2.   a set of plastic triangles
3.   a bevel protractor
4.   none of the above

Refer to Questions 166, 167, and 168 in Chapter 12, Product and Materials Control and Measurement Systems.

17.   Management has been receiving complaints from the field about the performance of its product. Although the quality system being used does require a final inspection for lot

acceptance, it also has been decided to do an end item (product) quality audit. Which sampling procedure would you recommend to your quality control manager?

1. ten percent of production
2. a fixed quantity per time period
3. a plan selected from MIL-STD-105E
4. a small sample
5. any of the above

Refer to Question 44 in Chapter 11, Quality Auditing.

18. Maintainability of equipment may be measured in terms of

1. maintenance man-hours
2. repair time
3. maintenance dollar cost
4. all of the above

Refer to Question 31 in Chapter 13, Reliability, Maintainability, and Product Safety.

19. When purchasing materials from vendors, it is sometimes advantageous to choose vendors whose prices are higher because

1. such a statement is basically incorrect; always buy at lowest bid price
2. such vendors may become obligated to bestow special favors
3. materials that cost more can be expected to be better, and "you get what you pay for"
4. the true cost of purchased materials, which should include items such as sorting inspection, contacting vendors, and production delays, may be lower

Refer to Question 58 in Chapter 9, Quality Practices and Applications and Question 69 in Chapter 11, Quality Auditing.

20. Your quality control manager has asked you to make a study of the costs of using variables sampling as against attribute sampling for a pipe fitting. After searching the literature you find that the following sampling plans will give equal protection over the range of quality levels in which you are interested

Types of plan	Sample size	Acceptance criterion
Attribute	450	Ac = 10, Re = 11
Variables, sigma unknown	100	k = 2.0
Variables, sigma known	33	k = 2.0

Upon investigating the possible costs involved in each type of sampling with your accounting, production, and inspection departments, you arrive at the following figures:

	Attributes $	Sigma known $	Sigma unknown $
Unit sampling cost	0.05	0.05	0.05
Unit inspection cost	0.05	0.35	0.35
Unit computation cost	0.00	0.02	0.01
Lot overhead cost	6.00	8.00	40.00

Which type of sampling would you advise your quality control manager to use based on the above information?

1.   use attribute sampling
2.   since they all give equal protection, it does not make any difference
3.   use continuous sampling
4.   usc variablcs sampling, sigma known
5.   use variables sampling, sigma unknown

Refer to Question 74 in Chapter 8, Acceptance Sampling.

21.   Specifying a tolerance by +0.000/−0.0001 is known as

1.   limit dimensioning
2.   manufacturing limits
3.   unilateral tolerancing
4.   bilateral tolerancing

Refer to Question 70 in Chapter 12, Product and Materials Control and Measurement Systems.

22.   The distinguishing feature of the optical comparator is that adjustments for measurements are observed on a

1.   screen
2.   reticle coordinator
3.   dial indicator
4.   rotating stage

Refer to Question 138 in Chapter 12, Product and Materials Control and Measurement Systems.

23.   The appropriate mathematical model for describing the sampling distribution of outcomes in samples of ten from a process which is five percent defective is

1.   the normal curve with mean 0.05
2.   the binomial distribution with $p' = 0.05$
3.   the hypergeometric distribution with mean 0.05
4.   the Poisson distribution with $np' = 0.05$

Refer to Question 168 in Chapter 3, Fundamental Concepts of Probability and Statistics.

24.   When selecting an audit sample size, which of the following rules should govern your choice?

1. Since quality may change over time, we should look at a fixed quantity each time period for audit purposes.
2. We need only a very small sample for audit purposes, as long as it is chosen at random.
3. Any size sample if randomly selected can be suitable for audit purposes, since we are not directly performing lot acceptance or rejection.
4. MIL-STD-105D is a scientific sampling procedure and we need scientific sampling for audit purposes.
5. In general, ten percent is a good sample size to use. Also it is easy to remember.

Refer to Question 45 in Chapter 11, Quality Auditing.

25. Select one sampling plan from MIL-STD-105D that meets the following requirements: lot size = 1000, AQL = 0.65%, inspection level II, tightened inspection.

1. sample size = 125, Ac = 1, Re = 2
2. sample size = 200, Ac = 1, Re = 2
3. sample size = 80, Ac = 1, Re = 2
4. sample size = 50, Ac = 0, Re = 2
5. sample size = 80, Ac = 8, Re = 9

Refer to Question 46 in Chapter 8, Acceptance Sampling.

26. In analyzing the cost data below

$ 20,000 = Final test
350,000 = Field warranty costs
170,000 = Reinspection and retest
45,000 = Loss or disposition of surplus stock
4,000 = Vendor quality surveys
30,000 = Rework

We might conclude that

1. internal failure costs can be decreased
2. prevention is too low a proportion of the quality costs shown
3. appraisal costs should be increased
4. nothing can be concluded

Refer to Question 61 in Chapter 10, Quality Cost Analysis.

27. When planning for quality functions, which one of the following is most directly related to production of a quality product?

1. process control and process capability
2. suitable blueprints
3. dimensional tolerances
4. product audit

Refer to Question 24 in Chapter 7, Statistical Process Control, and Question 70 in Chapter 9, Quality Practices and Applications.

28.   A random sample of 10 items was taken from lot A, 20 from lot B, and 30 from lot C. The three lots contained the same type of material. Each of the samples yielded the same mean. Which of the following statements is true concerning the standard deviation of the samples?

1.   The standard deviation of the lot C sample is the largest.
2.   The standard deviation of the lot A sample is the largest.
3.   The standard deviation of the lot C sample is three times as large as that of the lot A sample.
4.   None of the above statements can be made.

Refer to Question 123 in Chapter 3, Fundamental Concepts of Probability and Statistics.

29.   A quality audit can be used to

1.   measure the effectiveness of a quality program
2.   verify product quality
3.   determine inspection inefficiency
4.   any of the above

Refer to Question 4 in Chapter 11, Quality Auditing.

30.   Methods for predicting human reliability in production processes

1.   are represented by the many motivation programs in effect
2.   are inevitably correlated with monetary rewards
3.   are still in the developmental stages
4.   are based on the complexity of the process

Refer to Question 97 in Chapter 13, Reliability, Maintainability, and Product Safety.

31.   This month's quality cost data collection shows the following:

Adjustment of customer complaints	$ 3,500
Rework and repair	$ 10,700
Quality management salaries	$ 25,000
Downgrading expense	$ 1,800
Warranty replacement	$ 53,500
Calibration and maintenance of test equipment	$ 2,500
Inspection and testing	$ 28,000

For your action report to top management you select which one of the following as the percentage of "*external failure* to *total quality costs*" to show the true impact of field problems?

    1.   24%
    2.   65%
    3.   56%
    4.   46%

Refer to Question 62 in Chapter 10, Quality Cost Analysis.

32.   A supplier of cotton yarn claims that his product has an average breaking strength of 90 pounds. To test his claim, you select a random sample of 16 pieces of yarn. If the standard deviation of his process is unknown and you use the normal curve theory instead of t distribution theory to test the null hypothesis, you would

    1.   increase the risk of Type I error
    2.   decrease the risk of Type I error
    3.   increase the risk of Type II error
    4.   both 2 and 3
    5.   none of the above

Refer to Question 63 in Chapter 4, Statistical Inference and Hypothesis Testing.

33.   You just have conducted a designed experiment at three levels, A, B, and C, yielding the following coded data:

A	B	C
6	5	3
3	9	4
5	1	2
2		

As a major step in your analysis you calculate the degrees of freedom for the error sum of the squares to be

    1.   7
    2.   9
    3.   3
    4.   2
    5.   10

Refer to Question 57 in Chapter 6, Design of Experiments.

34.   Typically, total quality costs include

    1.   all costs incurred by the quality department
    2.   some costs incurred by production
    3.   some costs incurred by production engineering
    4.   all of the above

Refer to Question 7 in Chapter 10, Quality Cost Analysis.

35.   Which of the following cost elements is usually considered an appraisal cost?

    1.   screening rejected lots
    2.   receiving inspection
    3.   surveying suppliers
    4.   preparing inspection plans

Refer to Question 41 in Chapter 10, Quality Cost Analysis.

36.   When there is a bank of dials to be read on a monitoring panel, it helps to orient them in which one of the following arrangements?

    1.   a random unpatterned display for the normal indicating positions to reduce boredom
    2.   half in a patterned group for the normal position at the 12 o'clock position and half in a patterned group at the 6 o'clock position to minimize eye fatigue
    3.   all normal indication positions in a pattern so that normal readings are in the 9 o'clock or 12 o'clock position
    4.   each with the normal indicating position in a new position varying in a clockwise pattern
    5.   any of the above

Refer to Question 149 in Chapter 12, Product and Materials Control and Measurement Systems.

37.   Establishing the quality policy for the company is the responsibility of

    1.   the customer
    2.   quality control
    3.   the marketing department
    4.   top management

Refer to Question 24 in Chapter 9, Quality Practices and Applications.

38.   The most important activity of a material review board (MRB) would normally be

    1.   making sure that corrective action is taken to prevent recurrence of the problem
    2.   to provide a bonded or segregated area of holding discrepant material pending disposition
    3.   to prepare discrepant material reports for management
    4.   to accept discrepant material when "commercial" decisions dictate
    5.   none of these

Refer to Question 47 in Chapter 9, Quality Practices and Applications and Questions 60 and 61 in Chapter 12, Product and Materials Control and Measurement Systems.

39.   Color can be described as

    1.   photometric

2.   two dimensional
3.   one dimensional
4.   three dimensional

Refer to Question 151 in Chapter 12, Product and Materials Control and Measurement Systems.

40.   A shipping line product audit will directly measure

1.   the outgoing product quality
2.   the quality capability of production
3.   the adequacy of inspection methods
4.   the motivational level of the operators

Refer to Question 9 in Chapter 11, Quality Auditing.

41.   The modern approach to quality cost is to

1.   concentrate on external failures; they are important to the business since they represent customer acceptance
2.   consider the four cost segments and their general trends
3.   budget each cost element, such as amounts for inspection, quality control salaries, scrap, etc.
4.   reduce expenditures on each segment individually
5.   make annual budget cuts where cost elements show major variances

Refer to Question 10 in Chapter 10, Quality Cost Analysis.

42.   An essential element of a quality motivation program is

1.   the establishment of attainable goals
2.   the establishment of failure costs
3.   a stable environment
4.   the generation of a minimum level of defects

Refer to Question 10 in Chapter 15, Motivation and Human Factors.

43.   One of the most important techniques in making a training program effective is to

1.   concentrate only on developing knowledge and skills needed to do a good job
2.   transmit all of the information that is even remotely related to the function
3.   set individual goals instead of group goals
4.   give people meaningful measures of performance

Refer to Question 37 in Chapter 15, Motivation and Human Factors.

44.   In a scanning type of inspection task, inspection accuracy is likely to be greater if

1.   the product moves toward the inspector rather than laterally past him or her
2.   the inspector scans each item for all types of defects rather than the entire lot for one type of defect at a time
3.   the magnification is increased
4.   the product is inspected while it is stationary rather than while it is moving

Refer to Question 46 in Chapter 12, Product and Materials Control and Measurement Systems.

45.   In order to test whether the outputs of two machines were yielding the same average value or one was larger than the other, a sample of ten pieces was taken from each. The t value turned out to be 1.767. Using a level of significance of 0.05, one tailed test, we conclude that

1.   the obtained t-ratio does not fall within the critical region
2.   there was no significant difference between the means
3.   the null hypothesis was rejected
4.   the null hypothesis was accepted
5.   the question cannot be answered unless we know the standard deviations

Refer to Question 64 in Chapter 4, Statistical Inference and Hypothesis Testing.

46.   One of the best analytical methods for identifying those failure costs that should be attacked first for the greatest return on the invested prevention dollars is to

1.   perform an internal financial audit
2.   study the budget variance report
3.   apply the Gompertz curve technique
4.   apply the Pareto principle
5.   perform a breakeven analysis

Refer to Questions 69 and 70 in Chapter 10, Quality Cost Analysis.

47.   The AOQL for the single sampling plan with a sample size of 200, acceptance number of 14, and rejection number of 15 for a lot size of 4000 is approximately

1.   10.0%
2.   4.5%
3.   4.0%
4.   7.2%

Refer to Question 47 in Chapter 8, Acceptance Sampling.

48.   The controlled process has a mean of 50 and a standard deviation of 5. What is the probability that a random sample of 16 items yields a mean greater than 53?

1.   0.99
2.   0.01
3.   0.49

4.   0.58
5.   0.42

Refer to Question 143 in Chapter 3, Fundamental Concepts of Probability and Statistics, and Question 15 in Chapter 4, Statistical Inference and Hypothesis Testing.

49.   Suppose that you are blindfolded and five items are placed before you, each of which is either defective or nondefective. The probability that you will identify all items correctly is approximately

1.   1.000
2.   0.170
3.   0.200
4.   0.500
5.   0.030

Refer to Question 166 in Chapter 3, Fundamental Concepts of Probability and Statistics.

50.   When planning the specifications for product quality in the so-called "mechanical" industries,

1.   market research establishes economic tolerances
2.   product design assumes prime responsibility for establishing economic tolerances
3.   product research issues official product specifications
4.   quality control develops products possessing qualities that meet consumer needs
5.   all of these

Refer to Question 68 in Chapter 9, Quality Practices and Applications.

51.   In the planning of a new major manufacturing program, the greatest quality effort should be put logically in

1.   inspection of the product
2.   nondestructive testing equipment
3.   nonconformance to specifications
4.   prevention of occurrence of substandard quality

Refer to Question 25 in Chapter 9, Quality Practices and Applications.

52.   During the design review stage for new equipment you recommend that a human factors use test be performed under one of the following conditions:

1.   on a production model if possible
2.   not combined with engineering test on the same equipment
3.   it demonstrates the capability of personnel to perform the required functions using the equipment
4.   all of the above

Refer to Question 27 in Chapter 15, Motivation and Human Factors.

53.   The lengths of a certain bushing are normally distributed with mean $\overline{X}'$. How many standard deviation units symmetrical about $\overline{X}'$ will include 70% of the lengths?

       1.   ± 1.04
       2.   ± 0.52
       3.   ± 1.28
       4.   ± 0.84

       Refer to Question 135 in Chapter 3, Fundamental Concepts of Probability and Statistics.

54.   If the distribution of defectives among various lots is found to follow the laws of chance, we can conclude that

       1.   all lots should be accepted
       2.   all lots should be rejected
       3.   the product was well mixed before dividing into lots
       4.   the manufacturing process is not predictable

       Refer to Question 141 in Chapter 3, Fundamental Concepts of Probability and Statistics.

55.   In planning the staffing for your new quality control department, you use which of the following as the best justification for estimating the number of people required?

       1.   a given ratio of production employees to quality personnel, typical of the industry
       2.   a total salary budget as a given percent of sales dollars
       3.   the number of people in the engineering department
       4.   the quality objectives that have been set by top management
       5.   none of the above

       Refer to Question 26 in Chapter 9, Quality Practices and Applications.

56.   Failure effects mode analysis is primarily for the purpose of

       1.   learning as much about the item as possible after qualification test
       2.   determining, by extensive analysis, the reliability of an item
       3.   determining the way an item will most likely fail to help obtain design and procedural safeguards against such failure
       4.   determining the cause of a failure, by dissecting the item, to help obtain the corrective action

       Refer to Question 91 in Chapter 13, Reliability, Maintainability, and Product Safety.

57.   The operating characteristic curve (OC) of an acceptance sampling plan

1.   demonstrates the advantages of double sampling over single sampling
2.   demonstrates how the plan will reject all of the lots worse than AQL
3.   shows the relative cost of sampling for various levels of quality
4.   shows the ability of the plan to distinguish between good and bad lots

Refer to Question 7 in Chapter 8, Acceptance Sampling.

58.   The sequence of punched fields for punched cards generally should be the same as

1.   the data from previous reports with similar source data
2.   the data to be punched from the original documents
3.   prescribed from the output report
4.   no generally accepted practice can be prescribed

Refer to Question 29 in Chapter 14, Quality Information Systems.

59.   In the so-called process industries

1.   quality control has some responsibility in choosing the process
2.   process development issues process specifications
3.   quality control may help to establish process tolerances
4.   all of the above

Refer to Question 69 in Chapter 9, Quality Practices and Applications.

60.   Three trainees were given the same lots of 50 pieces and asked to classify them as defective or nondefective with the following results.

	Trainee #1	Trainee #2	Trainee #3	Total
Defective	17	30	25	72
Nondefective	33	20	25	78
Total	50	50	50	150

In determining whether or not there is a difference in the ability of the three trainees to properly classify the parts

1.   the value of chi-square is about 6.90
2.   using a level of significance of 0.05, the critical value of chi-square is 5.99
3.   since the obtained chi-square is greater than 5.99, we reject the null hypothesis
4.   all of the above
5.   none of the above

Refer to Question 76 in Chapter 4, Statistical Inference and Hypothesis Testing.

61.   Costs incurred in field testing of acceptance at the customer's site, prior to releasing a product for customer acceptance, are considered

    1.   prevention cost
    2.   appraisal cost
    3.   failure cost
    4.   none of the above

Refer to Question 42 in Chapter 10, Quality Cost Analysis.

62.   In planning for quality, an important consideration at the start is

    1.   the relation of the total cost of quality to the net sales
    2.   the establishment of company quality policy or objectives
    3.   deciding precisely how much money is to be sent
    4.   the selling of the quality program to the top management

Refer to Question 29 in Chapter 9, Quality Practices and Applications.

63.   What is the best estimate of the variance of the population from which the following sample came: 17, 20, 18, 22, 21?

    1.   3.44
    2.   4.3
    3.   5.00
    4.   2.10

Refer to Question 106 in Chapter 3, Fundamental Concepts of Probability and Statistics.

64.   A substance discontinuity in some purchased steel bar stock is a suspected cause for the high failure rate in your parts fabrication area, which of the following nondestructive test (NDT) methods would you not recommend as an effective screening device?

    1.   magnetic particle testing
    2.   radiographic testing
    3.   liquid penetrant testing
    4.   eddy current testing
    5.   ultrasonic testing

Refer to Question 104 in Chapter 12, Product and Materials Control and Measurement Systems.

65.   Fixed gages

    1.   measure one or more dimensions
    2.   measure only one dimension
    3.   are all made of tool steel
    4.   are a fast method of checking parts

Refer to Question 123 in Chapter 12, Product and Materials Control and Measurement Systems.

66. You have just been put in charge of incoming inspection and have decided to institute a sampling plan on a small gear which your company uses in considerable quantity. The vendor ships them to you in lots of 1000. You have decided to use MIL-STD-105D inspection level II and AQL = 4.0%. Naturally, your inspectors, never having used scientific sampling, are interested in seeing how it works. The first lot is inspected and accepted. One of the inspectors says "This means that the lot is not more than four percent defective." Assuming the sample was randomly taken and no inspection errors were made, which one of the following would you accept?

   1.   The inspector's statement is correct.
   2.   The probability of accepting the lot is about 0.99.
   3.   You should go to reduced sampling.
   4.   The lot may be 10% defective.
   5.   all of the above

   Refer to Question 48 in Chapter 8, Acceptance Sampling.

67. Management requests that you analyze the quality costs in department A, which produces an average of one large complex product every six months. After reviewing the alternatives, you select which of the following indexes as the most valid and reliable indicator for cost trends?

   1.   quality costs per net sales billed
   2.   quality costs per unit produced
   3.   quality costs per direct labor dollar
   4.   quality costs per total manufacturing costs
   5.   any of the above

   Refer to Question 82 in Chapter 10, Quality Cost Analysis.

68. Find the predicted system reliability for the three parts shown if the individual part reliability is 90% each for a specified mission time and mission conditions

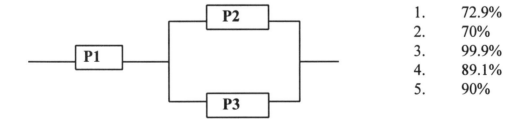

   1.   72.9%
   2.   70%
   3.   99.9%
   4.   89.1%
   5.   90%

   Refer to Question 66 in Chapter 13, Reliability, Maintainability, and Product Safety.

69. The reliability of the measuring instrument is linked to the U.S. National Standards by

   1.   traceability
   2.   confirmation
   3.   unification
   4.   capability

Refer to Question 94 in Chapter 12, Product and Materials Control and Measurement Systems.

70.   Gages that tell how much a dimension varies from specification are called

1.   accurators
2.   depth gages
3.   indicating gages
4.   tolerators

Refer to Question 124 in Chapter 12, Product and Materials Control and Measurement Systems.

71.   Each value below is the number of defects found in 25 groups of eight subassemblies inspected

77	61	59	22	54
64	49	54	92	22
75	65	41	89	49
93	45	87	55	33
45	77	40	25	20

Assume that a c chart is to be used for future protection. Calculate the preliminary three sigma control limits from the above data.

1.   65.7,   45.7
2.   78.2,   33.2
3.   15.6,   6.6
4.   82.5,   28.9

Refer to Question 87 in Chapter 7, Statistical Process Control.

72.   The primary responsibility for follow-up on corrective action commitments after an audit report usually rests with

1.   production management
2.   quality engineering
3.   the function being audited
4.   the audit group

Refer to Question 34 in Chapter 11, Quality Auditing.

73.   The finest reading possible with a vernier micrometer in inches is

1.   hundred-thousandths
2.   ten-thousandths
3.   micro lengths
4.   thousandths

Refer to Question 116 in Chapter 12, Product and Materials Control and Measurement Systems.

74.   Given $Z_{0.05} = \pm 1.96$, the mean of a sample as 30 and the standard error of the mean as 5, the lower limit of the interval that would include the population mean with probability 0.95 is

    1.   20.20
    2.   28.04
    3.   15.31
    4.   25.00
    5.   24.00

Refer to Question 23 in Chapter 4, Statistical Inference and Hypothesis Testing.

75.   You have been asked to appraise the new quality data system developed by your statistical services group. Which of the following measures need not be considered during your evaluation of the effectiveness of that quality data system?

    1.   The information is resulting in effective and timely corrective action.
    2.   The system is being adequately maintained.
    3.   The reports are being distributed monthly.
    4.   Paperwork is held to a minimum.

Refer to Question 79 in Chapter 9, Quality Practices and Applications and Question 53 in Chapter 11, Quality Auditing.

76.   The percentages of total quality cost are distributed as follows:

Prevention	10%
Appraisal	25%
Internal Failures	40%
External Failures	25%

We conclude

    1.   we should invest more money in prevention
    2.   the amount spent for appraisal seems about right
    3.   expenditures for failures are excessive
    4.   nothing

Refer to Question 53 in Chapter 10, Quality Cost Analysis.

77.   A vendor quality control plan has been adopted; which of the following provisions would you advise top management to be least effective?

    1.   product audits
    2.   source inspection
    3.   certificate of analysis
    4.   certificate of compliance

Refer to Question 56 in Chapter 9 Quality Practices and Applications and Question 66 in Chapter 11, Quality Auditing.

78. In the manufacture of airplane fuselage frame inspections, thousands of rivets are used to join aluminum sheets and frames. A study of the number of oversize rivet holes and the number of minor repairs on a unit yielded a correlation coefficient of ±1.08. This means

   1. the number of oversize rivet holes on a unit is good predictor of the number of minor repairs that will have to be made
   2. you should hire a new statistician
   3. the number of oversize rivet holes is a poor predictor of the number of minor repairs
   4. a large number of oversize rivet holes means that a small number of minor repairs will have to be made
   5. a large number of oversize rivet holes means that a large number of minor repairs will have to be made

Refer to Question 12 in Chapter 5, Regression and Correlation Analysis.

79. The method whereby several sizes of gage blocks can be conveniently combined to total a desired dimension is called

   1. magnetism
   2. interlocking
   3. wringing
   4. stacking

Refer to Question 126 in Chapter 12, Product and Materials Control and Measurement Systems.

80. A process is producing a material which is 40% defective. Four pieces are selected at random for inspection. What is the probability of exactly one defective piece being found in the sample?

   1. 0.870
   2. 0.575
   3. 0.346
   4. 0.130

Refer to Question 167 in Chapter 3, Fundamental Concepts of Probability and Statistics.

ANSWERS FOR OCTOBER 1974 EXAMINATION

PRINCIPLES

Q	A
1.	2
2.	4
3.	4
4.	2
5.	3
6.	3
7.	4
8.	2
9.	4
10.	4
11.	2
12.	4
13.	4
14.	2
15.	4
16.	1
17.	2
18.	3
19.	3
20.	2

Q	A
21.	3
22.	4
23.	1
24.	5
25.	1
26.	2
27.	4
28.	4
29.	4
30.	2
31.	2
32.	1
33.	1
34.	2
35.	2
36.	1
37.	2
38.	2
39.	1
40.	1

Q	A
41.	3
42.	2
43.	5
44.	2
45.	4
46.	3
47.	4
48.	4
49.	2
50.	2
51.	1
52.	2
53.	2
54.	4
55.	4
56.	4
57.	2
58.	4
59.	3
60.	1

Q	A
61.	2
62.	3
63.	4
64.	1
65.	4
66.	3
67.	3
68.	4
69.	2
70.	4
71.	4
72.	3
73.	2
74.	3
75.	1
76.	5
77.	2
78.	2
79.	2
80.	1

Q	A
81.	4
82.	5
83.	1
84.	4
85.	5
86.	2
87.	4
88.	3
89.	3
90.	2

COMMENTS / NOTES:

ANSWERS FOR OCTOBER 1974 EXAMINATION

APPLICATIONS

Q	A
1.	3
2.	4
3.	4
4.	5
5.	3
6.	2
7.	1
8.	3
9.	3
10.	2
11.	4
12.	2
13.	2
14.	1
15.	2
16.	1
17.	5
18.	4
19.	4
20.	4

Q	A
21.	3
22.	1
23.	2
24.	3
25.	1
26.	2
27.	1
28.	4
29.	4
30.	3
31.	4
32.	1
33.	1
34.	4
35.	2
36.	3
37.	4
38.	1
39.	4
40.	1

Q	A
41.	2
42.	1
43.	4
44.	4
45.	3
46.	4
47.	2
48.	2
49.	5
50.	2
51.	4
52.	3
53.	1
54.	3
55.	4
56.	3
57.	4
58.	2
59.	4
60.	4

Q	A
61.	2
62.	2
63.	2
64.	3
65.	4
66.	4
67.	2
68.	4
69.	1
70.	3
71.	2
72.	4
73.	2
74.	1
75.	3
76.	4
77.	4
78.	2
79.	3
80.	3

COMMENTS / NOTES:

CHAPTER 19

ASQC-CQE EXAMINATION, QUALITY PROGRESS, OCTOBER 1972

PRINCIPLES

Note: *This examination set originally used the alphabet letters and not the numbers for choices. However the following questions use the numerical choices for consistency with the previous three examination sets.*

Recent examinations and the study guides published in ASQC's recent certification brochures use letters, e.g., a, b, c, d, and e, for choices to a question in place of numbers. Hence letters are used in all individual subject matter chapters 3 through 15. Readers are advised to note this difference while referring to solutions in respective chapters.

1.   Accuracy is

      1.   getting consistent results repeatedly
      2.   reading to four decimals
      3.   using the best measuring device available
      4.   getting an unbiased true value

Refer to Questions 72 and 73 in Chapter 12, Product and Materials Control and Measurement Systems.

2.   Classification of characteristics

      1.   is the same as classification of defects
      2.   can only be performed after the product is produced
      3.   must have tolerances associated with it
      4.   is independent of defects

Refer to Question 6 in Chapter 12, Product and Materials Control and Measurement Systems.

3.   In planning EDP applications, which element is necessary to reduce computing costs:

      1.   selecting quality control applications having little input and output but extensive calculations
      2.   selecting applications with high volume input and output but simple calculations
      3.   a limited number of highly repetitive jobs
      4.   a group of jobs where output of one determines the input of another

Refer to Question 26 in Chapter 14, Quality Information Systems.

4.   A Latin Square design is an experiment design which

      1.   cannot be used when an estimation of the interaction effects is desired
      2.   affords a good estimate of interaction effects
      3.   is useful because the underlying distributions need not be normal
      4.   avoids the need to assume that the effects are additive

      Refer to Question 34 in Chapter 6, Design of Experiments.

5.   Measurement error

      1.   is the fault of the inspector
      2.   can be determined
      3.   is usually of no consequence
      4.   can be eliminated by frequent calibrations of the measuring device

      Refer to Question 76 in Chapter 12, Product and Materials Control and Measurement Systems.

6.   Precision is

      1.   getting consistent results repeatedly
      2.   reading to four or more decimals
      3.   distinguishing small deviations from the standard value
      4.   extreme care in the analysis of data

      Refer to Question 74 in Chapter 12, Product and Materials Control and Measurement Systems.

7.   The concept of accelerated cycling or a burn-in program of all devices for six months under
      normal operating conditions would

      1.   reduce premature failures in use
      2.   improve constant failure rate probability
      3.   be of little use
      4.   assure an acceptable quality to the customer

      Refer to Question 101 in Chapter 13, Reliability, Maintainability, and Product Safety.

8.   In the failure rate model shown in Fig. 19-1, the part of the curve identified as A represents

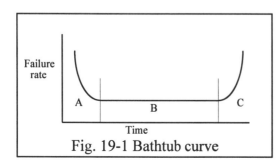

Fig. 19-1 Bathtub curve

      1.   the "bathtub" curve
      2.   random and independent failures fitting a
            Poisson model
      3.   the debugging period for complex
            equipment
      4.   the wearout period

Refer to Question 36 in Chapter 13, Reliability, Maintainability, and Product Safety.

9.   What results can you expect from QIE in the area of quality costs?

    1.   lowered equipment utilization factors
    2.   reduced percents defective for both scrap and rework
    3.   less extensive and complicated equipment maintenance
    4.   decreased quality control direct and indirect labor

Refer to Question 21 in Chapter 14, Quality Information Systems.

10.   The most effective tool for action in any quality control program is

    1.   the effect on profits
    2.   the type and scope of quality reporting
    3.   the dynamic nature of the quality manager
    4.   valid feedback

Refer to Question 15 in Chapter 9, Quality Practices and Applications.

11.   The application of human factors in a plant production environment

    1.   identifies reasons why errors are made
    2.   is a practical example of using psychological techniques on workers
    3.   is identified with a formal quality motivation program
    4.   relates attitudes and prejudices among plant personnel

Refer to Question 25 in Chapter 15, Motivation and Human Factors.

12.   A goal of the quality cost report should be to

    1.   get the best product quality possible
    2.   be able to satisfy MIL-Q-9858A
    3.   integrate two financial reporting techniques
    4.   indicate areas of excessive costs

Refer to Question 68 in Chapter 10, Quality Cost Analysis.

13.   The concept of quality cost budgeting

    1.   involves budgeting the individual elements
    2.   replaces the traditional profit and loss statement
    3.   does not consider total quality costs
    4.   considers the four categories of quality costs and their general trends

Refer to Question 86 in Chapter 10, Quality Cost Analysis.

14.   When a new manufacturing process is contemplated, an important reason for scheduling a trial production lot is

    1.   to prove engineering feasibility
    2.   to prove that the pilot plant results are the same as those in the production shop
    3.   to prove that the tools and processes can produce the product successfully with economic yields
    4.   that it is inexpensive

Refer to Question 71 in Chapter 9, Quality Practices and Applications.

15.   The effective supervisor

    1.   sees his or her role primarily as one of making people happy
    2.   sometimes does a job her or himself because she or he can do it better than others
    3.   has objectives of growth and increased profit by working through other people
    4.   assumes the functions of planning, decision making, and monitoring performance, but leaves personnel development to the personnel department

Refer to Question 30 in Chapter 15, Motivation and Human Factors.

16.   Sources of quality cost data do not normally include

    1.   scrap reports
    2.   labor reports
    3.   salary budget reports
    4.   capital expenditure reports

Refer to Question 85 in Chapter 10, Quality Cost Analysis.

17.   To achieve consistent lot by lot protection the receiving inspector should

    1.   allow no defective product into the shop
    2.   return all rejected lots to the vendor
    3.   not know how the vendor inspects the product
    4.   use a sampling plan based on LTPD

Refer to Question 56 in Chapter 8, Acceptance Sampling.

18.   Which one of the following would most closely describe machine process capability?

    1.   the process variation
    2.   the total variation over a shift
    3.   the total variation of all cavities of a mold, cavities of a die cast machine, or spindles of an automatic assembly machine
    4.   the variation in a very short run of consecutively produced parts

Refer to Question 59 in Chapter 7, Statistical Process Control.

19.   A correlation problem

1.   is solved by estimating the value of the dependent variable for various values of the independent variable
2.   considers the joint variation of two measurements, neither of which is restricted by the experimenter
3.   is the one case where the underlying distributions must be geometric
4.   is solved by assuming that the variables are normally and independently distributed with mean = 0 and variance = σ_e^2

Refer to Question 8 in Chapter 5, Regression and Correlation Analysis.

20.   The ratio $\dfrac{\text{probability density function (t)}}{\text{reliability (t)}}$ is called

1.   useful life
2.   failure rate
3.   MTBF
4.   median

Refer to Question 18 in Chapter 13, Reliability, Maintainability, and Product Safety.

21.   For the exponential model, the reliability at mean time to failure is about

1.   37%
2.   50%
3.   63%
4.   73%

Refer to Question 44 in Chapter 13, Reliability, Maintainability, and Product Safety.

22.   A p chart

1.   can be used for only one type of defect per chart
2.   plots the number of defects in a sample
3.   plots either the fraction or percent defective in order of time
4.   plots variations in dimensions

Refer to Question 70 in Chapter 7, Statistical Process Control.

23.   Maintainability is

1.   the probability that a system will not fail
2.   the process by which a system is restored to operation after failure
3.   a characteristic of design and installation
4.   the time required to restore a system to operation after failure

Refer to Question 30 in Chapter 13, Reliability, Maintainability, and Product Safety.

24.   The basic reason for randomness in sampling is to

        1.   make certain that the sample represents the population
        2.   eliminate personal bias
        3.   guarantee to reduce the cost of inspection
        4.   guarantee correct lot inferences

        Refer to Question 3 in Chapter 4, Statistical Inference and Hypothesis Testing.

25.   To state that the levels of a factor are fixed indicates that

        1.   the levels are to be set at certain fixed values
        2.   the equipment from which the data are collected must not be moved
        3.   the factors under consideration are qualitative
        4.   the levels were chosen from a finite population

        Refer to Question 8 in Chapter 6, Design of Experiments.

26.   When considering qualitative and quantitative factors in the same designed experiment

        1.   the sum of squares for the qualitative factors can still be calculated even though no
                numerical scale can be attached to the levels
        2.   tables of orthogonal polynomials do not apply because no numerical scale can be
                attached to one of the factors
        3.   the interactions between qualitative and quantitative factors no longer make sense
        4.   the tables of orthogonal polynomials apply to both types of factors if the levels of each
                are equally spaced

        Refer to Question 10 in Chapter 6, Design of Experiments.

27.   Quality information equipment (QIE) is the physical apparatus which is concerned with

        1.   data collection and analysis
        2.   data collection, storage, and retrieval
        3.   data collection and storage
        4.   data collection, analysis, and feedback

        Refer to Question 22 in Chapter 14, Quality Information Systems.
        This question is repeated with a slight change in Questions 9, 55, and 68 of the Principles section
        of this examination and in the August 1978 and October 1974 examinations.[1]

28.   When constructing a factorial experiment, one of the following is true

---

[1] *ASQC - CQE Examination*, Quality Progress, August 1978, Principles section, Question 81, and October 1974, Principles section, Question 49.

1. factorial experiments may not contain any number of levels per factor. They must be the same for each factor
2. confounding takes place in factorials when we run a fractional part of the complete experiment
3. contrasts and treatment combinations are the same
4. in factorials, the factors must be quantitative

Refer to Question 25 in Chapter 6, Design of Experiments.

29. Characteristics are often classified (critical, major, etc.) so that

1. equal emphasis can be placed on each characteristic
2. punitive action against the responsible individuals can be equitably distributed
3. an assessment of quality can be made
4. a quality audit is compatible with management desires

Refer to Question 3 in Chapter 12, Product and Materials Control and Measurement Systems. This question is repeated with a slight change in text in the October 1974 and August 1978 examinations.[2] Also refer to Question 2 in the Principles section of this examination.

30. True testing variability can be obtained in a destructive testing situation under one of these conditions

1. enough samples have been tested
2. it cannot be obtained
3. all samples are taken closely together
4. the same person and instrument are used

Refer to Question 113 in Chapter 12, Product and Materials Control and Measurement Systems.

31. Recognizing the nature of process variability, the process capability target is usually

1. looser than product specifications
2. the same as product specifications
3. tighter than product specifications
4. not related to product specifications

Refer to Question 51 in Chapter 7, Statistical Process Control.

32. There are two basic aspects of product quality:

1. in-process and finished product quality
2. appraisal costs and failure costs
3. quality of design and quality of conformance

---

[2] *ASQC - CQE Examination*, Quality Progress, October 1974, Principles section, Questions 15, 65, and 77, and in August 1978, Principles section, Question 39.

4.   impact of machines and impact of men
Refer to Question 4 in Chapter 9, Quality Practices and Applications.

33.   The error term ε_{ij} of the population model $\chi_{ij} = \mu + \tau_{ij} + \varepsilon_{ij}$ is usually considered

1.   normally and independently distributed with mean = 0 and variability = 1
2.   normally and randomly distributed with mean = 0 and variance = 1
3.   randomly distributed with mean = 0 and variance = σ_e^2
4.   normally and independently distributed with mean = 0 and variance = σ_e^2

Refer to Question 18 in Chapter 6, Design of Experiments.

34.   A random variable

1.   may be either discrete or variable
2.   is called random because it depends on the normal distribution
3.   is called variable because it refers to the variance
4.   is all of the above

Refer to Question 16 in Chapter 3, Fundamental Concepts of Probability and Statistics.

35.   Which one of the following is a true statement of probability?

1. $P(E \text{ and } F) = P(E) + P(F)$
2. $P(E \text{ or } F) = P(E) + P(E/F)$
3. $P(E \text{ or } F) = P(E) + P(F) - P(E \text{ and } F)$
4. $P(E \text{ and } F) = P(E) + P(F) - P(E \text{ and } F)$

Refer to Question 39 in Chapter 3, Fundamental Concepts of Probability and Statistics.

36.   When finding a confidence interval for mean μ based on a sample size of n

1.   increasing n increases the interval
2.   having to use s_x instead of σ decreases the interval
3.   the larger the interval, the better the estimate of μ
4.   increasing n decreases the interval

Refer to Question 19 in Chapter 4, Statistical Inference and Hypothesis Testing.

37.   A parameter is

1.   a random variable
2.   a sample value
3.   a population value
4.   the solution to a statistical problem

Refer to Question 8 in Chapter 3, Fundamental Concepts of Probability and Statistics.

38.   Which trigonometric function finds the most use in ordinary angular measurement?

       1.   sine
       2.   cosine
       3.   tangent
       4.   cotangent

       Refer to Question 166 in Chapter 12, Product and Materials Control and Measurement Systems.

39.   In the preproduction phase of quality planning, an appropriate activity would be to:

       1.   determine responsibility for process control
       2.   determine the technical depth of available people
       3.   establish compatible approaches for accumulation of process data
       4.   conduct the process capability studies to measure process expectations

       Refer to Question 73 in Chapter 9, Quality Practices and Applications.

40.   Process acceptance involves decision making with regard to

       1.   the type of equipment or machinery used to process items during manufacture
       2.   items not yet made, that is, approval of "first piece" and periodic checks during
             production run
       3.   items already made regardless of the technique used to control quality during
             processing
       4.   acceptance sampling using MIL-STD-105D

       Refer to Question 24 in Chapter 12, Product and Materials Control and Measurement Systems.

41.   The control chart that is most sensitive to variation in a measurement is the

       1.   p chart
       2.   pn chart
       3.   c chart
       4. $\overline{X}$ and R chart

       Refer to Question 48 in Chapter 7, Statistical Process Control.

42.   When one first analyzes quality cost data, he or she might expect to find that, relative to total
       quality costs,

       1.   costs of prevention are high
       2.   costs of appraisal are high
       3.   costs of failure are high
       4.   all of the above

Refer to Question 18 in Chapter 10, Quality Cost Analysis.

43.   The assumed probability distribution for the control chart for the number of defects is the

    1.   binomial distribution
    2.   Poisson distribution
    3.   normal distribution
    4.   Student's t distribution

Refer to Question 173 in Chapter 3, Fundamental Concepts of Probability and Statistics, and Question 81 in Chapter 7, Statistical Process Control.

44.   A statistic is

    1.   the solution to a problem
    2.   a population value
    3.   a positive number between 0 and 1, inclusive
    4.   a sample value

Refer to Question 2 in Chapter 3, Fundamental Concepts of Probability and Statistics.

45.   Sensitivity is

    1.   extreme care in data analysis
    2.   ability to distinguish differences in the response variable
    3.   getting the true result
    4.   using the best measuring device

Refer to Question 16 in Chapter 6, Design of Experiments.

46.   Quality costs should not be reported against which one of the following measurement bases:

    1.   direct labor
    2.   sales
    3.   net profit
    4.   unit volume of production

Refer to Question 74 in Chapter 10, Quality Cost Analysis

47.   A computer program is

    1.   the overall computer project for an entire company
    2.   a set of instructions to accomplish a given set of calculations
    3.   a subset of instructions later patched into a larger project
    4.   instructions written only in basic computer language

Refer to Question 10 in Chapter 14, Quality Information Systems.

48.   A 3² experiment indicates

    1.   two levels of three factors
    2.   three independent variables and two dependent variables
    3.   three levels of two factors
    4.   two go-nogo variables and three continuous variables

    Refer to Question 29 in Chapter 6, Design of Experiments.

49.   Information generated in a designed experiment

    1.   always results in an analysis of variance table
    2.   is based on the fact that "the variance of the sum is the sum of the variances"
    3.   must always be quantitative
    4.   may be based on values which are not necessarily numerical

    Refer to Question 11 in Chapter 6, Design of Experiments.

50.   Historically, under the sorting inspection type of quality control function,

    1.   when failure costs rise, appraisal costs fall
    2.   failure and appraisal quality costs trend together
    3.   when failure costs fall, appraisal costs rise
    4.   failure and appraisal costs generally remain unchanged

    Refer to Question 51 in Chapter 10, Quality Cost Analysis.

51.   A classification of characteristics makes it possible to

    1.   separate the "vital few" from the "trivial many" kinds of defects
    2.   direct the greatest inspection efforts to the most important quality characteristics
    3.   establish inspection tolerances
    4.   allow the inspector to choose what to inspect and what not to inspect

    Refer to Question 7 in Chapter 12, Product and Materials Control and Measurement Systems.
    This question is repeated with a slight change in text in the October 1974 and August 1978
    examinations.[3]

52.   A frequency polygon

    1.   is a plot of connected points whose ordinates are proportional to cell frequencies
    2.   is also known as a cumulative relative frequency graph
    3.   is also known as a sample distribution function
    4.   applies only to discrete random variables

---

[3] *ASQC - CQE Examination*, Quality Progress, October 1974, Principles section, Questions 15, 65, and 77, and in August
1978, Principles section, Question 39.

Refer to Question 66 in Chapter 3, Fundamental Concepts of Probability and Statistics.

53.　　The beta risk is the risk of

　　　1.　　selecting the wrong hypothesis
　　　2.　　accepting an hypothesis when it is false
　　　3.　　accepting an hypothesis when it is true
　　　4.　　rejecting an hypothesis when it is true

Refer to Question 48 in Chapter 4, Statistical Inference and Hypothesis Testing.

54.　　If two sigma limits are substituted for conventional three sigma limits on a control chart, one of the following occurs

　　　1.　　decrease in alpha risk
　　　2.　　increase in beta risk
　　　3.　　increase in alpha risk
　　　4.　　increase in sample size

Refer to Question 51 in Chapter 4, Statistical Inference and Hypothesis Testing.

55.　　What conditions are now developing which require the installation of QIE (quality information equipment) for continued quality control effectiveness?

　　　1.　　need for better vendor-vendee relations
　　　2.　　mechanization and automation of manufacturing operations
　　　3.　　automation and mechanization of data processing activities
　　　4.　　new and more accurate measurement methods

Refer to Question 23 in Chapter 14, Quality Information Systems. This question is repeated with a slight change in Questions 9, 27, and 68 of the Principles section of this examination, and also in the August 1978 and October 1974 examinations.[4]

56.　　The hypergeometric distribution is

　　　1.　　used to describe sampling without replacement from a finite population where there are several outcomes for each trial
　　　2.　　a continuous distribution
　　　3.　　a discrete distribution with its expected value equal to its variance
　　　4.　　the limiting distribution of the sum of several independent discrete random variables

Refer to Question 183 in Chapter 3, Fundamental Concepts of Probability and Statistics.

57.　　The two factors that have the most to do with determining an attribute sampling plan

---

[4] *ASQC - CQE Examination*, Quality Progress, August 1978, Principles section, Question 81, and October 1974, Principles section, Question 49.

(assuming a binomial distribution) are:

1.   sample size and rejection number
2.   lot size and sample size
3.   lot size and acceptance number
4.   none of the above

Refer to Questions 26, 27, and 28 in Chapter 8, Acceptance Sampling. This question is repeated in the July 1984, August 1978, and October 1974 examinations.[5]

58.   Ratio of two variances drawn from the same normal population are described by which one of the following distributions?

1.   F
2.   Student's "t"
3.   Chi-Square
4.   Normal

Refer to Question 68 in Chapter 4, Statistical Inference and Hypothesis Testing.

59.   Defining the required data output should be

1.   performed next after the use of a computer is economically justified
2.   performed next after input preparation
3.   done in such a way as to optimize computing formulas
4.   the first step in computer planning

Refer to Question 11 in Chapter 14, Quality Information Systems.

60.   Quality cost trend analysis is facilitated by comparing quality costs to

1.   manufacturing costs over the same time period
2.   appropriate measurement bases
3.   cash flow reports
4.   QC department budget

Refer to Question 78 in Chapter 10, Quality Cost Analysis.

61.   100 percent inspection is

1.   used to sort items
2.   at best only 60% effective
3.   assures a satisfactory outgoing quality level
4.   theoretically unsound but an excellent practice

---

[5] *ASQC - CQE Examination*, July 1984, Principles section, Question 16, August 1978, Principles section, Question 31, and October 1974, Principles section, Question 31.

Refer to Question 32 in Chapter 12, Product and Materials Control and Measurement Systems.

62.   The basic statistical principle in EVOP is the

      1.   Ability to find small, significant differences through large sample sizes
      2.   Operating with low levels of confidence
      3.   Making large changes in independent variables
      4.   None of these

Refer to Question 64 in Chapter 6, Design of Experiments.

63.   The following is an example of what type of response surface?

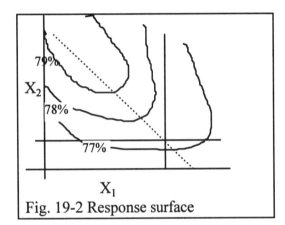

Fig. 19-2 Response surface

      1.   rising ridge
      2.   maximum or minimum
      3.   stationary ridge
      4.   minimax

Refer to Question 63 in Chapter 6, Design of Experiments.

64.   When considering a factorial experiment, observe that

      1.   this experiment cannot be used when complete randomization is necessary
      2.   a main effect may be confounded
      3.   this type of design is not encountered in industrial experiments
      4.   one of the advantages is that an exact test always exists for all effects

Refer to Question 27 in Chapter 6, Design of Experiments.

65.   The factor D_4 used in $\overline{\overline{X}}$ and R control charts is

      1.   the distance between the mean and the upper control limit of a range chart
      2.   the number of defects in a second sample
      3.   the constant which corrects the bias in estimating the population standard deviation from the average range of randomly drawn samples
      4.   the probability that $\overline{X}$ is in control

Refer to Question 30 in Chapter 7, Statistical Process Control.

66.   The power of efficiency in designed experiment lies in the

1.   random order of performance
2.   sequential and cyclical procedure of conjecture to design to analysis and back to analysis
3.   hidden replication
4.   large number of possible combinations of factors

Refer to Question 19 in Chapter 6, Design of Experiments.

67.   In planning process controls

1.   deciding whether the process runs or not is determined by whether the resulting product conforms or not
2.   the basic approach follows the servomechanism cycle so common in engineering
3.   collection of information goes hand in hand with decision making
4.   meeting process specification tolerances is the same as meeting product tolerances

Refer to Question 12 in Chapter 12, Product and Materials Control and Measurement Systems.

68.   In planning for quality information equipment, an appropriate activity would be to

1.   review present process capabilities to permit correlation with newer processes
2.   establish training plans as required for the operation of the equipment
3.   establish the routine for checkout and calibration tooling
4.   evaluate process cost relative to performance

Refer to Question 20 in Chapter 14, Quality Information Systems.

69.   The most important reason for a checklist in a process control audit is to

1.   assure that the auditor is qualified
2.   minimize the time required for audit
3.   obtain relatively uniform audits
4.   notify the audited function prior to audit

Refer to Question 39 in Chapter 11, Quality Auditing.

70.   In the analysis of variance

1.   the total sum of squares of deviations from the grand mean is equal to the sum of squares of deviations between treatment means and the grand mean minus the sum of squares of deviations within treatments
2.   the total standard deviation is equal to the sum of the standard deviation for the treatment effect plus the standard deviation of the random error
3.   the degrees of freedom are additive
4.   a basic population model can be constructed to represent the behavior of the experimentation

Refer to Question 43 in Chapter 6, Design of Experiments.

71.   It has been found that the more complex the inspection task, the less accurate the inspection becomes. This can be partially overcome by

    1.   using several inspectors in a team approach
    2.   reducing the inspection task to a scanning operation
    3.   providing inspectors with an unlimited amount of inspection time
    4.   restricting inspection time in order to encourage increased concentration on the part of the inspector

Refer to Question 23 in Chapter 12, Product and Materials Control and Measurement Systems.

72.   In linear measurement, what overriding consideration should guide the quality control engineer in specifying the measuring instrument to be used?

    1.   the ability of the instrument to be read to one decimal place beyond the places in the base dimension or tolerance
    2.   the ability of the instrument to meet an error design goal of 10%
    3.   the combination of base dimension and tolerance as they relate to measurement error
    4.   the ability of the instrument-inspector system to obtain the necessary correct information at minimum overall cost

Refer to Question 34 in Chapter 12, Product and Materials Control and Measurement Systems.

73.   Double sampling is better than single sampling because

    1.   it involves less inspection regardless of lot quality
    2.   if the first sample rejects the lot, the second sample will accept it
    3.   it is more economical except when lots are of borderline quality
    4.   it is easier to administer

Refer to Questions 63 and 64 in Chapter 8, Acceptance Sampling.

74.   In every experiment, there is experimental error. Which one of the following statements is true?

    1.   This error is due to lack of uniformity of the material used in the experiment and to inherent variability in the experimental technique.
    2.   This error can be changed statistically by increasing the degrees of freedom.
    3.   The error can be reduced only by improving the material.
    4.   In a well-designed experiment, there is no interaction effect.

Refer to Question 17 in Chapter 6, Design of Experiments.

75.   The intentional difference in the sizes of mating parts is the

    1.   Specification
    2.   Clearance
    3.   Natural tolerance

4.   Satisfactory functioning

Refer to Question 165 in Chapter 12, Product and Materials Control and Measurement Systems.

76.   The ultimate standard for U.S. units of measurement used to verify all masters is

1.   the official meter
2.   the imperial yard
3.   the length of light wave
4.   the Geiger Counter

Refer to Question 155 in Chapter 12, Product and Materials Control and Measurement Systems.

77.   The primary visual consideration in designing an inspection workplace is

1.   the environmental color decor because of its psychological effect
2.   the size and shape of the inspection table or bench
3.   the illumination and how it is provided
4.   the traffic flow in or near the inspection station

Refer to Question 26 in Chapter 12, Product and Materials Control and Measurement Systems.

78.   Let X be any random variable with mean μ and standard deviation σ. Take a random sample of size n. As n increases and as a result of central limit theorem

1.   The distribution of the sum $Sn = X_1 + X_2 + ... + X_n$ approaches a normal distribution with mean μ and standard deviation $\sigma / \sqrt{n}$
2.   The distribution of $Sn = X_1 + X_2 + ... + X_n$ approaches a normal distribution with mean μ and standard deviation $\dfrac{\sigma}{\sqrt{n}}$
3.   The distribution of X approaches a normal distribution with mean $n\mu$ and standard deviation $\dfrac{\sigma}{\sqrt{n}}$
4.   None of the above

Refer to Question 1 in Chapter 4, Statistical Inference and Hypothesis Testing.

79.   In the regression equation $y = mx + b$, y increases with x in all cases

1.   if b is positive
2.   if b is negative
3.   if m is positive
4.   if m is negative

Refer to Question 26 in Chapter 5, Regression and Correlation Analysis.

80.   The basic objective of a quality cost program is to

       1.   identify the source of quality failures
       2.   determine quality control department responsibilities
       3.   utilize accounting department reports
       4.   improve the profit posture of your company

       Refer to Question 5 in Chapter 10, Quality Cost Analysis.

81.   Management is constantly seeking new ways to make profitable use of their expensive
       computers. Which of the following computer applications promises to be the most beneficial
       from management's standpoint?

       1.   decision-making help in combination with simulation techniques
       2.   wider use as an accounting machine
       3.   high-density information storage and rapid retrieval rates
       4.   solution of complex mathematical formulas

       Refer to Question 5 in Chapter 14, Quality Information Systems.

82.   In comparing the philosophies of "tight tolerances loosely enforced" and "realistic tolerances
       rigidly enforced," we can conclude that

       1.   the first one is preferred
       2.   the second one is preferred
       3.   neither is really practical
       4.   both have a place in any production operation

       Refer to Question 62 in Chapter 9, Quality Practices and Applications.

83.   Good forms design and layout are essential in both manual and electronic data processing
       because

       1.   they are easier to read, check data, use, and file
       2.   they are cheaper (faster) to use although initial cost is higher than quickly made forms
       3.   they help to avoid typographical errors
       4.   all of the above

       Refer to Question 14 in Chapter 14, Quality Information Systems.

84.   Random selection of a sample

       1.   theoretically means that each item in the lot had an equal chance to be selected in the
             sample
       2.   assures that the sample average will equal the population average
       3.   means that a table of random numbers was used to dictate the selection
       4.   is a meaningless theoretical requirement

Refer to Question 17 in Chapter 3, Fundamental Concepts of Probability and Statistics, and Question 2 in Chapter 4, Statistical Inference and Hypothesis Testing.

85.   The binomial distribution is a discrete distribution and may be used to describe

    1.   sampling without replacement from a finite population
    2.   the case of n independent trials with probabilities constant from trial to trial
    3.   the case of n independent trials with several outcomes for each trial
    4.   sampling without replacement from a finite population where there are several outcomes for each trial

Refer to Question 156 in Chapter 3, Fundamental Concepts of Probability and Statistics.

86.   One defective is

    1.   an item that is unacceptable to the inspector
    2.   the same as one defect
    3.   a characteristic that may be unacceptable for more than one reason
    4.   an item that fails to meet quality standards and specifications

Refer to Question 157 in Chapter 3, Fundamental Concepts of Probability and Statistics.

87.   The permissible variation in a dimension is the

    1.   Clearance
    2.   Allowance
    3.   Tolerance
    4.   Measurement

Refer to Question 147 in Chapter 3, Fundamental Concepts of Probability and Statistics, and Question 59 in Chapter 9, Quality Practices and Applications.

88:     This expression $\dfrac{n!}{x!(n-x)!} p'^{x}(1-p')^{n-x}$ is the

    1.   general term for the Poisson distribution
    2.   general term for the Pascal distribution
    3.   general term for the binomial distribution
    4.   the general term for the hypergeometric distribution

Refer to Question 155 in Chapter 3, Fundamental Concepts of Probability and Statistics.

89.   The standard deviation as a percent of the mean is called

    1.   relative precision
    2.   coefficient of variability
    3.   standard deviation of the mean

4.   standard error

Refer to Question 111 in Chapter 3, Fundamental Concepts of Probability and Statistics.

90.   Monte Carlo method refers to a technique for

1.   the simulation of operations when random variations are an essential consideration
2.   programming roulette for maximum return
3.   random sampling from homogeneous population
4.   establishing quantitative values to unknown restrictive variables in linear programming

Refer to Question 98 in Chapter 13, Reliability, Maintainability, and Product Safety.

APPLICATIONS

1.   Given that random samples of process A produced 10 defective and 30 good units, while process B produced 25 defectives out of 60 units. Using chi-square test, what is the probability that the observed value of chi-square could result, under the hypothesis that both processes are operating at the same quality level?

    1.   less than 5%
    2.   between 5% and 10%
    3.   greater than 10%
    4.   50%

Refer to Question 77 in Chapter 4, Statistical Inference and Hypothesis Testing.

2.   How many degrees of freedom should you use in the above problem?

    1.   1
    2.   2
    3.   3
    4.   4

Refer to Question 78 in Chapter 4, Statistical Inference and Hypothesis Testing.

3.   On the basis of the data in the previous problem, what would you conclude?

    1.   Nothing. The facts involving the consequences of a wrong decision are unknown.
    2.   The two processes are comparable.
    3.   The two processes are significantly different.
    4.   Reject the null hypothesis.

Refer to Question 79 in Chapter 4, Statistical Inference and Hypothesis Testing.

4.   Color can be described as

    1.   one dimensional
    2.   two dimensional
    3.   three dimensional
    4.   photometric

Refer to Question 151 in Chapter 12, Product and Materials Control and Measurement Systems.

5.   Wear allowance on a go-plug gage permits gages to be

    1.   slightly smaller in diameter than the low limit of specification
    2.   slightly larger in diameter than the low limit of specification
    3.   right on the low limit of the specification

4.   slightly larger in diameter than the high limit of specification

Refer to Question 125 in Chapter 12, Product and Materials Control and Measurement Systems.

6.   To insure success of a quality audit program, the most important activity for a quality supervisor is

1.   setting up audit frequency
2.   maintenance of a checking procedure to see that all required audits are performed
3.   getting corrective action as a result of audit findings
4.   checking that the audit procedure is adequate and complete

Refer to Question 35 in Chapter 11, Quality Auditing.

7.   Measurement gaging is preferable to go-no-go gaging in a quality characteristic because

1.   it is more scientific
2.   it provides the most information per piece inspected
3.   it requires greater skills
4.   it requires a larger sample than gaging does

Refer to Question 127 in Chapter 12, Product and Materials Control and Measurement Systems.

8.   Characteristics of a good incoming inspection department are

1.   written and visual quality standards
2.   proper inspection equipment and gages
3.   inspector knowledge of sampling techniques
4.   all of the above

Refer to Question 36 in Chapter 12, Product and Materials Control and Measurement Systems.

9.   The technology of predicting human reliability in production processes

1.   is inevitably correlated with monetary rewards
2.   is represented by the many motivation programs in effect
3.   is still in the developmental stage
4.   is based on the determination of the workmanship error rate

Refer to Question 97 in Chapter 13, Reliability, Maintainability, and Product Safety.

10.   In planning for quality, an important consideration at the start is

1.   the relationship of the total cost of quality to the net sales
2.   the establishment of a company quality policy or objective
3.   deciding precisely how much money is to be spent
4.   the selling of the quality program to the top management

Refer to Question 29 in Chapter 9, Quality Practices and Applications.

11.   The sample size for a product quality audit should be

       1.   based on MIL-STD-105D
       2.   based on the lot size
       3.   a stated percentage of production
       4.   very small

Refer to Question 2 in Chapter 8, Acceptance Sampling.

12.   Which of the following nondestructive testing methods is best for rapid inspection of 1/2 in. diameter carbon steel rod one foot long for surface cracks'?

       1.   radiography
       2.   ultrasonic
       3.   magnetic particle
       4.   liquid penetrant

Refer to Question 98 in Chapter 12, Product and Materials Control and Measurement Systems.

13.   To measure an angle on a work piece, the most accurate method would involve the use of

       1.   a sine bar
       2.   a set of plastic triangles
       3.   a bevel protector
       4.   none of the above

Refer to Questions 166, 167, and 168 in Chapter 12, Product and Materials Control and Measurement Systems.

14.   Who has the initial responsibility for manufactured product quality?

       1.   the inspector
       2.   thc vice president
       3.   the operator
       4.   the quality manager

Refer to Question 35 in Chapter 12, Product and Materials Control and Measurement Systems.

15.   What type of gaging instrument would you use to determine the fractional part of an inch that can be read by multiplying the denominator of the finest subdivision on the scale by the total number of divisions on the second scale?

       1.   Vernier
       2.   Micrometer
       3.   Comparator

4.   Demonimeter

Refer to Question 115 in Chapter 12, Product and Materials Control and Measurement Systems.

16.   Given the following results obtained from a fixed factor randomized block designed experiment, in which the production outputs of three machines (A, B, C) were to be compared,

A	4	8	5	7	6
B	2	0	1	−2	4
C	−3	1	−2	−1	0

how many degrees of freedom are used to compute the error variance?
1.   2
2.   3
3.   12
4.   14

Refer to Question 59 in Chapter 6, Design of Experiments.

17.   What is the critical value of F at 0.05 risk for the data in the previous problem?

1.   3.89
2.   4.75
3.   3.49
4.   4.6

Refer to Question 60 in Chapter 6, Design of Experiments.

18.   What is the sum of the squares for the error term for the data in the previous problem?

1.   170
2.   130
3.   40
4.   14

Refer to Question 61 in Chapter 6, Design of Experiments.

19.   The purpose of such an experiment described in the previous question is to compare

1.   the output variances of the three machines
2.   the variance of the machines against the error
3.   the output averages of the three machines
4.   the process capabilities of the tree machines

Refer to Question 62 in Chapter 6, Design of Experiments.

20.   The term "random access" identifies information stored

        1.   when all parts of it are designed to be equally accessible when needed
        2.   someplace inside a computer, whose address only the computer's scanning device can
                locate
        3.   outside a computer, so it has to be sought by humans rather than electronically
        4.   in the special part of the processing unit for temporary storage only

        Refer to Question 28 in Chapter 14, Quality Information Systems.

21.   Assume a large lot contains exactly 4 percent defective items. Using the Poisson distribution,
        what is the probability that a random sample of 50 items will not reflect the true lot quality?

        1.   27%
        2.   73%
        3.   82%
        4.   67%

        Refer to Question 181 in Chapter 3, Fundamental Concepts of Probability and Statistics.

22.   When setting up a sorting operation for a visual defect, which one of the following is most
        important?

        1.   the importance of the defect
        2.   whether the operator or inspector does the job
        3.   the percent defective estimated to be in the lot
        4.   the quality standard

        Refer to Question 39 in Chapter 12, Product and Materials Control and Measurement Systems.

23.   A device used to measure viscosity or consistency is

        1.   Viscosimeter
        2.   Farinograph
        3.   Consistometer
        4.   all of the above

        Refer to Question 150 in Chapter 12, Product and Materials Control and Measurement Systems.

24.   Which one of the following tasks has been shown to have the most incentive or motivational
        value to the quality engineer?

        1.   attend defect control meetings
        2.   document action taken on special problems
        3.   investigate product quality problems
        4.   initiate corrective actions to solve nonroutine problems

Refer to Question 34 in Chapter 15, Motivation and Human Factors.

25.   When planning the specifications for product quality in the so-called "mechanical" industries

    1.   Market research helps to establish economic tolerances.
    2.   Quality control develops products possessing qualities which meet customer needs.
    3.   Product research issues official product specifications.
    4.   Product design assumes prime responsibility for establishing economic tolerances.

Refer to Question 67 in Chapter 9, Quality Practices and Applications.

26.   In the so-called *process* industries

    1.   quality control has some responsibility in choosing the process
    2.   quality control may help to establish process tolerances
    3.   process development issues process specifications
    4.   All of the above

Refer to Question 69 in Chapter 9, Quality Practices and Applications.

27.   Shewhart $\overline{X}$ control charts are designed with which one of the following objectives?

    1.   reduce sample size
    2.   fix risk of accepting poor product
    3.   decide when to hunt for causes of variation
    4.   establish an acceptable quality level

Refer to Question 5 in Chapter 7, Statistical Process Control.

28.   If the probability of a success on a single trial is 0.20 and 3 trials are performed, what is the probability of at least one success?

    1.   0.008
    2.   0.384
    3.   0.488
    4.   0.600

Refer to Question 165 in Chapter 3, Fundamental Concepts of Probability and Statistics.

29.   A process is acceptable if its standard deviation is not greater than 1.0. A sample of four items yields the values 52, 56, 53, and 55. In order to determine if the process be accepted or rejected, the following statistical test should be used:

    1.   t test
    2.   chi-square test
    3.   Z test

4.   none of the above

Refer to Question 80 in Chapter 4, Statistical Inference and Hypothesis Testing.

30.   When planning the quality aspects of packing and shipping, it is not usual that the

1.   product design department specify packaging and shipping procedures
2.   shipping department conduct packing and shipping operations
3.   inspection department determine packing specifications
4.   inspection department check the adequacy of packing and shipping operations

Refer to Question 37 in Chapter 12, Product and Materials Control and Measurement Systems.

31.   If the distribution of defectives among various lots is found to follow the laws of chance, we can conclude that

1.   the product was well mixed before dividing into lots
2.   the manufacturing process is not predictable
3.   all lots should be accepted
4.   none of the above is true

Refer to Question 38 in Chapter 12, Product and Materials Control and Measurement Systems.

32.   When purchasing materials from vendors, it is sometimes advantageous to choose vendors whose prices are higher because

1.   materials which cost more can be expected to be better, and "you get what you pay for"
2.   such vendors may become obligated to bestow special favors
3.   such a statement is basically incorrect; always buy at lowest bid price
4.   the true cost of purchased materials, which should include items such as sorting, inspection, contacting vendors, and production delays, may be lower

Refer to Question 58 in Chapter 9, Quality Practices and Applications.

33.   In a scanning type of inspection task, inspection accuracy is likely to be greater if

1.   the product moves toward the inspector rather than laterally past him or her
2.   the inspector searches the product, area by area, for all types of defects, rather than the entire product for one type of defect at a time
3.   the magnification is increased
4.   the product is scanned while it is stationary rather than while it is moving

Refer to Question 46 in Chapter 12, Product and Materials Control and Measurement Systems.

34. In which one of the following is the use of an $\overline{X}$ and R chart liable to be helpful as a tool to control a process?

1. The machine capability is wider than the specification.
2. The machine capability is equal to the specification.
3. The machine capability is somewhat smaller than the specification.
4. The machine capability is very small compared to the specification.

Refer to Question 64 in Chapter 7, Statistical Process Control.

35. The basic concept of MIL-STD-105D (now MIL-STD-105E) sampling tables and procedures is that

1. poor product is accepted frequently
2. good product is accepted rarely
3. poor product is accepted consistently
4. good product is accepted most of the time

Refer to Question 36 in Chapter 8, Acceptance Sampling.

36. In acceptance sampling, the probability of accepting a rejectable lot is called

1. beta
2. AQL
3. alpha
4. LTPD

Refer to Question 19 in Chapter 8, Acceptance Sampling.

37. When performing calculations on sample data

1. the cumulative relative frequency graph that is often used is called a histogram
2. rounding the data has no effect on the mean and standard deviation
3. coding the data has no effect on the mean and standard deviation
4. coding and rounding affect both the mean and standard deviation

Refer to Question 89 in Chapter 3, Fundamental Concepts of Probability and Statistics.

38. When analyzing quality costs, a helpful method for singling out the highest cost contributors is

1. a series of interviews with the line foreman
2. the application of the Pareto theory
3. an audit of budget variances
4. the application of breakeven and profit volume analysis

Refer to Questions 69 and 70 in Chapter 10, Quality Cost Analysis.

39.   One of the most effective techniques in making a training program effective is to

        1.   give people meaningful measures of performance
        2.   transmit all of the information that is even remotely related to the function
        3.   set individual goals instead of group goals
        4.   concentrate only on developing knowledge and skills needed to do a good job

        Refer to Question 37 in Chapter 15, Motivation and Human Factors.

40.   The Dodge-Romig sampling tables for AOQL protection

        1.   require sorting of rejected lots
        2.   are the same in principle as the MIL-STD-105D (now E) tables
        3.   do not depend upon the process average
        4.   require larger samples than MIL-STD-105D for equivalent quality assurances

        Refer to Question 57 in Chapter 8, Acceptance Sampling.

41.   EVOP should be used

        1.   when there is a manufacturing problem
        2.   when a process is not in statistical control
        3.   when an experimenter first begins working on a new product
        4.   when a process is producing satisfactory material

        Refer to Question 65 in Chapter 6, Design of Experiments.

42.   Three parts are additive in an assembly. Their design specifications for length and tolerance are
        0.240 ± 0.006, 0.3200 ± 0.0006, and 1.360 ± 0.003, respectively. Assume that each of the
        distributions is normal. Combine these dimensions statistically to give a final length and
        tolerance to three decimal places.

        1. 1.360 ± 0.006
        2. 0.799 ± 0.565
        3. 0.640 ± 0.010
        4. 1.920 ± 0.007

        Refer to Question 149 in Chapter 3, Fundamental Concepts of Probability and Statistics.

43.   If a process is out of control, the theoretical probability that four consecutive points on an $\overline{X}$
        chart will fall on the same side of the mean is

        1.   Unknown
        2. $(1/2)^4$
        3. $2(1/2)^4$
        4. $1/2\,(1/2)^4$

Refer to Question 34 in Chapter 7, Statistical Process Control.

44.   An incomplete block design may be especially suitable when

        1.   there is missing data
        2.   there is a need for fractional replication
        3.   it may not be possible to apply all treatments in every block
        4.   there is a need to estimate the parameters during the experimentation

        Refer to Question 20 in Chapter 6, Design of Experiments.

45.   A cost estimate associated with average outgoing quality protection is determined from the

        1.   average total inspection
        2.   average outgoing quality
        3.   average sample size
        4.   acceptable quality limit

        Refer to Question 61 in Chapter 8, Acceptance Sampling.

46.   Using a 10% sample of each lot, with an acceptance number of zero, regardless of lot size

        1.   results in a constant level of protection against a bad product
        2.   assures a constant producer's risk
        3.   abdicates the responsibility for predetermining quality requirements
        4.   provides an AQL of zero and an LTPD of 10%

        Refer to Question 22 in Chapter 8, Acceptance Sampling.

47.   Estimate the variance of the population from which the following sample data came: 22, 18, 17, 20, 21.

        1.   4.3
        2.   2.1
        3.   1.9
        4.   5.0

        Refer to Question 105 in Chapter 3, Fundamental Concepts of Probability and Statistics.

48.   The operating characteristics (OC) curve of an acceptance sampling plan

        1.   demonstrates how the plan will reject all of the lots worse than AQL
        2.   shows the ability of the plan to distinguish between good and bad lots
        3.   shows the relative cost of sampling for various levels of quality
        4.   demonstrates the advantages of double sampling over single sampling

        Refer to Question 7 in Chapter 8, Acceptance Sampling.

49.   The quality costs of writing instructions and operating procedures for inspection and testing should be charged to

       1.   appraisal costs
       2.   internal failure costs
       3.   prevention costs
       4.   external failure costs

       Refer to Question 32 in Chapter 10, Quality Cost Analysis.

50.   In a normal distribution, what is the area under the curve between +0.7 and +1.3 standard deviation units?

       1.   0.2930
       2.   0.7580
       3.   0.2580
       4.   0.1452

       Refer to Question 128 in Chapter 3, Fundamental Concepts of Probability and Statistics.

51.   A useful tool to determine when to investigate excessive variation in a process is

       1.   MIL-STD-105E
       2.   Control chart
       3.   Dodge-Romig AOQL sampling table
       4.   Process capability study

       Refer to Question 3 in Chapter 7, Statistical Process Control.

52.   Calculate the standard deviation of the following complete set of data: 52, 20, 24, 31, 35, 42.

       1.   10.8
       2.   11.8
       3.   12.8
       4.   13.8

       Refer to Question 100 in Chapter 3, Fundamental Concepts of Probability and Statistics.

53.   It is generally considered desirable that quality audit reports be

       1.   stated in terms different from those of the function being audited
       2.   simple but complete
       3.   sent to the general manager in all cases
       4.   quantitative in all cases

       Refer to Question 54 in Chapter 11, Quality Auditing.

54.   Establishing the quality policy of the company is typically the responsibility of

       1.   marketing management
       2.   top management
       3.   quality control
       4.   customer

       Refer to Question 24 in Chapter 9, Quality Practices and Applications.

55.   Two balance scales are to be compared by weighing the same five items on each scale, yielding the following results:

	Item #1	#2	#3	#4	#5
Scale A	110	99	112	85	99
Scale B	112	101	113	88	101

       The sharpest test comparing mean effects is obtained by using which one of the following?

       1.   paired data test of significance with 4 degrees of freedom
       2. $t = \dfrac{\overline{X}_A - \overline{X}_B}{S_p / \sqrt{n}}$ for 8 degrees of freedom
       3.   analysis of variance for randomized blocks
       4.   determining the correlation coefficient r

       Refer to Question 66 in Chapter 4, Statistical Inference and Hypothesis Testing.

56.   "Determine the flux meter reading of the part per specification." This inspection instruction violates which of the following guiding principles?

       1.   A specific objective should be established for each instruction.
       2.   Only necessary words should be used.
       3.   The correct inspection method should be stated in operational terms.
       4.   all of the above

       Refer to Question 42 in Chapter 12, Product and Materials Control and Measurement Systems.

57.   A value of 0.9973 refers to the probability that

       1.   the process is in control
       2.   a correct decision will be made as to control or lack of control of the process
       3.   the process is unstable
       4.   a point will fall inside the three sigma limits for an $\overline{X}$ chart if the process is in control

       Refer to Question 81 in Chapter 4, Statistical Inference and Hypothesis Testing, and Question 52 in Chapter 7, Statistical Process Control.

58.   A chart for number of defects is called

        1.   np chart
        2.   p chart
        3. $\overline{X}$ chart
        4.   c chart

        Refer to Question 84 in Chapter 7, Statistical Process Control.

59.   When considering EVOP as a statistical tool:

        1.   A change in the means indicates that we are using the wrong model.
        2.   An extreme estimate of the experiment error is necessary.
        3.   EVOP may be extended beyond the two level factorial case.
        4.   We are limited to one response variable at a time; a new EVOP should be run for each response.

        Refer to Question 66 in Chapter 6, Design of Experiments.

60.   The Dodge-Romig tables for AOQL protection are designed to provide

        1.   minimum average sampling costs
        2.   maximum protection against poor material
        3.   maximum risk of accepting good lots
        4.   minimum average total inspection for a given process average

        Refer to Questions 57, 58, and 59 in Chapter 8, Acceptance Sampling.

61.   Each value below is the number of defects found in a group of five subassemblies inspected

        | 77 | 61 | 59 | 22 | 54 |
        | 64 | 49 | 54 | 92 | 22 |
        | 75 | 65 | 41 | 89 | 49 |
        | 93 | 45 | 87 | 55 | 33 |
        | 45 | 77 | 40 | 25 | 20 |

        Assume that a c chart is to be used for future production. Calculate the preliminary three sigma control limits from the above data.

        1.   82.5, 28.9
        2.   15.6, 6.6
        3.   65.7, 45.7
        4.   78.2, 33.2

        Refer to Question 87 in Chapter 7, Statistical Process Control.

62.   Referring to the data in the preceding question, if points are outside of the control limits and we wish to set up a control chart for future production,

   1.   more data are needed
   2.   discard those points falling outside the control limits, for which you can identify an assignable cause, and revise the limits
   3.   check with production to determine the true process capability
   4.   discard those points falling outside the control limits and revise the limits

   Refer to Question 88 in Chapter 7, Statistical Process Control.

63.   Included as a "prevention quality cost" would be

   1.   salaries of personnel engaged in the design of measurement and control equipment that is to be purchased
   2.   capital equipment purchased
   3.   training costs of instructing plant personnel to achieve the production standards
   4.   sorting of nonconforming material, which will delay or stop production

   Refer to Question 33 in Chapter 10, Quality Cost Analysis.

64.   The modern concept of budgeting quality costs is to

   1.   budget each of the four segments: prevention, appraisal, internal and external failure
   2.   concentrate on external failures; they are important to the business since they represent customer acceptance
   3.   establish budget for reducing the total of the quality costs
   4.   reduce the expenditures on each segment

   Refer to Question 87 in Chapter 10, Quality Cost Analysis.

65.   The percentages of total quality cost are distributed as follows:

Prevention	2%
Appraisal	33%
Internal failure	35%
External failure	30%

   We can conclude

   1.   expenditures for failures are excessive
   2.   nothing
   3.   we should invest more money in prevention
   4.   the amount spent for appraisal seems about right

   Refer to Question 54 in Chapter 10, Quality Cost Analysis.

66.　　Specifying a tolerance by + 0.000/− 0.001 is known as

　　　1.　　Bilateral tolerance
　　　2.　　Limit dimensioning
　　　3.　　manufacturing limits
　　　4.　　unilateral tolerance

　　　Refer to Question 70 in Chapter 12, Product and Materials Control and Measurement Systems.

67.　　Component 1 has an exponential failure rate of 3×10^{-4} failures per hour. Component 2 normally is distributed with a mean of 600 hours and standard deviation of 200 hours. Assuming independence, calculate the reliability of the system after 200 hours.

　　　1.　　0.878
　　　2.　　0.918
　　　3.　　0.940
　　　4.　　0.977

　　　Refer to Question 60 in Chapter 12, Reliability, Maintainability, and Product Safety.

68.　　The main objection of designed experimentation in an industrial environment is

　　　1.　　obtaining more information for less cost than can be obtained by traditional experimentation
　　　2.　　getting excessive scrap as a result of choosing factor levels that are too extreme
　　　3.　　verifying that one factor at a time is a most economical way to proceed
　　　4.　　obtaining data and then deciding what to do with it

　　　Refer to Question 12 in Chapter 6, Design of Experiments.

69.　　Using the range method, calculate the machine capability standard deviation to nearest 0.0001 of the following

8 am	9 am	10 am	11 am
0.001	0.003	0.001	0.005
−0.001	0.004	−0.002	0.006
0.003	0.003	−0.003	0.005
0.002	0.004	0.002	0.005
0.001	0.002	0.000	0.006

　　　1.　　0.0024
　　　2.　　0.0470
　　　3.　　0.0013

4.   0.0030

Refer to Question 47 in Chapter 7, Statistical Process Control.

70.   The purpose of a written inspection procedure is to

1.   provide answers to inspection questions
2.   let the operator know what the inspector is doing
3.   errorproof the inspection function
4.   standardize methods and procedures of inspectors

Refer to Question 37 in Chapter 9, Quality Practices and Applications.

71.   The smallest size a 3 in. micrometer can measure is

1.   3 in.
2.   2 in.
3.   1 in.
4.   2.5 in.

Refer to Question 120 in Chapter 12, Product and Materials Control and Measurement Systems.

72.   Studies have shown that the most effective communications method for transferring information is

1.   oral only
2.   written only
3.   combined written and oral
4.   bulletin board

Refer to Question 35 in Chapter 15, Motivation and Human Factors.

73.   Maintainability of equipment may be measured in terms of

1.   maintenance dollars cost
2.   maintenance labor hours
3.   repair time
4.   all of the above

Refer to Question 31 in Chapter 13, Reliability, Maintainability, and Product Safety.

74.   Assume that the cost data available to you for a certain period are limited to the following:

$ 20,000	Final test
$350,000	Field Warranty costs
$170,000	Reinspection and retest
$ 45,000	Loss on disposition of surplus stock

$ 4,000   Vendor quality surveys
$ 30,000   Rework

The total of the quality costs is

1. $ 619,000
2. $ 574,000
3. $ 615,000
4. $ 570,000

Refer to Question 63 in Chapter 10, Quality Cost Analysis.

75.   In the previous problem, the total failure cost is

1. $ 550,000
2. $ 30,000
3. $ 350,000
4. $ 380,000

Refer to Question 64 in Chapter 10, Quality Cost Analysis.

76.   In analyzing the cost data in Question 74, we can conclude that

1.   prevention cost is too low a proportion of total quality cost
2.   total of the quality costs is excessive
3.   internal failure costs can be decreased
4.   appraisal costs should be decreased

Refer to Question 65 in Chapter 12, Quality Cost Analysis.

77.   The design function which assigns probability of failures between components or subsystems is called

1.   apportionment
2.   significance
3.   confidence
4.   qualification

Refer to Question 94 in Chapter 13, Reliability, Maintainability, and Product Safety.

78.   An important aid to the quality supervisor in the area of record keeping and data processing is

1.   adaptability of records to computer processing
2.   using well-designed forms and records
3.   getting sufficient copies of records and reports distributed to key personnel
4.   training inspectors to follow inspection instructions and procedures

Refer to Question 15 in Chapter 14, Quality Information Systems.

79.   What piece of data processing equipment can facilitate the handling of common quality control calculations on EDP equipment?

        1.   Boolean algebra calculator
        2.   Collator
        3.   Matrix converter
        4.   Tensor analyzer

Refer to Question 27 in Chapter 14, Quality Information Systems.

80.   Tabular arrays of data and graphs on the same page are especially useful in quality control work because

        1.   both are there for those who don't like graphs only
        2.   graphs help spot data transposition or errors
        3.   control limits can be easily applied
        4.   all of the above

Refer to Question 89 in Chapter 7, Statistical Process Control.

81.   For complex electronic equipments, the major contributor to repair time is generally

        1.   diagnosis
        2.   disassembly/reassembly
        3.   remove/replace
        4.   final checkout

Refer to Question 31 in Chapter 14, Quality Information Systems.

82.   What is the major drawback to using punch cards in a sophisticated information retrieval system?

        1.   They answer only one question in a complete pass of the file.
        2.   They do not store sufficient information.
        3.   They take up too much space.
        4.   They are not as fast as magnetic tape.

Refer to Question 30 in Chapter 14, Quality Information Systems.

83.   The sequence of punched fields for punched cards generally should be the same as

        1.   the data from previous reports with similar source data
        2.   prescribed from the output report
        3.   no generally accepted practice can be prescribed
        4.   the data to be punched from the original documents

Refer to Question 29 in Chapter 14, Quality Information Systems.

84.   A reliability test conducted during the preproduction stage is called

        1.   Demonstration test
        2.   Acceptance test
        3.   Significance test
        4.   Qualification test

        Refer to Question 77 in Chapter 13, Reliability, Maintainability, and Product Safety.

85.   How many standard deviation units, symmetrical about the mean, will span an area around the mean of 40 percent of the total area under the normal curve?

        1. ± 0.84
        2. ± 0.52
        3. ± 1.28
        4. -0.25

        Refer to Question 130 in Chapter 3, Fundamental Concepts of Probability and Statistics.

86.   A process is checked at random by inspection of samples of four shafts after a polishing operation and $\overline{X}$ and R charts are maintained. A person making a spot check measures two shafts accurately, and plots their range on the R chart. The point falls just outside the control limit. He or she advises the department foreman to stop the process. This decision indicated that

        1.   the process level is out of control
        2.   the process level is out of control but not the dispersion
        3.   the person is misusing the data
        4.   the process dispersion is out of control

        Refer to Question 42 in Chapter 7, Statistical Process Control.

87.   If X and Y are dependent random variables, and if X has variance 4 and Y has variance 3, then the variance of $5X - Y$ is

        1.   103
        2.   23
        3.   17
        4.   unknown

        Refer to Question 115 in Chapter 3, Fundamental Concepts of Probability and Statistics.

88.   Test and inspection equipment should be

        1.   replaced periodically

2.   covered when not in use
3.   calibrated periodically
4.   as sophisticated as possible

Refer to Question 92 in Chapter 12, Product and Materials Control and Measurement Systems.

89.   A process is in control with $\bar{p} = 0.10$ and n = 100. The three sigma limits of the np control chart are

1.   1 and 19
2.   9.1 and 10.9
3.   0.01 and 0.19
4.   0.07 and 0.13

Refer to Question 78 in Chapter 7, Statistical Process Control.

90.   The metric system

1.   is based upon the circumference of the earth's equator
2.   originated in England
3.   is better than the inch-pound system
4.   is legal in the United States

Refer to Question 154 in Chapter 12, Product and Materials Control and Measurement Systems.

ANSWERS FOR OCTOBER 1972 EXAMINATION

PRINCIPLES

Q	A	Q	A	Q	A	Q	A	Q	A
1.	4	21.	1	41.	4	61.	1	81.	1
2.	4	22.	3	42.	3	62.	1	82.	2
3.	3	23.	3	43.	2	63.	1	83.	4
4.	1	24.	2	44.	4	64.	2	84.	1
5.	2	25.	1	45.	2	65.	1	85.	2
6.	1	26.	1	46.	3	66.	3	86.	4
7.	1	27.	4	47.	2	67.	2	87.	3
8.	3	28.	2	48.	3	68.	2	88.	3
9.	4	29.	3	49.	4	69.	3	89.	2
10.	1	30.	2	50.	2	70.	3	90.	1
11.	1	31.	3	51.	2	71.	1		
12.	4	32.	3	52.	1	72.	4		
13.	4	33.	4	53.	2	73.	3		
14.	3	34.	1	54.	3	74.	1		
15.	3	35.	3	55.	2	75.	2		
16.	4	36.	4	56.	1	76.	3		
17.	4	37.	3	57.	1	77.	3		
18.	4	38.	1	58.	1	78.	4		
19.	2	39.	2	59.	4	79.	3		
20.	2	40.	2	60.	2	80.	4		

COMMENTS / NOTES:

ANSWERS FOR OCTOBER 1972 EXAMINATION

APPLICATIONS

Q	A	Q	A	Q	A	Q	A	Q	A
1.	2	21.	2	41.	4	61.	4	81.	1
2.	1	22.	4	42.	4	62.	2	82.	4
3.	1	23.	4	43.	1	63.	1	83.	4
4.	3	24.	3	44.	3	64.	3	84.	4
5.	2	25.	4	45.	1	65.	2	85.	2
6.	3	26.	4	46.	3	66.	4	86.	4
7.	2	27.	3	47.	1	67.	2	87.	4
8.	4	28.	3	48.	2	68.	2	88.	3
9.	3	29.	2	49.	3	69.	3	89.	1
10.	2	30.	3	50.	4	70.	4	90.	4
11.	4	31.	1	51.	2	71.	2		
12.	3	32.	4	52.	1	72.	3		
13.	1	33.	4	53.	2	73.	4		
14.	3	34.	3	54.	2	74.	2		
15.	1	35.	4	55.	1	75.	1		
16.	3	36.	1	56.	3	76.	1		
17.	1	37.	4	57.	4	77.	1		
18.	3	38.	2	58.	4	78.	2		
19.	3	39.	1	59.	3	79.	2		
20.	1	40.	1	60.	4	80.	4		

COMMENTS / NOTES:

APPENDIX

STATISTICAL TABLES

TABLE A Factors for Computing Control Chart Lines*

Observations in Sample, n	Chart for averages — Factors for control limits			Chart for standard deviations — Factors for central line		Chart for standard deviations — Factors for control limits				Factors for central line			Chart for ranges — Factors for control limits			
	A	A_2	A_3	c_4	$1/c_4$	B_3	B_4	B_5	B_6	d_2	$1/d_2$	d_3	D_1	D_2	D_3	D_4
2	2.121	1.880	2.659	0.7979	1.2533	0	3.267	0	2.606	1.128	0.8865	0.853	0	3.686	0	3.267
3	1.732	1.023	1.954	0.8862	1.1284	0	2.568	0	2.276	1.693	0.5907	0.888	0	4.358	0	2.574
4	1.500	0.729	1.628	0.9213	1.0854	0	2.266	0	2.088	2.059	0.4857	0.880	0	4.698	0	2.282
5	1.342	0.577	1.427	0.9400	1.0638	0	2.089	0	1.964	2.326	0.4299	0.864	0	4.918	0	2.114
6	1.225	0.483	1.287	0.9515	1.0510	0.030	1.970	0.029	1.874	2.534	0.3946	0.848	0	5.078	0	2.004
7	1.134	0.419	1.182	0.9594	1.0423	0.118	1.882	0.113	1.806	2.704	0.3698	0.833	0.204	5.204	0.076	1.924
8	1.061	0.373	1.099	0.9650	1.0363	0.185	1.815	0.179	1.751	2.847	0.3512	0.820	0.388	5.306	0.136	1.864
9	1.000	0.337	1.032	0.9693	1.0317	0.239	1.761	0.232	1.707	2.970	0.3367	0.808	0.547	5.393	0.184	1.816
10	0.949	0.308	0.975	0.9727	1.0281	0.284	1.716	0.276	1.669	3.078	0.3249	0.797	0.687	5.469	0.223	1.777
11	0.905	0.285	0.927	0.9754	1.0252	0.321	1.679	0.313	1.637	3.173	0.3152	0.787	0.811	5.535	0.256	1.744
12	0.866	0.266	0.886	0.9776	1.0229	0.354	1.646	0.346	1.610	3.258	0.3069	0.778	0.922	5.594	0.283	1.717
13	0.832	0.249	0.850	0.9794	1.0210	0.382	1.618	0.374	1.585	3.336	0.2998	0.770	1.025	5.647	0.307	1.693
14	0.802	0.235	0.817	0.9810	1.0194	0.406	1.594	0.399	1.563	3.407	0.2935	0.763	1.118	5.696	0.328	1.672
15	0.775	0.223	0.789	0.9823	1.0180	0.428	1.572	0.421	1.544	3.472	0.2880	0.756	1.203	5.741	0.347	1.653
16	0.750	0.212	0.763	0.9835	1.0168	0.448	1.552	0.440	1.526	3.532	0.2831	0.750	1.282	5.782	0.363	1.637
17	0.728	0.203	0.739	0.9845	1.0157	0.466	1.534	0.458	1.511	3.588	0.2787	0.744	1.356	5.820	0.378	1.622
18	0.707	0.194	0.718	0.9854	1.0148	0.482	1.518	0.475	1.496	3.640	0.2747	0.739	1.424	5.856	0.391	1.608
19	0.688	0.187	0.698	0.9862	1.0140	0.497	1.503	0.490	1.483	3.689	0.2711	0.734	1.487	5.891	0.403	1.597
20	0.671	0.180	0.680	0.9869	1.0133	0.510	1.490	0.504	1.470	3.735	0.2677	0.729	1.549	5.921	0.415	1.585
21	0.655	0.173	0.663	0.9876	1.0126	0.523	1.477	0.516	1.459	3.778	0.2647	0.724	1.605	5.951	0.425	1.575
22	0.640	0.167	0.647	0.9882	1.0119	0.534	1.466	0.528	1.448	3.819	0.2618	0.720	1.659	5.979	0.434	1.566
23	0.626	0.162	0.633	0.9887	1.0114	0.545	1.455	0.539	1.438	3.858	0.2592	0.716	1.710	6.006	0.443	1.557
24	0.612	0.157	0.619	0.9892	1.0109	0.555	1.445	0.549	1.429	3.895	0.2567	0.712	1.759	6.031	0.451	1.548
25	0.600	0.153	0.606	0.9896	1.0105	0.565	1.435	0.559	1.420	3.931	0.2544	0.708	1.806	6.056	0.459	1.541

*The above table is a copy of Table 27 in *ASTM Manual on Presentation of Data and Control Chart Analysis.* (1976). ASTM Publication STP15D. American Society for Testing and Materials. Philadelphia, pp. 134–135. Used with permission.

Notes: For $n > 25$, $A = 3/\sqrt{n}$, $A_2 = 3/c_4\sqrt{n}$, $A_3 \simeq 4(n - 1)/(4n - 3)$, $c_4 \simeq 4(n - 1)/(4n - 3)$; $B_3 = 1 - 3/c_4\sqrt{2(n - 1)}$, $B_4 = 1 + 3/c_4\sqrt{2(n - 1)}$,

$$B_5 = c_4 - 3/\sqrt{2(n - 1)}, \quad B_6 = c_4 + 3/\sqrt{2(n - 1)}$$

FORMULAS

Purpose of chart	Chart for	Central line	3-Sigma control limits
For analyzing past inspection data for control ($\overline{\overline{X}}$, $\overline{s}$, $\overline{R}$ are average values for the data being analyzed)	Averages	$\overline{\overline{X}}$	$\overline{\overline{X}} \pm A_3\overline{s}$, or $\overline{\overline{X}} \pm A_2\overline{R}$
	Standard deviations	$\overline{s}$	$B_3\overline{s}$ and $B_4\overline{s}$
	Ranges	$\overline{R}$	$D_3\overline{R}$ and $D_4\overline{R}$
For controlling quality during production ($\overline{X}_0$, σ_0, R_0, are selected standard values; $R_0 = d_2\sigma_0$ for samples of size n)	Averages	$\overline{X}_0$	$\overline{X}_0 \pm A\sigma_0$ or $\overline{X}_0 \pm A_2R_0$
	Standard deviations	s_0 or $c_4\sigma_0$	$B_5\sigma_0$ and $B_6\sigma_0$
	Ranges	R_0 or $d_2\sigma_0$	$D_1\sigma_0$ and $D_2\sigma_0$

TABLE B Normal Distribution*

Proportion of total area under the curve from $-\infty$ to $Z = \dfrac{X-\mu}{\sigma}$. To illustrate: when $Z = +2.0$, the probability is 0.9773 of obtaining a value equal to or less than X.

Z	0.00	0.01	0.02	0.03	0.04	0.05	0.06	0.07	0.08	0.09
−3.5	0.00023	0.00022	0.00022	0.00021	0.00020	0.00019	0.00019	0.00018	0.00017	0.00017
−3.4	0.00034	0.00033	0.00031	0.00030	0.00029	0.00028	0.00027	0.00026	0.00025	0.00024
−3.3	0.00048	0.00047	0.00045	0.00043	0.00042	0.00040	0.00039	0.00038	0.00036	0.00035
−3.2	0.00069	0.00066	0.00064	0.00062	0.00060	0.00058	0.00056	0.00054	0.00052	0.00050
−3.1	0.00097	0.00094	0.00090	0.00087	0.00085	0.00082	0.00079	0.00076	0.00074	0.00071
−3.0	0.00135	0.00131	0.00126	0.00122	0.00118	0.00114	0.00111	0.00107	0.00104	0.00100
−2.9	0.0019	0.0018	0.0017	0.0017	0.0016	0.0016	0.0015	0.0015	0.0014	0.0014
−2.8	0.0026	0.0025	0.0024	0.0023	0.0023	0.0022	0.0021	0.0021	0.0020	0.0019
−2.7	0.0035	0.0034	0.0033	0.0032	0.0031	0.0030	0.0029	0.0028	0.0027	0.0026
−2.6	0.0047	0.0045	0.0044	0.0043	0.0041	0.0040	0.0039	0.0038	0.0037	0.0036
−2.5	0.0062	0.0060	0.0059	0.0057	0.0055	0.0054	0.0052	0.0051	0.0049	0.0048
−2.4	0.0082	0.0080	0.0078	0.0075	0.0073	0.0071	0.0069	0.0068	0.0066	0.0064
−2.3	0.0107	0.0104	0.0102	0.0099	0.0096	0.0094	0.0091	0.0089	0.0087	0.0084
−2.2	0.0139	0.0136	0.0132	0.0129	0.0125	0.0122	0.0119	0.0116	0.0113	0.0110
−2.1	0.0179	0.0174	0.0170	0.0166	0.0162	0.0158	0.0154	0.0150	0.0146	0.0143
−2.0	0.0228	0.0222	0.0217	0.0212	0.0207	0.0202	0.0197	0.0192	0.0188	0.0183
−1.9	0.0287	0.0281	0.0274	0.0268	0.0262	0.0256	0.0250	0.0244	0.0239	0.0233
−1.8	0.0359	0.0351	0.0344	0.0336	0.0329	0.0322	0.0314	0.0307	0.0301	0.0294
−1.7	0.0446	0.0436	0.0427	0.0418	0.0409	0.0401	0.0392	0.0384	0.0375	0.0367
−1.6	0.0548	0.0537	0.0526	0.0516	0.0505	0.0495	0.0485	0.0475	0.0465	0.0455
−1.5	0.0668	0.0655	0.0643	0.0630	0.0618	0.0606	0.0594	0.0582	0.0571	0.0559
−1.4	0.0808	0.0793	0.0778	0.0764	0.0749	0.0735	0.0721	0.0708	0.0694	0.0681
−1.3	0.0968	0.0951	0.0934	0.0918	0.0901	0.0885	0.0869	0.0853	0.0838	0.0823
−1.2	0.1151	0.1131	0.1112	0.1093	0.1075	0.1057	0.1038	0.1020	0.1003	0.0985
−1.1	0.1357	0.1335	0.1314	0.1292	0.1271	0.1251	0.1230	0.1210	0.1190	0.1170

TABLE B (Continued)

Z	0.09	0.08	0.07	0.06	0.05	0.04	0.03	0.02	0.01	0.00
−1.0	0.1379	0.1401	0.1423	0.1446	0.1469	0.1492	0.1515	0.1539	0.1562	0.1587
−0.9	0.1611	0.1635	0.1660	0.1685	0.1711	0.1736	0.1762	0.1788	0.1814	0.1841
−0.8	0.1867	0.1894	0.1922	0.1949	0.1977	0.2005	0.2033	0.2061	0.2090	0.2119
−0.7	0.2148	0.2177	0.2207	0.2236	0.2266	0.2297	0.2327	0.2358	0.2389	0.2420
−0.6	0.2451	0.2483	0.2514	0.2546	0.2578	0.2611	0.2643	0.2676	0.2709	0.2743
−0.5	0.2776	0.2810	0.2843	0.2877	0.2912	0.2946	0.2981	0.3015	0.3050	0.3085
−0.4	0.3121	0.3156	0.3192	0.3228	0.3264	0.3300	0.3336	0.3372	0.3409	0.3446
−0.3	0.3483	0.3520	0.3557	0.3594	0.3632	0.3669	0.3707	0.3745	0.3783	0.3821
−0.2	0.3859	0.3897	0.3936	0.3974	0.4013	0.4052	0.4090	0.4129	0.4168	0.4207
−0.1	0.4247	0.4286	0.4325	0.4364	0.4404	0.4443	0.4483	0.4562	0.4562	0.4602
−0.0	0.4641	0.4681	0.4721	0.4761	0.4801	0.4840	0.4880	0.4920	0.4960	0.5000

Z	0.00	0.01	0.02	0.03	0.04	0.05	0.06	0.07	0.08	0.09
+0.0	0.5000	0.5040	0.5080	0.5120	0.5160	0.5199	0.5239	0.5279	0.5319	0.5359
+0.1	0.5398	0.5438	0.5478	0.5517	0.5557	0.5596	0.5636	0.5675	0.5714	0.5753
+0.2	0.5793	0.5832	0.5871	0.5910	0.5948	0.5987	0.6026	0.6064	0.6103	0.6141
+0.3	0.6179	0.6217	0.6255	0.6293	0.6331	0.6368	0.6406	0.6443	0.6480	0.6517
+0.4	0.6554	0.6591	0.6628	0.6664	0.6700	0.6736	0.6772	0.6808	0.6844	0.6879
+0.5	0.6915	0.6950	0.6985	0.7019	0.7054	0.7088	0.7123	0.7157	0.7190	0.7224
+0.6	0.7257	0.7291	0.7324	0.7357	0.7389	0.7422	0.7454	0.7486	0.7517	0.7549
+0.7	0.7580	0.7611	0.7642	0.7673	0.7704	0.7734	0.7764	0.7794	0.7823	0.7852
+0.8	0.7881	0.7910	0.7939	0.7967	0.7995	0.8023	0.8051	0.8079	0.8106	0.8133
+0.9	0.8159	0.8186	0.8212	0.8238	0.8264	0.8289	0.8315	0.8340	0.8365	0.8389
+1.0	0.8413	0.8438	0.8461	0.8485	0.8508	0.8531	0.8554	0.8577	0.8599	0.8621
+1.1	0.8643	0.8665	0.8686	0.8708	0.8729	0.8749	0.8770	0.8790	0.8810	0.8830
+1.2	0.8849	0.8869	0.8888	0.8907	0.8925	0.8944	0.8962	0.8980	0.8997	0.9015
+1.3	0.9032	0.9049	0.9066	0.9082	0.9099	0.9115	0.9131	0.9147	0.9162	0.9177
+1.4	0.9192	0.9207	0.9222	0.9236	0.9251	0.9265	0.9279	0.9292	0.9306	0.9319
+1.5	0.9332	0.9345	0.9357	0.9370	0.9382	0.9394	0.9406	0.9418	0.9429	0.9441

z	.00	.01	.02	.03	.04	.05	.06	.07	.08	.09
+1.6	0.9452	0.9463	0.9474	0.9484	0.9495	0.9505	0.9515	0.9525	0.9535	0.9545
+1.7	0.9554	0.9564	0.9573	0.9582	0.9591	0.9599	0.9608	0.9616	0.9625	0.9633
+1.8	0.9641	0.9649	0.9656	0.9664	0.9671	0.9678	0.9686	0.9693	0.9699	0.9706
+1.9	0.9713	0.9719	0.9726	0.9732	0.9738	0.9744	0.9750	0.9756	0.9761	0.9767
+2.0	0.9773	0.9778	0.9783	0.9788	0.9793	0.9798	0.9803	0.9808	0.9812	0.9817
+2.1	0.9821	0.9826	0.9830	0.9834	0.9838	0.9842	0.9846	0.9850	0.9854	0.9857
+2.2	0.9861	0.9864	0.9868	0.9871	0.9875	0.9878	0.9881	0.9884	0.9887	0.9890
+2.3	0.9893	0.9896	0.9898	0.9901	0.9904	0.9906	0.9909	0.9911	0.9913	0.9916
+2.4	0.9918	0.9920	0.9922	0.9925	0.9927	0.9929	0.9931	0.9932	0.9934	0.9936
+2.5	0.9938	0.9940	0.9941	0.9943	0.9945	0.9946	0.9948	0.9949	0.9951	0.9952
+2.6	0.9953	0.9955	0.9956	0.9957	0.9959	0.9960	0.9961	0.9962	0.9963	0.9964
+2.7	0.9965	0.9966	0.9967	0.9968	0.9969	0.9970	0.9971	0.9972	0.9973	0.9974
+2.8	0.9974	0.9975	0.9976	0.9977	0.9977	0.9978	0.9979	0.9979	0.9980	0.9981
+2.9	0.9981	0.9982	0.9983	0.9983	0.9984	0.9984	0.9985	0.9985	0.9986	0.9986
+3.0	0.99865	0.99869	0.99874	0.99878	0.99882	0.99886	0.99889	0.99893	0.99896	0.99900
+3.1	0.99903	0.99906	0.99910	0.99913	0.99915	0.99918	0.99921	0.99924	0.99926	0.99929
+3.2	0.99931	0.99934	0.99936	0.99938	0.99940	0.99942	0.99944	0.99946	0.99948	0.99950
+3.3	0.99952	0.99953	0.99955	0.99957	0.99958	0.99960	0.99961	0.99962	0.99964	0.99965
+3.4	0.99966	0.99967	0.99969	0.99970	0.99971	0.99972	0.99973	0.99974	0.99975	0.99976
+3.5	0.99977	0.99978	0.99978	0.99979	0.99980	0.99981	0.99981	0.99982	0.99983	0.99983

*Adapted with permission from Grant, Eugene L. and Leavenworth, Richard S. (1972). *Statistical Quality Control,* 4th ed. McGraw-Hill, New York, pp. 642–643.

TABLE C Exponential Distribution*

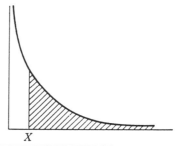

$\dfrac{X}{\mu}$	0.00	0.01	0.02	0.03	0.04	0.05	0.06	0.07	0.08	0.09
0.0	1.000	0.9900	0.9802	0.9704	0.9608	0.9512	0.9418	0.9324	0.9231	0.9139
0.1	0.9048	0.8958	0.8860	0.8781	0.8694	0.8607	0.8521	0.8437	0.8353	0.8270
0.2	0.8187	0.8106	0.8025	0.7945	0.7866	0.7788	0.7711	0.7634	0.7758	0.7483
0.3	0.7408	0.7334	0.7261	0.7189	0.7118	0.7047	0.6977	0.6907	0.6839	0.6771
0.4	0.6703	0.6637	0.6570	0.6505	0.6440	0.6376	0.6313	0.6250	0.6188	0.6126
0.5	0.6065	0.6005	0.5945	0.5886	0.5827	0.5769	0.5712	0.5655	0.5599	0.5543
0.6	0.5488	0.5434	0.5379	0.5326	0.5273	0.5220	0.5169	0.5117	0.5066	0.5016
0.7	0.4966	0.4916	0.4868	0.4819	0.4771	0.4724	0.4677	0.4630	0.4584	0.4538
0.8	0.4493	0.4449	0.4404	0.4360	0.4317	0.4274	0.4232	0.4190	0.4148	0.4107
0.9	0.4066	0.4025	0.3985	0.3946	0.3906	0.3867	0.3829	0.3791	0.3753	0.3716

	0.0	0.1	0.2	0.3	0.4	0.5	0.6	0.7	0.8	0.9
1.0	0.3679	0.3329	0.3012	0.2725	0.2466	0.2231	0.2019	0.1827	0.1653	0.1496
2.0	0.1353	0.1225	0.1108	0.1003	0.0907	0.0821	0.0743	0.0672	0.0608	0.0550
3.0	0.0498	0.0450	0.0408	0.0369	0.0334	0.0302	0.0273	0.0247	0.0224	0.0202
4.0	0.0183	0.0166	0.0150	0.0130	0.0123	0.0111	0.0101	0.0091	0.0082	0.0074
5.0	0.0067	0.0061	0.0055	0.0050	0.0045	0.0041	0.0037	0.0033	0.0030	0.0027
6.0	0.0025	0.0022	0.0020	0.0018	0.0017	0.0015	0.0014	0.0012	0.0011	0.0010

*Adapted with permission from Selby, S. M. (ed.) (1969). *CRC Standard Mathematical Tables,* 17th ed. The Chemical Rubber Co., pp. 201–207.

TABLE D • Distribution of t

Value of t corresponding to certain selected probabilities (i.e. tail areas under the curve). To illustrate: The probability is 0.975 that a sample with 20 degrees of freedom would have $t = +2.086$ or smaller.

DF	$t_{.60}$	$t_{.70}$	$t_{.80}$	$t_{.90}$	$t_{.95}$	$t_{.975}$	$t_{.99}$	$t_{.995}$
1	0.325	0.727	1.376	3.078	6.314	12.706	31.821	63.657
2	0.289	0.617	1.061	1.886	2.920	4.303	6.965	9.925
3	0.277	0.584	0.978	1.638	2.353	3.182	4.541	5.841
4	0.271	0.569	0.941	1.533	2.132	2.776	3.747	4.604
5	0.267	0.559	0.920	1.476	2.015	2.571	3.365	4.032
6	0.265	0.553	0.906	1.440	1.943	2.447	3.143	3.707
7	0.263	0.549	0.896	1.415	1.895	2.365	2.998	3.499
8	0.262	0.546	0.889	1.397	1.860	2.306	2.896	3.355
9	0.261	0.543	0.883	1.383	1.833	2.262	2.821	3.250
10	0.260	0.542	0.879	1.372	1.812	2.228	2.764	3.169
11	0.260	0.540	0.876	1.363	1.796	2.201	2.718	3.106
12	0.259	0.539	0.873	1.356	1.782	2.179	2.681	3.055
13	0.259	0.538	0.870	1.350	1.771	2.160	2.650	3.012
14	0.258	0.537	0.868	1.345	1.761	2.145	2.624	2.977
15	0.258	0.536	0.866	1.341	1.753	2.131	2.602	2.947
16	0.258	0.535	0.865	1.337	1.746	2.120	2.583	2.921
17	0.257	0.534	0.863	1.333	1.740	2.110	2.567	2.898
18	0.257	0.534	0.862	1.330	1.734	2.101	2.552	2.878
19	0.257	0.533	0.861	1.328	1.729	2.093	2.539	2.861
20	0.257	0.533	0.860	1.325	1.725	2.086	2.528	2.845
21	0.257	0.532	0.859	1.323	1.721	2.080	2.518	2.831
22	0.256	0.532	0.858	1.321	1.717	2.074	2.508	2.819
23	0.256	0.532	0.858	1.319	1.714	2.069	2.500	2.807
24	0.256	0.531	0.857	1.318	1.711	2.064	2.492	2.797
25	0.256	0.531	0.856	1.316	1.708	2.060	2.485	2.787
26	0.256	0.531	0.856	1.315	1.706	2.056	2.479	2.779
27	0.256	0.531	0.855	1.314	1.703	2.052	2.473	2.771
28	0.256	0.530	0.855	1.313	1.701	2.048	2.467	2.763
29	0.256	0.530	0.854	1.311	1.699	2.045	2.462	2.756
30	0.256	0.530	0.854	1.310	1.697	2.042	2.457	2.750
40	0.255	0.529	0.851	1.303	1.684	2.021	2.423	2.704
60	0.254	0.527	0.848	1.296	1.671	2.000	2.390	2.660
120	0.254	0.526	0.845	1.289	1.658	1.980	2.358	2.617
∞	0.253	0.524	0.842	1.282	1.645	1.960	2.326	2.576

*Adapted with permission from Dixon, W. J. and Massey, F. J., Jr. (1969). *Introduction to Statistical Analysis*, 3rd ed. McGraw-Hill, New York. Entries originally from Fisher, R. A. and Yates, F. *Statistical Tables*. Oliver & Boyd, London, Table III.

TABLE E Poisson Distribution*

1000 × probability of r or fewer occurrences of event that has average number of occurrences equal to np.

np \ r	0	1	2	3	4	5	6	7	8	9
0.02	980	1,000								
0.04	961	999	1,000							
0.06	942	998	1,000							
0.08	923	997	1,000							
0.10	905	995	1,000							
0.15	861	990	999	1,000						
0.20	819	982	999	1,000						
0.25	779	974	998	1,000						
0.30	741	963	996	1,000						
0.35	705	951	994	1,000						
0.40	670	938	992	999	1,000					
0.45	638	925	989	999	1,000					
0.50	607	910	986	998	1,000					
0.55	577	894	982	998	1,000					
0.60	549	878	977	997	1,000					
0.65	522	861	972	996	999	1,000				
0.70	497	844	966	994	999	1,000				
0.75	472	827	959	993	999	1,000				
0.80	449	809	953	991	999	1,000				
0.85	427	791	945	989	998	1,000				
0.90	407	772	937	987	998	1,000				
0.95	387	754	929	984	997	1,000				
1.00	368	736	920	981	996	999	1,000			
1.1	333	699	900	974	995	999	1,000			
1.2	301	663	879	966	992	998	1,000			
1.3	273	627	857	957	989	998	1,000			
1.4	247	592	833	946	986	997	999	1,000		
1.5	223	558	809	934	981	996	999	1,000		
1.6	202	525	783	921	976	994	999	1,000		
1.7	183	493	757	907	970	992	998	1,000		
1.8	165	463	731	891	964	990	997	999	1,000	
1.9	150	434	704	875	956	987	997	999	1,000	
2.0	135	406	677	857	947	983	995	999	1,000	

np \ r	0	1	2	3	4	5	6	7	8	9
2.2	111	355	623	819	928	975	993	998	1,000	
2.4	091	308	570	779	904	964	988	997	999	1,000
2.6	074	267	518	736	877	951	983	995	999	1,000
2.8	061	231	469	692	848	935	976	992	998	999
3.0	050	199	423	647	815	916	966	988	996	999
3.2	041	171	380	603	781	895	955	983	994	998
3.4	033	147	340	558	744	871	942	977	992	997
3.6	027	126	303	515	706	844	927	969	988	996
3.8	022	107	269	473	668	816	909	960	984	994
4.0	018	092	238	433	629	785	889	949	979	992
4.2	015	078	210	395	590	753	867	936	972	989
4.4	012	066	185	359	551	720	844	921	964	985
4.6	010	056	163	326	513	686	818	905	955	980
4.8	008	048	143	294	476	651	791	887	944	975
5.0	007	040	125	265	440	616	762	867	932	968
5.2	006	034	109	238	406	581	732	845	918	960
5.4	005	029	095	213	373	546	702	822	903	951
5.6	004	024	082	191	342	512	670	797	886	941
5.8	003	021	072	170	313	478	638	771	867	929
6.0	002	017	062	151	285	446	606	744	847	916

np \ r	10	11	12	13	14	15	16
2.8	1,000						
3.0	1,000						
3.2	1,000						
3.4	999	1,000					
3.6	999	1,000					
3.8	998	999	1,000				
4.0	997	999	1,000				
4.2	996	999	1,000				
4.4	994	998	999	1,000			
4.6	992	997	999	1,000			
4.8	990	996	999	1,000			
5.0	986	995	998	999	1,000		
5.2	982	993	997	999	1,000		
5.4	977	990	996	999	1,000		
5.6	972	988	995	998	999	1,000	
5.8	965	984	993	997	999	1,000	
6.0	957	980	991	996	999	999	1,000

np \ r	0	1	2	3	4	5	6	7	8	9
6.2	002	015	054	134	259	414	574	716	826	902
6.4	002	012	046	119	235	384	542	687	803	886
6.6	001	010	040	105	213	355	511	658	780	869
6.8	001	009	034	093	192	327	480	628	755	850
7.0	001	007	030	082	173	301	450	599	729	830
7.2	001	006	025	072	156	276	420	569	703	810
7.4	001	005	022	063	140	253	392	539	676	788
7.6	001	004	019	055	125	231	365	510	648	765
7.8	000	004	016	048	112	210	338	481	620	741
8.0	000	003	014	042	100	191	313	453	593	717
8.5	000	002	009	030	074	150	256	386	523	653
9.0	000	001	006	021	055	116	207	324	456	587
9.5	000	001	004	015	040	089	165	269	392	522
10.0	000	000	003	010	029	067	130	220	333	458

	10	11	12	13	14	15	16	17	18	19
6.2	949	975	989	995	998	999	1,000			
6.4	939	969	986	994	997	999	1,000			
6.6	927	963	982	992	997	999	999	1,000		
6.8	915	955	978	990	996	998	999	1,000		
7.0	901	947	973	987	994	998	999	1,000		
7.2	887	937	967	984	993	997	999	999	1,000	
7.4	871	926	961	980	991	996	998	999	1,000	
7.6	854	915	954	976	989	995	998	999	1,000	
7.8	835	902	945	971	986	993	997	999	1,000	
8.0	816	888	936	966	983	992	996	998	999	1,000
8.5	763	849	909	949	973	986	993	997	999	999
9.0	706	803	876	926	959	978	989	995	998	999
9.5	645	752	836	898	940	967	982	991	996	998
10.0	583	697	792	864	917	951	973	986	993	997

	20	21	22
8.5	1,000		
9.0	1,000		
9.5	999	1,000	
10.0	998	999	1,000

r / np	0	1	2	3	4	5	6	7	8	9
10.5	000	000	002	007	021	050	102	179	279	397
11.0	000	000	001	005	015	038	079	143	232	341
11.5	000	000	001	003	011	028	060	114	191	289
12.0	000	000	001	002	008	020	046	090	155	242
12.5	000	000	000	002	005	015	035	070	125	201
13.0	000	000	000	001	004	011	026	054	100	166
13.5	000	000	000	001	003	008	019	041	079	135
14.0	000	000	000	000	002	006	014	032	062	109
14.5	000	000	000	000	001	004	010	024	048	088
15.0	000	000	000	000	001	003	008	018	037	070

np	10	11	12	13	14	15	16	17	18	19
10.5	521	639	742	825	888	932	960	978	988	994
11.0	460	579	689	781	854	907	944	968	982	991
11.5	402	520	633	733	815	878	924	954	974	986
12.0	347	462	576	682	772	844	899	937	963	979
12.5	297	406	519	628	725	806	869	916	948	969
13.0	252	353	463	573	675	764	835	890	930	957
13.5	211	304	409	518	623	718	798	861	908	942
14.0	176	260	358	464	570	669	756	827	883	923
14.5	145	220	311	413	518	619	711	790	853	901
15.0	118	185	268	363	466	568	664	749	819	875

np	20	21	22	23	24	25	26	27	28	29
10.5	997	999	999	1,000						
11.0	995	998	999	1,000						
11.5	992	996	998	999	1,000					
12.0	988	994	997	999	999	1,000				
12.5	983	991	995	998	999	999	1,000			
13.0	975	986	992	996	998	999	1,000			
13.5	965	980	989	994	997	998	999	1,000		
14.0	952	971	983	991	995	997	999	999	1,000	
14.5	936	960	976	986	992	996	998	999	999	1,000
15.0	917	947	967	981	989	994	997	998	999	1,000

*Adapted with permission from Grant, E. L. and Leavenworth, Richard S. (1972). *Statistical Quality Control,* 4th ed. McGraw-Hill, New York.

TABLE F Binomial Distribution*

Probability of r or fewer occurrences of an event in n trials, where p is the probability of occurrence on each trial.

n	r	0.05	0.10	0.15	0.20	0.25	0.30	0.35	0.40	0.45	0.50
2	0	0.9025	0.8100	0.7225	0.6400	0.5625	0.4900	0.4225	0.3600	0.3025	0.2500
	1	0.9975	0.9900	0.9775	0.9600	0.9375	0.9100	0.8775	0.8400	0.7975	0.7500
3	0	0.8574	0.7290	0.6141	0.5120	0.4219	0.3430	0.2746	0.2160	0.1664	0.1250
	1	0.9928	0.9720	0.9392	0.8960	0.8438	0.7840	0.7182	0.6480	0.5748	0.5000
	2	0.9999	0.9990	0.9966	0.9920	0.9844	0.9730	0.9571	0.9360	0.9089	0.8750
4	0	0.8145	0.6561	0.5220	0.4096	0.3164	0.2401	0.1785	0.1296	0.0915	0.0625
	1	0.9860	0.9477	0.8905	0.8192	0.7383	0.6517	0.5630	0.4752	0.3910	0.3125
	2	0.9995	0.9963	0.9880	0.9728	0.9492	0.9163	0.8735	0.8208	0.7585	0.6875
	3	1.0000	0.9999	0.9995	0.9984	0.9961	0.9919	0.9850	0.9744	0.9590	0.9375
5	0	0.7738	0.5905	0.4437	0.3277	0.2373	0.1681	0.1160	0.0778	0.0503	0.0312
	1	0.9774	0.9185	0.8352	0.7373	0.6328	0.5282	0.4284	0.3370	0.2562	0.1875
	2	0.9988	0.9914	0.9734	0.9421	0.8965	0.8369	0.7648	0.6826	0.5931	0.5000
	3	1.0000	0.9995	0.9978	0.9933	0.9844	0.9692	0.9460	0.9130	0.8688	0.8125
	4	1.0000	1.0000	0.9999	0.9997	0.9990	0.9976	0.9947	0.9898	0.9815	0.9688
6	0	0.7351	0.5314	0.3771	0.2621	0.1780	0.1176	0.0754	0.0467	0.0277	0.0156
	1	0.9672	0.8857	0.7765	0.6554	0.5339	0.4202	0.3191	0.2333	0.1636	0.1094
	2	0.9978	0.9842	0.9527	0.9011	0.8306	0.7443	0.6471	0.5443	0.4415	0.3438
	3	0.9999	0.9987	0.9941	0.9830	0.9624	0.9295	0.8826	0.8208	0.7447	0.6562
	4	1.0000	0.9999	0.9996	0.9984	0.9954	0.9891	0.9777	0.9590	0.9308	0.8906
	5	1.0000	1.0000	1.0000	0.9999	0.9998	0.9993	0.9982	0.9959	0.9917	0.9844
7	0	0.6983	0.4783	0.3206	0.2097	0.1335	0.0824	0.0490	0.0280	0.0152	0.0078
	1	0.9556	0.8503	0.7166	0.5767	0.4449	0.3294	0.2338	0.1586	0.1024	0.0625
	2	0.9962	0.9743	0.9262	0.8520	0.7564	0.6471	0.5323	0.4199	0.3164	0.2266
	3	0.9998	0.9973	0.9879	0.9667	0.9294	0.8740	0.8002	0.7102	0.6083	0.5000
	4	1.0000	0.9998	0.9988	0.9953	0.9871	0.9712	0.9444	0.9037	0.8471	0.7734
	5	1.0000	1.0000	0.9999	0.9996	0.9987	0.9962	0.9910	0.9812	0.9643	0.9375

n	x										
	6	1.0000	1.0000	1.0000	1.0000	0.9999	0.9998	0.9994	0.9984	0.9963	0.9922
8	0	0.6634	0.4305	0.2725	0.1678	0.1001	0.0576	0.0319	0.0168	0.0084	0.0039
	1	0.9428	0.8131	0.6572	0.5033	0.3671	0.2553	0.1691	0.1064	0.0632	0.0352
	2	0.9942	0.9619	0.8948	0.7969	0.6785	0.5518	0.4278	0.3154	0.2201	0.1445
	3	0.9996	0.9950	0.9786	0.9437	0.8862	0.8059	0.7064	0.5941	0.4770	0.3633
	4	1.0000	0.9996	0.9971	0.9896	0.9727	0.9420	0.8939	0.8263	0.7396	0.6367
	5	1.0000	1.0000	0.9998	0.9988	0.9958	0.9887	0.9747	0.9502	0.9115	0.8555
	6	1.0000	1.0000	1.0000	0.9999	0.9996	0.9987	0.9964	0.9915	0.9819	0.9648
	7	1.0000	1.0000	1.0000	1.0000	1.0000	0.9999	0.9998	0.9993	0.9983	0.9961
9	0	0.6302	0.3874	0.2316	0.1342	0.0751	0.0404	0.0207	0.0101	0.0046	0.0020
	1	0.9288	0.7748	0.5995	0.4362	0.3003	0.1960	0.1211	0.0705	0.0385	0.0195
	2	0.9916	0.9470	0.8591	0.7382	0.6007	0.4628	0.3373	0.2318	0.1495	0.0898
	3	0.9994	0.9917	0.9661	0.9144	0.8343	0.7297	0.6089	0.4826	0.3614	0.2539
	4	1.0000	0.9991	0.9944	0.9804	0.9511	0.9012	0.8283	0.7334	0.6214	0.5000
	5	1.0000	0.9999	0.9994	0.9969	0.9900	0.9747	0.9464	0.9006	0.8342	0.7461
	6	1.0000	1.0000	1.0000	0.9997	0.9987	0.9957	0.9888	0.9750	0.9502	0.9102
	7	1.0000	1.0000	1.0000	1.0000	0.9999	0.9996	0.9986	0.9962	0.9909	0.9805
	8	1.0000	1.0000	1.0000	1.0000	1.0000	1.0000	0.9999	0.9997	0.9992	0.9980
10	0	0.5987	0.3487	0.1969	0.1074	0.0563	0.0282	0.0135	0.0060	0.0025	0.0010
	1	0.9139	0.7361	0.5443	0.3758	0.2440	0.1493	0.0860	0.0464	0.0232	0.0107
	2	0.9885	0.9298	0.8202	0.6778	0.5256	0.3828	0.2616	0.1673	0.0996	0.0547
	3	0.9990	0.9872	0.9500	0.8791	0.7759	0.6496	0.5138	0.3823	0.2660	0.1719
	4	0.9999	0.9984	0.9901	0.9672	0.9219	0.8497	0.7515	0.6331	0.5044	0.3770
	5	1.0000	0.9999	0.9986	0.9936	0.9803	0.9527	0.9051	0.8338	0.7384	0.6230
	6	1.0000	1.0000	0.9999	0.9991	0.9965	0.9894	0.9740	0.9452	0.8980	0.8281
	7	1.0000	1.0000	1.0000	0.9999	0.9996	0.9984	0.9952	0.9877	0.9726	0.9453
	8	1.0000	1.0000	1.0000	1.0000	1.0000	0.9999	0.9995	0.9983	0.9955	0.9893
	9	1.0000	1.0000	1.0000	1.0000	1.0000	1.0000	1.0000	0.9999	0.9997	0.9990

*Adapted with permission from Miller, Irwin and Freund, John E. (1965). *Probability and Statistics for Engineers*. Prentice-Hall, Englewood Cliffs, NJ, pp. 388–389.

For more extensive tables see The Staff of Harvard University Computation Laboratory (1955). *Tables of Cumulative Binomial Probability Distribution*. Harvard University Press, Cambridge, MA. See also Robertson, W. H. (1960). *Tables of the Binomial Distribution Function for Small Values of p*. Sandia Corp. Monograph, available from the Office of Technical Services, Department of Commerce, Washington, DC.

TABLE G • Distribution of F

Values of F corresponding to certain selected probabilities (i.e., tail areas under the curve). To illustrate: The probability is 0.05 that the ratio of two sample variances obtained with 20 and 10 degrees of freedom in numerator and denominator, respectively, would have F = 2.77 or larger. For a two-sided test, a lower limit is found by taking the reciprocal of the tabulated F value for the degrees of freedom in reverse. For the above example, with 10 and 20 degrees of freedom in numerator and denominator, respectively, F is 2.35 and 1/F is 1/2.35, or 0.43. The probability is 0.10 that F is 0.43 or smaller or 2.77 or larger.

$F_{.95}\ (n_1, n_2)$

n_2 \ n_1	1	2	3	4	5	6	7	8	9	10	12	15	20	24	30	40	60	120	∞
1	161.4	199.5	215.7	224.6	230.2	234.0	236.8	238.9	240.5	241.9	243.9	245.9	248.0	249.1	250.1	251.1	252.2	253.3	254.3
2	18.51	19.00	19.16	19.25	19.30	19.33	19.35	19.37	19.38	19.40	19.41	19.43	19.45	19.45	19.46	19.47	19.48	19.49	19.50
3	10.13	9.55	9.28	9.12	9.01	8.94	8.89	8.85	8.81	8.79	8.74	8.70	8.66	8.64	8.62	8.59	8.57	8.55	8.53
4	7.71	6.94	6.59	6.39	6.26	6.16	6.09	6.04	6.00	5.96	5.91	5.86	5.80	5.77	5.75	5.72	5.69	5.66	5.63
5	6.61	5.79	5.41	5.19	5.05	4.95	4.88	4.82	4.77	4.74	4.68	4.62	4.56	4.53	4.50	4.46	4.43	4.40	4.36
6	5.99	5.14	4.76	4.53	4.39	4.28	4.21	4.15	4.10	4.06	4.00	3.94	3.87	3.84	3.81	3.77	3.74	3.70	3.67
7	5.59	4.74	4.35	4.12	3.97	3.87	3.79	3.73	3.68	3.64	3.57	3.51	3.44	3.41	3.38	3.34	3.30	3.27	3.23
8	5.32	4.46	4.07	3.84	3.69	3.58	3.50	3.44	3.39	3.35	3.28	3.22	3.15	3.12	3.08	3.04	3.01	2.97	2.93
9	5.12	4.26	3.86	3.63	3.48	3.37	3.29	3.23	3.18	3.14	3.07	3.01	2.94	2.90	2.86	2.83	2.79	2.75	2.71
10	4.96	4.10	3.71	3.48	3.33	3.22	3.14	3.07	3.02	2.98	2.91	2.85	2.77	2.74	2.70	2.66	2.62	2.58	2.54
11	4.84	3.98	3.59	3.36	3.20	3.09	3.01	2.95	2.90	2.85	2.79	2.72	2.65	2.61	2.57	2.53	2.49	2.45	2.40
12	4.75	3.89	3.49	3.26	3.11	3.00	2.91	2.85	2.80	2.75	2.69	2.62	2.54	2.51	2.47	2.43	2.38	2.34	2.30
13	4.67	3.81	3.41	3.18	3.03	2.92	2.83	2.77	2.71	2.67	2.60	2.53	2.46	2.42	2.38	2.34	2.30	2.25	2.21
14	4.60	3.74	3.34	3.11	2.96	2.85	2.76	2.70	2.65	2.60	2.53	2.46	2.39	2.35	2.31	2.27	2.22	2.18	2.13
15	4.54	3.68	3.29	3.06	2.90	2.79	2.71	2.64	2.59	2.54	2.48	2.40	2.33	2.29	2.25	2.20	2.16	2.11	2.07
16	4.49	3.63	3.24	3.01	2.85	2.74	2.66	2.59	2.54	2.49	2.42	2.35	2.28	2.24	2.19	2.15	2.11	2.06	2.01
17	4.45	3.59	3.20	2.96	2.81	2.70	2.61	2.55	2.49	2.45	2.38	2.31	2.23	2.19	2.15	2.10	2.06	2.01	1.96
18	4.41	3.55	3.16	2.93	2.77	2.66	2.58	2.51	2.46	2.41	2.34	2.27	2.19	2.15	2.11	2.06	2.02	1.97	1.92
19	4.38	3.52	3.13	2.90	2.74	2.63	2.54	2.48	2.42	2.38	2.31	2.23	2.16	2.11	2.07	2.03	1.98	1.93	1.88
20	4.35	3.49	3.10	2.87	2.71	2.60	2.51	2.45	2.39	2.35	2.28	2.20	2.12	2.08	2.04	1.99	1.95	1.90	1.84
21	4.32	3.47	3.07	2.84	2.68	2.57	2.49	2.42	2.37	2.32	2.25	2.18	2.10	2.05	2.01	1.96	1.92	1.87	1.81
22	4.30	3.44	3.05	2.82	2.66	2.55	2.46	2.40	2.34	2.30	2.23	2.15	2.07	2.03	1.98	1.94	1.89	1.84	1.78
23	4.28	3.42	3.03	2.80	2.64	2.53	2.44	2.37	2.32	2.27	2.20	2.13	2.05	2.01	1.96	1.91	1.86	1.81	1.76
24	4.26	3.40	3.01	2.78	2.62	2.51	2.42	2.36	2.30	2.25	2.18	2.11	2.03	1.98	1.94	1.89	1.84	1.79	1.73
25	4.24	3.39	2.99	2.76	2.60	2.49	2.40	2.34	2.28	2.24	2.16	2.09	2.01	1.96	1.92	1.87	1.82	1.77	1.71
26	4.23	3.37	2.98	2.74	2.59	2.47	2.39	2.32	2.27	2.22	2.15	2.07	1.99	1.95	1.90	1.85	1.80	1.75	1.69
27	4.21	3.35	2.96	2.73	2.57	2.46	2.37	2.31	2.25	2.20	2.13	2.06	1.97	1.93	1.88	1.84	1.79	1.73	1.67
28	4.20	3.34	2.95	2.71	2.56	2.45	2.36	2.29	2.24	2.19	2.12	2.04	1.96	1.91	1.87	1.82	1.77	1.71	1.65
29	4.18	3.33	2.93	2.70	2.55	2.43	2.35	2.28	2.22	2.18	2.10	2.03	1.94	1.90	1.85	1.81	1.75	1.70	1.64
30	4.17	3.32	2.92	2.69	2.53	2.42	2.33	2.27	2.21	2.16	2.09	2.01	1.93	1.89	1.84	1.79	1.74	1.68	1.62
40	4.08	3.23	2.84	2.61	2.45	2.34	2.25	2.18	2.12	2.08	2.00	1.92	1.84	1.79	1.74	1.69	1.64	1.58	1.51
60	4.00	3.15	2.76	2.53	2.37	2.25	2.17	2.10	2.04	1.99	1.92	1.84	1.75	1.70	1.65	1.59	1.53	1.47	1.39
120	3.92	3.07	2.68	2.45	2.29	2.17	2.09	2.02	1.96	1.91	1.83	1.75	1.66	1.61	1.55	1.50	1.43	1.35	1.25
∞	3.84	3.00	2.60	2.37	2.21	2.10	2.01	1.94	1.88	1.83	1.75	1.67	1.57	1.52	1.46	1.39	1.32	1.22	1.00

Adapted with permission from Pearson, E. S. and Hartley, H. O. (eds.) (1958). Biometrika Tables for Statisticians, 2nd ed. Cambridge University Press, New York, vol. I.

Note: n_1 = degrees of freedom for numerator. n_2 = degrees of freedom for denominator.

TABLE G (Continued)

F.975 (n_1, n_2)

n_2 \ n_1	1	2	3	4	5	6	7	8	9	10	12	15	20	24	30	40	60	120	∞
1	647.8	799.5	864.2	899.6	921.8	937.1	948.2	956.7	963.3	968.6	976.7	984.9	993.1	997.2	1,001	1,006	1,010	1,014	1,018
2	38.51	39.00	39.17	39.25	39.30	39.33	39.36	39.37	39.39	39.40	39.41	39.43	39.45	39.46	39.46	39.47	39.48	39.49	39.50
3	17.44	16.04	15.44	15.10	14.88	14.73	14.62	14.54	14.47	14.42	14.34	14.25	14.17	14.12	14.08	14.04	13.99	13.95	13.90
4	12.22	10.65	9.98	9.60	9.36	9.20	9.07	8.98	8.90	8.84	8.75	8.66	8.56	8.51	8.46	8.41	8.36	8.31	8.26
5	10.01	8.43	7.76	7.39	7.15	6.98	6.85	6.76	6.68	6.62	6.52	6.43	6.33	6.28	6.23	6.18	6.12	6.07	6.02
6	8.81	7.26	6.60	6.23	5.99	5.82	5.70	5.60	5.52	5.46	5.37	5.27	5.17	5.12	5.07	5.01	4.96	4.90	4.85
7	8.07	6.54	5.89	5.52	5.29	5.12	4.99	4.90	4.82	4.76	4.67	4.57	4.47	4.42	4.36	4.31	4.25	4.20	4.14
8	7.57	6.06	5.42	5.05	4.82	4.65	4.53	4.43	4.36	4.30	4.20	4.10	4.00	3.95	3.89	3.84	3.78	3.73	3.67
9	7.21	5.71	5.08	4.72	4.48	4.32	4.20	4.10	4.03	3.96	3.87	3.77	3.67	3.61	3.56	3.51	3.45	3.39	3.33
10	6.94	5.46	4.83	4.47	4.24	4.07	3.95	3.85	3.78	3.72	3.62	3.52	3.42	3.37	3.31	3.26	3.20	3.14	3.08
11	6.72	5.26	4.63	4.28	4.04	3.88	3.76	3.66	3.59	3.53	3.43	3.33	3.23	3.17	3.12	3.06	3.00	2.94	2.88
12	6.55	5.10	4.47	4.12	3.89	3.73	3.61	3.51	3.44	3.37	3.28	3.18	3.07	3.02	2.96	2.91	2.85	2.79	2.72
13	6.41	4.97	4.35	4.00	3.77	3.60	3.48	3.39	3.31	3.25	3.15	3.05	2.95	2.89	2.84	2.78	2.72	2.66	2.60
14	6.30	4.86	4.24	3.89	3.66	3.50	3.38	3.29	3.21	3.15	3.05	2.95	2.84	2.79	2.73	2.67	2.61	2.55	2.49
15	6.20	4.77	4.15	3.80	3.58	3.41	3.29	3.20	3.12	3.06	2.96	2.86	2.76	2.70	2.64	2.59	2.52	2.46	2.40
16	6.12	4.69	4.08	3.73	3.50	3.34	3.22	3.12	3.05	2.99	2.89	2.79	2.68	2.63	2.57	2.51	2.45	2.38	2.32
17	6.04	4.62	4.01	3.66	3.44	3.28	3.16	3.06	2.98	2.92	2.82	2.72	2.62	2.56	2.50	2.44	2.38	2.32	2.25
18	5.98	4.56	3.95	3.61	3.38	3.22	3.10	3.01	2.93	2.87	2.77	2.67	2.56	2.50	2.44	2.38	2.32	2.26	2.19
19	5.92	4.51	3.90	3.56	3.33	3.17	3.05	2.96	2.88	2.82	2.72	2.62	2.51	2.45	2.39	2.33	2.27	2.20	2.13
20	5.87	4.46	3.86	3.51	3.29	3.13	3.01	2.91	2.84	2.77	2.68	2.57	2.46	2.41	2.35	2.29	2.22	2.16	2.09
21	5.83	4.42	3.82	3.48	3.25	3.09	2.97	2.87	2.80	2.73	2.64	2.53	2.42	2.37	2.31	2.25	2.18	2.11	2.04
22	5.79	4.38	3.78	3.44	3.22	3.05	2.93	2.84	2.76	2.70	2.60	2.50	2.39	2.33	2.27	2.21	2.14	2.08	2.00
23	5.75	4.35	3.75	3.41	3.18	3.02	2.90	2.81	2.73	2.67	2.57	2.47	2.36	2.30	2.24	2.18	2.11	2.04	1.97
24	5.72	4.32	3.72	3.38	3.15	2.99	2.87	2.78	2.70	2.64	2.54	2.44	2.33	2.27	2.21	2.15	2.08	2.01	1.94
25	5.69	4.29	3.69	3.35	3.13	2.97	2.85	2.75	2.68	2.61	2.51	2.41	2.30	2.24	2.18	2.12	2.05	1.98	1.91
26	5.66	4.27	3.67	3.33	3.10	2.94	2.82	2.73	2.65	2.59	2.49	2.39	2.28	2.22	2.16	2.09	2.03	1.95	1.88
27	5.63	4.24	3.65	3.31	3.08	2.92	2.80	2.71	2.63	2.57	2.47	2.36	2.25	2.19	2.13	2.07	2.00	1.93	1.85
28	5.61	4.22	3.63	3.29	3.06	2.90	2.78	2.69	2.61	2.55	2.45	2.34	2.23	2.17	2.11	2.05	1.98	1.91	1.83
29	5.59	4.20	3.61	3.27	3.04	2.88	2.76	2.67	2.59	2.53	2.43	2.32	2.21	2.15	2.09	2.03	1.96	1.89	1.81
30	5.57	4.18	3.59	3.25	3.03	2.87	2.75	2.65	2.57	2.51	2.41	2.31	2.20	2.14	2.07	2.01	1.94	1.87	1.79
40	5.42	4.05	3.46	3.13	2.90	2.74	2.62	2.53	2.45	2.39	2.29	2.18	2.07	2.01	1.94	1.88	1.80	1.72	1.64
60	5.29	3.93	3.34	3.01	2.79	2.63	2.51	2.41	2.33	2.27	2.17	2.06	1.94	1.88	1.82	1.74	1.67	1.58	1.48
120	5.15	3.80	3.23	2.89	2.67	2.52	2.39	2.30	2.22	2.16	2.05	1.94	1.82	1.76	1.69	1.61	1.53	1.43	1.31
∞	5.02	3.69	3.12	2.79	2.57	2.41	2.29	2.19	2.11	2.05	1.94	1.83	1.71	1.64	1.57	1.48	1.39	1.27	1.00

TABLE G (Continued)

$F_{.99}(n_1, n_2)$

n_2 \ n_1	1	2	3	4	5	6	7	8	9	10	12	15	20	24	30	40	60	120	∞
1	4,052	4,999.5	5,403	5,625	5,764	5,859	5,928	5,982	6,022	6,056	6,106	6,157	6,209	6,235	6,261	6,287	6,313	6,339	6,366
2	98.50	99.00	99.17	99.25	99.30	99.33	99.36	99.37	99.39	99.40	99.42	99.43	99.45	99.46	99.47	99.47	99.48	99.49	99.50
3	34.12	30.82	29.46	28.71	28.24	27.91	27.67	27.49	27.35	27.23	27.05	26.87	26.69	26.60	26.50	26.41	26.32	26.22	26.13
4	21.20	18.00	16.69	15.98	15.52	15.21	14.98	14.80	14.66	14.55	14.37	14.20	14.02	13.93	13.84	13.75	13.65	13.56	13.46
5	16.26	13.27	12.06	11.39	10.97	10.67	10.46	10.29	10.16	10.05	9.89	9.72	9.55	9.47	9.38	9.29	9.20	9.11	9.02
6	13.75	10.92	9.78	9.15	8.75	8.47	8.26	8.10	7.98	7.87	7.72	7.56	7.40	7.31	7.23	7.14	7.06	6.97	6.88
7	12.25	9.55	8.45	7.85	7.46	7.19	6.99	6.84	6.72	6.62	6.47	6.31	6.16	6.07	5.99	5.91	5.82	5.74	5.65
8	11.26	8.65	7.59	7.01	6.63	6.37	6.18	6.03	5.91	5.81	5.67	5.52	5.36	5.28	5.20	5.12	5.03	4.95	4.86
9	10.56	8.02	6.99	6.42	6.06	5.80	5.61	5.47	5.35	5.26	5.11	4.96	4.81	4.73	4.65	4.57	4.48	4.40	4.31
10	10.04	7.56	6.55	5.99	5.64	5.39	5.20	5.06	4.94	4.85	4.71	4.56	4.41	4.33	4.25	4.17	4.08	4.00	3.91
11	9.65	7.21	6.22	5.67	5.32	5.07	4.89	4.74	4.63	4.54	4.40	4.25	4.10	4.02	3.94	3.86	3.78	3.69	3.60
12	9.33	6.93	5.95	5.41	5.06	4.82	4.64	4.50	4.39	4.30	4.16	4.01	3.86	3.78	3.70	3.62	3.54	3.45	3.36
13	9.07	6.70	5.74	5.21	4.86	4.62	4.44	4.30	4.19	4.10	3.96	3.82	3.66	3.59	3.51	3.43	3.34	3.25	3.17
14	8.86	6.51	5.56	5.04	4.69	4.46	4.28	4.14	4.03	3.94	3.80	3.66	3.51	3.43	3.35	3.27	3.18	3.09	3.00
15	8.68	6.36	5.42	4.89	4.56	4.32	4.14	4.00	3.89	3.80	3.67	3.52	3.37	3.29	3.21	3.13	3.05	2.96	2.87
16	8.53	6.23	5.29	4.77	4.44	4.20	4.03	3.89	3.78	3.69	3.55	3.41	3.26	3.18	3.10	3.02	2.93	2.84	2.75
17	8.40	6.11	5.18	4.67	4.34	4.10	3.93	3.79	3.68	3.59	3.46	3.31	3.16	3.08	3.00	2.92	2.83	2.75	2.65
18	8.29	6.01	5.09	4.58	4.25	4.01	3.84	3.71	3.60	3.51	3.37	3.23	3.08	3.00	2.92	2.84	2.75	2.66	2.57
19	8.18	5.93	5.01	4.50	4.17	3.94	3.77	3.63	3.52	3.43	3.30	3.15	3.00	2.92	2.84	2.76	2.67	2.58	2.49
20	8.10	5.85	4.94	4.43	4.10	3.87	3.70	3.56	3.46	3.37	3.23	3.09	2.94	2.86	2.78	2.69	2.61	2.52	2.42
21	8.02	5.78	4.87	4.37	4.04	3.81	3.64	3.51	3.40	3.31	3.17	3.03	2.88	2.80	2.72	2.64	2.55	2.46	2.36
22	7.95	5.72	4.82	4.31	3.99	3.76	3.59	3.45	3.35	3.26	3.12	2.98	2.83	2.75	2.67	2.58	2.50	2.40	2.31
23	7.88	5.66	4.76	4.26	3.94	3.71	3.54	3.41	3.30	3.21	3.07	2.93	2.78	2.70	2.62	2.54	2.45	2.35	2.26
24	7.82	5.61	4.72	4.22	3.90	3.67	3.50	3.36	3.26	3.17	3.03	2.89	2.74	2.66	2.58	2.49	2.40	2.31	2.21
25	7.77	5.57	4.68	4.18	3.85	3.63	3.46	3.32	3.22	3.13	2.99	2.85	2.70	2.62	2.54	2.45	2.36	2.27	2.17
26	7.72	5.53	4.64	4.14	3.82	3.59	3.42	3.29	3.18	3.09	2.96	2.81	2.66	2.58	2.50	2.42	2.33	2.23	2.13
27	7.68	5.49	4.60	4.11	3.78	3.56	3.39	3.26	3.15	3.06	2.93	2.78	2.63	2.55	2.47	2.38	2.29	2.20	2.10
28	7.64	5.45	4.57	4.07	3.75	3.53	3.36	3.23	3.12	3.03	2.90	2.75	2.60	2.52	2.44	2.35	2.26	2.17	2.06
29	7.60	5.42	4.54	4.04	3.73	3.50	3.33	3.20	3.09	3.00	2.87	2.73	2.57	2.49	2.41	2.33	2.23	2.14	2.03
30	7.56	5.39	4.51	4.02	3.70	3.47	3.30	3.17	3.07	2.98	2.84	2.70	2.55	2.47	2.39	2.30	2.21	2.11	2.01
40	7.31	5.18	4.31	3.83	3.51	3.29	3.12	2.99	2.89	2.80	2.66	2.52	2.37	2.29	2.20	2.11	2.02	1.92	1.80
60	7.08	4.98	4.13	3.65	3.34	3.12	2.95	2.82	2.72	2.63	2.50	2.35	2.20	2.12	2.03	1.94	1.84	1.73	1.60
120	6.85	4.79	3.95	3.48	3.17	2.96	2.79	2.66	2.56	2.47	2.34	2.19	2.03	1.95	1.86	1.76	1.66	1.53	1.38
∞	6.63	4.61	3.78	3.32	3.02	2.80	2.64	2.51	2.41	2.32	2.18	2.04	1.88	1.79	1.70	1.59	1.47	1.32	1.00

TABLE H • Distribution of χ^2

Values of χ^2 corresponding to certain selected probabilities (i.e., tail areas under the curve). To illustrate: The probability is 0.95 that a sample with 20 degrees of freedom, taken from a normal distribution, would have $\chi^2 = 31.41$ or smaller.

VALUES OF $\chi^2{}_P$ CORRESPONDING TO P

DF	$\chi^2{}_{.005}$	$\chi^2{}_{.01}$	$\chi^2{}_{.025}$	$\chi^2{}_{.05}$	$\chi^2{}_{.10}$	$\chi^2{}_{.90}$	$\chi^2{}_{.95}$	$\chi^2{}_{.975}$	$\chi^2{}_{.99}$	$\chi^2{}_{.995}$
1	0.000039	0.00016	0.00098	0.0039	0.0158	2.71	3.84	5.02	6.63	7.88
2	0.0100	0.0201	0.0506	0.1026	0.2107	4.61	5.99	7.38	9.21	10.60
3	0.0717	0.115	0.216	0.352	0.584	6.25	7.81	9.35	11.34	12.84
4	0.207	0.297	0.484	0.711	1.064	7.78	9.49	11.14	13.28	14.86
5	0.412	0.554	0.831	1.15	1.61	9.24	11.07	12.83	15.09	16.75
6	0.676	0.872	1.24	1.64	2.20	10.64	12.59	14.45	16.81	18.55
7	0.989	1.24	1.69	2.17	2.83	12.02	14.07	16.01	18.48	20.28
8	1.34	1.65	2.18	2.73	3.49	13.36	15.51	17.53	20.09	21.96
9	1.73	2.09	2.70	3.33	4.17	14.68	16.92	19.02	21.67	23.59
10	2.16	2.56	3.25	3.94	4.87	15.99	18.31	20.48	23.21	25.19
11	2.60	3.05	3.82	4.57	5.58	17.28	19.68	21.92	24.73	26.76
12	3.07	3.57	4.40	5.23	6.30	18.55	21.03	23.34	26.22	28.30
13	3.57	4.11	5.01	5.89	7.04	19.81	22.36	24.74	27.69	29.82
14	4.07	4.66	5.63	6.57	7.79	21.06	23.68	26.12	29.14	31.32
15	4.60	5.23	6.26	7.26	8.55	22.31	25.00	27.49	30.58	32.80
16	5.14	5.81	6.91	7.96	9.31	23.54	26.30	28.85	32.00	34.27
18	6.26	7.01	8.23	9.39	10.86	25.99	28.87	31.53	34.81	37.16
20	7.43	8.26	9.59	10.85	12.44	28.41	31.41	34.17	37.57	40.00
24	9.89	10.86	12.40	13.85	15.66	33.20	36.42	39.36	42.98	45.56
30	13.79	14.95	16.79	18.49	20.60	40.26	43.77	46.98	50.89	53.67
40	20.71	22.16	24.43	26.51	29.05	51.81	55.76	59.34	63.69	66.77
60	35.53	37.48	40.48	43.19	46.46	74.40	79.08	83.30	88.38	91.95
120	83.85	86.92	91.58	95.70	100.62	140.23	146.57	152.21	158.95	163.64

*Adapted with permission from Dixon, W. J. and Massey, F. J., Jr. (1969). *Introduction to Statistical Analysis*, 3rd ed. McGraw-Hill, New York.

ABOUT THE AUTHOR

Jagdish Vani is a manager in the Dimensional
Management department with General Motors
Corporation's Midsize Car Division, where he is
responsible for the implementation of GM's Key
Characteristic Designation System (KCDS). He was
the chairman of the Greater Detroit Section of the
ASQC. He holds CQE, CRE, and CQA certifications.
He is an instructor for CQE, CQT, CQA, and CRE
refresher courses for ASQC's certification
examinations.